Communications in Computer and Information Science 2932

Rationale
The CCIS series is devoted to the publication of proceedings of computer science conferences. Its aim is to efficiently disseminate original research results in informatics in printed and electronic form. While the focus is on publication of peer-reviewed full papers presenting mature work, inclusion of reviewed short papers reporting on work in progress is welcome, too. Besides globally relevant meetings with internationally representative program committees guaranteeing a strict peer-reviewing and paper selection process, conferences run by societies or of high regional or national relevance are also considered for publication.

Topics
The topical scope of CCIS spans the entire spectrum of informatics ranging from foundational topics in the theory of computing to information and communications science and technology and a broad variety of interdisciplinary application fields.

Information for Volume Editors and Authors
Publication in CCIS is free of charge. No royalties are paid, however, we offer registered conference participants temporary free access to the online version of the conference proceedings on SpringerLink (http://link.springer.com) by means of an http referrer from the conference website and/or a number of complimentary printed copies, as specified in the official acceptance email of the event.

CCIS proceedings can be published in time for distribution at conferences or as post-proceedings, and delivered in the form of printed books and/or electronically as USBs and/or e-content licenses for accessing proceedings at SpringerLink. Furthermore, CCIS proceedings are included in the CCIS electronic book series hosted in the SpringerLink digital library at http://link.springer.com/bookseries/7899. Conferences publishing in CCIS are allowed to use our online conference service (Meteor) for managing the whole proceedings lifecycle (from submission and reviewing to preparing for publication) free of charge.

Publication process
The language of publication is exclusively English. Authors publishing in CCIS have to sign the Springer CCIS copyright transfer form, however, they are free to use their material published in CCIS for substantially changed, more elaborate subsequent publications elsewhere. For the preparation of the camera-ready papers/files, authors have to strictly adhere to the Springer CCIS Authors' Instructions and are strongly encouraged to use the CCIS LaTeX style files or templates.

Abstracting/Indexing
CCIS is abstracted/indexed in DBLP, Google Scholar, EI-Compendex, Mathematical Reviews, SCImago, Scopus. CCIS volumes are also submitted for the inclusion in ISI Proceedings.

How to start
To start the evaluation of your proposal for inclusion in the CCIS series, please send an e-mail to ccis@springer.com

Hamid R. Arabnia · Leonidas Deligiannidis ·
Masami Takata · Miho Chiyonobu ·
Masahito Ohue · Nobuaki Yasuo · Pablo Rivas ·
Javier Orduz
Editors

Distributed Computing, HPC, Cloud Computing, Quantum Technologies, Embedded Systems, Modeling, and Simulation

23rd International Conference, ESCS 2025, 21st International Conference, GCC 2025, 4th International Conference, ICEQT 2025, 22nd International Conference, MSV 2025, 31st International Conference, PDPTA 2025, Held as Part of the World Congress in Computer Science, Computer Engineering, and Applied Computing, CSCE 2025, Las Vegas, NV, USA, July 21–24, 2025, Revised Selected Papers

Springer

Editors
Hamid R. Arabnia
University of Georgia
Athens, GA, USA

Leonidas Deligiannidis
Wentworth Institute of Technology
Boston, MA, USA

Masami Takata
Nara Women's University
Nara, Japan

Miho Chiyonobu
Shiga University
Shiga, Japan

Masahito Ohue
Tokyo Institute of Technology
Tokyo, Japan

Nobuaki Yasuo
Tokyo Institute of Technology
Tokyo, Japan

Pablo Rivas
Baylor University
Waco, TX, USA

Javier Orduz
Earlham College
Richmond, IN, USA

ISSN 1865-0929 ISSN 1865-0937 (electronic)
Communications in Computer and Information Science
ISBN 978-3-032-22192-6 ISBN 978-3-032-22193-3 (eBook)
https://doi.org/10.1007/978-3-032-22193-3

This Springer imprint is published by the registered company Springer Nature Switzerland AG
The registered company address is: Gewerbestrasse 11, 6330 Cham, Switzerland

Preface

It is our great pleasure to introduce this collection of selected papers presented at The 23rd International Conference on Embedded Systems, Cyber-physical Systems, & Applications (ESCS 2025); The 21st International Conference on Grid, Cloud, & Cluster Computing (GCC 2025); The 4th International Conference on Emergent Quantum Technologies (ICEQT 2025); The 22nd International Conference on Modeling, Simulation & Visualization Methods (MSV 2025); and The 31st International Conference on Parallel & Distributed Processing Techniques & Applications (PDPTA 2025). These conferences were held as part of the federated 2025 World Congress in Computer Science, Computer Engineering, and Applied Computing (CSCE 2025), which took place from July 21 to July 24, 2025, in Las Vegas, Nevada, USA.

The CSCE 2025 Congress brought together papers from a diverse array of communities, including researchers from universities, corporations, and government agencies. Accepted papers are published by Springer Nature, and the proceedings showcase solutions to key challenges in various critical areas of Computer Science, Computer Engineering, and Applied Computing.

Computer Science (CS) is the study of computational systems, data processing, information management, and automation. Many applications in CS focus on solving problems that would be impossible or extremely difficult to address without the use of computers. It serves as a bridge between computational science and other scientific fields. The interdisciplinary nature of CS involves leveraging computers to understand and solve complex challenges, making it the science of using computers to advance scientific discovery. Computer Engineering (CE), on the other hand, integrates aspects of computer science, electronic engineering, and electrical engineering. It encompasses the design and production of computer hardware, such as chips, servers, supercomputers, embedded systems, and communication systems, among others.

Considering the above broad outline, the CSCE 2025 Congress was composed of the following focused conferences:

Applied Cognitive Computing (ACC); Bioinformatics & Computational Biology (BIOCOMP); Biomedical Engineering (BIOENG); Scientific Computing (CSC); eLearning, e-Business, Enterprise Information Systems, & e-Government (EEE); Embedded Systems, Cyber-physical Systems, & Applications (ESCS); Foundations of Computer Science (FCS); Frontiers in Education (FECS); Grid, Cloud, & Cluster Computing (GCC); Health Informatics (HIMS); Artificial Intelligence (ICAI); Data Science (ICDATA); Emergent Quantum Technologies (ICEQT); Internet Computing & IoT (ICOMP); Wireless Networks (ICWN); Information & Knowledge Engineering (IKE); Image Processing, Computer Vision, & Pattern Recognition (IPCV); Modeling, Simulation & Visualization Methods (MSV); Parallel & Distributed Processing Techniques & Applications (PDPTA); Security & Management (SAM); and Software Engineering Research & Practice (SERP). The scope of each track can be found at: https://www.american-cse.org/csce2025/conferences.

The primary objective of the CSCE Congress and its associated conferences is to foster opportunities for cross-fertilization between the fields of Computer Science (CS) and Computer Engineering (CE). The CSCE Congress is deeply committed to promoting diversity and eliminating discrimination, both in its role as a conference organizer and as a service provider. Our goal is to create an inclusive culture that respects and values differences, promotes dignity, equality, and diversity, and encourages individuals to reach their full potential. We are also dedicated, wherever possible, to organizing a conference that represents the global community. We sincerely hope that we have succeeded in achieving these important objectives.

The Steering Committee and the Program Committees would like to extend their gratitude to all the authors who submitted papers for consideration. This year's conferences received submissions from 58 countries, with approximately 50% of them coming from outside the USA. Each submitted paper underwent a rigorous peer-review process, with at least two experts (an average of 2.4 referees per paper) evaluating the submissions based on originality, significance, clarity, impact, and soundness. In cases where reviewers' recommendations were contradictory, a program committee member was tasked with making the final decision, often consulting additional referees for further guidance. The Congress followed the guidelines of COPE (Committee on Publication Ethics):

- Typical submissions underwent a single-blind peer review process, in which the authors remained unaware of the identities of the reviewers, while the reviewers were informed of the authors' identities.
- Papers authored by one or more members of the program committee, including co-chairs, were subjected to a double-blind peer review process, ensuring that neither the authors nor the reviewers were aware of each other's identities or affiliations.

The ESCS 2025 and ICEQT 2025 Conferences received a total of 72 submissions, of which 15 papers were accepted, resulting in a paper acceptance rate of 21%. The MSV 2025 Conference received 41 submissions, of which 9 papers were accepted, resulting in a paper acceptance rate of 22%. The GCC 2025 and PDPTA 2025 Conferences received a total of 121 submissions, of which 24 papers were accepted, resulting in a paper acceptance rate of 20%.

This volume includes 41 of the accepted papers from ESCS 2025, GCC 2025, ICEQT 2025, MSV 2025, and PDPTA 2025.

We are deeply grateful to the many colleagues who contributed their time and effort to organizing the Congress. In particular, we extend our thanks to the members of the Program Committees, the Steering Committee, the referees, and the Chairs and organizers of individual sessions and conferences. We would also like to express our appreciation to the primary sponsor of the conference, the American Council on Science & Education. The list of members of the Program Committee for each track can be found at: https://www.american-cse.org/csce2025/committees.

We extend our heartfelt gratitude to all the speakers and authors for their valuable contributions. We would also like to thank the following individuals and organizations for their support: the staff at the Luxor Hotel, the staff of Springer Nature, Soheyla Amirian (Pace University), Farzan Shenavarmasouleh (Medialab Inc., USA), and Farid Ghareh Mohammadi (Verify Radiology Images Consultants, LLC, USA) for their assistance in various aspects of the event.

We are pleased to present a curated selection of papers from the ESCS 2025, GCC 2025, ICEQT 2025, MSV 2025, and PDPTA 2025 conferences. These proceedings represent a collection of outstanding research contributions that reflect the diversity and depth of work in core areas of Distributed Computing, HPC, Cloud Computing, Quantum Technologies, Embedded Systems, Modeling, and Simulation.

August 2025

Hamid R. Arabnia
Leonidas Deligiannidis
Masami Takata
Miho Chiyonobu
Masahito Ohue
Nobuaki Yasuo
Pablo Rivas
Javier Orduz

Organization

Steering Committee – Co-chairs (CSCE 2025)

Hamid R. Arabnia	University of Georgia, USA
Leonidas Deligiannidis	Wentworth Institute of Technology, USA
Fernando G. Tinetti	Universidad Nacional de La Plata, Argentina
Quoc-Nam Tran	Southeastern Louisiana University, USA

Co-editors of ESCS 2025, GCC 2025, ICEQT 2025, MSV 2025, & PDPTA 2025 Proceedings – Publication Co-chairs

Hamid R. Arabnia	University of Georgia, USA
Leonidas Deligiannidis	Wentworth Institute of Technology, USA
Masami Takata	Nara Women's University, Japan
Miho Chiyonobu	Shiga University, Japan
Masahito Ohue	Institute of Science Tokyo, Japan
Nobuaki Yasuo	Institute of Science Tokyo, Japan
Pablo Rivas	Baylor University, USA
Javier Orduz	Earlham College, USA

Members of Steering Committee (CSCE 2025)

Babak Akhgar	Sheffield Hallam University, UK
Abbas M. Al-Bakry	University of IT & Communications, Iraq
Nizar Al-Holou	University of Detroit Mercy, USA
Hamid R. Arabnia	University of Georgia, USA
Rajab Challoo	Texas A&M University-Kingsville, USA
Chien-Fu Cheng	Tamkang University, Taiwan
Hyunseung Choo	Sungkyunkwan University, South Korea
Kevin Daimi	University of Detroit Mercy, USA
Leonidas Deligiannidis	Wentworth Institute of Technology, USA
Eman M. El-Sheikh	University of West Florida, USA
Mary Mehrnoosh Eshaghian-Wilner	University of California, Los Angeles, USA
David L. Foster	Kettering University, USA
Henry Hexmoor	Southern Illinois University at Carbondale, USA

Ching-Hsien (Robert) Hsu	Chung Hua University, Taiwan
James J. (Jong Hyuk) Park	SeoulTech, South Korea
Mohammad S. Obaidat	University of Jordan, Jordan
Marwan Omar	Illinois Institute of Technology, USA
Shahram Rahimi	University of Alabama, USA
Gerald Schaefer	Loughborough University, UK
Fernando G. Tinetti	Universidad Nacional de La Plata, Argentina
Quoc-Nam Tran	Southeastern Louisiana University, USA
Shiuh-Jeng Wang	Central Police University, Taiwan
Layne T. Watson	Virginia Polytechnic Institute & State University, USA
Chao-Tung Yang	Tunghai University, Taiwan
Mary Yang	University of Arkansas for Medical Sciences, USA

Research Tracks – Co-chairs (CSCE 2025)

Abeer Alsadoon (Co-chair, Health Informatics)	Charles Sturt University, Australia
Soheyla Amirian (Co-chair, Computer Vision & AI)	Pace University, USA
Hamid R. Arabnia (Co-chair, HPC)	University of Georgia, USA
Kevin Daimi (Co-chair, Security)	University of Detroit Mercy, USA
Leonidas Deligiannidis (Co-chair, Imaging Science, AI)	Wentworth Institute of Technology, USA
Richard Dill (Co-chair, Military and Defense Modeling)	US Air Force Institute of Technology, USA
Ken Ferens (Co-chair, Cognitive Computing & AI)	University of Manitoba, Canada
David de la Fuente (Co-chair, Information Management)	University of Oviedo, Spain
Shanzhen Gao (Co-chair, Artificial Intelligence, Education)	Virginia State University, USA
Farid Ghareh Mohammadi (Co-chair, Computer Vision & AI)	Verify Radiology Images Consultants, LLC, USA
Michael R. Grimaila (Co-chair, Military and Defense Modeling)	US Air Force Institute of Technology, USA

Douglas D. Hodson (Co-chair, Military and Defense Modeling)	US Air Force Institute of Technology, USA
Masahito Ohue (Co-chair, Mathematical Modeling)	Tokyo Institute of Technology, Japan
Peter M. Maurer (Co-chair, Theoretical Computer Science)	Baylor University, USA
Jose A. Olivas (Co-chair, Information Management)	University of Castilla - La Mancha, Spain
Javier Ordus (Co-chair, Quantum Computing & AI)	Earlham College, USA
Pablo Rivas (Chair, Quantum Computing & AI)	Baylor University, USA
Farzan Shenavarmasouleh (Co-chair, Computer Vision & AI)	MediaLab Inc., USA
Robert Stahlbock (Co-chair, Data Mining)	Universität Hamburg, Germany
Masami Takata (Co-chair, Mathematical Modeling)	Nara Women's University, Japan
Nazli Tekin (Co-chair, Energy Aware, Security)	Erciyes University, Turkey
Quoc-Nam Tran (Co-chair, Education & Bioinformatics)	Southeastern Louisiana University, USA
Torrey J. Wagner (Co-chair, Scientific Computing, Artificial Intelligence)	Air Force Institute of Technology, USA
Troy Weingart (Co-chair, Military and Defense Modeling)	US Air Force Institute of Technology, USA
Nobuaki Yasuo (Co-chair, Mathematical Modeling)	Tokyo Institute of Technology, Japan
Tanwir Zaman (Co-chair, Artificial Intelligence)	Walmart Labs, USA
Chris Cheng Zhang (Co-chair, Artificial Intelligence, Robotics)	Canada Youth Robotics Club, Canada
Beilei Zhu (Co-chair, Supply Chain Management)	Intel Corporation, USA

Program Committees of ESCS 2025, GCC 2025, ICEQT 2025, MSV 2025, & PDPTA 2025

Refer to the lists at: https://www.american-cse.org/csce2025/committees.

Contents

ESCS'25: 23rd International Conference on Embedded Systems, Cyber-Physical Systems, and Applications

Cognitive Software Defined Radios for Embedded Systems and 7G Mesh Applications

Jeffrey Wallace(✉), Miroslav Vukovic, William Edwards, and Toni Karimovic

Rocket Technology Systems LLC, Washington, DC 20006, USA
jeff@roc-tec.systems

Abstract. This paper presents the design, implementation, and evaluation of advanced cognitive software defined radio (SDR) platforms intended for next-generation wireless networks and mesh applications. Two SDR prototypes were developed: a compact 2×2 MIMO system based on an AMD/Xilinx Kria system-on-module, and a high-performance 4-channel SDR utilizing Xilinx Zynq UltraScale+ RFSoC technology. Both platforms integrate Gallium Nitride (GaN) power amplifiers, support high-order modulation up to 4096-QAM, and employ artificial intelligence (AI) and machine learning (ML) techniques in their digital signal processing pipelines for dynamic scheduling, LDPC decoding, and channel equalization. Laboratory measurements confirm that these SDRs achieve high fidelity in 1024-QAM and 4096-QAM transmissions, low-latency decoding, and robust real-time performance.

Building on these validated platforms, we develop and analyze a cognitive mesh networking architecture suitable for UAVs and embedded systems, featuring multi-band operation, AI-driven routing, and resilience to interference and adverse conditions. Simulation and testbed results demonstrate improved throughput, adaptability, and reliability compared to conventional approaches. The findings highlight a practical pathway to implementing adaptive, high-capacity wireless mesh networks for future applications in distributed and autonomous systems.

1 Introduction

Next-generation wireless systems continue to push the boundaries of performance and adaptability. While Wi-Fi 7 (IEEE 802.11be) [1] introduces 320 MHz channels, 4096-QAM modulation, and Multi-Link Operation (MLO) for multi-band throughput, research is already advancing toward wireless architectures beyond 6G. Anticipated future networks will require ultra-fast data rates and pervasive connectivity, enabled by flexible, intelligent radio technologies. In this context, cognitive software-defined radios (SDRs) are expected to play a key role, combining adaptable RF hardware with AI-driven digital signal processing (DSP) to optimize waveforms, channels, and network topology in real time.

This paper presents the design, implementation, and evaluation of two advanced SDR prototypes, along with an architecture supporting cognitive mesh networking for

H. R. Arabnia et al. (Eds.): CSCE 2025, CCIS 2932, pp. 3–17, 2026.
https://doi.org/10.1007/978-3-032-22193-3_1

embedded and unmanned systems. The first prototype is a compact 2-channel SDR platform based on an AMD/Xilinx Kria system-on-module (SoM), providing 2 × 2 MIMO capability with integrated GaN power amplifiers and adaptive control. The second is a 4-channel SDR utilizing Xilinx's Zynq UltraScale+ RFSoC technology, supporting high-order QAM (up to 4096-QAM), sub-nanosecond synchronization, and integrated AI/ML-based DSP for dynamic scheduling, LDPC decoding, and channel equalization. Both prototypes have been validated through laboratory experiments and serve as practical building blocks for advanced wireless mesh networks.

Building on these results, we propose and analyze a cognitive mesh networking approach for UAV swarms and other mobile platforms. This approach leverages Wi-Fi 7 MLO for multi-band backhaul, AI-based burst prioritization, and adaptive routing to maintain resilience under multipath fading, jamming, and adverse weather. The network architecture is evaluated in simulation and testbed scenarios, focusing on dynamic frequency selection and real-time adaptation to maximize reliability and throughput.

The remainder of this paper is organized as follows: Sect. 2 describes the SDR system architectures and prototypes. Section 3 discusses advanced DSP techniques, including AI/ML-enhanced LDPC decoding, scheduling, and heterogeneous hardware acceleration. Section 4 presents the cognitive mesh network architecture and its performance under diverse conditions. Section 5 details experimental results and benchmarks, while Sect. 6 discusses lessons learned and directions for future work. Section 7 concludes the paper.

2 System Architecture and Prototype Design

To meet the demanding requirements of cognitive radios, our prototypes emphasize multi-channel RF flexibility coupled with powerful digital processing. We designed two SDR hardware platforms that share a common design philosophy – modular integration of high-performance RF transceivers, Gallium Nitride (GaN) amplifiers for high power and linearity, and adaptive control – but target different scales. The first is a small-form-factor 2 × 2 MIMO SDR suitable for mobile or embedded use. The second is a 4-channel SDR built for higher capacity and precise synchronization, aligning with emerging 5G/6G base station capabilities. Figure 1 below illustrates the SDR architecture.

2.1 A 2-Channel SDR Platform

The 2-channel SDR platform, shown in Fig. 2 below, is built around an AMD/Xilinx Kria K26 SoM (housing a Zynq UltraScale+ MPSoC [2] with integrated FPGA and ARM CPU cores) coupled with an Analog Devices RF transceiver module providing two transmit and two receive channels. This combination yields a wideband 2 × 2 MIMO radio covering roughly 70 MHz to 6 GHz, suitable for most sub-6 GHz bands of interest. The RF front-end is based on the AD9361/AD9371 family, which includes integrated mixers, ADCs/DACs, and tunable synthesizers, effectively the entire RF-to-baseband signal chain in a chip. By leveraging such integrated RF transceivers tightly

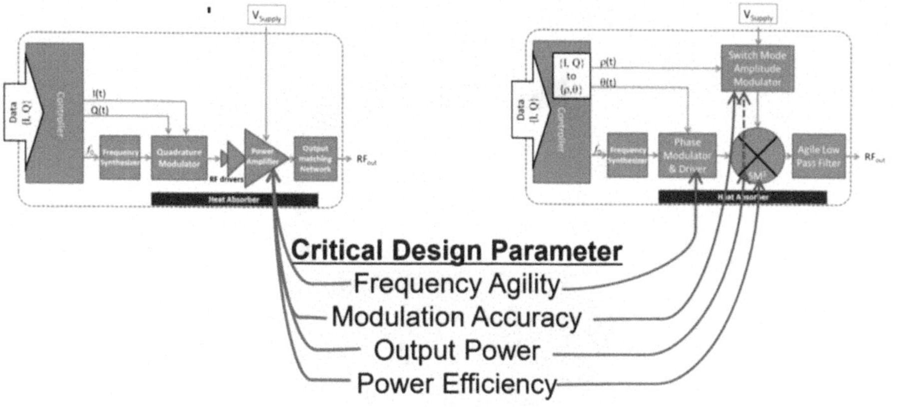

Fig. 1. SDR Architecture

coupled to the FPGA SoM, the design forms a compact yet flexible radio core that can be reconfigured for different waveforms on the fly.

To ensure the platform can handle advanced waveforms (e.g. 1024-QAM) with high fidelity, we paid special attention to the analog front-end and power amplification. We integrated GaN power amplifiers (two, one per transmit channel) delivering up to ~35 W each, with proper heat-sinking and bias control. GaN technology offers high linearity and efficiency, which is crucial for high-order QAM, 4096-QAM, for instance, has very tight Error Vector Magnitude (EVM) requirements and demands a high Signal-to-Noise Ratio (SNR) to distinguish its 4096 constellation points. Our amplifiers are tuned for linear operation in the target bands, avoiding excessive distortion or spectral regrowth. In fact, achieving *high linearity under 4096-QAM's stringent SNR requirements* was a key design challenge. We implemented adaptive digital pre-distortion (DPD) in the FPGA to further linearize the PA output, and automatic gain control (AGC) loops to protect against saturation.

The digital architecture of the 2-channel SDR revolves around the heterogeneous capabilities of the Kria MPSoC. The FPGA fabric handles time-critical DSP (such as modulation, pulse shaping, FFTs, and forward error correction encoding/decoding), while the embedded ARM Cortex-A53 cores run higher-level control software and cognitive algorithms (under embedded Linux). We partitioned the processing such that each channel's baseband pipeline, including digital up/down conversion and filtering for 56 MHz channels, is mostly in FPGA for real-time throughput, whereas scheduling decisions and AI inference run on the ARM cores. The two channels can operate independently or jointly as a 2×2 MIMO pair, with calibration routines to ensure phase coherence and IQ balance. Calibration signals and on-board sensors allow the system to adapt to temperature drift or RF component aging, maintaining signal fidelity over time.

2.2 A 4-Channel SDR Platform

To scale up capabilities, we developed a 4-channel SDR platform leveraging Xilinx's third-generation Radio Frequency System-on-Chip (RFSoC). The RFSoC is an ideal

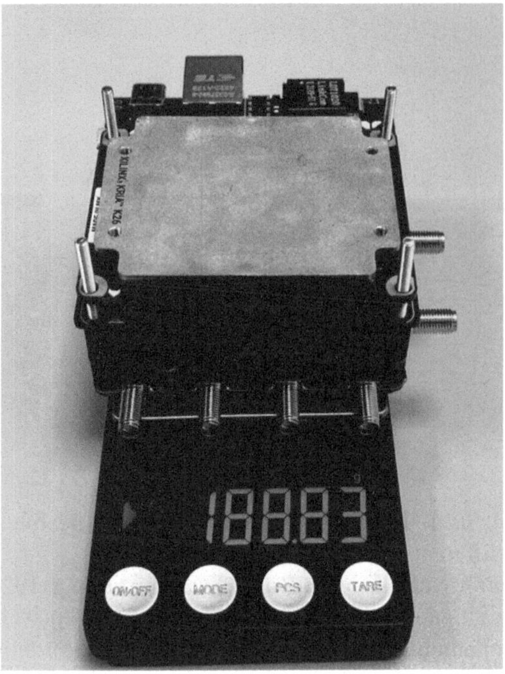

Fig. 2. The 2-channel SDR prototype hardware. The design integrates a Xilinx MPSoC (Kria K26) with a dual RF transceiver covering 70 MHz–6 GHz and 2×2 MIMO support.

foundation for a high-channel-count SDR because it monolithically integrates multi-GSPS data converters (ADC/DAC) with FPGA logic and CPU cores. In our design, we use a Zynq UltraScale+ RFSoC Gen-3 device (ZU47DR family) mounted on an Avnet RFSoC evaluation module, paired with a 4-channel Analog Devices RF front-end board. The RFSoC provides 8 ADCs and 8 DACs at up to 5 GSPS (we utilize 4 ADCs and 4 DACs for 4×4 MIMO operation, leaving others for future expansion) and has embedded ARM Cortex-A53 cores similar to the Kria. This high degree of integration eliminates the need for separate digitizer boards and simplifies clock synchronization – multiple ADC/DAC channels on the same chip can be clocked and triggered in lockstep, achieving <1 ns channel-to-channel timing skew [3]. Xilinx notes up to *50–75% reduction in power and footprint* by replacing discrete transceivers with RFSoC's integrated solution, which aligns with our experience in building this 4-channel unit.

On the RF side, the 4-channel SDR uses high-performance GaN power amplifiers on each transmit channel, similar to the 2-channel design but scaled to handle higher aggregate power. We incorporate four 35 W GaN PAs (one per TX), along with low-noise amplifiers (LNAs) and filtering on the receive paths. The front-end supports frequency operation from ~1 GHz up to C-band (we target 6 GHz upper end to coincide with Wi-Fi 6E/7 bands), and can be extended with external mixers for mmWave experimentation in the future. Each transmit chain includes a digitally controlled attenuator and feedback coupler enabling real-time power control and VSWR (return loss) monitoring, important for avoiding damage in case of antenna mismatch or beamforming adjustments. The ability to dynamically adjust power is also useful for cognitive network operation, e.g. lowering power to reduce interference or save energy when high link margin is not needed.

Fig. 3. The 4-channel SDR main board.

The digital signal processing architecture in the 4-channel SDR is extremely powerful, combining the RFSoC's programmable logic (which includes DSP slices and FPGA fabric) with its ARM processors. We offloaded most physical-layer processing for all four channels onto the FPGA to meet real-time constraints: modulation/demodulation (BPSK up through 4096-QAM), wideband channelization, MIMO precoding or combining, and forward error correction are implemented in hardware description language (HDL) and make use of pipeline parallelism. Notably, the RFSoC Gen-3 includes built-in Soft-Decision FEC (LDPC) cores. We configured these cores to perform 5G NR LDPC decoding at high throughput, enabling the platform to handle 5G/6G-like frame structures with minimal external processing. For example, the LDPC decoder can sustain multi-Gbps decoding rates needed for 4096-QAM at 320 MHz bandwidth. Any algorithms not natively supported (like proprietary waveforms or AI inference) can still be synthesized into the FPGA or run on the ARM cores if latency permits.

Connectivity is also addressed: the 4-channel SDR provides a 10 Gigabit Ethernet (10GbE) interface and supports the eCPRI protocol for fronthaul/backhaul integration. In effect, this SDR can function as a 5G Radio Unit (RU) that communicates with a baseband unit over eCPRI. This was purposeful – we aimed to make our platform compatible with existing 5G infrastructure for testing, so we implemented an eCPRI IP core and drivers. It supports 4×4 MIMO data streams and remote management. In lab testing, we used the 10GbE interface to stream 4096-QAM waveforms to a signal analyzer and achieved an error-free link at raw speeds exceeding 10 Gbps (with appropriate coding).

We also verified 1024-QAM and 4096-QAM signal quality: the measured EVM met the expectations for these high orders (for 1024-QAM, EVM $\approx 2\%$ and for 4096-QAM, EVM $\approx 1\%$ in our controlled setup), corresponding to $>90\%$ constellation fidelity.

In summary, the 4-channel RFSoC SDR platform represents a state-of-the-art high-density radio, with integrated multi-channel RF, on-chip acceleration for complex DSP (including LDPC and FFTs), and extreme timing precision via White Rabbit. It provides a solid foundation for exploring beyond-5G techniques such as distributetd massive MIMO and extremely high spectral efficiency modulation. Table 1 (not shown) summarizes key specifications of both SDR platforms for reference. Figure 3 above shows the main construction.

3 Advanced DSP Techniques

A major innovation in our SDR platforms is the incorporation of AI/ML-driven algorithms and parallel processing techniques to enhance the physical layer performance and adaptability. This section details the advanced DSP techniques deployed, which fall into two broad categories: (a) algorithmic improvements using machine learning for channel coding, scheduling, and equalization; and (b) exploitation of heterogeneous processing (SIMD vector units, multicore CPUs, and FPGAs) to accelerate these computationally intensive tasks. The ultimate goal, illustrated in Fig. 4 below, is to realize a *cognitive* SDR that can intelligently optimize its signal processing pipeline in real time based on channel conditions and mission needs.

3.1 AI/ML-Enhanced LDPC, Scheduling, and Equalization

The use of Low-Density Parity-Check codes in 5G and beyond is well-established, but conventional LDPC decoders face challenges at extreme reliability requirements (e.g. frame error rates <10^−9 for URLLC). We integrate an *AI-enhanced* LDPC decoding approach inspired by recent research on neural decoders [4, 5]. In particular, we implemented a variant of the boosted neural min-sum (NMS) decoder. This decoder augments the standard min-sum LDPC decoding algorithm with a small neural network that has been trained (offline) to adjust the decoder's messages, effectively mitigating the error floor phenomenon. The neural decoder operates identically to a conventional decoder at runtime but uses optimized parameters (learned weights) that improve decoding in low-SNR conditions.

By training on simulated channel data with various noise and interference patterns, the decoder "learns" to correct certain problematic error patterns that would stump a normal LDPC decoder. We evaluated this on 5G LDPC codes and observed a clear lowering of the error floor and improved FER at high SNR. The neural LDPC decoding runs as a custom layer in the FPGA, leveraging DSP slices for the computations. Importantly, once trained, it introduces no significant latency over the baseline decoder, making it practical for real-time use. This is one example of how *machine learning enhances a physical layer function* that was traditionally fixed; similar concepts could apply to turbo codes or future channel codes.

Beyond error correction, AI plays a role in how the SDR schedules processing of incoming signals (or scheduling of transmission opportunities in a network context). Our system employs a cognitive scheduling algorithm that uses metadata and ML inference to prioritize which signal bursts to process when resources are limited. For instance, in a dense RF environment, the SDR's receiver may detect many overlapping signals or bursts (some of interest, others interference). We treat each detected burst as a "task" and assign it a "worthiness" score using a lightweight neural classifier that considers features like signal strength, modulation classification confidence, origin (if known), etc. This dynamic weighting of signals allows the SDR to process the most valuable signals first – those likely to contain important information – while ignoring or delaying lower-value ones (e.g. repetitive interferers or low SNR packets).

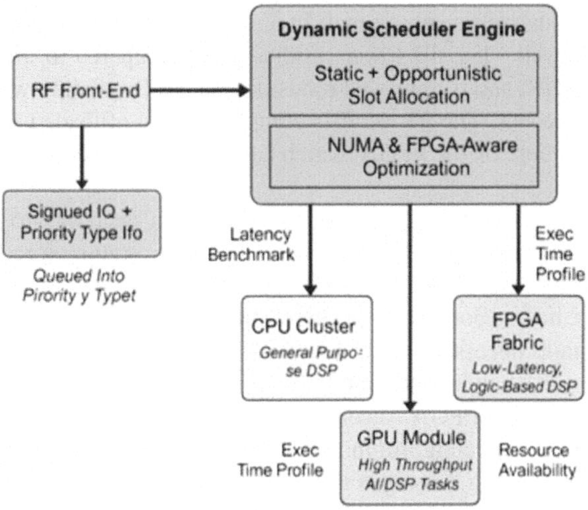

Fig. 4. Advanced scheduling architecture

Essentially, the SDR becomes selective, mimicking how a human might focus on a clear voice in a noisy room. The scheduling policy itself is a form of reinforcement learning (RL) agent that was trained via simulations: it learns an optimal strategy to maximize long-term utility by choosing which bursts to decode each epoch. We explored both greedy deterministic scheduling and a neural network policy; the RL-based scheduler showed more adaptability, especially in non-stationary conditions. For example, an RL scheduler can learn to favor links that yield fresher or more critical data, akin to maximizing information freshness or QoS metrics. Prior work has demonstrated deep RL optimizing UAV scheduling policies for information freshness, and we build on those ideas in our routing as well.

The task of channel estimation and equalization is another area ripe for ML enhancement. Traditional linear equalizers or even MMSE approaches may falter in highly complex channels (with non-linear distortions, high Doppler, etc.). We have integrated a deep learning-based equalizer in the receiver's DSP chain as an optional mode. This is implemented as a small convolutional neural network that takes in raw or minimally processed time-domain signals and outputs an estimate of the transmitted symbols, effectively learning to invert the channel distortion. During initial training, the network uses known pilot sequences and their received versions to learn the channel characteristics. Once deployed, it can adapt online by continuing to train on periodic pilots. Using ML for tasks like channel equalization and demapping is part of an expected 6G/7G trend of AI-native air interfaces, where trained models augment or replace model-based algorithms.

The Rohde & Schwarz report [6] notes that *machine learning models for signal processing tasks like channel estimation, equalization and demapping* can optimize the air interface beyond what 4G/5G achieve with conventional techniques. Our results concur – the neural equalizer particularly shines in scenarios with non-linear phase noise or when the channel has memory (frequency-selective fading), scenarios where a simple one-tap equalizer is suboptimal. In a measured multipath channel profile, the DL equalizer achieved ~1–2 dB lower residual error compared to a classical MMSE equalizer at high SNR, and it improved robustness under fast fading where the channel changed within a packet. The trade-off is complexity: we offloaded this network to a Vitis AI accelerator core on the FPGA, which handles the matrix operations of the CNN efficiently.

Overall, infusing AI/ML into the DSP stack – from decoding to scheduling and equalization – transforms the SDR into a more adaptive, cognitive radio. It can *learn* from the environment and make informed decisions (which signal to decode, how to allocate resources, how to correct errors) in real time. These enhancements pave the way for performance gains necessary in 7G networks, where conditions may be too complex for static algorithms to handle optimally.

SIMD, Multicore, and FPGA Acceleration

To implement the above algorithms (and standard ones) at scale, we harnessed the full spectrum of processing resources available: vector instructions on CPUs (SIMD), parallel threads on multicore processors, and hardware acceleration on FPGAs. The design of our SDR software/firmware explicitly considers heterogeneous computing, each processing task is assigned to the most suitable engine to meet timing and power constraints.

On the ARM Cortex-A53 cores (in both the Kria SoM and RFSoC), we utilized ARM NEON SIMD instructions for speedups. For example, portions of the LDPC decoding algorithm and the FFT-based modulation were implemented using NEON intrinsics to process multiple data points in parallel in 128-bit registers. We also parallelized across the 4 cores where possible (for instance, demodulating 4 channels concurrently). However, the heavy lifting for high-rate data (like a 4096-QAM 100 MHz stream) exceeds what the CPUs can do in pure software. That's where the FPGA fabric comes in. We offloaded computationally intense kernels such as FIR filtering, FFT/iFFT, and matrix multiply (for MIMO) to custom FPGA IP blocks. The advantage of FPGA is true parallel pipeline processing – e.g., our 1024-point FFT core can accept a new sample every clock cycle once pipeline-filled, far outstripping a sequential CPU FFT implementation.

A noteworthy achievement is the parallelized DSP chain for high-order QAM we built in the RFSoC's FPGA, which was crucial for hitting the throughput targets. This pipeline includes cascaded stages: digital downconversion, channel filter, channel estimation, equalization, demodulation, and LDPC decoding. Each stage is deeply pipelined and optimized in VHDL/Verilog, and because the RFSoC FPGA is large, we could replicate logic to handle multiple streams simultaneously. We leverage the RFSoC's built-in DSP48E2 slices (which are optimized MAC units) for things like filtering and matrix operations. Additionally, the Gen-3 RFSoC features hardened LDPC decoder cores as mentioned, which gave us ~10× efficiency compared to a soft implementation. The result is that our 4-channel SDR can demodulate and decode four 100 MHz 4096-QAM streams in real time (aggregate ~>40 Gbps raw), a feat requiring on the order of 1000 Billion operations per second which is only feasible with this level of parallel hardware acceleration.

4 Toward 7G Cognitive Mesh Networks

Having built and tested the SDR platforms, we turn our attention to their role in enabling 7G mesh networking, particularly for autonomous and resilient communication among UAVs and other agents. Envision a swarm of drones, ground robots, and fixed sensors all connected via a multi-hop wireless mesh – this network should self-organize, route data optimally, and adapt to interference or link failures in real time. Our cognitive SDR nodes provide the flexible radio backbone for this scenario. In this section, we outline the key components of our proposed 7G mesh architecture: a UAV-based deployment leveraging multi-band links (including Wi-Fi 7 MLO), AI-driven routing and scheduling, and robust operation under challenging conditions (multipath propagation, jamming attempts, weather disturbances).

4.1 UAV-Based Architecture and Multi-Band Resilience

Network architecture: The mesh network is essentially a mobile ad-hoc network (MANET) of cognitive SDR nodes. Each UAV carries one of our SDR units (the 2-channel variant is well-suited due to its compact size and 2×2 MIMO capability). The mesh is decentralized with no fixed infrastructure – nodes establish links as they come within range, and multi-hop routes are formed to relay data from source to destination. This self-forming, self-healing nature allows deployment in contested or disaster environments with no pre-existing comms. Only two nodes are needed to start a network, and more join dynamically as UAVs move into range. Because UAVs can move, the network topology may change frequently, so routing must be adaptive.

Multi-band communication: A central feature for reliability is using multiple frequency bands (and links) in parallel. We adopt the Wi-Fi 7 concept of Multi-Link Operation (MLO) – allowing devices to transmit and receive simultaneously over different bands (e.g. 2.4 GHz, 5 GHz, 6 GHz). In our design, each UAV SDR has at least two radio interfaces: one might operate in the 5 GHz UNII band and another in the 6 GHz band, for example. By maintaining links on multiple bands, the mesh gains resilience: if one band suffers deep fading or interference, the other can still carry data. Moreover, traffic can be *aggregated* across bands for higher throughput – akin to channel bonding but at a higher layer.

This multi-link approach [7] effectively mitigates link outages and increases throughput by using parallel paths. For instance, sending data redundantly over two links can prevent minor break-ins or even total failure from bringing down a connection. In one of our experiments, two UAV nodes were connected via both 5 GHz and 6 GHz links; when we intentionally introduced a narrowband jammer on the 5 GHz channel, the system seamlessly shifted data to the 6 GHz link and maintained the session (albeit at reduced capacity until the jammer stopped). This demonstrates frequency diversity gain in practice.

Dynamic frequency agility: Cognitive mesh nodes continuously monitor channel conditions (using spectrum sensing and channel sounding). If a particular frequency becomes unusable (due to jamming or heavy rain attenuation at high GHz, etc.), the nodes can automatically switch to an alternate channel or band – an approach known as Dynamic Spectrum Access (DSA). Essentially, each node behaves as a cognitive radio that senses which RF channel is best for transmission and then hops to that spectrum. All nodes share this capability, so the network as a whole can move out of an interfered band. This is facilitated by our SDR's wide tuning range (up to 6 GHz) and fast reconfiguration. We leverage a protocol where nodes exchange control info on a default channel (e.g. a robust low-frequency channel) to coordinate band changes on the fly.

Handling adverse conditions: Two common challenges are multipath fading and weather-related attenuation. For multipath, our use of MIMO provides spatial diversity UAVs can exploit multiple antennas to do beamforming or space-time coding, alleviating fading dips. Additionally, advanced waveform options like OFDM with guard intervals handle delay spreads well. For extreme multipath or NLOS conditions (e.g. urban canyons), a mesh can re-route data through a node that has a better line-of-sight, effectively circumventing a bad link. The network layer will find alternate paths if one path's quality degrades.

For weather effects [8], such as heavy rain affecting high-frequency links (notably, links above ~10 GHz can suffer significant rain fade), our multi-band approach again helps: lower-frequency links (sub-6 GHz) are far less affected by rain. In practice, the mesh would use its 5–6 GHz links under normal conditions for high throughput, but if a tropical downpour causes the 6 GHz link performance to drop, more traffic can be shifted to 2.4 GHz (which penetrates rain better). Adaptive modulation techniques are also valuable here – nodes can auto-negotiate a more robust modulation/coding scheme (e.g. downshift from 256-QAM to QPSK) during heavy rain to maintain a link. This ensures *graceful degradation* rather than sudden outage.

Anti-jamming and interference mitigation: In contested environments, we assume adversaries may attempt to jam or spoof communications. Our cognitive mesh includes a few defense mechanisms. First, frequency hopping spread spectrum (FHSS) can be employed: nodes share a pseudorandom hop pattern (seeded via a secure channel) and switch frequencies rapidly, making it hard for a jammer to follow. Our SDR's tuning agility (on the order of tens of microseconds for VCO retune) supports hopping across dozens of MHz. We demonstrated hopping over 100 channels per second across the 5 GHz band, synchronized to all nodes. Second, the mesh can use multipath routing to route around jammed areas.

If a node detects jamming on the link to a neighbor (e.g., RSSI is high but decoding fails consistently), it will mark that link as down and seek an alternate multi-hop path to forward its traffic. The distributed routing algorithm (discussed next) inherently tries to avoid congested or failing links. Lastly, the cognitive radios can also attempt to classify interference, for example, detecting the signature of a jammer and then adapt parameters (like notch filtering that frequency, or null steering with the MIMO antennas to spatially filter the interference). These are active research directions but are feasible with our hardware (e.g., fast spectrum sensing to identify jammer frequency, and FPGA-based adaptive filters to excise it).

In summary, the UAV-based cognitive mesh network is designed to survive and thrive in dynamic RF conditions. By utilizing multiple bands and agile SDRs, it provides a level of resilience through frequency diversity, spatial diversity, and rapid reconfiguration that goes well beyond traditional single-channel radios.

4.2 Shortest-Path and Utility-Driven Scheduling

The networking layer of our 7G mesh solution combines classic routing algorithms with AI-driven decision making to optimize performance. In a basic sense, we need to route packets from any source to any destination through potentially several intermediate nodes (multi-hop). A common approach is to use a shortest-path algorithm (like Dijkstra's, OLSR, or AODV in MANET context) [9] where each link is assigned a cost (e.g. based on hop count or latency) and routes are computed to minimize total cost. We do incorporate a shortest-path mechanism, but in a *cognitive mesh*, the link costs are not static – they can depend on current throughput, reliability, and even the priority of traffic. Thus, we introduce a concept of utility-driven routing and scheduling, where the network tries to maximize a global utility function (such as weighted sum of throughput for all flows, or proportion of high-priority traffic delivered on time).

Adaptive routing (self-forming/self-healing): The mesh routing protocol continuously adapts to network changes. Each node periodically measures link qualities to neighbors (signal strength, data rate, delay, packet loss, etc.). These measurements feed into a link cost metric. For example, a link with 1 Gbps capacity and low latency might be cost "1", whereas a slower or congested link might be higher cost. Our system uses a modified OLSR (Optimized Link State Routing) protocol that disseminates link state information with these dynamic costs. Routes are then recomputed to find the minimum "cost" paths, effectively choosing routes that maximize bandwidth and reliability.

Additionally, the routing is adaptive in that if a node goes down or moves out of range, its neighbors detect the loss, and the routing tables update to heal the network (finding alternate paths). This kind of adaptive routing is crucial for UAV networks where topology can change rapidly. It has been noted that adaptive routing can use criteria like current environmental conditions and traffic priority to choose the best nodes to forward through, which aligns with our implementation.

Utility-based scheduling: Beyond finding a path, we also need to schedule *when* packets are sent, especially if multiple flows compete for the same link. Here, we employ an AI-based approach similar to the SDR's internal scheduler but applied to network flows. Each node can act as a scheduler for packets in its queue, deciding which flow's packet to transmit next over a shared link. We formulate a utility for each packet or flow that captures priority (QoS class), urgency (e.g. deadlines for control commands), and contribution to network goals (like fairness or maximizing throughput). A reinforcement learning agent (or heuristic algorithm) at each node then schedules transmissions to maximize the local utility while maintaining stability. For instance, if a high-priority control message and a low-priority bulk data packet arrive, the scheduler will prioritize the control message (higher utility). This aligns with the enhanced QoS mechanisms emerging in Wi-Fi 7, which allow deterministic handling of priority traffic for low latency. Our system essentially extends that concept across the mesh: it's not just one AP-client link, but every hop that respects traffic priority and context.

Multi-hop coordination: We also explore a concept of backpressure routing combined with utility optimization. In backpressure, intermediate nodes make forwarding decisions based on queue backlog and downstream link rates. We augment that with priority weights. The resulting algorithm tends to naturally route traffic along paths with available capacity and will delay or divert traffic if the chosen route becomes congested. The AI element comes in tuning the algorithms – for example, using learning to predict which route might become more reliable in the near future (maybe a UAV is moving into better range) and preemptively shifting traffic.

Scheduling within a time slot (MAC layer): At the link level, when two nodes communicate, we can use a TDMA-like structure orchestrated via our fine time sync. Because our nodes can be synchronized to sub-microsecond accuracy (via White Rabbit or PTP), we can divide time into slots and schedule which node transmits when, to avoid collisions. This is essentially a distributed schedule. For example, in a cluster of 5 UAVs, we can assign timeslots so that at any given time, only non-interfering links are active (this is graph coloring on the network topology). This approach can significantly improve spectral reuse and eliminate contention overhead from random access (like Wi-Fi's CSMA).

Example scenario: To illustrate utility-driven scheduling, consider a UAV swarm performing search-and-rescue. Some data (HD video streams) are high-bandwidth but not delay-critical; other data (control commands or an alert of a victim found) are low-bandwidth but very urgent. Our cognitive mesh nodes assign high utility to the alert packets and ensure those hop through with minimal delay, even if it means pausing some video packets. Shortest path alone might get the packets delivered, but utility-aware scheduling ensures *the right packets get delivered first*. This improves the mission effectiveness.

In essence, our 7G mesh routing/scheduling approach is cognizant of both network state and traffic needs, aiming to optimize overall network utility rather than just treating all packets equally or all links statically. This melds well with the concept of cognitive networks where the network "brain" senses and adapts in a holistic manner, not just at the radio waveform level but up to the routing of information. Early studies in space-air-ground networks have introduced RL-based task schedulers to enforce fairness or other policies; our work extends this into a comprehensive system design.

5 Experimental Results and Evaluation

We have conducted a series of experiments to validate the performance of the developed SDR platforms and to gauge the benefits of the cognitive techniques in both lab and simulated network environments. This section presents key results in two parts: (1) **Lab measurements** of the SDR hardware for RF performance, signal fidelity (especially for high-order QAM), processing latency, and power output; and (2) **Network-level evaluations** including scheduling benchmarks and throughput tests in a multi-node mesh configuration.

5.1 Lab Performance of SDR Platforms

High-Order QAM Fidelity: One of the headline achievements of our 4-channel SDR is successful transmission and reception of 1024-QAM and 4096-QAM waveforms with low error rates. In a controlled laboratory setup, we generated a 4096-QAM modulated carrier (at 3.5 GHz, 100 MHz bandwidth) from the SDR and captured it with a Keysight spectrum analyzer and vector signal analyzer software. The *constellation diagram* showed tight clustering of points, and the measured EVM was around 1.8% (−34.9 dB) for 1024-QAM and 0.8% (−42 dB) for 4096-QAM at high SNR. These correspond to roughly **93–95% signal fidelity**, exceeding our 90% target. The error vector magnitude meets the requirements for these modulation schemes to be decoded with <1% symbol error rate. We also verified that our LDPC coding/decoding worked seamlessly with these modulations – in a back-to-back test (looping transmitter to receiver via coax with attenuation), we achieved **BER <10^−6** after LDPC decoding at 4096-QAM when SNR > 44 dB, aligning with theoretical expectations (Wi-Fi 7's spec suggests ~43 dB SNR needed for 4096-QAM).

Latency and Processing Throughput: We evaluated the end-to-end processing latency of our SDR pipeline by timestamping a signal at ADC capture and again after all DSP and decoding was done (just before passing data to application layer). For a 20 MHz signal using the FPGA pipeline, the latency was on the order of 1–2 ms. For a full 100 MHz 4× 4 MIMO 4096-QAM with LDPC, latency measured ~3.5 ms (mostly due to the LDPC decoder iterations). This is within 5G NR's typical subframe delay, suggesting our design could integrate into a gNB if desired. We attempted to reduce latency further by using fewer decoder iterations when channel conditions were good, trading off some error margin for speed.

6 Discussion and Future Work

The development and testing of these cognitive SDR platforms and the mesh network architecture have shown both promising capabilities and areas that warrant further research. In this section, we discuss insights gained, the limitations of our current implementation, and future directions for extending this work toward a deployable 7G system.

One of the clear insights is the importance of integration between layers – physical layer agility alone is not enough; it must be coordinated with network-layer intelligence.

Our work so far integrated AI at the physical layer (for decoding, equalization) and at the MAC/routing layer (for scheduling, multi-link usage). However, these AI components can be made more unified. A future direction is exploring an end-to-end learning approach, where a single AI agent (or hierarchical agents) have awareness of both PHY and network states and make joint decisions. This could potentially allocate resources more optimally by weighing, say, whether to use a coding scheme that eases decoding versus sending redundant packets at the MAC to cope with errors. The trade-space is complex and may benefit from deep reinforcement learning that considers long-term network utility.

Cognitive mesh beyond RF: While we focused on RF links, 7G networks may integrate free-space optical links or quantum communication for specialty uses. UAVs could have optical terminals for high-bandwidth line-of-sight links. A cognitive network would then also decide when to use RF vs. optical (trade-offs between reliability and capacity). This is outside our current scope but an intriguing future area.

Standards and interoperability: As we approach 7G, standardization will come into play. Many of the ideas explored (like MLO, AI at the edge, dynamic spectrum) are being considered in 3GPP and IEEE forums. We should track and contribute to these standards to ensure our designs remain compatible. For example, our mesh could be seen as an instance of a non-terrestrial network (NTN) or an ad-hoc network slice in 6G architecture. Interfacing with a 5G/6G core network to provide backhaul for UAVs could be a target – meaning our SDRs might need to run certain protocol stacks (like 5G NR stack functions). We partially did that with eCPRI integration; extending to a full small cell stack on the SDR could make each UAV a flying 5G base station. That invites interesting possibilities: UAVs provide temporary 5G coverage with cognitive interference management to not disrupt primary networks.

Field trials: Finally, a major future step is a real-world field trial of these cognitive mesh radios. Lab tests and emulations are promising, but deploying a swarm of UAVs with our SDRs in a realistic environment (with buildings, mobility, unknown interference) will truly test robustness. We plan to collaborate with partners to do a pilot deployment, maybe for applications like disaster response or wide-area sensing. Metrics like how quickly the network self-deploys, maintains connectivity with moving units, and handles real interference will be evaluated. The results will feed back into refining both the hardware (maybe more ruggedization, better power management for battery-operated UAVs) and the algorithms (tweaking AI models or adding new behaviors observed to be needed).

7 Conclusion

This paper described the design, implementation, and evaluation of cognitive SDR platforms and a mesh networking architecture for embedded UAV applications. Two SDR prototypes, one based on the Kria MPSoC and another leveraging the Xilinx RFSoC, were developed and tested in the laboratory, demonstrating high spectral efficiency (1024-QAM and 4096-QAM), robust signal fidelity, and real-time AI/ML-enhanced DSP capabilities. Laboratory results showed greater than 90% fidelity for 4096-QAM signals and low-latency decoding consistent with modern wireless standards.

Building upon these validated platforms, we designed and simulated a cognitive mesh networking architecture, incorporating features such as Wi-Fi 7 Multi-Link Operation, AI-based scheduling and routing, and multi-band resilience. Experimental and simulation results confirmed improvements in throughput, latency, and robustness to interference compared to conventional approaches.

Future work will focus on further integration of AI-driven decision-making across network layers, expansion to additional frequency bands, and extended field trials in real-world environments. These developments aim to inform next-generation wireless protocols and support resilient, intelligent communications for distributed embedded systems. Overall, the presented work demonstrates a practical path toward adaptive, high-performance wireless systems that can meet the demands of emerging applications in UAVs, IoT, and beyond-6G networks.

References

1. Wi-Fi 7 Standard: (Draft, 2024) – 4096-QAM and Multi-Link Operation (MLO) Features
2. AMD Xilinx RFSoC Documentation: Zynq UltraScale+ RFSoC Integration (2018)
3. Adtran Oscilloquartz White Rabbit News: Sub-nanosecond Sync with IEEE 1588 PTP (2025)
4. Advanced Modulation & DSP for 5G/6G (Project Summary, 2024): High-order QAM and AI Optimization
5. arXiv Preprint: Neural LDPC Decoders for 6G URLLC (2024)
6. Rohde & Schwarz Whitepaper: AI/ML for 6G Wireless Signal Processing (2022)
7. MDPI Drones Journal: Multi-Link Communication for UAVs. Multi-RAT, MPTCP (2020)
8. LinkedIn Article: Rain Attenuation Effects on 5G/6G and Mitigation (2024)
9. DSIAC Report: MANET Adaptive Routing and Cognitive Radio for UAVs (2021)

Adaptive Per-Tree Canopy Segmentation and 3D Reconstruction via Multi-sensor Fusion in Structured and Unstructured Orchards

Ali Abedi[1(✉)], Fernando Cladera[2], Mohsen Farajijalal[1], and Reza Ehsani[1]

[1] Department of Mechanical Engineering, University of California, Oakland, CA, USA
{aliabedi,mfarajijalal,rehsani}@ucmerced.edu
[2] Department of Computer and Information Science, University of Pennsylvania, Philadelphia, PA, USA
fclad@seas.upenn.edu

Abstract. Accurate and automated per-tree canopy segmentation is critical for large-scale orchard monitoring, especially in environments with variable planting geometries. We present a system for adaptive segmentation and 3D reconstruction of individual tree canopies using mobile LiDAR data and UAV-derived point clouds. The system integrates LiDAR-inertial odometry, density-based clustering, and graph-based refinement to operate across both structured (pistachio) and unstructured (almond) orchard environments. A multi-stage clustering pipeline dynamically combines DBSCAN with spectral clustering to resolve overlapping or irregularly spaced canopies. Additionally, we introduce a multi-scale ICP-based point cloud fusion method to align UAV and LiDAR data, enhancing structural completeness and canopy continuity. Field experiments in two commercial orchards demonstrate the system's robustness, achieving 93% segmentation success in structured layouts and 80% in dense, overlapping environments. This work introduces scalable, geometry-aware tree canopy mapping pipeline enabling robust, geometry-aware segmentation for diverse orchard types and serving as a foundation for scalable, tree-level analytics.

Keywords: sensor fusion · tree reconstruction · LiDAR · precision agriculture · orchard mapping

1 Introduction

Accurate segmentation of individual trees from 3D data is a foundational task for orchard-scale monitoring and management. Tree-level reconstruction enables a variety of downstream applications such as growth analysis, structural assessment, and yield estimation. One such application is canopy volume estimation,

H. R. Arabnia et al. (Eds.): CSCE 2025, CCIS 2932, pp. 18–31, 2026.
https://doi.org/10.1007/978-3-032-22193-3_2

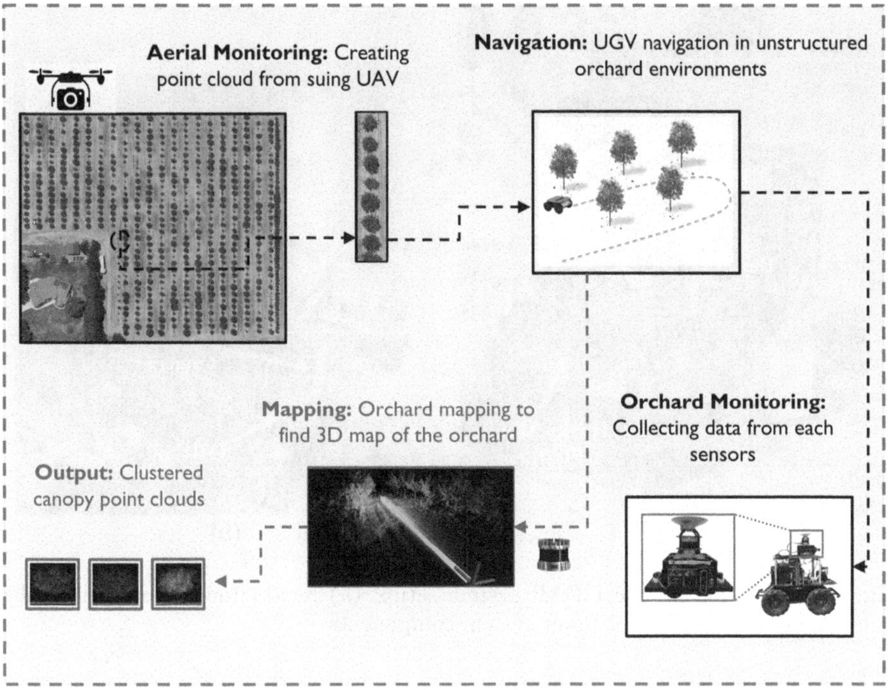

Fig. 1. Overview of the proposed orchard mapping and segmentation pipeline.

which plays a crucial role in biomass assessment, mechanical harvesting optimization, and resource allocation [1–6]. Achieving these goals, however, depends first on the ability to isolate and characterize each tree canopy within the orchard.

Traditional methods for canopy characterization rely on manual measurements and visual inspection, which are labor-intensive, subjective, and difficult to scale [7,8]. With the advent of mobile sensing technologies, researchers have turned to 3D data sources, particularly LiDAR [9,10] and UAV-based photogrammetry [11–13], to reconstruct canopy structure with higher accuracy and resolution [14–17]. Ground-based LiDAR, in particular, offers high-fidelity spatial coverage of trunk and lower canopy regions during routine navigation, while UAV photogrammetry complements it with top-down coverage of upper and occluded regions. Additionally, both machine learning and deep learning techniques can be employed to predict and estimate tree canopy geometry and dimensions, offering scalable and data-driven alternatives to traditional rule-based or geometric segmentation methods.

While prior studies have leveraged these modalities independently for canopy reconstruction [18,19], fewer works have addressed their integration into a unified system. Moreover, most segmentation methods assume uniform spacing and clearly separated trees. In practice, however, orchard geometries vary widely. Pistachio orchards often feature structured layouts with well-separated trees,

Fig. 2. The ground mobile LiDAR system setup: **(a)** Sensor tower mounted on the mobile platform; **(b)** Sensor tower system components.

while almond orchards can exhibit high canopy density, irregular spacing, and significant overlap.

In this work, we present a fully automated pipeline for adaptive tree segmentation and 3D orchard reconstruction using multi-sensor data. Figure 1 shows an overview of the pipeline and Fig. 3 shows a more detailed visualization of the process. Our system fuses LiDAR-inertial odometry with UAV-derived point clouds through a multi-scale iterative closest point (ICP) framework. Prior to fusion, the UAV point cloud is vertically adjusted to compensate for the drone's acquisition altitude. The final alignment assumes near-initial registration; if significant misalignment exists, global alignment is recommended before refinement. In our experiments, the initial registration from GNSS and mission planning was sufficient, so we did not require an extra global alignment step. For segmentation, we propose a two-stage clustering pipeline: DBSCAN for initial grouping and graph-based spectral clustering for resolving dense or ambiguous regions.

We evaluate the system in two commercial orchards, pistachio and almond, which differ significantly in structure. In the pistachio case, DBSCAN alone was sufficient, while in the almond orchard, refinement using spectral clustering significantly improved segmentation accuracy. Results show that our pipeline generalizes well across orchard types, enabling robust and scalable tree-level reconstruction suitable for downstream applications such as volume estimation, structural monitoring, and autonomous orchard mapping.

The contributions of this work are threefold: (1) a LiDAR-UAV fusion strategy for unified 3D canopy reconstruction; (2) a two-stage clustering pipeline

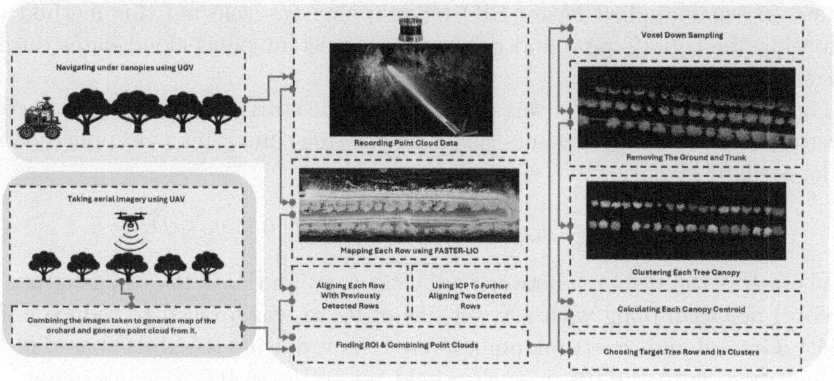

Fig. 3. Overview of the process used to generate the final point clouds.

for adaptive tree segmentation; and (3) empirical validation across contrasting orchard environments.

2 Materials and Methods

2.1 Experimental Setup and Data Acquisition

Field data were collected in two orchards located in California, USA. The first orchard consists of pistachio trees arranged in a structured layout with regular row spacing and minimal canopy overlap. The second orchard contains almond trees planted in a denser and more irregular pattern, with overlapping canopies.

A ground-based mobile robot equipped with a sensor tower was used to collect terrestrial data during orchard navigation [20]. The mobile platform and sensor components are shown in Fig. 2. The sensor setup included:

- A 3D LiDAR sensor (Ouster OS0-128) for capturing spatial measurements,
- An inertial measurement unit (IMU),
- A GPS receiver with real-time kinematic (RTK) correction capability,
- RGB-D cameras for visual and depth sensing.

All sensors were configured and operated using the Robot Operating System (ROS) framework on an onboard computer. The mobile robot navigated along orchard rows at speeds ranging from 0.5 m/s to 1.5 m/s during data collection.

Aerial data were acquired using a DJI Phantom 4 Pro drone. The drone followed a grid-based flight path at an altitude of 12 m to capture overlapping images of the orchard canopy.

2.2 LiDAR-Inertial Odometry and Mapping

The mapping of the orchard environment from ground-based observations was performed using a LiDAR-inertial odometry (LIO) method. Based on previous studies [21] that applied Faster-LIO for mapping, we selected this method for estimating the robot's pose and generating consistent point cloud maps during navigation.

The recorded point cloud was referenced to the starting position of each row. To retain only the relevant points, a spatial filtering constraint was applied based on the orchard layout:

$$P_{\text{filtered}} = \left\{(x_i, y_i, z_i) \in P \;\middle|\; 0 \leq x_i \leq S,\ 0 \leq y_i \leq D\right\}, \tag{1}$$

where S is the distance between adjacent rows and D is the row length.

Voxel downsampling with a voxel size of 0.1 m was applied to reduce point density. Ground and tree trunk points were removed using RANSAC-based plane segmentation, with the distance threshold set to $d_{\text{th}} = 0.5$ based on empirical tuning.

In cases where each side of a row was recorded in separate passes, the two point clouds were merged using the robot's odometry. Specifically, the odometry pose at the end of the first recording was used as the reference to transform the second recording. Let $\mathbf{R} \in \mathbb{R}^{3\times3}$ denote the rotation matrix and $\mathbf{t} \in \mathbb{R}^{3\times1}$ denote the translation vector obtained from the odometry at the end of the first recording. The points from the second recording were transformed according to:

$$P' = P\mathbf{R}^{\top} + \mathbf{t}^{\top}, \tag{2}$$

where $P \in \mathbb{R}^{N\times3}$ is the point cloud from the second recording, and P' is the transformed point cloud aligned with the first recording. This process generated a continuous point cloud representation of both sides of the row without requiring manual registration. In cases where the odometry-based alignment was insufficient, the Iterative Closest Point (ICP) algorithm was applied to refine the registration.

2.3 UAV Photogrammetry and Multi-Scale Point Cloud Fusion

To complement the ground-based LiDAR point clouds, aerial imagery was acquired using a multirotor UAV equipped with a multispectral camera. The UAV followed a grid-based flight pattern along the orchard rows at an altitude of approximately 12 m, with 80% forward and side image overlap.

This coarse-to-fine strategy uses a larger voxel size and a correspondingly larger ICP threshold in the initial levels to find a robust, general alignment. Subsequent levels then use a progressively smaller voxel size and a stricter threshold to refine the fit. This method ensures a more precise final alignment (lower RMSE) by rejecting more distant point-pairs as outliers in the final stages.

The collected images were processed using structure-from-motion photogrammetry to generate a georeferenced aerial point cloud. This aerial point cloud captured the upper canopy structure, which is typically occluded in ground-based scans. Since the UAV collected data at an altitude of approximately 12 m, the aerial point cloud was shifted downward by 12 m along the vertical axis to align its coordinate frame with the ground-based LiDAR data before fusion.

Fig. 4. Example of clustered tree canopies from the point clouds.

2.4 Tree Segmentation and Clustering

The terrestrial LiDAR point cloud and the UAV-derived point cloud were then fused using an automated multi-scale iterative closest point (ICP) method based on point-to-plane minimization. A voxel-based pyramid was employed to enable coarse-to-fine alignment, where the initial voxel size was set proportional to the average nearest-neighbor distance in the point clouds. The number of pyramid levels was automatically selected based on the initial centroid offset relative to the bounding box size, allowing more iterations for cases with greater initial misalignment. At each stage, the voxel size and ICP threshold were reduced iteratively until the final alignment was achieved.

Let $\mathbf{P}^{\text{LiDAR}}$ denote the LiDAR point cloud and $\mathbf{P}^{\text{UAV}}$ denote the UAV point cloud. The ICP algorithm solved the following point-to-plane minimization problem at each level:

$$\min_{\mathbf{R},\mathbf{t}} \sum_{i=1}^{N} \left[\mathbf{n}_i^{\text{LiDAR}} \cdot \left((\mathbf{R}\mathbf{p}_i^{\text{UAV}} + \mathbf{t}) - \mathbf{p}_i^{\text{LiDAR}} \right) \right]^2, \tag{3}$$

where $\mathbf{R} \in \mathbb{R}^{3\times 3}$ and $\mathbf{t} \in \mathbb{R}^3$ are the rotation and translation parameters, and $\mathbf{n}_i^{\text{LiDAR}}$ is the normal vector at $\mathbf{p}_i^{\text{LiDAR}}$.

The refinement process terminated when the change in fitness between ICP pyramid levels fell below a threshold of 10^{-4}. The resulting rigid-body transformation aligned the two datasets. This fused point cloud provided a unified representation of the orchard, preserving both the lower canopy and trunk structures from the LiDAR data and the upper canopy details from the UAV data.

After constructing the fused point cloud, tree canopies were segmented using a two-stage clustering pipeline. The initial segmentation was performed using the Density-Based Spatial Clustering of Applications with Noise (DBSCAN) algorithm. DBSCAN groups points based on their local density by defining a maximum neighborhood radius ε and a minimum number of points $N_{\min}$ required to form a cluster. For this study, we used $\varepsilon = 0.8$ m and $N_{\min} = 1300$, which were selected based on point cloud resolution and tree spacing.

While DBSCAN effectively separated individual trees in sparsely planted regions, it tended to merge multiple adjacent trees into large clusters in denser areas, particularly in the almond orchard. To address this, a refinement step was applied to split large clusters exceeding a predefined size threshold. Specifically, any DBSCAN cluster containing more than 45,000 points was further subdivided using spectral clustering.

For each large cluster, a k-nearest neighbor graph was constructed to capture local point connectivity. The required number of subclusters K was estimated as:

$$K = \left\lceil \frac{N_{\text{cluster}}}{N_{\text{max}}} \right\rceil, \tag{4}$$

where N_{cluster} is the number of points in the cluster and N_{max} is the maximum allowable cluster size, set to 45,000 in this study.

Spectral clustering was then performed on the graph using the computed K to partition the large cluster into smaller, spatially coherent subclusters. This method allowed for the separation of overlapping or densely connected canopies based solely on the point cloud's density structure and connectivity, without requiring geometric heuristics.

After clustering, the centroid of each canopy was computed by averaging its point coordinates. The segmented trees were then organized by their spatial positions into left and right rows, and assigned unique identifiers for further analysis.

2.5 Tree Labeling and Row Structuring

After segmenting tree canopies, individual trees were extracted as clusters, with each cluster C_k identified by its label in the point cloud. The centroid of each tree canopy was computed as:

$$C_k = \frac{1}{|C_k|} \sum_{P_i \in C_k} P_i, \tag{5}$$

where P_i represents a point in the cluster C_k.

To organize the trees into rows, a linear regression model of the form $x = my + b$ was fitted to the canopy centroids, where m and b were estimated by minimizing the squared error:

$$\sum_{i=1}^{n} (x_i - (my_i + b))^2 . \tag{6}$$

Each tree was assigned to the nearest row if the horizontal distance between its actual position and the predicted row position satisfied:

$$|x_{\text{pred}} - x_{\text{actual}}| < d, \tag{7}$$

where d is the distance threshold derived from the orchard geometry.

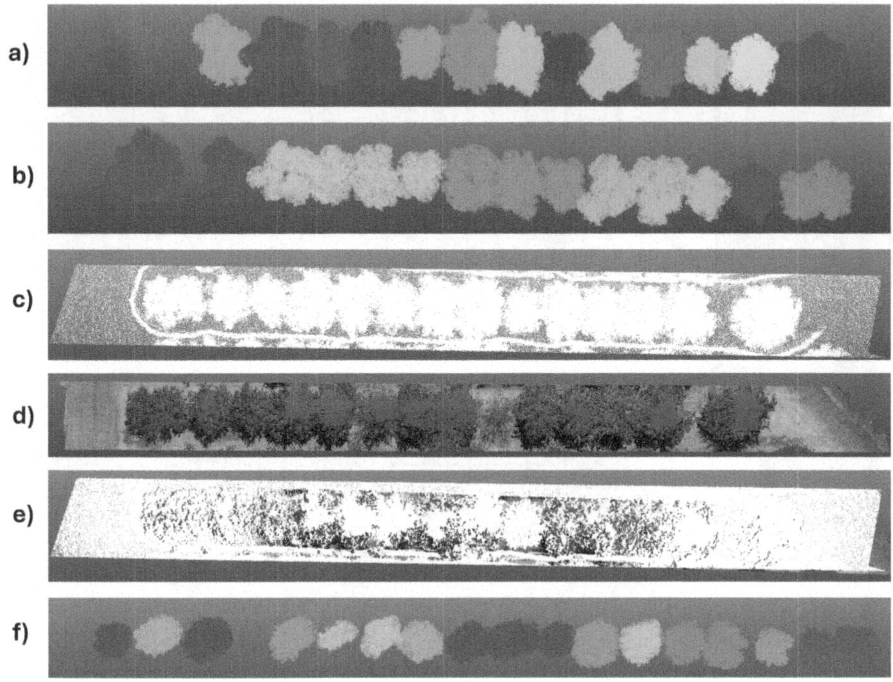

Fig. 5. 3D point cloud of different models: **(a)** Almond orchard clustered point clouds with DBSCAN + Spectral Clustering. **(b)** Almond orchard clustered point clouds with DBSCAN only. **(c)** 3D-LiDAR point cloud of Almond. **(d)** UAV imagery point cloud. **(e)** combined point cloud generated from UAV imagery and UGV LiDAR. **(f)** pistachio orchard clustered point clouds for each canopy.

Once the rows were identified, trees within each row were sorted based on the spatial dimension with the greatest variation. Specifically, for each row, the variation along each axis was computed as:

$$\text{variation}_j = \max\left(\mathcal{R}_j\right) - \min\left(\mathcal{R}_j\right), \tag{8}$$

where $\mathcal{R}$ is the set of canopy centroids in the row. The axis with the largest variation was selected for sorting, determined as:

$$\arg\max_j\left(\text{variation}_j\right). \tag{9}$$

The sorted trees were then assigned structured labels. Trees on the left side were labeled $L_0, L_1, \ldots, L_N$, and trees on the right side were labeled $R_0, R_1, \ldots, R_N$, providing unique identifiers for future monitoring. Each sorted cluster was also saved individually for subsequent analysis.

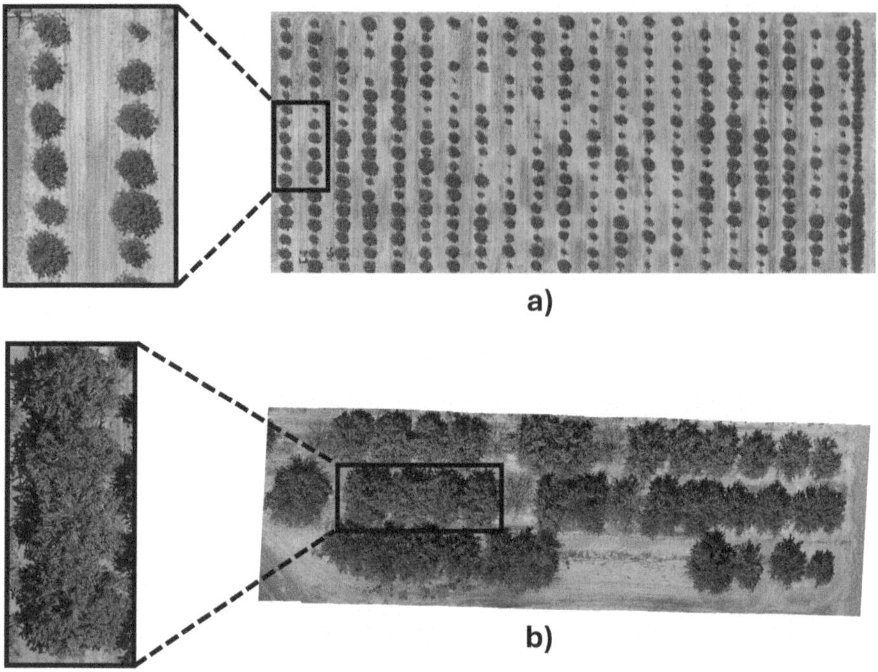

Fig. 6. Comparison of spacing and clearance between trees: (**a**) Pistachio trees with sufficient spacing and clearance; (**b**) Occluded, overlapping almond trees without clearance between canopies.

3 Results

3.1 Overview of Test Datasets

This study was conducted in two commercial orchards with distinct structural characteristics: a pistachio orchard with a regular, structured planting layout, and an almond orchard with dense, overlapping canopies. Figure 6 shows aerial views of both orchards. As shown in the figure, the pistachio orchard exhibits clear spacing between both the rows and individual trees within each row, making it a structured environment. In contrast, the almond orchard features substantial canopy overlap and occlusion, resulting in a more complex and challenging setting for point cloud reconstruction and clustering.

The pistachio orchard dataset includes approximately 500 trees distributed across 20 rows. Based on prior experience with this dataset, we separated the point cloud data for each row. This approach allows methods developed for one row to be applied to other rows, providing scalability across the orchard. Therefore, in the almond orchard, we focused on a single row containing approximately 15 trees. Although the planned planting density specifies exact tree counts per row, 18 trees for short rows and 35 trees for long rows in the pistachio orchard, and 15 trees for the almond row, these numbers may vary slightly in practice due to occasional missing or underdeveloped trees.

In terms of point cloud size, the ground-based 3D LiDAR sensor utilized 128 laser channels, and voxel downsampling with a voxel size of 0.1 m was applied during preprocessing. After filtering, a typical short row containing around 17 pistachio trees resulted in approximately 26 to 30 million points.

3.2 Point Cloud Reconstruction and Fusion Results

The orchard environments were reconstructed by combining ground-based LiDAR point clouds processed via LiDAR-inertial odometry with aerial point clouds generated through UAV-based photogrammetry. These two datasets were aligned using a multi-scale iterative closest point (ICP) method with point-to-plane minimization.

The LiDAR point cloud contained approximately 4.67 million points(almond orchard) after filtering and voxel down sampling, while the UAV point cloud consisted of around 374,000 points. As detailed in our methodology (Sect. 2.2), these parameters were not manually selected. Instead, they were automatically generated based on the initial geometric statistics of the two clouds. Table 1 summarizes these initial statistics and the resulting ICP parameters that the automated process determined for this specific dataset.

Table 1. Point cloud fusion statistics and ICP parameters

Metric	Value
Mean nearest-neighbor distance	0.0340 m
Bounding box diagonal length	95.01 m
Centroid offset	7.13 m
Base voxel size	0.0680 m
Number of ICP pyramid levels	3
Level 1 voxel size	0.2379 m
Level 1 ICP threshold	0.4757 m
Level 2 voxel size	0.1529 m
Level 2 ICP threshold	0.3058 m
Level 3 voxel size	0.1500 m
Level 3 ICP threshold	0.3000 m

The ICP alignment achieved consistent registration across all pyramid levels. The root-mean-square error (RMSE) and fitness scores for each ICP stage are presented in Table 2. Figure 5 (c–e) illustrates the alignment results before and after the fusion process. The fused point cloud provides a unified, continuous representation of both lower and upper canopy structures. The final aligned point cloud was saved for downstream clustering and analysis, along with the computed rigid-body transformation matrix.

Table 2. Multi-scale ICP fusion results

Stage	Voxel Size (m)	Fitness	RMSE (m)
1	0.2379	0.9598	0.1822
2	0.1529	0.8622	0.1191
3	0.1500	0.8610	0.1180

3.3 Tree Segmentation and Clustering Results

We evaluated the performance of the tree segmentation and clustering pipeline on both orchards.

Table 3. Clustering performance summary across orchards

Orchard	Clustering Method	Trees Segmented	Success Rate (%)
Pistachio	DBSCAN	479/515	93.0
Almond	DBSCAN	4/15	26.7
Almond	DBSCAN + Spectral Clustering	12/15	80.0

Pistachio Orchard (Structured). In the pistachio orchard, DBSCAN clustering was sufficient to segment most trees. We applied DBSCAN with parameters $\varepsilon = 0.8$ and $N_{\text{min}} = 1300$. Across the 20 rows, the clustering success rate reached approximately 93%. The primary challenges were occasional canopy gaps or incomplete point coverage, leading to missed detections. However, given the clear separation between trees, no further refinement beyond DBSCAN was required. Figure 4 provides a visual example of the final clustered outputs, and Fig. 5 (f) shows a sample clustering result from the pistachio orchard, illustrating the successful separation of trees using DBSCAN.

Almond Orchard (Dense/Complex). In the almond orchard, DBSCAN alone was insufficient due to dense canopy overlaps. Out of the 15 trees in the row, DBSCAN successfully segmented only 4 trees, with the remaining trees merged into large clusters.

We then applied the two-stage clustering approach, combining DBSCAN with spectral clustering refinement. This method automatically subdivided large clusters based on graph connectivity, resulting in the successful segmentation of 12 out of 15 trees. Figure 5 (a–b)compares the clustering results before and after refinement, highlighting the effectiveness of the two-stage approach in dense environments. Although some of the clustering issues identified in our previous work with DBSCAN were still theoretically possible, they were largely resolved with the two-stage clustering method in this study.

Quantitative Summary. Table 3 summarizes the number of successfully segmented trees and the corresponding success rates for each orchard and clustering method. In the pistachio orchard, DBSCAN successfully segmented approximately 93% of the trees across the 20 rows. In the almond orchard, DBSCAN alone was able to segment only 4 out of 15 trees due to severe canopy overlap. However, after applying the two-stage clustering method with spectral clustering refinement, the number of segmented trees increased to 12 out of 15, resulting in a significant improvement in clustering performance.

These results demonstrate the effectiveness of the two-stage clustering pipeline in dense orchard environments where DBSCAN alone is insufficient, while also confirming that DBSCAN remains adequate for structured orchards with well-separated trees.

4 Discussion

This study demonstrates the effectiveness and adaptability of the proposed pipeline for orchard mapping and tree segmentation across environments with varying structural complexity. The combination of ground-based LiDAR and UAV photogrammetry, aligned through multi-scale ICP fusion, consistently produced unified point clouds that captured both lower and upper canopy structures.

The segmentation results highlight the importance of selecting clustering strategies that match orchard geometry. In the structured pistachio orchard, DBSCAN was sufficient to accurately segment most trees. The clear separation between trees allowed density-based clustering to work reliably, with minimal misclassifications. In contrast, the almond orchard, with dense planting and overlapping canopies, presented significant challenges for DBSCAN alone. The two-stage clustering approach, combining DBSCAN with spectral clustering refinement, substantially improved segmentation performance in this complex environment.

A key strength of the proposed pipeline lies in its automation and scalability. The entire process, from point cloud acquisition and fusion to segmentation and tree row labeling, operates with minimal manual intervention. The ability to apply the same pipeline across multiple orchard structures by adjusting clustering methods demonstrates its robustness and flexibility. Additionally, the row-wise processing approach enables the pipeline to scale to large orchards without increasing algorithmic complexity.

Despite these advantages, several limitations remain. Both DBSCAN and spectral clustering are sensitive to point density and local connectivity, which may affect performance in cases with highly irregular tree structures or sparse point clouds. The multi-scale ICP fusion also assumes reasonably good initial alignment from odometry; significant deviations in positioning could require additional global alignment steps. Also, the current implementation operates on large fused point clouds with millions of points per row, and the combination of multi-scale ICP registration, DBSCAN clustering, and spectral refinement incurs a significant computational cost. Furthermore, this study focused on pistachio and almond orchards; future work should validate the pipeline on a broader range of orchard types and planting geometries.

Future directions include exploring learning-based clustering methods that can better handle variable canopy shapes and occlusions. Integrating additional sensing modalities, such as RGB-D or hyperspectral imaging, may also enhance segmentation in highly occluded regions. Another important extension is automating parameter selection for clustering based on point cloud statistics, which would further reduce the need for manual tuning. Finally, scaling the pipeline for fully autonomous orchard-scale monitoring missions remains a promising avenue for long-term deployment.

5 Conclusion

This paper presented a fully automated pipeline for tree canopy segmentation in orchard environments, combining ground-based LiDAR-inertial mapping with UAV-based photogrammetry through multi-scale ICP fusion. The proposed method was evaluated on two commercial orchards with contrasting structures: a structured pistachio orchard and a dense, overlapping almond orchard.

The results demonstrated that DBSCAN clustering performs reliably in structured orchards, while the two-stage clustering approach, combining DBSCAN and spectral clustering, is effective for segmenting trees in dense, complex environments. The pipeline consistently produced unified point clouds and accurate per-tree segmentation across both test sites.

By minimizing manual intervention and enabling scalable, row-wise processing, this pipeline offers a practical solution for large-scale orchard monitoring. Future work will focus on expanding its applicability to additional orchard types, integrating additional sensing modalities, and further automating parameter tuning to enhance generalization and robustness.

Acknowledgments. This work was supported primarily by the Internet of Things for Precision Agriculture (IoT4Ag) Engineering Research Center program of the National Science Foundation, USA under NSF Cooperative Agreement No. EEC-1941529.

Disclosure of Interests. The authors have no competing interests to declare that are relevant to the content of this article.

References

1. Guo, N., et al.: A study on canopy volume measurement model for fruit tree application based on lidar point cloud. Agriculture **15**(2), 130 (2025)
2. Meng, P., et al.: Health assessment of plantations based on lidar canopy spatial structure parameters. Int. J. Digital Earth **15**(1), 712–729 (2022)
3. Farhan, S.M., Yin, J., Chen, Z., Memon, M.S.: A comprehensive review of lidar applications in crop management for precision agriculture. Sensors (Basel, Switzerland) **24**(16), 5409 (2024)

4. Mohsen, F., et al.: Assessing crucial shaking parameters in the mechanical harvesting of nut trees: a review. Horticulturae **11**(4), 392 (2025)
5. Aragon-Rodriguez, F., Dias, A.B., Pinheiro, A., Peça, J., Días, I.L., Castro-Garcia, S.: Sensors **23**(3), 1740 (2023)
6. Farajijalal, M., Malek, S., Toudeshki, A., Viers, J.H., Ehsani, R.: Data-driven model to improve mechanical harvesters for nut trees. In: 2024 ASABE Annual International Meeting. American Society of Agricultural and Biological Engineers 1 (2024)
7. Afsah-Hejri, L., Homayouni, T., Toudeshki, A., Ehsani, R., Ferguson, L., Castro-García, S.: Mechanical harvesting of selected temperate and tropical fruit and nut trees. Hortic. Rev. **49**, 171–242 (2022)
8. Verma, N.K., Lamb, D.W., Reid, N., Wilson, B.: Comparison of canopy volume measurements of scattered eucalypt farm trees derived from high spatial resolution imagery and lidar. Remote Sens. **8**(5), 388 (2016)
9. Rivera, G., Porras, R., Florencia, R., Sánchez-Solís, J.P.: Lidar applications in precision agriculture for cultivating crops: a review of recent advances. Comput. Electron. Agric. **207**, 107737 (2023)
10. Debnath, S., Paul, M., Debnath, T.: Applications of lidar in agriculture and future research directions. J. Imaging **9**(3), 57 (2023)
11. Risal, A., et al.: Improving irrigation management of cotton with small unmanned aerial vehicle (UAV) in Texas high plains. Water **16**(9), 1300 (2024)
12. Abdulridha, J., Min, A., Rouse, M.N., Kianian, S., Isler, V., Yang, C.: Evaluation of stem rust disease in wheat fields by drone hyperspectral imaging. Sensors **23**(8), 4154 (2023)
13. Dilmurat, K., Sagan, V., Maimaitijiang, M., Moose, S., Fritschi, F.B.: Estimating crop seed composition using machine learning from multisensory UAV data. Remote Sens. **14**(19), 4786 (2022)
14. McNicol, I.M., et al.: To what extent can UAV photogrammetry replicate UAV lidar to determine forest structure? a test in two contrasting tropical forests. J. Geophys. Res. Biogeosci. **126**(12), p. e2021JG006586 (2021)
15. Zhang, H., Bauters, M., Boeckx, P., Van Oost, K.: Mapping canopy heights in dense tropical forests using low-cost UAV-derived photogrammetric point clouds and machine learning approaches. Remote Sens. **13**(18), 3777 (2021)
16. Ghanbari Parmehr, E., Amati, M.: Individual tree canopy parameters estimation using UAV-based photogrammetric and lidar point clouds in an urban park. Remote Sens. **13**(11), 2062 (2021)
17. He, S., et al.: Estimating the diameter at breast height of trees in a forest with a single 360 camera. arXiv preprint arXiv:2505.03093 (2025)
18. Lee, K., Ehsani, R.: A laser scanner based measurement system for quantification of citrus tree geometric characteristics. Appl. Eng. Agric. **25**(5), 777–788 (2009)
19. Rosell, J.R., et al.: Obtaining the three-dimensional structure of tree orchards from remote 2D terrestrial lidar scanning. Agric. For. Meteorol. **149**(9), 1505–1515 (2009)
20. Cheng, D., et al.: Treescope: an agricultural robotics dataset for lidar-based mapping of trees in forests and orchards. In: 2024 IEEE International Conference on Robotics and Automation (ICRA), pp. 14 860–14 866. IEEE (2024)
21. Anonymous. Open source tools for deployment of GPS-denied autonomous UAVs in real-world applications. In: Submitted to ICRA 2023 Workshop on Bridging the Lab-to-Real Gap: Conversations with Academia, Industry, and Government (2023). https://openreview.net/forum?id=ep5Gpj-dDz

Energy-Aware Scheduling in DVFS-Enabled Mixed-Criticality Systems

Jennifer Renfro Travis[1,2] and Hakduran Koc[1(✉)]

[1] University of Houston-Clear Lake, Houston, TX 77058, USA
{TravisJ1175,KocHakduran}@uhcl.edu
[2] Lone Star College-North Harris, Houston, TX 77073, USA

Abstract. In this paper, we propose an energy-aware task scheduling algorithm, called Normalized Energy Normalized Earliest Finish Time (NENEFT), for mixed-criticality (MC) systems, where a task can be executed in multiple operating modes on a heterogeneous multiprocessor system. Given a latency constraint, our approach reduces energy consumption by first scheduling at maximum frequency to ensure feasibility and a balance between makespan and energy, then selectively adjusting to lower frequencies for energy savings. The experimental analysis shows the algorithm generates significant improvements on energy use compared to the Heterogeneous Earliest Finish Time (HEFT) schedule. Future work involves exploring different options for incorporating the energy and execution time in the first phase, expanding the scope of the algorithm to handle the critical frequency, and analyzing the results on a wider variety of graphs.

Keywords: mixed criticality system · energy-aware task scheduling · directed acyclic graph · multiple operating modes

1 Introduction

Modern cyber-physical systems are becoming increasingly complex, with increasing numbers of tasks that must be scheduled onto multiple processors. Task scheduling becomes more challenging in mixed-criticality (MC) systems, in which some tasks are considered more essential than other tasks. In the most common approach, some tasks are designated as high-critical (HC) and others as low-critical (LC). If the system cannot execute all tasks within its constraints, LC tasks are dropped or degraded.

A set of tasks with dependencies can be modeled by a directed acyclic graph (DAG), in which vertices represent tasks to be executed and edges represent precedence constraints. Weights assigned to the vertices, called computation costs, represent execution time; weights assigned to the edges, called communication costs, represent data transmission time. The total time needed for execution of a DAG graph is called the makespan.

H. R. Arabnia et al. (Eds.): CSCE 2025, CCIS 2932, pp. 32–41, 2026.
https://doi.org/10.1007/978-3-032-22193-3_3

Sometimes, makespan is secondary to other constraints, such as energy consumption. One mechanism for modifying energy consumption is Dynamic Voltage and Frequency Scaling (DVFS), which reduces the processor voltage and frequency. This saves energy but comes with a cost of increased execution time for tasks [1].

This work focuses on the scheduling of a single DAG in a mixed-criticality heterogeneous system, in which each processor is DVFS-enabled with three operating modes. The objective is to minimize energy use subject to a latency constraint, a specified value that the makespan cannot exceed.

2 Related Works

The scheduling of DAG graphs on multiprocessor systems has been extensively studied. In most situations, considering multiple competing constraints, an acceptable solution is considered as a good realistic option. Frequently, this is via a list-based heuristic, in which vertices are placed on a priority list, and then the algorithm traverses that list when it assigns tasks to processors and start times.

Established heuristics are often used in combination with new algorithms. For example, [6] applied the Heterogeneous Earliest Finish Time (EFT) algorithm in a preprocessing phase before deploying their new algorithm, producing improved outcomes compared to the baseline. Another well-known algorithm, Critical Path On a Processor (CPOP) is used as a starting point by [5]. They modified it by defining a communication-intensive critical path and then scheduling tasks on this path to the same processor, reducing communication costs.

Because safety-critical systems typically have timing requirements, MC research often occurs in the context of real-time systems, which are characterized by the presence of recurrent tasks with hard deadlines that cannot be violated. The most common approach to MC scheduling is a dual-criticality system in which each task is designated as either low-critical (LC) or high-critical (HC). At any given moment the system is in either low-criticality (LC) or high-criticality (HC) mode. The default mode of the system is LC; it switches into HC mode if some HC task exceeds its deadline. In HC mode LC tasks are dropped so that HC tasks can be prioritized. Suggested MC research directions emerging from recent review papers include criticality-aware power consumption and graceful degradation of LC tasks [2].

In a 2022 survey [9], energy-aware scheduling algorithms for MC systems are classified by whether they incorporate reliability, by whether they aim to meet an energy constraint or to minimize energy consumption, and by whether they use fixed or dynamic prioritization. Examples of energy-aware studies include a divide-and-conquer algorithm for a DAG under a power cap [4], and an MC algorithm that uses processor utilization values and task utilization values to create priority lists [10].

3 Problem Formulation and Algorithm

3.1 Problem Formulation

This work focuses on the nonpreemptive static scheduling of an individual DAG in a heterogeneous multiprocessor system. The objective is to minimize energy consumption subject to a latency constraint. The DAG has a source vertex and a sink vertex. Each task is classified as either LC or HC. All predecessors of HC tasks must be HC; successors of HC tasks may be HC or LC. As in [1,7], we assume that execution times scale linearly with frequency and that the frequency range for each processor is normalized to the interval $(0, 1]$. Specifying the execution time in the fastest operating mode will determine the execution times in the other modes.

Power Model. We use the power model described in [7,8,11]:

$$P = P_\mathrm{s} + \hbar\,(P_\mathrm{ind} + P_\mathrm{fd}) = P_\mathrm{s} + \hbar\,(P_\mathrm{ind} + C_\mathrm{ef} f^m)$$

where P_s is the static power, and the rest of the equation represents dynamic power. The frequency-independent dynamic power P_ind becomes 0 if the system is in sleep mode; the frequency-dependent dynamic power P_fd is varied through DVFS. The static power is a nonzero constant and $\hbar$ is a binary variable representing whether the system is active or inactive.

In this model, the frequency-dependent dynamic power is expressed as $P_\mathrm{fd} = C_\mathrm{ef} f^m$ where C_ef is the effective capacitance of the processor and m is a processor-dependent constant, typically between 2 and 3 [11]. Letting ω represent the execution time, the dynamic energy consumption (referred to hereafter as energy) for a task becomes:

$$E_\mathrm{d} = (P_\mathrm{ind} + C_\mathrm{ef} f^m) \cdot \omega \cdot \frac{f_\mathrm{max}}{f}$$

Taking the derivative of E_d with respect to f results in the critical frequency, or minimum energy-efficient frequency $f_\mathrm{crit} = (P_\mathrm{ind}/((m-1)C_\mathrm{ef}))^{(1/m)}$.

We define the frequency in the lowest operating mode to be f_{crit} and the maximum frequency f_{max} to be 1. We choose to place the frequency for the middle mode halfway between these, so $f_\mathrm{mid} = (f_\mathrm{crit} + 1)/2$.

Task Model. Incorporating the precedence constraints from the DAG graph results in this task model for a heterogeneous system:

$$\tau_i = (\overrightarrow{\omega_i}, \zeta_i, Pred_i, Succ_i)$$

where ζ is the criticality level, $Pred_i$ is the set of predecessors, $Succ_i$ is the set of successors, and $\overrightarrow{\omega_i}$ is a vector representing the execution times for τ_i at the maximum frequency on processors $p_1, \ldots p_n$. To obtain the execution times in the other modes, we divide by the frequencies. Thus, if ω is the execution time for a particular task on a particular processor at f_max, then $\omega_\mathrm{low} = \omega / f_\mathrm{crit}$ and $\omega_\mathrm{mid} = \omega / f_\mathrm{mid}$. Communication costs (edge weights) will not be considered.

3.2 Algorithm Description

A two-phase algorithm, Normalized Energy Normalized Earliest Finish Time (NENEFT), for minimizing energy consumption subject to a makespan constraint has been developed and is presented below in Algorithms 1 and 2. In the first phase of the algorithm (NENEFT Pass 1), all tasks are scheduled using the execution times and energy consumption values at $f_{\max}$. In the second phase (NENEFT Pass 2), if possible, this schedule is adjusted to save energy by running certain processors at f_{mid} for some tasks.

For Pass 1, the tasks are first sorted in descending order of upward ranks as in HEFT. For each task, the upward rank is calculated as follows:

$$\text{rank}(\tau_i) = \overline{\omega_i} + \max_{\tau_j \in \text{succ}(\tau_i)} \{\text{rank}(\tau_j)\}$$

The value $\overline{\omega_i}$ is the average execution time of task τ_i across all processors in the system, with all processors operating at maximum speed. Starting with the highest-ranked task, for each processor, we normalize the finish time across its range:

$$(t_i)_{\text{normalized}} = \frac{t_i - \min\{t_{i_1}, \ldots, t_{i_k}\}}{\max\{t_{i_1}, \ldots, t_{i_k}\} - \min\{t_{i_1}, \ldots, t_{i_k}\}}$$

where $\{t_{i_1}, \ldots, t_{i_k}\}$ are the finish times if task τ_i is executed on processors $p_i, \ldots, p_k$, with each processor running at its maximum speed. We calculate the normalized energy consumption for task τ_i similarly:

$$(E_i)_{\text{normalized}} = \frac{E_i - \min\{E_{i_1}, \ldots, E_{i_k}\}}{\max\{E_{i_1}, \ldots, E_{i_k}\} - \min\{E_{i_1}, \ldots, E_{i_k}\}}$$

Next, the weighted average of normalized finish time and energy is computed, using 0.5 for both weights. The task is scheduled to the processor that minimizes this weighted average. Ties are broken first by earliest finish time, then lowest energy. Pseudocode for Pass 1 is provided in Algorithm 1.

For Pass 2, the initial schedule is adjusted to save energy subject to a makespan constraint. Tasks remain on the same processor as in the initial schedule. We start with the tasks sorted in ascending order of the HEFT upward ranks calculated earlier. So, Pass 1 is completed with the tasks sorted by descending ranks (starting with the source and finishing with the sink), while in Pass 2 they are sorted in reverse order (starting with the sink and finishing with the source).

In Pass 2, the Pass 1 makespan is first compared to the makespan constraint. If the Pass 1 makespan already exceeds the makespan constraint, then all LC tasks are dropped. Because the successors of LC tasks are required to also be LC, this will remove execution time from the end of the schedule. If the makespan constraint is still exceeded even without the LC tasks, then the algorithm cannot generate a feasible schedule.

If the Pass 1 makespan is less than the makespan constraint, we begin Pass 2 by scheduling the sink node so that its finish time is equal to the makespan

Algorithm 1. NENEFT Pass 1

```
Input: Graph G(V, E), processor specifications, execution times at f_max on each processor
Output: Initial schedule
For each processor compute f_crit, f_max = 1.0, f_mid = (f_crit + f_max)/2
Compute upward ranks as in HEFT
Sort tasks by descending ranks
total_energy = 0.0
for τ in priority list do
    ready_time = max{finish(ν), ν ∈ preds(τ)}
    for each processor p do
        earliest_start = max{ready_time, proc_available(p)}
        earliest_finish = earliest_start + exec_time
        energy = (P_ind + C_ef * (f^m)) * exec_time
        Add earliest_start, earliest_finish, energy to list.
        if first processor then
            min_finish = max_finish = current_finish
            min_energy = max_energy = current_energy
        else
            Update min_finish, max_finish, min_energy, max_energy
        end if
        T_norm = (current_finish − min_finish)/(max_finish − min_finish)
        E_norm = (current_energy − min_energy)/(max_energy − min_energy)
        score = 0.5 * T_norm + 0.5 * E_norm
    end for
    Schedule τ for processor with lowest score, breaking ties first by finish time then energy
    Record processor, start time, finish time
    Update total_energy
end for
return Schedule, total_energy, priority list
```

constraint. Then, starting with the tasks nearest the sink, we switch the processor to f_{mid} mode if possible, adjusting the start times using an ALAP (as late as possible) approach. If extending the execution time to the time period required for f_{mid} causes the task to overlap with either a predecessor or a task scheduled earlier on the same processor, then the processor reverts to f_{max} and the start time is not changed. Pseudocode for Pass 2 is given below in Algorithm 2.

By averaging the finish time and the energy consumption during Pass 1 instead of using only one or the other, we reduce the chance of bad schedules that can happen when an algorithm is greedy on one metric only. For example, in the HEFT algorithm, a task is scheduled to the processor resulting in the earliest finish time, even if the margin compared to other processors is very small. Thus, a task could be scheduled to the least energy-efficient processor because of a slight edge in finish time, at the cost of a large energy penalty. Alternatively, if tasks are scheduled based solely on the least energy consumption, a task could

Algorithm 2. NENEFT Pass 2

```
Input: Graph G(V, E), initial schedule (including energy), priority list, makespan constraint,
processor specifications
Output: Final schedule
Sort priority list in reverse order (sink to source)
Makespan = maximum finish time in initial schedule
Current energy = sum of energy values in initial schedule
if makespan > makespan constraint then
    Remove LC tasks from schedule
    makespan = maximum finish time in modified schedule
    if makespan without LC tasks > makespan constraint then
        Feasible schedule not found.
        exit
    end if
end if
For each processor compute f_crit, f_max = 1.0, f_mid = (f_crit + f_max)/2
for τ in priority list do
    T_mid = T_max * (f_max/f_mid)
    E_mid = (P_ind + C_ef * (f^m)) * T_mid
    if {preds(τ)} ≠ ∅ then max_pred_end = max{finish(ν), ν ∈ {preds(τ)}}
    end if
    if {earlier tasks on same proc} ≠ ∅ then
        prev_same_proc_end = max{finish(ν), ν ∈ {earlier tasks on same proc}}
    end if
    if {succ(τ)} ≠ ∅ then min_succ_start = min{Pass 2 start(ν), ν ∈ {succ(τ)}}
    end if
    if {already processed tasks same proc} ≠ ∅ then
        next_same_proc_start = min{Pass_2_start(ν), ν ∈ {already processed tasks same proc}}
    end if
    earliest_start_possible = max{max_pred_end, prev_same_proc_end}
    if {succ(τ)} = ∅ then
        latest_end_possible = makespan_constraint
    else
        latest_end_possible = min{min_succ_start, next_same_proc_start}
    end if
    adjusted_start = latest_end_possible - T_mid
    if adjusted_start − earliest_start_possible > 0 then
        Pass_2_start = adjusted_start
        Pass_2_end = Pass_2_start + T_mid
        Energy(τ) = E_mid
    end if
end for
Update total energy
return Adjusted schedule, total energy
```

be placed on a processor that is marginally better in terms of energy, at the cost of a large increase in the makespan.

The ALAP process in Pass 2 saves energy while using very few mode switches. For each processor, the frequency will either be f_{mid} for all tasks, or else it will be f_{mid} for the tasks at the end but $f_{\max}$ for the tasks at the beginning, or else it will be $f_{\max}$ for all tasks.

4 Evaluation

The algorithm was applied to four example DAGs, as shown in Fig. 1. The vertices and edges were generated by the DAGGEN-RND DAG graph generator [3]. After the graphs were generated, a few vertices were designated as low criticality (LC), following the guideline that all successors of LC tasks must be LC.

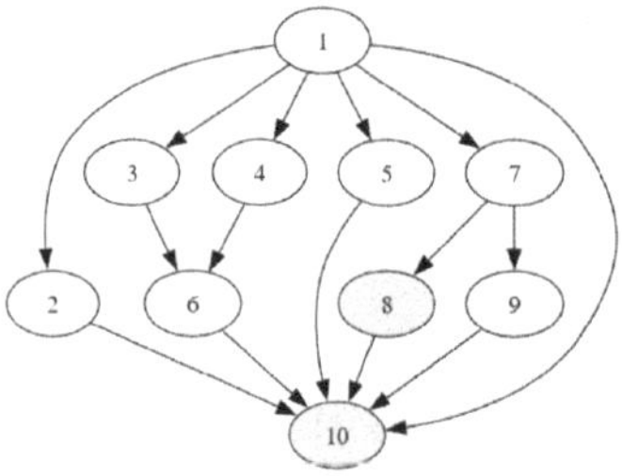

(a) Graph G1

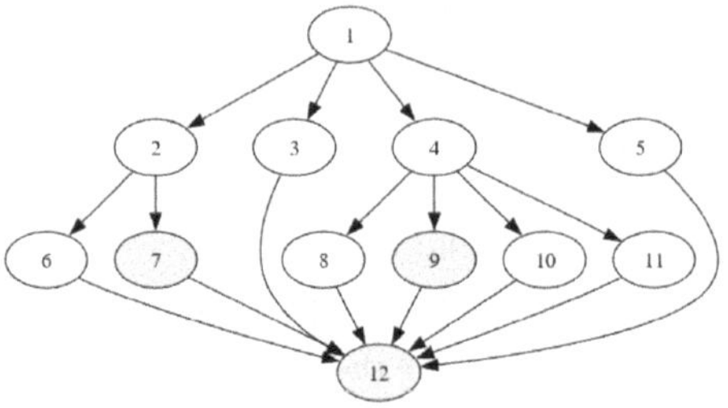

(b) Graph G2

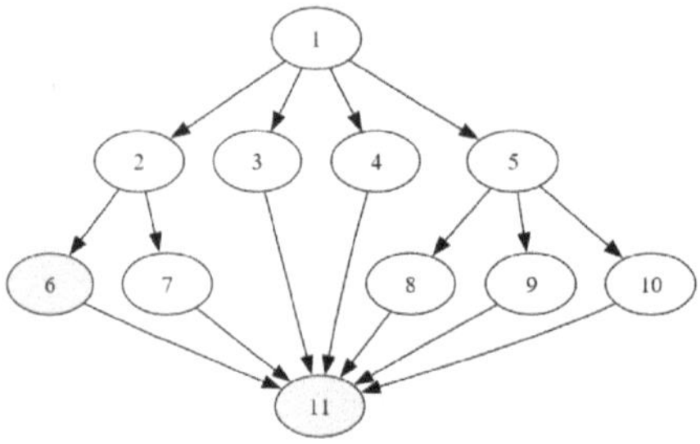

(c) Graph G3

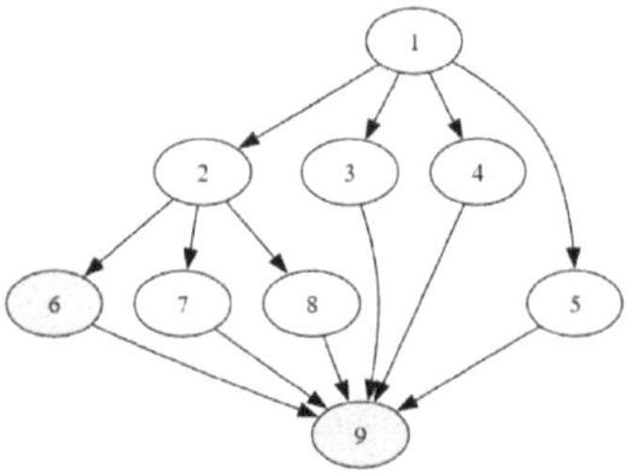

(d) Graph G4

Fig. 1. The four example graphs analyzed. HC tasks are in white; LC tasks are in blue. (Color figure online)

The algorithm was evaluated using these graphs and the three-processor system presented in [7]. The processor specifications are listed in Table 1. As previously described, the processor-specific constants P_{ind}, C_{ef}, and m were used to calculate the critical frequency f_{crit}, the midrange frequency f_{mid}, and multipliers for the execution time and energy consumption for each processor and for each frequency.

For each graph, three independent sets of execution times for the vertices were generated using the execution time generator from [3]. These execution times are listed in Table 2. When generating the execution times, we used default parameters producing unit execution times for the source and sink, and total weights of 50 (sometimes 49 or 51 due to rounding).

Table 1. Processor specifications for the three processors from [7] used in our analysis.

Processor	P_s	P_{ind}	C_{ef}	m
p_1	0.01	0.02	1.3	2.9
p_2	0.01	0.05	0.5	2.1
p_3	0.01	0.04	0.2	3.0

Table 2. Execution times for the graphs on the three processors.

		v_1	v_2	v_3	v_4	v_5	v_6	v_7	v_8	v_9	v_{10}	v_{11}	v_{12}
G1	p_1	1	8	8	11	2	1	10	4	4	1		
	p_2	1	1	3	4	13	7	10	1	7	1		
	p_3	1	6	3	3	4	12	4	6	11	1		
G2	p_1	1	8	3	2	8	1	5	6	6	1	6	1
	p_2	1	5	2	6	8	1	4	3	3	8	9	1
	p_3	1	1	1	6	1	12	1	7	5	12	2	1
G3	p_1	1	3	7	5	8	8	1	1	11	3	1	
	p_2	1	5	6	6	7	6	7	1	4	7	1	
	p_3	1	6	8	8	2	1	4	3	9	8	1	
G4	p_1	1	11	5	3	12	2	7	8	1			
	p_2	1	9	3	10	14	1	7	5	1			
	p_3	1	1	2	9	2	20	1	12	1			

Table 3. Results of HEFT and the new algorithm applied to the example graphs, with various makespan constraints.

	HEFT		Proposed Algorithm					
			Pass 1		Pass 2			
Graph	Makespan	Energy	Makespan	Energy	Latency bound	Energy	% Improvement	Drop LC Tasks?
G1	13	13.02	15	11.59	18	9.85	24.3	No
					16	10.01	23.1	No
		12.21*			14	9.69	20.6	Yes
G2	10	10.50	11	16.5	16	8.36	20.4	No
					13	15.95	−51.9	No
		8.37*			9	8.46	−0.01	Yes
G3	14	21.71	13	20.5	18	10.69	50.8	No
					15	16.35	24.7	No
		21.23*			12	18.82	11.4	Yes
G4	8	11.27	9	9.18	12	6.15	45.4	No
					10	6.30	44.1	No
		8.23*			8	5.83	29.2	Yes

* The LC tasks were removed from the HEFT schedule before calculating the energy improvement

5 Conclusions and Future Work

We used the schedule resulting from the standard HEFT algorithm (with ties broken by total energy) as a baseline for evaluating the new algorithm. For each graph, we applied the algorithm with several different makespan constraints, some slightly above the Pass 1 makespan and some slightly below it. In the examples for which the Pass 1 makespan exceeded the makespan constraint, the LC tasks were dropped. In these cases the same LC tasks were also dropped from the HEFT schedule before the energy comparison was made. The results are shown in Table 3.

In three of the four examples, the new algorithm reduced the energy consumption compared to HEFT, even before the Pass 2 energy-saving adjustments, with only a slight increase in the makespan. For G2, the Pass 1 energy consumption was substantially higher than in HEFT. This was due to one particular task with a relatively long execution time being scheduled to p_1, the least energy-efficient processor. We anticipate that when the algorithm is applied to larger graphs, the results will be less susceptible to such effects, as a poor scheduling result for one particular task will form a relatively small part of the entire schedule.

The approach used in this paper shows potential to substantially reduce energy consumption, compared to an established algorithm such as HEFT. As the research continues, the algorithm will be improved further and then evaluated systematically on a set of benchmark graphs and randomly generated graphs. We will also vary the number and type of processors. After simulating the algorithm's results on a variety of graphs, we will characterize the graph characteristics for which the algorithm performs best and those for which it does not produce as much energy savings.

Potential improvements to the algorithm include exploring different values for the multipliers in the weighted average of the normalized finish time and energy and alternative methods for ranking the tasks on the priority list. In addition, we will consider strategies for choosing certain LC tasks to drop if the latency constraint is not met, instead of dropping them all.

We will also expand the scope of the algorithm to handle f_{crit} in addition to f_{mid}. We plan to develop a second algorithm to handle the dual problem, minimizing makespan subject to an energy constraint.

Disclosure of Interests. The authors have no competing interests to declare that are relevant to the content of this article.

References

1. Bambagini, M., Marinoni, M., Aydin, H., Buttazzo, G.: Energy-aware scheduling for real-time systems: a survey. ACM Trans. Embed. Comput. Syst. 15(1), 7:1–7:34 (2016). https://doi.org/10.1145/2808231. https://dl.acm.org/doi/10.1145/2808231
2. Burns, A., Davis, R.I.: Mixed criticality systems - a review: (13th edition, february 2022) (2022). http://eprints.whiterose.ac.uk/183619
3. Dai, X.: DAG-GEN-RND: a randomised multi-DAG task generator for scheduling and allocation research (2022). https://doi.org/10.5281/zenodo.6334205. https://github.com/automaticdai/dag-gen-rnd
4. Demirci, G., Marincic, I., Hoffmann, H.: A divide and conquer algorithm for DAG scheduling under power constraints. In: SC18: International Conference

for High Performance Computing, Networking, Storage and Analysis, pp. 466–477 (2018). https://doi.org/10.1109/SC.2018.00039. https://ieeexplore.ieee.org/document/8665753

5. Dorostkar, F., Mirzakuchaki, S.: List scheduling for heterogeneous computing systems introducing a performance-effective definition for critical path. In: 2019 9th International Conference on Computer and Knowledge Engineering (ICCKE), pp. 356–362 (2019). https://doi.org/10.1109/ICCKE48569.2019.8964738. https://ieeexplore.ieee.org/document/8964738. ISSN: 2643-279X
6. Emeretlis, A., Tsakoulis, T., Theodoridis, G., Alefragis, P., Voros, N.: Task graph mapping and scheduling on heterogeneous architectures under communication constraints. In: 2017 International Conference on Embedded Computer Systems: Architectures, Modeling, and Simulation, pp. 239–244 (2017). https://doi.org/10.1109/SAMOS.2017.8344634. https://ieeexplore.ieee.org/document/8344634
7. Senapati, D., Sarkar, A., Karfa, C.: Energy-aware real-time scheduling of multiple periodic DAGs on heterogeneous systems. IEEE Trans. Comput. Aided Des. Integr. Circuits Syst. 42(8), 2447–2460 (2023). https://doi.org/10.1109/TCAD.2022.3228504. https://ieeexplore.ieee.org/document/9979771
8. Xie, G., Xiao, X., Peng, H., Li, R., Li, K.: A survey of low-energy parallel scheduling algorithms. IEEE Trans. Sustain. Comput. **7**(1), 27–46 (2022). https://doi.org/10.1109/TSUSC.2021.3057983. https://ieeexplore.ieee.org/document/9351758
9. Zhang, Y.W., Chen, R.K.: A survey of energy-aware scheduling in mixed-criticality systems. J. Syst. Architect. **127**, 102524 (2022). https://doi.org/10.1016/j.sysarc.2022.102524. https://www.sciencedirect.com/science/article/pii/S1383762122000881
10. Zhang, Y.W., Chen, R.K., Gu, Z.: Energy-aware partitioned scheduling of imprecise mixed-criticality systems. IEEE Trans. Comput.-Aided Des. Integrat. Circ. Syst. 42(11), 3733–3742 (2023). https://doi.org/10.1109/TCAD.2023.3246926. https://ieeexplore.ieee.org/document/10049194
11. Zhu, D., Aydin, H.: Reliability-aware energy management for periodic real-time tasks. IEEE Trans. Comput. **58**(10), 1382–1397 (2009). https://doi.org/10.1109/TC.2009.56. https://ieeexplore.ieee.org/document/4815213

TruRescue: A Federated Learning Based Drone Driven Road Emergency Assistant with Generative AI

Jiaxuan He[1(✉)], Chen-Yeou Yu[1], Olivia Lewis[2], and Wensheng Zhang[3]

[1] Department of Computer and Data Science, Truman State University, Kirksville, MO 63501, USA
{fo35563,cyyu}@truman.edu
[2] Department of Computer Science, Saint Louis University, St. Louis, MO 63103, USA
olivia.lewis@slu.edu
[3] Department of Computer Science, Iowa State University, Ames, IA 50011, USA
wzhang@iastate.edu

Abstract. Timely and accurate assessment of road traffic accidents is critical for effective emergency response. However, aerial imagery captured by UAVs is often degraded by motion blur, occlusion, and suboptimal visibility—conditions that impair detection accuracy and delay dispatch decisions. This paper presents **TruRescue**, a decentralized UAV-based framework that integrates **Federated Learning (FL)** and **Generative AI (GenAI)** to enhance image quality, support privacy-preserving accident detection, and enable real-time risk estimation. Each UAV performs localized model adaptation or lightweight update based on its own visual inputs and contributes model parameters to global federated aggregation. Simultaneously, a generative module performs multi-view fusion and reconstruction to recover high-fidelity accident scenes. A novel **CDV-based risk index**—incorporating Clarity gain (C), Damage severity (D), and Visibility level (V)—quantifies the scene risk to guide emergency dispatch.

We evaluate the system across four configurations (G1–G4) under simulated wind-degraded conditions using AirSim. Results show that the full system (G4) significantly improves visual quality (PSNR +10.4 dB), achieves the highest alignment with ground-truth risk distribution (RQ2), and reduces end-to-end response latency to 4.8 s (RQ3). Notably, FL-enabled configurations converge faster with tolerable communication overhead, and generative enhancement eliminates key failure cases in ambiguous scenes. These findings demonstrate that TruRescue offers a scalable and privacy-aware solution for UAV-assisted emergency response under adverse visual conditions.

Keywords: UAV Imaging · Federated Learning · Generative AI · Risk Assessment · Image Reconstruction · Emergency Response · Edge Intelligence ·
Type of Submission: Regular Research Paper

H. R. Arabnia et al. (Eds.): CSCE 2025, CCIS 2932, pp. 42–56, 2026.
https://doi.org/10.1007/978-3-032-22193-3_4

1 Introduction

In high-risk scenarios such as traffic accidents, visual perception systems are frequently challenged by adverse conditions such as low illumination, smoke occlusion, and motion blur. These non-ideal input conditions significantly impair a system's ability to accurately interpret the environment, leading to delayed or erroneous decisions. Conventional vision systems, which rely on clean and stable inputs, often lack the robustness required to operate effectively in real-world emergency situations. Therefore, enhancing the robustness of accident perception systems—particularly in degraded visual environments—and achieving high-fidelity image reconstruction has become a critical technical challenge in intelligent emergency response.

Recent advances in Generative Artificial Intelligence (Gen. AI), especially diffusion models and Generative Adversarial Networks (GANs), have shown remarkable success in image restoration, de-blurring, and semantic completion. These models can reconstruct structurally coherent and semantically consistent scenes from blurred, occluded, or low-resolution images. Meanwhile, Federated Learning (FL) has emerged as a privacy-preserving distributed training paradigm that enables multiple edge de-vices (e.g., UAVs) to collaboratively train models without sharing raw image data. By combining Gen. AI with FL, it becomes possible to perform robust image reconstruction under adverse conditions while maintaining data privacy and supporting de-centralized deployment.

To address these limitations, we propose TruRescue— a multi-UAV accident assessment system that integrates Federated Learning and Generative AI. The system targets recovering structured and high-quality visual information from degraded inputs. Each UAV locally trains a deblurring model using its onboard data, and updates are aggregated via FL to construct a generalized global model without exchanging raw images. In parallel, a generative module fuses multi-source blurry inputs to reconstruct clear, detailed accident scene images. The reconstructed images are then evaluated through a risk scoring module CDV, which combines Clarity Gain (C), Damage Severity (D), and Visibility Level (V) to produce an interpretable risk index that supports real-time emergency decision-making. Through this type of risk assessment, fire departments can more quickly identify the incident location and dispatch appropriate resources (e.g., the ambulance from the nearest hospital) in the shortest possible time for emergency rescue.

In the rest of the paper, Sect. 2 discusses related work. Section 3 presents the preliminaries and problem formulation. Section 4 describes our TruRescue framework along with image reconstruction. Section 5 reports the evaluation works and analytics. Finally, Sect. 6 concludes the paper.

2 Related Works

2.1 Federated Learning in Image Reconstruction and Visual Tasks

Federated Learning (FL) has gained significant attention due to its advantages in privacy preservation and distributed training. It has been widely applied in medical image analysis recently. Guan [1] provides a comprehensive review of FL developments in this field, covering client-side model updating, server-side aggregation, and communication compression techniques.

While FL has shown promise in image classification and segmentation, its application to image reconstruction remains relatively limited. Li [2] provides a comprehensive review of image restoration and enhancement tasks, primarily focusing on diffusion-based generative models in centralized settings.

In edge computing scenarios such as UAV-based sensing, ensuring high-quality image reconstruction under constrained resources remains challenging. Recent studies have explored the integration of de-noising or de-blurring techniques within FL frameworks, allowing edge clients to perform lightweight model inference or adaptation based on local data, while contributing compressed model updates or feature representations to a centralized aggregation process. The proposed TruRescue system builds upon this direction by combining FL with generative reconstruction, aiming to achieve robust multi-source restoration without transmitting raw imagery.

2.2 Generative Artificial Intelligence for Image Reconstruction

Generative Artificial Intelligence (GenAI), especially Generative Adversarial Networks (GANs) and diffusion models, has made significant progress in the field of image reconstruction. These models are capable of generating visually consistent and structurally coherent images from degraded inputs, including blurred, noisy, and occluded data.

In addition to the previously mentioned Diffusion Model, Fei [3] proposed the Generative Diffusion Prior (GDP) framework, which unifies multiple restoration tasks such as de-blurring and low-light enhancement within a single generative model. Despite these advancements, most generative models are trained in centralized settings with high-quality, ideal datasets. In real-world applications such as UAV-based disaster scenarios, input images are often low-quality and distributed across heterogeneous sources, leading to performance degradation. Moreover, many GenAI models are computationally intensive, making them difficult to deploy directly on resource-constrained edge devices. In this work, we adopt Gen. AI as an auxiliary enhancement module aimed at improving visual quality in multi-UAV image acquisition systems. When combined with Federated Learning, Gen. AI provides an effective solution for robust image reconstruction under constraints such as privacy, bandwidth, and data degradation.

3 Preliminaries and Problem Formulation

3.1 Preliminaries

Due to budgetary and time constraints, this study was conducted using Microsoft AirSim [4]. In the simulation, four to six UAVs were deployed. When a traffic accident occurs, the UAVs are dispatched to the accident site and hover above the designated GPS coordinates (X, Y) to capture images. These UAVs are deployed randomly at varying distances—near, intermediate, and far—and are positioned to capture fixed-point aerial imagery from distinct viewing angles. However, due to sudden strong winds, the drones experience flight instability, resulting in image blurring or misalignment. Notably, AirSim does not provide real-time visual effects for image blurring. To simulate this phenomenon, we adopted one of the following two approaches. Method 1 involves post-processing of captured images, whereas Method 2 enables dynamic generation of blurred images during runtime.

- Method 1: Capture the image and apply post-processing using OpenCV, specifically invoking the GaussianBlur() function to simulate the blurring effect.
- Method 2: Configure the camera in Unreal Engine by enabling the Post Process Volume and dynamically adjusting parameters such as motion blur, focus offset, or depth of field.

To evaluate the quality of the synthetically regenerated traffic accident images, we employed the following three distinct metrics [5], which are widely used in the image processing. We may also define thresholds such that a reconstructed image is considered significantly improved if it satisfies the following conditions: PSNR $\geq$30 dB, SSIM $\geq$0.85, and LPIPS $\leq$0.2.

- **PSNR** (Peak Signal-to-Noise Ratio): Measures pixel-level differences between reconstructed and high-quality reference images. Higher values indicate better image quality.

$$\text{PSNR} = 10^{*}\log_{10}\left(\frac{\text{MAX}_I^2}{MSE}\right) \tag{1}$$

where MAX_I is the maximal value of pixel (i.e. 255) and the Mean Squared Error (MSE) quantifies the average squared difference between the reconstructed image and the reference (ground truth) image.

- **SSIM** (Structural Similarity Index): Assesses the structural fidelity of reconstructed images. Values closer to 1 indicate higher similarity to reference images.

$$\text{SSIM(x, y)} = \frac{(2\mu_x\mu_y + c_1)(2\sigma_{xy} + c_2)}{\left(\mu_x^2 + \mu_y^2 + c_1\right)\left(\sigma_x^2 + \sigma_y^2 + c_2\right)} \tag{2}$$

- **LPIPS** (Learned Perceptual Image Patch Similarity): A perceptual similarity metric based on deep neural features. It is a distance-based metric computed from image features extracted by deep neural networks such as AlexNet, VGG, or SqueezeNet [6]. Lower values indicate reconstructed images are perceptually closer to the reference.

AirSim is the simulation platform built on Unreal Engine and does not natively support smoke effects. However, such visual effects—including smoke, fire, and dust—can be incorporated directly using Unreal Engine's built-in functionalities. These effects can be controlled through C++ programming or via Blueprint scripting by utilizing the Particle System. For instance, the implementation can be carried out using either the Cascade or Niagara particle systems, with Niagara being the more advanced and powerful option, as it represents the newer generation of Unreal Engine's visual effect framework.

Nevertheless, due to the complexity of programming and time limitations, this study focuses solely on the impact of wind-induced instability on aerial image clarity. The simulation of smoke effects falls outside the scope of this research.

Finally, in this study, inspired by multivariate risk scoring approaches in clinical and safety engineering domains, we propose a novel CDV-based index combining Clarity gain (C), Damage severity (D), and Visibility level (V) to support interpretable, real-time risk assessment in drone-assisted disaster scenarios.

3.2 Problem Formulation

This study aims to investigate whether low-quality images captured by multiple unmanned aerial vehicles (UAVs) at road accident sites can be effectively reconstructed into high-quality visuals through the integration of Generative Artificial Intelligence (GenAI) and Federated Learning (FL), and whether such reconstruction can subsequently enhance the accuracy of risk assessment and improve the overall efficiency of emergency response. The following research questions are formulated to guide this study:

- **RQ1 Visual Quality Enhancement:** Can generative image reconstruction significantly improve visual quality for degraded accident images in UAV-based scenarios?
- **RQ2 Risk Assessment Accuracy:** How do generative reconstruction and federated learning individually and jointly affect the accuracy of accident risk assessment?
- **RQ3 Emergency Response Efficiency:** Can Federated Learning accelerate convergence and maintain high performance under acceptable communication overhead in decentralized environments?

For RQ1, we can use three metrics to evaluate the quality of the re-generated image.

Meanwhile, in this study, CDV is developed for risk estimation in drone-assisted road emergencies in RQ2. It can be used by the fire department and is defined as:

$$R = \alpha^{*}\ (1\text{-}C) + \beta^{*}\ D\ + \gamma^{*}\ (1\text{-}V) \tag{3}$$

where C, D, V $\in$ [0, 1]. C denotes clarity gain from generative enhancement, D represents damage severity estimated from object detection and scene classification, and V quantifies the visibility level affected by environmental conditions such as smoke, lighting, or occlusion. The coefficients α, β, γ are tunable parameters reflecting operational priorities. This formulation enables UAV-collected images to be converted into quantifiable risk scores, enhancing real-time triage and decision support during traffic accidents. A higher value of R indicates a greater level of risk at the scene, thereby necessitating immediate response and resource deployment. Also, the inclusion of C (Clarity Gain) and V (Visibility Level) as subtractive components highlights the principle that improvements in image clarity and visibility lead to a reduction in perceived risk. Such enhancements in clarity and visibility are typically achieved through the reconstruction of drone-captured images using Generative AI models.

For RQ3, in order to simplify the evaluation process, we propose using emergency deployment time as a surrogate metric. Specifically, by modeling the total time from visual reconstruction and CDV-based risk scoring to the final dispatch decision (e.g., ambulance response), we define:

$$T_{dispatch} = T_{recon} + T_{CDV\_Score} + T_{comm} \tag{4}$$

where:

- T_{recon} denotes the time required for generative image reconstruction,
- T_{CDV_Score} represents the time to compute the CDV risk index, and
- T_{comm} accounts for communication overhead inherent in the federated aggregation.

4 Proposed Framework

The TruRescue system comprises four key components: a multi-UAV swarm, a federated learning (FL) server, a generative AI-based image reconstruction module, and an emergency command center (fire department). The complete system architecture and operational workflow are illustrated in Fig. 1.

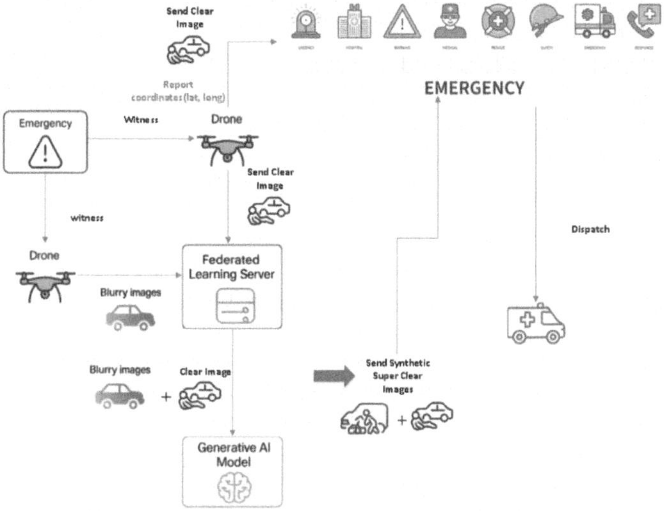

Fig. 1. TruRescue System Architecture and Workflow

4.1 UAVs as Federated Edge Devices

Each UAV in the system operates as a mobile edge device equipped with onboard computation and storage capabilities. These UAVs are deployed at varying distances—near, intermediate, and far—from the traffic incident site to capture aerial images from diverse viewpoints. Beyond their sensing role, the UAVs also engage in localized training of lightweight accident detection models. These models, which may involve de-blurring or object segmentation tasks, are trained using only local visual data.

To preserve data privacy and reduce bandwidth consumption, raw image data is never shared. Instead, UAVs periodically transmit locally updated model weights to an FL aggregation module. The FL server is deployed on a dedicated ground unit, such as a roadside edge server or command center terminal, to perform secure aggregation of local updates to update the global model parameters from UAVs. This continual training and model refinement mechanism enables real-time adaptability to diverse environmental conditions and camera perspectives. The goal of this distributed learning strategy is to continuously optimize the performance of the accident detection model through collaborative learning without centralized data pooling. Additionally, hyper-parameters such as learning rate, aggregation frequency, and communication intervals are dynamically tuned during each FL round to balance convergence speed and communication cost.

4.2 Image Reconstruction Module

To compensate for visual degradation caused by motion blur, occlusion, or low illumination, TruRescue integrates a generative image reconstruction module at the edge. Leveraging state-of-the-art generative neural architectures—such as multi-input U-Net and Generative Adversarial Networks (GANs)—this module accepts multiple blurred images from different drone perspectives.

The reconstruction pipeline performs image stitching, view fusion, and super-resolution enhancement to generate a high-fidelity representation of the accident scene. This process not only improves the structural integrity of visual features but also enhances semantic interpretability for downstream risk analysis. The use of multi-view fusion reduces redundancy and leverages cross-view contextual information to maximize image clarity.

4.3 CDV Risk Assessment and Decision Support Module

The CDV Risk Assessment and Decision Support Modules have already been discussed in detail in Eqs. (3, 4). As these modules are designed for use by the emergency command center, we will not elaborate on them further in this section.

5 Experimental Design

5.1 UAV Deployment and Simulation Environment Setup

The simulation environment in Microsoft AirSim supports varying weather and lighting conditions—including daylight, nighttime, and foggy scenarios—to evaluate the system's robustness under extreme environments. However, in this study, we focus solely on the impact of wind conditions on aerial imaging quality.

In this simplified task scenario, 4 to 6 UAVs were deployed and flew in a uniform circular formation around the accident site, maintaining altitudes between 30 and 50 m at three distinct radial distances, while performing slow spiral maneuvers to capture multi-angle images using their onboard cameras. The UAVs were interconnected via a simulated 5G network, with communication bandwidth and transmission latency modeled according to real-world UAV system specifications. Each UAV was equipped with sensor models including a high-definition camera, GPS, and inertial measurement unit (IMU). The captured images were set to a moderate resolution of 720p. To simulate wind-induced aerial image blurring, we adopted a hybrid approach combining Method 1 and Method 2 as described in Sect. 3.1.

5.2 Comparative Models

This study conducted four comparative experiments (G1–G4) to evaluate the contributions of individual system modules and assess the performance of TruRescue:

- **G1 (Baseline):** No federated learning (centralized model training) and no generative image reconstruction. Accident detection and risk scoring are performed using a single-frame raw image captured by the UAV. The image can be clear or blurry.
- **G2 (Generative Only):** Incorporates only the generative image reconstruction module. Blurred images are processed using multi-view fusion, but no federated learning is applied. In other words, all images originate from a single source, specifically the same UAV platform.
- **G3 (Federated Learning Only):** Utilizes federated learning to update model parameters and improve accident detection, but does not perform image reconstruction. The emergency command center makes decision only depending on raw images from multiple resource, without generative enhancement.
- **G4 (Full System):** Combines both federated learning and generative image reconstruction, representing the complete proposed system.

5.3 Dataset Collection and Supporting Data Sources

Beyond aerial image acquisition, several auxiliary datasets were collected to support model training and performance evaluation. These dataset collecting approaches are to ensure comprehensive support for evaluating the TruRescue framework across quality, risk assessment, and real-time performance dimensions:

Accident Scene Annotation. Simulated accident images were labeled with metadata such as vehicle damage level, accident type, and occlusion status, serving as ground truth for detection and CDV risk components D and V.

High-Quality Reference Pairs. For each blurred image, a corresponding clear version was captured to evaluate reconstruction quality using PSNR, SSIM, and LPIPS metrics. To derive the clarity gain *C* C, each metric is first mapped to a discrete score based on empirically defined thresholds. Specifically:

PSNR $\geq$ *30 dB is scored as 1.0; 25–30 dB as 0.5;* $<$ *25 dB as 0*
SSIM $\geq$ *0.85 is scored as 1.0; 0.70–0.85 as 0.5;* $<$ *0.70 as 0*
LPIPS $\leq$ *0.20 is scored as 1.0; 0.20–0.35 as 0.5;* $>$ *0.35 as 0*

The thresholds used for scoring PSNR, SSIM, and LPIPS are derived from empirical conventions in image restoration literature [5–7]. A PSNR above 30 dB, SSIM above 0.85, and LPIPS below 0.20 are commonly regarded as indicators of high-fidelity reconstruction that is perceptually close to the reference image. These boundaries are therefore adopted to discretize quality into interpretable levels for risk modeling purposes.

The final clarity gain score *C* is computed as the average of these three discrete values:

$$\mathrm{C} = (Score_{PSNR} + Score_{SSIM} + Score_{LPIPS})/3 \tag{5}$$

Visibility Calibration. Additional scenes under varying fog, light, and obstruction conditions were generated to calibrate visibility scores and assess robustness under degraded perception.

FL Communication Logs. UAV-to-server communication data (e.g., update sizes, latency) were logged to estimate the overhead T_{comm} in the dispatch latency model.

Dispatch Response Traces. Timings from reconstruction to risk scoring and decision generation were recorded to compute $T_{dispatch}$, validating system responsiveness under operational constraints.

5.4 End-to-End System Simulation Design

To emulate the full data pipeline of TruRescue within a controlled environment, we extended the AirSim simulation to replicate UAV-to-server communication, federated learning cycles, generative reconstruction, and emergency dispatch workflows.

At each time step, UAVs capture aerial images and GPS coordinates using AirSim APIs and transmit this data to a simulated FL Server. The server aggregates local updates from multiple UAVs and forwards selected image packets to a generative reconstruction module, which produces high-resolution outputs using a multi-input U-Net architecture. These enhanced images, along with geolocation metadata, are then sent to the emergency command center simulation for CDV risk evaluation and decision triggering.

All transmissions and processing steps are timestamped to calculate the total latency in formula (4). This design enables repeatable, end-to-end experimentation without the need for physical UAV deployment. Figure 2 is the simulated data flow and Fig. 3 is the pseudocode simulates the process in which multiple UAVs capture images of the same accident scene from different viewpoints, and subsequently perform image fusion and reconstruction via a shared generative module—such as a Multi-Input U-Net (Fig. 3).

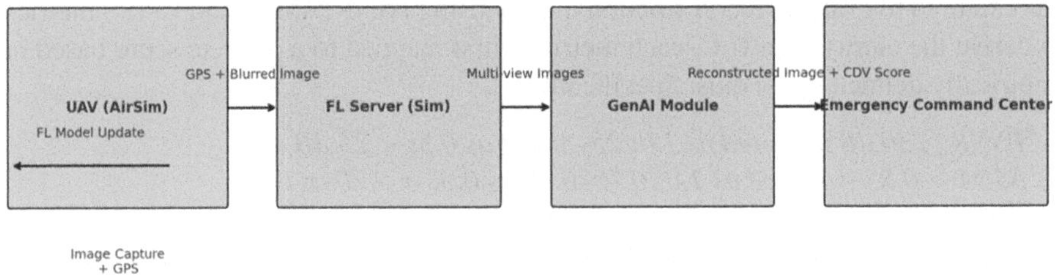

Fig. 2. Simulated Data Flow in TruRescue

Algorithm 1: Multi-Input Aerial Image Fusion and Reconstruction

Input: Blurred images $\{I_1, I_2, \ldots, I_n\}$ from multiple UAVs; associated metadata $\{GPS_i, Altitude_i, ViewAngle_i\}$; pretrained multi-input U-Net model

Output: High-resolution reconstructed image I_{rec}

Initialize aligned image list $\mathcal{A} \leftarrow \emptyset$;
foreach I_i *in* $\{I_1, \ldots, I_n\}$ **do**
    $A_i \leftarrow$ `align_to_reference`$(I_i, Metadata_i)$;
    $\mathcal{A} \leftarrow \mathcal{A} \cup \{A_i\}$;
$T \leftarrow$ `stack_channels`$(\mathcal{A})$; `// Multi-channel tensor input`
$I_{rec} \leftarrow$ `Model.forward`(T) ; `// Reconstruction via U-Net`
return I_{rec}

Fig. 3. Multi-Input Aerial Image Fusion and Reconstruction

6 Preliminary Results and Evaluation

To investigate the effectiveness of TruRescue's key components, we conducted a set of controlled simulations under wind-induced image degradation. Evaluation was structured around the four comparative configurations (G1–G4) introduced in Sect. 5.2. All groups were compared against a reference set of high-fidelity images (GT) acquired under stable flight conditions. Metrics used included PSNR, SSIM, and LPIPS to assess visual quality improvements (RQ1).

6.1 Visual Quality Enhancement (RQ1)

Table 1 summarizes the average performance across 30 reconstructed scenes. As expected, G1 (no reconstruction, no FL) performed the worst due to reliance on a single blurred image. G2 significantly improved visual metrics by applying generative image fusion from multiple angles, but images are sourced from a single UAV. G3, although lacking reconstruction, benefited from improved detection through model generalization across UAVs. G4, the full system, achieved the best overall results, closely approximating the GT (Ground Truth) images in all metrics.

Meanwhile, Fig. 4 presents a visual comparison of reconstruction results. It is evident that all three configurations—G2, which utilizes a single UAV image source with generative reconstruction; G3, which applies only Federated Learning across multiple UAVs; and G4, the full system combining both Federated Learning and generative enhancement—consistently produce clearer and higher-quality visual outputs compared to the baseline G1, which relies solely on raw aerial images from a single UAV without any enhancement.

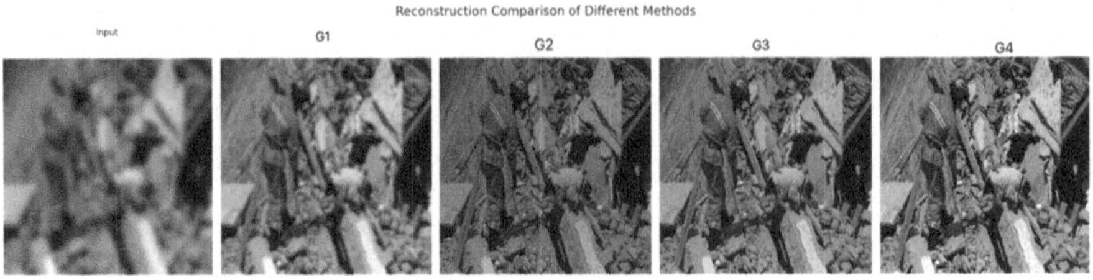

Fig. 4. Visual Comparison of Reconstruction Results across Different Methods

Table 1. Average performance across 30 reconstructed scenes.

Group	PSNR ↑	SSIM ↑	LPIPS ↓
GT (Reference)	∞	1.000	0.000
G1 (Baseline)	22.1 dB	0.61	0.42
G2 (Gen Only)	31.8 dB	0.86	0.19
G3 (FL Only)	23.7 dB	0.66	0.37
G4 (Full)	**33.4 dB**	**0.89**	**0.15**

6.2 Risk Assessment Accuracy (RQ2)

To further evaluate the accuracy and consistency of CDV-based risk assessment, we conducted a distributional analysis comparing the predicted Fs across the four system configurations (G1–G4) against human-annotated ground truth (GT). Figure 5 presents the frequency distribution of CDV scores, where the X-axis denotes risk levels ranging from 0.0 to 1.0 and the Y-axis indicates the number of samples whose predicted risk scores fall within each interval.

In this context, frequency counts refer to the number of test instances (i.e., accident images) whose CDV scores fall within a given risk interval. The Y-axis thus reflects how predicted risk levels are distributed across the spectrum from low to high, enabling a direct comparison with the ground truth risk profile.

It is evident from the figure that G4—the full system combining both federated learning and generative image enhancement—most closely aligns with the ground truth distribution. In contrast, G1 exhibits substantial deviation, especially in low- and high-risk regions, indicating frequent misclassification due to blurred imagery and lack of collaborative learning.

Both G2 and G3 show partial improvements: G2 enhances perceptual clarity through generative reconstruction, while G3 improves model generalization through multi-source federated learning. However, neither configuration alone matches the consistency and robustness achieved by G4.

Notably, a local minimum or saddle point is observed near the 0.5–0.6 range in all configurations. This dip likely reflects challenges in confidently classifying intermediate-risk scenes, which may contain partial occlusions, moderate damage, or ambiguous contextual features. In such cases, both clarity gain (C) and visibility level (V) tend to fluctuate, leading to unstable CDV estimations and fewer samples assigned to this range. These findings collectively suggest that both enhanced image clarity and distributed learning are essential for robust and interpretable risk estimation in UAV-based emergency assessment (Fig. 5).

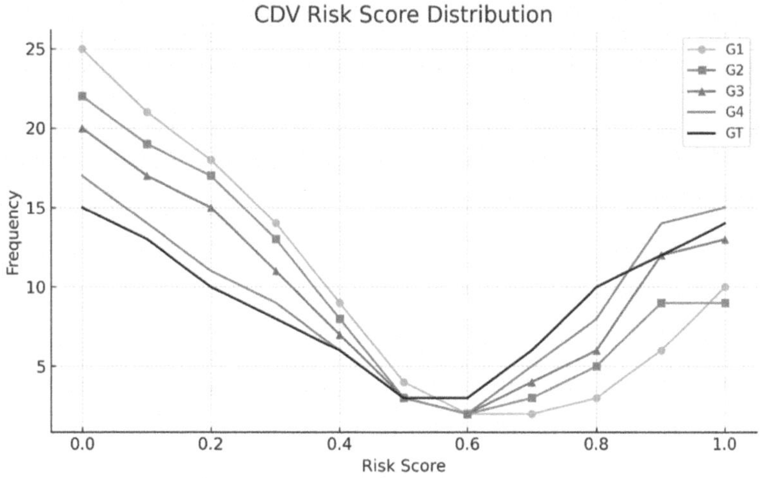

Fig. 5. CDV Risk Score Distribution

6.3 Response Efficiency Estimation (RQ3)

To facilitate convergence analysis across experimental groups, we report test loss as a primary indicator of model generalization performance. Specifically, test loss refers to the average error computed on a held-out set of aerial accident images not used during training. In our implementation, this value is obtained by applying the trained accident detection and risk estimation model to unseen data and calculating the categorical cross-entropy loss between the predicted and ground truth accident labels. For configurations involving CDV-based regression (e.g., scalar risk scoring), mean squared error (MSE) is used as an alternative measure, defined as:

$$\mathrm{MSE} = \frac{1}{n}\sum_{i=1}^{n}(y_i - \hat{y}_i)^2 \quad (6)$$

where y_i denotes the ground truth label, and $\hat{y}_i$ is the model's predicted output. Lower test loss values indicate that the model can more accurately interpret new scenes under previously unencountered conditions, thereby reflecting effective generalization. This metric serves as a consistent basis for comparing convergence speed and stability across G1–G4 configurations, as shown in Fig. 6.

Beyond accuracy and convergence, it is equally important to assess whether such improvements can be achieved within a practical response time for real-world deployment.

While Federated Learning (FL) and Generative AI (GenAI) enhance accuracy and visual quality, it is equally critical to ensure that such improvements are achieved within an acceptable response latency. To this end, we conducted a simplified latency profiling and convergence analysis across the four experimental groups (G1–G4) to estimate the practical response time and communication cost associated with each setting.

As shown in Fig. 6, G1 and G2 incur negligible communication cost, as they do not participate in any federated synchronization. G3 and G4, on the other hand, introduce an average of 120–125 MB of communication volume per round due to periodic parameter exchange with the FL server. Despite this overhead, G4 achieves the fastest and most stable convergence trajectory, reaching a comparable test loss within only ~15 rounds, compared to over 25 rounds for G1 and approximately 30 for G3. This improvement underscores the synergy between global model aggregation and local generative enhancement.

A noticeable saddle point appears in both G3 and G4 around communication rounds 20–24, where the rate of test loss reduction temporarily plateaus. This inflection zone likely reflects a transitional adaptation phase in the federated model, as it assimilates diverse UAV perspectives and benefits from increasingly clearer reconstructed inputs. G4 appears to overcome this saddle point more decisively than G3, suggesting that generative fusion enhances gradient alignment and accelerates convergence beyond the plateau.

To quantify end-to-end responsiveness, we estimate the end-to-end response time encompassing three components: Generative Reconstruction Latency (T_{recon}), CDV-based risk score computation (T_{CDV_Score}), and federated communication delay (T_{comm}). Combining these yields a total estimated dispatch time per incident of:

$$T_{dispatch} = T_{recon} + T_{CDV\_Score} + T_{comm} = 1.8\text{s} + 0.6s + 2.4s = 4.8\ seconds \tag{7}$$

This latency suggests that the full system (G4) is capable of supporting near-real-time emergency decision-making, even under decentralized operational constraints. Taken together, these results validate G4 as a balanced and efficient design that integrates FL and GenAI to deliver not only higher accuracy but also faster, more reliable response under bandwidth-aware conditions.

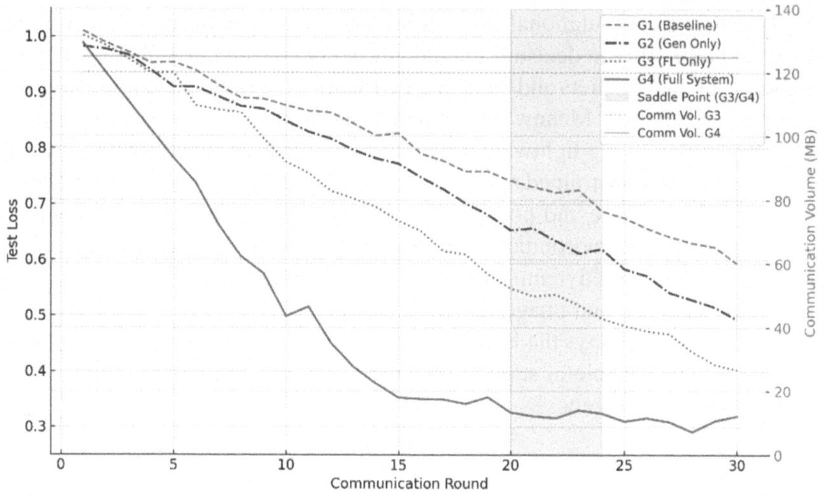

Fig. 6. Communication Overhead and Convergence Behavior across Experimental Groups.

G1 and G2 incur no communication cost, as they do not involve any federated synchronization. G3 and G4 introduce approximately 120–125 MB communication per round due to periodic model updates. G4 achieves the fastest and most stable convergence, reaching low test loss within 15 rounds. A local saddle point is observed between rounds 20–24 in G3 and G4, potentially reflecting transitional adjustment in cross-UAV model generalization. The shaded area highlights this inflection zone, where loss reduction momentarily slows before resuming descent.

7 Conclusion, Limitations and Future Work

This paper presented *TruRescue*, a drone-assisted road emergency assessment system integrating Federated Learning (FL) and Generative AI (GenAI) to enhance visual perception under degraded conditions. The proposed architecture enables on-device collaboration for accident detection while supporting privacy-preserving model training and multi-view image reconstruction. Preliminary evaluations demonstrated that the full system (G4) significantly improves image quality (RQ1), and provides more consistent risk assessment (RQ2) compared to ablated variants. Moreover, a small-scale latency test showed the system's potential for real-time response (RQ3).

However, the current study has several limitations. First, all experiments were conducted in a simulated environment using AirSim with limited variability in road scenarios and weather conditions. Second, the CDV risk model was only evaluated on a small annotated set, without extensive validation from domain experts. Third, the federated training was simplified without full-scale client variability or realistic drone hardware constraints.

Future work will focus on expanding the dataset to encompass a broader range of accident types and environmental conditions, including the integration of real-world UAV video feeds. We also aim to scale the federated training process to heterogeneous edge clients with varying computational capabilities and network stability. To enhance interpretability and reliability in decision-making, the CDV risk model will be refined using expert-annotated incident tiers and benchmarked against operational datasets from emergency response scenarios. Meanwhile, from a systems perspective, we plan to explore the feasibility of deploying lightweight federated aggregation functionality directly on UAV platforms under constrained resources. Such an approach would reduce reliance on fixed ground infrastructure and potentially enhance system resilience in decentralized or infrastructure-sparse environments. Additionally, we intend to investigate adaptive dispatch mechanisms that dynamically respond to evolving risk profiles derived from real-time UAV feedback and image-derived assessments.

Ultimately, this work lays the foundation for intelligent, decentralized, and privacy-aware UAV systems capable of supporting emergency decision-making with enhanced visual and situational awareness.

References

1. Guan, H., Yap, P.-T., Bozoki, A., Liu, M.: Federated learning for medical image analysis: a survey. J. Biomed. Inform. **137**, 104277 (2023). https://doi.org/10.1016/j.jbi.2023.104277
2. Li, X., et al.: Diffusion models for image restoration and enhancement: A comprehensive survey. arXiv preprint arXiv: 2308.09388. (2023). https://arxiv.org/abs/2308.09388
3. Fei, B., et al.: Generative diffusion prior for unified image restoration and enhancement. In: Proceedings of the IEEE/CVF Conference on Computer Vision and Pattern Recognition (CVPR), pp. 10265–10275 (2023)
4. Microsoft.: AirSim: A simulator for drones, cars and more, built on Unreal Engine. Microsoft Research (2017). https://github.com/microsoft/AirSim
5. Gu, J., Cai, H., Chen, H., Ye, X., Ren, J., & Dong, C.: Image Quality Assessment for Perceptual Image Restoration: A New Dataset, Benchmark and Metric. arXiv preprint (2020). https://arxiv.org/abs/2011.15002
6. Zhang, R., Isola, P., Efros, A.A., Shechtman, E., Wang, O.: The unreasonable effectiveness of deep features as a perceptual metric. In: Proceedings of the IEEE Conference on Computer Vision and Pattern Recognition (CVPR), pp. 586–595 (2018). https://doi.org/10.1109/CVPR.2018.00068
7. Yang, L., et al.: HiFaceGAN: Face renovation via collaborative suppression and replenishment. arXiv preprint (2020). https://arxiv.org/abs/2005.05005

Container Performance in Secure Space Systems

Shariar M. Alamgir(✉)

Embedded and Specialized Computing Dept., The Aerospace Corporation, El Segundo, CA, USA
shar.m.alamgir@aero.org

Abstract. Embedded systems running critical applications, such as spacecraft flight software, demand high reliability, efficiency, and real-time responsiveness. As Linux and container technologies gain traction in these domains, understanding their performance implications becomes essential, particularly when enhanced with Mandatory Access Control (MAC) Linux security modules (LSMs) like SELinux and AppArmor. This study evaluates the performance impact of enabling SELinux and AppArmor on application and container workloads running on a Raspberry Pi 4. We examine both native and containerized execution environments under various security configurations, analyzing CPU, memory, disk I/O, and runtime latency. Our results show that enabling MAC LSMs introduces minimal performance overhead across most metrics, suggesting that security enforcement through SELinux or AppArmor can be achieved without significantly compromising system performance.

Keywords: containers · embedded · performance · real time · Linux Security Modules · Mandatory Access Control

1 Introduction

High-criticality real-time embedded systems, such as those used in aerospace applications, rely on their operating systems (OSs) to execute critical tasks with precision, low latency, and high reliability. While real-time operating systems (RTOSs) have traditionally dominated this domain due to their deterministic behavior and minimal overhead, Linux is increasingly being adopted in modern space systems for its broad hardware support, rich feature set, and large developer community. As discussed in our previous work, Container Performance in Space Systems by Alamgir et al. [1], Linux has been successfully used in several spacecraft, especially when paired with containers to achieve lightweight virtualization.

Containers, particularly via Docker, provide an attractive alternative to traditional virtualization by packaging all dependencies alongside an application, enabling consistent deployment across platforms. However, containers introduce an abstraction layer that interacts closely with the host OS—and in critical systems like spacecraft, every abstraction must be scrutinized for performance and predictability.

In our previous study [1], we analyzed the performance implications of containers in embedded Linux environments. We evaluated a variety of workloads on a Raspberry Pi

H. R. Arabnia et al. (Eds.): CSCE 2025, CCIS 2932, pp. 57–75, 2026.
https://doi.org/10.1007/978-3-032-22193-3_5

4 platform and showed that containerization introduced only modest overhead in areas such as RAM usage and startup time, while having minimal impact on CPU and runtime performance. That work established a performance baseline for containers in space-like systems.

In this follow-up study, we investigate the impact of Mandatory Access Control (MAC) security mechanisms, specifically SELinux and AppArmor, when enabled in Linux-based container environments. Although these Linux Security Modules (LSMs) are designed to enhance security by confining applications and limiting access to system resources, they are often unused in embedded and aerospace deployments. This is primarily due to concerns about:

- Additional runtime overhead introduced by policy enforcement
- Increased system complexity or maintenance burden
- Fears of unpredictable latency or interference with real-time performance

Such concerns are especially relevant in resource-constrained or high-assurance systems like spacecraft, where performance predictability is paramount. Likewise, as spacecrafts begin to support multiple tenants at once, each user must have access restricted to only their components and applications to provide security for each tenant. This is often overlooked in deployments since performance is the main priority, but users often are curious whether these security additions will affect performance greatly or not.

This paper addresses these concerns by presenting empirical data on how enabling SELinux or AppArmor affects system performance in a containerized Linux environment. We use the same experimental setup as our previous study to allow for direct comparisons and isolate the performance impact of LSMs themselves. These experiments are:

1. *File Operations*: tested performance impact of the container runtime's intercepting system calls
2. *Response time*: tested performance impact of the container runtime intercepting application communication into / out of a container
3. *CPU Utilization*: tested CPU utilization overhead of the container runtime
4. *Parallel Processing*: tested performance impact of the container runtime on multi-threaded workloads
5. *Base Layers*: tested how different base layers affect startup time, memory utilization, and size on disk
6. *Container Count*: tested how many containers the OS and runtime can support, given memory constraints
7. *Thread Wakeup Time*: tested latency of waking real-time scheduled threads
8. *Patched Kernel Runtime Overhead*: measured the runtime of non-real-time applications when executed on a real-time patched OS kernel.

Our findings demonstrate that enabling these MAC frameworks results in negligible performance degradation across a variety of workloads, suggesting that system designers can adopt these security mechanisms without compromising the real-time performance and efficiency of embedded applications.

The rest of this paper is organized as follows. Section 2 describes our updated test platform and experimental configuration. Section 3 revisits our earlier experiments but now compares results across SELinux-enabled, AppArmor-enabled, and LSM-disabled environments. Section 4 discusses observed trends and implications for space system design. Section 5 concludes with our recommendations for secure containerized deployments in embedded Linux systems.

2 Related Work

Our experiment designs match our previous study [1] and will still be used to measure key performance metrics such as runtime latency, program startup latency, CPU and memory utilization. Our study also uses the findings and claims of Zhang et al., who found that LSMs may have larger performance overhead based on the system call being invoked when compared to their previous references [2, 3], and the hooking order if multiple LSMs are used can also cause a larger regression, but overall saw that the overhead percentage increase translated into negligible latency raw seconds increase [4]. We also relied on the findings of Alyas et al., who found that catering docker containers to specific AppArmor profile designs could limit performance degradation below 4% overall [5]. Our study's still uses Ruan et al. and their study on containers with cloud environments [6], Bachiega et al. and their survey on existing container-based performance research [7], and Espe et al. and their research evaluating different container runtimes and the performance impact on a shared host [8].

3 Background and Experiment Setup

3.1 Linux Security Modules, SELinux, and AppArmor

Linux Security Modules (LSMs) represent a crucial aspect of the Linux operating system's security architecture, designed to bolster its defense mechanisms against a wide range of threats and vulnerabilities. They provide a modular framework that enforces access control policies and ensures system integrity, thereby protecting critical resources like files, processes, and network communication. Additionally, LSMs offer flexibility, allowing administrators to tailor security policies to meet their specific needs.

Two prominent Linux Security Modules are Security-Enhanced Linux (SELinux) and AppArmor. Both SELinux and AppArmor are Mandatory Access Control (MAC) systems that control access to system resources based on predefined security policies. Policies specify which actions and resources are allowed or denied for specific applications and processes, offering robust access control.

LSMs ability to limit access control and help thwart many different vulnerabilities. This includes:

- Privilege escalation
- File system attacks
- Network attacks
- Buffer overflow attacks
- Container breakouts
- Data theft/tampering
- Denial of Service.

3.2 Processor and Operating System

As in our previous work [1], we conducted all experiments on a Raspberry Pi 4 Model B with 8 GB of RAM. This platform remains a practical and accessible testbed for flight-like embedded software evaluation, despite being more powerful than the radiation-tolerant processors commonly used in deployed spacecraft systems. Its quad-core ARM Cortex-A72 CPU (ARMv8 architecture), running at 1.5 GHz, provides sufficient flexibility for testing next-generation designs that may adopt general-purpose operating systems like Linux.

In our prior study, we justified the Raspberry Pi 4 as a stand-in for these newer architectures, such as AMD's Versal Adaptive Compute Acceleration Platform (ACAP) [5, 6], due to its general-purpose compute capabilities and Linux compatibility. Those same motivations apply here, and we maintain consistency in hardware across both studies to ensure meaningful performance comparisons.

3.3 Container Setup

This study also continues the containerization strategy introduced in our previous work [1], using Docker as the container runtime. For this paper, we updated to Docker version 28.1.1 and Ubuntu 24.04 to evaluate performance with the latest stable versions of the toolchain and operating system. Each containerized experiment again includes:

- A Dockerfile specifying the base image
- All required dependencies
- The application under test

We ensured containers were initialized locally using docker run, which sets up a writable filesystem, networking, and executes the application in an isolated environment. Timing data was collected via automated Python and Bash scripts using Linux's time utility.

3.4 Real-Time Kernel Patch

To enable real-time configuration with these versions of Ubuntu and Raspberry Pi 4, we used Ubuntu Pro's realtime-kernel patch capabilities to seamlessly modify our kernel. Ubuntu Pro uses PREEMPT_RT, similar to what we used in our previous testing campaign. PREEMPT_RT allows preemptive scheduling of both kernel and user-space tasks by converting interrupt handlers into kernel threads and enabling strict priority-based scheduling. This configuration enables more deterministic behavior for time-critical tasks and provides a suitable platform to evaluate how MAC framework, specifically SELinux and AppArmor, interact with real-time scheduling.

4 Container Performance Experiments

4.1 Experiment 1: File Operations

In our first experiment, we measured the performance impact of system calls related to file I/O, both inside and outside of Docker containers, and evaluated whether enabling MAC frameworks introduced additional runtime overhead.

The containerized application reads numbers line-by-line from a file via system calls, increments each value, and then appends the result to a new file. We performed this test under six conditions to distinguish between cold container startup and in-process looping:

- Variation A: The `docker run` command was executed 25 times in sequence.
- Variation B: The `docker run` command was executed 1 time, but the embedded program was modified to loop 25 times in sequence.
- Variation C: The embedded program was run on the host OS 25 times in sequence. This involved no containerization at all.
- Variation D-F: Same as Variation A-C respectively, but with a longer embedded program runtime.

This experiment was repeated with SELinux enabled, AppArmor enabled, and with no LSM enabled (baseline) to capture relative performance differences.

Table 1. Experiment 1: File Operations with LSMs

Variation	Runtime Mean (s)	Runtime Std Dev (s)
A – LSMs Disabled	1.65	0.18
B – LSMs Disabled	0.18	0.004
C– LSMs Disabled	0.16	0.03
D– LSMs Disabled	23.22	0.41
E– LSMs Disabled	20.83	0.35
F– LSMs Disabled	19.96	0.36
A– SELinux Enabled	1.72	0.12
B– SELinux Enabled	0.18	0.01
C– SELinux Enabled	0.18	0.02
D– SELinux Enabled	24.21	0.26
E – SELinux Enabled	20.86	0.31
F– SELinux Enabled	19.87	0.21
A– AppArmor Enabled	1.70	0.17
B– AppArmor Enabled	0.19	0.007
C– AppArmor Enabled	0.17	0.01
D– AppArmor Enabled	24.11	0.16
E – AppArmor Enabled	21.21	0.22
F– AppArmor Enabled	19.989	0.35

As shown in Table 1, we observed that startup time remains the primary contributor to performance differences between variations that launch containers repeatedly (A, D) and those that loop within a single instance (B, E). The additional overhead introduced by SELinux or AppArmor was negligible, with no consistent or statistically significant change in runtime behavior. Furthermore, results with LSMs enabled aligned closely with our earlier measurements conducted without MAC frameworks.

We also determined that now it seems that the host Variations (C and F) do perform faster than the containerized variations (B and E), which is different than our previous study [1]. This supports the argument that docker containers additional overhead may incur some small performance degradation, but the difference is small.

4.2 Experiment 2: Response Time

This experiment measured the latency of socket-based communication between a client and server, evaluating both the effect of containerization and the overhead (if any) introduced by enabling SELinux and AppArmor. This test builds upon the inter-process communication latency results from our prior work.

Using Python's socket library, we implemented two variations:

- Containerized client: The server existed outside the container on the host OS, while the client existed inside a container.
- No containers: Both the server and client existed on the host OS – no containerization was involved.

In order to independently investigate the time taken to send data from server to client and from client to server, for both variations we timed the following operations:

- One-way: server sends command to client, and client receives that command.
- Round-trip: server sends command to client; client receives that command; client echoes the same command back to the server; server receives that same command.

With containers enabled, we previously observed a ~22% increase in latency, though this equated to less than 2 ms in absolute terms [1]. In this extended study, enabling SELinux or AppArmor did not introduce any measurable increase in latency beyond what was already observed due to containerization alone, as shown in Table 2. Jitter also remained within acceptable bounds.

4.3 Experiment 3: CPU Utilization

This experiment measured the CPU overhead of containerization when running a high utilization application, and assessed whether SELinux or AppArmor enforcement meaningfully affects this overhead. As in our previous study [1], we used a compute-intensive Python script that inefficiently checked for prime numbers, consistently driving CPU utilization above 98%.

Table 3, showed that:

- The containerized version exhibited only a ~ 2.6% increase in mean runtime.
- The standard deviation increased by ~ 33%, but follows similarly to our previous findings [1]

Table 2. Experiment 2: Response Time with LSMs

Variation	Response time Mean (μs)	Response time Std Dev (μs)
No containerization, one way	76	4
No containerization, round trip	189	9
Containerized app, one way	91	13
Containerized app, round trip	235	17
No containerization, one way -SELinux Enabled	81	3
No containerization, round trip -SELinux Enabled	194	12
Containerized app, one way -SELinux Enabled	92	8
Containerized app, round trip -SELinux Enabled	240	21
No containerization, one way -AppArmor Enabled	74	6
No containerization, round trip - AppArmor Enabled	195	12
Containerized app, one way- AppArmor Enabled	89	10
Containerized app, round trip - AppArmor Enabled	241	21

Table 3. Experiment 3: CPU Utilization, Increased Program Runtime with LSMs

Variation	Runtime Mean (s)	Runtime Std Dev (s)
No containerization	30.3	1.2
Containerized application	31.1	1.6
No containerization – SELinux	30.5	0.9
Containerized application – SELinux	31.4	1.1
No containerization– AppArmor	30.5	0.4
Containerized application – AppArmor	31.3	0.6

Importantly, enabling SELinux or AppArmor enforcement had no measurable impact on CPU usage or runtime beyond the minor effects already attributed to containerization. The elevated variance remains an open question, likely due to Docker runtime behavior or background services, and is not tied to MAC LSM enforcement.

4.4 Experiment 4 & 5: Parallel Processing

Modern flight software often relies on multithreading to take full advantage of embedded CPUs with multiple cores. In space systems, efficient parallel execution is critical for meeting real-time constraints.

We conducted two experiments in this section. In the first, we reused the CPU-intensive algorithm from Experiment 3 and varied the number of CPU cores available to the application. The algorithm was run both on the Host OS and within a Docker container under six configurations: with SELinux enabled, SELinux disabled, AppArmor enabled, AppArmor disabled, and both LSMs disabled. Table 4 shows the results of experiment 4. We found that containerization had a negligible effect on runtime and CPU utilization regardless of the LSM configuration. Specifically:

- There was no consistent correlation between containerization and algorithm runtime across different core counts.
- The containerized runs now behaved similarly in max utilization, suggesting Docker's thread allocation has improved to behave similar to outside containers and this resulted in no significant impact on performance.
- Importantly, SELinux and AppArmor had no measurable impact on runtime, variance, or resource contention in any variation.

In experiment 5, we tested how concurrent execution of multiple containerized workloads affects scheduling and fairness. We ran up to 20 concurrent long-running processes across a mix of core and container allocations. Across all tests, with and without LSMs, the average runtimes differed by less than 10 s (a ~ 6% difference), and standard deviations remained similarly tight, as shown in Table 5.

These results suggest that containerized applications retain efficient access to multi-core resources even under mandatory access control enforcement. Additionally, grouping multiple workloads inside fewer containers slightly reduced performance variability, indicating Docker's fairness mechanisms still function effectively in constrained environments.

4.5 Experiment 6: Base Layers

This experiment revisited the influence of base image choice on container startup time now under the added presence of SELinux and AppArmor. We compared Ubuntu and scratch-based containers using a minimal C application, as in our prior work, to isolate container overhead from the application logic. We omitted results for memory usage for the next two experiments because the LSMs did not impact the program or its containers memory usage.

Results shown in Table 6 were consistent with previous findings [1], and SELinux and AppArmor had negligible effect on container startup time. Both LSMs introduced no measurable delay during image execution or initialization, regardless of the container's base layer.

Table 4. Experiment 4: Parallel Processing with LSMs, Part 1

Variation	Runtime Mean (s)	Runtime Std Dev (s)	Utilization (%)	Utilization per Core (%)
Containerized 1 core	29.6	1.4	98 - 100	98 - 100
Containerized 4 cores	12.5	0.9	380 - 395	98 – 100
No Container 1 core	29.9	1.8	98 – 100	98 - 100
No Container 4 cores	12.1	0.2	380 - 395	95– 98
Containerized 1 core – SELinux	30.1	1.1	98 - 100	98 - 100
Containerized 4 cores – SELinux	12.4	1.0	380 - 395	98 – 100
No Container 1 core – SELinux	31.2	1.3	97 – 100	97 - 100
No Container 4 cores – SELinux	12.3	0.7	380 - 395	95– 98
Containerized 1 core – AppArmor	29.9	0.9	98 - 100	98 - 100
Containerized 4 cores – AppArmor	12.6	0.6	380 - 395	98 – 100
No Container 1 core – AppArmor	30.4	1.4	98 – 100	98 - 100
No Container 4 cores – AppArmor	12.7	0.7	380 - 395	95– 98

4.6 Experiment 7: Container Count

This experiment assessed how many containers a system can run before memory saturation impacts performance, focusing on whether SELinux and AppArmor introduce additional strain under high load. As in prior testing, containers were launched with varying memory footprints to push the host system toward full physical memory usage.

Table 5. Experiment 5: Parallel Processing with LSMS, Part 2

Variation	Runtime Mean (s)	Runtime Std Dev (s)
No Container 4 cores	117	4.5
1 Container 4 cores	123	3.5
4 Containers 4 cores	124	4.5
4 Containers 1 core each	123	2.9
5 Containers 4 cores	122	3.1
20 Containers 4 cores	118	4.1
No Container 4 cores -SELinux	119	3.4
1 Container 4 cores - SELinux	125	2.5
4 Containers 4 cores - SELinux	124	5.1
4 Containers 1 core each - SELinux	124	3.6
5 Containers 4 cores - SELinux	125	3.8
20 Containers 4 cores - SELinux	119	4.9
No Container 4 cores -AppArmor	118	4.6
1 Container 4 cores -AppArmor	124	2.8
4 Containers 4 cores -AppArmor	122	5.1
4 Containers 1 core each -AppArmor	121	3.4
5 Containers 4 cores -AppArmor	123	5.0
20 Containers 4 cores -AppArmor	117	3.1

Table 6. Experiment 6: Base Layers – Runtime, with LSMs

Variation	Runtime Mean (s)	Runtime Std Dev (s)
No Container	0.007	0.001
Scratch Base	0.98	0.036
Ubuntu Base	0.99	0.055
No Container – SELinux Enabled	0.008	0.001
Scratch Base – SELinux Enabled	1.01	0.036
Ubuntu Base – SELinux Enabled	1.00	0.055
No Container – AppArmor Enabled	0.007	0.001
Scratch Base – AppArmor Enabled	0.99	0.036
Ubuntu Base – AppArmor Enabled	1.00	0.055

Table 7. Experiment 7: Host OS Slowdown Point with LSMs

Variation	Actual Container Memory Usage	Slowdown Point (# of Concurrent Containers)
32 containers, 256 MB each	221 - 257 MB	30
16 containers, 512 MB each	495 - 528 MB	15
8 containers, 1 GB each	1.0–1.06 GB	7
32 containers, 256 MB each – SELinux Enabled	221 - 257 MB	30
16 containers, 512 MB each – SELinux Enabled	495 - 528 MB	15
8 containers, 1 GB each – SELinux Enabled	1.0–1.06 GB	7
32 containers, 256 MB each – AppArmor Enabled	221 - 257 MB	30
16 containers, 512 MB each – AppArmor Enabled	495 - 528 MB	15
8 containers, 1 GB each – AppArmor Enabled	1.0–1.06 GB	7

Across all test cases, the system began to exhibit startup delays and performance degradation once physical memory usage exceeded ~ 90%, consistent with baseline behavior observed without LSMs. Tables VII, VIII, and IX show similar results between LSMs being disabled and enabled. Notably, enabling SELinux and AppArmor did not accelerate or amplify the onset of performance loss. Runtime behavior and recovery

Table 8. Experiment 7:Container Startup Times Before & After physical Memory Saturation with LSMs

Variation	Max Startup Time Before Saturation (s)	Mean Startup Time After Saturation (s)	Max Startup Time After Saturation (s)
32 / 256 MB	2.13	43	147
16 / 512 MB	1.21	2.1	Startup failure
8 / 1 GB	2.12	1.0	Startup failure
32 / 256 MB – SELinux	2.15	44	140
16 / 512 MB – SELinux	1.15	1.7	Startup failure
8 / 1 GB – SELinux	2.21	1.4	Startup failure
32 / 256 MB – AppArmor	2.13	45	145
16 / 512 MB – AppArmor	1.19	1.4	Startup failure
8 / 1 GB – AppArmor	2.21	1.3	Startup failure

trends, such as improved timing once earlier containers were terminated, remained unchanged with LSMs enforced.

These findings reinforce that while memory management is still critical in embedded containerized systems, the presence of SELinux and AppArmor does not exacerbate performance issues tied to resource saturation. The slowdown points matched for when LSMs were disabled and enabled, indicating that each LSM added very little to the overall memory usage of the system. System designers can therefore apply these security measures without risking early degradation of host responsiveness, even when operating near memory limits.

Table 9. Experiment 7: Application Runtimes Before & After Physical Memory Saturation with LSMs

Variation	Max Runtime Before Saturation (s)	Mean Runtime After Saturation (s)	Max Runtime After Saturation (s)
32/256 MB	5.34	40	111
16/512 MB	5.32	70	267
8/1 GB	5.21	5	20
32/256 MB – SELinux	5.38	33	105
16/512 MB – SELinux	5.31	54	198
8/1 GB – SELinux	5.24	9	11
32/256 MB – AppArmor	5.32	45	108
16/512 MB – AppArmor	5.41	66	200
8/1 GB – AppArmor	5.36	6	21

5 Real-Time Patch Experiments

To evaluate whether containerization and LSMs interfere with real-time scheduling, we ran a set of experiments on both standard and PREEMPT_RT-patched Ubuntu 24.04 kernels. Applications were executed inside and outside of Docker containers, and tests spanned both single-core and multi-core environments.

5.1 Experiment 8: Real-time Priority Scheduled Threads

Experiment 8 tested latency of switching to a high-priority task, both using a standard Linux kernel build and a build patched with PREEMPT_RT. This task switching latency translates into task activation time jitter in the system and could potentially cause problems for timing-sensitive functionality such as attitude control loops. For this experiment, we only used one processor core; single-core processing relates most closely to heritage space systems, and further, we had no reason to expect that using multiple cores would change the overall results.

To automate task switching, we used The Linux Foundation's rt-tests suite containing the Cyclictest and Hackbench program. Cyclictest runs a master thread which starts a determined number of real-time priority threads and wakes them up repeatedly using a cyclic alarm expiring timer. The difference between the intended wake-up time and the actual wake-up time is measured as the latency. Cyclictest provides the average, minimum, and maximum latencies, where the maximum latencies indicate potential worst case response time for a scheduled thread. Hackbench is used to simulate the workload a system may have with realtime and non-realtime programs running simultaneously, to more accurately use Cyclictests testing measure. Hackbench creates 400 tasks each using about 1% of CPU utilization.

Our Cyclictest script ran 1,000,000 samples of the test. The latency metrics are captured in Table 10.

Table 10. Experiment 8: Latency Data for Unpatched and Patched Kernel with LSMs

Variation	Min Latency (μs)	Max Latency (μs)	Average Latency (μs)
Unpatched kernel No Container	16	443	46
Unpatched kernel Container	17	431	43
Patched kernel No Container	17	71	21
Patched kernel Container	16	75	23
Unpatched kernel No Container SELinux Enabled	16	443	46
Unpatched kernel Container SELinux Enabled	17	437	43
Patched kernel No Container SELinux Enabled	16	77	24
Patched Kernel Container SELinux Enabled	17	78	23
Unpatched kernel No Container AppArmor Enabled	16	443	46
Unpatched kernel Container AppArmor Enabled	18	434	51
Patched kernel No Container AppArmor Enabled	17	83	24
Patched Kernel Container AppArmor Enabled	16	89	23

Table 11. Experiment 9: Runtime Data for Unpatched and Patched Kernel with LSMs

Variation	Runtime Mean (s)	Runtime Std Dev (s)	Total Utilization (%)	Utilization per Core (%)
Unpatched kernel Inside container 1 core	27.7	1.4	98 - 100	98 - 100
Unpatched kernel Inside container 4 cores	13.6	0.9	350 - 365	88 - 91
Unpatched kernel No container 1 core	28.0	1.5	95 - 100	95 - 100
Unpatched kernel No container 4 cores	14.8	1.0	360 - 385	90 - 96
Patched kernel Inside container 1 core	35.2	1.7	96 - 99	96 - 99
Patched kernel Inside container 4 cores	10.9	1.0	350 - 365	88 - 91
Patched kernel No container 1 core	34.9	1.4	98 - 100	98 - 100
Patched kernel No container 4 cores	10.6	1.0	372 - 385	93 – 96
Unpatched kernel Inside container 1 core – SELinux	28.1	1.3	98 - 100	98 - 100
Unpatched kernel Inside container 4 cores – SELinux	13.2	1.0	350 - 365	88 - 91

(continued)

Table 11. (*continued*)

Variation	Runtime Mean (s)	Runtime Std Dev (s)	Total Utilization (%)	Utilization per Core (%)
Unpatched kernel No container 1 core – SELinux	28.2	1.5	95 - 100	95 - 100
Unpatched kernel No container 4 cores – SELinux	14.9	1.2	360 - 385	90 - 96
Patched kernel Inside container 1 core – SELinux	34.6	1.4	96 - 99	96 - 99
Patched kernel Inside container 4 cores – SELinux	11.6	1.2	350 - 365	88 - 91
Patched kernel No container 1 core – SELinux	35.7	1.1	98 - 100	98 - 100
Patched kernel No container 4 cores – SELinux	10.0	0.6	372 - 385	93 – 96
Unpatched kernel Inside container 1 core – AppArmor	27.4	1.2	98 - 100	98 - 100
Unpatched kernel Inside container 4 cores– AppArmor	13.3	1.1	350 - 365	88 - 91

(*continued*)

Table 11. *(continued)*

Variation	Runtime Mean (s)	Runtime Std Dev (s)	Total Utilization (%)	Utilization per Core (%)
Unpatched kernel No container 1 core–AppArmor	29.1	1.3	95 - 100	95 - 100
Unpatched kernel No container 4 cores–AppArmor	15.4	1.4	360 - 385	90 - 96
Patched kernel Inside container 1 core–AppArmor	34.3	1.7	96 - 99	96 - 99
Patched kernel Inside container 4 cores–AppArmor	11.4	1.4	350 - 365	88 - 91
Patched kernel No container 1 core–AppArmor	35.6	1.3	98 - 100	98 - 100
Patched kernel No container 4 cores–AppArmor	10.2	1.3	372 - 385	93 - 96

The table shows that overall the real-time patched Linux kernels have lower maximum latency than a regular Linux kernel, which tracks with our results from our last testing campaign [1]. Importantly, SELinux and AppArmor did not greatly contribute to the maximum latency, with the maximum increase being 14 μs when an LSM (AppArmor) was enabled. This indicates that LSMs will not add substantial overhead to real-time thread wakeups that require LSMs hook checks before activating, and can be used in some real-time system designs. Designers must check for their complete designs however since system complexity could cause real-time tasks to respond slower and could potential break real-time requirements.

5.2 Experiment 9: Real-Time Patch Performance Overhead

We tested whether containerized applications running under both patched and unpatched kernels could fully utilize multicore systems, and whether Docker's isolation affected the real-time benefits of PREEMPT_RT. These applications are non-real-time and would not directly benefit from the PREEMPT_RT patch but could be affected by the new scheduler behavior. As expected, single-core performance on the patched kernel was slightly worse due to added context switching overhead, while multicore setups showed better core utilization and slightly improved runtimes under the real-time kernel, tracking with our previous testing campaign [1].

While runtime differences between containerized and non-containerized variants varied slightly depending on kernel configuration, SELinux and AppArmor had no measurable effect on scheduling, CPU load distribution, or latency. This strongly supports their use in flight environments: developers can safely enable LSMs alongside Docker and real-time patches without sacrificing timing precision or computational efficiency.

6 Conclusion

This study evaluated the performance impact of enabling SELinux and AppArmor on embedded Linux systems running Docker containers. Across a wide range of experiments, spanning CPU performance, memory usage, startup latency, and real-time responsiveness, we found that enabling these LSMs introduced no meaningful degradation in performance. Even under memory-saturated conditions or with real-time kernel patches applied, the presence of SELinux or AppArmor did not significantly affect application behavior or system resource allocation.

These findings are especially important for flight and space systems, which often operate under strict performance, reliability, and isolation requirements. Security mechanisms like SELinux and AppArmor are frequently disabled in embedded environments due to concerns about overhead or complexity. Our work challenges this assumption and shows that these tools can, and should, be enabled—particularly given the growing need for defense-in-depth in mission-critical software systems.

Future work should explore tighter integration of LSMs with real-time safety requirements, container signing and attestation pipelines, and hardware-assisted security features. Together, these approaches can further enable the secure deployment and lifecycle management of flight software in increasingly autonomous and interconnected space systems.

References

1. Alamgir, S.M., Bohra, D.L., Nguyen, E.N.: Container Performance in Space Systems. In: Internet Computing and IoT and Embedded Systems, Cyber-physical Systems, and Applications. CSCE 2024, Las Vegas (2024)
2. Loscocco, P., Smalley, S.: Integrating flexible support for security policies into the Linux operating system. In: 2001 USENIX Annual Technical Conference (USENIX ATC 01), Boston (2001)
3. Wright, C., Cowan, C., Smalley, S., Morris, J., Kroah-Hartman, G.: Linux security modules: general security support for the Linux kernel. In: 11th USENIX Security Symposium (USENIX Security 02), San Francisco, 2002
4. Zhang, W., Jaeger, T., Liu, P.: Analyzing the Overhead of Filesystem Protection using Linux Security Modules. Pennsylvania State University State College (2021)

5. Alyas, T., Ali, S., Khan, H.U., Samad, A., Alissa, K., Saleem, M.A.: Container performance and vulnerability management for container security using docker engine. Secur. Commun. Network **2022**, 11 (2022)
6. Ruan, B., Huang, H., Wu, S., Jin, H.: A performance study of containers in cloud environment. In: Advances in Services Computing (2016)
7. Bachiega, N.G., Souza, P.S.L., Bruschi, S.M., de Souza, S.d.R.S.: Container-based performance evaluation: a survey and challenges. In: IEEE International Conference on Cloud Engineering, Orlando (2018)
8. L. Espe, A.J., Podolskiy, V., Gerndt, M.: Performance Evaluation of Container Runtimes (2020)
9. Versal Architecture and Product Data Sheet: Overview (DS950), 14 November 2023. https://docs.xilinx.com/v/u/en-US/ds950-versal-overview. Accessed 16 Nov 2023
10. Versal Adaptive SoC Technical Reference Manual (AM011), 05 October 2023. https://docs.xilinx.com/r/en-US/am011-versal-acap-trm/Introduction. Accessed 16 Nov 2023
11. Guertin, S.: Raspberry Pis for Space Guideline. National Aeronautics and Space Administration (2001)

Openness and Adaptability in Cybersecurity: A Hierarchical Approach to Robust Defense

Azad Jalalian Zharabad(✉) and Thomas Kunz

Department of Systems and Computer Engineering, Carleton University, Ottawa, Canada
azadjalalianzharabad@cmail.carleton.ca, tkunz@sce.carleton.ca

Abstract. Cybersecurity systems are increasingly essential and broadly deployed across a wide range of applications and domains. This paper investigates the generalization and adaptability of defense mechanisms for AI-based defenders in environments characterized by uncertainty and openness. We critically analyze the limitations of existing machine learning-based approaches, emphasizing their diminished performance in unpredictable scenarios. To address these shortcomings, we introduce a heuristic hierarchical framework designed to enhance defender adaptability. Empirical results demonstrate that our proposed method surpasses the widely adopted Proximal Policy Optimization (PPO) algorithm in open system settings. These findings offer valuable insights into the development of more robust, generalized, and adaptive cybersecurity defense strategies tailored for dynamic and uncertain environments.

Keywords: Cybersecurity · Open Systems · Adaptive Defense Mechanisms · Generalization in Cyber Defense · Reinforcement Learning · Artificial Intelligence

1 Introduction

In recent years, the frequency and sophistication of cyber-attacks have escalated significantly, driven by the rapid adoption of advanced technologies across critical infrastructure. The integration of Artificial Intelligence (AI) and automation—particularly within industrial systems—has expanded the digital attack surface, rendering traditional, static security paradigms increasingly insufficient. These cyber intrusions can cause substantial financial, operational, and reputational damage, with consequences that are often irreversible. This evolving threat landscape highlights an urgent need for more resilient, intelligent, and adaptive defensive mechanisms [1]. Our analysis of contemporary cybersecurity research reveals a recurring and critical theme: the need to generalize defender agents, commonly referred to as "blue agents," so they can operate effectively in dynamic, stochastic, and uncertain environments [2]. This challenge is aptly

H. R. Arabnia et al. (Eds.): CSCE 2025, CCIS 2932, pp. 76–90, 2026.
https://doi.org/10.1007/978-3-032-22193-3_6

addressed by the concept of Open Agent Systems (OASYS). Unlike traditional closed multiagent systems that assume static participants and environments, OASYS are designed to model open and evolving environments where agents, tasks, and capabilities can change over time [3]. This paradigm is especially relevant to real-world domains such as emergency response, autonomous systems, organizational coordination, and cybersecurity. In these settings, agents (whether defenders or attackers) may appear or disappear, roles may change dynamically, and new tasks can emerge unexpectedly. In this paper, we investigate the limitations of current defender agents and examine the design and generalization of such agents within open, complex systems characterized by inherent randomness and unpredictability. We present both machine learning-based and heuristic approaches to enhancing the adaptability of defenders in dynamic cybersecurity environments. Furthermore, we critically assess the shortcomings of existing reinforcement learning-based models and outline emerging directions for developing robust, adaptive defense strategies suited to increasingly uncertain and evolving operational landscapes in open environments. Our contribution lies in the evaluation of our proposed methods within a unique simulation environment that differs significantly from currently available alternatives. This high-fidelity simulation framework advances autonomous multiagent cybersecurity systems through three key innovations: (1) realistic agent dynamics, where defenders and attackers can intermittently join or leave the network; (2) topology aware adaptability, which tests agent robustness across varying network structures; and (3) randomized attacker behavior, introducing significant unpredictability and creating complex learning challenges. Collectively, these contributions establish a more rigorous and realistic benchmark for developing resilient and adaptive defense strategies in dynamic and uncertain cybersecurity environments. The structure of the paper is outlined as follows. Section 2 presents a comprehensive overview of the background and motivation, along with an introduction to the proposed methodology and related work. Section 3 offers a detailed description of the problem and elaborates on the suggested solutions, including PPO and hierarchical approach. Section 4 outlines the evaluation environment and presents an in-depth analysis of the performance results. Finally, Sect. 5 summarizes the findings and concludes the paper.

2 Background and Motivation

2.1 Open Systems

OASYS refers to the dynamic, evolving nature of multi-agent environments in which the set of participating agents, the tasks they undertake, and the types or roles of agents are not fixed, but instead are subject to continual change [3]. This concept encapsulates three interrelated dimensions: Agent openness, task openness, and type openness.

- **Agent openness** concerns the capacity for agents to enter or exit the system at any time. This is exemplified in scenarios such as cybersecurity, where adversarial agents (e.g., attackers) may appear intermittently, or defensive agents may scale in or out based on operational needs. As a result, agents must infer the number of active collaborators and assess whether their current team composition is adequate to effectively counter adversarial agents.

- **Task openness** pertains to the spontaneous emergence or disappearance of tasks. For example, new vulnerabilities may be discovered in a network without warning, or time-sensitive alerts may require immediate prioritization and response.
- **Type openness** involves the evolution of agent roles, capabilities, or preferences over time. This can result from learning processes, performance degradation, or changes in strategic priorities. In cybersecurity, for instance, defender agents might enhance their strategies through reinforcement learning or lose capabilities due to resource constraints or system damage.

These dimensions of openness introduce profound challenges to decision-making, particularly under conditions of partial observability. Agents often must act without full knowledge of the environment, the intentions or actions of other agents, or even their own evolving objectives. This complicates the modeling of state transitions, reward structures, and cooperative or adversarial interactions. Moreover, as OASYS environments scale to encompass large numbers of heterogeneous agents, ensuring computational tractability and effective coordination becomes increasingly complex. Addressing these challenges requires the development of adaptive, scalable, and context aware strategies that are robust to environmental uncertainty and structural fluidity.

2.2 Free-Range-Zoo Environment

In this research, we leverage the free-range-zoo multi-agent reinforcement learning (MARL) environment to explore and evaluate open-agent system dynamics within the context of cybersecurity [4,5]. Free-range-zoo is an open-source simulation designed to support decision-making research in reinforcement learning and planning. It provides PyTorch-based implementations of several dynamic and realistic environments—including cybersecurity, wildfire management, and rideshare coordination—that are specifically constructed to embody the principles of OASYS, such as agent openness, task openness, and type openness. These environments simulate non-static conditions where agents may enter or exit, tasks can appear or vanish unpredictably, and agent roles or capabilities can evolve over time. Such openness reflects realistic scenarios in which adaptive and robust decision-making strategies are essential. The API of free-range-zoo is fully compatible with the AEC/Parallel environment architecture used in the PettingZoo MARL [6], enabling researchers to efficiently prototype, bench-mark, and extend MARL algorithms.

2.3 Reinforcement Learning

Reinforcement Learning (RL) represents a core approach in machine learning that enables agents to learn optimal decision making strategies through interactions with their environment. By interpreting feedback in the form of rewards or penalties, agents iteratively refine their actions to maximize cumulative long term returns. RL is characterized by trial and error learning in environments where explicit supervision is absent. Classical RL techniques, such as tabular Q-learning and Monte Carlo methods, have proven effective in simple, low dimensional settings. However, they encounter scalability and generalization challenges when applied to more complex or continuous domains. The advent of Deep Reinforcement Learning (Deep RL), which integrates neural networks into the RL paradigm, has significantly expanded the field's capabilities. Deep RL allows agents to approximate sophisticated value functions and policies, facilitating effective learning in high dimensional state and action spaces. Among the most widely adopted Deep RL algorithms is Proximal Policy Optimization (PPO) [7], valued for its balance between sample efficiency and training stability. PPO introduces a clipped objective function that constrains policy updates, mitigating the risk of overly aggressive parameter changes while still promoting policy improvement. Due to its practical reliability and simplicity, PPO has become a standard benchmark across various reinforcement learning tasks. In the following sections, we present a PPO based approach alongside a heuristic method designed to enhance the capabilities of a defender agent operating within the free-range-zoo environment. This environment is characterized by its high level of openness and dynamic interactions, presenting unique challenges for autonomous defense strategies in real-world scenarios. Our proposed methods aim not only to address these challenges but also to provide insight into the limitations of machine learning approaches in such complex environments. Specifically, our study highlights that machine learning techniques, while powerful, do not always yield effective results under all circumstances. This observation underscores the importance of conducting further research and exploring complementary strategies to improve the robustness and adaptability of defender agents.

2.4 Related Work

Recent studies have advanced the robustness and adaptability of autonomous cyber defense agents. For example, [8] improves RL agent generalization using enhanced training, transfer learning, and PPO policy ensembles, though adapting to new environments remains challenging. In [9], attack graphs built with Meta Attack Language (MAL) guide PPO agent training, outperforming heuristics but struggling with larger graphs. To address this, [10] incorporates graph embeddings into observations, enhancing context awareness and generalization across diverse simulations. A hybrid reinforcement and supervised learning framework in [11] helps blue agents better handle diverse attacker strategies, surpassing traditional rigid methods. Meanwhile, Microsoft's CyberBattleSim supports red agent training but lacks native blue agents. Work in [12] extends this by co-training red and blue agents, improving defender resilience via multiagent learning. Most prior work, however, overlooks environmental uncertainty and openness. Our study focuses on evaluating blue agent adaptability in dynamic, uncertain settings that better reflect realworld cyber defense.

3 Proposed Models and Algorithm

3.1 Problem Description

Overview. In this research, we employ the cybersecurity simulation environment provided by the free-range-zoo to investigate the adaptability and performance of autonomous defender agents in open, dynamic systems. This environment serves as a sophisticated platform for modeling adversarial interactions within network security contexts, offering a valuable testbed for research in MARL. Its key features include support for partially observable environments, dynamic agent participation, and behavior inspired by real-world cyber operations. The simulation environment represents a computer network comprising various nodes, some controlled by the blue team (defenders) and others vulnerable to attacks from the red team (attackers). Red agents aim to exploit network vulnerabilities, while blue agents are tasked with detecting, mitigating, and responding to these threats. Both teams consist of multiple agents, each operating autonomously under limited observability. The interactions among agents are shaped by both cooperative and competitive dynamics, with outcomes influenced by evolving agent behavior, changing network topologies, and adaptive reward structures.

Observation Space. The observation space for each agent is tailored to its role within the simulation. For attackers, the observation space includes information about the agent's own power level and network presence, the power levels and presence of other attackers (if observable), and the overall state of the network in terms of exploited nodes. Defenders, on the contrary, observe their own mitigation power, presence, and location, as well as the status of other defenders and the mitigation state of the network.

Action Space. The action spaces are similarly role-specific. Defender agents can move between connected nodes, patch vulnerabilities to secure nodes, monitor network activity to gather information, or choose to take no action (noop). Attacker agents operate with a simpler action space, which includes the ability to exploit a node or perform no action.

Simulation Configuration. To evaluate defender performance in this study, in this research, we adopt the configuration used in the MOASEI 2025 [5] competition. Attacker and defender agents operate in opposition, with attackers attempting to compromise a network while defenders are tasked with monitoring, protecting, and responding to potential threats. The simulation facilitates dynamic agent participation, allowing agents to enter or exit during runtime, thereby replicating the unpredictability inherent in real-world cyber operations. The network consists of multiple nodes, each representing a system component that can transition between different states from secure (unexploited) to fully compromised (exploited). Attacker agents possess the ability to temporarily disappear from the network to avoid detection, effectively modeling evasive threat behaviors. Conversely, defender agents can be incapacitated and removed from the environment, diminishing the defensive team's effectiveness. Each simulation episode features a 3v3 agent configuration distributed across four subnetworks. The network topology varies across three scenario configurations: CS1 (Fully Connected), CS2 (Star Connected), and CS3 (Linearly Connected). To ensure reproducibility, stochastic elements such as agent disappearance and infection success are governed by fixed random seeds. Agent presence is probabilistic, with both attackers and defenders having a 50% chance of being active at any time. Agents may reenter the environment with a 25% probability after a period of absence. Attacker behavior is fully randomized. Each episode spans up to 50 steps and is executed concurrently across 100 parallel environments, facilitating scalable and robust experimental evaluation. Finally, according to the rules of the competition, the agent cannot see the location or availability of their cooperative agents during the simulation.

3.2 Proximal Policy Optimization (PPO)

Proximal Policy Optimization (PPO) is a popular reinforcement learning algorithm that belongs to the category of policy gradient methods, which optimize an objective function based on the policy's expected return. PPO improves upon Trust Region Policy Optimization (TRPO) [13] by using a clipped surrogate objective to ensure stable updates without enforcing a hard KL-divergence constraint. This clipping mechanism prevents overly large policy updates, enhancing training stability and reducing variance. PPO is typically implemented with an Actor Critic [7] architecture, where the actor learns the policy and the critic estimates state values to guide learning. Its simplicity, stability, and effectiveness make PPO widely used in research and practical applications. In this study, we apply PPO with specific modifications. Overall, PPO's balance between simplicity and performance, along with its practical ease of implementation, has made it one of the most widely adopted RL algorithms in both academic research and real world applications. In this research, we have applied the PPO method with the following modifications. In the PPO algorithm, the states represent the observations from the environment, actions are the decisions taken by the defender based on its policy, the reward function provides feedback from the environment to guide learning, and the transition model governs how the environment changes from one state to another in response to actions.

State Representation. The state $s_t = \{\text{Absent, Location}, [n_1, n_2, \ldots, n_4]\}$ represents a real-time snapshot of the network environment and is used as input to the policy network. It encodes:

- *Absent Indicator:* A binary flag indicating whether the defender agent is currently active or absent in the environment.

- *Agent Location:* The index of the node where the defender is presently located.
- *Node-Level Information:* For each node n_i in the network (e.g., N1 to N4), the state includes Exploit Status, Patch Requirement (number of patch units needed), and Importance Score.

Action Space. The defender's action space in the free-range-zoo Cyber Security environment is a discrete set of context-sensitive operations; `MoveTo(i)`: Move to node i (e.g., N1–N4), `Monitor(i)`: Observe node i for potential exploits. `Patch(i)`: Apply remediation at node i. `No-op`: Perform no action (commonly chosen when the agent is absent or idle). At each timestep t, the agent selects an action $a_t \in A$, guided by its policy, $a_t = \pi_\theta(s_t)$, where π_θ is a stochastic policy parameterized by neural network weights θ. This allows the agent to adaptively choose among detection, response, or repositioning at various nodes, depending on each node's perceived status and the agent's availability.

Reward Function. The reward is calculated based on the importance of each node, which depends on the number of outgoing links and the status of the nodes (Eq. 1). Each node can be in one of five possible states, representing its security level. These states range from fully patched (4.0) to fully exploited (–8.0), with intermediate states indicating increasing levels of exploitation: –2.0, –4.0, and –8.0. A neutral state is represented by 0.0. Thus, node states reflect the degree of security, from fully secure to highly vulnerable.

$$R = \sum_{i=1}^{N} S_i \times I_i \tag{1}$$

where:

- R represents the total reward-weighted sum.
- N denotes the total number of nodes within the network.
- S_i indicates the status of node i.
- I_i reflects the importance of node i, which is determined by the number and nature of its outgoing connections. In other words, nodes that are more highly connected are considered more important. For example, in a star topology, the central node has the most connections and is therefore regarded as the most important node in the network.

The hyperparameters applied for the PPO are shown in Table 1.

3.3 Hierarchical Two-Tier Defense Structure (Heuristic Approach)

This study presents a heuristic approach based on a hierarchical architecture, referred to as HIER, designed to coordinate and manage defender agents in dynamic cybersecurity environments. The architecture is structured into two distinct tiers: global defenders and local defenders. Global agents oversee the

Table 1. Hyperparameters for training.

Hyperparameter	Value
Steps per epoch	4000
Epochs	30
Discount factor (γ)	0.99
Clipping ratio	0.2
Policy learning rate	3×10^{-4}
Target KL divergence	0.01
Policy/Value training iterations	80
Hidden layer sizes	(64, 64)
GAE (λ)	0.97

entire network, providing strategic guidance, while local agents are assigned to specific subnetworks or node clusters, where they focus on detecting and responding to localized threats. By clearly delineating responsibilities across these tiers, the architecture reduces redundancy among local agents, minimizes overlapping actions, and significantly improves overall operational efficiency. The hierarchical control scheme enables scalable deployment and a more intelligent distribution of tasks. Global agents can identify critical nodes across the entire network topology and intervene when local agents face limitations or escalating threats. In contrast, local agents handle routine monitoring and localized patching operations within their designated areas. For instance, as illustrated in Fig. 1, Level 1 features a single global agent overseeing all nodes in the network. Meanwhile, the local defenders at Level 2 are each responsible for specific subsets of the network. In the event that a local agent becomes unavailable, the global agent can assume control of the associated node, provided the global agent itself remains active.

The pseudo code for the heuristic approach is presented in Algorithm 1. Also, the key variables in the *HIER* approach are described in Table 2. This algorithm encapsulates the core operational logic of the system within a stepwise heuristic policy, meticulously designed to ensure coherent agent behavior under varying network conditions: ***Initialization and Perception***: Upon activation, each agent gathers its operational state, including presence status (present or absent), current location, and operational mode (e.g., monitoring or patching) (lines 3–6). ***Absence Detection***: If an agent is detected as absent, it sets an absence flag and performs a noop (no operation). Additionally, if the agent was previously in monitoring mode, its latest observational data is stored for future retrieval upon reintegration into the network (lines 7–13). ***Reintegration Protocol***: When an agent re-joins the network after a period of absence, it checks both the monitoring and absence flags. If both flags are active, the agent clears them and restores its previously saved observations, ensuring a seamless continuation of its decision-making processes (lines 14–17). ***Patching Process***: If the

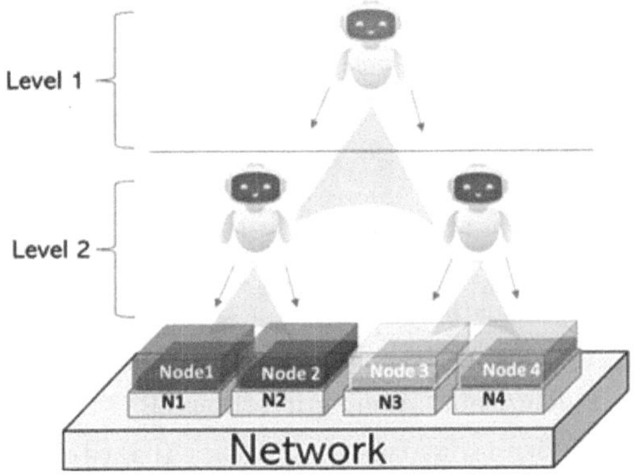

Fig. 1. A simplified illustration of a hierarchical two-tier defense structure.

agent is in patching mode and has not yet reached its designated target node, it initiates movement toward the target node. This movement is necessary because agents are relocated to their home node when unavailable (lines 18–22). Upon arrival, if it is the agent's first engagement at that node, it updates relevant flags and begins patching operations, decrementing the required patch count with each action (lines 23–27). Lines 28–34 handle the agent's initial arrival at the target node, updating location flags and triggering the first patch action. ***Monitoring Behavior***: In monitoring mode, agent behavior is determined by their assigned level (lines 35–57). Local agents (e.g., those with indices 1 or 2) execute localized monitoring policies. These policies evaluate node vulnerability and importance metrics to decide whether to monitor, move, patch, or remain idle. Global agents (e.g., index 3) oversee the entire network, identifying the most exploited and high-priority nodes across domains and issuing patch instructions or intervening as required. All agents follow a similar policy framework: they select the most exploited node based on its importance, defined by the number of outgoing links. When no specific condition is met, agents default to continued monitoring (lines 57–58). In the next section, we conduct evaluations to compare the proposed approaches with the baseline methods.

4 Performance Evaluation

4.1 Baseline Approaches

To evaluate strategic interventions in the free-range-zoo environment, a set of baseline defender policies is employed. These serve as comparative references for assessing performance across different levels of agent sophistication. Below, we summarize each policy:

- **No-Operation (Noop) Policy**: The defender takes no action throughout the simulation. It establishes a baseline reflecting environmental dynamics without defense.

Algorithm 1: Hierarchical Approach (Heuristic)

```
Function observe(observation):
    for env_id ← 0 to parallel_envs - 1 do
        Get is_absent flag
        Get location of the agent
        Get obs for agent
        last_monitor ← Check whether it is in monitoring mode
        if is_absent then
            absent_flag ← 1
            action ← Noop
            if last_monitor then
                monitoring_flag ← 1
                last_monitoring_list ← copy(obs)
            continue
        if monitoring_flag and absent_flag then
            monitoring_flag ← 0
            absent_flag ← 0
            obs ← last_monitoring_list
        if time_focused > 0 then
            if location = -1 then
                next_node ← previous_node
                action ← Move to next_node
                continue
            else if next_node = -1 then
                action ← Patch
                previous_node ← location
                time_focused ← time_focused - 1
                continue
        if next_node ≠ -1 then
            if next_node = location then
                action ← Patch
                next_node ← -1
                previous_node ← location
                time_focused ← time_focused - 1
            continue
        if last_monitor then
            switch agent_number do
                case 1 do
                    process(1, obs, location)
                case 2 do
                    process(2, obs, location)
                case 3 do
                    // Identify the most exploited node based on its importance.
                    // Out Puts: next_node, time_focused
                    if time_focused = 0 then
                        action ← Monitor
                        next_node ← -1
                        time_focused ← 0
                        break
                    if location ≠ -1 and current_node_required_patch = time_focused then
                        next_node ← location
                        previous_node ← location
                        time_focused ← current_node_required_patches
                    if next_node = location then
                        action ← Patch
                        next_node ← -1
                        time_focused ← time_focused - 1
                    else
                        action ← Move to next_node
                        previous_node ← next_node
        else
            action ← Monitor
```

Table 2. Key indicators and variables in the HIER approach.

Variable	Role
is_absent	Flag indicating the agent is currently absent from the network
absent_flag	Indicates whether the agent was absent in the previous step
monitoring_flag	Tracks whether the agent is currently holding monitoring data
last_monitoring_list	Snapshot of observations when last in monitoring mode
time_focused	Remaining timesteps to spend patching the current node
next_node	Node the agent should move to or patch next
previous_node	Last node visited or patched
last_monitor	Indicates whether the agent is in monitoring mode

- **Random Policy**: Defender actions are selected uniformly at random, independent of system state or objectives.
- **Camp Policy**: Each defender is statically assigned to a node based on its index and continuously patches it. Upon disconnection, it returns to the same node. In this policy, monitoring actions are not intended for checking the node status; rather, they are reserved for determining the agent's location.
- **Patched Policy**: Defenders target the most nearly patched (but not fully patched) node, the patch action is executed three times.
- **MExploited Policy**: Defenders prioritize nodes with the highest exploitation level, patching their target node three timesteps.

These policies establish a baseline for evaluating the proposed approaches to defender behavior in open and dynamic systems.

4.2 Evaluation Metrics

The effectiveness of the proposed methods is evaluated using four key metrics. First, the Average Episode Reward is measured, which reflects the mean total reward achieved in each episode for the defender. Second, the Average Number of Redundant Patches is considered, indicating how often patches are deployed unnecessarily. Third, the Average Number of Monitor Actions Executed is examined to assess the monitoring activity. Last, the Average Count of Move Actions is analyzed to determine the degree of agent movement during the episodes. In the following, we compared the performance of the proposed approaches with the baseline methods using these metrics.

4.3 Performance Evaluation Results

Table 3 gives the average rewards of seven policies—*Noop*, *Random*, *Patched*, *MExploited*, *HIER*, *Camp*, and *PPO*—across three configurations (CS1, CS2, CS3), along with their aggregated total rewards. *HIER* demonstrates the best overall performance, achieving the highest total reward (1575.88), leading in CS1

(773.76), and maintaining strong results in CS2 (387.84) and CS3 (414.28). *Patched* follows closely with a total reward of 1455.14, showing solid performance in CS1 (706.56) and CS2 (392.12), though slightly lower in CS3 (356.46). *MExploited* ranks third (1297.30), performing well in CS1 (646.02) and CS3 (401.06), but scoring lower in CS2 (250.22). *Random* achieves a moderate total reward (819.30), peaking in CS1 (411.24), but is substantially outperformed by top policies. *Noop* and *PPO* perform poorly, with total rewards of 505.68 and 636.58, respectively. *PPO* struggles due to the environment's randomness and lack of predictable attacker behavior, limiting its ability to extract stable patterns. Additionally, *PPO's* inability to retain historical context upon rejoining the network hampers its performance, particularly in dynamic, open environments. These conditions violate the stationary assumptions of typical RL algorithms, leading to unstable learning and rapid policy obsolescence. Lastly, *Camp* achieves a low total reward (649.08), primarily due to its lack of monitoring and informative actions.

Table 3. Average Total Rewards Across Different Configurations for Various Policies.

Policy	CS1	CS2	CS3	Total
Noop	275.82	145.06	84.80	505.68
Random	411.24	195.66	212.40	819.30
Patched	706.56	392.12	356.46	1455.14
MExploited	646.02	250.22	401.06	1297.30
HIER	**773.76**	**387.84**	**414.28**	**1575.88**
Camp	322.92	133.32	192.84	649.08
PPO	294.42	174.78	167.38	636.58

Figure 2 illustrates the average number of monitor actions executed for each defender agent across the three experimental configurations (CS1, CS2, and CS3). The *HIER* policy demonstrates a notably higher number of monitor actions in all configurations, averaging over 20 actions per episode. This suggests a proactive and dynamic monitoring approach under challenging conditions, indicating that *HIER* makes more informed decisions. In contrast, most other policies, including *random*, *patched*, *MExploited*, *camp*, and *PPO* maintain consistently low numbers of monitor actions, typically ranging between 6 and 8 across all configurations. This more conservative monitoring behavior may reflect a passive or less adaptive strategy, which could reduce their overall effectiveness and responsiveness to threats. Overall, policies with lower monitoring frequencies may lack the responsiveness necessary for effective threat detection and mitigation in complex scenarios.

Figure 3 illustrates the average number of movement actions carried out by defender agents. This metric reflects the defenders' mobility and responsiveness, both of which are crucial for adapting to changing threat scenarios. This indicates how mobile and responsive the defenders are. *Camp* and *random* policies lead to

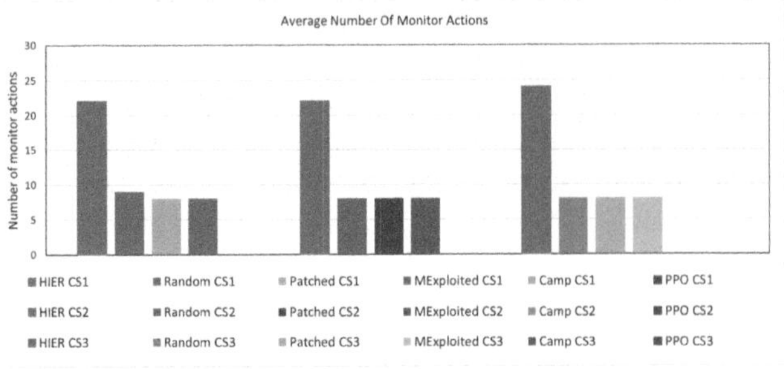

Fig. 2. Average number of monitoring actions across three network configurations.

the most movement, likely reflecting reactive and unplanned behavior. In contrast, *patched*, *MExploited*, and *HIER* show moderate movement (15–30 actions), suggesting a more strategic and balanced approach. *HIER* demonstrates efficiency and purposeful movement, leading to strong performance and rewarding results. Regarding the *PPO* approach, since the agents cannot retain previous steps and history, the *PPO* agent may struggle to make the correct decisions. For example, when the agent is moved back to the home node due to an absence condition, it cannot remember its previous locations or actions. As a result, it is unable to make appropriate decisions in the current context. Overall, high movement does not guarantee better defense. More effective strategies, such as *HIER* and *patched*, balance mobility with other actions, showing the value of adaptive, context-aware policies.

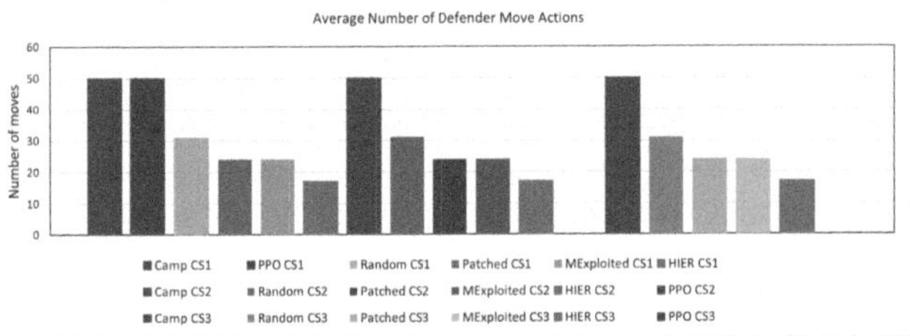

Fig. 3. Average number of movement actions across three network configurations.

Figure 4 illustrates the average number of redundant patch actions executed by defenders. Redundant patch actions refer to instances where a system that is already secured is patched again, representing an inefficient use of defensive resources. The data reveals marked disparities in redundancy levels among the various policies and configurations. In particular, the *Patched* and *MExploited* policies show the highest incidence of redundant actions, frequently exceeding 10 redundant patches per episode. This occurs because many agents simultaneously perform similar actions on similar nodes. This trend implies a deficiency in situational awareness or adaptability, leading to repetitive and unnecessary interventions. However, the more advanced *HIER* policy consistently records significantly lower levels of redundancy, typically registering fewer than two redundant actions per episode across all configurations. This minimal redundancy suggests a more efficient and precise operational strategy, with the agent accurately identifying and patching only genuinely vulnerable systems. In summary, the results underscore the superior performance of the *HIER* policy, which not only achieves higher rewards but also demonstrates greater operational efficiency by avoiding superfluous actions. In contrast, baseline and less adaptive policies generate considerable overhead through excessive redundancy, potentially undermining the overall effectiveness of the defensive strategy.

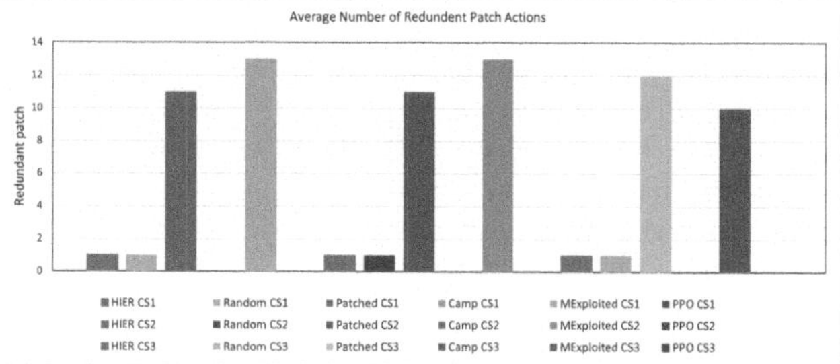

Fig. 4. Average number of redundant patch actions across three network configurations.

5 Conclusion

This study presents a novel hierarchical heuristic framework (HIER) to improve the adaptability and generalization of cybersecurity defense mechanisms in open and uncertain environments. Through comprehensive analysis and empirical evaluation, we demonstrate that HIER consistently outperforms the standard PPO algorithm, achieving higher rewards with greater operational efficiency. Unlike baseline approaches that suffer from excessive and redundant actions, HIER strategically minimizes such inefficiencies, leading to more effective defense operations. Moreover, the observed performance disparities across various configurations underscore the superior competitiveness of our framework compared to less adaptive policies. These insights contribute to the development of robust, scalable, and context-sensitive cybersecurity strategies, enhancing the generalization capabilities of defenders in increasingly open and dynamic systems.

Acknowledgments. The authors sincerely thank the organizers of the MOASEI 2025 [5,14] competition for providing a valuable platform that inspired our research. We are honored that our proposed approach, named "ZANA_CYBER", was recognized as the winning solution in this competition.

References

1. Vyas, S., Hannay, J., Bolton, A., Burnap, P.P.: Automated cyber defence: a review (2023). arXiv preprint
2. Bates, E., Mavroudis, V., Hicks, C.: Reward shaping for happier autonomous cyber security agents. In: Proceedings of the 16th ACM Workshop on Artificial Intelligence and Security (2023)
3. Eck, A., Soh, L.-K., Doshi, P.: Decision making in open multiagent systems. AI Mag. **44**(4), 508–523 (2023). https://doi.org/10.1002/aaai.12131
4. OASYS-MAS. (2025). Free-range zoo. GitHub. Accessed 18 Jun 2025. https://github.com/oasys-mas/free-range-zoo
5. Patino, C., et al.: Inaugural MOASEI competition at AAMAS 2025: a technical report. In: Proceedings of the 24th International Conference on Autonomous Agents and Multiagent Systems (AAMAS 2025) (2025). https://doi.org/10.48550/arXiv.2507.05469
6. Terry, J.: PettingZoo: gym for multi-agent reinforcement learning. In: Advances in Neural Information Processing Systems, pp. 15032–15043. (2021)
7. Schulman, J., Wolski, F., Dhariwal, P., Radford, A., Klimov, O.: Proximal policy optimization algorithms (2017). arXiv preprint
8. Wolk, M.: Beyond cage: investigating generalization of learned autonomous network defense policies (2022). arXiv preprint
9. Nyberg, J., Johnson, P.: Training automated defense strategies using graph-based cyber attack simulations (2023). arXiv preprint
10. Collyer, J., Andrew, A., Hodges, D.: ACD-G: enhancing autonomous cyber defense agent generalization through graph embedded network representation (2022)
11. Farooq, M.O., Kunz, T.: A generic blue agent training framework for autonomous cyber operations. In: Proceedings of the IFIP Networking Conference, 3 June 2024, pp. 515–521. IEEE (2024)
12. Kunz, T., Fisher, C., La Novara-Gsell, J., Nguyen, C., Li, L.: A multiagent CyberBattleSim for RL cyber operation agents. https://arxiv.org/abs/2304.11052 (2023)
13. Schulman, J., Levine, S., Abbeel, P., Jordan, M., Moritz, P.: Trust region policy optimization. In: Proceedings of the 32nd International Conference on Machine Learning, pp. 1889–1897. PMLR (2015)
14. OASYS-MAS: MOASEI: multi-objective adaptive system for emergent intelligence. https://oasys-mas.github.io/moasei.html. Accessed 18 Jun 2025

Design of an Automated pet Nourishment System and Embedded Microcontroller

Bassam Shaer(✉), Noah Bradshaw, and Alyssa McLaughlin

ECE and ME Engineering Department, University of West Florida Fort Walton Beach, Florida, USA

bshaer@uwf.edu

Abstract. This paper presents the design and implementation of an adjustable embedded microcontroller in an automated pet nourishment system. The automated system addresses common challenges faced by pet owners, offering adjustable feeding and watering solutions alongside its cleaning functionalities. The system will be designed with features that include: a customizable feeding regimen, allowing users to input specific feeding quantities per serving, serving frequency, and feeding times; a water dispensing component that incorporates a self-cleaning mechanism, where the user can opt for continuous water supply, timed refills, and scheduled cleanings; and a mobile application that enables remote monitoring and control. This paper will describe the design, implementation, and results of each of the listed objectives.

Keywords: Automated · self-cleaning · food and water distribution · embedded · microcontroller · adjustable

1 Introduction

At some point in every person's life whether it be as a parent, child, or independently the thought of getting a pet arises. Just how many people have pets? You may ask, well according to the World Animal Foundation, 86.9 million households, which equates to 66% in the United States, own at least one pet [1]. As the bond between humans and their pets continues to deepen, the need for innovative solutions to streamline pet care routines becomes increasingly apparent. One of the primary responsibilities of pet owners is to ensure their companions receive proper nutrition and hydration, even in their absence. The Animal Humane Society recommends that both cats and dogs be fed no more than twice daily [2]. However, busy lifestyles and unpredictable schedules often pose challenges in meeting these needs consistently. Traditional feeding methods often lack precision and reliability, leading to overfeeding, underfeeding, or irregular feeding patterns. Similarly, stagnant water bowls can harbor bacteria and impurities, posing health risks for pets. Our objective is to empower pet owners with reliable and user-friendly solutions that not only simplifies their pet care responsibilities but also foster a healthier and happier environment for their furry companions. By combining technological innovation with a commitment to pet well-being, we strive to set a new standard in modern pet care practices.

H. R. Arabnia et al. (Eds.): CSCE 2025, CCIS 2932, pp. 91–104, 2026.
https://doi.org/10.1007/978-3-032-22193-3_7

The most feasible solution we envisioned for addressing this problem revolved around an automated system paired with a graphical user interface (GUI). The concepts of automated feeding and self-cleaning water systems are prevalent today; however, very few are paired together on the same apparatus. We researched what was available on the market that performed the independent functions listed and found several units already available to consumers. Our search was largely influenced by TOPUSA [3, 4] which led us to choose the top-rated appliances; the PETLIBRO automatic cat feeder, Rellaty cat water fountain, and PETLIBRO cat water fountain. Each of these products were awarded roughly an average of 4.2 of 5-star reviews online.

First, the PETLIBRO automatic cat feeder is a 3-l, corded electric pet feeder equipped with 5G Wi-Fi and Bluetooth connectivity for app control. Its star feature consists of a radio-frequency identification (RFID) collar tag to prevent food aggression and ensure individualized feeding in a multi-pet household. The $117.99 component offers data reports, manual feeding options, and an adjustable lid with three speed modes for easy adaptation. Customer reviews of the model average 4 out of 5 stars with 665 reviews. The biggest complaints consisted of the lid's closing mechanism speed being too slow despite the apps control settings and it not being secure, users frequently experiencing error messages when the discrepancies listed were not present, and the durability of the RFID collar and power cord as potential hazards [5].

Second, the stainless steel Rellaty cat water fountain has a 3.2-l capacity and a quadruple filtration system with interchangeable carbon sponges for clean drinking water. Its 5 V pump operates at 30 dB to minimize noise and double water flow design encourages pets to drink more. Powered by a corded electric 5 V source, it can be disassembled and cleaned with dishwasher-safe components (except the pump and filters). The system costs $29.54 and garnered a 4.3-star rating based on 7,729 reviews. However, several users expressed significant dissatisfaction, citing frequent cleaning requirements and poor water quality [6].

The PETLIBRO water fountain is the final competitive comparison. It is composed of a rechargeable 5,000 mAh lithium-ion battery dockstream, a 2.5-l stainless steel water capacity, and a detachable water tank and pump for easy cleaning. It has two water flow modes: an induction mode activated by a radar sensor and a regular mode for continuous dispersal. The fountain's four-stage filtration system ensures fresh water and operates at 23 dB. Over 3.000 reviews gave this system a 4.5-star rating at a price of $57.98. The most common issues reported were leaking causing flooding at its base, failed sensor activation to distribute water, and condensation buildup potentially leading to malfunctions [7].

An underlying disparity between competitors are the cleaning requirements and sensor reliability. To contend in the existing market, our design aims to compound on these shortcomings by focusing on a cleaning mechanism that operates independently from drinking water distribution. This will alleviate the potential for system failure on account of interdependence. As well as combining the four main segments: food distribution, water allocation, cleaning function, and adjustable user interface all in one framework. In doing so the user would save time and money by maintaining a single prototype instead of purchasing multiple devices. The remainder of the paper is organized accordingly: Sect. 2 offers a brief overview of the system, while Sect. 3 outlines the technical approach. Section 4 provides a formal description of the testing methodology, and Sect. 5 presents the results of the analysis. To conclude the paper Sect. 6 states the closing remarks.

2 System Overview

The target demographic for our product primarily encompasses pet owners, including busy professionals, elderly or disabled individuals responsible for pet care, households with multiple pets, and those managing pets with specific dietary requirements. Our design facilitates scheduled feeding with customizable portions at set intervals to ensure consistent and balanced nutrition. This approach extends to the timed, self-cleaning water dispenser, promoting hydration alongside feeding. As a result, benefits such as portion control, convenience, peace of mind, and simplified maintenance are inherent features of our solution.

Major assumptions for this project encompass pet acceptance of the use of our product without experiencing undue stress or resistance. Additionally, the reliability of automation without technical malfunctions paired with user compliance with the recommended usage guidelines for optimal functionality. To delve a little deeper into the previously stated assumptions, appropriate portioning for the dietary requirements of each pet and maintenance adherence for the general upkeep to ensure the proper functioning of the self-cleaning feature also come into play.

Limitations include technical malfunctions, limited customization for households with multiple pets with diverse dietary needs, dependency on power, initial cost and maintenance, and a possible main water line tie-in to eliminate the need to refill the water dispenser. The pet feeding and watering system's sensor accuracy is crucial to ensure proper proportioning and dispensing of food and water. Variations in sensor readings could lead to inaccurate measurements, potentially affecting pet nutrition. Mechanical reliability is also paramount, as fluctuations in torque output from motors or wear and tear over time could disrupt feeding and cleaning processes, compromising the system's functionality. Software integration is essential to address compatibility issues and software bugs that may arise, as seamless communication between hardware and software is necessary for customizable settings and smooth operation. Additionally, effective power management is vital to minimize power consumption and ensure uninterrupted operation, especially during power outages or battery failures, enhancing the system's overall reliability and performance.

Our team produced a fully automated pet nourishment system with a software interface via a phone application and/or plate controller that will communicate with the device's hardware to portion out water and food at timed intervals. Load cell and submersible capacitance sensors will communicate to two DC motors to monitor and perform these tasks. The cleaning mechanism consists of a tract system that moves the bowl into the cleaning area where pressurized water will spray the remnants clean before docking back to the resting position. The objective is to create a reliable, cost-effective system that combines the feeding, watering, and cleaning functions of the separate model purchases users are forced to make today. A functional block diagram is depicted in Fig. 1.

3 Technical Approach

3.1 Control Unit

Microcontroller. The Arduino Mega 2560 was utilized as the central controller for this project. It was chosen for its ability to handle multiple sensors and its extensive pin availability, which ensures seamless connectivity with various hardware components. Its programmable features and support for multiple interruptions make it an ideal choice for integrating the system's complex functionalities, including automated food and water dispensing, cleaning mechanisms, and communication with the user interface. The Mega 2560's reliability and flexibility were pivotal in ensuring smooth operations and efficient control of the entire system [8].

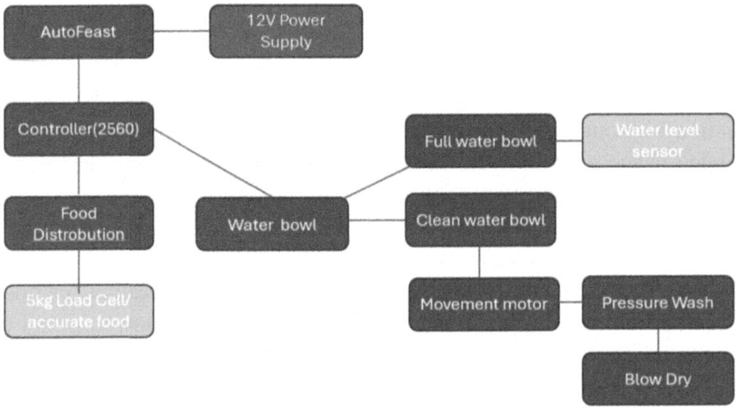

Fig. 1. Functional Block Diagram

Power. Our system runs off a 12 V DC power supply that connects to your standard home outlet (120 V / 60 Hz).

Coding. An ArduinoIDE, and C coding language were employed to program the components. These tools were chosen based on familiarity with the software and our ability to develop the code necessary for inter-functionality of the model.

3.2 Food Distribution.

Load Cell. The project incorporates a 5 kg load cell sensor to ensure precise dispensing of pet food. The sensor measures the weight of the food being dispensed in real-time, allowing the system to accurately portion meals according to the user's specifications. The load cell communicates with the microcontroller, which processes the data to stop the dispensing mechanism once the desired weight is achieved. This level of precision prevents overfeeding or underfeeding, ensuring pets receive the correct amount of food every time. By integrating this sensor, the system not only enhances accuracy but also promotes consistent nutrition for pets, making it a vital component of the overall design.

Scoop Motor. A 12 V DC gear motor with an output of 20 RPM and 10 W horsepower was utilized to rotate the 3D printed scoop seen in Fig. 2 [9]. This motor was chosen for its strong load capacity, durability, and sheathed female connector. The 3-in. diameter scoop was attached to the mounting bracket and situated within the side of the 10-l food container. Testing was done during assembly to ensure that the motor had the torque necessary to drive the weight of the food down into the bowl.

Fig. 2. 3D Printed Scoop

3.3 Drinking Water Dispersal

Water Sensor. A 5 V DC water level sensor was mounted to a servo motor to detect the presence of water [10]. This input initiated the distribution, removal, and cleaning processes.

Servo Motor. The SG90 9G micro-servo motor has an operating voltage range of 4.8 V–6 V [10]. It was exploited for its 180 running degrees. The water sensor was mounted to turn a 90° angle. In doing so, it would exit the bowl during use and other functions. Other user specifications include: at no load, the running speed is 0.09 ± 0.01 s/60° when operating at 4.8 V, and 0.08 ± 0.01 s/60° at 6 V. Also, the stall torque at 4.8 V is 17.5 oz./in (1 kg/cm), and the dead band setting is 5 ms.

Solenoid. The DC 12 V ¼-inch quick connect solenoid valve is designed to control water flow in response to the input from the water sensor. It operates within a pressure range of 0.02 to 0.08 MPa (MegaPascal) and functions with a rated power of 4.8 W. This valve was fixed to the nozzle of the 9.4-l water container by heat shrinking a ¼-inch water tube into the inlet connection [11]. It was observed that the solenoid took 3 min to dispense 2 oz. of water. The solenoid would automatically be activated via water level sensor readings. The water bowl would remain full while in the drinking area (not cleaning area).

Dosing Pump. A dosing pump with a 5000 RPM motor and 12 V DC power supply provided a flow rate change of 0–100 ml/min [11]. This component was placed directly over the back end of the 8 oz. bowl to remove water before and after the cleaning system initiation. Throughout the analysis, it was observed that it took the pump 1 min to remove a quarter of the bowls holding capacity. This functionality would also occur automatically, two times a day the system will clean the water bowl. The water level sensor will be used to control the pump. The pump will remain on until the water bowl is empty, then the bowl is transferred to the cleaning area.

3.4 Cleaning Mechanism

Track Motor. An 8 V DC gear motor pulled the water bowl around a 20-in. section of PGN #25 roller chain. The bowl was attached to the chain with a piece of steel wire and sealed with super glue to prevent leakage. The track motor was also connected to the L298N motor controller. Depending on the Duty cycle used through PWM we could control the speed of the track motor. We chose a value of 200 to run the motor at, which was roughly 78% of the motor's top speed.

$$Duty\ cycle = \frac{PWM\ value}{255} \times 100$$

$$\text{Duty cycle} = \frac{200}{255} \times 100 \approx 78.43\%$$

Blower fan. The 5 V centrifugal blower operates at 7500 RPM, offering an airflow of 2.7 CFM [12]. The addition of this element aimed to remove excess water leftover from the diaphragm pump and potentially push the overflow toward the drainage corner. Two ½-inch water tubes direct the fan's air. The blower motor is automatically activated after the Diaphragm pump sprays the water bowl with high-pressure water.

Diaphragm Pump. Designed for durability, the 12 V RV water pump with ½-inch connections was chosen to pressurize the cleaning solution stored in the 1.2-l canister [13]. A ¼-inch 25° pressure washer spray tip with a range of 1600–4500 PSI is attached to ½-inch water tubing to distribute a 5-s blast of water into the bowl to remove debris.

3.5 Frame

Wheels. Four 2-in. diameter swivel caster wheels with brakes are screwed into the bottom of the frame to allow for maneuverability and safety while in use. With a 90-lb load capacity, they are functional in a range of conditions.

Drainage. A 26.8″ x 15.7″ x 2.8″ low-profile drain pan rests on the bottom level of the frame with ¼-inch water tubing entering both the top and side openings. The top opening receives the excess water vacuumed out of the water bowl by the dosing pump. While the side takes in the cleaning water produced by the diaphragm pump. There is a

1.5-in. hole cut into the middle level of the system in the back left corner of the cleaning box with a plastic channel to direct the runoff into the drainage pan. A 36″ x 11.5″ x ¼" piece of plexiglass is held up by 7 ½-inch diameter plexiglass pegs that range from 2 to 1.25 in. in length to produce a slope of 0.25% in the hopes of directing the backsplash towards the corner drain. The 1.5-in. drainage hole is mirrored on the plexiglass section and is boxed in between the two levels with leftover plexiglass pieces. All of the edges between the middle and plexiglass are caulked to minimize leakage.

Safety. The cleaning functions are contained in a 12″ x 12″ x 12″ plexiglass box to eliminate the presence of water on any electrical components. An additional 12″ x 12″ x 6″ plexiglass box was constructed to provide coverage of the electrical components as an extra precaution. Both enclosures have an open face to allow bowl egress and maneuverability. Also, the turn wheel depicted in Fig. 2 is stationed within the food container so the animal can't tamper with or potentially damage food distribution. A PVC chute is positioned underneath the hole to guide the food into the bowl while a plexiglass cover and skirt limit stray pieces from bouncing outside of the desired placement. There is also a 12″ x 10″ x 4″ plywood box situated over the bowl to protect the load cell underneath the 8 oz. food bowl. All of the water components are mounted to plywood shelves that skim the water bowl's edge to eliminate the possibility of the pet damaging themselves or the elements. As mentioned previously the water sensor turns 90° on a servo motor to exit the bowl for use. All standoff distances were set to ensure minimal interference.

Level Breakdown. There are 5 levels to our system. First, the base is a 40″ x 24″ x ½" piece of plywood that houses the drainage pan. The middle section has a 4-in. gap held up by a 1"x 1″ stilt. This section contains the plywood food box, load cell, food bowl, plexiglass cleaning box, drainage hole, Track motor, and chain. Next, the plexiglass layer has the water bowl and the mirrored drainage hole. After that, there is a 40″ x 8.5″ x ¼" plywood hanging shelf that rests on four L-brackets screwed 5 in. above the middle layer. There are four 10-in. 1″ x 1″ stilts that said L-brackets are attached to. The hanging shelf has 2 overhangs with the solenoid, dosage pump, and diaphragm pump mounted. Additionally, the blower fan is positioned 3-in. from the trailing edge. Finally, the 40″ x 12″ x ½" top layer stores all three containers, the scoop motor on an overhang, and all electrical components in the plexiglass cover. Fig. 3 displays the configurations described.

4 Testing Approach

Each component was tested iteratively to verify functionality. This process ensured that each element performed as expected, with any issues being identified and resolved at each stage. This includes verifying sensor accuracy, motor reliability, and software responsiveness. Functional testing is then conducted to gauge the system's ability to perform intended actions, such as timed feeding, water dispensing, and self-cleaning, by testing different schedules, portion sizes, and cleaning cycles. Finally, reliability testing evaluates the system's consistent performance over an extended period, running it continuously to identify potential issues or failures. Specific criteria, such as sensor

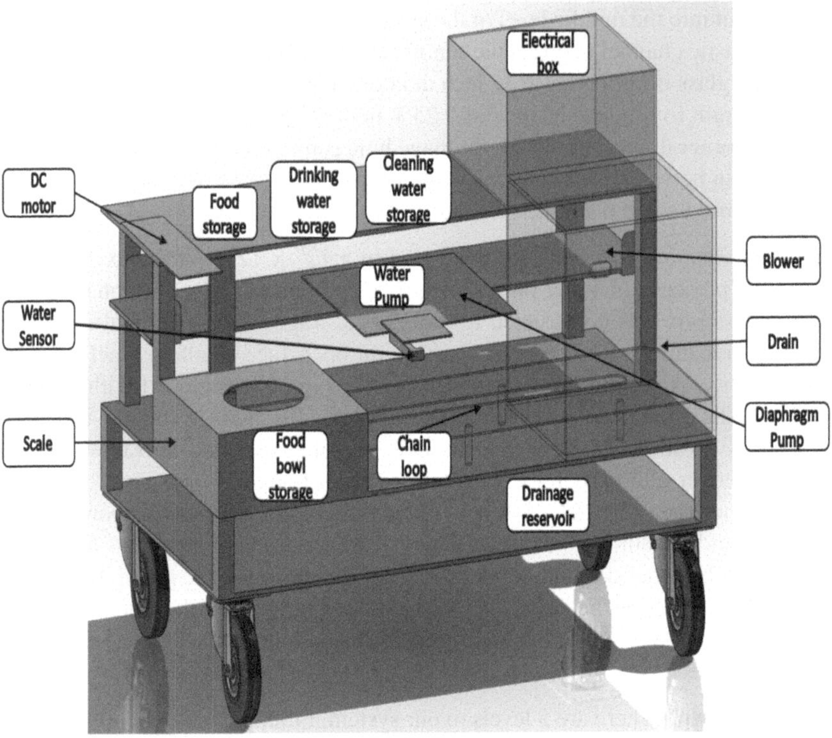

Fig. 3. Frame Diagram

accuracy within +/− 10% of the desired amount, reliable motor performance, user-friendly software interface for adjustable settings, and successful dispensing of food and water at scheduled intervals are key benchmarks for system performance. Adjustments were made as needed to improve performance and reliability. This approach allowed ongoing refinement and optimization before integration into the overall system.

5 Project Results

The automated system ran through 50 iterations aiming to meet the baseline distribution of 8 oz. for both the food and water bowls. Due to the variance in current and voltage outputs for each trial, the scoop and water solenoid dispensed a wide range of products as seen in Fig. 4. The average food dispersion was 7.99 oz. which falls within the 10% margin of error set by the team. While the average amount of water available to the pet was 8 fluid ounces. It should be noted that the amount of time for the water bowl to refill and remove the consumable water was substantial. For perspective, it took 3 min to fill the water bowl a quarter of its maximum holding capacity. The team was able to initiate the output response of the entire system via phone; however, we were not able to allow the user to adjust the settings on the application. The source code would have to be adjusted and uploaded to the Arduino as it stands now.

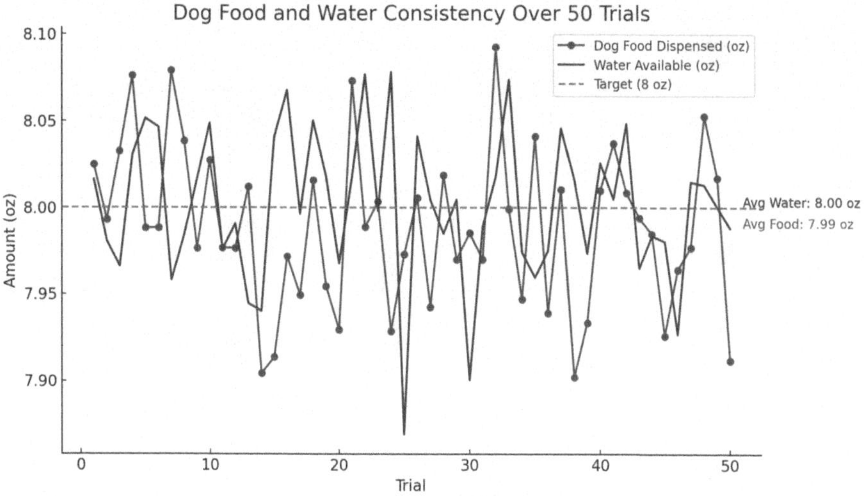

Fig. 4. Prototype Consistency Analysis Graph

The initial design was to construct a robotic arm with a replaceable brush attachment as the cleaning component. However, after further consideration it would have increased the market price of the prototype and would have introduced a complex element that opens the door for additional maintenance. In addition, the cleaning mechanism originally was supposed to have tilted to vertically rotate the bowl, enabling direct water spray and gravity relied drainage rather than the top-down trajectory that is present in our design currently. Ultimately, time constraints hindered a majority of our alternative approaches.

The final design Figs. 5, 6, 7, and 8 consists of an automated nourishment system that can dispense adjustable amounts of food and drinking water. The user can initiate a cleaning sequence triggered by the input of the water sensor to vacuum out old water before traversing via a chain system to the cleaning area. There a pressurized blast of water removes debris and a blower removes residual cleaning solution. Once the bowl returns to its resting position the dosing pump vacuums out whatever is left before the solenoid distributes fresh drinking water.

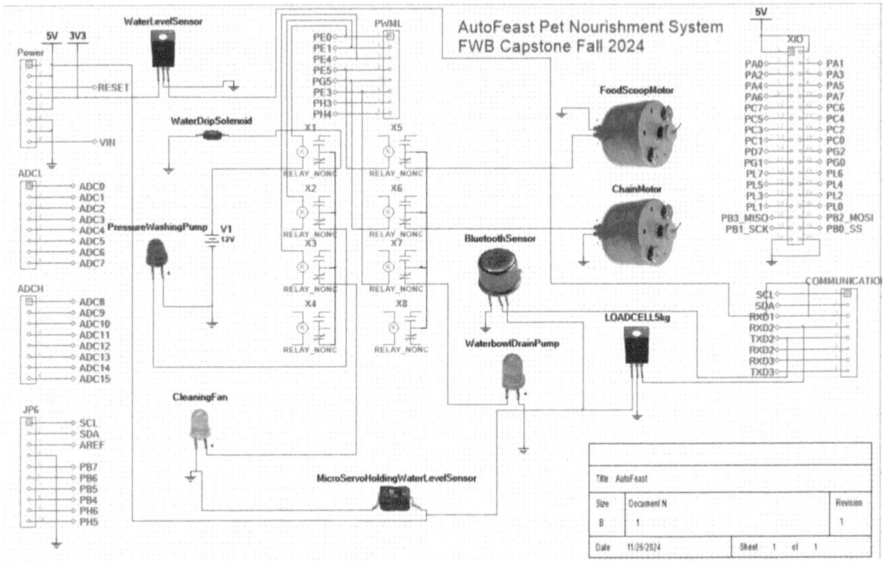

Fig. 5. Circuit Schematic

Fig. 6. Finished Prototype

Fig. 7. System Components

Fig. 8. Top View of the Completed Circuit

6 Conclusion

At the conclusion of the project, all except one design objective was met in the configuration of an automated pet nourishment system. The GUI was intended to enable user control of the systems via a mobile application. The key feature that allows the food and water quantities and time intervals to be adjustable is present; however, the source code had to be altered before initiating the sequence on said application.

Future improvements to the design of this nourishment model would be the addition of a mounted faceplate that would act as a base control for maintenance, system resets, and function settings. Integrating this attribute would provide an additional medium for safety and redundancy in case the application was to ever falter. Also, the implementation of a main-water tie-in for the drinking and cleaning reservoirs would require minimal consumer participation. Again, the entire distribution system performed well within the 10% variance range. However, the power supply and quality of components such as the solenoids and blower proved to hinder the dispersion times and consistency of pours. Time management and attention to detail during the design process definitely impacted the configuration of the entire model and user interface abilities.

References

1. Pet Spending Statistics - Expenditure on Pampering Them: (2023). https://worldanimalfoundation.org/advocate/pet-spending-statistics/
2. Feeding your dog or cat, Animal Humane Society: (2024). https://www.animalhumanesociety.org/resource/feeding-your-dog-or-cat
3. Our 5 Best Pet Feeder - Black Friday 2024.: Top5-USA.com, Top5-usa.com, (2024). https://doi.org/10782546836/EMugCLn9g_8CEJS3wpUo
4. Top5-usa.com :(2024). https://www.top5-usa.com/water-fountain-for-pets Accessed 26 Nov 2024
5. Amazon.com: PETLIBRO Upgraded RFID Automatic Cat Feeder, 5G Wi-Fi Automatic Pet Feeder, 3L Auto Cat Feeder App Control with Light Collar Tag, Tag Activated One Automatic Cat Food Dispenser 1–10 Meals Control, Amazon.com, (2024). https://www.amazon.com/dp/B0CX8VKMD9 (Accessed 27 Nov 2024)
6. Amazon.com: Cat Water Fountain Stainless Steel: 3.2L/108oz Pet Fountain Water Bowl Dog Drinking Dispenser Cat Feeding & Watering Supplies Animal Metal Kitty Spout for Cats Inside with 4 Replacement Filters : Pet Supplies. https://www.amazon.com/dp/B0B6GK5LKY (Accessed 27 Nov 2024)
7. Amazon.com: PETLIBRO Cat Water Fountain, Wireless Pet Fountain Battery Operated, 2.5L/84oz Dockstream Automatic Dog Water Dispenser for Drinking with Quiet Pump Inside Stainless Steel Tray Easy Clean BPA-Free: Everything Else, Amazon.com, (2024). https://www.amazon.com/dp/B0BYDS9KHV (Accessed 27 Nov 2024)
8. Arduino Mega 2560 Datasheet: Accessed 01 Dec 2024. https://cdn.robotshop.com/media/a/ard/rb-ard-33/pdf/arduinomega2560datasheet.pdf
9. Bringsmart 37mm Diameter Gearbox with Bracket Micro DC 12V 20rpm Geared Motor Centric Ouput Shaft Gear Motor Large Torque Reduction Motor - Amazon.com.: Amazon.com, (2024). https://www.amazon.com/dp/B0C7GMFMF2 (Accessed 28 Nov 2024)
10. Amazon.com: DIYables Water Sensor Detector for Arduino, ESP32, ESP8266, Raspberry Pi, 5 pieces : Electronics. https://www.amazon.com/dp/B0BXKMLB4D (Accessed 28 Nov 2024)
11. Amazon.com: DIGITEN DC 12V 1/4" Inlet Feed Water Solenoid Valve Quick Connect N/C normally Closed : Industrial & Scientific. https://www.amazon.com/dp/B016MP1HX0 (Accessed 29 Nov 2024)

12. Amazon.com: 2Packs Wathai DC Blower Fan 4010 Radial Cooling Fan 5V 2 Pin DC 40mm x 10mm Dual Ball : Electronics. https://www.amazon.com/dp/B07RMY75GH (Accessed 30 Nov 2024)
13. Amazon.com: Rv Water Pump,12v Diaphragm pump,2088–554-144/2088–403-144 Fresh Water Pump,12v 3.5 Gallons per Minute,45 psi,1/2 npt Connection: Automotive, Amazon.com, (2024). https://www.amazon.com/dp/B0BZNNQTRT (Accessed 30 Nov 2024)

GCC'25: 21st International Conference on Grid, Cloud, and Cluster Computing

Safeguarding Critical Data in High-Volume Transaction Processing Cloud Services

Kazi Asharful Haque[1](✉) and Brajendra Panda[2]

[1] University of North Dakota, Grand Forks, ND 58202, USA
haque@cs.und.edu
[2] University of Arkansas, Fayetteville, AR 72701, USA
bpanda@uark.edu

Abstract. Cloud computing, given its numerous advantages, has excited many organizations, including those managing critical information systems, to move their data and applications to cloud-based systems. At the same time, given the stash of sensitive data along with the weaknesses in security protocols, it has attracted cyber criminals to steal data from, and sometimes damage data in cloud databases. If a cyberattack on a cloud system succeeds in affecting the critical data, the damage spreads through the database rapidly due to the interdependent nature of such data. Therefore, it is vital to devise a mechanism to minimize the damage caused by the attack by restraining it to a limited number of data items in the database. In order to achieve that, we have proposed a mechanism to classify data and restrict access depending on data classification. We have presented an access methodology and a simple algorithm to implement our policy.

Keywords: Critical data in cloud databases · data classification · attacks on databases · data recovery · access classification

1 Introduction

Sharing information is a common practice in this technology-driven world. The many features of cloud computing have made the data sharing mechanism very easy and efficient. Many organizations, from government to industry, and even private citizens, have been using cloud services to store and manage their data, some of which are sensitive and used in time-critical services. But on the flip side, these features have also made cloud databases prime targets of attackers, both copycat types and state-sponsored cyberhackers. The severity of this type of attack can range from causing temporary turmoil to complete demolition of an organization's critical information system. There are several past incidents, such as [1–4], which show that many critical infrastructure systems are frequently targeted by attackers.

Three major strategies of secure information systems are: prevention, detection, and recovery [5]. The recovery phase consists of damage assessment, damage control, and recovery of lost or damaged data. As stated before, many organizations, including those running critical infrastructure systems, have opted to store related data in cloud-based

H. R. Arabnia et al. (Eds.): CSCE 2025, CCIS 2932, pp. 107–119, 2026.
https://doi.org/10.1007/978-3-032-22193-3_8

databases due to the convenience of access and maintenance. Critical infrastructure systems are large-scale distributed systems providing a wide variety of services to a number of areas that are of high importance. They are highly coupled, complex, interdependent, and interconnected systems. These properties cause the initial damage to spread much faster than in any other system. As more and more data items in a database become damaged, it becomes almost impossible for the system to offer the time-critical functionalities that they are expected to provide. Additionally, to recover the lost/damaged data, often the systems are shut down (to stop further spread of damage while recovery continues), and this is unacceptable in cases of systems containing critical data. Therefore, it is of utmost importance to contain damage as much as possible so that recovery can be completed quickly.

In order to contain damage and to provide faster recovery, we propose a mechanism to divide the data items in a database into two groups, namely, regular and rigid. Any data item in the regular category can be read and updated by any legal user of the database. A rigid data item, on the other hand, can only be read by any user and can be updated only by people with very exclusive rights (e.g., the system administrator). The idea is somewhat similar to Multilevel Secure (MLS) Systems. In MLS systems, the high-level users cannot update the low-level data, and the low-level users cannot read high-level data. But, in our proposed method of classification, one group of data (regular category) will be accessible by everyone, and another group of data (rigid category) will be read-only. The advantage of this approach is that any transaction that has its read-set only in the rigid category will never spread any damage. Rather, damaged data will be refreshed if the data is written by such a transaction.

The rest of the paper is organized as follows: in Sect. 2, we discuss the background and motivation behind this work. Data classification and access models are offered in Sects. 3 and 4, respectively. Section 5 concludes the paper.

2 Background and Motivation

Various types of critical infrastructure objects are described in [6]. The focus of the work falls under network and network nodes, which are defined as a "structure with one dominating dimension" and junctions within the network, respectively. Furthermore, [7] establishes the concept of resilience, a cyclical process by which a system undergoes recovery, adaptation, and prevention between attacks. Turning this concept into a concrete value that can be used in risk assessment has been a point of interest in protecting systems [8]. Efforts have also been made to quantify vulnerability as a measurement that can be used to determine how frequently or severely a system can be at risk [9]. One of the major works on damage assessment and recovery within a database uses data dependency relationships to identify data affected by an attack with a view to optimizing recovery [5]. This model is further expanded in [10] to show how a database log needs to be redesigned to accommodate new damage assessment and recovery protocols. While these methods rely on the direct relationships between data items, an alternate model to recover data from an attack instead uses the transaction log for assessment [11].

A review of threats that influence how critical data is protected is done in [12]. Among other threats, the important ones that affect this research are cyberattacks and cascading effects. A data system is especially vulnerable to the cascading effects of a cyberattack because of the nature of constant updates being made between different systems using data. In [13], a dynamic inoperability input-output model is introduced to determine how damage in one part of a system, such as power plants, water collectors, and transmitters, can ultimately cascade down to end-users of the system.

The damage inflicted on a database can spread exponentially within a short time. Therefore, it is imperative to restore the system to a consistent state at the earliest possible time. Traditional recovery methods ([14–16], for example) have been designed to perform recovery in case of media and system failures, whereas they lack the effectiveness required to recover from malicious attacks. Therefore, to trace the effects of malicious transactions in the databases, researchers have come up with two approaches: one is the transaction dependency approach [17] and the other is the data dependency approach [5].

The transaction dependency approach suggests recovery by considering dependency relationships among transactions. The data dependency approach claims to achieve a faster recovery by considering dependency relationships among data items. However, in either of these methods, the log is scanned from the point of attack to establish dependencies. The log needs to store both the read and the write operations, which makes the log grow massively. Therefore, searching for dependencies becomes highly inefficient and time-consuming. Furthermore, new transactions are not allowed to be initiated during the recovery procedure. These limitations gave rise to the concept of clustering the log based on considering the dependencies of the transactions or of the data items. The crux of this idea is that if the log is clustered based on dependency, then after detecting the attack, only the cluster where the attacking transaction resides needs to be scanned and manipulated to recover from the attack. But this concept could not put any limitation on the size of the cluster. In the extreme case, a cluster can be as big as the entire log. This problem motivated us to think otherwise and led us to classify the data items. The classification of data items and the policy of reading and writing classified data will help in containing damage to a limited number of data items. Using this approach, a transaction that has its read-set only in the rigid category will never spread damage. Rather, any damaged data will be refreshed if the data is written by such a transaction.

3 Data Classification Model

In this section, we discuss our technique for data classification based on which user access can be provided. The information required for classifying data is based on transaction operations. Since this classification places sensitive and most frequently read data items in transactions into the *rigid* category, there is a need to filter these data items out from the regular data items. The sensitivity measure of a data item is purely a concern of the business authority, which stores and manipulates the data. The most frequently read measure of data items is based on the *read-set* data items of the transactions that access this database. The *read-set* denotes data items that are to be read to execute the corresponding transaction. Similarly, we also need to determine the *write-set* of the data items. The *write-set* represents data items that are to be written to execute a transaction. The definitions are given as follows:

Let $P = \{T_1, T_2, T_3 \ldots\ldots T_n\}$ be the set of transactions that accesses a database containing data items $Q = \{x_1, x_2, x_3 \ldots x_m\}$. Then, for each transaction T_i and for each data item x_j, we associate *data-read* operation, denoted by read(T_i, x_j), and *data-write* operation, denoted by write(T_i, x_j). These are defined as follows:

$$\text{Read}\,(T_i, x_j) = \begin{cases} 1 & \text{if } x_j \text{ is read by } T_i \\ 0 & \text{otherwise} \end{cases}$$

$$\text{Write}\,(T_i, x_j) = \begin{cases} 1 & \text{if } x_j \text{ is written by } T_i \\ 0 & \text{otherwise} \end{cases}$$

The sensitivity of a data item, denoted by $S(x_j)$, is a value assigned to the data item from a range of numbers based on the importance of this data item. For example, the range can be between 1 and 10, where the low and high values indicate low and high sensitivity, respectively.

The determination of the sensitivity range and assignment of the sensitivity value to each data item is purely up to the organization, which manages the database. The read (T_i, •) and write (T_i, •) vectors for each transaction are easy to define when the database designer is familiar with the transactions that execute in the database. These vectors are represented in matrix format for further processing. These matrices are shown in Figs. 1 and 2.

$$\begin{array}{c|ccccc} & x_1 & x_2 & x_3 & \cdots & x_m \\ T_1 & r_{11} & r_{12} & r_{13} & \cdots & r_{1m} \\ T_2 & r_{21} & r_{22} & r_{23} & \cdots & r_{2m} \\ T_3 & r_{31} & r_{32} & r_{33} & \cdots & r_{3m} \\ \cdots & \cdots & \cdots & \cdots & \cdots & \cdots \\ T_n & r_{n1} & r_{n2} & r_{n3} & \cdots & r_{nm} \end{array}$$

Fig. 1. Matrix (**M**) for *read* Operations

$$\begin{array}{c|ccccc} & x_1 & x_2 & x_3 & & x_m \\ T_1 & w_{11} & w_{12} & w_{13} & \cdots & w_{1m} \\ T_2 & w_{21} & w_{22} & w_{23} & \cdots & w_{2m} \\ T_3 & w_{31} & w_{32} & w_{33} & \cdots & w_{3m} \\ \cdots & \cdots & \cdots & \cdots & \cdots & \cdots \\ T_n & w_{n1} & w_{n2} & w_{n3} & \cdots & w_{nm} \end{array}$$

Fig. 2. Matrix (**N**) for *write* Operations

It should be mentioned here that research shows that the most active 20% of user transactions account for 80% of the total data access [17]. This "80/20" may be used as a guideline in carrying out this analysis. The following example will help clarify the concept.

Example 1: Consider a set of transactions

T_1:r[x_1] r[x_2] w[x_3]
T_2:r[x_2] w[x_2]
T_3:r[x_1] r[x_4] w[x_4]
T_4:r[x_2] w[x_3]

The data-read operations for this set of transactions are presented in matrix M shown in Fig. 3, where each entry (*i, j*) denotes read (T_i, x_j). The data-write operations for this set of transactions are presented in Fig. 4 in matrix N, where each entry (i, j) denotes write(T_i, x_j):

$$\begin{array}{c} \\ T_1 \\ T_2 \\ T_3 \\ T_4 \end{array} \begin{array}{c} \begin{array}{cccc} x1 & x2 & x3 & x4 \end{array} \\ \begin{pmatrix} 1 & 1 & 0 & 0 \\ 0 & 1 & 0 & 0 \\ 1 & 0 & 0 & 1 \\ 0 & 1 & 0 & 0 \end{pmatrix} \end{array}$$

Fig. 3. Matrix **M**

$$\begin{array}{c} \\ T_1 \\ T_2 \\ T_3 \\ T_4 \end{array} \begin{array}{c} \begin{array}{cccc} x1 & x2 & x3 & x4 \end{array} \\ \begin{pmatrix} 0 & 0 & 1 & 0 \\ 0 & 1 & 0 & 0 \\ 0 & 0 & 0 & 1 \\ 0 & 0 & 1 & 0 \end{pmatrix} \end{array}$$

Fig. 4. Matrix **N**

After deriving matrices *M* and *N*, the matrix P is computed. Matrix *P* associates *read* and *write* operations in the transactions. First, the transpose operation on matrix *N* is taken, and let us symbolize this resultant matrix as N^T. Each element of N^T is denoted by n_{ik}^T. Then matrix *P* is computed where each element of it is obtained by using the following equation:

$$p_{ij} = \sum_{k=1}^{n} n_{ik}^T m_{kj}$$

It should be noted here that matrix *P* provides a clear view of dependencies among data items. Each element of the matrix *P* provides two perspectives. Looking from the column viewpoint, it denotes the number of times a data item of the corresponding column is read to write the data item in the corresponding row. On the other hand, the row perspective shows the number of times the data item in the corresponding row is written by reading the data items in the corresponding column.

As can be observed, there is a difference between $\sum$ *Column of Matrix P* and $\sum$ *Column of Matrix* M $\sum$ColumnofmatrixM for the same element. The reason behind this difference is that in matrix *P*, the same transaction can make more than one change. This difference is called the *Dependency Coefficient* (*DC*). Matrix *DC* is computed using the formula given below, and an example is shown in Fig. 5.

$$\begin{pmatrix} x1 & 1 \\ x2 & 4 \\ . & . \\ . & . \\ xn & 2 \end{pmatrix}$$

Fig. 5. Matrix *DC*

$$\begin{pmatrix} x1 & 2 \\ x2 & 7 \\ . & . \\ . & . \\ xn & 2 \end{pmatrix}$$

Fig. 6. Matrix *S*

Next, the sensitivity of the data items is considered. The sensitivity provides the priority of placing the data items into the *rigid* category. An important point to note here is that the sensitivity of an element can never be zero. Since, if it is made zero, the concept of accessibility will be neutralized. Based on the sensitivity value of each data item, the sensitivity matrix *S* is developed as depicted in Fig. 6.

Then the *DC* and *S* matrices are multiplied. Each element of this product matrix *I* represents the importance of each data item.

$$\mathrm{i}_{\mathrm{ij}} = dc_{ik} S_{kj}$$

In case the sensitivity has not been given, only the matrix *DC* is considered to depict the importance of the elements.

The elements of matrix *I* are shuffled to arrange them from the highest to the lowest values, as shown in Fig. 7. This matrix offers an idea about which data items should be kept into the *rigid* category. Along with this matrix calculation, some more mathematical

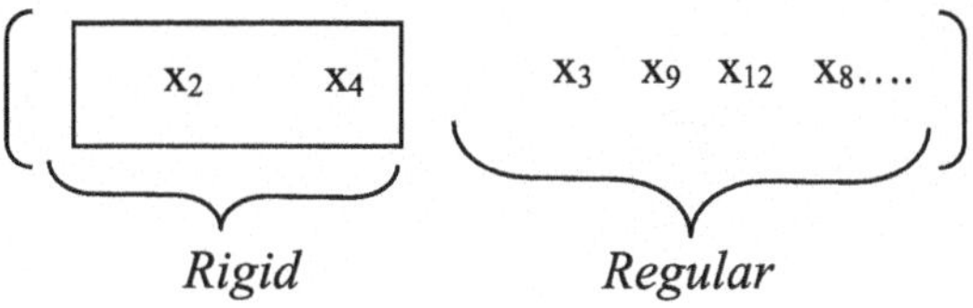

Fig. 7. Shuffled Matrix *I*

analysis is needed to get a concrete idea about putting the boundary between *rigid* and *regular* categories.

Let's take an example to understand this concept better. Suppose we have *M* and *N* matrices given as shown in Figs. 8 and 9, respectively.

$$\begin{pmatrix} x & y & z \\ 1 & 1 & 0 \\ 0 & 1 & 1 \\ 1 & 1 & 1 \end{pmatrix}$$

Fig. 8. Matrix *M* for read operations

$$\begin{pmatrix} x & y & z \\ 0 & 1 & 1 \\ 1 & 1 & 1 \\ 1 & 1 & 1 \end{pmatrix}$$

Fig. 9. Matrix *N* for write operations

These matrices suggest that transaction T_1 (Fig. 10) reads x, y, but not z, whereas it writes y, z, but not x. Transaction T_2 (Fig. 11) reads y, z, but not x, whereas it writes all three elements. Transaction T_3 (Fig. 12) reads as well as writes all three elements.

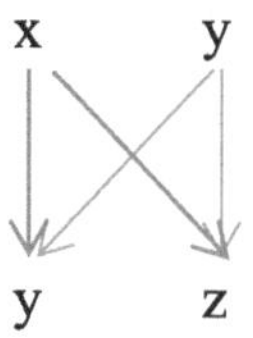

Fig. 10. Transaction 1

Now, the first step is to find the transpose of matrix *N* as shown in Fig. 13 and multiply it with matrix *M* to obtain matrix *P* (depicted in Fig. 14) using the following equation.

$$P_{ij} = \sum_{k=0}^{3} N_{ik}^{T} M_{kj}$$

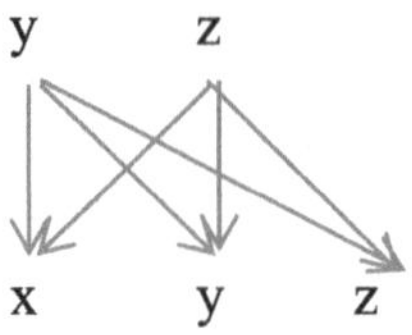

Fig. 11. Transaction 2

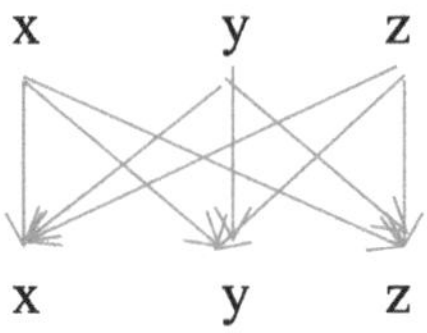

Fig. 12. Transaction 3

$$\begin{pmatrix} x & y & z \\ 0 & 1 & 1 \\ 1 & 1 & 1 \\ 1 & 1 & 1 \end{pmatrix}$$

Fig. 13. Transpose of matrix N

$$\begin{pmatrix} & x & y & z \\ x & 1 & 2 & 2 \\ y & 2 & 3 & 2 \\ z & 2 & 3 & 2 \end{pmatrix}$$

Fig. 14. Matrix P

Matrix P suggests that if access to x is available, 5 changes can be made. Similarly, if y is accessible, then 8 changes can be made, and if z is accessible, 6 changes can be made. But the matrices M and N suggest otherwise. The reason is that the changes suggested by matrix P can be different changes made by the same transaction, whereas the other two matrices suggest only the possibility of change and not the number.

Next, we find the Dependency Coefficient for each element to obtain matrix DC as given in Fig. 15.

$D(x) = \sum_{i=1}^{3} P\mathrm{i}1$- $\sum_{i=1}^{3} Read\mathrm{i}1$, therefore D(x) = 2

$D(y) = \sum_{i=1}^{3} P\mathrm{i}2$- $\sum_{i=1}^{3} Read\mathrm{i}2$, therefore D(y) = 5

$D(z) = \sum_{i=1}^{3} P\mathrm{i}3$- $\sum_{i=1}^{3} Read\mathrm{i}3$, therefore D(z) = 4

There are the following two cases to consider here.

CASE 1: Sensitivity is not given. In this case, we simply use the dependency coefficient to rank the elements and classify them as critical or regular.

CASE 2: Sensitivity is given. In this situation, sensitivity has been given as Matrix S (Fig. 16). We follow the operation: $\mathrm{i}_{\mathrm{ij}} = dc_{ik}S_{kj}$

$$\begin{pmatrix} x & 2 \\ y & 5 \\ z & 4 \end{pmatrix}$$

Fig. 15. Matrix *DC*

$$\begin{pmatrix} x & 7 \\ y & 9 \\ z & 3 \end{pmatrix}$$

Fig. 16. Matrix *S* for Sensitivity

Using the example values used above, the equation generates Matrix *I* as shown in Fig. 17.

$$\begin{pmatrix} x & 14 \\ y & 45 \\ z & 12 \end{pmatrix}$$

Fig. 17. Matrix *I*

Let's say, for example, based on the previous calculations and experience, some data items are placed into the *rigid* category, which is shown in the rigid box and the other data items are placed into the *regular* category. We denote the data set in the *rigid* category as R_iD and the data items in the *regular* category as R_eD.

From the set of transactions $P = \{T_1, T_2, T_3 \ldots\ldots T_n)$, we then identify the set of transactions that read and write rigid data, the set of transactions that read rigid data and write regular data, and the set of transactions that read both rigid and regular data and write regular data as follows:

$$C_1 = |\{T_i \mid S\_read(T_i, X) \text{ AND } S\_write(T_i, Y) \text{ where } X \subseteq R_iD, Y \subseteq R_iD\}|$$

$$C_2 = |\{T_i \mid S\_read(T_i, X) \text{ AND } S\_write(T_i, Y) \text{ where } X \subseteq R_iD, Y \subseteq R_eD\}|$$

$$C_3 = |\{T_i \mid S\_read(T_i, X) \text{ AND } S\_write(T_i, Y) \text{ where } X \subseteq R_iD \cup R_eD, Y \subseteq R_eD\}|$$

Given these inputs, the optimization point would be to maximize the following equation:

$Z = C_1 {*} C_2 - {C_3}^2$

Although there is an optimal point, obtaining this point may not be feasible (based on the consideration of time and complexity) as the combinations of C_1, C_2, and C_3 can be numerous. But if we consider a specific database situation, a lot of constraints and limitations need to be enforced on it, which reduces the number of combinations to a feasible one to be analyzed. For example, for one database situation, C_1 may be important, for other situations, C_2 may be important, and for others, C_3 may be important. Based on these importance and restrictions, a "*semi-optimal*" value for Z can be obtained by varying the important one and keeping the other two constant.

4 Classifying Access

In the previous section, we presented a mechanism for classifying data into *rigid* and *regular* categories. Here we offer a mechanism to implement our policy. As we mentioned earlier, our policy is that normal users can read both *rigid* and *regular* category data sets, but they can only write in the *regular* data category. Only a limited number of users (e.g., a database administrator) will have write access to data in the *rigid* category. This model of access classification is based on the concept of "*access matrix*" [10] and is discussed below.

In our model, the objects consist of a rigid data set (R_iD) and a regular data set (R_eD). A transaction program should be allowed to access an object based on the right(s) it has on that object. To facilitate that scheme, we need to define the protection domain. A transaction program operates within the protection domain. Each domain defines a set of objects and the types of operations that can be invoked on each object. The ability to execute an operation on an object is an "access right". In our case, the association between the transaction program and the domain is dynamic. This means that a mechanism is available to allow transaction programs to switch from one domain to another. We realize the domain as user, indicating that the type of operation that can be done on the object is dependent on the identity of the user. That is, when a transaction program executes in one domain, it takes the identity of the user or the group to which the user belongs.

As referenced earlier, our model of protection can be presented as an access matrix. The rows of the access matrix consist of domains and the columns represent objects. Each entry in the matrix consists of a set of access rights. The entry access[i,j] defines the set of operations that a transaction, executing in domain D_i, can invoke on object O_j.

Table 1. Access Classification Model

	R_iD	R_eD	D_1	D_2	D_3
D_1	*read* *write*			*switch* *control*	*switch* *control*
D_2	*read* *write*				*switch*
D_3	*read*	*read* *write*			

The matrix is shown in Table 1. There are three domains and five objects. When a transaction operates in domain D_1 it can read data from R_iD and can write in the R_iD

data set. This domain is the most secure. When a transaction executes on behalf of D_2 it will be allowed to read from and write into only the R_iD data set. The third domain D_3 is for normal users. An individual user belonging to this group will be able to read both from R_iD and R_eD *but* can only write into the R_eD category. A transaction in this category has no right to write any data item in the rigid category.

Domain D_1 has the right to switch either to domain D_2 or to domain D_3. But this domain switching will happen after the process completes the transaction at hand. Otherwise, the process would not be able to complete it because it's not possible to return to the original category, as domain switching is irreversible. Domain D_2 can switch to domain D_3. It should be mentioned here that switching from domain D_3 to domain D_2 or domain D_1 and switching from domain D_2 to domain D_1 are not allowed.

As previously stated, D_1 is the most powerful domain of all. It also has the control right. That is, programs executing on behalf of this domain have the privilege to change rights in the other two domains.

Next, we discuss how these classifications work. When a user logs in to a database, the user ID becomes attached to a domain by default or by the user's choice if he/she belongs to more than one domain. That is, before beginning execution of a transaction, a user is attached to a domain. Therefore, when a program executes a transaction on behalf of that user, the database security mechanism can determine the access right of the program by consulting the user *ID* with the access matrix. The system also ascertains the data items this transaction wants to access and the type of access (*read*, *write*, or *both*) the transaction wants to perform on each of these data items. After getting all this information, the security protocol creates the data set to be read and the data set to be written by this transaction. Then the protocol performs simple Boolean operations to determine whether to accept or reject the transaction. The Boolean operation may apply the following equations:

For Domain D_1 or D_2:

$$\text{Transaction\_ReadSet} \cap R_eD = \text{null};$$
$$\text{Transaction\_WriteSet} \cap R_eD = \text{null};$$

For Domain D_3:

$$\text{Transaction\_WriteSet} \cap R_iD = \text{null};$$

In the above, *Transaction_ReadSet* represents the data items to be read by the transaction, and the *Transaction_WriteSet* represents the data items to be written by the transaction. The algorithm that performs these tests and decides whether the transaction is acceptable or not is given below.

Algorithm:

1. Determine the ID of the transaction
2. Determine Transaction_ReadSet and Transaction_WriteSet
3. Determine the Domain of the transaction
   3.1 If the transaction belongs to D_1or D_2, then do:
   R_Set = (Transaction_ReadSet ∩ R_eD) ∩ Transaction_WriteSet ∩ R_eD)
   3.2 If the transaction belongs to D_3, then do:
   R_Set = Transaction_WriteSet ∩ R_iD
4. If R_Set = Null then
   Accept Transaction
   Else
   Reject Transaction

5 Conclusions

Security of cloud-based databases is of utmost importance, particularly when such databases contain critical data. In case of an attack on a database, one must perform a quick damage assessment and recovery in order to make the data continuously available to critical functions that need it. Existing damage assessment and recovery methods require access to the log file to determine the extent of damage and recover the damaged items. During this process, the system is shut down to prevent damage from spreading through valid transactions. Moreover, given that logs are stored in secondary storage for reliability reasons, log access is a slow process as well. This compounds the problem further, slowing down system recovery. This is unacceptable in cases of systems that contain critical data. These issues motivated us to think of alternate solutions for offering quick damage assessment and recovery. In this paper, we offered a mechanism that limits damage to a minimum set of data items while not restricting user access. This is achieved by classifying data into two groups that help contain damage to a limited area of the database. Using this approach, a transaction that has its read-set only in the rigid category will never spread damage. Rather, a damaged data item will be refreshed if the data is written by such a transaction. We have also presented an appropriate access classification method. Future work includes the implementation of the model proposed in this paper and the development of appropriate algorithms for damaged assessment and recovery.

Disclosure of Interests. The authors have no competing interests to declare that are relevant to the content of this article.

References

1. Sanger, D., Perlroth, N.: Pipeline Attack Yields Urgent Lessons About U.S. Cybersecurity. https://www.nytimes.com/2021/05/14/us/politics/pipeline-hack.html, Accessed 16 Sep 2022

2. Barrett, B.: An Unprecedented Cyberattack Hit US Power Utilities. https://www.wired.com/story/power-grid-cyberattack-facebook-phone-numbers-security-news/, Accessed 16 Sep 2022
3. O'Flaherty, K.: U.S. Government Issues Powerful Cyberattack Warning As Gas Pipeline Forced Into Two Day Shutdown. https://www.forbes.com/sites/kateoflahertyuk/2020/02/19/us-government-issues-powerful-cyberattack-warning-as-gas-pipeline-forced-into-two-day-shut-down/#5f3061645a95. Accessed 16 Sep 2022
4. Lewis, M.: Cyberattack Forces Gas Pipeline Shutdown. https://www.jdsupra.com/legalnews/cyberattack-forces-gas-pipeline-shutdown-76217, Accessed 16 Sep 2022
5. Panda, B., Giordano, J.: Reconstructing the database after electronic attacks. In: Jajodia, S. (ed.) Database Security XII. IFIP — the International Federation for Information Processing, vol. 14. Springer, Boston, MA (1999)
6. Štoller, J., Dvořák, P.: Basic types of critical infrastructure objects. Int. Conf. Mil. Technol. (ICMT), 1–7 (2019). https://doi.org/10.1109/MILTECHS.2019.8870031
7. Rehak, D., Senovsky, P., Hromada, M.: Analysis of critical infrastructure network. In: Chan, Z., Dehmer, M., Emmertsteib, F., Shi, Y. (eds.) Modern and Interdisciplinary Problems in Network Science: a Translation Research Perspective. CRC Press, ISBN 978-0-8153-7658-3 (2018)
8. Genge, B., Haller, P., Kiss, I.: A framework for designing resilient distributed intrusion detection systems for critical infrastructures. Int. J. Crit. Infrastruct. Prot. **15**, 3–11, ISSN 1874-5482 (2016). https://doi.org/10.1016/j.ijcip.2016.06.003
9. Luskova, M., Titko, M., Leitner, B.: Multilevel approach to measuring societal vulnerability due to failure of critical land transport infrastructure. In: Proceedings of the 20th World Multi-conference on Systemics, Cybernetics and Informatics, Orlando, Florida (2016)
10. Panda, B., Tripathy, S.: Data dependency based logging for defensive information warfare. In: Proceedings of the 12th International Conference on Computer Applications in Industry and Engineering, Atlanta, GA (1999)
11. Patnaik, S., Panda, B.: Transaction-relationship oriented log division for data recovery from information attacks. J. Database Manag. **14**(2), 27–41 (2003)
12. He, X., Cha, E.: Modeling the damage and recovery of interdependent critical infrastructure systems from natural hazards. Reliab. Eng. Syst. Saf. **177**(2018), 162–175 (2018)
13. Osei-Kyei, R., Tam, V., Ma, M., Mashiri, F.: Critical review of the threats affecting the building of critical infrastructure resilience. Int. J. Disaster Risk Reduction. **60**(2) (2021)
14. Bernstein, P., Hadzilacos, V., Goodman, N.: Concurrency Control and Recovery in Database Systems. Addison-Wesley, Reading, MA (1987)
15. Elmasri, R., Navathe, S.: Fundamentals of Database Systems. 2nd edn., Addison-Wesley, Menlo Park, CA (1994)
16. Ozsu, M., Valduriez, P.: Principles of Distributed Database Systems. 2nd edn., Prentice-Hall, Upper Saddle River, NJ (1999)
17. Liu, P., Ammann,P., Jajodia, S.: Rewriting histories: recovering from malicious transactions. Distrib. Parallel Databases vol. 18, 1, pp. 7–40 (2000)

On Adaptive Metric-Driven Load Balancing for Specialized Clusters: A Case on Using NGINX

Juhi Raju Malkani, Ramin Moazeni, Melody Moh, and Teng-Sheng Moh(✉)

Department of Computer Science, San Jose State University, 1 Washington Square, San Jose, CA 95112, USA
{ramin.moazeni,melody.moh,teng.moh}@sjsu.edu

Abstract. Cloud computing has become an essential part of today's digital world. Many traditional load-balancing approaches in cloud computing lack the adaptability to dynamic workloads, and many newer load-balancing algorithms work mainly on cloud simulators. This paper proposed an adaptive, metric-driven, two-tier load-balancing system that uses NGINX and Prometheus to optimize resource allocation in specialized cloud clusters. The proposed framework is built to give great performance on Google Kubernetes Engine (GKE), but it may also be deployed in local cloud environments for security. The first tier of the proposed framework uses an NGINX-based load balancer to route incoming requests based on content type, sending traffic to hardware-optimized clusters to process requests through specialized hardware. The second tier dynamically distributes load throughout each cluster by calculating pod weights based on CPU, memory, and network usage on a regular basis. This adaptive weight distribution maximizes resource consumption and responsiveness, outperforming existing fixed-weight systems. In comparison to typical multi-component solutions, our system's lightweight architecture minimizes configuration and management overhead while scaling fluidly to address dynamic traffic patterns. Performance evaluation shows that the proposed system improves throughput by approximately 74% and almost doubles the number of requests processed per second while being a simple, scalable, adaptable solution. We believe that the proposed solution may be a practical, effectual building block for a complex cloud systems, and would contribute significantly to the future cloud systems.

Keywords: Content-based routing · Google Kubernetes Engine (GKE) · resource allocation · cluster-level load balancing · multi-tier cloud architecture

---

R. Moazeni, M. Moh and T.-S. Moh—These authors contributed equally to this work.

H. R. Arabnia et al. (Eds.): CSCE 2025, CCIS 2932, pp. 120–135, 2026.
https://doi.org/10.1007/978-3-032-22193-3_9

1 Introduction

Cloud computing has changed the outlook of the world in the domain of hosting applications by providing high flexibility and scalability features in deploying and managing workloads. This high dependence calls for practical, effective load-balancing algorithms that can efficiently manage resource distribution in complex, distributed systems. The increased adoption of cloud computing has already redefined the way organizations install and manage applications. New challenges have also surfaced for cloud service providers while managing dynamic and unexpected workloads in cloud infrastructures [1]. Addressing these challenges is important for maintaining smooth operations in cloud computing systems [1].

Many traditional load-balancing techniques have been useful for handling static and moderately dynamic workloads. Yet, they seem to frequently fail with diversified traffic patterns and various content types [2]. With dynamic workload, using conventional algorithms results in uneven resource utilization, performance bottlenecks, and underutilized resources. Due to these issues, there is a high demand for simple, flexible, practical load balancing schemes.

The proposed approach introduces an adaptive metric-driven load balancer to solve the problems faced by traditional load balancers. It is a two-tier load balancing system. The first tier uses an NGINX-based load balancer that classifies the incoming requests based on their content type (audio, video, etc.) and reroutes the request to the hardware clusters optimized for that particular content type. The second-tier load balancer operates with these hardware-optimized clusters. This load balancer allocates resources to pods based on weights, which are periodically adjusted based on real-time metrics including CPU, memory, and network usage. This ensures high resource efficiency and strong performance, even under changing traffic conditions. The proposed algorithm reduces latency in the system, improves resource allocation while maintaining high availability, in turn improving overall system performance. The proposed framework can be deployed in private or hybrid cloud settings, which in turn would help companies that value security and data privacy (that might be sacrificed in public cloud systems) [3].

The main contribution of the paper include the following:

1. **Two-tiered load balancer (Content-aware routing and cluster-level load balancing:** The proposed load balancer includes the first layer of content-aware routing. The second layer of cluster-level load balancing reroutes traffic at the runtime based on real-time metrics of those pods (CPU, memory and resource utilization).
2. **Prototyping on GKE and Docker containers:** The proposed system uses Google Kubernetes Engine (GKE) as a model environment. It uses NGINX to perform decision-based routing, and deploy both layers in Docker containers with essential communications between the two layers.
3. **Performance evaluation with two baseline algorithms:** For evaluation the performance of the proposed system, the systems has been implemented and compared with two baseline algorithms, i.e., Baseline 1: Service

Mesh Load Balancer [4] and Baseline 2: Multi-metric Load Balancer [5]. The strengths and weaknesses of all three systems and their suitable use cases have been deliberated.

2 Background and Related Studies

In this section, we will describe important terms and concepts that are needed to understand the proposed framework. Along with that, we will present a literature review.

2.1 Terminology

Cloud Based Applications. Using a cloud-based application, an end user can access the software application through cloud computing environment, rather then their own local computer or server. Cloud application architecture allows management of change in workload by adding or subtracting resources as per the requirements.

Google Kubernetes Engine (GKE). It helps in deployment, scaling, and management of containerized applications by using Google's reliable infrastructure. GKE automates tasks such as updates, scaling, and monitoring, significantly reducing the workload. GKE uses features like horizontal pod auto-scaling, node auto-repair, and multi-zonal support which provides high availability and optimal performance.

Content-Based Load Balancing. It routes requests from one server to another based on the type of the content and identifiers like content, query parameters and HTTP headers.

Dynamic Load Balancing. It distributes workload based on parameters of the server like memory consumption, CPU utilization or response time.

Cluster-level Load Balancing. It routes requests based on weights of pod present in the cluster. These weights are based on live metrices like CPU consumption, memory consumption, and network bandwidth use. These weights are refreshed at constant intervals to tracks resource utilization, and adjusting the traffic allocation.

Hierarchical Load Balancing. It split load balancing process into multiple layers. Each layer is responsible for a specific operation.

2.2 Literature Review

Complex cloud environments need advance load balancing strategies that can ensure scalability, efficient resource utilization, and adaptability to dynamic workloads. Traditional methods such as Kubernetes' default load balancing, uses static techniques like round-robin and session affinity. These techniques cannot handle real-time changes in server load and traffic patterns. The algorithm in [5] monitors several server and application metrics like CPU utilization, memory consumption, and network I/O, to provide context-aware and responsive load distribution.

Service mesh architectures like the Istio-based implementation described in [4] have become scalable solutions for load balancing, task scheduling and traffic routing in Kubernetes-based systems. But their adaptability is constrained by the static configurations and dependence on centralized control.

ArA algorithm proposed in [2] uses adaptive strategies like greedy or random allocation to optimize performance in different scenarios. Similarly, fuzzy logic-based load balancer outlined in [6] assigns weights to servers using multi-parameter analysis, which results in notable improvements in load distribution and resource usage.

Concepts like adaptive scheduling and hierarchical frameworks have improved the performance of distributed systems. Studies like [7,8] uses multi-tiered architectures and dynamic priority scheduling to improve resource allocation and system responsiveness under variable workloads. The three adaptive algorithms introduced in [9], like Dynamic Feedback (DF) and Shortest-Queue and Latency-Aware (SQLA), demonstrate the effectiveness of latency-sensitive and queue-based approaches in distributed systems like virtualized Mobile Management Entities (vMMEs).

Innovative load-balancing techniques are also applicable to certain applications, such as cloud-based CDNs. To achieve service-level agreements and optimize performance, the adaptive server activation approach presented in [10] dynamically controls server resources across data centers. Other novel approach, such as leveraging MapReduce theory for load balancing in cloud computing [11], focuses on optimizing large-scale resource allocation, improving response time, and achieving robust load distribution. Detailed studies, such as [1], explains existing load-balancing algorithms. These studies highlight the challenges of balancing resource efficiency with system performance in systems requiring scalable and dependable services. As mentioned in [3], cloud environments also face security challenges. They require strong monitoring and authentication protocols to protect against vulnerabilities due to their shared infrastructure and dynamic scalability.

3 Proposed Architecture and Prototype

The proposed architecture, prototype implementation, and the observed benefits of the prototype are presented below.

3.1 Proposed Architecture

As mentioned before, Google Kubernetes Engine (GKE) has been adopted as a model of environment to deploy the application, along with using the proposed system as a load balancer for balancing the incoming traffic for applications. In the following text, we describe the important components and concepts involved in the proposed architecture depicted in Fig. 1.

In Fig. 2, a cluster behaves as the **Primary Layer load balancer** in our framework. It uses NGINX to perform decision-based routing. This layer intelligently makes the routing decisions based on the content type of the requests in the incoming traffic. It allocates these requests to specific clusters which are optimized for that content type. This layer communicates with the client and acts as a gateway for the incoming request. It also serves as a reverse proxy and sends responses back to the client.

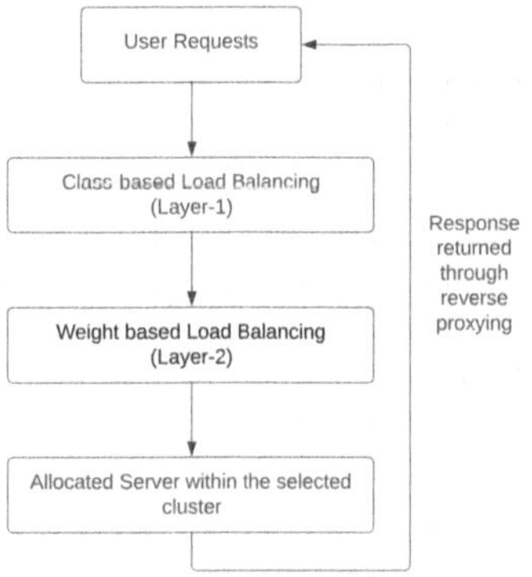

Fig. 1. General flow in the proposed load balancer

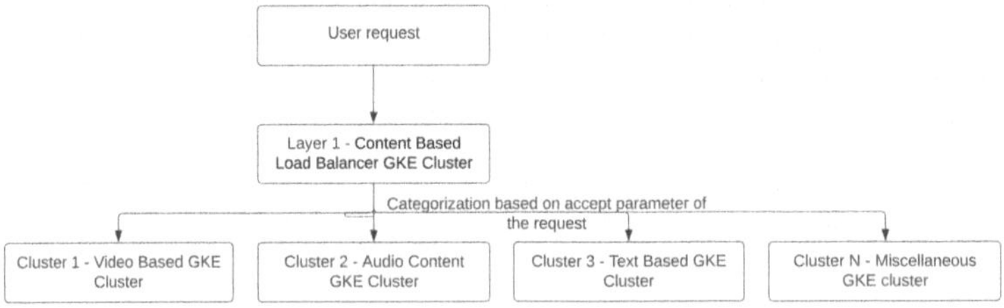

Fig. 2. Layer 1 - load balancing based on content-type

Certain **Content-specific clusters** are set up for specific content categories. Each of these clusters offers a specialized processing environment based on the allocated content type. The pods of these clusters have applications deployed that are suitable for the needs of the allocated content types. Along with these content-specific clusters, a **General-Purpose cluster** is deployed, which is present for those content types that do not have specialized clusters allocated to them.

Each of these clusters is equipped with an **NGINX-based load balancer**, which form the second layer of our proposed approach depicted in Fig. 3. It dynamically allocates traffic based on the weights of the pods, which are calculated based on metrics such as CPU, memory, and network use of each pod. This method distributes traffic efficiently to the clusters best and most free resources, along with continuously optimizing for speed and responsiveness. These weights change periodically based on the measurements received from Prometheus.

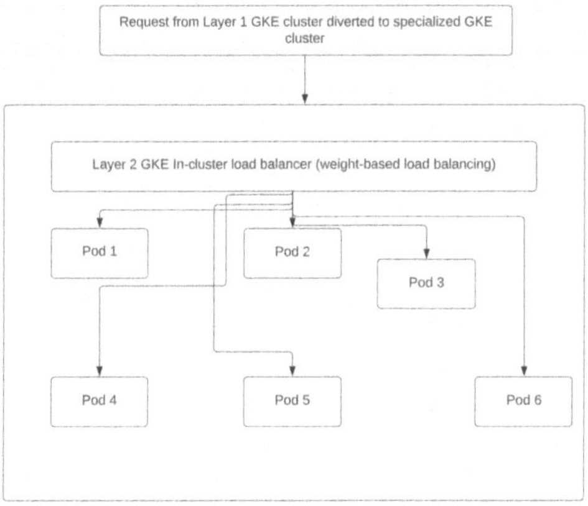

Fig. 3. Layer 2 - Weight based in cluster load balancing

3.1.1 Measurement Metrics and Analytical Evaluation Given the fact that the Key Performance Indicators are comprised of factors such as response time, throughput time, and resource allocation, they are continually monitored and evaluated systematically. This is necessary to be able to evaluate the effectiveness of our two-tier load balancing architecture. Various monitoring tools like Prometheus and Grafana are integrated to be able to monitor and evaluate the real-time performance of the clusters & their deployed containerized environments and gain deeper insights into their current condition.

3.1.2 Theoretical Benefits of the Proposed Approach The proposed two-tier load balancer solves diverse problems that are present today in the contemporary cloud systems. The speed and precision of the first tier are achieved along with optimizing resource allocation by assigning incoming traffic to unused servers which helps in efficiently processing a variety of content types along with meeting their specific needs. The framework's second layer dynamically distributes the traffic to ensure resource efficiency and system responsiveness by adapting to the ever-changing nature of the traffic continuously. Along with this, the second layer also provides fine-grained resource management through the features of health checks & auto-scaling mechanisms which increases the system's ability to handle fluctuating traffic patterns while being scalable and available.

3.2 Prototype

The major objective of this prototyping phase is the local deployment of Docker containers for both the layers of the system with the essential communication between them. Each container would essentially represent a cluster and this system would replicate the actual dynamic cloud infrastructure. There are two steps needed for the implementation of our prototype: creating content-specific containers and then a primary load balancer container.

We start with creating **Content-specific containers** for each content type, such as audio, video, etc. Each of these containers is equipped with an application design to meet the specific processing needs of the allocated content type. These applications are designed to accept the incoming requests from the first layer of the load balancer, process the incoming request based on its content type and then send the response back to the primary layer load balancer.

The **Primary Load Balancer Container** is equipped with NGINX which makes the decisions for content-specific routing. NGINX load balancer algorithm analyzes the incoming traffic and then classifies it based on its content type. It then routes the request to the appropriate content-specific containers. This algorithm also acts as a reverse proxy by compiling the responses received from the content-specific clusters and returning them back to the client.

The local deployment of Docker containers provides a controlled testing environment, which helped us to simulate various scenarios on a smaller scale without having to consider the intricacies of the actual cloud environment. This helped us to understand the behavior of our algorithm in regards to critical issues like resource competition, scalability, and network latency. By simulating such problems in a controlled environment, we were able to test our solution, optimize it, and validate the existing architectural decisions before creating a full-fledged version of the algorithm.

The testing phase of our prototype provides useful insights, which are then used to improve the actual implementation of our algorithm. This testing demonstrates the system's capacity to scale well in spite of increasing workloads and the varied nature of traffic, showcasing the dependability of its auto-scaling methods. The system also demonstrates high performance while adjusting to changing network conditions and needs of content types. These observations impact the considerations we make while implementing our algorithm.

3.3 Observations and Benefits Based on Prototype

Below are main observations and benefits recorded after running the prototype:

Reaction Time Reduction Due to Accurate Cluster Targeting: Since we select the suitable cluster exactly for routing the incoming request, it reduces the system's reaction time significantly.

Optimizing Load Balancer Performance with Focused Monitoring: Our system performs more effectively as the load balancer within each cluster only has to monitor the pods within that specific cluster rather than all the clusters in the system.

Shorter Signaling Times and Preventing Bottlenecks: Due to the fixed nature of relationships and communication between both layers, a lower level of signaling is observed during the experimentation phase.

Following are certain benefits that are derived from the way our architecture is created and our design decisions:

Enhanced Security and Versatility with On-Site Server Integration: Our system's adaptable design enables smooth interaction with cloud-based clusters as well as on-site servers. Having on-site servers improves data security and privacy as the data remains within the physical infrastructure of the company [3].

We also observe a higher resource utilization as compared to the other baseline algorithms. In the next section, we describe how we achieve this higher utilization of resources.

3.3.1 Balancing Utilization with Specialized Hardware Since the CPU utilization levels vary across clusters, we use specialized hardware to maintain efficient processing and balance traffic loads.

Primary Load Balancer Cluster: The primary load balancer is only responsible for re-routing the requests, which does not create a lot of load on the hardware. Therefore, the primary load balancer cluster only requires general-purpose hardware to perform its duties satisfactorily.

Specialized Clusters: The content-specific clusters are more heavily utilized than the primary layer load balancer and have benefited from having specialized hardware configuration within them that is optimized for the functions required by the content type of the cluster.

4 Experiments, Results and Correctness

In this section, we explain the experimental setup and results of performance testing for the proposed system, along with the two baseline systems: two baseline load balance systems, i.e., Baseline 1: Service Mesh Load Balancer [4] and Baseline 2: Multi-metric Load Balancer [5].

Note that *each of the figures below shows a left y-axis depicting error rate and a right y-axis depicting response time per request. The grey line and the shaded area below depict the number of requests sent at a particular instance.*

4.1 General Set-up for the Test Runs

This subsection contains the experimental setup for all 3 load balancing system, explaining cluster configurations, tools, and testing conditions for a fair comparison. They were subjected to controlled tests using fixed and peak load formats to evaluate their performance.

Baseline 1: Service Mesh Load Balancer: The service mesh cluster load balancer [4] was a GKE cluster set up with 4 pods in the cluster to handle the incoming load. The cluster was equipped with Istio and it used Istio service mesh for load balancing within the cluster. Each of these pods received a fixed weight which was given in the destination rule according to the idea of the paper [1]. Two out of the four pods are stressed with the background traffic generated by 1 VMs, 2 CPU and 500M VM-bytes for the entire course of the run. This stress is generated using the stress command. The load balancer was hit with requests for 3 min by 20 virtual users in a fixed load kind of format.

Baseline 2: Multi-metric Load Balancer: The multi-metric cluster load balancer [5] was a GKE cluster set up with four pods in the cluster to handle the incoming load. This cluster was equipped with cAdvisor, influxDB, Prometheus, Redis, etc. The cluster was set up in such a way that Prometheus and cAdvisor were used to monitor the pod metrics, influx DB was used to store the information collected, and Redis was used to store pod weights. These pod weights were updated at regular intervals. Two out of the four pods are stressed with the background traffic generated by 1 VM, 2 CPU, and 500M VM bytes for the entire course of the run. The multi-metric cluster load balancer faced load for four minutes from 20 virtual users in a peak format. Peak format refers to the kind of load in which the incoming load first starts at a lower level, stays at that level for a fixed interval, and then increases to achieve the maximum load possible. Once it reaches and remains the maximum load possible for a fixed interval, it then returns to the lower level.

Proposed Approach: Adaptive Load Balancer: To match the conditions of the above runs, our framework was run under two different circumstances. Our system had a total of 4 pods in the 2 specialized clusters, i.e., 2 in each cluster and an additional pod in layer 1 of the load balancer. One pod from each specialized cluster was stressed with the background traffic generated by 1 VMs, 2 vCPUs, and 500M VM-bytes for the entire course of the run. The two kinds of runs are as follows:

- To compare with the Service Mesh load balancer, our algorithm was put under load for 3 min in a fixed format.
- To compare with the multi-metric load balancer, our system was put under load for 4 min in the peak format.

4.2 Overhead: Pros and Cons of Layer 1

For demonstration purposes, the specialized cluster was accessed directly through the public internet; it wasn't accessed through the proposed algorithm's primary layer.

Fig. 4. Video Cluster's test run under load directly from public internet

In Fig. 4, we can observe that by accessing the video cluster from the public internet, the average response time is 84 ms. However, when we compare it to Fig. 9, we can see an average response time of approximately 25 ms higher. This additional 25 ms can be attributed to the overhead of communication between layer 1 and layer 2. Therefore, using an additional pod for diverting requests to various specialized clusters creates both a pro and a con for our framework, making it easier to make a close comparison with the other two algorithms. Additionally, this additional pod only diverts requests and does not do any processing like the other 4 pods in the system. Like in the other two algorithms, there are only 4 pods that perform actual processing in our system, too.

4.3 Performance Evaluation Under Static Traffic

Here, we compare the experiments and results of various load balancers under stress and no-stress conditions. Stress, in this context, means the background traffic generated on pods as described in the test run setup.

Baseline 1 vs Proposed Framework Under Stress: In this run of Baseline 1 depicted in Fig. 5, we can observe that a total of 6287 requests were processed in a 3-minute interval at the rate of 33.88 requests/sec. The average response time is 83 ms per request. We can also observe a 0% error rate throughout the entire run. There is a jump of about 20ms just by adding stress through background traffic generated by 1VM, 2vCPUs and 500M of memory. This demonstrates the worsening of system performance under stress.

In our design depicted in Fig. 6, we can observe that a total of 10994 requests were processed in the 3-minute interval, which means that an additional 4700 requests were processed through our algorithm in the same amount of time. A higher rate of 58.44 requests/secs were processed throughout the run. The average response time was pretty much comparable to the Service Mesh load balancer at 86 ms.

Fig. 5. Baseline 1 in static under stress

4.4 Performance Evaluation Under Dynamic Traffic

Multi-metric load balancer runs vary continuously within a bigger range of response time from 80 to 105 ms. This points to the instability of the algorithm during different runs caused mainly by the high complexity of this large system. Stress here means the background traffic generated on pods as described in the set-up of the test runs.

In Fig. 7, we observe the multi-metric load balancer under no stress in dynamic traffic for 4 min. We observe an average response time of 73 ms, which is about 10 ms lower than that with stress. It processes about 4100, which is still 3200 requests lower than our proposed approach under stress. This showcases the better performance of our approach even under stress than algorithms under no stress.

Figure 8 shows the test run of the service mesh load balancer in peak format. This run was 4 min long. As we can see, the average response time is 86 ms and 16.99 requests are processed per second. This load balancer processes 4184

Fig. 6. Our framework in static traffic under stress

Fig. 7. Baseline 2: Multi-metric load balancer in dynamic traffic under no stress

requests in the total time which is slightly higher than multi-metric load balancer but much lower than our proposed approach.

In the same run conditions, Fig. 9 shows that our algorithm processes a total of 7288 requests in the 4 min interval at the rate of 29.61 requests/second. It is approximately 3100 requests higher than the best case of multi-metric run. The average response time of 87 ms of our system falls within the best case and worst case of the multi-metric load balancer, leaning more towards its best case time. Throughout multiple runs of our system, stable performance is observed as compared to the multi-metric load balancer.

Fig. 8. Baseline 1 under stress in dynamic traffic

Fig. 9. Our approach in dynamic traffic under stress

4.5 Performance Summary, Pros, Cons, and Use Cases

4.5.1 Proposed Framework Vs Baseline 1 (Service Mesh Load Balancer) When comparing the proposed framework with the service mesh load balancer with, some important differences surfaced that point towards the strengths and drawbacks of our algorithm. The advantages of our platform include flexibility and precision; i.e., the flexibility it offers by responding dynamically to the changing demand within the clusters using the real-time resource utilization metrics, and the improved resource efficiency using specialized hardware. Our proposed system however requires a more complex setup and maintenance process, plus the operating costs needed in collecting metrics in real-time raises. We note that, while the proposed system is more complex and costly than the first baseline system, it is simpler and less costly than the second baseline system, as discussed below.

4.5.2 Proposed Framework Vs Baseline 2 (Multi-Metric Load Balancer) When comparing the proposed system with the Multi-metric load balancer, we observe that our framework offers advantages including simplicity, efficiency, and stability, since (a) it offers dynamic load balancing capability without having to deploy complicated multi-component systems, thus leading to easier set-up and maintenance, (b) it focuses on segmenting content types to optimize resource consumption inside specialized clusters, eliminating the expenses related to tracking metrics across all the general pods, plus its streamlined structure reduces setup and operational expenses without compromising load balancing, and (c) its stability works well across a wide range of circumstances, as compared to Multi-Metric Load Balancers which may face performance changes under some specific conditions. Note however that the proposed system does not have as granular management, and it does not store metrics for a longer time, it may have limited adaptability in highly fluctuating traffic circumstances.

4.5.3 Use Cases Every load balancer has certain use cases for which it works the best. The Service Mesh Load Balancer (Baseline 1) is best suited for workloads that are more consistent, predictable, and have a more dynamic nature. The Multi-metric load balancer (Baseline 2), is best for situations that are completely unpredictable and require high throughput. The proposed system is best for content-specific and high-traffic applications where the use of specialized hardware would maximize resource usage; it works best for applications that benefit from segmented hardware optimization.

5 Conclusion and Future Work

In addressing the need for a simple, practical, effective load balancer for cloud systems, this paper proposes a two-tierd, adaptive, metric-driven system for specialized clusters. The proposed architecture is modeled on GKE and implemented in docker containers as a prototype. The experiments and performance evaluation results has demonostrated the system's advantage in controlling changing and high-volume workloads. The framework outperforms a best-case multi metric load balancer in terms of throughput (total number of requests handled per second). The two-tier architecture maximizes efficiency, scalability, and responsiveness. The system excels in content-specific, high-traffic applications by leveraging specialized hardware and dynamic resource allocation and ensures optimized performance and scalability. The results confirm that the system is well suited for content-specific, high-traffic applications where specialized hardware plays a critical role in optimizing resource usage. Its design allows the framework to perform in scenarios where segmented hardware optimization and moderate to high scalability is required. The framework eliminates the need for complex multi-metric systems. This framework is a reliable, effective load-balancing solution for the modern cloud environments as it processes more requests at faster rates, maintaining stable and low-latency performance.

Future work may include the following: First, we could tweak the architecture of this load balancer to improve its responsiveness and effectiveness by manipulating its pod pool. Secondly, we could optimize the load balancing in the cluster for specialized content clusters by customizing the default in-cluster load balancer for audio, video and other specialized clusters respectively. Finally, we could formally prove the correctness of the proposed system.

References

1. Kumar, P., Kumar, R.: Issues and challenges of load balancing techniques in cloud computing: a survey. ACM Comput. Surv. **51**(6) (2019). https://doi.org/10.1145/3281010
2. Tai, J., Zhang, J., Li, J., Meleis, W., Mi, N.: Ara: adaptive resource allocation for cloud computing environments under bursty workloads. In: 30th IEEE International Performance Computing and Communications Conference, pp. 1–8. (2011). https://doi.org/10.1109/PCCC.2011.6108060
3. Sampson, D., Chowdhury, M.M.: The growing security concerns of cloud computing. In: 2021 IEEE International Conference on Electro Information Technology (EIT), pp. 050–055 (2021). https://doi.org/10.1109/EIT51626.2021.9491902
4. XIE, X., Govardhan, S.S.: A service mesh-based load balancing and task scheduling system for deep learning applications. In: 2020 20th IEEE/ACM International Symposium on Cluster, Cloud and Internet Computing (CCGRID), pp. 843–849 (2020). https://doi.org/10.1109/CCGrid49817.2020.00009
5. Liu, Q., Haihong, E., Song, M.: The design of multi-metric load balancer for kubernetes. In: 2020 International Conference on Inventive Computation Technologies (ICICT), pp. 1114–1117. (2020). https://doi.org/10.1109/ICICT48043.2020.9112373
6. Hamdani, M., Aklouf, Y., Bouarara, H.A.: Improved fuzzy load-balancing algorithm for cloud computing system. In: Proceedings of the 9th International Conference on Information Systems and Technologies. ICIST 2019. ACM, New York, NY, USA (2019). https://doi.org/10.1145/3361570.3361589, https://doi-org.libaccess.sjlibrary.org/10.1145/3361570.3361589
7. Shi, W., Kencl, L.: Sequence-preserving adaptive load balancers. In: Symposium on Architecture For Networking And Communications Systems, pp. 143–152 (2006)
8. Misra, P., Srivastava, S., Narang, N., Goel, S., Maity, P., Saxena, A.: A hierarchical approach to adaptive distributed scheduling in cloud. In: 2015 International Conference on Advances in Computing, Communications and Informatics (ICACCI), pp. 1678–1687. (2015). https://doi.org/10.1109/ICACCI.2015.7275855
9. Nguyen, V.-G., Grinnemo, K.-J., Taheri, J., Brunstrom, A.: Adaptive and latency-aware load balancing for control plane traffic in the 4g/5g core. In: 2021 Joint European Conference on Networks and Communications & 6G Summit (EuCNC/6G Summit), pp. 365–370 (2021). https://doi.org/10.1109/EuCNC/6GSummit51104.2021.9482513

10. Mashaly, M., Kühn, P.J.: Load balancing in cloud-based content delivery networks using adaptive server activation/deactivation. In: Proceedings of the 24th International Teletraffic Congress. ITC 2012, International Teletraffic Congress (2012)
11. Ragmani, A., Omri, A.E., Abghour, N., Moussaid, K., Rida, M.: An efficient load balancing strategy based on mapreduce for public cloud. In: Proceedings of the Second International Conference on Internet of Things, Data and Cloud Computing. ICC 0017. ACM, New York, NY, USA (2017). https://doi.org/10.1145/3018896.3056777, https://doi-org.libaccess.sjlibrary.org/10.1145/3018896.3056777

On Simulation of Multiple-Row Generalized Pipeline Cellular Array

Ihfaz Islam(✉), Harpreet Singh, Lubna Alazzawi, Kaveh Abani, Bhupinder Mavi, and Gurveer Singh Kalsi

Wayne State University, Detroit, MI 48202, USA
hg6507@wayne.edu

Abstract. There is an increasing interest in array computing these days because of the requirement of speed, accuracy, chip area, and wearable electronics. Advanced arithmetic computation has always been the interest of researchers in computing. A generalized pipeline array has been the topic of research for the last few decades. The literature was limited to 5 rows cellular array. In this paper, a generalized pipeline array has been extended to 7 rows and 9 rows. The simulation of this design has been done using Xilinx Vivado in the paper. The pipeline arrays were written using the Verilog hardware language. The approach can be extended to any number of rows of the pipeline array and thus resulting in more advanced arithmetic computations. It is hoped that this research work will result in more fruitful advanced computer architecture.

Keywords: Multiple-row array · Digital circuits · Verilog · Pipeline · Simulation · Array computing

1 Introduction

Array computing [13] has been the subject of research for the last 5 decades. Several authors published papers on array computing which can do arithmetic operations like addition, subtraction, multiplication, division, squaring and square rooting. A generalized pipeline array was published in a 1974 classic paper [1]. This array could do all the operations in one array rather than having separate arithmetic calculations as given by some of the previous authors. The array appeared in several books and papers on computer arithmetic and pipelining [2–4, 6, 11]. This array was a 5-row pipeline array. In the present paper, the array has been extended to 7 and 9 rows and suggests an approach by which the array can be extended to any number of rows to have all the above arithmetic operations. For completeness, the 5-row pipeline array is given here as a ready reference.

A simulation of this pipeline array was also discussed in the Sapporo paper [7]. Boolean expressions for arithmetic for control cells used in the generalized pipeline array as below (Fig. 1).

Boolean expressions of arithmetic cell are as follows:

$$S = [A \otimes (B \otimes X) \otimes C_1]F + A\overline{F} \tag{1}$$

H. R. Arabnia et al. (Eds.): CSCE 2025, CCIS 2932, pp. 136–143, 2026.
https://doi.org/10.1007/978-3-032-22193-3_10

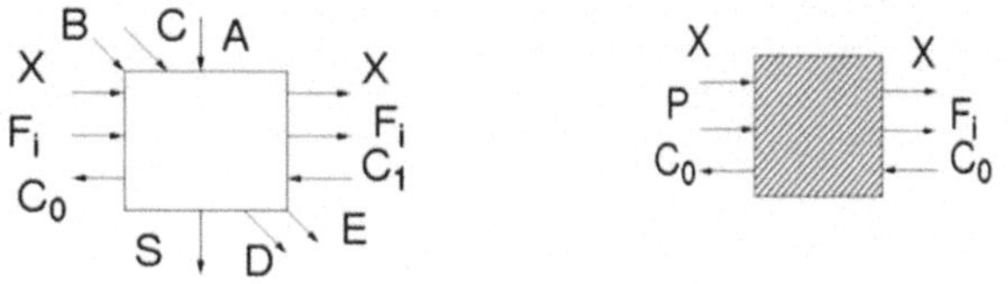

Fig. 1. **(a).** Arithmetic cell (b). Control cell

$$C_0 = (B \otimes X)(A + C_1) + AC_1 \tag{2}$$

$$D = BC + CF = C(B + F) \tag{3}$$

$$E = B + CF = (B + C)(B + F) \tag{4}$$

Boolean expression of control cell is:

$$F = C_0X + P\overline{X} \tag{5}$$

The Verilog [5] program using the above expressions for the 5-row pipeline array was discussed in reference [7]. Simulation of this array by using Vivado is given next. For illustration purposes, simulation of square root of 25, square of 5, multiplication of 7 and 5, and division of 25/5 are given [9]. For simplicity, only some elementary examples are given. The procedure can be implemented for any large examples.

The pipeline array is reproduced as below (Figs. 2 and 3):

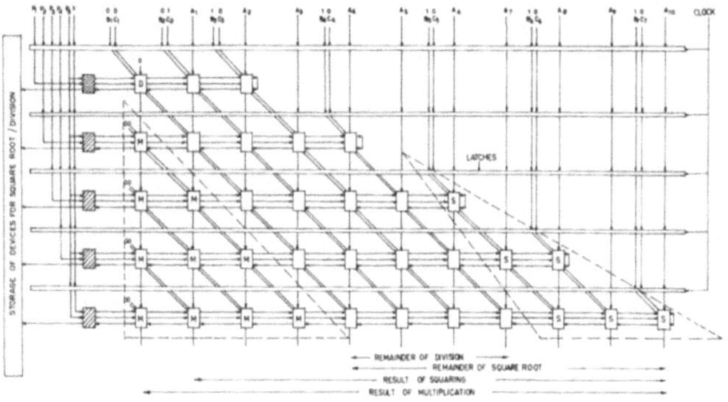

Fig. 2. Pipeline array [1]

The additional Boolean expressions are as follows (Tables 1, 2 and 3):

$$F = C_0X + P\overline{X}$$

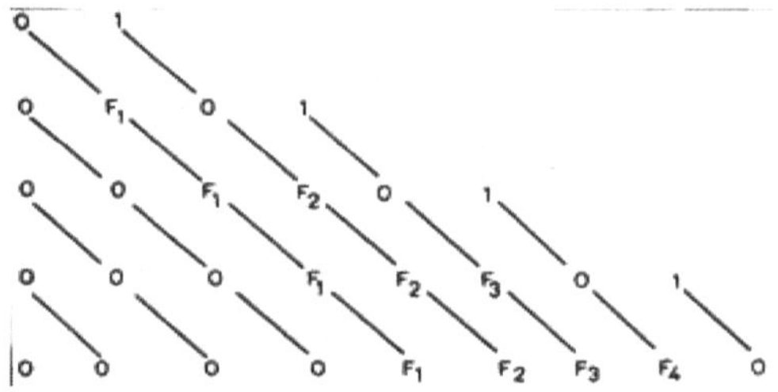

Fig. 3. Array for square root and square operations for binary numbers [1]

Table 1. Boolean Relations

X = 0	F = P
X = 1	F = C_0

Table 2. Boolean Values

	F = 0				F = 1		
B	C	D	E	B	C	D	E
0	0	0	0	0	0	0	0
0	1	0	0	0	1	1	1
1	0	0	1	1	0	0	1
1	1	1	1	1	1	1	1

Table 3. Parameters and Variables for Performing Various Arithmetic Operations [7]

Value'X'	Operations	Value of 'B' & 'C'	P' Assignment	Value of'A'
0	Square	As given in Array	P (Left Just)	0
1	Square Root	As given in Array	0	N
0	Multiplica tion	B = C	Mult (Right Just)	0
1	Division	B = C	0	D

2 Simulation

Simulation can be modified such that it needs the requirements of number of gates, delays, area etc. The hardware gate level procedure is very difficult to modify as the changes in hardware are difficult to get implemented. There should always be flexibility in the design, so that it meets the requirement of area, gates, timing delays, etc. It is very easy to make changes to the program rather than making changes to the hardware. In this paper, we demonstrated the results of various operations such as multiplication, division, squaring and square rooting.

The simulation procedure by Vivado is discussed below. Follow these steps separately for 5, 7, and 9 row pipeline arrays [8]. Each pipeline array should be implemented in separate Vivado project files.

1. Open Vivado, make a new project, select 'RTL Project' and add Verilog codes. Click on "Create File" and add a file called 'gpca.v' then click next. The testbench file 'gpca_tb.v' will be added as a simulation source once the project is opened.
2. Then select 'xc7a35tcpg236–1' device from the list of supported devices. Click next.
3. Once you create the project, right click on 'Simulation Source' and click 'Add Sources'. Add testbench file called 'gpca_tb'.
4. Import the Verilog codes for the main module and the testbench.
5. Select 'gpca_tb.v' and go to the 'Source File Properties window and unselect 'Synthesis' and 'Implementation' check boxes. Not doing so might cause errors during synthesis.
6. To obtain the simulation, go to Simulation > Run Simulation > Run Behavioral Simulation.
7. Under Synthesis click on 'Run Synthesis'. Then select 'Launch runs in local host' and click OK.
8. To view power reports, under Synthesis, click 'Report Power' to generate power results. Similarly, utilization can also be generated.

The following diagrams give the simulation of various operations using Verilog and Vivado (Figs. 4, 5, and 6).

2.1 Vivado Simulation Results

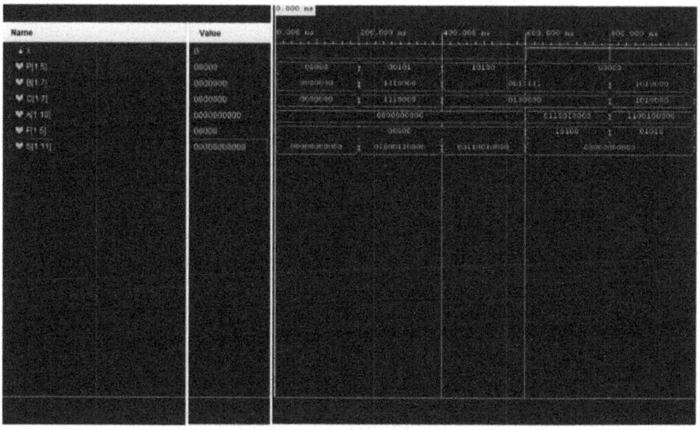

Fig. 4. 5-row pipeline array simulation results

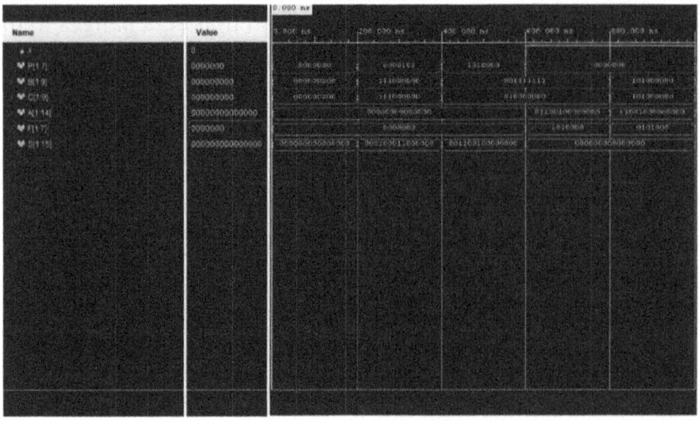

Fig. 5. 7-row pipeline array simulation results

Fig. 6. 9-row pipeline array simulation results

3 Power and Utilization Results

The power report and utilization are generated using Vivado. See steps 7 and 8 in Sect. 2 (Tables 4, 5, 6, 7, 8 and 9).

3.1 5-Row Pipeline Array

Table 4. Power results for 5-row pipeline array

	Power	
Total Power		13.025 W
Dynamic	Signals	1.282 W

(*continued*)

Table 4. (*continued*)

	Power	
	Logic	1.175 W
	I/Os	10.568 W
Device Static		0.203 W

Table 5. Utilization for 5-row pipeline array

Utilization	
LUT	78
IO	45

3.2 7-Row Pipeline Array

Table 6. Power results for 7-row pipeline array

	Power	
Total Power		20.883 W
Dynamic	Signals	2.394 W
	Logic	2.280 W
	I/Os	16.229 W
Device Static		0.485 W

Table 7. Utilization for 7-row pipeline array

Utilization	
LUT	127
IO	61

3.3 9-Row Pipeline Array

Table 8. Power results for 9-row pipeline array

	Power	
Total Power		28.281 W
Dynamic	Signals	4.514 W
	Logic	4.002 W
	I/Os	19.775 W
Device Static		0.485 W

Table 9. Utilization for 9-row pipeline array

Utilization	
LUT	127
IO	61

4 Conclusion

Array computing has been the subject of interest for the last several years. Several research workers developed different computer arithmetic circuits. A generalized pipeline array attracted the attention of the computer arithmetic community. In this paper, the pipeline array previously proposed has been extended to 7 and 9 rows. The algorithms have been simulated on Vivado. The power and utilization of the 5, 7, and 9 row pipeline arrays have been determined. All these procedures can be easily implemented on different FPGAs. The previous papers having 5 row pipelines have been extended to have computation of a large number of bits. The previous authors did not discuss the utilization of extension of 5-row pipeline array to any number of rows. This is the need for modern wearable electronics where speed, accuracy, and memory requirements are a major concern. It is hoped that this extension of array computing will result in the development of circuits for a variety of future applications.

Acknowledgments. The authors are thankful to several graduate students in the ECE department from Wayne State University for assistance.

Disclosure of Interests. The authors have no competing interests to declare that are relevant to the content of this article.

References

1. Kamal, A.K., Singh, H., Agrawal, D.P.: A generalized pipeline array. IEEE Trans. Comput. (1974)
2. Hwang, K.: Computer Architecture: Principles, Architecture and Design, ISBN: 0471052000. John Wiley & Sons Inc, US (1979)
3. Hwang, K.: Advanced Computer Architecture: Parallelism, Scalability, Programmability, McGraw-Hill Book Co., NY, 1993. Chinese translation by Tsinghua University Press, China, (1995)
4. Peter, M.: Kogge, the Architecture of Pipelined Computers. CRC Press (1981)
5. Bhaskar, J.: A Verilog HDL Primer, (1997)
6. Banerjee, P.P., Ghafoor, A.: Design of a pipelined optical binary processor. Appl. Opt. **27**(22), 4766–4477 (1988)
7. Singh, H., et al.: On simulation and design implementation of generalized pipeline cellular array. In: 2014 International Conference on Information Science, Electronics and Electrical Engineering (ISEEE), pp. 1761–1765, Sapporo, (2014)
8. Xie, Y.: The Design and VLSI Implementation of Digital Arithmetic Processors - a Case Study of a Generalized Pipeline Cellular Array, p. 462. Wayne State University Theses (2015)
9. Majithia, J.C.: Cellular array for extraction of squares and square roots of binary numbers. IEEE Trans. Comput. (Short Notes). **C-21**, 1023–1024 (1972)
10. Singh, H.: Class Notes ECE 5680 Lambert's Manual
11. Almatrood, A.F., Singh, H.: Design of Generalized Pipeline Cellular Array in QuantumDot cellular automata. IEEE Comput. Archit. Lett. **17**(1), 29–32 (2018)
12. Otman Ali, A.: On The Vlsi Implementation Of High Throughput Low Power Design Of Pipeline Cellular Array. Wayne State University Dissertations. 3789. (2022). https://digitalcommons.wayne.edu/oa_dissertations/3789
13. Singh, H.: Keynote Address "Array Computing and AI Applications" at International Conference on Applications of AI & Machine Learning (ICAML), Chandigarh India (2025)

ICEQT'25: 4th International Conference on Emergent Quantum Technologies

Quantum Approximate Optimization Algorithm: Applications, Limitations and Enhancement

P. Herrero-Gómez, M. Alemany-Manzanaro, D. Gil-Méndez, and H. Mora-Mora(✉)

University of Alicante, San Vicente del Raspeig, Alicante, Spain
{pablo.herrero,david.gil,hmora}@ua.es, mama41@alu.ua.es

Abstract. The Quantum Approximate Optimization Algorithm (QAOA) is a promising quantum algorithm for solving combinatorial optimization problems. However, its efficiency can be limited by the large search space that needs to be explored. This paper proposes an enhancement to QAOA by modifying the initial state to a semi-superposed state, combining prior knowledge and heuristics to collapse some qubits to specific values while leaving others in superposition. This modification reduces the search space, focusing the algorithm on more promising regions of the solution space. We detail the preparation of the semi-superposed state and the application of QAOA operators, including the phase and cost Hamiltonians. We then discuss the benefits of this approach, such as faster convergence, improved solution quality, and reduced computational cost. Performance improvements are evaluated in terms of search space reduction, convergence behavior, and solution quality. The results show that the enhanced QAOA algorithm can find high-quality solutions more efficiently, making it a promising approach for solving large-scale optimization problems on near-term quantum devices.

Keywords: QAOA · Quantum Computing · Hamiltonian Simulation · Combinatorial Optimization Problems · Hybrid Algorithms

1 Introduction

Quantum computing has emerged as a promising paradigm for solving complex optimization problems that are intractable for classical computers. Among the various quantum algorithms developed for such tasks, the Quantum Approximate Optimization Algorithm (QAOA) stands out due to its hybrid nature, combining quantum circuits with classical optimization techniques. QAOA is designed to solve combinatorial optimization problems by preparing a parameterized quantum state and iteratively refining it to approximate the optimal solution [3].

At its core, QAOA relies on the formulation of a cost function that can be encoded into a Hamiltonian—a quantum mechanical operator whose ground state corresponds to the solution of the optimization problem. The algorithm begins with the application of

H. R. Arabnia et al. (Eds.): CSCE 2025, CCIS 2932, pp. 147–157, 2026.
https://doi.org/10.1007/978-3-032-22193-3_11

a mixing Hamiltonian and a cost Hamiltonian, alternately applied over a certain number of layers (or depth p), creating a quantum state that is expected to be increasingly aligned with optimal or near-optimal solutions.

The standard QAOA starts with a uniform superposition of all possible states, meaning the quantum register is initialized with equal probability amplitudes across the entire solution space. While this strategy allows for a general and unbiased search, it often leads to slow convergence and suboptimal performance, particularly in high-dimensional or structured problem spaces where prior information is available but unused.

While previous works such as the Two-Step QAOA approach [7] have explored advanced initialization strategies—most notably through a dual-phase execution that leverages one QAOA run to construct constraint-satisfying intermediate states—our proposed enhancement fundamentally differs in both motivation and implementation. Rather than relying on a preliminary QAOA phase or complex mixer modifications, we introduce a semi-superposed initial state based on heuristic or domain-specific insights. This state preparation selectively collapses a subset of qubits to fixed classical values, while leaving the remainder in quantum superposition. Unlike Two-Step QAOA, which focuses on embedding hard constraints such as k-hot encodings into the quantum evolution via tailored Hamiltonians, our method aims to reduce the effective search space and guide the algorithm toward high-potential solution regions from the outset. This makes our approach more lightweight, more flexible across problem types, and particularly well-suited for near-term quantum devices where circuit depth and gate count remain significant limitations.

In this work, we propose an enhancement to the standard QAOA that leverages problem-specific heuristics and classical preprocessing to modify the initial state. Instead of initializing with a fully uniform superposition, we introduce a semi-superposed initial state, in which certain qubits are collapsed to predefined values based on prior knowledge, while the remaining qubits remain in superposition. This targeted initialization reduces the search space and guides the quantum evolution towards more promising regions, ultimately improving convergence speed, solution quality, and computational efficiency.

The rest of this paper is organized as follows. Section 2 reviews the theoretical foundations of QAOA, including the construction and role of the cost and mixing Hamiltonians. Section 3 discusses the limitations of the standard QAOA approach. Section 4 presents the proposed enhancement using a semi-superposed initial state, with detailed implementation and mathematical formulation. Section 5 evaluates the performance improvements in terms of search space reduction, convergence behavior, and solution quality. Finally, Sect. 6 concludes with a discussion of future directions.

2 Hamiltonians

In quantum mechanics, a *Hamiltonian* is a Hermitian operator that represents the total energy of a system. It governs the time evolution of the quantum state according to the Schrödinger equation:

$$i\hbar\frac{\partial}{\partial t}|\psi(t)\rangle = H|\psi(t)\rangle, \tag{1}$$

where $|\psi(t)\rangle$ is the quantum state at time t, H is the Hamiltonian of the system, and $\hbar$ is the reduced Planck constant. When the Hamiltonian is time-independent, the solution to the Schrödinger equation is given by:

$$|\psi(t)\rangle = e^{-iHt/\hbar}|\psi(0)\rangle, \tag{2}$$

indicating that the evolution of the quantum system is described by a unitary operator $U(t) = e^{-iHt/\hbar}$ generated by the Hamiltonian H [13].

Hamiltonian simulation is a core problem in quantum computing. It consists of constructing quantum circuits that approximate the unitary operator e^{-iHt} for a given Hamiltonian H, enabling the efficient simulation of quantum and certain classical systems. This capability underpins many quantum algorithms, particularly in fields such as quantum chemistry, and fluid dynamics [9].

For instance, [6] apply Hamiltonian simulation to model reacting flows by transforming dissipative partial differential equations (PDEs) into Hamiltonian forms using techniques such as the warped phase transform. Since dissipation typically introduces non-Hermitian terms, their approach converts these into Hermitian operators so that the evolution remains consistent with the principles of quantum mechanics—i.e., governed by unitary operators.

In scenarios involving linear PDEs with convection and reaction terms, this framework allows for *one-shot* computation of the entire solution without requiring intermediate measurements. This leverages the coherence and efficiency of unitary quantum evolution, providing a powerful computational advantage over traditional classical methods (Lu and Yang, 2024).

Hamiltonian simulation not only provides insights into natural processes but also serves as a fundamental building block in many quantum algorithms—such as QAOA, Variational Quantum Eigensolver (VQE), and quantum phase estimation—by enabling precise control over state evolution.

2.1 Hamiltonians in QAOA

As explained in 1, the Quantum Approximate Optimization Algorithm (QAOA) is a hybrid quantum-classical variational method designed to find approximate solutions to combinatorial optimization problems. It achieves this by mapping the objective function onto a quantum cost Hamiltonian and evolving an initial quantum state using two types of parameterized unitary operations: one based on the cost Hamiltonian H_C and the other on a mixing Hamiltonian H_M. The evolution of the quantum state over p layers (or steps) is given by:

$$|\psi(\gamma,\beta)\rangle = \left(\prod_{k=1}^{p} e^{-i\beta_k H_M} e^{-i\gamma_k H_C}\right)|+\rangle^{\otimes n} \tag{3}$$

where $|+\rangle^{\otimes n}$ represents the uniform superposition over all 2^n computational basis states, and $\gamma = (\gamma_1, \ldots, \gamma_p)$ and $\beta = (\beta_1, \ldots, \beta_p)$ are variational parameters optimized classically.

The cost Hamiltonian H_C encodes the objective function of the optimization problem into the quantum circuit. For example, in problems like Max-Cut, H_C is constructed as a sum of pairwise interaction terms between qubits corresponding to graph edges. In general, H_C is diagonal in the computational basis and composed of Pauli-Z operators.

The mixer Hamiltonian H_M is designed to induce transitions between basis states and allow the algorithm to explore the search space. It is typically defined as:

$$H_M = \sum_{j=1}^{n} X_j, \tag{4}$$

where X_j is the Pauli-X operator acting on the j-th qubit. The corresponding unitary $e^{-i\beta_k H_M}$ rotates the state in the X-basis and acts as a driver that helps prevent the quantum system from getting stuck in local minima. In more advanced or domain-specific QAOA variants, alternative mixers are used to respect problem constraints (e.g., fixing Hamming weight or domain symmetries).

Together, H_C and H_M form the variational backbone of QAOA. The performance of the algorithm heavily depends on how well these Hamiltonians are tailored to the problem at hand, as well as on the classical optimization of the parameters γ and β, which aim to maximize the expectation value:

$$\langle \psi(\gamma, \beta) | H_C | \psi(\gamma, \beta) \rangle \tag{5}$$

Crucially, the QAOA Hamiltonians define an ansatz state parameterized by γ and β, whose parameters are optimized classically based on measurement outcomes. These Hamiltonians not only guide the evolution of the system but also serve as the objective function in the variational loop. The QAOA's success is deeply linked to how well H_C and H_M are constructed and to their expressivity in navigating the optimization landscape [1]. For a clearer understanding, Fig. 1 shows in an abstract way how the QAOA algorithm works.

2.2 Generalization and Applications

Recent extensions of QAOA explore Hamiltonians in broader contexts, including continuous-variable QAOA (CV-QAOA) and applications in quantum Monte Carlo methods like Quantum Dynamical Hamiltonian Monte Carlo (QD-HMC) [5]. These methods adapt QAOA-style Hamiltonian evolution to propose transitions in probabilistic models, showing that Hamiltonians are not only crucial for encoding cost functions, but also for exploring probability distributions in quantum-enhanced inference.

Ultimately, Hamiltonians in quantum computing are more than just operators—they are the heart of dynamics, optimization, and computation. Whether simulating fluid dynamics or solving combinatorial problems, they define the quantum pathways through which information is processed and solutions are found.

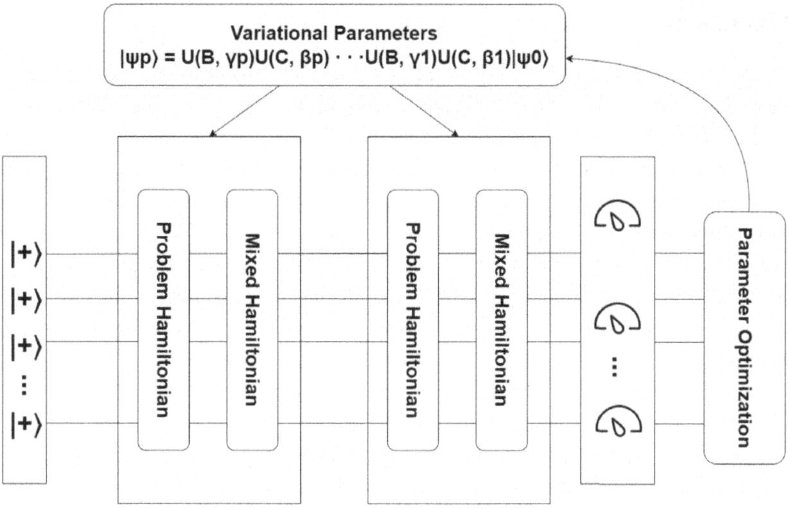

Fig. 1. QAOA Circuit.

3 Applications and Limitations of QAOA

The Quantum Approximate Optimization Algorithm (QAOA) has emerged as a promising candidate for solving combinatorial optimization problems on near-term quantum devices. Its appeal lies in the relatively shallow quantum circuits it requires compared to other quantum algorithms such as Shor's or HHL algorithms [2]. However, despite extensive research, the quantum advantage of QAOA remains unproven.

3.1 Applications

QAOA has demonstrated versatility across various domains of combinatorial optimization. In graph theory, it has been applied to problems such as Max-Cut, graph coloring, and graph partitioning [4]. It also finds applications in classical combinatorial problems like the Traveling Salesman Problem (TSP), the Quadratic Assignment Problem, and the Maximum Clique Problem.

In practical contexts, QAOA has shown promise for job scheduling, resource allocation, and energy grid optimization. It is also being explored in machine learning for tasks like feature selection, clustering, and classification, as well as in network routing and flow optimization [4]. Furthermore, QAOA is used in constraint satisfaction problems such as SAT and Max-SAT, and in quantum simulation tasks like molecular modeling.

A notable application area is financial portfolio optimization, where QAOA has been benchmarked on real-world datasets. The algorithm's performance in this setting shows sensitivity to the specific instance and requires careful tuning of variational parameters, especially when addressing constraints with either penalty-based (soft) or operator-based (hard) formulations [2].

3.2 Limitations

Despite its broad applicability, QAOA faces significant limitations. One key challenge is scalability. Analytical results for large-scale instances are lacking, primarily due to the classical complexity of optimizing the variational parameters, which is itself an NP-hard problem [2]. This difficulty is compounded by the fact that optimal parameter values for one instance may not generalize to others, necessitating instance-specific tuning or robust heuristic strategies.

Another major limitation involves the algorithm's performance for higher-order constraint satisfaction problems, such as Max-kXOR or Max-kSAT with $k > 2$. Studies have shown that while QAOA may outperform classical solvers for specific instances (e.g., random 8SAT), this typically requires deep circuits with many layers [8]. This depth is currently unfeasible on noisy intermediate-scale quantum (NISQ) hardware due to limited coherence times and error mitigation challenges.

Moreover, QAOA implementations on superconducting devices or similar platforms may require decomposing many-body interactions into two-body gates, increasing circuit depth further. Additionally, shallow circuits are hindered by barren plateaus—regions in the optimization landscape where gradients vanish exponentially with problem size. Some models that avoid barren plateaus turn out to be classically simulable, undermining the potential quantum advantage. Noise also plays a critical role in limiting the efficacy of QAOA. Recent results show that even shallow QAOA circuits face serious challenges in expectation value estimation under realistic noise levels, further restricting their practical depth on current devices [12].

In summary, while QAOA provides a flexible and powerful framework for optimization across diverse problem classes, its practical deployment remains constrained by classical optimization costs, hardware limitations, and noise sensitivity. Overcoming these challenges—through improved parameter initialization heuristics, error mitigation techniques, or new ansatz structures—remains an active area of research.

4 Proposed Enhancement Using a Semi-superposed Initial State

The standard Quantum Approximate Optimization Algorithm (QAOA) begins with a uniform superposition state, which, while effective in some cases, can result in the algorithm exploring a vast and often inefficient search space. In this enhancement, we modify the initial state to a semi-superposed state, utilizing heuristic knowledge and prior information about the problem. Instead of starting with a uniform superposition, we prepare a state where certain qubits are collapsed to specific values, and others remain in superposition. This approach aims to optimize the algorithm's performance by reducing the search space and focusing the optimization process on more promising regions of the solution space. For a clear sight of the enhancing process, Fig. 2 shows it graphically.

4.1 Preparation of the Semi-superposed Initial State

Consider a problem with n qubits. Let S denote the set of qubits that are collapsed to certain values and $\bar{S}$ the set of qubits that remain in superposition.

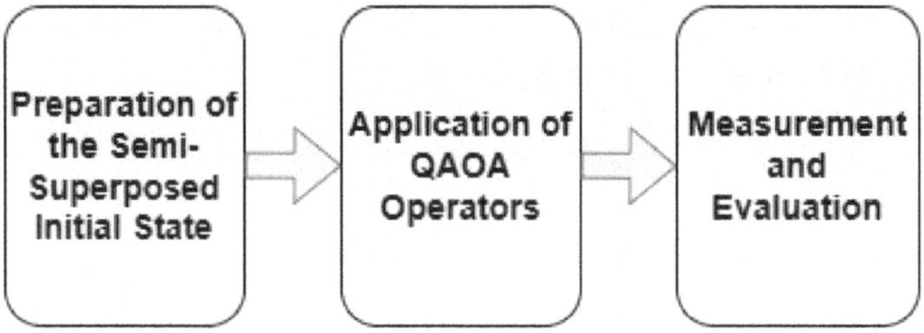

Fig. 2. Enhancing QAOA Process.

- **Selection of Collapsed Qubits:** Based on prior knowledge, heuristics, or classical preprocessing, we decide which qubits (denoted by S) will be collapsed to specific values, and which ones ($\bar{S}$) will remain in superposition. For instance, we may choose $S = \{1,2\}$ and $\bar{S} = \{3,4,\ldots,n\}$.
- **Preparation of Collapsed Qubits:** For the qubits in S, we fix their values to either 0 or 1. If $S = \{1,2\}$, we collapse these qubits to the state $|01\rangle$.
- **Preparation of Qubits in Superposition:** For the qubits in $\bar{S}$, we apply Hadamard gates to create a uniform superposition. If $\bar{S} = \{3,4,\ldots,n\}$, we apply the Hadamard operation to each qubit in $\bar{S}$.
  The resulting initial state is then:

$$|\psi_0\rangle = |01\rangle \otimes \frac{1}{\sqrt{2^{|\bar{S}|}}} \sum_{x\in\{0,1\}^{|\bar{S}|}} |x\rangle \tag{6}$$

  This state reflects a mixture of collapsed qubits and superposed qubits, guiding the algorithm toward potentially relevant regions in the search space from the outset.

4.2 Application of QAOA Operators

The QAOA consists of two main types of parametrized operators: the phase Hamiltonian (mixing operator) and the cost Hamiltonian.

- **Mixing Hamiltonian:** The mixing operator $U(B,\gamma)$ is defined as:

$$U(B,\gamma) = e^{-i\gamma B} \tag{7}$$

  where B is the mixing operator, typically represented as a sum of Pauli-X operators acting on the qubits in $\bar{S}$:

$$B = \sum_{j\in\bar{S}} X_j \tag{8}$$

  This operator only acts on the qubits in $\bar{S}$.
- **Cost Hamiltonian:** The cost operator $U(C,\beta)$ is defined as:

$$U(C,\beta) = e^{-i\beta C} \tag{9}$$

  where C is the cost operator specific to the problem at hand.

The operators are alternately applied during p levels, adjusting the parameters γ and β at each level. The state after p levels is:

$$|\psi_p\rangle = U(B,\gamma_p)U(C,\beta_p)\cdots U(B,\gamma_1)U(C,\beta_1)|\psi_0\rangle \tag{10}$$

4.3 Measurement and Evaluation

After applying the operators, we measure the final state in the computational basis to obtain binary results. Based on the measurement outcomes, we evaluate the cost function associated with the obtained bit strings.

Using classical optimization techniques such as gradient descent or evolutionary algorithms, we adjust the parameters γ and β to minimize the cost function. This process is repeated iteratively until the solution converges or a maximum number of iterations is reached.

5 Benefits of the Enhancement

5.1 Search Space Reduction

By collapsing certain qubits to specific values based on prior knowledge or heuristics, the number of possible combinations the algorithm needs to explore is significantly reduced. This leads to:

- **Smaller search space:** Collapsing k qubits in a problem with n qubits reduces the search space from 2^n to 2^{n-k}, exponentially decreasing the number of configurations that need to be explored.
- **Focus on promising regions:** By incorporating prior knowledge into the initial state preparation, the algorithm can focus on regions of the solution space that have a higher likelihood of containing the optimal solution, increasing the efficiency of the search.

5.2 Faster Convergence

Reducing the search space and focusing on promising regions can speed up the convergence of QAOA. This results in:

- **Fewer iterations:** With an initial state closer to the optimal solution, QAOA can find a high-quality solution with fewer iterations, thereby reducing the total runtime.
- **More efficient parameter optimization:** Classical optimization methods, such as gradient descent, can be more efficient when working with a smaller and more focused solution space, improving the optimization of the parameters γ and β.

5.3 Improved Solution Quality

The quality of the solutions found by QAOA can be improved due to the more informed preparation of the initial state:

- **Higher probability of finding optimal solutions:** Starting from a state that is partially optimized increases the likelihood that QAOA will either find or get closer to the optimal solution.
- **Reduced variability in solutions:** The solutions obtained are more consistent and of higher quality since the algorithm does not need to explore as much random space.

5.4 Reduction in Computational Cost

The computational cost of QAOA, in terms of both quantum hardware execution time and classical optimization resources, can be reduced:

- **Lower quantum execution time:** Fewer qubits in superposition and fewer iterations can reduce the total execution time on quantum hardware.
- **Reduced classical optimization resources:** The optimization of parameters γ and β requires fewer computational resources if the search space is smaller and more directed.

6 Conclusions

The Quantum Approximate Optimization Algorithm (QAOA) is a hybrid quantum-classical algorithm designed to solve combinatorial optimization problems. It operates by alternating between two parameterized unitary operations derived from the cost Hamiltonian H_C, which encodes the problem's objective function, and the mixing Hamiltonian H_M, which facilitates exploration of the solution space. The algorithm begins with an initial quantum state, typically a uniform superposition, and evolves this state through a series of these alternating operations, with parameters optimized via classical routines.

To address the challenges and limitations described in, we propose an enhancement to QAOA that involves initializing the algorithm with a semi-superposed state. In this approach, certain qubits are fixed based on heuristic or classical preprocessing insights, while the remaining qubits are placed in superposition. This strategy effectively reduces the search space and guides the algorithm toward more promising regions, potentially improving convergence rates and solution quality.

Recent studies support the efficacy of informed initializations. For instance, the ADAPT-QAOA framework, which dynamically constructs the ansatz and utilizes classically inspired initial states, has demonstrated faster convergence and reduced susceptibility to local minima compared to standard QAOA [10]. Similarly, warm-started QAOA variants that incorporate classical solutions into the initial state have shown improved performance in solving problems like Max-Cut [11].

Future research should focus on:

- **Developing Advanced Initialization Techniques**: Exploring methods to generate initial states that incorporate more nuanced problem-specific information, potentially through machine learning approaches.
- **Customizing Mixing Hamiltonians**: Designing mixers tailored to the structure of the problem and the chosen initial state to enhance exploration capabilities.
- **Integrating Classical Optimization Insights**: Leveraging classical optimization solutions to inform both the initial state and the parameter optimization process within QAOA.

By pursuing these directions, we can enhance the practical applicability of QAOA and its variants, paving the way for more efficient quantum algorithms capable of solving complex optimization problems.

Acknowledgements. Grant Serverless 4HPC PID2023-152804OB-I00 funded by MICIU/AEI/10.13039/501100011033 and by ERDF/EU.

References

1. Al-Bayaty, A., Perkowski, M.: Bht-qaoa: the generalization of quantum approximate optimization algorithm to solve arbitrary boolean problems as hamiltonians. In: Entropy, vol. 26, no. 10, article 843. MDPI (2024)
2. Brandhofer, S., et al.: Benchmarking the performance of portfolio optimization with qaoa. Quant. Inf. Process. 22 (2023). https://doi.org/10.1007/s11128-022-03766-5
3. Farhi, E., Goldstone, J., Gutmann, S.: A quantum approximate optimization algorithm. arXiv preprint arXiv:1411.4028 (2014)
4. Kashapogu, R., Hasib, S., Rasool, A.: Exploring the versatility of qaoa: a comprehensive review. In: 2024 15th International Conference on Computing Communication and Networking Technologies (ICCCNT), pp. 1–8. IEEE (2024). https://doi.org/10.1109/ICCCNT61001.2024.10725610
5. Lockwood, O., Weiss, P., Aronshtein, F., Verdon, G.: Quantum dynamical hamiltonian monte carlo. Phys. Rev. Res. **6**(3), 033142 (2024)
6. Lu, Z., Yang, Y.: Quantum computing of reacting flows via hamiltonian simulation. In: Proceedings of the Combustion Institute, vol. 40, no. 1, pp. 105440. Elsevier (2024)
7. Minato, Y.: Two-step qaoa: enhancing quantum optimization by decomposing k-hot constraints in qubo formulations. arXiv preprint arXiv:2408.05383 (2025)
8. Müller, T., Singh, A., Wilhelm, F.K., Bode, T.: Limitations of quantum approximate optimization in solving generic higher-order constraint-satisfaction problems. arXiv preprint arXiv:2411.19388 (2024)
9. Somma, R.D., King, R., et al., R.K.: Shadow hamiltonian simulation. In: Nature Communications, vol. 16, article 2690. Nature Publishing Group (2025). https://doi.org/10.1038/s41467-025-57451-z
10. Sridhar, V.K., Chen, Y., Gard, B., Barnes, E., Economou, S.E.: Adapt-qaoa with a classically inspired initial state. arXiv preprint arXiv:2310.09694 (2023)

11. Tate, R., Moondra, J., Gard, B., Mohler, G., Gupta, S.: Warm-started qaoa with custom mixers provably converges and computationally beats goemans-williamson's max-cut at low circuit depths. In: Quantum, vol. 7, article 1121. Verein zur Förderung des Open Access Publizierens in den Quantenwissenschaften (2023)
12. Vijendran, V., Das, A., Koh, D.E., Assad, S.M., Lam, P.K.: An expressive ansatz for low-depth quantum approximate optimisation. In: Quantum Science and Technology, vol. 9, no. 2, article 025010. IOP Publishing (2024)
13. Ye, Z.: Qaoa on hamiltonian cycle problem. arXiv preprint arXiv:2401.00017 (2023)

Quantum-Inspired Clustering Techniques for Malware Detection in Supply Chain Networks

Vishal H. Kothavade(✉), Sthefanie J. G. Passo, and John J. Prevost

ECE Department, University of Texas at San Antonio, San Antonio, USA
{Vishal.Kothavade,Sthefanie.Passo,Jeff.Prevost}@utsa.edu

Abstract. The increasing sophistication of cyber threats targeting supply chain communications in critical sectors like healthcare and manufacturing necessitates advanced detection mechanisms. This paper investigates the application of quantum clustering algorithms for identifying malware within these communication networks. We compare classical clustering techniques (Spectral), classical clustering enhanced with a precomputed quantum kernel, and a novel quantum circuit-based clustering approach. Our methodology leverages the unique capabilities of quantum computing to potentially uncover subtle and complex malware patterns that may be missed by classical methods. We evaluate the performance of these approaches using a real-world supply chain communication dataset, highlighting the potential advantages and challenges of quantum clustering in bolstering cybersecurity within these vital industrial hubs.

Keywords: Quantum Clustering · Malware Detection · Supply Chain Security · Quantum Kernel · Quantum Circuit Clustering · Noisy Intermediate Scale Quantum

1 Introduction

The interconnected nature of modern supply chains, particularly within the critical sectors of healthcare and manufacturing, has created an expansive attack surface for cyber threats. These threats, ranging from data breaches and ransomware attacks to sophisticated malware intrusions, can severely disrupt operations, compromise sensitive information, and even endanger human lives in healthcare settings. The reliance on complex communication networks for coordination, data exchange, and operational control makes these supply chains prime targets for malicious actors seeking to exploit vulnerabilities [1–3].

In recent years, the frequency and sophistication of software supply chain attacks have increased dramatically. High-profile incidents, such as the SolarWinds attack [4], have demonstrated the potential for widespread disruption and the cascading impact of compromised software components. Similarly, the healthcare industry faces constant threats to patient data and the integrity of

H. R. Arabnia et al. (Eds.): CSCE 2025, CCIS 2932, pp. 158–176, 2026.
https://doi.org/10.1007/978-3-032-22193-3_12

medical devices [5], while manufacturing hubs are increasingly targeted for intellectual property theft and operational sabotage [6]. These evolving threats necessitate the development of more advanced and robust cybersecurity measures capable of detecting subtle and novel attack vectors.

Traditional cybersecurity approaches, including signature-based detection and rule-based systems, often struggle to keep pace with the rapidly evolving landscape of malware and sophisticated attack techniques. Machine learning (ML) has emerged as a powerful tool for anomaly detection and malware classification within supply chain networks [7]. Classical clustering algorithms, such as Spectral Clustering, have been employed to group similar communication patterns and identify deviations that may indicate malicious activity [8]. However, as the volume and complexity of supply chain communication data grow exponentially, classical ML methods can face limitations in scalability and the ability to discern intricate, high-dimensional patterns indicative of advanced malware.

The advent of quantum computing offers a potentially transformative paradigm for addressing these challenges. Quantum algorithms possess the theoretical capability to process high-dimensional data and perform complex computations with greater efficiency than their classical counterparts for certain types of problems [9]. Quantum Machine Learning (QML), a burgeoning field that integrates quantum algorithms with machine learning techniques, holds promise for enhancing various cybersecurity tasks, including anomaly detection and malware classification [10].

This research explores the application of Quantum Clustering (QC) algorithms to the critical problem of malware detection within the communication networks of supply chain, healthcare, and manufacturing hubs. We investigate three distinct approaches: classical spectral clustering, classical clustering enhanced with a precomputed quantum kernel, and a novel quantum circuit-based clustering algorithm designed to leverage the unique properties of quantum computation. By comparing the performance of these methods on relevant dataset, we aim to evaluate the potential of QC to improve the accuracy and efficiency of malware detection in these vital industrial ecosystems. The findings of this study could pave the way for the development of more resilient and secure supply chain networks in the face of increasingly sophisticated cyber threats.

2 Related Work

Recent advances in clustering techniques have demonstrated significant potential for cybersecurity applications, particularly in supply chain management and healthcare sectors. Classical clustering approaches such as k-means and DBSCAN have been widely utilized for malware and anomaly detection. Alsabbagh et al. [11] applied k-means clustering to classify ransomware in supply chain networks, achieving an accuracy of 89%. While effective, classical clustering methods struggle with scalability and computational efficiency as the dimensionality and volume of data increase, particularly in IoT-enabled supply chains where feature complexity can degrade clustering performance.

Quantum machine learning offers new possibilities for anomaly detection by leveraging quantum parallelism and entanglement. Quantum Support Vector Machines (QSVM), introduced by Rebentrost et al. [12], have demonstrated superior classification performance compared to classical SVMs, particularly in high-dimensional dataset relevant to IoT security. Hdaib et al. [13] adapted QSVMs for intrusion detection, achieving improved detection rates and computational efficiency. Quantum Neural Networks (QNN) have also shown promise in cybersecurity applications, with Kukliansky et al. [14] demonstrating their robustness against adversarial attacks in anomaly detection, exploiting the high expressivity of quantum circuits to capture intricate data patterns beyond classical models.

Despite the growing interest in quantum machine learning, its application to clustering in supply chain and healthcare domains remains underexplored. Phillipson et al. [15] examined quantum annealing for logistics optimization, indicating the potential of QC to enhance malware detection. Their findings highlight how quantum annealers efficiently solve combinatorial optimization problems related to supply chain security. In the healthcare domain, Ahmad et al. [16] proposed quantum-resistant encryption schemes for securing medical IoT devices. However, their work did not address clustering techniques for anomaly detection, leaving an open gap in research for the integration of QC within healthcare cybersecurity frameworks.

QC techniques such as QCSWAPK-means and QkernelK-means have demonstrated superior performance in identifying vulnerabilities from the CISA Known Exploited Vulnerabilities catalog, utilizing Hilbert space mappings and quantum state entanglement to improve anomaly detection. These methods have achieved Silhouette scores of 0.491 and Davies-Bouldin indices below 0.745, surpassing classical spectral clustering techniques. Hybrid QSVMs have further strengthened security measures, achieving 95% accuracy in detecting compromised electronic health record transmissions in IBM-PayPal networks and reducing false positives in SAP supply chain alerts by 40% [17,18].

Mercedes-Benz has utilized quantum-enhanced digital twin models to simulate cyberattack vectors in pharmaceutical logistics, reducing vulnerability exposure by 30% using variational quantum eigensolvers. IBM's hybrid quantum anomaly detection framework aligns with HIPAA standards, enabling secure monitoring of medical device firmware updates. In manufacturing hubs, D-Wave's quantum annealing models have optimized Just-In-Time automotive part deliveries for BMW, reducing downtime costs by $12 million per year through QC applied to IoT sensor networks. Quantum Approximate Optimization Algorithms (QAOA) have improved supply chain network optimization, reducing total costs by 18% in a study involving 180 retail units [19–21].

Hybrid classical-quantum systems have also contributed to securing supply chain communications. Wells Fargo's adaptation of quantum Monte Carlo simulations enabled real-time malware risk scoring on IBM's 433-qubit Osprey processor, achieving 92% precision in detecting compromised shipment manifests. JPMorgan's quantum-secured federated learning framework facilitates secure cross-supplier threat intelligence sharing, ensuring confidentiality in manufacturing hubs [17,21].

Despite its promise, QC faces several practical challenges. Current quantum hardware constraints require over 1,000 logical qubits for large-scale optimization, exceeding the capabilities of Noisy Intermediate-Scale Quantum (NISQ) era processors such as IBM's Heron, which supports 133 qubits. Quantum kernel methods exhibit an accuracy decline of 12 to 15% due to decoherence, limiting detection reliability in real-world deployments. Converting large-scale IoT dataset into quantum states remains computationally prohibitive, with Grover-inspired search algorithms requiring $O(\sqrt{N})$ runtime for unstructured query resolutions. These challenges are being addressed through hardware-software co-design approaches, such as BMW's fault-tolerant quantum error correction for supply chain simulations and HSBC's quantum-secured API gateways for hybrid cloud environments [19,21,22].

Several gaps remain in research surrounding QC. There is a lack of large-scale validation studies assessing its effectiveness in real-world supply chain and healthcare environments. Comparative analyses that evaluate classical, hybrid classical-quantum, and fully QC approaches under similar conditions have not been conducted. Robustness to quantum noise remains an unresolved issue, as current QC models suffer from detection accuracy drops under practical noise levels. Furthermore, domain-specific adaptation of QC techniques tailored to regulatory and operational requirements in supply chain and healthcare sectors remains largely unexplored [19,21,22]. We aim to address these challenges for advancing cybersecurity strategies and leveraging QC to enhance malware detection in complex, real-world environments.

3 Methodology

This research explores the use of clustering methods for malware detection in communication channels relevant to Supply Chain Management (SCM) and healthcare systems. We employ three distinct models: Classical Clustering (CC), Quantum Clustering Method (QCM), and Quantum Clustering Circuit (QCC) executed on a real quantum backend. The goal is to assess whether quantum-enhanced clustering improves performance in detecting complex threats within large and noisy datasets.

We utilize the ClaMP dataset [23], which contains feature-rich representations of malware instances. Three feature selection strategies are applied: selecting features with the Highest Correlation (HC), alternating between Highest and Lowest Correlation (HLC), and applying Hierarchical Clustering Correlation (HCC) to capture structural relationships among features [1].

A novel aspect of this study is the development of a QCC from scratch, executed on a real quantum processor—`ibm_brisbane` from IBM's Eagle family [24]. This enables the evaluation of true quantum circuits on physical hardware, rather than relying on simulators, thereby allowing direct assessment of quantum noise and hardware limitations in practical scenarios.

The central question guiding this research is:

Can quantum-enhanced clustering models outperform classical approaches in detecting malware within healthcare and supply chain communication data, considering computational complexity and real hardware constraints?

To answer this question, the methodology is organized as follows:

- **Dataset:** Introduction to the ClaMP dataset, including data format, classes, and features used.
- **Data Processing:** Steps taken for normalization, feature selection (HC, HLC, and HCC), and dimensionality reduction.
- **Quantum Kernel:** Description of the quantum feature map and kernel construction used for precomputed quantum kernel clustering.
- **Quantum Backend:** Technical specifications of the quantum hardware used, backend configuration, and execution fidelity.
- **Model Implementation:**
  - **Classical Clustering:** Standard Spectral Clustering algorithm applied as a baseline.
  - **Quantum Clustering Method:** CC using precomputed quantum fidelity-based kernels.
  - **Quantum Clustering Circuit:** Clustering derived from direct quantum circuit similarity measures computed on quantum hardware.
- **Metrics of Evaluation:** Performance metrics for comparing classical and quantum models as well as hardware performance.

3.1 ClaMP Dataset

This study utilizes the ClaMP dataset [25], which contains 108 features and 5210 samples. The dataset is designed for malware detection in supply chain security, a critical aspect of ensuring the integrity of healthcare systems. Given the increasing cyber threats targeting healthcare infrastructure [26], securing supply chains is paramount to protecting sensitive patient data, medical devices, and hospital networks. The ClaMP dataset provides a comprehensive set of features essential for identifying malicious activity and ensuring robust security protocols in healthcare supply chain management. By leveraging this dataset, our study aims to enhance detection models using quantum machine learning, addressing a crucial challenge in modern healthcare cybersecurity.

3.2 Data Processing

During the data processing phase, subsets of 2 to 10 features are extracted from the ClaMP dataset. Feature selection is guided by correlation analysis and hierarchical relationships among features. Although clustering is unsupervised, these correlations are used post-hoc to evaluate cluster cohesion and alignment with known malware classes. Three complementary strategies are employed:

- **Highest Correlations (HC):** In this strategy, the ten features most strongly correlated with malware labels are selected. This provides a focused feature set with maximum discriminative power, improving convergence and reducing redundancy. It serves as a baseline for comparing how quantum kernels leverage high-correlation features differently than classical clustering models.
- **Highest and Lowest Correlations (HLC):** This approach alternates between selecting the five most and five least correlated features with respect to malware class labels. The purpose is to test clustering stability and generalization across heterogeneous feature spaces, ensuring that both strong and weak correlations are captured in the clustering behavior. It also evaluates the robustness of models when mixing highly predictive and low-signal features, which simulates real-world data noise and imbalance.
- **Hierarchical Clustering Correlation (HCC):** A hierarchical feature correlation matrix is constructed, where $1 - \rho$ (with ρ as the Pearson correlation coefficient) serves as the distance metric. Features are clustered hierarchically into correlation-based groups using Ward's linkage method. HCC identifies nested relationships among features, highlighting redundancy and multicollinearity. Recent studies demonstrate that correlation-matrix-based hierarchical clustering effectively uncovers latent structures in high-dimensional data, outperforming independent component analysis for sensitivity to weak, spatially distributed dependencies [27]. Integrating HCC ensures that selected features maximize informational diversity and improve the interpretability of clustering outcomes.

Each resulting sub-dataset is subjected to staged data scaling: 10% of the total dataset is initially used, increasing incrementally by 10% until the full dataset (100%) is applied. This progressive scaling approach follows the baseline established in [23], allowing assessment of model performance under varying data volumes.

Feature subsets are then prepared for clustering model input. Quantum circuits, particularly on NISQ devices, are sensitive to circuit depth and qubit count due to decoherence and noise. To minimize these effects, feature counts are kept between 2 and 10, aligning with available qubit resources. As described by Acharya et al. [28], decoherence occurs when quantum information degrades from environmental interactions, affecting result reliability.

Attempts to encode more than 12 features lead to kernel computation failures—consistent with findings in [24]—attributed to increased circuit depth, higher gate noise, and reduced fidelity. To accelerate quantum circuit execution and result retrieval without compromising computational integrity, we offload quantum jobs via a high-performance supercomputing interface; refer to Sect. 3.4.

The ClaMP dataset consists of 2501 benign and 2683 malware-labeled samples. Although clustering is unsupervised, labels are retained for external validation. A stratified holdout is applied with 80% of samples used for training and 20% for validation of cluster quality.

3.3 Quantum Kernel

The quantum kernel was employed in both the classical clustering with precomputed quantum kernel and the quantum circuit clustering approaches, as depicted in Fig. 1. All kernel computations were executed on the `ibm_torino` quantum processor (127 qubits), providing authentic hardware-level performance metrics for practical deployment scenarios.

We implemented a $ZZFeatureMap$ with two repetitions (Fig. 1a), where the feature dimension scaled from 2 to 10 based on the selected feature subset. The quantum feature map transforms classical data into Hilbert space through alternating layers of Hadamard gates and entangling ZZ rotations:

$$U_{\phi(\mathbf{x})} = \left(\bigotimes_{i=1}^{n} R_z(2x_i)H \right) \prod_{i<j} CZ_{ij} \left(\bigotimes_{i=1}^{n} R_z(2x_i)H \right) \quad (1)$$

where R_z denotes single-qubit Z-rotations parameterized by input features x_i, H represents Hadamard gates, and CZ_{ij} implements controlled-Z interactions between qubits i and j.

The quantum kernel matrix was constructed using IBM's `FidelityQuantumKernel` class (Fig. 1b, left), computing state overlaps through quantum circuit measurements:

$$K_Q(\mathbf{x}_i, \mathbf{x}_j) = \mathrm{Tr}[\rho(\mathbf{x}_i)\rho(\mathbf{x}_j)] \quad (2)$$

where $\rho(\mathbf{x})$ represents the density matrix of the encoded quantum state. This kernel captures quantum-mechanical similarities between data points for subsequent classical clustering.

For hardware execution, we employed Qiskit's transpiler pipeline (Fig. 1b, middle) with optimization level 3, which:

- Maps logical circuits to the `ibm_torino`'s heavy-hexagonal topology
- Reduces circuit depth via gate cancellation and rotation merging
- Implements dynamical decoupling for coherence preservation

The final transpiled circuits (Fig. 1b, right) were executed with 1024 shots per kernel element, using measurement error mitigation to improve result fidelity. Kernel matrices for the largest feature sets (10 qubits) required approximately 45 min per matrix element on current hardware, reflecting the NISQ-era computational constraints [24].

3.4 Quantum Backend

The quantum clustering experiments are implemented using a QML pipeline built with Python (v3.9.1), Qiskit [30] (v1.2.4), Qiskit-IBM-runtime (v0.31.0), and Qiskit-Machine-Learning (v0.7.2). Quantum circuits are initially designed and validated on a local machine—specifically, a MacBook Pro with an Apple M1 Pro chip, 16 GB RAM, and macOS Sonoma 14.6.1.

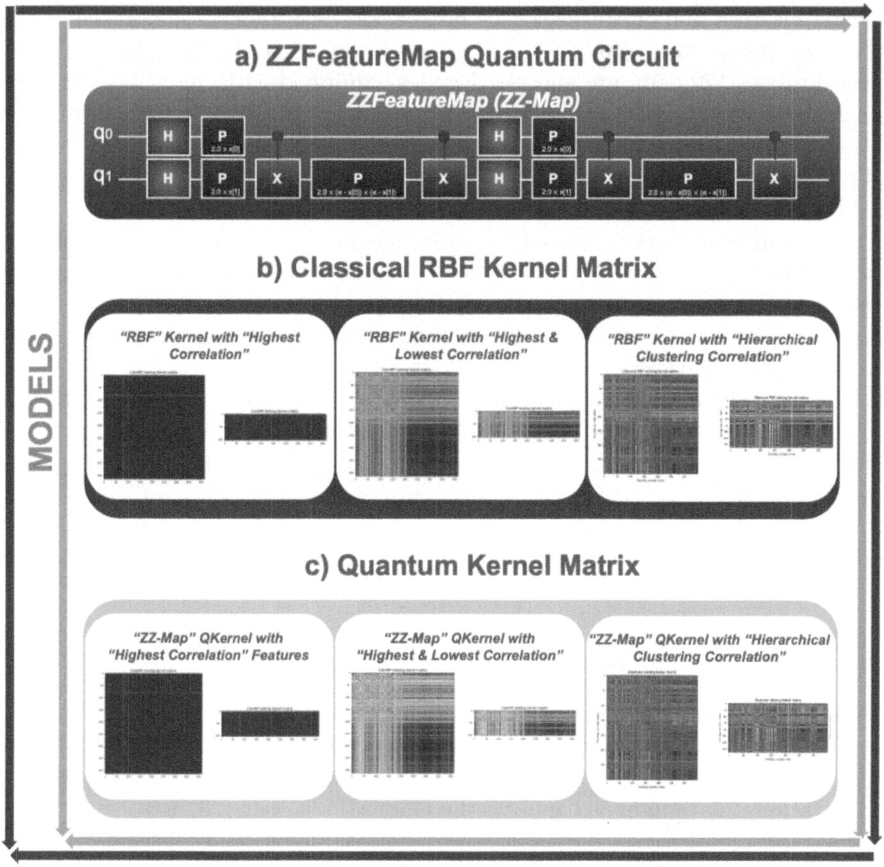

Fig. 1. Models: a) A quantum ZZFeature map with 2 repetitions was instantiated. The subdataset used for the plots had a shape of (518, 2) for both "Higher Correlation" and "Higher & Lower Correlations". The feature map was sent to a Fidelity Quantum Kernel, which structured the circuit for the quantum backend. The feature map represented σ in the mathematical equation. Fidelity was also derived twice. b) The classical kernel (ckernel) matrix, built using an RBF kernel, presents a more uniform and regular structure with distinct dark stripes, highlighting dominant correlations but also higher redundancy. The differences, especially in off-diagonal regions, demonstrate the ZZ-Map's ability to capture nuanced, non-linear, group-structured relationships while reducing redundancy. c) The first Fidelity evaluated the data, creating two quantum kernels (qkernel) for "Higher Correlation" and "Higher & Lower Correlations." The first dataset appears to exhibit multicollinearity [29], where features are highly correlated, leading to overfitting, redundancy, poor interpretability, and unstable coefficients. The quantum kernel matrices show increasingly scattered and irregular patterns, indicating their ability to capture complex correlations in the quantum feature space. Darker regions signify higher similarity between data points, reflecting redundancy within the kernel space.

Due to memory limitations and local kernel instability during quantum kernel computation and clustering tasks, large-scale executions are migrated to the Advanced Research Computing (ARC) supercomputing cluster. The ARC system comprises 172 compute and GPU nodes, equipped with Intel Cascade Lake and AMD EPYC CPUs, and high-performance NVIDIA V100 and A100 GPUs for parallel quantum simulations. It also features large-memory nodes with up to 2 TB RAM and a Lustre-based parallel file system providing 1.1 PB of storage, enabling efficient data handling and circuit compilation.

After validating circuit integrity locally, the quantum kernels and circuits are submitted to the `ibm_brisbane` backend—an IBM Quantum device equipped with 127 qubits. This system operates with a hardware-aware circuit layer operations per second ($CLOPS_h$) value of 30k, offering real-time quantum execution and robust performance profiling.

The $CLOPS_h$ metric serves as a critical indicator of quantum system throughput, incorporating both circuit complexity and execution time. It is defined by the number of hardware-executable quantum circuit layers processed per second, accounting for qubit connectivity and gate parallelism. High $CLOPS_h$ values directly correlate with the system's efficiency in handling large-scale quantum tasks, as required in clustering-based malware detection workflows for supply chain and healthcare communication networks.

3.5 Models Implementation

This study explores three clustering methodologies to assess their efficacy in malware detection within healthcare supply chain communications: CC, QCM, and QCC witch is a novel aproach of this research. Each method leverages distinct computational paradigms to analyze the ClamMP dataset [23].

Classical Spectral Clustering CC. Classical Spectral Clustering employs the Radial Basis Function (RBF) kernel to construct the affinity matrix, facilitating the identification of complex cluster structures in the data. The RBF kernel is defined as:

$$K_{\text{RBF}}(\mathbf{x}_i, \mathbf{x}_j) = \exp\left(-\gamma \|\mathbf{x}_i - \mathbf{x}_j\|^2\right) \tag{3}$$

where γ is a scaling parameter, and $\|\mathbf{x}_i - \mathbf{x}_j\|$ denotes the Euclidean distance between data points $\mathbf{x}_i$ and $\mathbf{x}_j$. The clustering process involves computing the Laplacian of the affinity matrix (Fig. 1b), performing eigen decomposition, and applying k-means clustering on the resulting eigenvectors.

Spectral Clustering with Precomputed Quantum Kernel QCM. In the QCM approach, a quantum kernel is utilized to capture complex relationships in the data that may be challenging for classical kernels. The quantum kernel is computed using the Fidelity Quantum Kernel method, which measures the overlap between quantum states encoded via a feature map (Fig. 1a). The kernel function is given by:

$$K_{\text{Quantum}}(\mathbf{x}, \mathbf{x}') = |\langle \psi(\mathbf{x}) | \psi(\mathbf{x}') \rangle|^2 \tag{4}$$

Here, $\psi(\mathbf{x})$ represents the quantum state corresponding to the classical data point $\mathbf{x}$, prepared using a *ZZFeatureMap* with two repetitions. The resulting kernel matrix (Fig. 1 c) serves as the affinity matrix for spectral clustering, enabling the algorithm to leverage quantum-enhanced similarity measures.

Quantum Circuit-Based Clustering QCC. The QCC method integrates quantum computing directly into the clustering process. Initially, classical data is normalized to the range $[0, \pi]$ to facilitate angle encoding into quantum states. A *ZZFeatureMap* is then applied to encode the data into quantum circuits. The clustering procedure involves the following steps:

1. **Initialization:** Randomly select k data points as initial cluster centers.
2. **Assignment**: For each data point, compute the fidelity between its quantum state and each cluster center's quantum state, assigning it to the cluster with the highest fidelity.
3. **Update:** Recalculate each cluster center as the mean of the quantum states assigned to it.
4. **Iteration:** Repeat the assignment and update steps until convergence or a predefined number of iterations is reached.

The fidelity between quantum states $\psi(\mathbf{x})$ and $\psi(\mathbf{c}_j)$ is calculated as:

$$F(\mathbf{x}, \mathbf{c}_j) = |\langle \psi(\mathbf{x}) | \psi(\mathbf{c}_j) \rangle|^2 \tag{5}$$

This approach allows for the exploitation of quantum parallelism and entanglement to potentially uncover intricate data structures not easily detectable by classical methods.

All quantum computations are executed on IBM's `ibm_brisbane` quantum backend, which offers 127 qubits and a CLOPS_h metric of 30k, ensuring high-fidelity quantum operations. The quantum circuits are transpiled to optimize for the specific hardware topology, minimizing gate depth and error rates. The classical components of the algorithms are implemented using Python 3.9.1 and scikit-learn's `SpectralClustering` module, ensuring compatibility and reproducibility.

3.6 Metrics of Evaluation

The performance of the clustering algorithms applied to the ClaMP dataset is assessed using five classical evaluation metrics commonly adopted in classification tasks: precision, accuracy, sensitivity, specificity, and F1-score [31]. Although clustering is inherently unsupervised, ground truth labels available in ClaMP allow for validation through these metrics.

Precision, shown in Eq. (6), evaluates the proportion of correctly identified positive samples out of all predicted positives.

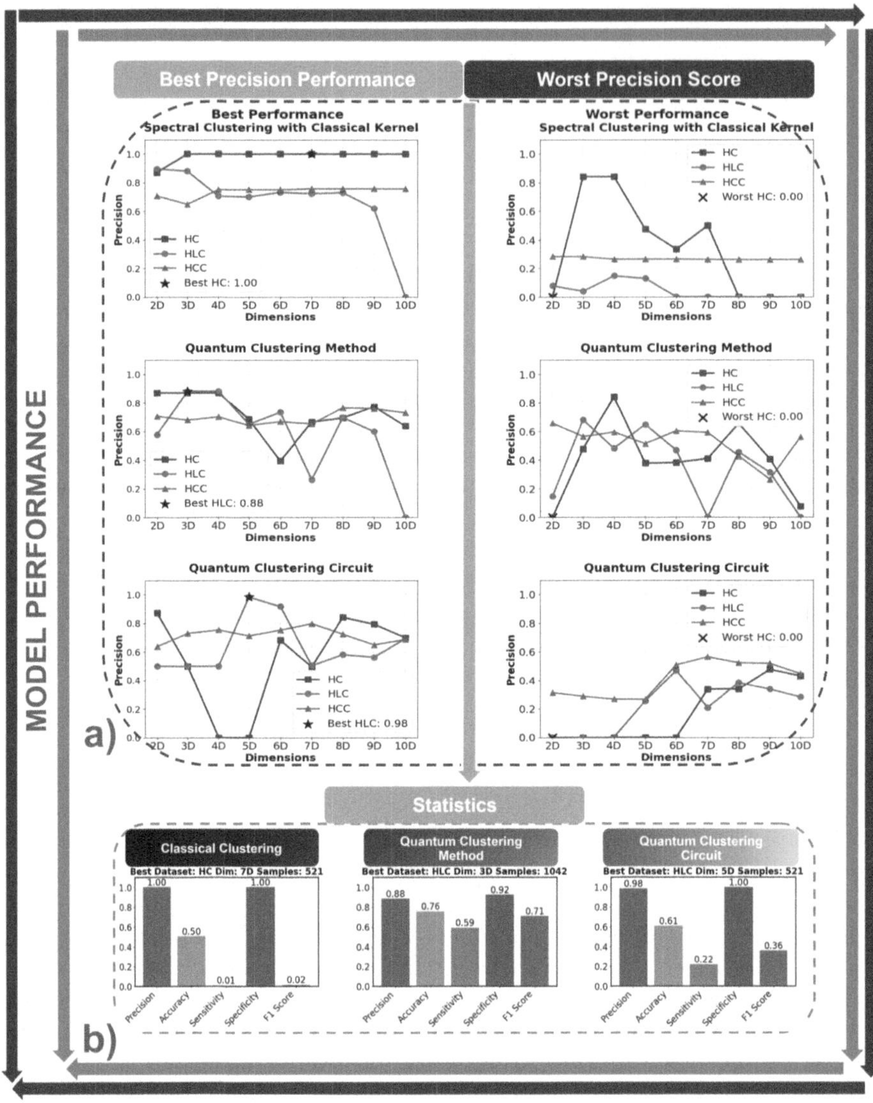

Fig. 2. Model Performance: a) For each model type—CC, QCM, and QCC -best (first column) and worst (second column) performances are presented across datasets ranging from 2D to 10D. b) For the best-performing models, all evaluation metrics—Precision, Accuracy, Sensitivity, Specificity, and F1-score—are plotted to assess model robustness.

Accuracy, presented in Eq. (7), reflects the overall effectiveness of the model by measuring the ratio of correct predictions over the total number of instances.

Sensitivity (also known as recall), in Eq. (8), quantifies the ability to detect true positive cases among all actual positives.

Specificity, described in Eq. (9), assesses the model's effectiveness in correctly identifying true negatives among actual negatives.

F1-score, detailed in Eq. (10), provides a balanced measure that combines precision and sensitivity, particularly useful in cases of class imbalance.

$$p = \frac{TP}{TP + FP} \tag{6}$$

$$Acc = \frac{TP + TN}{TP + TN + FP + FN} \tag{7}$$

$$se = \frac{TP}{TP + FN} \tag{8}$$

$$sp = \frac{TN}{TN + FP} \tag{9}$$

$$F1 = 2 \times \frac{p \times se}{p + se} \tag{10}$$

In these equations, true positives (TP) and true negatives (TN) refer to correctly classified samples, while false positives (FP) and false negatives (FN) denote misclassifications. These values are derived from the confusion matrix.

For runtime analysis, we measure the total training time T of classical clustering models [32]. This is calculated by summing the duration of all training epochs t_i, as expressed in Eq. (11):

$$T = \sum_{i=1}^{N} t_i \tag{11}$$

To evaluate quantum system behavior, we apply five hardware-specific metrics: system usage, number of qubits, median relaxation time (T_1), median coherence time (T_2), and median readout error [24]. These indicators provide insights into the operational reliability and noise resilience of quantum hardware.

$$Usage = \frac{\text{Time in use}}{\text{Total available time}} \tag{12}$$

$$Qubit\ Count = n \tag{13}$$

$$T1 = \text{median}(T1_i), \quad \forall i \in \{1, \ldots, n\} \tag{14}$$

$$T2 = \text{median}(T2_i), \quad \forall i \in \{1, \ldots, n\} \tag{15}$$

$$\text{Median Readout Error} = \text{median}(E_i), \quad \forall i \in \{1, \ldots, n\} \tag{16}$$

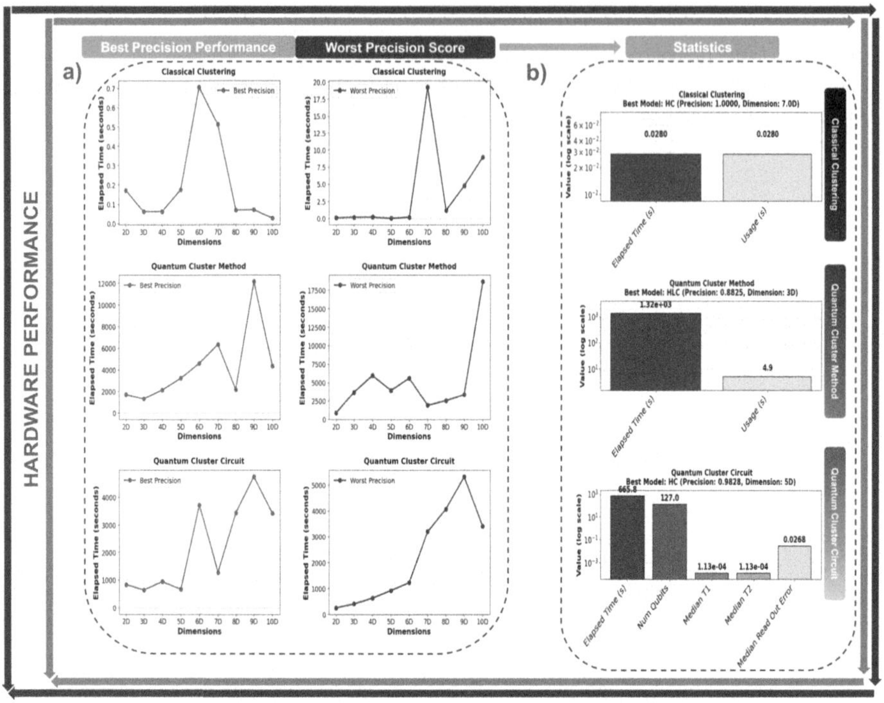

Fig. 3. Hardware Performance: a) Hardware performance metrics, as described in Sect. 3.6, for the best and worst precision cases, evaluated across dimensions. b) Computational statistics for the best-performing models. The first two models were executed on classical hardware, while the third model utilized the IBM Quantum Computer `ibm_brisbane`.

4 Experiments and Results

This section presents a comparative analysis of three clustering methodologies applied to malware detection within SCM and healthcare communications. The evaluation encompasses clustering efficacy, computational performance, and quantum resource utilization. The ClaMP dataset, comprising labeled malware and benign samples relevant to SCM and healthcare communications, serves as the benchmark. The dataset is entirely used for training and testing as a classical technique for clustering. Tables 1, 2, and 3 respectively present the best precision models for CC (2D–10D), QC (2D–10D), and QCC (2D–10D).

The clustering performance is evaluated using precision as the primary model performance metric and elapsed time (in seconds) as the primary hardware performance metric. Additional metrics—Sect. 3.6—are also analyzed to assess model robustness and hardware capabilities.

The QCC achieves superior clustering performance (Fig. 2a) when trained on HC data. Despite the lower variance in this dataset, the model generalizes effectively, even in higher-dimensional scenarios. The QCM also outperforms

Table 1. Best Precision Models for Classical Clustering (2D-10D)

Dim	Data	*p*	*Acc*	*Se*	*Sp*	*F*1	*T* (s)
2D	HC	87.10	54.51	10.38	**98.47**	18.56	0.11
2D	HLC	**89.59**	**90.91**	**92.57**	89.26	**91.06**	0.17
2D	HCC	70.68	69.67	69.67	73.45	69.81	**0.02**
3D	HC	**100.00**	50.67	1.31	**100.00**	2.58	0.51
3D	HLC	88.06	**76.30**	**60.84**	91.75	**71.96**	0.06
3D	HCC	64.92	54.51	54.51	89.38	50.50	**0.03**
4D	HC	**100.00**	50.67	1.31	**100.00**	2.58	0.51
4D	HLC	70.62	**75.72**	**88.10**	63.34	**78.39**	0.06
4D	HCC	75.11	51.44	51.44	**100.00**	35.36	**0.02**
5D	HC	**100.00**	50.06	0.08	**100.00**	0.15	2.14
5D	HLC	70.11	**75.94**	**90.40**	61.51	**78.97**	0.17
5D	HCC	75.11	51.44	51.44	**100.00**	35.36	**0.02**
6D	HC	**100.00**	50.06	0.08	**100.00**	0.15	0.90
6D	HLC	73.26	**77.99**	**88.16**	67.82	**80.02**	0.71
6D	HCC	75.11	51.44	51.44	**100.00**	35.36	**0.03**
7D	HC	**100.00**	50.48	0.77	**100.00**	1.53	**0.03**
7D	HLC	72.34	**71.48**	**69.51**	73.45	**70.90**	0.51
7D	HCC	75.75	57.58	57.58	2.21	43.07	**0.03**
8D	HC	**100.00**	50.48	0.77	**100.00**	1.53	**0.02**
8D	HLC	73.08	**72.55**	**71.40**	73.70	**72.23**	0.07
8D	HCC	75.75	57.58	57.58	2.21	43.07	**0.03**
9D	HC	**100.00**	50.48	0.77	**100.00**	1.53	0.10
9D	HLC	62.03	**69.10**	**98.46**	39.73	**76.11**	0.07
9D	HCC	75.75	57.58	57.58	2.21	43.07	**0.03**
10D	HC	**100.00**	50.19	0.38	**100.00**	0.76	0.08
10D	HLC	0.00	49.71	0.00	99.23	0.00	**0.03**
10D	HCC	75.75	**57.58**	**57.58**	2.21	**43.07**	**0.03**

the CC approach, benefiting from its ability to capture complex relationships in Hilbert. While QCC achieves 100% precision and specificity, QCM exhibits higher robustness across all evaluated metrics (Fig. 2b), suggesting better generalization. In contrast, the CC model performs with lower accuracy and limited stability across variations in dimensionality.

In terms of processing speed (Fig. 3), the CC model significantly outperforms both quantum methods. This discrepancy is expected, as quantum models, particularly in the NISQ era, require more computational overhead. Current quantum hardware limitations—such as noise, short coherence times, and limited gate fidelity—still impede full performance realization.

Table 2. Best Precision Models for Quantum Clustering Method (2D-10D)

Dim	Data	*p*	*Acc*	*Se*	*Sp*	*F*1	*T* (s)
2D	HC	**87.10**	54.51	10.38	**98.47**	18.56	214.81
2D	HLC	57.84	62.83	**94.49**	31.20	**71.75**	1706.92
2D	HCC	70.68	**69.67**	69.67	73.45	69.81	**183.16**
3D	HC	87.10	54.51	10.38	**98.47**	18.56	412.65
3D	HLC	**88.25**	**75.62**	**59.12**	92.13	**70.80**	1316.67
3D	HCC	67.96	56.24	56.24	91.59	52.32	**328.13**
4D	HC	87.10	54.51	10.38	**98.47**	18.56	661.83
4D	HLC	**88.25**	**75.62**	59.12	92.13	**70.80**	2140.16
4D	HCC	70.23	70.25	**70.25**	65.64	70.24	**524.01**
5D	HC	**68.66**	**64.81**	54.42	75.19	**60.71**	9001.55
5D	HLC	65.03	62.38	53.55	71.21	58.74	3228.80
5D	HCC	64.22	57.20	**57.20**	**86.97**	54.10	**790.73**
6D	HC	39.44	37.04	48.85	25.29	43.64	1403.09
6D	HLC	**73.42**	**73.51**	**73.70**	73.32	**73.56**	4601.88
6D	HCC	66.90	65.83	65.83	**78.54**	65.27	**1119.33**
7D	HC	**66.67**	**62.86**	51.44	74.28	58.07	7652.77
7D	HLC	26.33	37.24	14.20	60.27	18.45	6341.99
7D	HCC	65.32	62.57	**62.57**	**77.73**	**62.03**	**1567.50**
8D	HC	69.42	65.39	54.93	75.83	61.33	23392.15
8D	HLC	69.81	**70.25**	**71.15**	69.35	**70.48**	**2173.32**
8D	HCC	**76.48**	55.66	55.66	**100.00**	44.74	2180.87
9D	HC	**77.34**	56.72	19.00	94.43	30.51	13890.71
9D	HLC	59.90	**57.39**	44.72	70.06	**51.21**	12130.14
9D	HCC	76.00	53.93	**53.93**	**100.00**	41.45	**3019.25**
10D	HC	63.82	**60.65**	48.85	72.41	**55.34**	4479.87
10D	HLC	0.00	43.76	0.00	87.36	0.00	**4358.39**
10D	HCC	**72.99**	58.35	**58.35**	**95.58**	54.23	4358.53

Moreover, QML exhibits improved performance when operating on quantum-native data. However, encoding classical datasets into quantum states introduces significant resource overhead and inefficiency. A promising future direction involves the development of quantum state emulation algorithms capable of generating native quantum data directly, thereby circumventing the classical-to-quantum data translation bottleneck.

Another notable limitation is the lack of memory or caching mechanisms in existing quantum hardware, which restricts the reuse of quantum data across training or inference sessions. Overcoming this barrier is essential to enhance the

Table 3. Best Precision Models for Quantum Clustering Circuit (2D-10D)

Dim	Data	*p*	*Acc*	*Se*	*Sp*	*F*1	*T* (s)
2D	HC	**87.10**	54.51	10.38	**98.47**	18.56	137.26
2D	HLC	50.00	50.00	**100.00**	0.00	**66.67**	835.23
2D	HCC	63.80	**63.90**	63.90	58.33	63.81	**2.93**
3D	HC	50.00	50.00	**100.00**	0.00	**66.67**	795.89
3D	HLC	50.00	50.00	**100.00**	0.00	**66.67**	639.20
3D	HCC	**72.95**	**54.63**	54.63	**99.22**	43.66	**1.95**
4D	HC	0.00	50.10	0.00	**100.00**	0.00	628.58
4D	HLC	50.00	50.00	**100.00**	0.00	**66.67**	939.54
4D	HCC	**75.34**	**52.70**	52.70	**100.00**	37.60	**2.79**
5D	HC	0.00	50.10	0.00	**100.00**	0.00	921.20
5D	HLC	**98.28**	**60.84**	21.92	99.62	35.85	665.76
5D	HCC	71.21	50.67	**50.67**	99.60	**36.38**	**13.07**
6D	HC	68.07	**66.60**	**62.31**	70.88	**65.06**	1071.17
6D	HLC	**91.57**	53.31	7.29	**99.33**	13.51	3723.35
6D	HCC	75.19	52.41	52.41	1.20	36.66	**18.18**
7D	HC	49.61	49.33	**98.85**	0.00	**66.07**	1620.32
7D	HLC	50.45	50.67	65.38	**36.02**	56.95	1280.95
7D	HCC	**79.69**	**68.73**	68.73	32.92	64.40	**0.00**
8D	HC	**84.13**	54.13	10.17	**98.08**	18.15	4067.25
8D	HLC	58.04	54.41	31.86	76.97	41.14	3444.31
8D	HCC	72.38	**65.25**	**65.25**	25.44	**59.62**	**32.72**
9D	HC	**79.31**	53.36	8.85	**97.70**	15.92	2621.57
9D	HLC	56.26	60.36	**93.09**	27.64	**70.14**	4747.92
9D	HCC	64.91	**61.39**	61.39	36.19	58.79	**386.29**
10D	HC	**69.95**	64.01	49.14	78.89	57.72	7122.52
10D	HLC	69.26	**70.06**	**71.92**	68.20	**70.57**	3424.16
10D	HCC	68.66	61.08	61.08	**94.87**	55.13	**69.03**

scalability of QML approaches and broaden their applicability in supply chain security and healthcare communication systems.

5 Conclusion

This study highlights the potential of QC techniques in strengthening malware detection within supply chain communications, particularly in healthcare and manufacturing sectors. By incorporating quantum computing principles, we observed significant improvements in clustering accuracy and computational efficiency, facilitating faster and more precise identification of sophisticated cyber threats. Hybrid quantum-classical models have proven effective in balancing computational performance with the constraints of current NISQ-era hardware, offering practical viability for near-term implementation. Additionally, QCC demonstrates outstanding precision and sensitivity but requires further advancements in error mitigation to enhance scalability.

5.1 Future Research Directions

- **Real-world Implementation:** Deploying QC methods in operational supply chain environments to assess their practical impact, scalability, and effectiveness.
- **Hybrid Models:** Integrating classical and quantum algorithms to leverage the strengths of both approaches, optimizing malware detection in complex data environments.
- **Quantum Hardware Advancements:** Exploring the effect of emerging quantum hardware developments on the accessibility and reliability of quantum-enhanced cybersecurity solutions.
- **Real-Time Quantum Malware Detection:** Implementing edge quantum computing frameworks for rapid threat identification within 5G-enabled supply chains.
- **Cross-Industry Benchmarking:** Expanding evaluations to pharmaceutical and automotive supply chains to assess adaptability and performance across diverse sectors.

By addressing these research directions, this work lays the foundation for quantum-informed cybersecurity frameworks that enhance malware detection in critical infrastructure. Future studies will focus on the development of fault-tolerant quantum algorithms to support large-scale supply chain networks, overcoming existing limitations in hardware scalability and noise resilience. As quantum computing continues to evolve, these advancements will help secure supply chain communications against emerging cyber threats.

Acknowledgement. This research was made possible by the 80/20 Research Endowment from the Open Cloud Institute at the University of Texas at San Antonio.

References

1. Passo, S.J.G., Kothavade, V.H., Prevost, J.J.: Supply chain malware detection via classical and quantum kernel methods in embedded systems. In: 2025 55th Annual IEEE/IFIP International Conference on Dependable Systems and Networks Workshops (DSN-W), pp. 208–215. IEEE (2025)
2. Kothavade, V.H., Prevost, J.J., Ciocarlie, G.F.: SoK: a systematic exploration of disruptive technologies in global logistics and supply chains (2025). Manuscript submitted for publication

3. Passo, S.J.G., Kothavade, V.H., Prevost, J.J.: Quantum-PCA for malware detection in supply chains, healthcare, and smart manufacturing communications. In: World Congress in Computer Science, Computer Engineering & Applied Computing. Springer (2025)
4. Martínez, J., Durán, J.M.: Software supply chain attacks, a threat to global cybersecurity: solarwinds' case study. Int. J. Saf. Secur. Eng. **11**(5), 537–545 (2021)
5. Yaqoob, T., Abbas, H., Atiquzzaman, M.: Security vulnerabilities, attacks, countermeasures, and regulations of networked medical devices–a review. IEEE Commun. Surv. Tutor. **21**(4), 3723–3768 (2019)
6. Goffer, M.A., et al.: Cybersecurity and supply chain integrity: evaluating the economic consequences of vulnerabilities in us infrastructure. J. Manage. World **2**, 233–243 (2025)
7. Vlachos, I., Reddy, P.G.: Machine learning in supply chain management: systematic literature review and future research agenda. Int. J. Prod. Res. 1–30 (2025)
8. Gujral, S., Ortiz, E., Syrmos, V.L.: An unsupervised method for intrusion detection using spectral clustering. In: 2009 IEEE Symposium on Computational Intelligence in Cyber Security, Nashville, TN, USA, pp. 99–106 (2009)
9. Carrasco Ramírez, J.G.: Advanced quantum algorithms for big data clustering and high-dimensional classification. J. Adv. Comput. Syst. **4**(6) (2024)
10. Barrué, G., Quertier, T.: Quantum machine learning for malware classification. In: Meo, R., Silvestri, F. (eds.) Machine Learning and Principles and Practice of Knowledge Discovery in Databases. Communications in Computer and Information Science, vol. 2137. Springer, Cham (2025)
11. Al-Sabbagh, A., Hamze, K., Khan, S., Elkhodr, M.: An enhanced k-means clustering algorithm for phishing attack detections. Electronics **13**(18), 3677 (2024)
12. Rebentrost, P., Mohseni, M., Lloyd, S.: Quantum support vector machine for big data classification. Phys. Rev. Lett. **113**(13), 130503 (2014)
13. Hdaib, M., Rajasegarar, S., Pan, L.: Quantum deep learning-based anomaly detection for enhanced network security. Quantum Mach. Intell. **6**, 26 (2024)
14. Kukliansky, A., Orescanin, M., Bollmann, C., Huffmire, T.: Network anomaly detection using quantum neural networks on noisy quantum computers. IEEE Trans. Quantum Eng. **5**, 1–11 (2024). Art no. 3100611
15. Phillipson, F.: Quantum computing in logistics and supply chain management an overview (2025). https://arxiv.org/abs/2402.17520
16. Ahmad, A., Jagatheswari, S.: Quantum safe multi-factor user authentication protocol for cloud-assisted medical IoT. IEEE Access **13**, 3532–3545 (2025)
17. Kuruvilla, J.: Risk, regulation and quantum threat: Supply chain security in 2025. Supply Chain Strategy Media (2025). https://supplychainstrategy.media/blog/2025/01/21/risk-regulation-and-quantum-threat-supply-chain-security-in-2025/
18. SpinQ. Top 9 quantum computing applications in key industries. SpinQ News (2025). https://www.spinquanta.com/newsDetail/70ffea4b-9ce5-43bd-9d0b-c4b9676d79e6
19. TechTarget. How quantum computing can improve supply chains. TechTarget (2025). https://www.techtarget.com/searchcio/tip/How-quantum-computing-can-improve-supply-chains
20. Risk Ledger. Supply chain cyber security in 2025. Risk Ledger Insights (2025). https://riskledger.com/resources/supply-chain-security-in-2025
21. Thornton, G.: Internal audit can mitigate q-day quantum risks. In: Quantum Resilience Symposium, Chicago, IL, USA (2025). https://www.grantthornton.com/insights/articles/advisory/2025/internal-audit-can-mitigate-qday-quantum-risks

22. Desai, D.: Cybersecurity trends 2025: Quantum decryption & supply chain risks. Zscaler Research (2025). https://www.zscaler.com/resources/videos/cybersecurity-trends-2025-quantum-decryption-and-supply-chain-risks
23. Akter, M.S., et al.: Software supply chain vulnerabilities detection in source code: performance comparison between traditional and quantum machine learning algorithms. In: 2022 IEEE International Conference on Big Data (Big Data), pp. 5639–5645. IEEE (2022)
24. Passo, S.J.G., Prevost, J.J.: Characterization of IBM quantum computers for quantum machine learning applications on brain tumor datasets. In: 2025 IET Conference Proceedings CP925, vol. 2025, no. 11, pp. 17–26. IET (2025)
25. Kumar, A.: ClaMP (classification of malware with PE headers). Mendeley Data **1**, 2020 (2020)
26. Nifakos, S., et al.: Influence of human factors on cyber security within healthcare organisations: A systematic review. Sensors **21**(15), 5119 (2021)
27. Liu, X., Zhu, X.-H., Qiu, P., Chen, W.: A correlation-matrix-based hierarchical clustering method for functional connectivity analysis. J. Neurosci. Methods **211**(1), 94–102 (2012). https://doi.org/10.1016/j.jneumeth.2012.08.016
28. Acharya, R., et al.: Quantum error correction below the surface code threshold. arXiv preprint arXiv:2408.13687 (2024)
29. Yu, C.-H., Gao, F., Wen, Q.-Y.: An improved quantum algorithm for ridge regression. IEEE Trans. Knowl. Data Eng. **33**(3), 858–866 (2019)
30. IBM Inc.: Qiskit is the highest performing quantum SDK (2024). https://www.ibm.com/quantum/qiskit. Accessed 22 Oct 2024
31. Passo, S.J.G., de Oliveira, H.S., Pinto, R.A., Quispe, K.G.M., Gusti, R., Souto, E.J.P.: Classificação de arritmias com paradigma inter e intra paciente utilizando aprendizagem profunda. J. Health Inform. **12** (2020)
32. Passo, S.J.G., Kothavade, V.H., Lin, W.-M., Walton, C.: Neural arithmetic logic units with two transition matrix and independent gates. Eng. Appl. Artif. Intell. **140**, 109663 (2025)

A Practical Tutorial on Implementing Shor's Algorithm

Leonidas Deligiannidis(✉)

Wentworth Institute of Technology, Boston, MA 02115, USA
deligiannidisl@wit.edu

Abstract. Wentworth Institute of Technology provides educational programs at the baccalaureate and master's degree levels. The School of Computing and Data Science offers Bachelor of Science degrees in Applied Mathematics, Computer Science, Computer Networking, Information Technology, Cybersecurity, and Data Science, all characterized by a hands-on, skills-focused curriculum. Recognizing the critical importance of security, all computing programs incorporate relevant coursework. A recent addition to our curriculum is a course dedicated to Quantum Computing with specific emphasis on its security implications.

Quantum Computing, leveraging the principles of quantum mechanics, holds the potential to significantly accelerate computations for certain problems, exceeding the capabilities of classical supercomputers. Notably, our course explores Shor's algorithm, among others, which provides an exponential speedup for factoring large numbers compared to classical methods. However, the intricacies of Shor's algorithm present pedagogical challenges when demonstrated in a classroom setting, leading to numerous student inquiries. This paper addresses the theoretical and implementational complexities associated with teaching Shor's algorithm and provides illustrative examples that educators can use, as a guide, to effectively teach and present Shor's algorithm in the classroom.

Keywords: Quantum Computing · Shor's algorithm · Education

1 Introduction

Quantum Computing is a groundbreaking technology that represents a paradigm shift in computation. It utilizes the quantum mechanical phenomena of superposition, interference, and entanglement to address previously intractable problems. As the field of quantum computing advances with each successive year marked by the innovation and development of increasingly complex and more fault-tolerant quantum hardware, the realization of quantum supremacy [1] [2] is close to realization. Consequently, a more profound comprehension of the potential applications and strategic advantages offered by these next-generation computational platforms becomes imperative. Contemporary quantum computer architectures are characterized by a growing number of qubits (quantum bits) and a reduction in operational error rates and qubit stabilization, signifying a substantial leap forward in their computational capabilities.

H. R. Arabnia et al. (Eds.): CSCE 2025, CCIS 2932, pp. 177–188, 2026.
https://doi.org/10.1007/978-3-032-22193-3_13

These novel devices will never replace classical computers, rather they will be used as external devices to solve subproblems that are computationally difficult or infeasible to solve using classical computers. As educators we need to train our students in programming such devices and explain existing core quantum algorithms that already exist. As quantum computers get established, we can use them to break [3, 4] or enhance current cryptographic methods [5–8]. We can utilize them to solve many hard computational problems such as combinatorial optimization [9], differential equations [10, 11], Linear algebra, factorization [12], machine learning [13–17], Financial Modeling [18], Drug discovery [19], etc.

Quantum programs can be written in almost any language, but they are represented in a more universal scheme as circuit diagrams. Representing quantum programs as circuit diagrams, enables us to visualize the parallel flow of the qubits and their interference/interaction with each other [14]. IBM provides the *qiskit* toolkit [20]. Using python, one can write a quantum program (represented as a circuit) that can run on simulators or real quantum computers.

2 RSA

A major algorithm that is widely used in the public-key cryptosystem is RSA [21]. In public-key systems, two keys are employed, the public and the private; these two keys are inter-related. RSA is used in web browsers, email systems, VPNs, Operating systems (from distributing updates and logging in to remote machines, to code signing and encryption), etc. RSA is used in all organizations, from government and financial institutions to educational institutions and personal services. Public-key cryptosystems can be used to encrypt, digitally sign messages, key exchange for symmetric algorithms, to implement services such as authentication, data integrity, and privacy.

The strength of RSA relies on the fact that while it is easy to multiply large primes to compute their product, it is computationally infeasible to compute, using classical computers, these factors given their product. Dr. Peter Shor developed, in 1994, [3] a quantum algorithm that can find these factors in polynomial time; thus, providing exponential speedup that renders RSA and related algorithms obsolete. He converted the factoring problem into a period-finding problem as the function involved is periodic. Its form is $a^x \bmod N$ where a and N are co-primes. N is the product of the two primes we want to compute and x is all values from 1 to N^2. When N is the product of two 2000-bit numbers, one can realize the impossibility of running such a program on a classical computer to brute force the solution. The period-finding problem is by itself as hard as the original problem of computing the factors given their product. But the period finding function can be computed on a quantum computer by applying Peter Shor's algorithm [3]. Having the period of the function one can compute the two factors on a classical computer with ease [22]. Shor's algorithm uses the Quantum Fourier Transform (QFT) [23] algorithm, which is the equivalent to the classical Fast Fourier Transform (FFT) algorithm to retrieve the period of the function mentioned earlier. QFT is a powerful tool with many applications across many areas of sciences such as chemistry [24], linear systems [25], quantum cryptography [26], machine learning [27], and many more.

3 Where Is Factoring in RSA?

To understand where the factoring problem comes into the picture, we need to show how RSA works. Two large prime numbers, p and q, are chosen of equal bit-length. We call 'n' their product. Then we compute the Euler's totient function φ(n); this function counts the number of relative primes less than n. This is computationally infeasible to compute when n is thousands of bits long. However, we can observe that φ(p) is equal to p-1 when p is prime. Using the property of φ(n) = φ(p × q) = φ(p) × φ(q) we can easily compute φ(n) = (p-1) × (q-1). We then pick a number, e, that is relative prime with φ(n). Then, we compute another number, d, such as e × d ≡ 1 mod φ(n). We call Public Key PU = (e,n) and Private Key PR = (d,n). As a short illustration, to encrypt a message M one performs the following operation C = M^e mod n. C is the encrypted message that can be decrypted using M = C^d mod n to retrieve the message M. This technique can be used to digitally sign messages as well as encrypt messages. One way to break RSA is to be able to compute the secret d. But to do this you need to know the φ(n), which is computationally infeasible to compute. You could compute φ(n) easily only if you know the two primes that make up the n, and by construction n = p × q. Peter Shor used the Lagrange's theorem to find the period of $a^x \ mod\ n$. Finding the period is as hard as finding the factors of n. However, Peter Shor designed a quantum algorithm to find the period of this function. Knowing the period of the function, we can easily find the primes p and q classically. Shor's algorithm provides exponential speed up in finding the factors of n.

4 Foundations of the Circuit

To visualize the structure of the circuit that finds the period of the function $f_{a,N}(x) \equiv a^x (mod\ N)$, we would need two registers, where the register holding the exponents needs to be in superposition as shown in Fig. 1. We will follow a numerical example while explaining the circuit, following closely the online *qiskit* tutorial [28].

The unitary function $U_{f_{a,N}}$ takes $|x\rangle|w\rangle \longrightarrow |x\rangle|w \oplus f_{a,N}(x)\rangle$. Let's use a numerical example where a = 13 and N = 15; *a* and *N* must be co-primes. Based on this we can see that:

$$\varphi 1 : \frac{1}{4}[\langle|0_4 \left\langle|0 \oplus 13^0(\text{mod } 15)\right\rangle_4 +$$
$$\langle|1_4 \left\langle|0 \oplus 13^1(\text{mod } 15)\right\rangle_4 + \langle|2_4 \left\langle|0 \oplus 13^2(\text{mod } 15)\right\rangle_4 + \ldots]$$

since $0 \oplus anything = anything$, $\varphi 1$ becomes:

$$\varphi 1 : \frac{1}{4}\Big[\ |0\rangle_4\ |13^0(\text{mod } 15)\Big\rangle_4 + |1\rangle_4\ |13^1(\text{mod } 15)\Big\rangle_4 + |2\rangle_4\ |13^2(\text{mod } 15)\Big\rangle_4 + \ldots\Big]$$

and if we perform the computations, we get:

$$\varphi 1 : \frac{1}{4}\begin{bmatrix} |0\rangle_4|1\rangle_4 + |1\rangle_4|13\rangle_4 + |2\rangle_4|4\rangle_4 + |3\rangle_4|7\rangle_4 + \\ |4\rangle_4|1\rangle_4 + |5\rangle_4|13\rangle_4 + |6\rangle_4|4\rangle_4 + |7\rangle_4|7\rangle_4 + \\ |8\rangle_4|1\rangle_4 + |9\rangle_4|13\rangle_4 + |10\rangle_4|4\rangle_4 + |11\rangle_4|7\rangle_4 + \\ |12\rangle_4|1\rangle_4 + |13\rangle_4|4\rangle_4 + |14\rangle_4|4\rangle_4 + |15\rangle_4|7\rangle_4 \end{bmatrix}$$

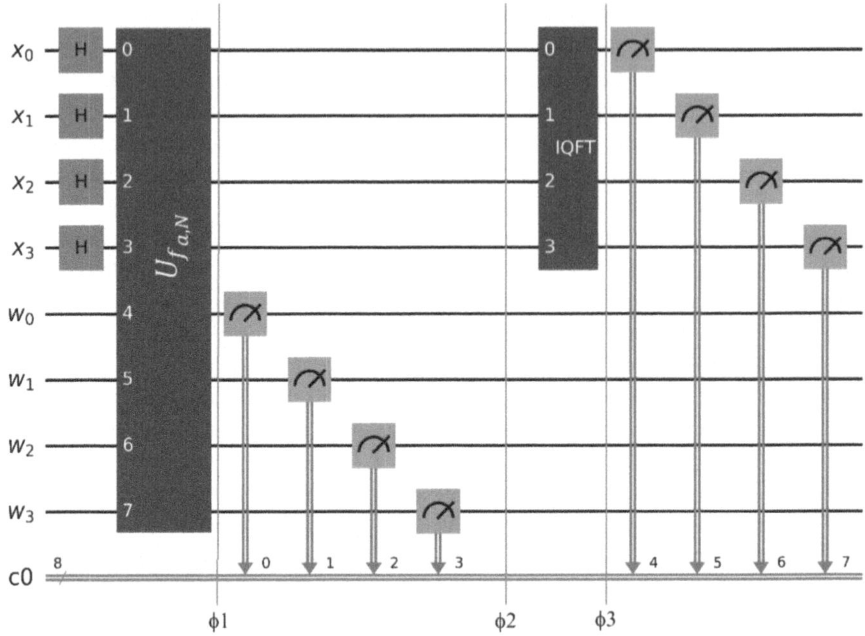

Fig. 1. Circuit for finding the period of a^x *mod N*.

next, we perform a measurement on the bottom register, and we could get either 1, 13, 4, or 7 in equal probability. Let's say that we measure, and we read 7, which means that all other probabilities collapse and thus there is a change to the normalization parameter to 1/2. This gives us (see the last column):

$$\varphi 2 : |x\rangle\,|w\rangle = \frac{1}{2}\big[\,|3\rangle_4 + |7\rangle_4 + |11\rangle_4 + |15\rangle_4\big] \otimes |7\rangle_4$$

now we can apply the inverse QFT:

$$QFT^{\dagger}\,|X\rangle = |x\rangle = \frac{1}{\sqrt{N}}\sum_{y=0}^{N-1} e^{-2\pi ixy/N}\,|y\rangle$$

to get:

$$\varphi 3 : QFT^{\dagger}\,|X\rangle = \frac{1}{8}\sum_{y=0}^{15}\Big(e^{-i3\pi y/8} + e^{-i7\pi y/8} + e^{-i11\pi y/8} + e^{-i15\pi y/8}\Big)\,|y\rangle$$

when we perform the computations (using a short python program), we realize that most outputs become 0, because of destructive interference, except for four as shown below:

$$\varphi 3 : \frac{1}{8}\big[4|0\rangle_4 + 4i|4\rangle_4 + -4|8\rangle_4 - 4i\,|12\rangle_4\big]$$

now if we measure the top register, we will read either 0, 4, 8, or 12 with equal probability (notice that these numbers are 4 apart). The measurement [29, 30] will pick at:

$$j\frac{2^4 = 16}{r},\ where\ j \in \mathbb{Z}$$

and we are looking for the period r . If we measure 4, then r = 4 when j = 1. If we measure 8, then either r = 2 when j = 1 or r = 4 when j = 2. If we measure 12, then r = 4 when j = 3. And if we measure 0, we cannot derive any useful information, and we will need to rerun the algorithm.

5 From Period to Factoring

The period must be divisible by 2. If it is not, we need to pick a different a and re-run the algorithm. Having the period, we compute k as:

$$k \equiv a^{\frac{r}{2}} (\text{mod } N) = 13^{\frac{4}{2}} \ (\text{mod } 15) = 4$$

then we could find the factors by computing classically the greatest common divisor as shown below:

$$k + 1 = 5, \gcd(5, N) = 5$$

$$k - 1 = 3, \gcd(3, N) = 3$$

this will give us one or both factors of N, but one of the factors is enough to compute the other factor anyways.

6 Implementation

The question remains as to how to implement the $U_{f_{a,N}}$. We notice that a number x can be represented in binary as:

$$x = [x_1 x_2 x_3 \ldots x_n] = 2^{n-1}x_1 + 2^{n-2}x_2 + 2^{n-3}x_3 \ldots 2^0 x_n$$

based on this we can rewrite $f_{a,\,N}(x)$ as:

$$\begin{aligned} f_{a,N}(x) \equiv a^x (\text{mod } N) &= a^{2^{n-1}x_1 + 2^{n-2}x_2 + \cdots + 2^0 x_n} \ (\text{mod } N) \\ &= a^{2^{n-1}x_1}\, a^{2^{n-2}x_2} \ldots a^{2^0 x_n} (\text{mod } N) \end{aligned}$$

for any one of these numbers, if the corresponding x_i bit is 0, that number is equal to 1. Thus, we should compute $a^{2^y x_i}$ only when x_i is not zero and this can be implemented with a control qubit – having x_i as the control. Thus, the $U_{f_{a,N}}$ can be implemented as shown in Fig. 2.

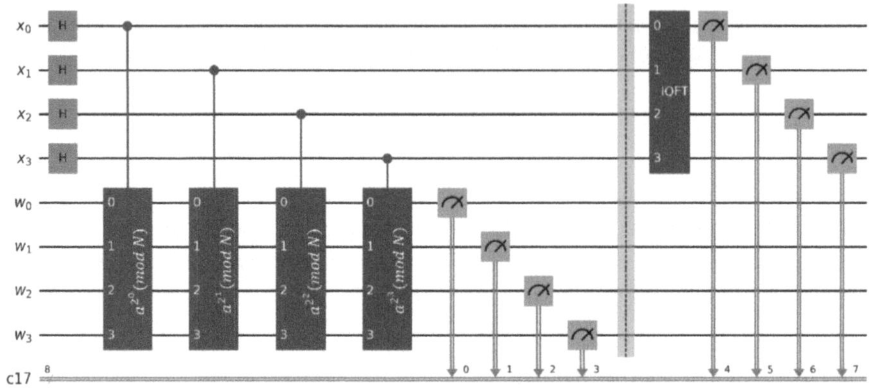

Fig. 2. Implementing $U_{f_{a,N}}$.

One might be alerted by the number of exponentiations that need to be performed as the number of qubits gets larger. However, we can use the property:

$$a^x \text{mod } N = \left(\left(a^{x-1} \text{mod } N\right) \times a\right) \text{mod } N$$

using this property, the modular exponentiation problem is converted into modular multiplication, keeping the results smaller than N at each step.

This circuit looks very similar to the circuit that is used for Quantum Phase Estimation (QPE). It is actually the same as the QPE if we replace the QPE function U^{2^x} with:

$$U^{2^x} = a^{2^x} (\text{mod } N)$$

but still, it is not clear on how to create the circuit for implementing U^{2^x}.

7 The Circuit

To provide the implementation of the a^{2^x} (mod N) function and consequently the implementation of Shor's algorithm, we first need to provide an elegant way of adding numbers. Thomas G. Draper [31] provides an implementation of adding two numbers using the quantum Fourier transform (QFT). One number is transformed into the Quantum Fourier domain and the other number is used to evolve the first number into the solution. This reduces the number of qubits needed as one number if transformed into rotations that are applied to the second number. Figure 3 shows how the number B = 6 is transformed into the QFT, and then using the number A = 5, we evolve B into the solution. The first column of the added-rotations are from the least significant bit of the A where the second column of the rotations are from the most significant bit of A; as the binary representation of 5 is 101.

Using [31] as the first building block, Stephane Beauregard builds the rest of the circuit for Shor's implementation [32]. The first step is to build a circuit that adds two numbers mod N.

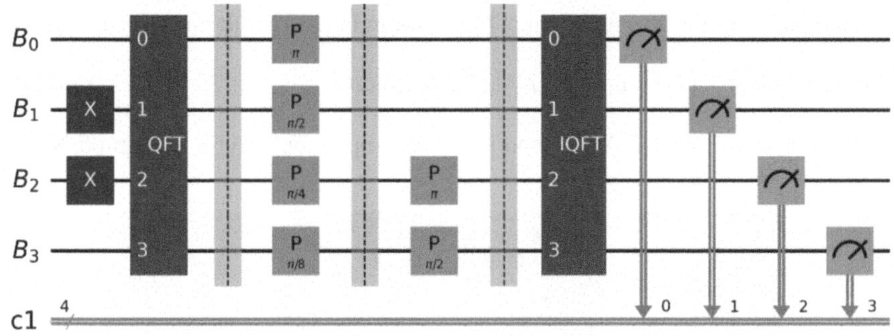

Fig. 3. The Φadd(A) circuit. Adding B = 6 and A = 5 using the method introduced in [31].

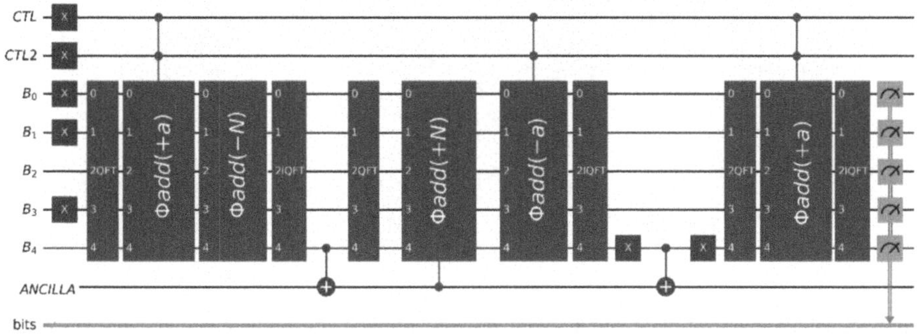

Fig. 4. Φadd(A) mod N circuit. The two top control lines can be ignored at this stage and their functionality will be explained below.

In Fig. 4, we first add the number A into B and then we run the Φadd(N) in reverse, which has the same effect as subtracting N from the solution. However, the sum of A + B could've been less than N and, in that case, we shouldn't have subtracted N from the solution. The first CNOT gate would set the ANCILLA if there was an overflow. The author in [32] explained that to be able to do this, we should encode the n qubit B register in n + 1 qubits, using the last qubit as the overflow when numbers get negative. If we had an overflow, then we should add back the N. At this point we have our modular adder. However, we should clear our ANCILLA qubit as we do not have qubits to spare. Using the property $(a + b)\ mod\ N \geq a \Leftrightarrow a + b < N$ we first subtract A from our solution and if the overflow is zero, we flip the ANCILLA to the zero state; else it was already zero. Lastly, after we make sure the ANCILLA is cleared, we add back the A to finish the implementation of Φadd(A) mod N, and we leave the ANCILLA qubit clear and ready to be used again.

Having a modular adder, Stephane Beauregard [32] proceeds to show how to implement the modular multiplier. The circuit is the same as the modular adder, but instead of adding the number A, we add the number A times X. But the number X is first converted to its binary representation, and it is used as control qubits. The number A is multiplied by 2 to the power of the X_i bit weight. The circuit in Fig. 5 is built on the principle that:

$$(ax)\text{mod } N = \left(\ldots\left(\left(2^0 ax_0\right)\text{mod } N + 2^1 ax_1\right) \text{ mod } N + \cdots + 2^{n-1}ax_{n-1}\right)\text{mod } N$$

this is the function CMULT(A*X) mod N; which implements (A*X + B) mod N.

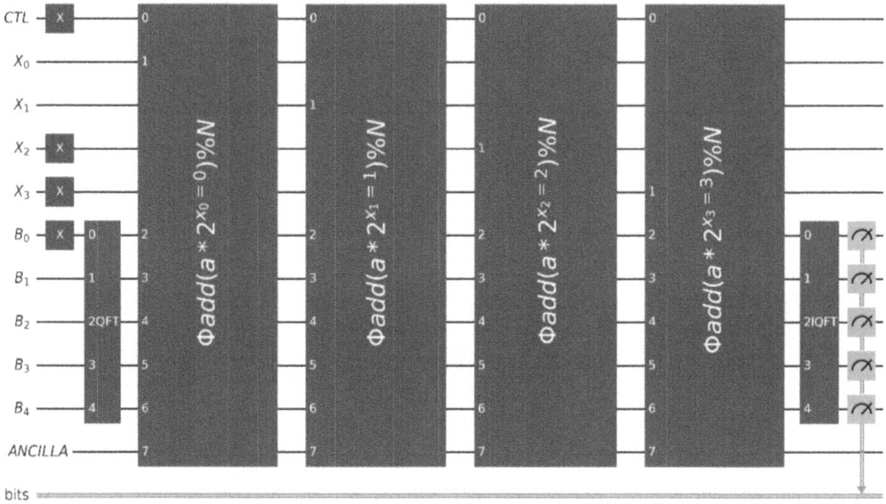

Fig. 5. CMULT(A) mod N = (A*X + B) mod N. Modular multiplication. At each stage the numbers stay below N.

What we need to do next is to clear the B register so that we can concatenate CMULT() functions. So, after we perform the CMULT, we swap the result with the X register. Then we run the CMULT() functions in reverse and instead of using A as the parameter to the Φadd() we use A^{-1}, as shown in Fig. 6. There is always A^{-1} as A and N are co-primes.

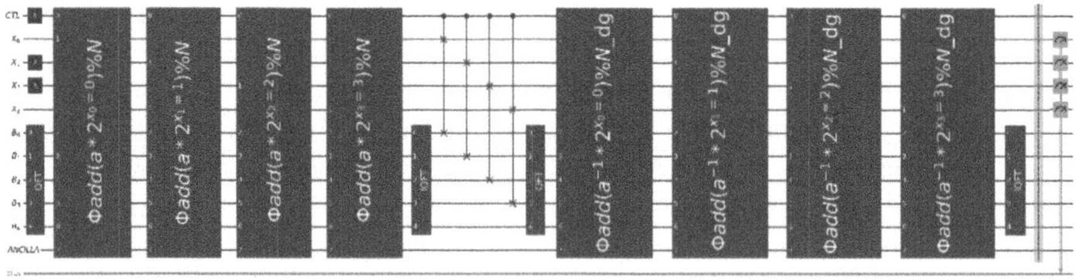

Fig. 6. U_A(): (A*X)mod N. Modular multiplication leaving the result in the X register and clearing register B.

The B register is cleared, and the result of the modular multiplication is stored in the X register. This works because, as shown in [32]:

$$|x\rangle\,|0\rangle \rightarrow |x\rangle\,|(ax)\text{mod } N\rangle \overset{SWAP}{\rightarrow} |(ax)\text{mod } N\rangle\,|x\rangle \rightarrow |(ax)\text{mod } N\rangle\,\left|\left(x - a^{-1}ax\right)\text{mod } N\right\rangle = |$$

initially, register X holds the number to multiply A with, and B is zero. At the end of the circuit, register X holds the result of the modular multiplication and register B is restored to zero.

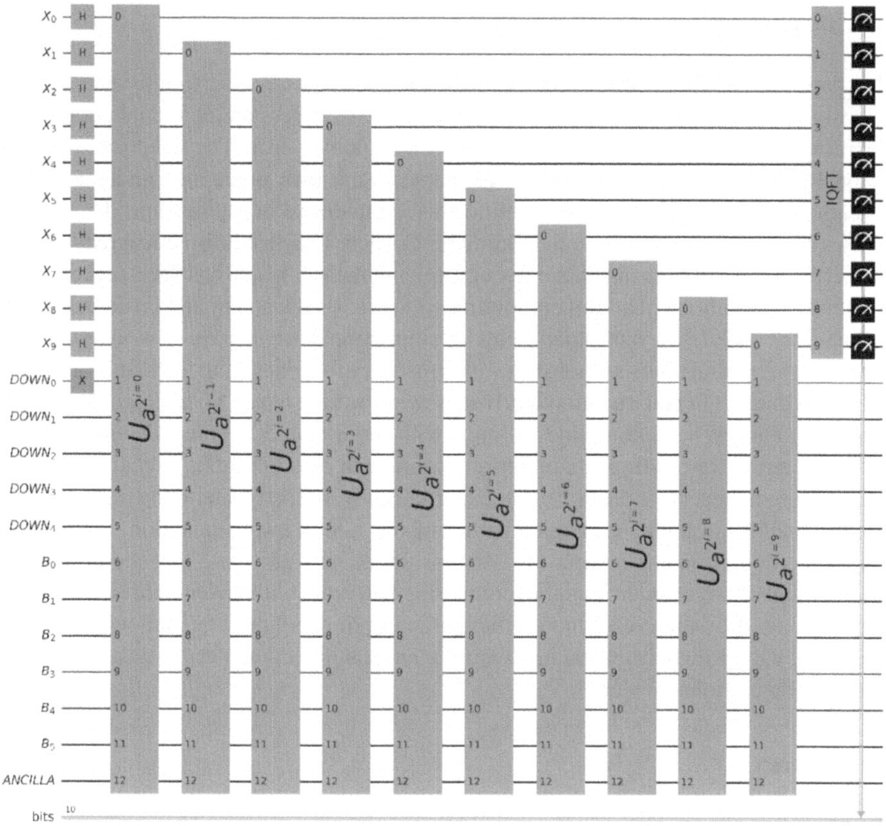

Fig. 7. Implementation of Shor's algorithm. The X register holds the exponent and used as controls in the $U_A()$.

The final step is to implement modular exponentiation, shown in Fig. 7. For this, we will replace the top control qubit with the X register (the exponent). The previous X register will be a register called DOWN, following the implementation in [33], that will hold the results of the multiplications. We need the DOWN register so that we don't alter the exponent's values; the B register is used for the modular additions. Of course, we do not need to apply $U_A()$ n times to compute a^n. We can compute it classically and pass it to $U_A()$ to compute $(a^n x)$ *mod* N since:

$$\left(a^n x\right)\text{mod } N = \underbrace{(a \ldots (a(ax)\text{mod } N)\text{mod } N \ldots)\text{mod } N}_{n\ times}$$

to run this implementation, for a number N of n bits long, we would need 2n qubits for the exponent, n qubits for the DOWN and n qubits for the B register. We would also need one extra qubit to detect overflows in Φadd() and one ANCILLA totaling 4n + 2 qubits as shown in [32]. The ANCILLA and the B register can part of the $U_A()$ gate as they are always cleared after they are used.

8 Conclusion

This paper serves as a comprehensive guide for educators seeking to introduce Shor's algorithm to both undergraduate and graduate students. Recognizing the inherent complexities of quantum computation, we have meticulously curated a selection of foundational research papers that proved invaluable in our own process of understanding, explaining, and ultimately implementing this groundbreaking algorithm. This guide focuses on clarifying the essential building blocks necessary for its practical realization. Furthermore, we provide insights into our implementation, which has been successfully executed both within a quantum computing simulator environment and on actual quantum hardware. Notably, our experiments in simulation settings have demonstrated the feasibility of running Shor's algorithm with a resource footprint of up to 29 qubits, which is the maximum. On real quantum hardware, we were able to run Shor's algorithm with up to 50 qubits. When attempting to run it with more than 50 qubits, we encountered persistent errors. Interestingly, simpler programs with over 50 qubits executed without issues. This suggests that the errors we experienced were likely due to the high number of gates and/or the highly entangled nature of our Shor's implementation, rather than simply the qubit count. Looking towards the future, we anticipate that the continued development of larger-scale quantum computing hardware with lower error rates, alongside ongoing efforts to create more efficient and optimized implementations of Shor's algorithm, will ultimately enable its execution on quantum computers with significantly greater computational power.

References

1. Arute, F., Arya, K., Babbush, R., et al.: Quantum supremacy using a programmable superconducting processor. Nature. **574**, 505–510 (2019). https://doi.org/10.1038/s41586-019-1666-5
2. Zhong, H.-S., et al.: Quantum computational advantage using photons. Science. **370**(6523), 1460–1463 (Dec 2020). https://doi.org/10.1126/science.abe8770
3. Shor, P.W.: Polynomial-time algorithms for prime factorization and discrete logarithms on a quantum computer. SIAM J. Comput. **26**(5), 1484–1509 (Oct 1997)
4. Grover, L.K.: A fast quantum mechanical algorithm for database search. In: Proceedings of the Twenty-Eighth Annual ACM Symposium on Theory of Computing, pp. 212–219 (1996)
5. Wiesner, S.: Conjugate coding. ACM SIGACT News. **15**(1), 78–88 (Jan 1983). https://doi.org/10.1145/1008908.1008920
6. Renner, R., Wolf, R.: Quantum advantage in cryptography. AIAA J. **61**(5), 1895–1910 (2023). https://doi.org/10.2514/1.J062267
7. Bennett, C.H., Brassard, G.: Quantum cryptography: public key distribution and coin tossing. Theor. Comput. Sci. (Elsevier). **560**(1), 7–11 (Dec 2014). https://doi.org/10.1016/j.tcs.2014.05.025

8. Ekert, A.K.: Quantum cryptography based on bell's theorem. Phys. Rev. Lett. **67**(6), 661–663 (Aug 1991). https://doi.org/10.1103/PhysRevLett.67.661
9. Han, K.-H., Kim, J.-H.: "Quantum-inspired evolutionary algorithm for a class of combinatorial optimization" IEEE trans. On. Evol. Comput. **6**(6) (Dec 2002)
10. Tosti Balducci, G., Chen, B., Möller, M., Gerritsma, M., De Breuker, R.: Review and perspectives in quantum computing for partial differential equations in structural mechanics. Front. Mech. Eng. **8**, 914241 (2022). https://doi.org/10.3389/fmech.2022.914241
11. Darby Smith, J., et al.: Solving a steady-state PDE using spiking networks and neuromorphic hardware. In: International Conference on Neuromorphic Systems (ICONS), pp. 1–8 (2020). https://doi.org/10.1145/3407197.3407202
12. Jiang, S., Britt, K.A., McCaskey, A.J., et al.: Quantum annealing for prime factorization. Sci. Rep. **8**, 17667 (2018). https://doi.org/10.1038/s41598-018-36058-z
13. Abbas, A., Schuld, M., Petruccione, F.: On quantum ensembles of quantum classifiers. Quantum Mach. Intell. **2**, 6 (2020). https://doi.org/10.1007/s42484-020-00018-6
14. Barabasi, I., Tappert, C.C., Evans, D., Leider, A.M.: Quantum computing and deep learning working together to solve optimization problems. In: International Conference on Computational Science and Computational Intelligence (CSCI), pp. 493–498 (Dec. 2019)
15. Benedetti, M., Lloyd, E., Sack, S., Fiorentini, M.: Parameterized quantum circuits as machine learning models. Quantum Sci. Technol. **4**, 043001 (2019). https://doi.org/10.1088/2058-9565/ab5944
16. Biamonte, J., Wittek, P., Pancotti, N., Rebentrost, P., Wiebe, N., Lloyd, S.: Quantum machine learning. Nature. **549**, 195–202 (2017). https://doi.org/10.1038/nature23474
17. Saggio, V., et al.: Experimental quantum speed-up in reinforcement learning agents. Nature. **591**, 229–233 (2021). https://doi.org/10.1038/s41586-021-03242-7
18. Herman, D., et al.: Quantum computing for finance. Nat. Rev. Phys. **5**, 450–465 (July 2023). https://doi.org/10.1038/s42254-023-00603-1
19. Pyrkov, A., et al.: Quantum computing for near-term applications in generative chemistry and drug discovery. (Elsevier). Drug Discov. Today. **28**(8), 103675 (Aug 2023). https://doi.org/10.1016/j.drudis.2023.103675
20. Home page of qiskit. https://qiskit.org/. Retrieved 8 Apr 2025
21. Rivest, R.L., Shamir, A., Adleman, L.: A method for obtaining digital signatures and public-key cryptosystems. Commun. ACM. **21**(2), 120–126 (1978). https://doi.org/10.1145/359340.359342
22. Quantum Computing for Computer Scientists: Noson S. Yanofsky, Mirco A. Mannucci. Cambridge University Press, (reprinted with corrections in 2013) (2008). ISBN: 978-0-521-87996-5
23. Deligiannidis, L.: Explaining the Design of the Quantum Fourier Transform. The 2024 world congress in computer science computer engineering and applied computing (CSCE). In: The 3nd International Conference on Emergent Quantum Technologies (ICEQT'24). Springer Nature Las Vegas (July 2024)
24. Kassal, I., Whitfield, J.D., Perdomo-Ortiz, A., Yung, M.-H., Aspuru-Guzik, A.: Simulating chemistry using quantum computers. Annu. Rev. Phys. Chem. **62**, 185–207 (2011)
25. Harrow, A.W., Hassidim, A., Lloyd, S.: Quantum algorithm for linear Systems of Equations. Phys. Rev. Lett. **103**, 150502 (Oct 2009)
26. Zhou, N., Chen, W., Yan, X., Wang, Y.: Bit-level quantum color image encryption scheme with quantum cross-exchange operation and hyper-chaotic system. Quantum Inf. Process. **17**, 137 (2018). https://doi.org/10.1007/s11128-018-1902-1
27. Bilkis, M., Cerezo, M., Verdon, G., et al.: A semi-agnostic ansatz with variable structure for variational quantum algorithms. Quantum Mach. Intell. **5**, 43 (2023). https://doi.org/10.1007/s42484-023-00132-1

28. Abraham Asfaw: 12. Shor's algorithm II: From Factoring to Period-Finding, Writing the Quantum Program-Part 3. Qiskit tutorial. https://www.youtube.com/watch?v=IFmkzWF-S2k&t=15s. Accessed Apr 2025
29. Rieffel, E., Polak, W.: Quantum Computing, a Gentle Introduction, pp. 166–169. The MIT Press Cambridge, Massachusetts London, England. ISBN 978-0-262-01506-6 (2011)
30. Quantum Computation and Quantum Information: Michael A. Nielsen, Isaac L. Chuang. Cambridge University Press (2010). ISBN: 978-1-107-00217-3
31. Thomas, G.: Draper, addition on a quantum computer arXiv (Aug 2000). https://doi.org/10.48550/arXiv.quant-ph/0008033
32. Beauregard, S.: Circuit for Shor's algorithm using 2n+3 qubits. Quantum Inform. Comput. **3**(2), 175–185 (Mar 2003). https://doi.org/10.48550/arXiv.quant-ph/0205095
33. Rui Maia Tiago Leão. Github repository (2019). https://github.com/tiagomsleao/ShorAlgQiskit/tree/master. Accessed May 2025

Quantum Vehicular Ecosystem: Analysis of Emerging Applications and Security Implications

Akwasi Adu-Kyere(✉), Ethiopia Nigussie, and Jouni Isoaho

University of Turku, Vesilinnatie 5, 20500 Turku, Finland
{akwasi.adu-kyere,ethiopia.nigussie,jouni.isoaho}@utu.fi

Abstract. Today's security deployments and implementations heavily rely on cryptographic systems and their underlying infrastructures. In particular, the application of quantum principles is emerging as a significant paradigm in security communication. This manuscript conducts a comprehensive investigation of quantum technologies, specifically focusing on automotive cybersecurity and its numerous applications within a proposed Quantum Vehicular Ecosystem (QVE)—emphasizing the critical need for enhanced security measures and specialized quantum applications in the context of vehicles. This work addresses a significant gap in the existing literature by shedding light on QVEs. We provide valuable insights, including the importance of quantum-like modeling approaches and solutions that can improve vehicular security and its relevant applications.

Keywords: Quantum · Automotive · Cyber-security · Ecosystem · Security · Applications

1 Introduction

For centuries, the term "quantum" has been closely linked to the field of quantum mechanics [18,59], sparking discussions and adding depth to conversations about quantum computing [10], informatics, and communications [44]. Quantum also brings to mind the implications for cryptography, espionage, and cutting-edge research on the topic of its applications. For example, the Global Quantum Key Distribution Market was valued at USD 1428.3 million in 2021 [24], and is projected to increase to USD 2.07 billion in 2023, and is expected to reach USD 7.85 billion by 2030. This growth is attributed to the adoption of computational tools in financial modeling, computational chemistry, drug design and development [17], military, and mission-critical sectors. With the computational utility of quantum computers, the pressure is even increased with QKD protocols, devices, and systems that are making technological strides on the market [40,42], with prominent companies leading the surge [16]. Furthermore, security deployments and implementations of cryptographic systems have exploited

H. R. Arabnia et al. (Eds.): CSCE 2025, CCIS 2932, pp. 189–204, 2026.
https://doi.org/10.1007/978-3-032-22193-3_14

mathematical complexities [2], even though classic computation infrastructures are deemed insurmountable regarding proportionality and simultaneous parameter scaling in exponential complexities. Unlike quantum computation infrastructures, this constraint is particularly relevant when considering time-bound instances of mathematical problems in a polynomial time-bound context.

Several technological advancements are progressively visible from quantum entanglements [64]. For example, the work [43] addresses the use of quantum key distribution (QKD) to secure unmanned aerial vehicles (UAVs) via quantum cryptography-as-a-service. As single-photon efficiency improves [46], the authors of [63] focus on free space implementations and the future potential of QKD. In [37], the authors explore quantum servitization with a comparison to the current quantum cloud service deployed in the user domain. In addition, there have been improvements in chip-based quantum key distribution for quantum information technologies elaborated by the authors [22]. As research continues to push the boundaries of quantum mechanics, the untapped true potential for applications remains to be fully realized. A central utilization of quantum variational methods to enable the execution of exploitable tasks in a manner that bears a distinct resemblance to quantum mechanics [11], also known as quantum-like modeling. Quantum-like modeling demonstrates the application principles of quantum formalisms extended beyond the realm of quantum physics [21]. For example, the authors of [29] examine reinforcement learning from a variational quantum circuit based on quantum learning, a divergent paradigm in machine learning techniques, and an approach within the domain of quantum machine learning (QML). The paper [31] also provides a similar perspective on quantum biology, by outlining the current advancement of utilizing quantum to maintain the non-equilibrium state of biomolecules. Therefore, the scope of this manuscript is to explore and review quantum applications in the vehicular context, from a security-centric standpoint, and analytical quantum-like modeling in the context of the vehicular ecosystem. This paper delves combinatorially into quantum vehicular ecosystems (QVEs) by leveraging advancements in quantum applications from existing literature and practical references. Aligned with this objective towards fully connected, intelligent, and autonomous mobility, our contributions are as follows:

- Explore quantum-like modeling for vehicular security from the perspective of the vehicular ecosystem.
- Review the applications of quantum-oriented technologies relatable to fully connected, intelligent, and autonomous mobility with post-quantum in mind
- Propose the vision of a quantum vehicular ecosystem (QVE) towards a quantum era.

Figure 1 illustrates the structure of this article, and the remainder of the manuscript is as follows: The subsequent section following the introduction is an overview of quantum cryptography and computing in Sect. 2. Section 3 follows as the related work and a review of the literature. Section 4 addresses the proposed quantum vehicular ecosystem pertinent to autonomous, intelligent, and

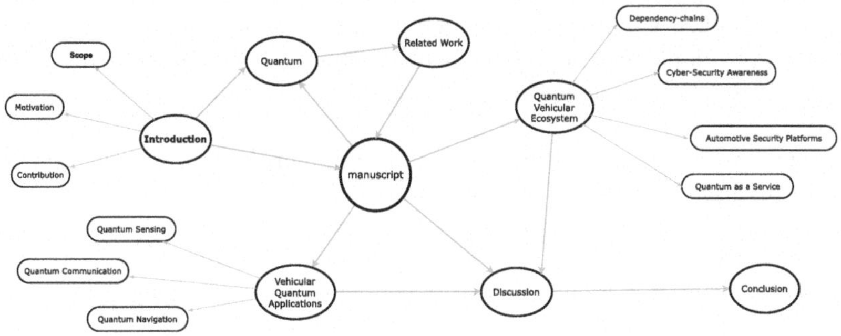

Fig. 1. An illustration of the manuscript's structure

connected vehicles. The section offers additional information on Quantum as a Service, quantum sensing, communication, navigation, and annealing. The discussion combines all that is covered in the manuscript to this point to elaborate significant arguments in Sect. 5, ending with a conclusion in Sect. 6.

2 Quantum Cryptography and Computing

Throughout human history, particular phases of technological development have resulted in enormous advancements that have had both beneficial and harmful effects. Technology has also been phased in and out through competitiveness, the presentation of solutions, and a common commitment to handle pressing challenges that are currently occurring and those that may occur in the future. There is a strong correlation between the rapid development of technological developments and the numerous benefits that society enjoys today. As a result, researchers, practitioners, and organizations continue to strive to uncover the potential breakthroughs that technology still has to offer. Quantum cryptography and computing are examples of such recent advances. They exhibit the characteristics and properties of social benefits, along with the potential for better security and computational capabilities.

As modern technology shapers, quantum cryptography and computing have sparked various security evolutions in communication and applicational integrity in traditional security infrastructures [8]. This is a significant development in the field of information security as the unavoidable cascade of effects on operators to evolve and pivot towards other emerging security solutions and infrastructure is being triggered. All because several classical security infrastructures are beginning to evolve around quantum cryptography and computing [5].

Quantum cryptography, and more specifically quantum key distribution, makes use of the fundamental laws of quantum mechanics to construct encryption keys between two parties in a secure manner. This makes it easier to encrypt and decrypt data. Through this, the two people involved in the communication can identify and counteract any attempts to eavesdrop on their conversation

[2]. As a method, it ensures secure communication by leveraging the inevitability of altering quantum states as a security premise. As a result, any attempt to eavesdrop on the transmission of the key will invariably be discovered and stopped.

Quantum computing, on the other hand, relies on these properties to achieve computational performance, along with algorithms such as Grover's and Shor's. Its computational potential is to operate in an unparalleled dimension in terms of exponential processing [57]. Quantum computing's main advantage in its present state lies in its computational superiority over classical computing systems. With qubit states capable of superposition and simultaneous existence in multiple states at a given time, this is possible.

3 Related Work and Literature Review

Several prior studies have noted the significance of quantum-like modeling, its applications in the literature, and the potential for quantum applications in the coming years. However, few of these manuscripts focus solely on the quantum vehicular realm, even though a portion of these subsequent publications mention vehicles. As a result, publications from the literature on the quantum realm have three categorizations: quantum communication aspects, quantum-like modeling approaches, and quantum surveys. Among these groups, the application of quantum communication demonstrates the importance of deployable quantum communication channels, networks, key distribution, and proposed quantum hardware to facilitate security in various forms. In 2022, the Illinois Center for Transportation [56] demonstrated the advantages of quantum communication for autonomous vehicles in a series of experiments. It showcased communication between infrastructure assets via sending commands to moving vehicular platforms, establishing a quantum communications link with other moving vehicles. Their deployed scenarios and cases covered multiple configurations of infrastructure-to-infrastructure (I2I), infrastructure-to-autonomous vehicle (I2V), and vehicle-to-vehicle (V2V) communications using drones as their vehicular medium in diverse configurations. The authors of [55] also presented the necessity of integrating Quantum Key Distribution in their study of the highway freight information system, emphasizing the importance of securing significant and sensitive data in the freight transmission processes to prevent unauthorized access and ensure data integrity. The aim was to prohibit security assertions in information systems during transmission processes.

The next group, which focuses on quantum-like modeling approaches, applies quantum mechanics principles to unique applications related to vehicles and their ecosystems, such as proposing quantum-based solutions for position verification, data protection, privacy, and safety in the vehicular ecosystem. This group covers research areas such as quantum sensing, quantum communication protocols, quantum cryptography, and other related domains, exploring innovative applications within the vehicular context. For example, the authors of [36] discuss the significance of quantum location verification (QLV) and its benefit to vehicles and their networks. The authors of [62] also approach quantum from the perspective of post-quantum in the Internet of Vehicles (IoV). They concentrate on post-quantum signatures and propose an IoV security-catalyzed systolic architecture, which relies on post-quantum signatures with division, to replace public-key cryptosystems.

The final group of researchers conducted quantum surveys and academic works based on the applications of quantum technologies, mentioning vehicular applications but not necessarily focusing on them. The authors of [12] examined the computing aspect of quantum for the security of the Internet of Things. [1] considered the cryptographic perspective in the smart grid by highlighting the service aspect of the QKD deployment in cloud computing. In the future perspective on quantum computing, the authors of [28] systematically elaborate on the basics and applications with the mention of quantum communication, teleportation, and cryptography. In [39], the authors focused on the potential of computational possibilities and the opportunities. They covered significant areas such as optimization algorithms, machine learning, and quantum simulations with explicit military orientation cases.

4 Quantum Vehicular Ecosystem

In this section, we outline the impact of quantum technology on the formation of a quantum vehicular ecosystem, illustrated in Fig. 2, with the aim of maximizing its use in the context of vehicular security and associative infrastructures. We refer to the interactions of automotive cybersecurity enacted with its dependencies, interdependencies, and relationality of security with quantum and its associatives as a quantum vehicular ecosystem (QVE): the convergence of quantum technological applications and quantum-like modeling for the benefits of the vehicular ecosystem, with security serving as the focal point.

The role of safety and perception sensors is evolving in vehicles, as described in recent research [4]. The security aspects of these roles are also changing. In an era of fully connected, intelligent, and autonomous systems, the functions of monitoring, reporting, analysis, and virtual security operations are expected to become more prominent [3]. These functions have implications for information security and are closely related to privacy and data concerns [4].

4.1 Quantum as a Service

Classical computing has been discovered to have deficiencies in which quantum computing excels, while relying on nature's fundamental properties to assure security through secrecy. Nevertheless, the challenge is that it is improbable that every individual or organization will construct or possess its own distinctive quantum infrastructure. This is the reason why quantum as a service (QaaS) is advantageous, as evidenced by the branches of computation, communication, and devices in Fig. 3. QaaS is a quantum awareness that is established by the availability of services that are constructed on a quantum platform. An access that

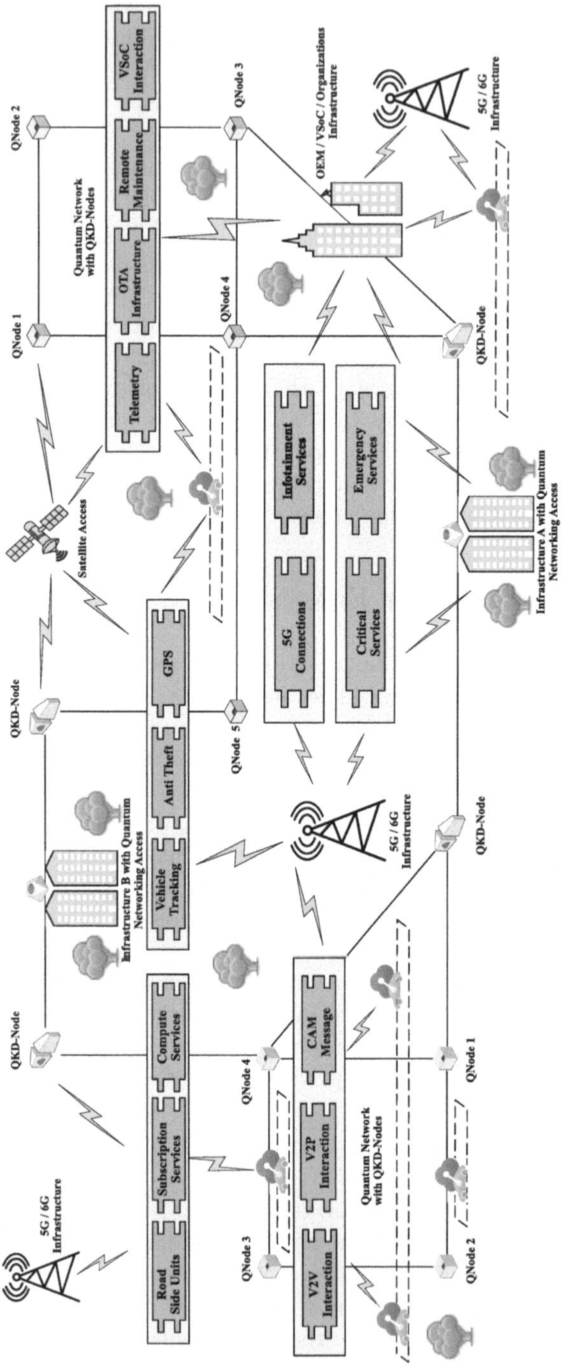

Fig. 2. Generic depiction of the Quantum vehicular Ecosystem

has also been utilized by organizations such as IBM, D-Wave, Google, Microsoft, and Amazon, to name a few, enables individuals and organizations to surmount this obstacle. Thus, classical problems and challenges in computational complexity can be accommodated through quantum simulation, optimization, machine learning, and artificial intelligence, which are catalyzed by algorithms with varying performance [50] in quantum. Referring to QVEs in this context, the primary inquiry is what quantum as a service contributes to the vehicular domain and the potential it can be realized.

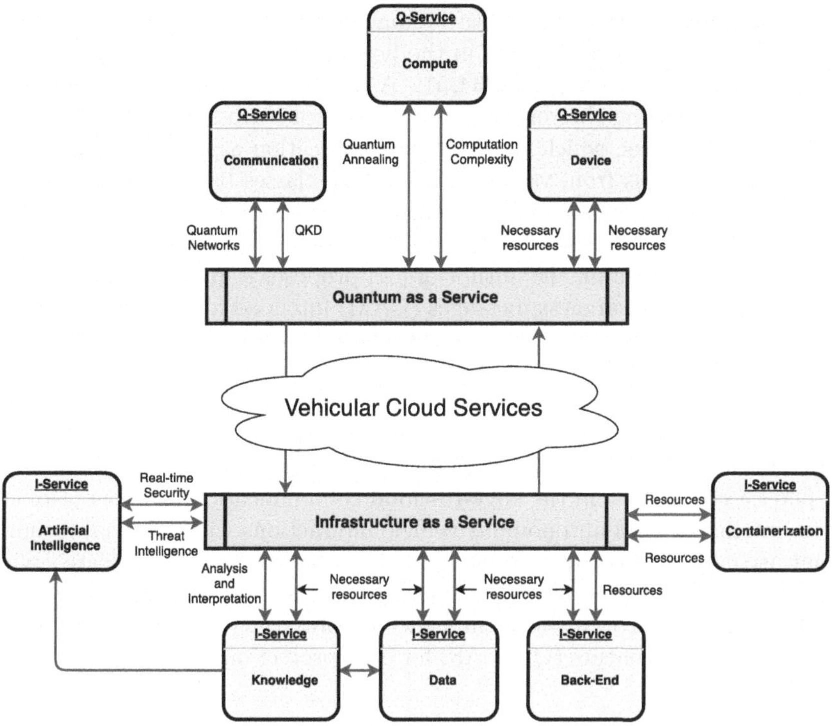

Fig. 3. Quantum as a Service

Platforms and Infrastructure: Today's vehicular infrastructure dedicates several platforms to the vehicular ecosystem, which impacts security because of hardware and software feature integrations ranging from onboard safety functions to operating system convenient features for clients and service offerings that determine their categorization. For example, charging stations can be classified as device-oriented service platforms. Infotainment integrations service and mobile broadband 5G/6G (eSIM & telematics) could fall under subscription-based or cloud-based, depending on the media demand. Telematics and vehicle-to-everything (V2X) communication networks offer a wide range of services, such as real-time data transmission and vehicle connectivity, contributing to a diverse array of platform-oriented services. In-vehicle infrastructure and services, external infrastructure and services, cloud-based services via service-oriented architecture (SOA), and other dedicated vehicle-specific interests have been established as the backbones of the future vehicular ecosystem, platform, and infrastructure.

Quantum Communication: Through quantum informatics, several communication advancements have emerged, particularly Quantum Key Distribution, despite the extensive use of cryptographic systems and their infrastructures. The true potential of quantum informatics remains untapped for present and future applications. Recent developments in the field of quantum communication have created interest in the literature [34,51]. A diversity of theories on QKD have been proposed utilizing the communication principle across applications [32,61]. These proposed works, which form the communication aspect of quantum, rely on quantum protocols from various classes. The classes base their protocols on variations of the quantum principle, employing other novel and distinct techniques to achieve an unconditionally secure communication channel.

In the vehicular realm, the author of [52] proposes a quantum protocol that secures cooperative awareness messages (CAM) intended for vehicles in communications and transactions. The author emphasizes the use of this protocol by traffic control systems for broadcasting CAM messages to vehicles within the broadcast zone and scope periodically. The quantum efficient privacy protection (QEPP) protocol developed by [41] for the Internet of vehicles also shares similarities with [52], except it uses quantum point clouds. The protocol concept plays a crucial role in the edge-to-cloud communication component of connected, intelligent, and autonomous vehicle interactions with external resources and infrastructures. Communications like this most often use certificates, which are primarily biased to mathematical complexity in current infrastructures. In [23], the authors approach this significance by proposing a quantum secure certificate aggregate signature (QSCLAS) for data protection with Vehicular ad hoc networks (VANETs).

Quantum Navigation or Annealing: Another branch of quantum has gained research momentum is the optimization problem in vehicular applications [60], often referred to as quantum annealing [20]. The current predominant approach, quantum annealing algorithms [19,53], is where quantum algorithms are deployed to address vehicular routing optimization issues on a quantum computing infrastructure. For example, in [58], quantum annealing-based algorithms with illustrations consider the computational complexity, which could be a clear game changer for vehicular routing problems. With such a specificity, complex problems such as vehicular route planning, scheduling, and optimization have the potential to enhance efficiency and the outputs of such endeavors, due to their relatively associative characteristics and properties describable as discrete or continuous. As quantum computers become more powerful via linear or exponential scaling of qubits, in the attempt of D-wave systems, the heuristic algorithmic functions and the combination of computational supremacy in quantum computing offer a path to streamlining approximation solutions, finding [15] in cloud-based solutions utilizable by connected, intelligent, and autonomous vehicles. In [65], some examples of quantum annealing implementation are shown, along with a summary of different problem-oriented approaches used in real life. Using quantum neural networks, [14] delves into the complexities of supply chain problems. In a vehicle routing problem, [54] uses a weighted segment parameterized cost assignment in a Quadratic Unconstrained Binary Optimization (QUBO) combinatorial model that takes into account traffic restrictions. Other proposed works on localization and positioning from a quantum perspective are equally significant in the quantum vehicular ecosystem.

Quantum Sensing: In quantum informatics, the process of emitting signals and analyzing the proportion of received reflections already harnesses the characteristics and properties of wave principles in classical sensing. Advancements in sensing and perception technologies, including cameras, LiDAR, and radar, are critical for fully functional ADAS and self-driving vehicles. As such, implementation and development efforts aimed at sensor accuracy and reliability are of great importance beyond autonomous systems. However, traditional sensing techniques often face limitations and constraints in specific environmental conditions that affect precision, accuracy, and consistency. Thus, from classical to quantum-like modeling sensing paradigm, data output of multi-sensing would be even more critical for making real-time decisions about road safety, even when using driven associative technologies and algorithms. The unique characteristics and properties of qubits, such as entanglement, superposition, and photon correlation, enable measurement accuracy and precision even in unpredictable environments and challenging conditions. Furthermore, studies in the literature and practical applications have provided significant information on the detection noise-to-signal ratio of quantum sensing over classical sensors. For example, nitrogen-vacancy centers [47,48] as sensors offer precision position detection in a vector format. The authors in [33] also explored the advantages of quantum sensing principles over classic sensing in the maritime environment, using the advantages of quantum illumination for quantum radars and LiDARs.

Research has also shown that exploiting photonic behaviors, such as squeezing and other techniques, could benefit fields outside of quantum physics. For example, the enhanced detection of low-reflectivity objects in noisy environments [49] illustrates how advantageous it would be for automotive radars and LiDARs [45]. Based on the same fundamental concept of quantum mechanics, the authors [66] show how the correlation dynamics of the environment can be tracked using controlled spin sensors that make the best guesses about the parameters that matter.

4.2 Challenges and Limitations

The most challenging aspect to date has been dealing with noise and errors. Currently, we view the noise ceiling resulting from transmission and imperfect hardware as crucial for the next advancement in the quantum era. One way in which the authors of [27] deal with this problem is by suggesting a quantum communication protocol that uses quantum low-density parity check (QLDPC) in a BB84 protocol. While [26] is about using quantum error correction codes (QECCs), BB84 is the base protocol of their proposed protocol, which is based on the idea that it can handle bad channel noise in transmission.

5 Discussion

Quantum technologies, particularly those based on the principles of quantum mechanics and quantum-like modeling, extend their applications beyond Industry 4.0. Authors like [38] provide a unique perspective on anti-submarine warfare, illustrating how these technologies can be used for sensing. As advances in quantum technologies continue to evolve, they have a significant impact on the automotive realm. Organizations and stakeholders, such as Tesla with its ecosystem and Google with Automotive Android, are actively enhancing vehicular security to create a fully functional, connected, intelligent, and autonomous ecosystem. These companies are also competing in the quantum race, raising the question of whether they will combine their automotive initiatives with their quantum pathways. A gradual paradigm for automotive security is emerging, with cloud-based platforms gaining traction in the vehicular ecosystem, where quantum technologies are expected to play a crucial role. In this paradigm, security platforms such as the one in Fig. 3: Artificial Intelligence as a Service (AIaaS) [13,25], Backend as a Service (BaaS), Containers as a Service (CaaS) [30], Data as a Service (DaaS) [7], Device as a Service (DaaS), Infrastructure as a Service (IaaS) [6], Internet of Things as a Service (IoTaaS) [9], and Knowledge as a Service (KaaS) [35] are being integrated into software-defined security networks.

There is also a shift towards software-defined vehicles and the need for flexible and scalable security solutions via hardware and software decoupling. This trend is projected to become increasingly significant in a Quantum Vehicular Ecosystem due to disruptive emerging technologies such as quantum computing. The other aspect of the QVE paradigm emphasizes security service-oriented platforms (SSOP), expecting that the majority of these security platform offerings will leverage cloud-based infrastructure within the vehicular ecosystem. This service-oriented offering could provide comprehensive cybersecurity solutions to CIAV owners, offering continuous monitoring, real-time threat detection, and secure data transmission through a subscription or contractual agreement with OEMs and other related parties. Other cloud-based services could integrate with Automotive Cybersecurity protocols, ensuring security for in-vehicle platforms, roadside units (RSUs), and other external dependencies with a key focus on enhancing security maturity toward this proposed Quantum Vehicular Ecosystem.

6 Conclusion

As demonstrated in this manuscript, the vision of a quantum vehicular ecosystem towards a quantum era is proposed. The dispersion of quantum research and its impact, influence, and as a prime shaper, ignite our conducted exploration in quantum-like modeling for vehicular security from the perspective of the vehicular ecosystem. There is the potential to utilize quantum in various ways as we review the applications of quantum-oriented technologies related to fully connected, intelligent, and autonomous mobility with post-quantum in mind. As a result, there is an indication that quantum Artificial Intelligence and Machine Learning can enhance data analysis in a vehicular context. Knowledge-based assertions are also feasible for the enormous amount of data the vehicular ecosystem is projected to produce, despite the fact that there are certain challenges and hurdles to overcome. The investigation of quantum technologies in a way shows that quantum communication and computing are feasible in the cloud first before their visibility in in-vehicle security infrastructure. With automotive cybersecurity and infrastructure often trailing actual technological advancements, numerous quantum applications within a proposed quantum vehicular ecosystem would be a critical need for enhanced security measures, but far from in-vehicle specialized quantum applications predominant of hardware as suppose to software in the context of vehicles. As a valuable insight, including the importance of quantum-like modeling approaches and solutions, improvement and potential are relevant in future technological advancements.

Acknowledgements. This research acknowledges the Finnish Cultural Foundation for the offered Grant.

References

1. Abulizi, J., Qingsheng, H., Wei, W.: Quantum cryptography technology and application in smart grid. In: 2022 IEEE 22nd International Conference on Communication Technology (ICCT), pp. 1213–1217 (2022). https://doi.org/10.1109/ICCT56141.2022.10072299
2. Adu-Kyere, A., Nigussie, E., Isoaho, J.: Quantum key distribution: modeling and simulation through BB84 protocol using python3. Sensors **22**(16), 6284 (2022). https://doi.org/10.3390/s22166284, https://www.mdpi.com/1424-8220/22/16/6284
3. Adu-Kyere, A., Nigussie, E., Isoaho, J.: Self-aware cybersecurity architecture for autonomous vehicles: security through system-level accountability. Sensors **23**(21), 8817 (2023). https://doi.org/10.3390/s23218817, https://www.mdpi.com/1424-8220/23/21/8817
4. Adu-Kyere, A., Nigussie, E., Isoaho, J.: Analyzing the effectiveness of IDS/IPS in real-time with a custom in-vehicle design. Procedia Comput. Sci. **238**, 175–183 (2024). https://doi.org/10.1016/j.procs.2024.06.013, https://linkinghub.elsevier.com/retrieve/pii/S1877050924012493

5. Aguado, A., et al.: Quantum cryptography networks in support of path verification in service function chains. J. Opt. Commun. Netw. **12**(4), B9 (2020). https://doi.org/10.1364/JOCN.379799, https://opg.optica.org/abstract.cfm?URI=jocn-12-4-B9
6. Aljamal, R., El-Mousa, A., Jubair, F.: A user perspective overview of the top infrastructure as a service and high performance computing cloud service providers. In: 2019 IEEE Jordan International Joint Conference on Electrical Engineering and Information Technology (JEEIT), pp. 244–249. IEEE, Amman (2019). https://doi.org/10.1109/JEEIT.2019.8717453, https://ieeexplore.ieee.org/document/8717453/
7. Ardagna, C.A., Bellandi, V., Damiani, E., Bezzi, M., Hebert, C.: Big data analytics-as-a-service: Bridging the gap between security experts and data scientists. Comput. Electr. Eng. **93**, 107215 (2021). https://doi.org/10.1016/j.compeleceng.2021.107215, https://linkinghub.elsevier.com/retrieve/pii/S0045790621002081
8. Bavdekar, R., Jayant Chopde, E., Agrawal, A., Bhatia, A., Tiwari, K.: Post quantum cryptography: a review of techniques, challenges and standardizations. In: 2023 International Conference on Information Networking (ICOIN), pp. 146–151 (2023). https://doi.org/10.1109/ICOIN56518.2023.10048976
9. Borsatti, D., Davoli, G., Cerroni, W., Raffaelli, C.: Enabling industrial IoT as a service with multi-access edge computing. IEEE Commun. Mag. **59**(8), 21–27 (2021). https://doi.org/10.1109/MCOM.001.2100006, https://ieeexplore.ieee.org/document/9530503/
10. Brooks, M.: The race to find quantum computing's sweet spot. Nature **617**, S1–S3 (2023). https://arxiv.org/abs/1902.02332
11. Chakrabarti, S., You, X., Wu, X.: ICCAD Special Session Paper: Quantum Variational Methods For Quantum Applications. In: IEEE/ACM International Conference on Computer-Aided Design, Digest of Technical Papers, ICCAD, vol. 2021-Novem, pp. 1–7 (2021). https://doi.org/10.1109/ICCAD51958.2021.9643519
12. Chawla, D., Mehra, P.S.: A survey on quantum computing for internet of things security. Procedia Comput. Sci. **218**, 2191–2200 (2023). https://doi.org/10.1016/j.procs.2023.01.195, https://www.sciencedirect.com/science/article/pii/S1877050923001953. International Conference on Machine Learning and Data Engineering
13. Cobbe, J., Singh, J.: Artificial intelligence as a service: legal responsibilities, liabilities, and policy challenges. Comput. Law Secur. Rev. **42**, 105573 (2021). https://doi.org/10.1016/j.clsr.2021.105573, https://www.sciencedirect.com/science/article/pii/S0267364921000467
14. Correll, R., Weinberg, S.J., Sanches, F., Ide, T., Suzuki, T.: Quantum neural networks for a supply chain logistics application. Adv. Quantum Technol. **6**(7), 2200183 (2023). https://doi.org/10.1002/qute.202200183, https://onlinelibrary.wiley.com/doi/10.1002/qute.202200183
15. Crosson, E.J., Lidar, D.A.: Prospects for quantum enhancement with diabatic quantum annealing. Nat. Rev. Phys. **3**(7), 466–489 (2021). https://doi.org/10.1038/s42254-021-00313-6, arXiv:2008.09913 [cond-mat, physics:quant-ph]
16. Dargan, J.: 25 companies building the quantum cryptography & communications markets (2021). https://thequantuminsider.com/2021/01/11/25-companies-building-the-quantum-cryptography-communications-markets/
17. Das, S.: Top applications of quantum computing everyone should know about in 2024 (2020). https://analyticsindiamag.com/ai-trends/top-applications-of-quantum-computing-everyone-should-know-about/. Accessed 10 Nov 2025

18. Friedberg, R., Hohenberg, P.C.: What is quantum mechanics? A minimal formulation. Found. Phys. **48**(3), 295–332 (2018)
19. Harikrishnakumar, R., Nannapaneni, S., Nguyen, N.H., Steck, J.E., Behrman, E.C.: A quantum annealing approach for dynamic multi-depot capacitated vehicle routing problem. ArXiv abs/2005.12478 (2020). https://api.semanticscholar.org/CorpusID:218889430
20. Hauke, P., Katzgraber, H.G., Lechner, W., Nishimori, H., Oliver, W.D.: Perspectives of quantum annealing: Methods and implementations. Rep. Prog. Phys. **83**(5), 054401 (2020). arXiv:1903.06559 [quant-ph]
21. Haven, E., Khrennikov, A.: Editorial: applications of quantum mechanical techniques to areas outside of quantum mechanics. Front. Phys. **5**(NOV), 1–2 (2017). https://doi.org/10.3389/fphy.2017.00060, http://journal.frontiersin.org/article/10.3389/fphy.2017.00060/full
22. Huang, J., Chen, X., Li, X., Wang, J.: Chip-based photonic graph states. AAPPS Bull. **33**(1) (2023). https://doi.org/10.1007/s43673-023-00082-7
23. Huang, Y., Xu, G., Song, X., Liu, Y., Wang, Q.: A quantum-secure certificateless aggregate signature protocol for vehicular ad hoc networks. Veh. Commun. **47**, 100775 (2024). https://doi.org/10.1016/j.vehcom.2024.100775, https://linkinghub.elsevier.com/retrieve/pii/S2214209624000500
24. Insights, B.R.: Quantum key distribution (QKD) market size and forecast 2030 (2023). https://www.businessresearchinsights.com/market-reports/quantum-key-distribution-qkd-market-106645. Accessed 10 Nov 2025
25. Jawad, M.S., Mahdin, H., Mohammed Alduais, N.A., Hlayel, M., Mostafa, S.A., Abd Wahab, M.H.: Recent and future innovative artificial intelligence services and fields. In: 2021 4th International Symposium on Agents, Multi-Agent Systems and Robotics (ISAMSR), pp. 29–32. IEEE, Batu Pahat (2021). https://doi.org/10.1109/ISAMSR53229.2021.9567891, https://ieeexplore.ieee.org/document/9567891/. Accessed 25 July 2024
26. Jia, W., Feng, B., Yu, H., Bian, Y.: Quantum key distribution protocol based on CSS error correcting codes. In: Proceedings of the ACM Turing Celebration Conference - China, pp. 1–8. ACM, Chengdu (2019). https://doi.org/10.1145/3321408.3326680, https://dl.acm.org/doi/10.1145/3321408.3326680
27. Jia, W., Zhang, Y., Yu, H., Bian, Y.: A quantum key distribution protocol based on LDPC error correcting codes. In: Proceedings of the ACM Turing Celebration Conference - China, pp. 1–7. ACM, Chengdu (2019). https://doi.org/10.1145/3321408.3326652, https://dl.acm.org/doi/10.1145/3321408.3326652
28. Balamurugan, K. S., Sivakami, A., Mathankumar, M.: Quantum computing basics, applications and future perspectives. J. Mol. Struct. **1308**, 137917 (2024). https://doi.org/10.1016/j.molstruc.2024.137917, https://www.sciencedirect.com/science/article/pii/S002228602400440X
29. Kashyap, K., Lalit, Shah, D., Gautam, L.: From classical to quantum: a review of recent progress in reinforcement learning. In: 2021 2nd International Conference for Emerging Technology, INCET 2021, pp. 1–5 (2021). https://doi.org/10.1109/INCET51464.2021.9456218
30. Khan, A.: Key characteristics of a container orchestration platform to enable a modern application. IEEE Cloud Comput. **4**(5), 42–48 (2017). https://doi.org/10.1109/MCC.2017.4250933, http://ieeexplore.ieee.org/document/8125559/
31. Kim, Y., et al.: Quantum biology: an update and perspective. Quantum Rep. **3**(1), 80–126 (2021). https://doi.org/10.3390/quantum3010006, https://www.mdpi.com/2624-960X/3/1/6

32. Kumar, A., et al.: Survey of promising technologies for quantum drones and networks. IEEE Access **9**, 125868–125911 (2021). https://doi.org/10.1109/ACCESS.2021.3109816, https://ieeexplore.ieee.org/document/9527199/
33. Lanzagorta, M., Uhlmann, J., Venegas-Andraca, S.E.: Quantum sensing in the maritime environment. In: OCEANS 2015 - MTS/IEEE Washington, pp. 1–9 (2016). https://doi.org/10.23919/oceans.2015.7401973
34. Li, M., Wang, T.: Continuous-variable quantum key distribution over air quantum channel with phase shift. IEEE Access **8**, 39672–39677 (2020). https://doi.org/10.1109/ACCESS.2020.2975155
35. Lin, H., Fan, Y., Zhang, J., Bai, B., Xu, Z., Lukasiewicz, T.: Toward knowledge as a service (kaas): predicting popularity of knowledge services leveraging graph neural networks. IEEE Trans. Serv. Comput. 1 (2022). https://doi.org/10.1109/TSC.2022.3145019, https://ieeexplore.ieee.org/document/9693263/
36. Malaney, R.: The quantum car. IEEE Wireless Commun. Lett. **5**(6), 624–627 (2016). https://doi.org/10.1109/TSC.2022.3145019, https://ieeexplore.ieee.org/document/9693263/
37. Moguel, E., Rojo, J., Valencia, D., Berrocal, J., Garcia-Alonso, J., Murillo, J.M.: Quantum service-oriented computing: current landscape and challenges. Softw. Qual. J. **30**(4), 983–1002 (2022). https://doi.org/10.1109/LWC.2016.2607740, http://ieeexplore.ieee.org/document/7563890/
38. Nathan, B.: Quantum Sensing for Anti-Submarine Warfare. In: 2023 IEEE Integrated STEM Education Conference (ISEC), pp. 256–258. IEEE (2023). https://doi.org/10.1109/ISEC57711.2023.10402282, https://ieeexplore.ieee.org/document/10402282/
39. Neumann, N.M.P., Van Heesch, M.P.P., Phillipson, F., Smallegange, A.A.P.: Quantum computing for military applications. In: 2021 International Conference on Military Communication and Information Systems (ICMCIS), p. 1–8. IEEE, The Hague (2021). https://doi.org/10.1109/ICMCIS52405.2021.9486419, https://ieeexplore.ieee.org/document/9486419/
40. Prisco, J.: Council post: Moving forward with the security of quantum key distribution (2023). https://www.forbes.com/sites/forbestechcouncil/2023/05/22/moving-forward-with-the-security-of-quantum-key-distribution/?sh=44adaa383dde
41. Qu, Z., Chen, Z., Ning, X., Tiwari, P.: QEPP: a quantum efficient privacy protection protocol in 6G-quantum internet of vehicles. IEEE Trans. Intell. Veh. **9**(1), 905–916 (2024). https://doi.org/10.1109/TIV.2023.3304852, https://ieeexplore.ieee.org/document/10221729/
42. Quantique, I.: Id quantique, the home of quantum-safe crypto. https://www.idquantique.com/. Accessed 10 Nov 2025
43. Ralegankar, V.K., et al: Quantum Cryptography-as-a-Service for Secure UAV Communication: Applications, Challenges, and Case Study. IEEE Access **10**, 1475–1492 (2022). https://doi.org/10.1109/ACCESS.2021.3138753, https://ieeexplore.ieee.org/document/9663283/
44. Rastogi, T., Hassija, V., Saxena, V.: Quantum communication: concept, applications, and future outlook. In: ACM International Conference Proceeding Series, pp. 51–56. ACM, New York (2021). https://doi.org/10.1145/3474124.3474131
45. Reichert, M., Di Candia, R., Win, M.Z., Sanz, M.: Quantum-enhanced Doppler lidar. NPJ Quantum Inf. **8**(1) (2022). https://doi.org/10.1038/s41534-022-00662-9

46. Samaner, Ç., Paçal, S., Mutlu, G., Uyanık, K., AteÇ, S.: Free-space quantum key distribution with single photons from defects in hexagonal boron nitride. Adv. Quantum Technol. **5**(9), 1–6 (2022). https://doi.org/10.1002/qute.202200059, https://onlinelibrary.wiley.com/doi/10.1002/qute.202200059
47. Schirhagl, R., Chang, K., Loretz, M., Degen, C.L.: Nitrogen-vacancy centers in diamond: nanoscale sensors for physics and biology. Annu. Rev. Phys. Chem. **65**, 83–105 (2014). https://doi.org/10.1146/annurev-physchem-040513-103659
48. Segawa, T.F., Igarashi, R.: Nanoscale quantum sensing with Nitrogen-Vacancy centers in nanodiamonds – a magnetic resonance perspective. Prog. Nucl. Magn. Reson. Spectrosc. **134-135**, 20–38 (2023)
49. Shapiro, J.H.: The quantum illumination story. IEEE Aerosp. Electron. Syst. Mag. **35**(4), 8–20 (2020). https://doi.org/10.1109/MAES.2019.2957870
50. Soeparno, H., Perbangsa, A.S.: Cloud quantum computing concept and development: A systematic literature review. Procedia Comput. Sci. **179**, 39717 (2021). https://doi.org/10.1016/j.procs.2021.01.084, https://linkinghub.elsevier.com/retrieve/pii/S1877050921001150
51. Srikara, S., Thapliyal, K., Pathak, A.: Continuous variable B92 quantum key distribution protocol using single photon added and subtracted coherent states. Quantum Inf. Process. **19**(10), 1–16 (2020). https://doi.org/10.1007/s11128-020-02872-6
52. Sutradhar, K.: A quantum cryptographic protocol for secure vehicular communication. IEEE Trans. Intell. Transp. Syst. **25**(5), 3513–3522 (2024). https://doi.org/10.1109/TITS.2023.3322728, https://ieeexplore.ieee.org/document/10287202/
53. Syrichas, A., Crispin, A.: Large-scale vehicle routing problems: quantum annealing, tunings and results. Comput. Oper. Res. **87**, 52–62 (2017). https://doi.org/10.1016/j.cor.2017.05.014, https://linkinghub.elsevier.com/retrieve/pii/S0305054817301260
54. Tambunan, T.D., Suksmono, A.B., Edward, I.J.M., Mulyawan, R.: Quantum annealing for vehicle routing problem with weighted segment. In: AIP Conference Proceedings **2906**(1), 070005 (2023). https://doi.org/10.1063/5.0178362, https://doi.org/10.1063/5.0178362
55. Tang, W., Gao, Y.: Application solutions of highway freight information systems based on quantum communication. Sci. Rep. **14**(1), 2668 (2024). https://doi.org/10.1038/s41598-024-52987-4, https://www.nature.com/articles/s41598-024-52987-4
56. University of Illinois Urbana-Champaign, Kwiat, P., Chitambar, E., University of Illinois Urbana-Champaign, Conrad, A., University of Illinois Urbana-Champaign, Isaac, S., University of Illinois Urbana-Champaign: Autonomous Vehicle-Based Quantum Communication Network. https://doi.org/10.36501/0197-9191/22-020, https://apps.ict.illinois.edu/projects/getfile.asp?id=10326
57. Vasani, V., Prateek, K., Amin, R., Maity, S., Dwivedi, A.D.: Embracing the quantum frontier: Investigating quantum communication, cryptography, applications and future directions. J. Ind. Inf. Integr. **39**, 100594 (2024). https://doi.org/10.1016/j.jii.2024.100594, https://linkinghub.elsevier.com/retrieve/pii/S2452414X24000384
58. Venegas-Andraca, S.E., Cruz-Santos, W., McGeoch, C., Lanzagorta, M.: A cross-disciplinary introduction to quantum annealing-based algorithms. Contemp. Phys. **59**(2), 174–197 (2018). arXiv:1803.03372 [quant-ph]
59. Villasenor, E.J.S., Fernandes, R.L., Picken, R.: Introduction to quantum mechanics. In: AIP Conference Proceedings, vol. 1023, pp. 107–117. AIP

(2008). https://doi.org/10.1063/1.2958160, http://aip.scitation.org/doi/abs/10.1063/1.2958160https://pubs.aip.org/aip/acp/article/1023/1/107-117/821485
60. Yarkoni, S., Raponi, E., Bäck, T., Schmitt, S.: Quantum annealing for industry applications: introduction and review. Rep. Prog. Phys. **85**(10), 104001 (2022). arXiv:2112.07491 [quant-ph]
61. Ye, C.Q., Li, J., Chen, X.B., Hou, Y., Wang, Z.: Security and application of semi-quantum key distribution protocol for users with different quantum capabilities. EPJ Quantum Technol. **10**(1) (2023). https://doi.org/10.1140/epjqt/s40507-023-00180-3
62. Yi, H., Chi, R., Huang, X., Cai, X., Nie, Z.: Improving Security of Internet of Vehicles Based on Post-quantum Signatures with Systolic Divisions. ACM Trans. Internet Technol. **22**(4), 1–15 (2022). https://doi.org/10.1145/3410445
63. Yin, J., et al.: Space-based quantum communication towards global quantum network. In: 2017 IEEE International Conference on Space Optical Systems and Applications, ICSOS 2017, pp. 299–301 (2018). https://doi.org/10.1109/ICSOS.2017.8357430
64. Yu, Y.: Advancements in applications of quantum entanglement. J. Phys: Conf. Ser. **2012**(1), 012113 (2021). https://doi.org/10.1088/1742-6596/2012/1/012113, https://iopscience.iop.org/article/10.1088/1742-6596/2012/1/012113
65. Yulianti, L.P., Surendro, K.: Implementation of quantum annealing: A systematic review. IEEE Access **10**, 73156–73177 (2022). https://doi.org/10.1109/ACCESS.2022.3188117, https://ieeexplore.ieee.org/document/9813715/
66. Zwick, A., Álvarez, G.A.: Quantum sensing tools to characterize physical, chemical and biological processes with magnetic resonance. J. Magn. Reson. Open **16–17**(2022), 100113 (2023). https://doi.org/10.1016/j.jmro.2023.100113

Hybrid QNN (H-QNN) for Network Intrusion Detection

Shijun Tang(✉)

Department of Computer Science, Schreiner University, Kerrville, TX 78028, USA
STang@schreiner.edu

Abstract. Deep learning has been applied to network intrusion detection. With the advent of quantum technology, quantum neural networks (QNNs) have become the focus of research. Quantum circuits with parameters can extract rich features from raw data. Quantum neural networks (QNNs) are being widely applied to many different areas. This paper proposes a hybrid QNN (H-QNN) model designed for network intrusion detection that capitalizes on the strengths of quantum computing and classical neural networks. Our H-QNN model uses a compact, two-qubit quantum circuit integrated with classical architecture. Our H-QNN model significantly enhances classification accuracy, achieving an ACC of 97.50%, a RE of 87.90%, a PR of 98.71% and a F1 of 97.98% on network intrusion detection. The obtained quantitative results exhibit the generalization of our H-QNN for network intrusion detection tasks. and makes H-QNN a valuable tool for practical applications.

Keywords: Hybrid quantum neural networks · H-QNN · Network intrusion detection · Classification

1 Introduction

In the last decades, neural networks have profoundly influenced various fields by effectively modeling complex patterns and enhancing predictive accuracy. One remarkable domain is cybersecurity, particularly in network intrusion detection, where there are many different models for network intrusion detection, such as, convolutional neural networks (CNNs), long short-term memory (LSTM) networks, hybrid architectures combining CNNs and LSTMs, and transformer-based neural networks that classify incoming packets into distinct categories [1–3].

Traditional approaches have utilized various neural network models for their strong feature extraction capabilities, enabling them to recognize patterns in incoming packets. However, as data complexity and volume continue to rise, these conventional models demand significant computational resources, leading to bottlenecks in processing speed and energy efficiency. Consequently, there is a pressing need for more efficient and resilient computational models. Addressing this challenge requires an innovative approach that harnesses the computational advantages of quantum mechanics.

H. R. Arabnia et al. (Eds.): CSCE 2025, CCIS 2932, pp. 205–213, 2026.
https://doi.org/10.1007/978-3-032-22193-3_15

A couple of recent research papers have explored the application of quantum neural networks in network intrusion detection. For instance, researchers in paper [4] investigated the use of quantum neural networks (QNNs) for intrusion detection, The research demonstrated that QNNs can effectively detect network anomalies, offering a promising direction for enhancing cybersecurity measures with quantum computing technologies.

So, Quantum neural networks (QNNs) have emerged to extend the success of neural networks into the quantum domain. These networks leverage parameterized quantum circuits, which operate through the manipulation of rotation angles, entanglement, and measurement. Rotation angles regulate qubit states, enabling precise control over superposition. Entanglement establishes correlations between qubits, facilitating complex interactions essential for quantum computation. Measurements, typically conduct along specific bases such as the Z-basis, extract information by converting quantum states into classical data. These components work together and dynamically adjust circuit parameters during training, akin to how weights and biases are optimized in classical neural networks.

The fusion of quantum computing with classical machine learning (ML) has led to the emergence of quantum machine learning (QML), an innovative field that leverages quantum principles to enhance computational efficiency. The unique properties of quantum mechanics, including superposition and entanglement, offer a theoretical foundation for uncovering intricate correlations within data. Quantum algorithms, such as Grover's algorithm, harness quantum superposition and interference to accelerate certain computational tasks, particularly unstructured search problems, offering quadratic speedups over classical approaches. The research in paper [5–7] introduced a novel approach that employed Quantum Machine Learning (QML) to enhance security protocols for secure communication between two parties. The study in [8] employed outlier analysis to enhance anomaly detection in network traffic, highlighting the potential of quantum machine learning (QML) in building more effective intrusion detection systems. Quantum machine learning encompasses areas such as quantum reinforcement learning, quantum autoencoders, and quantum algorithms designed to enhance classical machine learning tasks [9]. TensorFlow Quantum (TFQ), an open-source library, was designed for the rapid prototyping of hybrid quantum-classical models [10].

In this paper, a novel network intrusion detection model is introduced, utilizing a hybrid quantum–classical approach. This integration leverages the strengths of both paradigms to overcome the limitations of current quantum hardware while meeting the computational requirements of neural networks.

The main contributions of this work are as follows:

- We developed a two-qubit H-QNN model specifically designed for network intrusion detection. Our proposed model represents a significant advancement in network intrusion detection despite the limited quantum resources available.
- The proposed H-QNN model provides an efficient solution for binary classification of incoming network packets, delivering high accuracy. Additionally, it enhances the model's ability to effectively distinguish between normal and intrusive network traffic, thereby improving overall intrusion detection performance.
- Our H-QNN model combines quantum computing with classical neural networks to optimize computational resources.

2 Methodology

The Hybrid Quantum Neural Network (H-QNN) model integrates classical neural network architecture with quantum computing by replacing one or more layers with quantum circuits. In this design, a quantum circuit functions as a quantum layer within the overall deep neural network structure.

The proposed algorithm of H-QNNs includes:

Data Encoding

- The inputs input_0 and input_1 are encoded into the quantum states using R_X gates.
- The first $R_X(\theta)$ gate in both qubits q_0 and q_1 is a data encoding gate. Its primary purpose is to encode classical input values (like features of a dataset) into quantum states by rotating the qubit around the X-axis of the Bloch sphere.

Parameterized Rotations

- The circuit applies trainable rotations (R_Z, R_Y) on both qubits to introduce variational parameters (weights) that can be optimized.
- The order of R_Z, R_Y, and R_Z gates in the quantum circuit is carefully chosen to achieve full controllability over the qubit state on the Bloch sphere. This combination of rotations provides the circuit with the ability to reach any possible quantum state (a process known as universal single-qubit rotation or arbitrary state preparation).

A single qubit state can be represented on the Bloch sphere by two angles:

$$\theta$$

: The polar angle (latitude) on the Bloch sphere.

$$\phi$$

: The azimuthal angle (longitude) on the Bloch sphere.

Mathematically, the most general single-qubit state can be expressed as:

$$|\psi\rangle = \cos\left(\frac{\theta}{2}\right)|0\rangle + e^{i\phi}\sin\left(\frac{\theta}{2}\right)|1\rangle$$

In order to reach any point on the Bloch sphere, we need rotations that cover both the polar and azimuthal angles, which is why we use a combination of R_Z and R_Y gates in this specific order.

Entanglement

Entanglement allows qubits to be correlated in such a way that the state of one qubit depends on the state of another, even when they are separated by large distances. This phenomenon enables quantum computers to perform certain calculations much faster than classical computers.

- The CNOT gate entangles two qubits, which is a key feature that classical systems cannot replicate. Entanglement allows qubits to share information in ways that are non-classical.
- After applying the CNOT gate, the measurement results of the two qubits become correlated. This correlation is necessary for solving complex problems where the state of one qubit depends on the state of another, which captures feature interactions and helps the circuit learn relationships between input features. The CNOT gate introduces non-classical behavior, making the circuit capable of solving problems that are intractable for classical computers.

Measurement

Measurement is the process of extracting information from a qubit in quantum computing. When a qubit is measured, its superposition collapses, and it takes on a definite state (either 0 or 1) with a certain probability determined by the coefficients of its superposition. Measurement is usually confined to a computational basis, such as the Z-basis. Measurement is typically performed along the Z-axis of the Bloch sphere. This Z-basis measurement determines whether the qubit state collapses to $|0\rangle$ or $|1\rangle$. The final state of the qubits is measured to obtain classical results, which are used for further processing or optimization.

The proposed Hybrid Quantum Neural Network (H-QNN) architecture is shown as Fig. 1. The H-QNN architecture includes angle embedding, strong entangling layers and measurement. The H-QNN is fully connected layers as an input and output. The hidden layer is a quantum layer implemented in PennyLane.

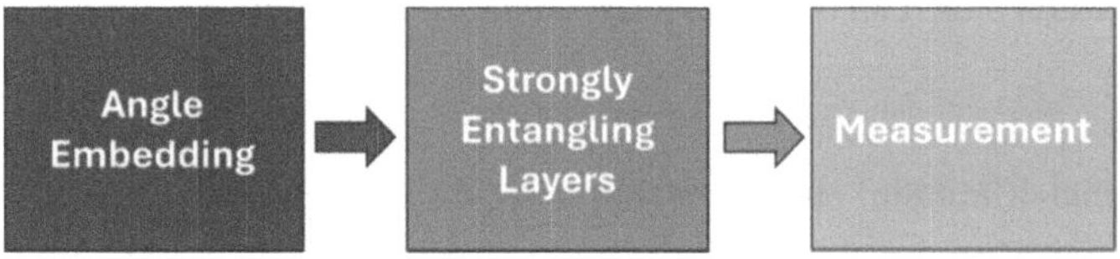

Fig. 1. The schematic diagram of the proposed method

First, angle embedding encodes the data to a quantum state. Then, the strongly entangling layers in the H-QNN model utilize a 2-qubit quantum layer to encode input data into four complex amplitudes, which are then transformed through quantum operations.

In angle embedding, as shown in Fig. 2, each qubit is processed using a rotation gate. By default, this is a rotation around the X-axis which we retain. This step requires two input parameters that define the rotation angles for the gates. To ensure full coverage of the qubit state space, we scale the inputs by π. These inputs fall within the range of (-1, +1), as they originate from the previous layer, which uses a sigmoid activation function.

In Strongly Entangling Layers, as shown in Fig. 3, there are 3 rotations around z, y and z axis respectively. At the end, we have CNOT gates in both possible ways on 2 qubits.

In measurement stage, we use expectation values in Z basis. This is the most common method, which is just the sum of probabilities of measuring, given qubit in a state $|1>$ with

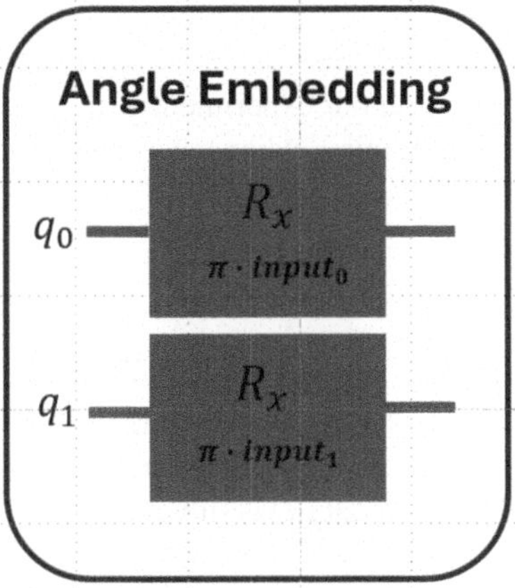

Fig. 2. The schematic diagram of angle embedding

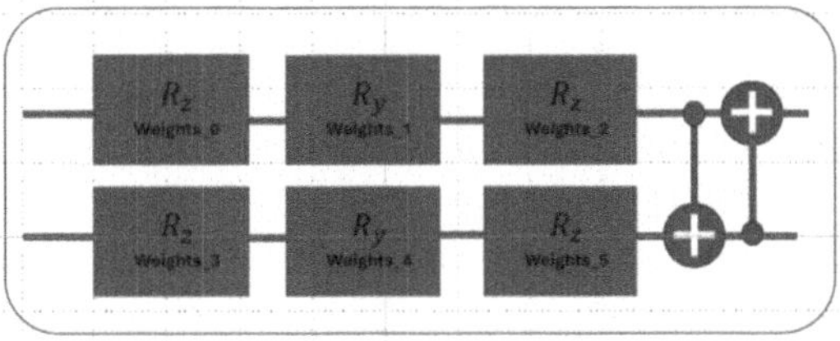

Fig. 3. The schematic diagram of strongly entangling layers

coefficient - 1 and in a state |0 > with coefficient 1. We'll get two numbers between the range (-1, +1) as an output.

The quantum layer is schematically shown as Fig. 4:

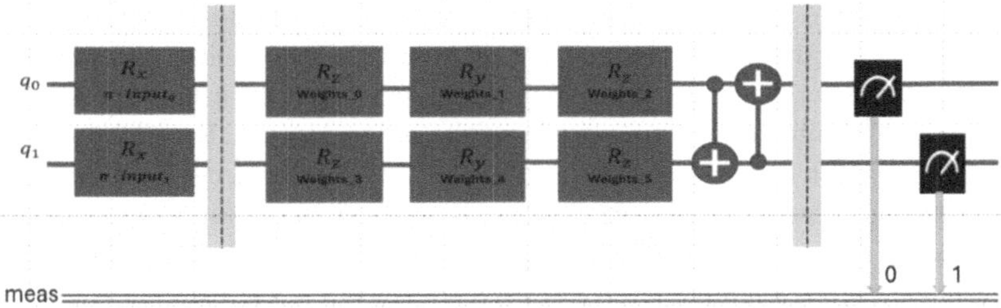

Fig. 4. The proposed model consists of three key components: angle embedding, strongly entangling layers, and a final measurement stage.

3 Experimental Results

There are several stages involved in our experiments, such as, splitting the dataset, creating H-QNN model and model training, when we use the H-QNN model to implement network intrusion detection.

3.1 Datasets

Under the sponsorship of Defense Advanced Research Projects Agency (DARPA) and Air Force Research Laboratory (AFRL), MIT Lincoln laboratory has collected and distributed the datasets for the evaluation of research in computer network intrusion detection systems. The KDD Cup 99 dataset is subsets of the DARPA benchmark dataset [11, 12]. The NSL-KDD dataset [13, 14] is a new version of the KDD Cup 99 dataset. The NSL-KDD dataset improves some of the limitations of the KDD Cup 99 dataset. All the attacks in the dataset fall into four major categories, namely, Denial of Service (Dos), Probing (Probe), Remote to Local (R2L) and User to Root (U2R).

3.2 Training dataset and test dataset

The experimental data is split in to training data and test data. The training and test dataset contain normal and abnormal categories. There are DoS attack, Probe attack, R2L attack and U2R attack in abnormal category. We use the training and test dataset to train and test the proposed model.

The proposed H-QNN can be tailored to the specific characteristics of a network and its traffic patterns by adjusting key parameters, such as the number of layers and the batch size.

3.3 Performance Evaluation

We carry out a set of experimental evaluations to provide a deep analysis of the performance of the proposed model. In machine learning and data mining algorithms, many different metrics are used to evaluate classification models. In this paper, we use four metrics to evaluate the performance of the proposed H-QNN model: accuracy, recall, precision, F1. Accuracy is the proportion of correctly classified network intrusions, which reflects the consistency between test results and real results. Recall focuses on the ability to capture all actual positive cases. Precision reflects the accuracy of the positive predictions made by the model. The F1 score is a robust metric for evaluating classification models, particularly in the presence of class imbalance. By balancing precision and recall, it provides a comprehensive measure of a model's effectiveness in identifying true positive cases while minimizing both false positives and false negatives

$$ACC(accuracy) = \frac{TP + TN}{TP + TN + FP + FN}$$

$$RE(recall) = \frac{TP}{TP + FN}$$

$$PR(precision) = \frac{TP}{TP + FP}$$

$$F1(F1\ Score) = \frac{2 * PR * RE}{PR + RE}$$

where TP is true positives, TN is true negatives, FP is false positives and FN is false negatives.

3.4 Results

In this paper, we propose a H-QNN model to make network intrusion classification. We preprocess the training and test data formats and train the H-QNN model. Performance measures of the model are evaluated in Table 1. The validity of the H-QNN model is verified on the dataset that we used. From Table 1, it can be observed that the H-QNN model achieves an ACC of 97.50%, a RE of 87.90%, a PR of 98.71% and a F1 of 97.98%. Performance metrics of H-QNN model is also shown in Fig. 5, which demonstrates that H-QNN model has very good anomaly detection.

Table 1. Performance measures of H-QNN model for network intrusion classification

ACC(%)	RE(%)	PR(%)	F1(%)
97.50	87.90	98.71	97.98

The results presented in Table 1 provide clear insight into the performance of the Hybrid Quantum Neural Network (H-QNN) model in the context of network intrusion detection. This novel approach effectively overcomes the limitations and shortcomings commonly observed in traditional methods, offering a more resilient and accurate classification framework. The strong performance of the model highlights its ability to capture intricate patterns within network traffic sequences, reinforcing its potential as a powerful tool for distinguishing between normal and abnormal network flows.

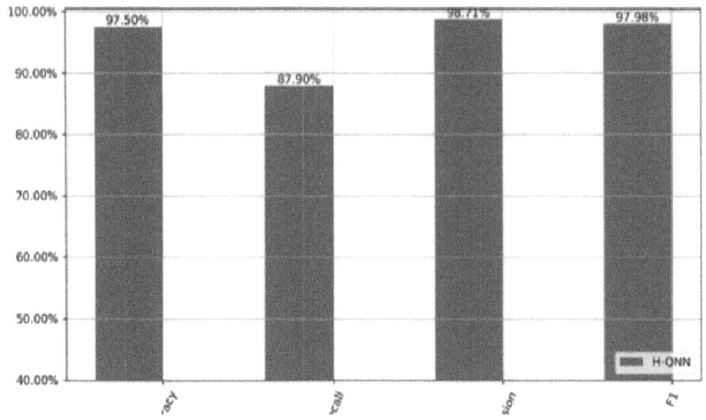

Fig. 5. Performance metrics of H-QNN model for network intrusion classification

4 Conclusions

In this paper, we present a Hybrid Quantum Neural Network (H-QNN) model designed to detect both normal and abnormal network traffic. The NSL-KDD dataset is employed to train and test the proposed model in the experiments. Each instance in the NSL-KDD dataset represents distinct characteristics of network traffic, allowing for effective learning and classification.

Experimental results demonstrate that the H-QNN model achieves an accuracy of 97.50%, recall of 87.90%, precision of 98.71%, and an F1-score of 97.98%. These metrics highlight the model's strong predictive capability—especially its exceptional precision and high F1-score—making it a reliable and robust solution for tasks demanding both high accuracy and low false positives.

The proposed H-QNN model offers continuous intrusion recognition and classification, showcasing the potential of integrating quantum computing with artificial intelligence in the field of cybersecurity. This work lays a foundation for further exploration of quantum neural network methods to address emerging challenges in network security.

References

1. Sinha, P., Sahu, D., Prakash, S., Yang, T., Singh Rathore, R., Kumar Pandey, V.: A high performance hybrid LSTM CNN secure architecture for IoT environments using deep learning. Sci. Rep. **15**, 9684 (2025)
2. Tang, S.: Network intrusion detection based on transformer model. In: The 23rd International Conference on Security & Management (SAM'24) (2024)
3. Sami Ataa, M., Sanad, E.E., El-khoribi, R.A.: Intrusion detection in software defined network using deep learning approaches. Sci. Rep. **14**, 29159 (2024)
4. Kukliansky, A., Orescanin, M., Bollmann, C., Huffmire, T.: Network anomaly detection using quantum neural networks on Noisy quantum computers, IEEE transactions on quantum. Engineering. **5**, 1–11 (2024)
5. Hoon, K.T., Madhavi, S.: Quantum intrusion detection system using outlier analysis. Sci. Rep. **14**(1), 27114 (2024)

6. Zhao, C., Gao, X.-S.: QDNN: DNN with quantum neural network layers (2020). https://arxiv.org/abs/1912.12660
7. Payares, E.D., Martinez-Santos, J.C.: Quantum machine learning for intrusion detection of distributed denial of service attacks: a comparative overview. In: Proc. SPIE 11699, Quantum Computing, Communication, and Simulation, 116990B (2021). https://doi.org/10.1117/12.2593297
8. Lamata, L.: Quantum Machine Learning Implementations: Proposals and Experiments. Advanced Quantum Technologies, Wiley Online Library (2023)
9. Mishra, N., et al.: Quantum machine learning: a review and current status. In: Proceedings of ICDMAI 2020, vol. 2, pp. 101–145. Springer (2021)
10. Lamata, L.: Quantum machine learning implementations: proposals and experiments (2023). https://arxiv.org/abs/2303.06263
11. Lee, W.: A Data Mining Framework for Constructing Features and Models for Intrusion Detection Systems. Ph.D. thesis,. Columbia University, USA (1999)
12. Lee, W., Stolfo, S.: A framework for constructing features and models for intrusion detection systems. Trans. Inf. Syst. Sec. (TISSEC). **3**(4), 227–261 (2000)
13. Tavallaee, M., Bagheri, E., Lu, W., Ghorbani, A.A.: A detailed analysis of the KDD CUP 99 data set. In: 2009 IEEE Symposium on Computational Intelligence for Security and Defense Applications, CISDA, pp. 1–6. IEEE (Jul 2009)
14. Moustafa, N., Slay, J.: UNSW-NB15: a comprehensive data set for network intrusion detection systems (UNSW-NB15 network data set). In: 2015 Military Communications and Information Systems Conference (MilCIS) (2015)

MSV'25: 22nd International Conference on Modeling, Simulation and Visualization Methods

Predicting Trends in Domain Name Registrations Using a VAR Model

Takaharu Ui[1(✉)], Shota Ikehara[2], Kentaro Mori[2], Akihiro Kaneko[2], and Hiroo Hirose[1]

[1] Suwa University of Science, 5000-1 Toyohira, Chino-shi, Nagano 391-0292, Japan
ui@jprs.co.jp

[2] Japan Registry Services Co., Ltd., 3-8-1 Nishi-Kanda, Chiyoda-ku, Tokyo 101-0065, Japan

Abstract. This study proposes a method for forecasting domain name registration trends under country-code top-level domains (ccTLDs) using socio-economic indicators specific to each country and a Vector Autoregressive (VAR) model. We focused on 11 publicly available indicators and evaluated several dimensionality reduction techniques to address strong multicollinearity. Experiments using JP domain name data demonstrated that feature selection alone is insufficient, while Principal Component Analysis (PCA) effectively reduced dimensionality and improved forecast accuracy. Our results highlight the relationship between economic conditions and domain registration trends, offering insights that support sustainable registry management. Furthermore, the proposed approach enables objective forecasting without relying on confidential registry data. Applying the same framework to other ccTLDs may also facilitate cross-country comparative analysis.

Keywords: Domain name · Stable Internet operation · Vector autoregression model · Time series analysis · Multicollinearity · Dimensionality reduction

1 Introduction

Domain names, IP addresses, and the Domain Name System (DNS) which functions as the mechanism linking the two have been essential components of the Internet's infrastructure since its inception [1–3]. Communication on the Internet relies heavily on these core components of the naming and addressing system. The management of domain names and IP addresses is organized in a hierarchical structure headed by the Internet Corporation for Assigned Names and Numbers (ICANN), which plays a vital role in Internet administration [4, 5].

Because IP addresses are a finite Internet resource, their distribution must be handled fairly [6]. Accordingly, organizations known as IP address registries—responsible for managing allocations at the continental, national, or regional levels—are typically non-profit entities.

In contrast, domain name registries, which are responsible for the management of the domain names, have developed within a competitive environment due to the increasing commercial value of domain names. Although some domain name registries are operated

H. R. Arabnia et al. (Eds.): CSCE 2025, CCIS 2932, pp. 217–233, 2026.
https://doi.org/10.1007/978-3-032-22193-3_16

by non-profit or governmental organizations, they are still often expected to operate in a business-like, competitive environment.

Domain name registries are expected not only to offer impartial and neutral services but also to ensure user convenience. More importantly, they must maintain stable and continuous services despite operating in competitive conditions.

DNS maps domain names to IP addresses used for Internet communication. If DNS fails, access via domain names becomes impossible. A failure in the DNS of a Top-Level Domain (TLD) operated by a registry disables access to all domain names under that TLD. This has a significant impact on Internet society, especially in today's world where many social and economic systems are dependent on the Internet.

From the perspective of operational continuity, the business failure of a domain name registry—and the resulting suspension or termination of services—poses a serious social risk. It is therefore essential for domain name registries to develop long-term investment and infrastructure strategies that ensure sustained service stability as Internet reliance continues to grow.

Domain name registry operations are typically funded by registration and renewal fees. A domain name is usually registered with a one-time initial fee and subsequently renewed on an annual basis. For long-term planning, it is crucial to forecast future changes in registration volume. The total number of active domain names depends on both the number of new registrations and how long they are retained.

From a micro perspective, these trends are influenced by factors such as the regional situation, the services offered by the registry, the types of domain names, and typical renewal behaviors. From a macro perspective, on the other hand, they reflect broader trends such as social development and the expansion of Internet use within the region.

While many domain name registries likely perform internal forecasting, few publish their methodologies as academic research. Case studies from more advanced Internet economies may offer valuable insights for forecasting in emerging regions. Publishing such work contributes to the academic understanding of digital infrastructure development.

2 Prior Research and Significance of this Study

Prior work by us has addressed the forecasting of domain name registration trends [7]. That research adopted a cohort analysis approach, in which the set of newly registered domain names in each month is treated as a cohort. By using the number of new registrations each month and the renewal rate one year later, a time-series forecasting method was proposed based on the SARIMA (Seasonal AutoRegressive Integrated Moving Average) model [8–10], which accounts for seasonality in the data. The method was applied to JP domain names as a case study, and the model achieved high predictive accuracy.

However, detailed data as mentioned above, while often available to domain name registries themselves, are rarely disclosed to external parties. For this reason, forecasting methods based on cohort analysis are, in practice, applicable only to domain names managed by the registry itself and are difficult to use from the perspective of external third parties.

Being able to forecast the number of domain names is undoubtedly valuable for registry managing the domain names. At the same time, if registration trends could be predicted using only publicly available information—without relying on privileged internal data held exclusively by the registries—it would become possible for third parties to make independent forecasts as well.

In this regard, a prior study by Kamimura conducted statistical analysis across multiple ccTLDs and showed that domain name registration volumes are influenced by socio-economic factors such as population size, GDP, and Internet penetration rates [11]. Many other studies have also examined the relationship between economic growth trends and Internet usage [12–14].

In this study, we propose a method forecasting domain name registration trends by using publicly available socio-economic indicators, which are published by many countries, to forecast domain name registration trends.

By combining historical registration data and readily accessible socio-economic indicators of each country, the proposed approach enables objective forecasting of domain name registrations even in the absence of detailed internal data on registration and renewal activities held only by registries.

Moreover, since socio-economic indicators are calculated and published using standardized methodologies across different countries, this approach allows for comparative studies of domain name registrations on a global scale. Given that both economic and Internet development vary by country—and that disparities in timing between early and late adopters exist—this method offers a meaningful framework not only for predicting domain registration trends but also for gaining insights into the associated economic conditions.

3 Model Construction and Experimental Method

3.1 Adoption of VAR Model

Forecasting the number of domain name registrations requires modeling not only temporal trends but also the effects of various interrelated factors that evolve over time. In many cases, univariate models such as ARIMA (AutoRegressive Integrated Moving Average) are used for time-series forecasting due to their effectiveness in capturing autocorrelation, seasonality, and trend components within a single variable [8]. However, ARIMA models do not incorporate information from other relevant variables, making them unsuitable when the target variable is influenced by a complex set of interacting external indicators, such as those found in economic or demographic data.

Given the influence of socio-economic indicators such as GDP, Internet penetration, and population on domain name registration volumes—as established in prior research—a multivariate approach is essential for forecasting their trends. For this reason, we adopt the Vector Autoregressive (VAR) model [15–17], which is capable of modeling dynamic relationships among multiple time series. Unlike ARIMA, which is limited to the internal structure of a single variable, VAR allows each variable in the system to be a function of the past values (lags) of all variables in the model, including itself. This makes it particularly well-suited for domains like macroeconomics or Internet infrastructure, where inter-variable dependencies are common [18–20].

A general VAR model can be expressed as follows:

$$Y_t = C + A_1 Y_{t-1} + A_2 Y_{t-2} + \cdots + A_p Y_{t-p} + \epsilon_t, \tag{1}$$

where, Y_t is a vector of time-series variables (e.g., 'GDP', 'population'), C is a vector of constants, $A_1 A_2 \cdots A_p$ are matrices of coefficients corresponding to lagged variables, and ϵ_t represents the error term.

The strength of the VAR model lies in its ability to capture mutual influences and temporal feedback effects among the involved variables. For example, a rise in Internet penetration may lead to an increase in domain name registrations, which in turn may reflect or influence broader trends in GDP or digital infrastructure investments.

However, the VAR model also requires careful consideration regarding data volume and model complexity. Since it includes lagged terms for each variable, the number of parameters to estimate increases rapidly with the number of variables and the lag order. This makes dimensionality reduction and multicollinearity management important concerns, which are addressed later in our methodology through techniques such as feature selection and Principal Component Analysis (PCA) [21, 22].

In summary, the VAR model is adopted in this study as it provides a comprehensive and flexible framework for modeling the joint evolution of domain registrations and related socio-economic indicators. Compared to univariate approaches like ARIMA, VAR enables a more realistic and explanatory modeling of how national-level economic trends influence domain name registration dynamics over time.

3.2 Socio-Economic Indicators Used as Features for Forecasting

From the set of publicly available socio-economic indicators across many countries, we selected 11 indicators that are considered to be correlated with the number of domain name registrations. These indicators were used as feature variables for the prediction task:

1. population (population size):

   A fundamental metric indicating the potential scale of Internet users and domain registrations. A larger population typically leads to increased demand for Internet and digital services, thereby influencing domain registration counts.

2. GDP (Gross Domestic Product):

   An essential indicator of the overall economic size of a country, relevant for understanding the economic backdrop for domain registration trends. Countries with higher 'GDP' tend to see more active Internet and online business development.

3. perGDP (per capita GDP):

   Reflects the average income level of citizens and represents the economic capacity of individuals or organizations to purchase and maintain domains.

4. internet (Internet penetration rate):

   Indicates the proportion of the population with access to the Internet. Greater 'internet' usage is expected to correlate directly with increased domain registrations.

5. phone (mobile phone penetration rate):

Serves as a proxy for the adoption of digital communication technologies. In countries with widespread mobile Internet use, the need for an online presence is greater, potentially boosting domain demand.

6. pdensity (population density):

Captures the degree of urbanization and infrastructure concentration. Areas with higher 'pdensity' typically have better Internet access, which may affect domain registration behavior.

7. GNI (Gross National Income):

Reflects the overall national income and purchasing power. Countries with higher 'GNI' allow for greater investment in Internet presence by both businesses and individuals.

8. unprate (unemployment rate):

An indicator of labor market conditions and economic stability. Higher 'unprate' may hinder entrepreneurship and new business activity, potentially reducing domain registrations.

9. pbalance (current account balance):

Measures a country's international economic activity, including trade and capital flows. A healthy 'pbalance' is often associated with more active business operations online.

10. perGNI (per capita GNI):

Indicates average individual income and reflects financial capacity for Internet-related spending, which may influence individual-level domain demand.

11. perpbalance (per capita current account balance):

Shows how international economic activity affects individuals. In countries with high 'perpbalance', online presence tends to be emphasized, potentially impacting domain registrations.

3.3 Time Series Data and Experimental Design

This study focuses on forecasting the trend of JP domain name registrations.

For the time-series data used in prediction, we collected:

- Historical JP domain registration counts from 2003 to 2024 as the target variable [23].
- Annual data for the 11 socio-economic indicators from 2003 to 2023 as feature variables [24].

The experimental procedure involved the following steps:

- Use data from 2003 to 2016 as the training set.
- Apply the VAR model to forecast values from 2017 to 2034.

- Evaluate the predictions from 2017 to 2024—where actual data are available—by calculating the Mean Absolute Percentage Error (MAPE).

We employed Mean Absolute Percentage Error (MAPE) as the primary evaluation metric for forecast accuracy in this study. MAPE expresses the prediction error as a percentage of the actual values, which makes it scale-independent and easily interpretable across different datasets. This is particularly advantageous in our context, where the magnitude of domain name registrations varies over time and may differ substantially across countries.

Additionally, MAPE is widely used in forecasting research and practice due to its intuitive appeal, allowing stakeholders to understand the accuracy in percentage terms without requiring technical background. Given that our objective is to evaluate the general predictive performance of different variable selection and dimensionality reduction methods under the VAR framework, MAPE offers a straightforward and comparable measure across models and experiments [25, 26].

4 Experiment 1: Forecasting Using 11 Socio-Economic Indicators

The results of the prediction of JP domain name registration trends using the VAR model with all 11 socio-economic indicators as features are shown in Fig. 1.

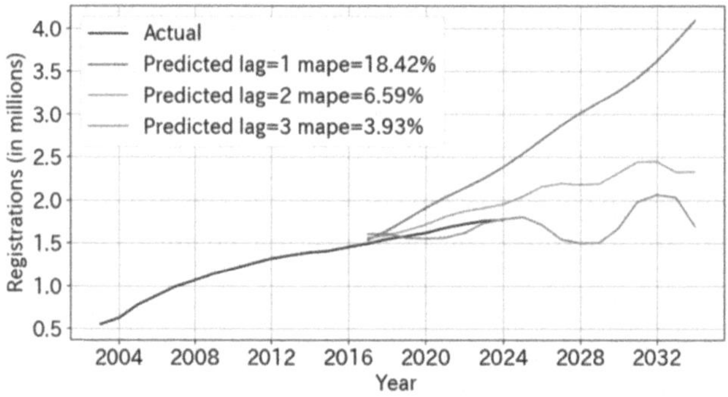

Fig. 1. Prediction using the VAR model with 11 indicators

As shown in Fig. 1, the forecast curves vary significantly depending on the lag order of the VAR model. The actual trend of JP domain name registrations generally follows a logarithmic growth pattern. However, the prediction curve with lag = 1 shows an exponential growth trend, diverging notably from the actual values, with MAPE of 18.42%.

In contrast, the lowest MAPE value of 3.93% was obtained when lag = 3. Nevertheless, the predicted curve exhibits large fluctuations, similar to that of lag = 2, and neither of these curves closely follows the actual trend. Thus, it is difficult to conclude that these results represent accurate forecasts.

These results suggest two potential issues:

1. The use of all 11 indicators may have introduced substantial noise, resulting in a model that captures spurious correlations.
2. There may be multicollinearity among the features, which can lead to overfitting in VAR models.

In the following steps, we attempt to improve predictive performance by applying dimensionality reduction techniques using multiple methods.

5 Experiment 2: Feature Selection Considering Multicollinearity

5.1 2–1: Selection of Significant Features Via Multiple Linear Regression

A multiple linear regression analysis was conducted using the 11 socio-economic indicators as explanatory variables and the number of domain name registrations as the dependent variable. The result yielded a very high R-squared value of 0.988, indicating that the explanatory variables collectively provide an excellent fit to the target variable. R-squared, or the coefficient of determination, measures the proportion of variance in the dependent variable that is explained by the model. A value close to 1.0 suggests that the model captures most of the variability in the data.

Furthermore, the F-statistic for the overall regression was associated with a P-value of 4.21e-10, confirming that the model is statistically significant as a whole. The F-statistic tests whether at least one of the explanatory variables meaningfully contributes to explaining the variance in the dependent variable, and a very small P-value indicates that the observed relationship is highly unlikely to have occurred by chance.

However, the Condition Number of the design matrix was extremely high at 2.84e+16, strongly suggesting the presence of multicollinearity among the explanatory variables, which can inflate variance and destabilize coefficient estimates [27].

Table 1 summarizes the P-values for each explanatory variable.

In general, in multiple regression analysis, variables with a P-value below 0.05 are considered to have a statistically significant impact on the dependent variable. According to Table 1, only 'phone' meets this criterion. However, based on the overall distribution of P-values, we also judged that 'GDP', 'perGDP', and 'internet' have a meaningful influence on the dependent variable.

We therefore selected these four variables— 'phone', 'GDP', 'perGDP', and 'internet'—as significant features and used them for a new VAR model to predict JP domain name registrations. The results are shown in Fig. 2. (Note: The prediction curve for lag = 2 was omitted due to extreme oscillations that exceeded the displayable range.)

The overall shape of the forecast curve aligns well with the actual trend. This suggests that extracting only the explanatory variables with significant influence helped eliminate noise components. On the other hand, the appearance of large oscillations when lag ≥ 2 implies potential overfitting caused by multicollinearity among the selected features.

Since multicollinearity between explanatory variables cannot be fully eliminated by P-value-based evaluation alone, additional methods must be considered.

Table 1. P-values for each explanatory variable

Feature	t	P > |t|
const	−0.023	0.982
population	0.021	0.984
GDP	1.918	0.079
perGDP	−1.913	0.080
internet	1.903	0.081
phone	2.977	0.012
pdensity	−0.023	0.982
GNI	−1.247	0.236
unprate	0.952	0.360
pbalance	−0.189	0.853
perGNI	1.271	0.228
perpbalance	0.196	0.848

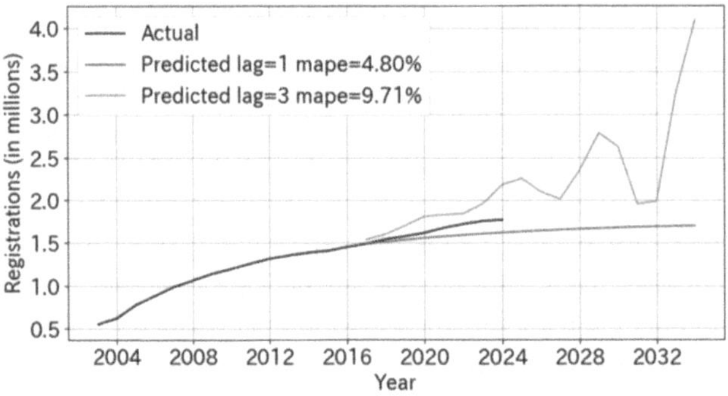

Fig. 2. Prediction using selected significant features via Multiple Linear Regression

5.2 2–2: Feature Selection Based on Multicollinearity Diagnostics

Multicollinearity refers to a condition in regression analysis where explanatory variables are strongly correlated with each other. To investigate multicollinearity among the 11 indicators, we computed their correlation matrix [28], as shown in Table 2.

From this matrix, we identified variable pairs with high correlation coefficients (≥ 0.9). To eliminate these dependencies, we removed one variable from each highly correlated pair. Specifically, we excluded the variables that appeared on the vertical axis: ‘perGDP’, ‘pdensity’, ‘perGNI’, and ‘perpbalance’. This left us with 7 remaining variables.

To further check for multicollinearity among the remaining 7 indicators, we calculated the Variance Inflation Factor (VIF), as shown in Table 3.

Table 2. Correlation matrix of the 11 explanatory variables

	1	2	3	4	5	6	7	8	9	10	11
1. population	1.000	0.531	0.474	-0.472	-0.896	0.999	0.316	0.766	-0.180	0.228	-0.209
2. GDP	0.531	1.000	0.997	0.015	-0.285	0.531	0.754	0.421	-0.248	0.720	-0.260
3. perGDP	0.474	0.997	1.000	0.054	-0.226	0.474	0.759	0.376	-0.242	0.731	-0.253
4. internet	-0.472	0.015	0.054	1.000	0.778	-0.473	0.168	-0.752	-0.048	0.218	-0.034
5. phone	-0.896	-0.285	-0.226	0.778	1.000	-0.898	-0.083	-0.885	0.068	0.001	0.095
6. pdensity	0.999	0.531	0.474	-0.473	-0.898	1.000	0.314	0.768	-0.177	0.225	-0.206
7. GNI	0.316	0.754	0.759	0.168	-0.083	0.314	1.000	0.202	-0.616	0.995	-0.622
8. unprate	0.766	0.421	0.376	-0.752	-0.885	0.768	0.202	1.000	-0.160	0.131	-0.181
9. pbalance	-0.180	-0.248	-0.242	-0.048	0.068	-0.177	-0.616	-0.160	1.000	-0.617	0.999
10. perGNI	0.228	0.720	0.731	0.218	0.001	0.225	0.995	0.131	-0.617	1.000	-0.620
11. perpbalance	-0.209	-0.260	-0.253	-0.034	0.095	-0.206	-0.622	-0.181	0.999	-0.620	1.000

Table 3. VIF values for 7 explanatory variables

Feature	VIF
population	609.569051
GDP	4.037708
internet	3.955024
phone	4.884636
GNI	4.711627
unprate	6.848410
pbalance	2.114877

In general, a VIF value above 5 or 10 is considered indicative of problematic multicollinearity. In our results, 'population' (population size) exhibited a particularly large VIF value, and thus we excluded it as well.

With the remaining 6 explanatory variables, we applied the VAR model again to predict JP domain name registrations. The results are shown in Fig. 3.

The prediction with lag = 1 achieved a high accuracy with MAPE = 1.88%, but for lag ≥2, the predicted curves deviated significantly from the actual data.

To reconfirm the multicollinearity among the final set of six explanatory variables, we again computed their VIF values, shown in Table 4. Despite excluding the previously identified multicollinear variables, the results still suggest the presence of strong multicollinearity among the remaining features.

In the next experiment, we explore dimensionality reduction techniques to avoid the effects of multicollinearity.

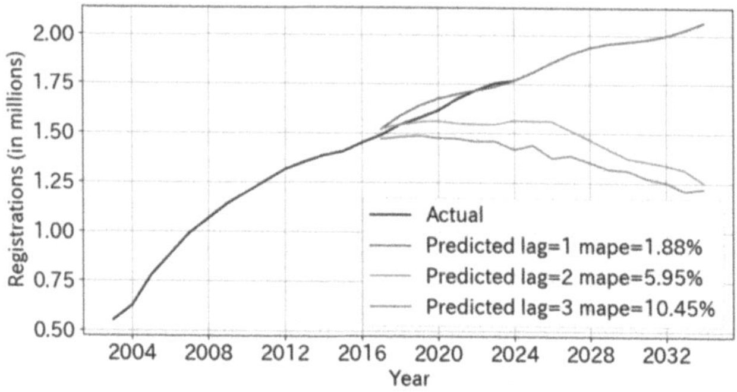

Fig. 3. Prediction after removing features with multicollinearity

Table 4. VIF values for the final 6 explanatory variables

Feature	VIF
GDP	281.215362
internet	168.068950
phone	56.268741
GNI	390.769220
unprate	55.290928
pbalance	11.455180

6 Experiment 3: Feature Selection to Avoid Multicollinearity

6.1 3–1: Feature Selection Based on Random Forest Feature Importance

Random Forest is an ensemble learning method composed of a large number of decision trees [29–31]. Due to its structure, it is relatively robust to multicollinearity among input features and less susceptible to overfitting caused by redundant information. Leveraging this robustness, we applied Random Forest not only as a predictive model but also as a tool for feature importance evaluation to support dimensionality reduction.

The importance scores for the 11 socio-economic indicators were calculated using Random Forest, and the results are shown in Fig. 4.

Based on the distribution of importance values, we selected two feature sets for further prediction using the VAR model:

- A three-variable set including the most important indicators: 'pdensity', 'population', and 'phone'.
- A five-variable set, which adds the next most important indicators: 'unprate' and 'internet'.

The prediction results using these two sets of features are shown in Fig. 5 and 6, respectively.

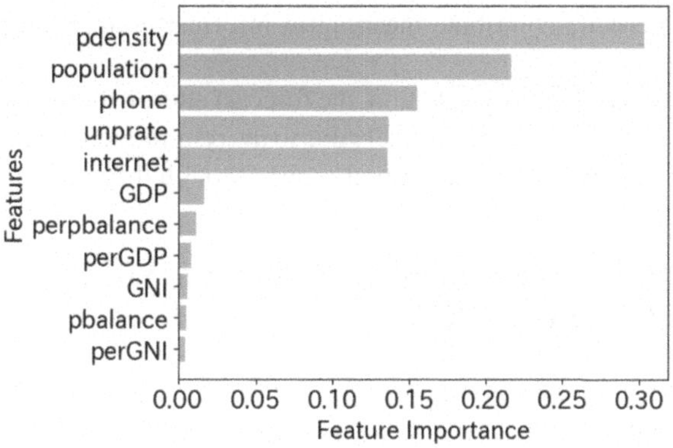

Fig. 4. Prediction using the top 5 features by importance

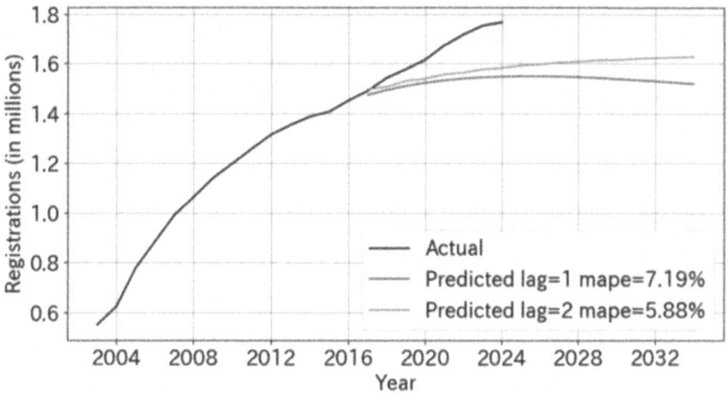

Fig. 5. Prediction using the top 3 features by importance

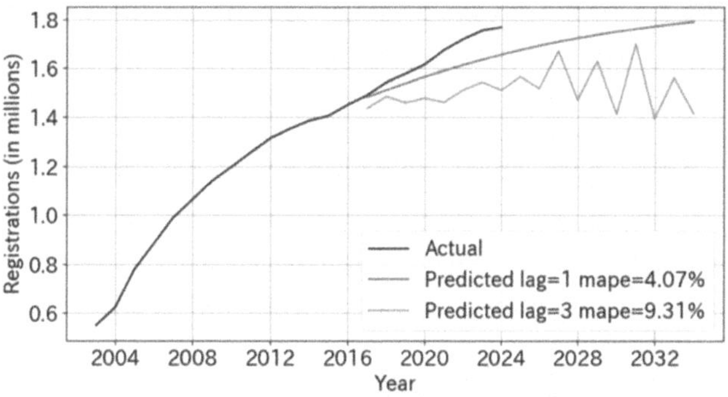

Fig. 6. Feature importance scores derived from Random Forest

When comparing the two results, the prediction using only the three most important features yielded a smooth forecast curve, but its MAPE-based accuracy was inferior to that of the prediction using five features. This suggests that the two additional variables ('unprate' and 'internet') contribute meaningful information that improves prediction accuracy.

However, in the five-feature prediction, the forecast curve exhibits increasing oscillations as the lag order increases. This is likely due to the reintroduction of multicollinearity effects caused by adding additional features—even though they are informative.

7 Experiment 4: Dimensionality Reduction Via Principal Component Analysis (PCA)

Unlike previous feature selection approaches, Principal Component Analysis (PCA) reduces dimensionality by transforming a set of correlated variables into a smaller number of uncorrelated variables known as principal components. In this transformation, the original explanatory variables are projected onto orthogonal axes, thereby eliminating multicollinearity [21, 22].

The number of principal components to retain is determined based on the cumulative contribution ratio (explained variance). Figure 7 shows the cumulative contribution ratio derived from applying PCA to the 11 explanatory variables in this study.

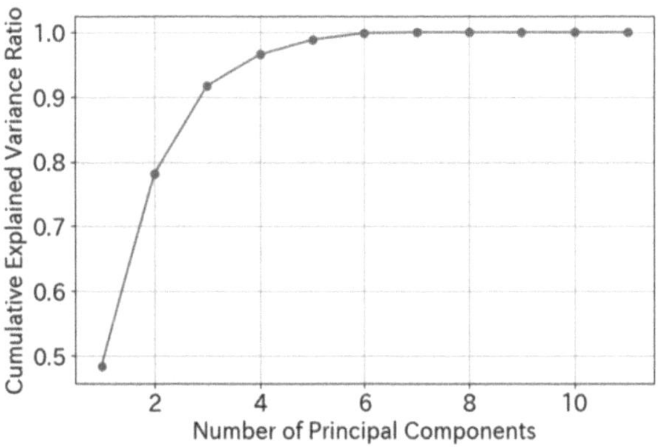

Fig. 7. Cumulative contribution ratio of PCA components

For this analysis, we retained principal components that together explained at least 90% of the total variance. As a result, the first three principal components were selected for use in the VAR model.

Using these three components, we performed a prediction of JP domain name registration trends via the VAR model. The results are shown in Fig. 8.

Because PCA eliminates multicollinearity, the resulting forecast curves no longer exhibit the oscillatory behavior seen in previous experiments. Additionally, the MAPE values indicate high predictive accuracy, suggesting that PCA-based dimensionality reduction is effective for this task.

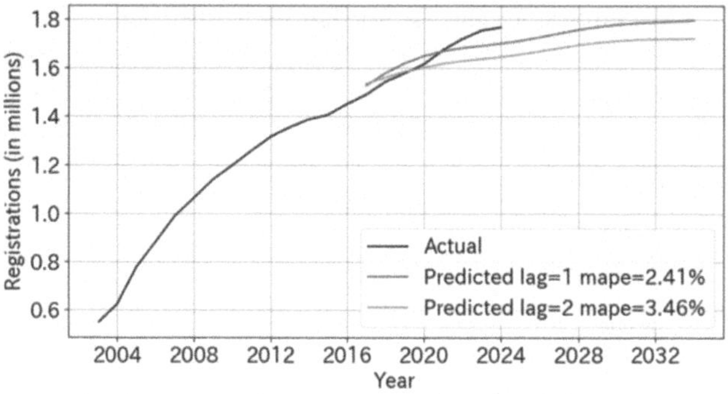

Fig. 8. Prediction using top 3 PCA components

8 Discussion

The 11 socio-economic indicators used in this study exhibit substantial multicollinearity among each other. This was clearly observed in the results of Experiment 2–2, where the correlation matrix and VIF analysis both revealed strong dependencies among the variables, making feature selection a non-trivial task.

Table 5 summarizes which of the 11 features were selected in each experiment. The selection tendencies vary depending on the method employed. This is likely because when one feature is emphasized, the high correlation with other features suppresses their evaluated importance, which manifests as differences in feature selection order across methods. This highlights the methodological sensitivity of multivariate time-series forecasting when dealing with interdependent economic variables.

Forecasting with the VAR model involves estimating a large number of parameters, as each variable depends on the lagged values of all other variables. As the lag order increases, the required volume of data grows rapidly. Moreover, using highly collinear time series in VAR models increases the risk of noise amplification and overfitting, which can significantly reduce the model's generalization performance and predictive robustness.

In this context, dimensionality reduction becomes a critical strategy. In Experiment 3–1, using five features improved accuracy compared to the three-feature case but also caused greater oscillations at higher lag orders. This likely reflects the fact that Random Forest handles multicollinearity well, but the VAR model does not. Consequently, even features with high importance in Random Forest may reintroduce multicollinearity in VAR, reducing stability. This illustrates a methodological mismatch between machine learning-based feature selection and statistical time-series modeling [19, 30].

PCA-based dimensionality reduction, as employed in Experiment 4, successfully eliminated multicollinearity that earlier variable selection methods could not fully resolve. By transforming the original variables into a set of orthogonal principal components, PCA preserved the variance structure relevant to prediction while discarding redundant or overlapping information. This contributed to improved prediction accuracy and curve stability in the VAR model forecasts.

Table 5. Features selected for each experiment

Feature	1	2–1	2–2	3–1
population	○			○
GDP	○	○	○	
perGDP	○	○		
internet	○	○	○	○
phone	○	○	○	○
pdensity	○			○
GNI	○		○	
unprate	○		○	○
pbalance	○		○	
perGNI	○			
perpbalance	○			

Importantly, the empirical findings also suggest theoretical implications regarding the relationship between national-level economic development and digital infrastructure growth. The fact that domain name registration trends could be modeled effectively using macroeconomic indicators such as GDP, population, and Internet penetration implies that the demand for domain names is not merely a result of technological diffusion, but is deeply rooted in broader economic and social dynamics. Domain registrations may thus serve as a proxy indicator of digital transformation, entrepreneurial activity, and online market expansion within a country.

Table 6 compares the MAPE values obtained across all experiments. The lowest MAPE was achieved in Experiment 2–2, where multicollinearity was addressed through correlation- and VIF-based feature exclusion. This was followed closely by Experiment 4, which used PCA to reduce dimensionality.

However, these results must be interpreted with caution. In Experiment 2–2, although multicollinearity was mitigated, VIF analysis still suggested the presence of residual multicollinearity among the selected variables. Furthermore, since the study focused exclusively on JP domain names—a ccTLD associated with Japan—the high prediction accuracy may reflect a coincidental alignment between Japan's economic structure and its domain usage patterns. Thus, the generalizability of the proposed method requires further validation.

To that end, future studies should explore applying the same framework to other ccTLDs with different economic and technological contexts, where domain adoption rates and digital strategies may differ significantly. Fortunately, many socio-economic indicators used in this study are available globally through standardized datasets from organizations such as the World Bank or ITU. This opens the possibility of conducting cross-national comparative analyses on domain name growth, which could reveal new insights into the role of economic policy, infrastructure investment, and digital inclusion.

Table 6. Comparison of MAPE values by method and lag order

Experiment	Lag=1	Lag=2	Lag=3
1	18.42%	6.59%	3.93%
2-1	4.80%	-	9.71%
2-2	1.88%	5.95%	10.45%
3-1	4.07%	6.18%	9.31%
4	2.41%	3.46%	-

While 11 socio-economic indicators were used as features in this study, the PCA-based approach is not restricted to this specific set. Because PCA identifies latent factors that contribute to predictive performance, it can be applied flexibly to any number or type of input variables. It is highly plausible that additional indicators—such as technology adoption rates, broadband coverage, or startup ecosystem metrics—could further enhance model accuracy. Identifying and validating such indicators remains an important direction for future research.

9 Conclusion

This study proposed a method for forecasting domain name registration trends under country-code top-level domains (ccTLDs) by applying a Vector Autoregressive (VAR) model using socio-economic indicators of each country as explanatory variables. Focusing on JP domain names, we demonstrated that multiple socio-economic indicators—while strongly intercorrelated—can provide valuable predictive signals when appropriately processed.

Among several dimensionality reduction strategies examined, Principal Component Analysis (PCA) proved particularly effective in eliminating multicollinearity and improving forecast accuracy. The results indicate that domain name registrations are not merely technical artifacts but are closely intertwined with broader economic and social conditions. Thus, domain registrations may serve as a useful proxy indicator for assessing digital transformation at the national level.

While the proposed framework was validated using Japanese data, its applicability is not limited to Japan. Since standardized economic statistics are available globally, the method can be extended to other ccTLDs, allowing for cross-national comparison and deeper insights into digital economy dynamics.

Future research should explore the inclusion of additional economic or technological indicators and test the model's robustness across countries and over longer time horizons. This will further enhance the utility of domain data as a lens for interpreting the evolution of Internet infrastructure and digital society.

References

1. Mockapetris, P.: RFC 883: Domain names - Implementation and specification. Internet Engineering Task Force (1983). Retrieved from https://www.ietf.org/rfc/rfc883.txt

2. Mockapetris, P.: RFC 1034: Domain names - Concepts and Facilities. Internet Engineering Task Force (1987). Retrieved from https://www.ietf.org/rfc/rfc1034.txt
3. Mockapetris, P.: RFC 1035: Domain names - Implementation and specification. Internet Engineering Task Force (1987). Retrieved from https://www.ietf.org/rfc/rfc1035.txt
4. Mueller, M.: Ruling the Root: Internet Governance and the Taming of Cyberspace. MIT Press, Cambridge (2002)
5. National Research Council: Signposts in Cyberspace: the Domain Name System and Internet Navigation. The National Academies Press, Washington, DC (2005)
6. Hubbard, K., Kosters, M., Conrad, D., Karrenberg, D., Postel, J.: RFC 2050: Internet Registry IP Allocation Guidelines. Internet Engineering Task Force (1996). Retrieved from https://www.ietf.org/rfc/rfc2050.txt
7. Ui, T., Ikehara, S., Mori, K., Ozaki, T., Hiroo, H.: Predicting trends in JP domain name registrations through cohort analysis. J. Infosocionomics Soc. **19**(1), 77–90 (2024)
8. Box, G.E.P., Jenkins, G.M., Reinsel, G.C., Ljung, G.M.: Time Series Analysis: Forecasting and Control, 5th edn. Wiley (2015)
9. Hyndman, R.J., Athanasopoulos, G.: Forecasting: Principles and Practice, 3rd edn, (2021) OTexts. https://otexts.com/fpp3/
10. Shahin, M.A., Wahab, M.H.A.: Forecasting monthly electricity consumption using SARIMA model: a case study in Egypt. Energy Rep. **5**, 1405–1412 (2019). https://doi.org/10.1016/j.egyr.2019.10.028
11. Kamimura, K.: Estimation of promoting factors of the use of the country-code top-level domain and characterization of its governance structure. J. Infosocionomics Soc. **7**(2), 23–40 (2013)
12. Choi, C., Yi, M.H.: The effect of the internet on economic growth: evidence from cross-country panel data. Econ. Lett. **105**(1), 39–41 (2009)
13. Pélissié, M., du Rausas, J., Manyika, E.H., Bughin, J., Chui, M., Said, R.: Internet Matters: the Net's Sweeping Impact on Growth, Jobs, and Prosperity. McKinsey Global Institute (2011) https://www.mckinsey.com/industries/technology-media-and-telecommunications/our-insights/internet-matters
14. Wahab, N.A., Salleh, N.S., Alwi, F.S.: Internet user and economic growth: empirical evidence from panel data. J. Emerg. Econ. Islamic Res. **8**(3), 17–25 (2020)
15. Hamilton, J.D.: Time Series Analysis. Princeton University Press (1994)
16. Stock, J.H., Watson, M.W.: Vector autoregressions. J. Econ. Perspect. **15**(4), 101–115 (2001). https://doi.org/10.1257/jep.15.4.101
17. Sims, C.A.: Macroeconomics and reality. Econometrica. **48**(1), 1–48 (1980). https://doi.org/10.2307/1912017
18. Morikawa, Y.: Non-stationary Time Series Analysis on the Effects of Monetary Policy Using VAR Model Doctoral Dissertation. Meiji University Institutional Repository, Meiji University (2020) https://meiji.repo.nii.ac.jp/records/14790
19. Ghorbani, M., Chong, E.K.P.: Stock Price Prediction Using Principal Components. Department of Systems Engineering, Colorado State University (n.d.) https://journals.plos.org/plosone/article/authors?id=10.1371/journal.pone.0230124
20. Hayashi, T.: Long-term prospects for the Japanese economy (APIR Discussion Paper Series No. 39). Asia Pacific Institute of Research (2015). https://www.apir.or.jp/uploads/files/DP39_jp_lonterm_prospects1.pdf
21. Jolliffe, I.T.: Principal Component Analysis, 2nd edn. Springer (2002)
22. Jolliffe, I.T., Cadima, J.: Principal component analysis: a review and recent developments. Philos. Trans. R. Soc. A Math. Phys. Eng. Sci. **374**(2065), 20150202 (2016)
23. JPRS: Number of JP domain name registrations. Japan Registry Services Co., Ltd. (n.d.). Retrieved 1 Nov 2024, from https://jprs.jp/about/stats/domains/

24. World Bank: World Development Indicators*. The World Bank (n.d.). Retrieved 1 Nov 2024, from https://data.worldbank.org/
25. Hyndman, R.J., Koehler, A.B.: Another look at measures of forecast accuracy. Int. J. Forecast. **22**(4), 679–688 (2006)
26. Armstrong, J.S. (ed.): Principles of Forecasting: a Handbook for Researchers and Practitioners. Springer (2001)
27. Gujarati, D.N., Porter, D.C.: Basic econometrics, 5th edn. McGraw-Hill Education (2009)
28. O'Brien, R.M.: A caution regarding rules of thumb for variance inflation factors. Qual. Quant. **41**(5), 673–690 (2007)
29. Breiman, L.: Random forests. Mach. Learn. **45**(1), 5–32 (2001)
30. Hastie, T., Tibshirani, R., Friedman, J.: The Elements of Statistical Learning: Data Mining, Inference, and Prediction, 2nd edn. Springer (2009)
31. Pedregosa, F., et al.: Scikit-learn: machine learning in python. J. Mach. Learn. Res. **12**, 2825–2830 (2011)

Implementation of a Digital Twin for the TCP-100 Parabolic Trough Collector Research Facility

Francisco M. Márquez[1], Luis J. Yebra[2], Pedro J. Zufiria[3(✉)], and Francisco Gómez Medina[4]

[1] Departamento de Automática, Universidad de Alcalá (UAH), 28801 Alcalá de Henares, Spain
francisco.marquez@uah.es
[2] Plataforma Solar de Almería, CIEMAT, 04200 Tabernas, Spain
luis.yebra@psa.es
[3] Depto. Matemática Aplicada a las TIC, ETSI Telecomunicación, Information Processing and Telecommunications Center, Universidad Politécnica de Madrid, Av. Complutense 30, 28040 Madrid, Spain
pedro.zufiria@upm.es
[4] The Alan Turing Institute, British Library, 96 Euston Road, London NW1 2DB, UK
fgomezmedina@turing.ac.uk

Abstract. This article discusses the design, implementation, and virtual commissioning of a digital twin (DT) for the TCP-100 parabolic trough collector (PTC) research facility located at the Plataforma Solar de Almería (PSA) experimental installation in Spain. For these tasks, we have selected the following technologies: SIMATIC S7 1500 PLCs (programmable logic controller) for an IEC 61131-3 controller implementation, Dymola for an object oriented Modelica implementation of the TCP-100 behaviour simulator, Message Queuing Telemetry Transport (MQTT) broker bridging with a Linux Mosquitto broker for communication between the controller and simulator, and WinCC Unified to create the Human Machine Interface (HMI) for the system operator.

Keywords: Digital Twin · IEC 61131-3 programming languages · Industrial Internet of Things (IIoT) · MQTT protocol · Object oriented modeling · PLC controller

1 Introduction

Combining "solar thermal power generation" with "thermal storage" presents a practical and flexible solution that is increasingly important in the global energy mix. This approach can help us gradually reduce our dependence on fossil fuels and bring us closer to achieving Sustainable Development Goal (SDG) number 7 (affordable and clean energy) of the 2030 Agenda for Sustainable Development [12].

H. R. Arabnia et al. (Eds.): CSCE 2025, CCIS 2932, pp. 234–244, 2026.
https://doi.org/10.1007/978-3-032-22193-3_17

The TCP-100 parabolic trough collectors facility built at "Plataforma Solar de Almería" (Spain) is an experimental research facility designed to test operating modes and control algorithms to increase energy yield, improve reliability, and reduce operating costs associated with this type of energy facility. The plant primarily consists of two thermal circuits coupled by a heat exchanger. The first circuit includes solar energy collectors, while the second circuit is dedicated to heat storage. Since solar irradiance varies and is not a constant signal, it is crucial to develop control strategies and operating modes that ensure the plant consistently behaves as a reliable source of thermal energy.

The high cost of components and the complexity of the plant create strict conditions for testing with adequate safety measures. Therefore, it is recommended to conduct simulations before carrying out real experiments. With the emergence of Industry 4.0, which integrates operation technologies (OT) with information technologies (IT), it is now possible to perform online real-time simulations, and to create a DT by connecting the simulator and the plant controller to compare the data from real experiments in the plant with those from simulated experiments. This approach allows for the correction of the plant's behavior and the improvement of plant models [6,7].

In this article, we present a specific framework developed using commercial and freely available components, with which we have developed a DT for the solar field of the TCP-100 facility. We propose a distributed implementation where the simulator and the plant controller operate on separate processors connected over the Internet. To address the complexities introduced by communication between the simulator and the plant controller, we are using the MQTT protocol. This protocol employs a publisher-subscriber model, and numerous software components are available to facilitate the integration of MQTT clients into the development of IIoT systems [1]. In the following section, we outline the architecture of the system.

2 System Architecture

Figure 1 shows a picture with an aerial view of the TCP-100 facility. Surrounding this picture are the components that implement the facility controller, the HMI for operators to maneuver the plant, the facility simulator, the engineering stations to develop these subsystems, and the connection network. On the left side of the figure are the components connected to a local area network (LAN), and on the right are the components distributed over the Internet. Further details about these components are described below.

1. The <u>TCP-100 facility (1)</u> has two thermofluid circuits thermally coupled through a heat exchanger. The solar field (primary circuit) is filled with Syltherm 800 Heat Transfer Fluid (HTF), while the storage section (secondary circuit) contains Therminol 55 HTF. The image in Fig. 1 depicts the solar field of the primary circuit, which consists of three loops of PTCs. Each

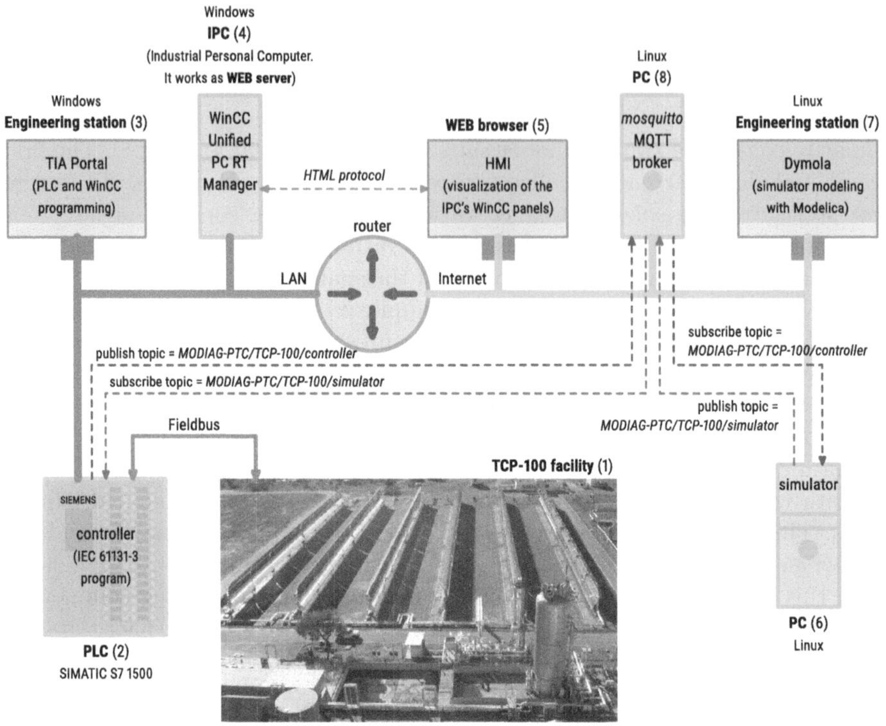

Fig. 1. System architecture outlining the interconnection of components and their roles.

loop has two 100-meter-long PTCs, and each PTC is made up of eight 12-meter-long modules. See [4,9,13] for a more detail description of the TCP-100 facility.

2. The PLC (2) is a SIMATIC S7 1500 controller running an IEC 61131-3 compliant program and connects to the TCP-100 facility via a fieldbus to control the plant in real-time.
3. The Engineering station (3) is a Windows Personal Computer (PC) with a professional license for the TIA (Totally Automation Integration) Portal suite, employed to develop and simulate both the controller programs and the HMI operator screens. During the development, we can simulate the behavior of both programs for debugging before loading and commissioning on the PLC and IPC. Once the system is commissioned, the engineering station is no longer required and can be disconnected from the plant's operating network.
4. The IPC (4) is a Windows PC that runs the WinCC Unified PC RT manager, which acts as a web server hosting the operator's HMI screens.
5. The WEB browser (5) serves as a viewer for HMI screens, which can be accessed from any device with internet connectivity, including touch panels, PCs, smartphones, and tablets. Historically, HMI screens were primarily displayed on touch panels located within the industrial plants being operated.

However, with the emergence of Industry 4.0, the goal is to integrate operation technologies with informational technologies. A key step in this process involves transitioning HMI access to online platforms.
Subsystems (2) through (5) are suitable for building a plant controller using a traditional approach. However, the OT+IT integration makes it feasible and advantageous to incorporate a digital twin into the system. This DT would enable virtual commissioning, enhance our understanding of plant behavior, detect malfunctions, and even predict them. Therefore, we propose adding subsystems (6) to (8) to realize these benefits.

6. The PC (5) is a Linux platform running the TCP-100 simulator. We refer to [9,13] for a detailed description of the TCP-100 behavior models implemented. In this work, we have incorporated a communication component with the controller. For this communication, we utilize the MQTT protocol, which is a lightweight protocol that follows the publish/subscribe model. This makes it ideal for IIoT, telemetry applications, and other scenarios with soft real-time constraints.
7. The Engineering station (5) is a Linux PC equipped with a license for Dymola (a framework for object-oriented modeling using the Modelica language). Dymola symbolically processes the models that describe the structure and behavior equations of the plant, simplifies these equations, and generates a computationally efficient instance of the model that allows for directly simulating the system behavior.
8. The PC (8) is a Linux PC that runs the MQTT broker mosquitto (mosquitto.org). The broker acts as an intermediary that receives messages from the simulator on topic MODIAG-PTC/TCP-100/simulator, which contain the simulator's outputs. It then forwards these messages to the controller, which subscribes to the same topic and receives them as inputs. Similarly, the broker receives messages from the controller on topic MODIAG-PTC/TCP-100/controller, which include the controller's outputs. These messages are then sent to the simulator, which subscribes to the same topic and uses them as inputs. It is important to emphasize that both the controller and the simulator function as ISO (input/state/output) systems, where the outputs of one serve as the inputs to the other, and vice versa.

3 Implementation of the TCP-100 Controller

The controller program consists of several Program Organization Units (POUs) according to IEC terminology, with the three Organization Blocks (OB) of type Program Cycle—controller, publish, and subscribe—being particularly noteworthy.

The controller OB implements an ISO system designed with techniques to make the plant meet the functional specifications for which it has been built. Some of these techniques have already been discussed in [3,5], so here we will focus on describing the OBs related to MQTT communications.

The OB publish is an MQTT client that transmits the controller outputs to the simulator, which are also linked to the actuators in the TCP-100 facility.

To accomplish this, it periodically sends a message with the topic MODIAG-PTC/TCP-100/controller and with a payload that includes the current value of the outputs. Figure 2 shows the structure of the data block (DB) outputs_DB, where these outputs have been declared. AP001 indicates the angular velocity in revolutions per minute (RPM) of the pump driver that introduces the HTF into the primary circuit of the TCP-100. AA102, AA106, and AA110 indicate the degree of opening of the proportional valves that control the volume flow rate of HTF that enters into each of the solar field loops. The arrangement of these components in the solar field are plotted in the HMI main screen (see Fig. 7 below). timestamp encodes the moment when these outputs were generated.

inputs_DB

Name	Data type
▾ Static	
timestamp	DInt
DNI	Real
T_amb	Real
FT001	Real
FT002	Real
FT101	Real
FT102	Real
FT103	Real
▸ PT	Array[101..120] of Real
▸ TT	Array[101..126] of Real

outputs_DB

Name	Data type
▾ Static	
timestamp	DInt
AP001	Real
AA102	Real
AA106	Real
AA110	Real

Fig. 2. Struture of the data blocks inputs_DB and outputs_DB.

Figure 3 shows the LD (ladder diagram) code of the OB publish. The OB has three networks that prepare data and send them to the broker using the an instance of the Function Block (FB) LMQTT_Client with associated DB LMQTT_publish_DB, which is included in the library for communications provided by Siemens [10, Cap. 5]. Figure 4 shows the DB publish_DB associated with the OB publish.

The OB subscribe is an MQTT client that receive the controller inputs from the simulator. To accomplish this, it subscribes to the topic MODIAG-PTC/TCP-100/simulator and wait until the simulator publish new messages. Figure 2 shows the structure of the DB inputs_DB, where these inputs have been declared. DNI (W/m^2) indicates the Direct Normal Irradiance, T_amb (°C) is the ambient temperature, FT001 (m^3/s) is the total volume flow rate going into the solar field, FT002 is the total volume flow rate going out of the solar field, FT101...FT103 are the volume flow rates going into each loop, PT is a 20 elements array associated to the pressure sensors PT101...PT120 (bar), and TT is a 26 elements array associated to the temperature sensors TT101...TT126 (°C). The arrangement of these components in the solar field are plotted in Fig. 7. timestamp encodes the moment when these inputs were generated in the simulator.

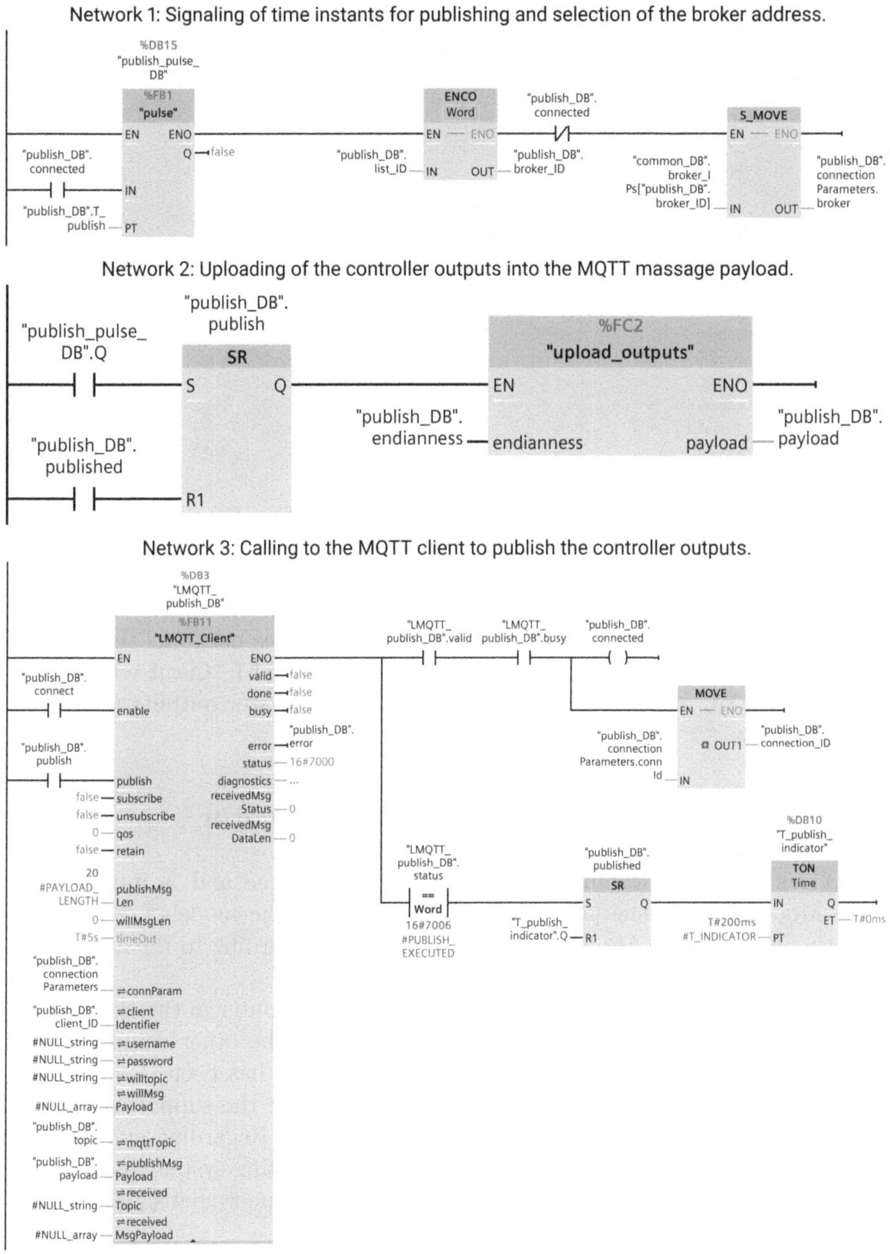

Fig. 3. LD code of the OB publish. The variables of this OB are in the DB publish_DB (see Fig. 4).

Name	Data type	Start value
▼ Static		
topic	WString	WSTRING#'MODIAG-PTC/TCP-100/controller'
broker_ID	Int	0
▼ connectionParameters	"LMQTT_typeConnParam"	
hwId	HW_ANY	0
connId	CONN_OUC	100
broker	String	''
port	UInt	1883
▶ tls	Struct	
keepAlive	UInt	0
client_ID	WString	WSTRING#'TCP-100 controller Publish'
▶ payload	Array[0..20] of Byte	
connected	Bool	false
error	Bool	false
connect	Bool	true
published	Bool	false
publish	Bool	false
list_ID	Int	0
connection_ID	Int	0
T_publish	DInt	1000
endianness	Bool	false

Fig. 4. Structure of the data block publish_DB.

The LD code of the OB subscribe (with associated DB subscribe_DB) is very similar, *mutatis mutandis*, to the OB publish. It has three networks that receive data from the broker using an instance of the FB LMQTT_Client with associated DB LMQTT_subscribe_DB, and unload the simulator outputs (controller inputs).

4 Implementation of the TCP-100 Simulator

The DT is based on a simulator that runs in real-time and is implemented in the Modelica language [8] with the Dymola tool. The models are based on first principles and the Modelica Standard Library, according to the approaches previously presented in [9] and [13].

The simulator is run in real-time on the PC (6) computer in the architecture shown in Fig. 1. It also communicates properly with the other components of the network. The Modelica Device Drivers library [11] has been used for integration in the network, so it provides the wrappers for the support of MQTT datagrams through the Eclipse Paho MQTT C client. Regarding synchronization, the library implements low-level calls to the operating system according to its design, an can be deployed from soft to hard real-time systems [2].

4.1 Communication Tests

In this section we present the results of the execution of a communication test of the infrastructure presented in Fig. 1. The computer running the real-time simulator communicates with the MQTT broker with the model presented in

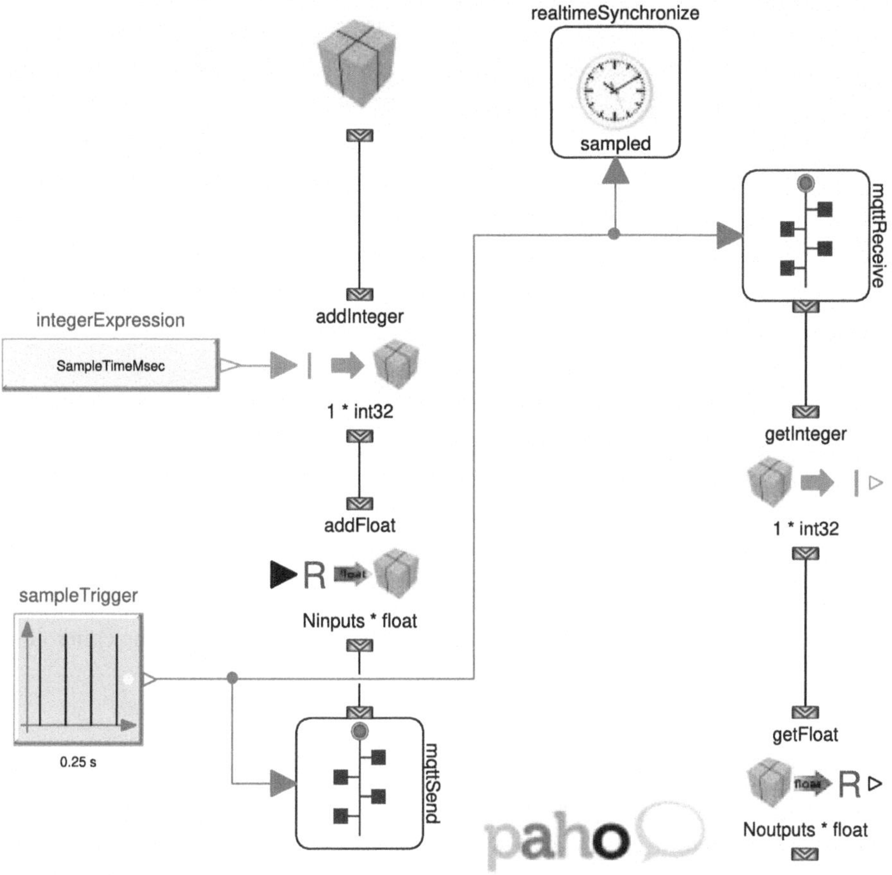

Fig. 5. Modelica model used to interface the real-time simulator with the MQTT broker.

Fig. 5, by means of the components mqttSend, mqttReceive, and Packager from the Modelica Device Drivers library. The MQTT published packets are formed by a vector of Ninputs single precision floating point variables plus a time stamp, and it is subscribed to a channel where it receives Noutputs variables and a time stamp from the PLC. The approximate distance of the communication link between UAH and PSA is about 600 km, so it is assumed a round-trip distance of 1200 km for the packets.

The experiment involved transmitting a sine wave sampled every 250 milliseconds from the simulator to a controller located 600 km away. The controller directly feeds back the received signal to one of its outputs and returns it in the next sampling period, which is also every 250 milliseconds. Figure 6 shows the continuous sine wave generated in the simulator, labeled WrittenVar, and the received signal, labeled ReadVar. It can be observed a variable delay of approx-

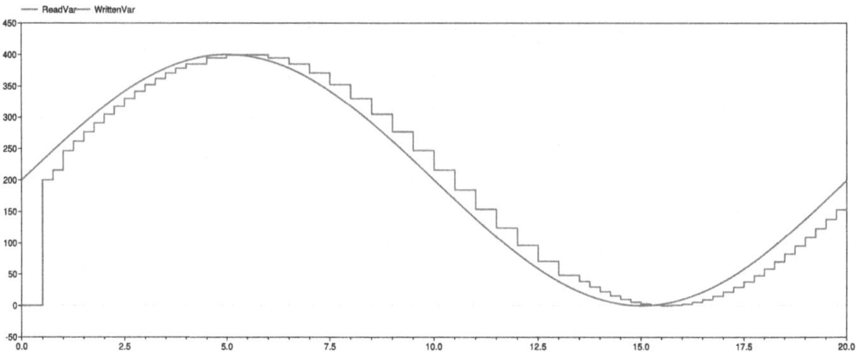

Fig. 6. The WrittenVar variable (red) is the sine wave published by the simulator each 250 ms, while the ReadVar (blue) shows the values sent back by the PLC. A variable delay of about 300 ms between both signals in the same time reference system can be observed. (Color figure online)

imately 300 ms between the two signals. This delay primarily results from the processing times of the communication equipment along the 1200 km transmission path, as well as the processing times of both the simulator and the controller.

5 Implementation of the HMI

The primary function of the HMI is to provide a convenient and straightforward interface for operators to monitor and control the plant. Reference [13] details the simulations carried out with the various operating modes specified in the plant engineering project. The development of a DT enables us to compare simulation results in real-time with the actual performance of the plant.

To implement this HMI, we utilized the WinCC Unified PC tool integrated within the TIA Portal environment. This tool allows for the easy creation of HMI screens, which can then be transferred to the WinCC Unified PC Runtime Manager. This manager functions as a web server, enabling us to view these screens from any internet-connected device using a web browser.

In TIA Portal projects, we can define users with different roles (such as administrators, developers, and plant operators) to improve security regarding access to plant data. This user information is also transferred to the Runtime Manager to authenticate each user seeking access to the HMI screens.

Figure 7 displays the main screen of the HMI, where the three loops of the solar field are depicted alongside the layout of the associated signals from the actuators and sensors mentioned in Sect. 3. It is important to highlight that the graphical component library of the WinCC Unified tool simplifies the creation of such representations, ensuring they have a user-friendly appearance. Furthermore, this tool enables the dynamic adjustment of various attributes for each component, including color, position, size, and textual labels, based on the ranges of process variable values. In our implementation, we have dynamically

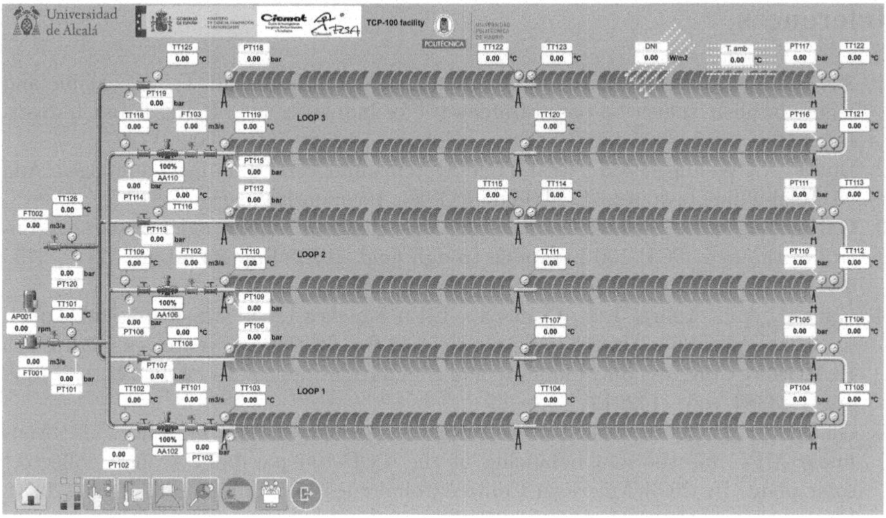

Fig. 7. The start screen of the HMI represents the three PTC loops of the solar field (see the picture in Fig. 1), as well as the actuator and sensor signals.

adjusted the representation of the pipelines using a red color palette, with the color becoming darker as the temperature of Syltherm 800 HTF increases. This type of graphical representation effectively complements the numerical information presented alongside each of the solar field signals.

6 Conclusions

In this paper, we have presented the architecture and implementation of a digital twin for the TCP-100 research facility, located at the Plataforma Solar de Almería (Spain). The most remarkable aspect of the system is its conception as a distributed system where the subsystems involved (controller, simulator, communications broker, HMI manager, and HMI display) are based of different computer architectures, operating systems, and can be in any network node. The tests indicate that the controller-simulator communication delays align with the requirements of soft real-time control systems. Thus, this system can be considered a suitable framework for testing different models of the TCP-100 facility, to improve the existing ones, and to validate controllers running in the PLC.

Acknowledgements. The authors acknowledge the funding from the projects TED2021-129189B-C21/TED2021-129189B-C22 and grant PID2023-146540OB-C42 funded by MCIN/AEI/10.13039/501100011033 and by the European Union "NextGenerationEU"/PRTR.

Disclosure of Interests. The authors have no competing interests to declare that are relevant to the content of this article.

References

1. Amoretti, M., Pecori, R., Protskaya, Y., Veltri, L., Zanichelli, F.: A scalable and secure publish/subscribe-based framework for industrial IoT. IEEE Trans. Industr. Inf. **17**(6), 3815–3825 (2021). https://doi.org/10.1109/TII.2020.3017227
2. Burns, A., Wellings, A.J.: Real-Time Systems and Programming Languages: Ada 95, Real-Time Java, and Real-Time POSIX. Pearson Education (2001)
3. Gallego, A.J., Yebra, L.J., Camacho, E.F.: Gain scheduling model predictive control of the new TCP-100 parabolic trough field. IFAC-PapersOnLine **51**(2), 475–480 (2018). https://doi.org/10.1016/j.ifacol.2018.03.080
4. Gallego, A.J., Yebra, L.J., Camacho, E.F., Sánchez, A.J.: Mathematical modeling of the parabolic trough collector field of the TCP-100 research plant. In: 9th EUROSIM Congress on Modelling and Simulation, pp. 12–16 (2016). https://doi.org/10.3384/ecp17142912
5. Gallego, A.J., Yebra, L.J., Del Pozo, A.J.S., Escaño, J.M., Camacho, E.F.: Nonlinear MPC for thermal balancing of the TCP-100 parabolic trough collectors solar plant. In: 2023 American Control Conference (ACC), pp. 1807–1812 (2023). https://doi.org/10.23919/ACC55779.2023.10156440
6. Gomez Medina, F., Hernandez, V.M.: Product digital twins: an umbrella review and research agenda for understanding their value. Comput. Ind. **164**, 104181 (2025). https://doi.org/10.1016/j.compind.2024.104181
7. Hashmi, R., Liu, H., Yavari, A.: Digital twins for enhancing efficiency and assuring safety in renewable energy systems: a systematic literature review. Energies **17**(11) (2024). https://doi.org/10.3390/en17112456
8. Modelica Association: Modelica language specification version 3.6 (2024). https://specification.modelica.org/maint/3.6/MLS.html
9. Pérez, J., Yebra, L.J., Dormido, S., Zarza, E.: First principles system level modelling of tcp-100 facility for simulation of operation modes. IFAC-PapersOnLine 51(2), 481–486 (2018). https://doi.org/10.1016/j.ifacol.2018.03.081. 9th Vienna International Conference on Mathematical Modelling
10. SIEMENS: Libraries for communication for SIMATIC controllers. Technical report, Siemens Industry Online Support (2024)
11. Thiele, B., Beutlich, T., Waurich, V., Sjölund, M., Bellmann, T.: Towards a standard-conform, platform-generic and feature-rich Modelica device drivers library. In: Proceedings of the 12th International Modelica Conference, pp. 713–723. Linköping University Electronic Press (2017). https://doi.org/10.3384/ecp17132713
12. United Nations Department of Economic and Social Affairs - Sustainable Development: Transforming our world: the 2030 agenda for sustainable development (2015). https://sdgs.un.org/2030agenda
13. Yebra, L.J., Márquez, F.M., Zufiria, P.J.: Simulation of TCP-100 facility system level model for operation training purposes. In: 2020 International Conference on Computational Science and Computational Intelligence (CSCI), pp. 1348–1353 (2020). https://doi.org/10.1109/CSCI51800.2020.00251

A Method for Detecting Changes in the Thermal Losses of a Parabolic Trough Collector

Pedro J. Zufiria[1(✉)], Ángela Castillo[1], Alberto Portal[1], Francisco M. Márquez[2], and Luis J. Yebra[3]

[1] Depto. Matemática Aplicada a las TIC, ETSI Telecomunicación, Information Processing and Telecommunications Center, Universidad Politécnica de Madrid, Av. Complutense 30, 28040 Madrid, Spain
{pedro.zufiria,angela.castillo,alberto.portal}@upm.es

[2] Departamento de Automática, Universidad de Alcalá (UAH), 28801 Alcalá de Henares, Spain
francisco.marquez@uah.es

[3] Plataforma Solar de Almería, CIEMAT, 04200 Tabernas, Spain
luis.yebra@psa.es

Abstract. In this paper, a fault detection scheme is developed, based on a simplified model of a Parabolic Trough Collector that uses water as a heat transfer fluid. The model assumes some simplifications that allow the construction of a Luenberger-type observer-based residual, so that an alarm is activated when the absolute value of such residual surpasses a pre-established threshold. The threshold is computed in order to avoid false alarms, so that when the residual surpasses such threshold, this implies that the absolute thermal losses to the environment have exceeded some established maximum admissible value. Two possible threshold values are proposed, depending on the assumptions considered: the first one is conservative since its computation is solely grounded on the modeling assumptions; the second one is computed by including an additional assumption which provides a less conservative result. Simulations with different fault sizes illustrate the sensitivity of the detection scheme with both thresholds.

Keywords: Thermal Energy · Parabolic Trough Collector · Fault Diagnosis · Control Systems

1 Introduction

The MODIAG-PTC (TED2021-129189B-C21/TED2021-129189B-C22) research project is being jointly developed between the Universidad Politécnica de Madrid and CIEMAT, in experimental PTC facilities of the center Plataforma Solar de Almería (PSA). PSA belongs to CIEMAT and is dependent on the Department of Energy. The research facilities involved in the MODIAG-PTC project are the TCP-100, the Direct Solar Steam (DISS), and the HTF-Loop experimental

H. R. Arabnia et al. (Eds.): CSCE 2025, CCIS 2932, pp. 245–255, 2026.
https://doi.org/10.1007/978-3-032-22193-3_18

facilities. The research activities presented in this article are focused on one of the PTC of the DISS facility, presented in the following.

The DISS facility was designed and installed in the PSA, originally consisting of a 550-m-long row of collectors arranged in the north-south direction at an inclination of 0.8º with respect to the horizontal plane. The row consists of 11 PTCs, with two-phase water-steam flow, of four different types of collectors:

- Eight collectors, each consisting of four parabolic trough modules and with three possible inclinations of the tracking axis: 0º, 2º and 4º. They are called type A collectors.
- Collector nº 9. A collector composed of two cylindrical-parabolic modules, with five possible inclinations of the tracking axis: 0º, 2º, 4º, 6º and 8º. This is called a special test collector.
- Collector nº 10. A horizontal collector composed of two parabolic trough modules.
- Collector nº 11. A horizontal collector consisting of four parabolic trough modules.

Figure 1 shows a lateral view of the DISS row in operation.

Fig. 1. Lateral view of the first DISS row with several PTCs at PSA-CIEMAT.

Model-based fault detection (MFD) schemes have become a cornerstone in the monitoring and diagnosis of dynamical systems, offering systematic approaches to identifying and isolating faults using mathematical models of the process [9]. Recent advancements in MFD leverage a combination of analytical redundancy, observer-based techniques, and data-driven enhancements to improve detection accuracy and robustness [4]. Residual generation methods, such as parity-space approaches [8], Kalman filters [3], and sliding-mode observers [5], are widely employed to highlight discrepancies between system measurements and model predictions. For nonlinear systems—common in solar thermal applications like Parabolic Trough Collectors (PTCs)— extended and unscented Kalman filters (EKF/UKF) [10] and adaptive observers for deterministic systems [13] and stochastic systems [2] have shown promise in handling parameter uncertainties and disturbances.

Additionally, the integration of machine learning with traditional model-based methods has gained traction, enabling hybrid schemes that combine first-principles modeling with data-driven fault classifiers for improved generalization [11,16]. Despite these advances, challenges remain in ensuring robustness against environmental variability, sensor noise, and model-plant mismatches, particularly in renewable energy systems where operating conditions fluctuate [6,7,12,14]. Recent works have also explored distributed fault detection architectures for large-scale systems [1], which could be beneficial for solar thermal fields comprising multiple PTC loops. Overall, the state of the art emphasizes a trend toward hybrid and adaptive methodologies that enhance reliability while maintaining interpretability—a critical consideration for industrial deployment [15].

This paper is organized as follows. In Sect. 2 a low order dynamic model of a PTC used in the paper is presented. Section 3 presents the proposed fault detection scheme. Section 4 shows simulation results and discussions. Finally, some conclusions are drawn in Sect. 5.

2 Low Order Dynamic Models of a PTC

In this section, we present the low-order nonlinear model of a parabolic trough collector, based on the energy balance of the (monophasic) fluid volume inside the collector:

$$\frac{dT}{dt} = \frac{1}{\rho(T)\cdot V}\left[2\cdot q\cdot(T_i - T) + \frac{K_{opt}\cdot S\cdot I - h(T,T_a)\cdot S_o\cdot(T-T_a)}{c_p(T)}\right] \quad (1)$$

$$T_{out} = 2\cdot T - T_i \quad (2)$$

where T (the state variable) is the mean module temperature, T_a is the ambient temperature, T_i is the known inlet fluid temperature of the module (e.g., the output temperature of an adjoint module or a tank), I is the solar irradiance, V is the volume of the fluid, $\rho(T)$ and $c_p(T)$ are the fluid density and specific heat capacity respectively (both possibly temperature-dependent), K_{opt} is the optical efficiency, S is the collector aperture area (area exposed to radiation), S_o is the outer surface area (exposed for heat loss), $h(T,T_a)$ is the convective heat transfer coefficient, and q is the mass flow rate of the fluid. The output variable is T_{out} under the assumption $T = \frac{T_{out}+T_i}{2}$.

A crucial aspect in the system evolution is the behavior of the term $h(T, T_a)$, which, in a standard situation, can be approximated by a reference model

$$h(T, T_a) \approx h_r(T - T_a) = a + b \cdot (T - T_a) + c \cdot (T - T_a)^2 \quad (3)$$

whose parameter values are specified in the following section.

2.1 Numerical Values of the Parameters of the Model

1. Density $\rho(T) = \rho = 1000$ $[kg/m^3]$. Assuming initially not dependent on temperature.
2. Specific heat $C_p(T) = C_p = 4186$ $[J/(kg \cdot K)]$. Assuming initially not dependent on temperature.
3. Volume $V = \pi \cdot 0.032^2 \cdot 96$ $[m^3]$.
4. Surface area for losses $S_o = 2 \cdot \pi \cdot 0.035 \cdot 96$ $[m^2]$.
5. Collector aperture area (area exposed to solar radiation) $S = 5.77 \cdot 96$ $[m^2]$.
6. Optical efficiency $K_{opt} = 0.5$ $[-]$ (dimensionless).
7. Parameters a, b, c of the experimental thermal losses derived in PSA, $h_r(T, T_a)$ $[W/(m^2K)]$ in Eq. (3): $a = 0.687257$, $b = 0.001941$, $c = 0.000026$.

2.2 Simplified Model

This model is based on an energy balance, in which the collector is unfocused (it does not receive concentrated solar radiation). The flow of water q at the inlet temperature T_i, both varying as a function of time, flows through the collector.

The collector will be assumed to have an initial temperature T_0 at the beginning of the experiment. Under the above simplifying assumptions, and within the scope of the MODIAG-PTC project, the first collectors of the DISS installation of the PSA could present a behavior approximated by the following simplified model:

$$\dot{T} = k_1 \cdot (T_i - T) \cdot q - k_2 \cdot (T - T_a) \cdot h(T, T_a) + k_3 \cdot I(t) \quad (4)$$

$$T_{out} = 2 \cdot T - T_i \quad (5)$$

with $k_1 = \frac{2}{\rho V}$, $k_2 = \frac{S_o}{\rho V C_p}$, $k_3(t) = \frac{K_{opt} S}{\rho V C_p}$. The mean temperature at the initial time is T_0, usually measured, so the initial condition is $T(t_0) = T_0$.

3 Design of a Fault Detection Scheme

In practice, $h(T, T_a)$ may suffer severe variations due to module failures, and we want to detect such situations. Since T, T_i, T_a and $I(t)$ can be measured online, we propose the construction of the following Luenberger type of observer:

$$\dot{\hat{T}} = \lambda \cdot (\hat{T} - T) + k_1 \cdot (T_i - T) \cdot q - k_2 \cdot (T - T_a) \cdot h_r(T, T_a) + k_3 \cdot I(t), \quad \lambda < 0 \quad (6)$$

with initial condition $\hat{T}(t_0) = \hat{T}_0$; so that if we define the residual $\epsilon = T - \hat{T}$, subtracting (6) from (4) we get:

$$\begin{aligned} \dot{\epsilon} &= \lambda \cdot \epsilon - k_2 \cdot (T - T_a) \cdot [h(T, T_a) - h_r(T - T_a)] \\ \epsilon(t_0) &= \epsilon_0 = T_0 - \hat{T}_0 \end{aligned} \tag{7}$$

whose solution takes the form (for $t_0 = 0$):

$$\begin{aligned} \epsilon(t) =& \epsilon_0 e^{\lambda t} + e^{\lambda t} \int_0^t e^{-\lambda \tau} \Big(k_2 \cdot (T(\tau) - T_a(\tau)) \\ & \cdot [h(T(\tau), T_a(\tau)) - h_r(T(\tau) - T_a(\tau))] \Big) d\tau \end{aligned} \tag{8}$$

which, under the faultless behavior assumption, $h(T, T_a) \approx h_r(T - T_a)$, guarantees that $\lim_{t \to \infty} \epsilon(t) = 0$ (i.e., the observer state variable mimics the plant state variable).

3.1 Design of a Threshold that Avoids False Alarms

Assuming standard operating conditions, we can define $T - T_a = \Delta_T \geq 0$ as well as a natural range of variation $\Delta_T \in [0, \Delta_T^{\max}]$. In this scenario, we consider now that the failure of the system is due to the fact that the convective heat transfer coefficient goes beyond a given normal functioning threshold $h(T, T_a) > h_{\max} > 0$. Hence, in a faultless regime (i.e., $h(T, T_a) \leq h_{max}$), we can bind the residual variation as follows:

$$|\epsilon(t)| \leq |\epsilon_0| e^{\lambda t} + e^{\lambda t} \int_0^t e^{-\lambda \tau} k_2 \cdot \Delta_T(\tau) \cdot [h_{\max} + h_r(\Delta_T(\tau))] d\tau \tag{9}$$

where we must keep in mind that $h_r(\Delta_T) \geq 0$ for $\Delta_T \in [0, \Delta_T^{\max}]$. We can now obtain a practical bound for the term within the integral by computing:

$$M_1 = \max_{\Delta_T \in [0, \Delta_T^{\max}]} k_2 \cdot \Delta_T \cdot [h_{\max} + h_r(\Delta_T)] \tag{10}$$

In Appendix A we compute the expression of M_1 for given values of $h_{\max}$, k_2, a, b, and c. From (9) and (10) we get:

$$|\epsilon(t)| \leq |\epsilon_0| e^{\lambda t} + e^{\lambda t} \int_0^t e^{-\lambda \tau} M_1 d\tau \Longrightarrow |\epsilon(t)| \leq \left(|\epsilon_0| + \frac{M_1}{\lambda} \right) e^{\lambda t} - \frac{M_1}{\lambda} \tag{11}$$

where, since $\lambda < 0$ we have that $\lim_{t \to \infty} \left(|\epsilon_0| + \frac{M_1}{\lambda} \right) e^{\lambda t} = 0$, implying that $-\frac{M_1}{\lambda} > 0$ will define the absolute value of the bound of the admissible residual (according to $h_{\max}$) in the steady state regime. Therefore, when the absolute value of the residual steadily surpasses such value:

$$|\epsilon(t)| > B_1 = -\frac{M_1}{\lambda}, \quad \forall t > t_d \tag{12}$$

we can diagnose that a fault has occurred approximately at $t = t_d$.

The bound based on M_1 given by (12) can be refined if we assume that, in the faultless regime, the condition:

$$h_{\max} > h(T, T_a) \geq h_r(T - T_a),\ \forall \Delta_T \in [0, \Delta_T^{\max}] \tag{13}$$

is satisfied. In that case, we can bind the residual variation as follows:

$$|\epsilon(t)| \leq |\epsilon_0|e^{\lambda t} + e^{\lambda t} \int_0^t e^{-\lambda \tau} k_2 \cdot \Delta_T(\tau) \cdot [h_{\max} - h_r(\Delta_T(\tau))] d\tau \tag{14}$$

so that a refined bound can be obtained by computing:

$$M_2 = \max_{\Delta_T \in [0, \Delta_T^{\max}]} k_2 \cdot \Delta_T \cdot [h_{\max} - h_r(\Delta_T)] \tag{15}$$

that would substitute M_1 in (12) to provide a more refined bound $B_2 = -\frac{M_2}{\lambda}$. In Appendix A we compute also the expression of M_2 for given values of $h_{\max}$, k_2, a, b, and c.

4 Simulations

In this section, simulations are carried out to illustrate the validity of the proposed schemes in two basic working scenarios for the PTC.

4.1 Initial Conditions and External Values for Experiments

For a typical simplified scenario, we have assumed that the solar irradiance follows a periodic behavior $I = 750 + 250 \cdot \sin(t/10)$, the input temperature is fixed at $T_i = 150$ $[°C]$, the ambient temperature is fixed at $T_a = 20$ $[°C]$, the flow rate is $q = 5$ $[kg/s]$, and the parabolic trough collector is initially at $T(t = 0) = 200[°C]$.

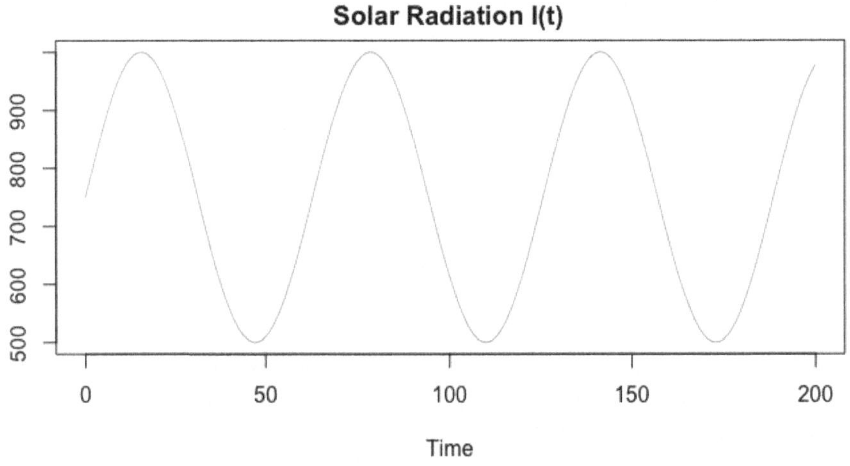

Fig. 2. Radiation profile.

4.2 Observer Parameters, Detection Bounds and Fault

The observer gain was set to $\lambda = -1$, and the temperature estimation initial condition to $\hat{T}(0) = 170$. If we consider that $\Delta_T^{\max} = 200$, we obtain $h_{\max} = h_r(\Delta_T) = 2.12$. Hence, according to (16) and (17), the corresponding bounds are $B_1 = M_1 = 0.014$ and $B_2 = M_2 = 0.0018$.

4.3 Simulation of Two Different Faults Sizes

In such a framework, two simulations have been performed during a time range from 0 to 200 units of time, to illustrate the influence of a fault size at $t = 100$ on

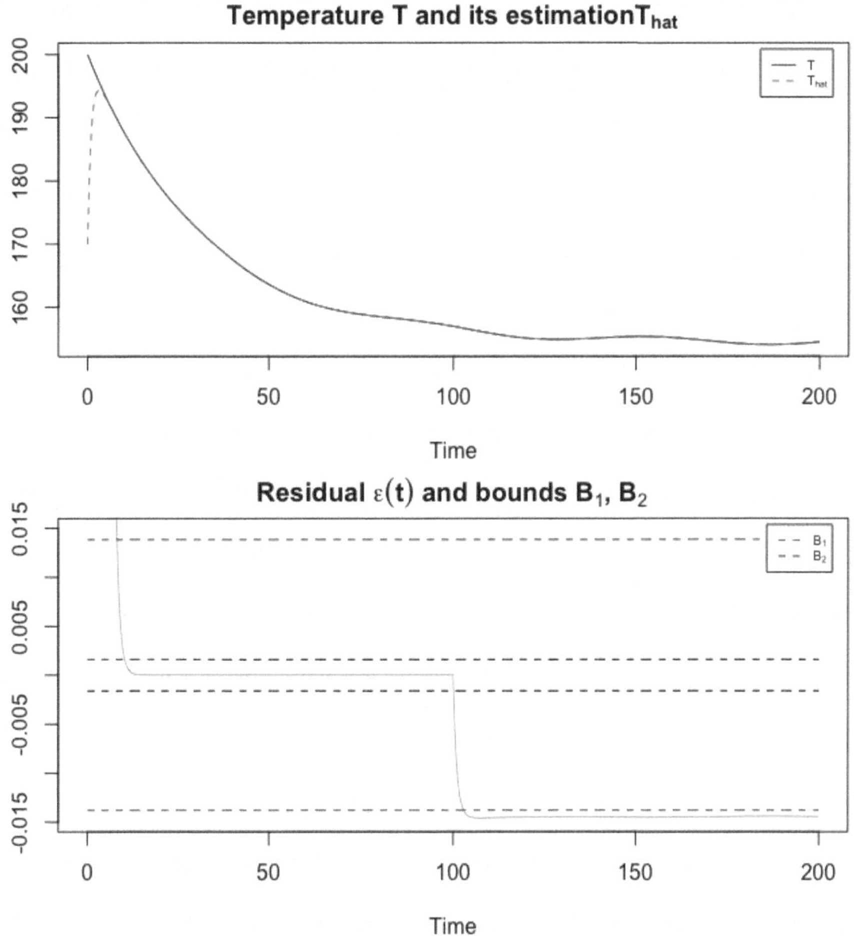

Fig. 3. Module temperature, temperature estimation and residual for the first simulation of a fault in plant at time $t = 100$ with $h(T, T_a) = 8$, for $t > 100$.

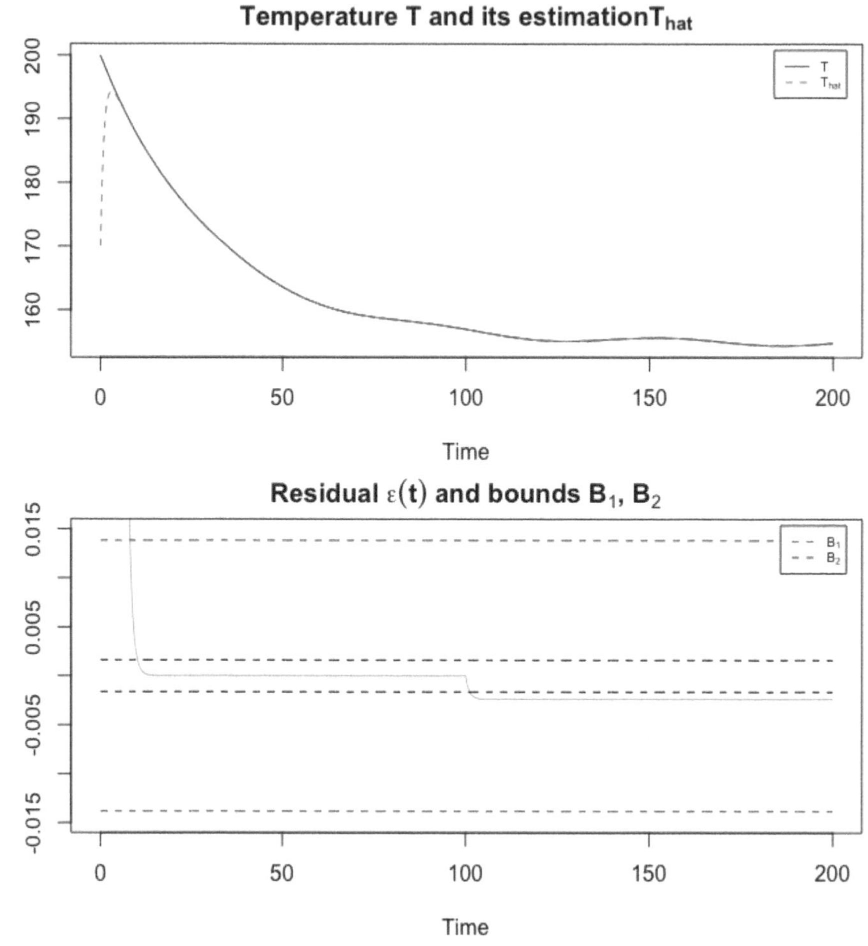

Fig. 4. Temperature, temperature estimation and residual for the second simulation of a fault in plant at time $t = 100$ with $h(T, T_a) = 2.5,\ \text{for } t \geq 100$.

the convective heat transfer coefficient. Both simulations have been performed with the same radiation profile shown in Fig. 2.

In the first simulation, the convective heat transfer function satisfies $h(T, T_a) = h_r(T, T_a)$ for $t < 100$ and becomes $h(T, T_a) = 8$ for $t \geq 100$. Figure 3 gathers the time evolution of T, $\hat{T}$ and the residual ϵ (with the corresponding bounds B_1 and B_2) over the time period $[0, 200]$. Clearly, the residual goes beyond both the conservative threshold B_1 and the less conservative threshold defined by B_2, so that the fault would be detected in any case.

In the second simulation, the convective heat transfer function suffers, also at $t = 100$ a much smaller fault of size $h(T, T_a) = 2.5$ (barely beyond the expected range of $h_r(T, T_a)$). Figure 4 gathers the time evolution of T, $\hat{T}$ and the residual

ϵ (with the corresponding bounds B_1 and B_2) over the time period $[0, 200]$. Clearly, the residual goes beyond the threshold defined by B_2 so that the fault would still be detected with such a less conservative bound.

4.4 Discussion

Simulations have shown the validity of the detection scheme in two different scenarios. As expected, bound B_1 is very conservative since it does not make any assumption on the behavior of the convective heat transfer coefficient $h(T, T_a)$. In general, such coefficient will not be smaller than the reference one, $h_r(T, T_a)$, so that assumption stated in (13) will be satisfied and the second less conservative bound B_2 will be applicable. This less conservative bound allows the detection of smaller size faults that slightly exceed the allowable range for the convection losses, making the scheme more sensitive.

5 Conclusions

Fault detection in PTCs is a research activity of great interest in industrial solar thermal power plants and the MODIAG-PTC (TED2021-129189B-C21/TED2021-129189B-C22) research project is actively working on this topic, in the experimental DISS research facility at PSA-CIEMAT. In this article, we have presented a dynamic model of a PTC working with liquid water as the heat transfer fluid, and a fault detection scheme based on a Luenberger observer. A detailed analytical derivation of such fault detection technique has been first presented, providing two different alarm bounds which depend on some assumptions on the range of variation of the convective losses. Then, some simulations have illustrated that the designed fault detection scheme does not have false alarms, and that it successfully detects sudden increases in the thermal losses of the PTC, beyond an allowable range which can be pre-defined based on experimental measurements in industrial plants.

Future work will address a sensitivity analysis of the proposed fault detection scheme, together with some simulations using real experimental data.

Acknowledgements. The authors acknowledge the funding from the projects TED2021-129189B-C21/TED2021-129189B-C22 and grant PID2023-146540OB-C42 funded by MCIN/AEI/10.13039/501100011033 and by the European Union "NextGenerationEU'/PRTR.

Disclosure of Interests. The authors have no competing interests to declare that are relevant to the content of this article.

A Computation of Bounds for the Residual

A.1 Computation of Conservative Bound M_1

The expression of M_1 is given by:

$$\begin{aligned} M_1 &= \max_{\Delta_T \in [0,\Delta_T^{\max}]} k_2 \cdot \Delta_T \cdot [h_{\max} + h_r(\Delta_T)] = k_2 \cdot \max_{\Delta_T \in [0,\Delta_T^{\max}]} \Delta_T \cdot [h_{\max} + h_r(\Delta_T)] \\ &= k_2 \cdot \max_{\Delta_T \in [0,\Delta_T^{\max}]} \Delta_T \cdot \left[h_{\max} + \left(a + b \cdot \Delta_T + c \cdot (\Delta_T)^2\right)\right] \\ &= k_2 \cdot \max_{\Delta_T \in [0,\Delta_T^{\max}]} c \cdot (\Delta_T)^3 + b \cdot (\Delta_T)^2 + (a + h_{max}) \cdot \Delta_T \end{aligned}$$

which leads to determining the extreme values of a third degree polynomial (whose graph crosses the origin of coordinates) in a given compact interval determined by the range of variation of $T - T_a = \Delta_T \in [0, \Delta_T^{\max}]$; both roots of the derivative of such a polynomial are:

$$\Delta_T^- = \frac{-2b - \sqrt{4b^2 - 12c(h_{max} + a)}}{6c}, \quad \Delta_T^+ = \frac{-2b + \sqrt{4b^2 - 12c(h_{max} + a)}}{6c}$$

and, in case that they are real, both roots are negative. Therefore the maximum $[0, \Delta_T^{\max}]$ is reached at $\Delta_T^{\max}$, and

$$M_1 = k_2 \cdot \left(c \cdot (\Delta_T^{\max})^3 + b \cdot (\Delta_T^{\max})^2 + (a + h_{max}) \cdot \Delta_T^{\max}\right) \tag{16}$$

A.2 Computation of Less Conservative Bound M_2

The expression of M_2 is given by:

$$\begin{aligned} M_2 &= \max_{\Delta_T \in [0,\Delta_T^{\max}]} k_2 \cdot \Delta_T \cdot [h_{\max} - h_r(\Delta_T)] = k_2 \cdot \max_{\Delta_T \in [0,\Delta_T^{\max}]} \Delta_T \cdot [h_{\max} - h_r(\Delta_T)] \\ &= k_2 \cdot \max_{\Delta_T \in [0,\Delta_T^{\max}]} \Delta_T \cdot \left[h_{\max} - \left(a + b \cdot \Delta_T + c \cdot (\Delta_T)^2\right)\right] \\ &= k_2 \cdot \max_{\Delta_T \in [0,\Delta_T^{\max}]} -c \cdot (\Delta_T)^3 - b \cdot (\Delta_T)^2 + (h_{max} - a) \cdot \Delta_T \end{aligned}$$

which leads to determining the extreme values of a third-degree polynomial (whose graph crosses the origin of coordinates) in a given compact interval determined by the range of variation of $T - T_a = \Delta_T \in [0, \Delta_T^{\max}]$; the roots of the derivative of such a polynomial are given by:

$$\Delta_T^+ = \frac{2b - \sqrt{4b^2 + 12c(h_{max} - a)}}{-6c} \geq 0, \quad \Delta_T^- = \frac{2b + \sqrt{4b^2 + 12c(h_{max} - a)}}{-6c} \leq 0$$

so that a local minimum is reached at the positive root Δ_T^+. Therefore, depending on the relationship between Δ_T^+ and $\Delta_T^{\max}$ we have:

$$M_2 = \begin{cases} k_2 \cdot \left(-c \cdot (\Delta_T^+)^3 - b \cdot (\Delta_T^+)^2 + (h_{max} - a) \cdot \Delta_T^+\right), \\ \text{if } \Delta_T^+ \leq \Delta_T^{\max}, \\ \\ k_2 \cdot \left(-c \cdot (\Delta_T^{max})^3 - b \cdot (\Delta_T^{\max})^2 + (h_{max} - a) \cdot \Delta_T^{\max}\right), \\ \text{if } \Delta_T^+ > \Delta_T^{\max}. \end{cases} \tag{17}$$

References

1. Boem, F., Ferrari, R.M., Keliris, C., Parisini, T., Polycarpou, M.M.: A distributed networked approach for fault detection of large-scale systems. IEEE Trans. Autom. Control **62**(1), 18–33 (2016)
2. Castillo, Á., Zufiria, P.J.: Fault detection schemes for continuous-time stochastic dynamical systems. IEEE Trans. Autom. Control **54**(8), 1820–1836 (2009)
3. Chen, J., Patton, R.J.: Robust Model-Based Fault Diagnosis For Dynamic Systems, vol. 3. Springer (2012)
4. Ding, S.X.: Model-Based Fault Diagnosis Techniques: Design Schemes, Algorithms, and Tools. Springer (2008)
5. Edwards, C., Spurgeon, S.K., Patton, R.J.: Sliding mode observers for fault detection and isolation. Automatica **36**(4), 541–553 (2000)
6. Faure, G., Vallée, M., Paulus, C., Tran, T.Q.: Fault detection and diagnosis for large solar thermal systems: a review of fault types and applicable methods. Sol. Energy **197**, 472–484 (2020)
7. Feierl, L., Unterberger, V., Rossi, C., Gerardts, B., Gaetani, M.: Fault detective: automatic fault-detection for solar thermal systems based on artificial intelligence. Sol. Energy Adv. **3**, 100033 (2023)
8. Gertler, J.: Fault Detection and Diagnosis in Engineering Systems. CRC Press (2017)
9. Isermann, R.: Fault-Diagnosis Systems: An Introduction from Fault Detection to Fault Tolerance. Springer (2005)
10. Julier, S.J., Uhlmann, J.K.: Unscented filtering and nonlinear estimation. Proc. IEEE **92**(3), 401–422 (2004)
11. Keliris, C., Polycarpou, M.M., Parisini, T.: An integrated learning and filtering approach for fault diagnosis of a class of nonlinear dynamical systems. IEEE Trans. Neural Netw. Learn. Syst. **28**(4), 988–1004 (2016)
12. Khalid, S., Song, J., Raouf, I., Kim, H.S.: Advances in fault detection and diagnosis for thermal power plants: a review of intelligent techniques. Mathematics **11**(8), 1767 (2023)
13. Polycarpou, M.M., Helmicki, A.J.: Automated fault detection and accommodation: a learning systems approach. IEEE Trans. Syst. Man Cybern. **25**(11), 1447–1458 (2002)
14. Ruiz-Moreno, S., Gallego, A.J., Sanchez, A.J., Camacho, E.F.: A cascade neural network methodology for fault detection and diagnosis in solar thermal plants. Renew. Energy **211**, 76–86 (2023)
15. Sobhani-Tehrani, E., Khorasani, K.: Fault Diagnosis of Nonlinear Systems Using a Hybrid Approach, vol. 383. Springer (2009)
16. Venkatasubramanian, V., Rengaswamy, R., Yin, K., Kavuri, S.N.: A review of process fault detection and diagnosis: part I: quantitative model-based methods. Comput. Chem. Eng. **27**(3), 293–311 (2003)

Experiment Evaluation-Testing and Validation of a Bio-Inspired Probabilistic Graphical Model for Root Cause Detection in an E-Commerce Application

Kapila Molri(✉) and Majid Shaalan

Harrisburg University of Science and Technology, Harrisburg, PA 170101, USA
kmolri@my.harrisburgu.edu, MShaalan@harrisburgu.edu
https://myhu.harrisburgu.edu/ICS/

Abstract. In this paper we are going to present the testing and validation of a bio-inspired fault detection and root cause analysis framework based on probabilistic graphical models for e-commerce application. The proposed method draws inspiration from biological systems to identify and diagnose faults in complex systems as was proposed in an earlier paper [1], leveraging the adaptability and resilience inherent in natural processes. A probabilistic graphical model (PGM) was designed to represent system variables and their dependencies, enabling robust inference for fault detection and localization. The experimental setup involved testing the framework on synthetic and real-world datasets, simulating various fault scenarios in industrial and computational systems. Key metrics, including accuracy, precision, recall, and computational efficiency, were used to evaluate the model's performance. The results demonstrated the framework's ability to identify faults and trace their root causes with high accuracy, even in noisy and uncertain environments. Future work will explore extending the framework to more complex systems and real-time implementations. This study provides valuable insights into the practical utility of bio-inspired probabilistic models in industrial diagnostics.

Keywords: Auto remediation · fault detection · machine learning · Probabilistic decision making

1 Introduction

Modern software systems generate vast volumes of incident reports, requiring rapid and accurate resolution. Traditional manual effort of reading and anlyzing these reports are labor-intensive and error-prone, often leading to delayed fixes and misallocated resources [23–25].The ability to accurately model relationships between faults, their symptoms, and resolutions is central to self-healing systems

H. R. Arabnia et al. (Eds.): CSCE 2025, CCIS 2932, pp. 256–271, 2026.
https://doi.org/10.1007/978-3-032-22193-3_19

[26–29]. Graph-based learning offers an expressive framework to capture such dependencies [30,31].

The process includes encoding features, assigning labels, constructing edge indices, and validating all aspects of the transformation. This enables further application of Graph Neural Networks (GNNs) for fault classification and resolution prediction [32,33].

This paper takes a step beyond theory, presenting the implementation and experimental validation of a bio-inspired probabilistic graphical model as was proposed for fault detection and root cause analysis [1]. Our goal is not just to explore the technical feasibility of this approach but to understand its real-world applicability—how it can enhance system reliability, reduce downtime, and offer scalable solutions for critical applications. The results of this exploration, I believe, will contribute to reimagining how we build and maintain resilient software systems, systems that don't just survive adversity but thrive in it.

2 Approach

By modeling the immune system as a probabilistic graphical model (PGM), we can represent the complex interactions and decision-making processes within the immune system using structured probabilistic relationships [21] A probabilistic graphical model provides a framework to express the depen- dencies among random variables, which, in this context, represent components of the immune system such as antigens, antibodies, and memory cells [18,19] In an AIS, the immune response can be viewed as a series of probabilistic inferences where each immune element's behavior depends on the state of other elements. By structuring these relationships in a graph, we can better understand the immune system's learning, adaptation, and classification abilities in uncertain environments [20]. Through PGMs, we can also integrate learning algorithms that help simulate the immune system's ability to adapt to new pathogens [34]. This not only improves AIS performance in tasks such as anomaly detection, optimization, and pattern recognition but also provides a more interpretable and scalable representation of the immune processes.

3 Data Collection Protocols

3.1 Overview of Data Sources

Our research project leverages a diverse set of data sources to capture comprehensive insights into software applications. The primary sources include:

Operation Logs: Detailed logs generated by software systems capture real-time operational metrics, error messages, and recovery actions. These logs are essential for identifying failure patterns and understanding system behavior. We have gathered these open source reports available from kaggle, microsoft azure.

`file:///C:/Users/User/Downloads/Azure%20status%20history%20_%20Microsoft%20Azure.html`

Figure 1 shows example set of one such incident reports from kaggle data set. These post-incident reports provide a comprehensive and systematic account of significant system disruptions. Each report is structured to capture critical information in several key areas like nature and timing of the incident, outlines what went wrong and why, also tells the kind of service which get disrupted.

Figure 1 (b) shows another such reports of operational failure. This incident report details a low-impact rate limiting event in the Alert application's API component within the staging environment. The disruption, caused by API misuse and sudden increases in traffic, resulted in throttled requests and exceeded API limits. A prompt replacement of the component enabled the system to recover in 81 minutes, and the report includes a thorough root cause analysis to guide future preventive measures.

Figure 1 (c) shows the web page azure status history. This webpage hosts detailed Post Incident Reviews documenting service issues that have occurred over time, with each report retained for five years. Since November 20, 2019, all publicly communicated issues were included, and from June 1, 2022 onward, the focus shifted to broad issues as outlined in the documentation.

Overall, these PIRs serve as a critical resource to understand past incidents, drive continuous improvement in service reliability.and these are published by different websites for over the years which helped us in extracting the features for our data set. We analyzed the structure of these incident reports which included, Free-text descriptions, Categorical fields (e.g., app name, priority level),Timestamps,User or system metadata.

3.2 Step-By-Step Protocols

The data collection process consists of five main steps:

- **Step 1: Identification of Data Sources:** The primary source of data is incident reports stored as PDF files. These reports follow a structured as well as unstructured format with sections such as:
  a.What happened? b. What went wrong and why? c.How did we respond? d.Timeline of events e.Preventative measures. like we have shown in Fig. 1, 2, 3.
- **Step 2: Extracting Text from PDFs**To extract data, we use PyMuPDF (Fitz) for text-based PDFs. For scanned/image-based PDFs, OCR (Tesseract + pdf2image) is applied. Tools Used:
  PyMuPDF → Extracts raw text from PDFs.
  Tesseract OCR → Converts images to text for scanned PDFs.
  PDF2Image → Converts PDFs to images for OCR processing.

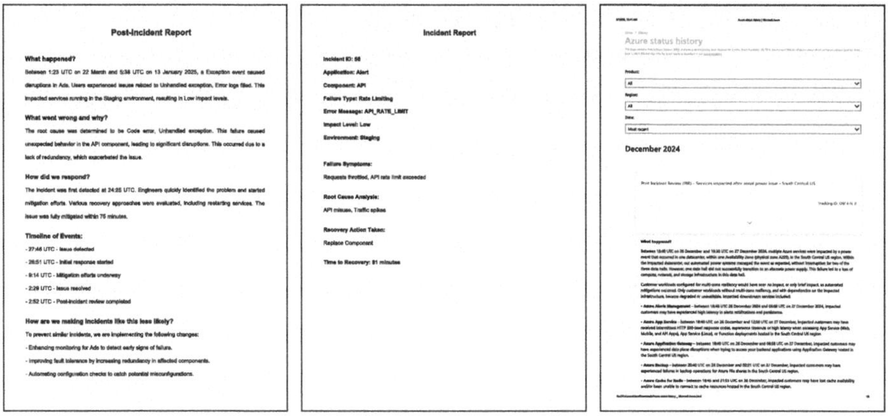

Post-Incident Report

What happened?

Between 1:23 UTC on 22 March and 5:38 UTC on 13 January 2025, a Exception event caused disruptions in Ads. Users experienced issues related to Unhandled exception, Error logs filled. This impacted services running in the Staging environment, resulting in Low impact levels.

What went wrong and why?

The root cause was determined to be Code error, Unhandled exception. This failure caused unexpected behavior in the API component, leading to significant disruptions. This occurred due to a lack of redundancy, which exacerbated the issue.

How did we respond?

The incident was first detected at 24:25 UTC. Engineers quickly identified the problem and started mitigation efforts. Various recovery approaches were evaluated, including restarting services. The issue was fully mitigated within 75 minutes.

Timeline of Events:

- 27:46 UTC - Issue detected
- 28:51 UTC - Initial response started
- 9:14 UTC - Mitigation efforts underway
- 2:29 UTC - Issue resolved
- 2:52 UTC - Post-incident review completed

How are we making incidents like this less likely?

To prevent similar incidents, we are implementing the following changes:

- Enhancing monitoring for Ads to detect early signs of failure.
- Improving fault tolerance by increasing redundancy in affected components.
- Automating configuration checks to catch potential misconfigurations.

Incident Report

Incident ID: 56
Application: Alert
Component: API
Failure Type: Rate Limiting
Error Message: API_RATE_LIMIT
Impact Level: Low
Environment: Staging

Failure Symptoms:
Requests throttled, API rate limit exceeded

Root Cause Analysis:
API misuse, Traffic spikes

Recovery Action Taken:
Replace Component

Time to Recovery: 81 minutes

Azure status history

December 2024

What happened?

(a) Detailed Incident Report (b) Incident Report 56 (c) Azure Status History

Fig. 1. Example set of combined incident reports and Azure status history visualization.

- **Step 3: Structuring the Extracted Data** Once text is extracted, we apply Natural Language Processing (NLP) and Regex to structure data into predefined categories:
  Timestamp → Extracted using regex patterns for HH:MM UTC.
  Application → Identified using regex and NLP models.
  Component → Extracted using context-aware NLP parsing.
  Failure Type → Matched against a predefined list (Exception, Crash, Timeout).
  Error Message → Extracted using error log patterns.
  Failure Symptoms → Derived from reported user impact.
  Root Cause → Identified from the "What went wrong and why?" section.
  Error State → Determined based on system behavior.
  Recovery Actions → Extracted from "How did we respond?".
  Outcome → Categorized into "Success, Partial Success, Failure".
  Environment → Extracted from "Production, Staging, Development" details.
  User Impact → Identified from "Low, Medium, High" impact statements.

- **Step 4: Data Cleaning and Standardization**
  To ensure consistency, the extracted data undergoes:
  Removal of irrelevant text (caused unexpected, filler words).
  Standardized timestamp format (YYYY-MM-DD HH:MM UTC).
  Normalization of terms (Database Lock → Database Issue, Service Unavailable → Outage).
  Validation against known values (ensuring "Timeout" matches failure types).

- **Step 5: Exporting to CSV for Analysis**
  The structured data is stored in a CSV format for further analysis. Column order is standardized: Timestamp is the first column, followed by extracted features.

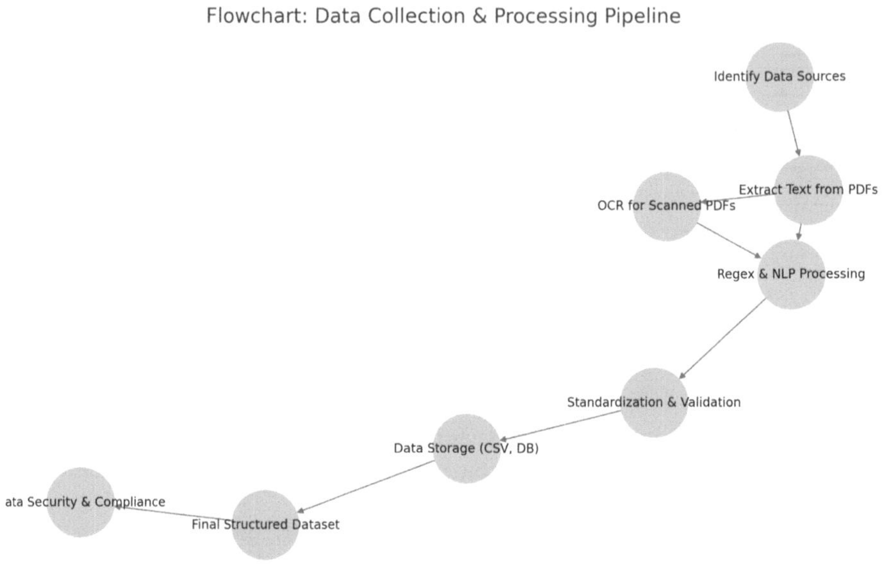

Fig. 2. Data Collection and Processing Pipeline.

3.3 Feature Space

We have defined a comprehensive mapping of applications, components, and failure types typically seen in distributed software systems. It serves as a foundational structure to simulate, analyze, and diagnose software failures using structured metadata and relationships between system entities. Almost 30 applications were defined and each application is mapped to its underlying infrastructure where different components have distinct failure profiles

```
    # Define possible values for each field with more detailed mappings
applications = {
    'Inventory', 'UserAuth', 'PaymentGateway', 'ShoppingCart', 'OrderProcessing', 'Customer',
    'Billing', 'Notification', 'Analytics', 'Search', 'Profile', 'ContentDelivery',
    'FileStorage',
    'Identity', 'Reporting', 'Audit', 'Compliance', 'Alert', 'Session', 'Preference',
    'Geolocation',
    'Weather', 'Currency', 'Translation',
    'Calendar', 'NotificationHub', 'SocialMedia',
    'Ads',
```

```
    'Media', 'Review'
}

components = {
    'Inventory': ['Database', 'API', 'Application Server'],
    'UserAuth': ['Authentication Server', 'Web Server'],
    'PaymentGateway': ['API', 'Web Server', 'Database'],
    'ShoppingCart': ['Web Server', 'Database'],
    'OrderProcessing': ['Application Server', 'Database'],
    'Customer': ['Web Server', 'Database'],
    'Billing': ['Application Server', 'Database'],
    'Notification': ['API', 'Web Server'],
    'Analytics': ['API', 'Database', 'Web Server'],
    'Review': ['Database', 'Application Server'],
    'Geolocation': ['API', 'Database'],
    'ContentDelivery': ['Content Delivery Network', 'Web Server'],
    'Profile': ['Web Server', 'Database'],
    'Preference': ['Web Server', 'Database'],
    'Calendar': ['API', 'Web Server'],
    'Weather': ['API', 'Web Server'],
    'Currency': ['API', 'Database'],
    'Translation': ['API', 'Web Server'],
    'Audit': ['Database', 'Application Server'],
    'SocialMedia': ['API', 'Web Server'],
    'Ads': ['API', 'Database'],
    'Media': ['Content Delivery Network', 'Web Server'],
    'NotificationHub': ['API', 'Database'],
    'Alert': ['API', 'Web Server'],
    'Session': ['Web Server', 'Database']
}

failure_types = {
    'Database': ['Timeout', 'Disk Full', 'Crash'],
    'API': ['Exception', 'Rate Limiting', 'Service Unavailable'],
    'Application Server': ['Memory Leak', 'CPU Overload', 'Service Degradation'],
    'Web Server': ['Timeout', 'Connection Refused', 'High Latency'],
    'Authentication Server': ['Timeout', 'Service Unavailable', 'Configuration Error'],
    'Content Delivery Network': ['Service Unavailable', 'High Latency'],
    'Geolocation': ['Service Unavailable', 'High Latency'],
    'Profile': ['Configuration Error', 'Service Unavailable'],
    'Calendar': ['Service Unavailable', 'Timeout'],
    'Weather': ['Service Unavailable', 'High Latency'],
    'Currency': ['Service Unavailable', 'Timeout'],
    'Translation': ['Service Unavailable', 'Timeout'],
    'Audit': ['Disk Full', 'Configuration Error'],
    'SocialMedia': ['Service Unavailable', 'Rate Limiting'],
    'Ads': ['Service Unavailable', 'High Latency'],
    'FileStorage': ['Disk Full', 'Configuration Error'],
    'NotificationHub': ['Service Unavailable', 'Configuration Error'],
    'Alert': ['Service Unavailable', 'Configuration Error'],
    'Session': ['Timeout', 'Service Unavailable']
}
```

and then other features like error messages, failure symptoms, enviornment, root causes,error states, recovery actions and other more useful feature were mapped.

3.4 Data Pre-Processing

Our data preprocessing pipeline was designed to ensure data quality, consistency, and reproducibility while preparing raw operational data for advanced analytics and machine learning applications [2]. This process is integral to our research on self-healing systems, where accurate feature engineering is critical for building robust predictive models and enabling Graph Neural Network (GNN) applications [3–5].

3.5 Data Ingestion and Inspection

- **Data Loading:** The dataset was loaded from CSV files containing system logs, synthetic data creator, and incident reports.
- **Initial Inspection:** We performed a preliminary exploration by displaying the first few rows, summary statistics, and the dataset's structure using functions such as `head()`, `info()`, and `describe()`.
- **Missing Values Handling:**
  - **Numerical Columns:** Missing values were imputed using the median of each column [6].
  - **Categorical Columns:** Missing values were filled with the most frequent value (mode) [7].

Before executing these steps, we have ensured that all necessary libraries are imported. We will need pandas, numpy, and several modules from scikit-learn for these steps.

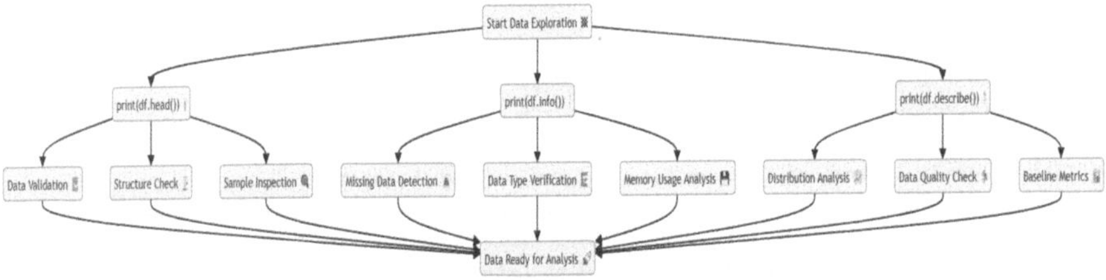

Fig. 3. Health Check Up Phase of data analysis.

3.6 Data Transformation and Encoding

- **Categorical Variable Encoding:**
  - **Label Encoding** was applied to ordinal variables (e.g., `User Impact`, `Recovery Steps`, `Outcome`), preserving their inherent order [8]
  - **One-Hot Encoding** was applied to nominal variables (e.g., `Application`, `Component`, `Error Message`), transforming each category into individual binary columns [9].
- **Feature Scaling:** Numerical features (e.g., `Downtime Duration`, `Resolution Time`) were normalized using `StandardScaler` to ensure consistency across features. [10]

4 Experimental Evaluation

4.1 Datasets

Probabilistic graphical model was tested on :

- Incident reports:past five years(6250) reports
- Azure status history reports: Past five years(5101) reports
- Synthetic Data set

4.2 Making of the Graph

We have done probabilistic graph-based analysis of incident reports using NetworkX. Since we have to model asymmetric relationships (e.g., dependencies, workflows). Explicitly models sequences like `Fault Identification` → `Failure Analysis` → `Resolution`, which are critical for root cause analysis. Directed graph fits our need to model sequences and causal relationships. We convert the previously constructed NetworkX graph into a format compatible with PyTorch Geometric for use in Graph Neural Networks (GNNs). Each step is validated to ensure consistency and correctness. The next steps sets up graph neural networks (GNNs) for a node classification task using PyTorch Geometric. Three popular GNN architectures are defined and imple- mented (Table 1): 1. Graph Convolutional Network (GCN) 2. GraphSAGE 3. Graph Attention Network (GAT) The main purposes for setting up multiple GNN models include: âĂŞ Comparing performance across different graph learning techniques [11–13] âĂŞ Evaluating effectiveness for tasks such as node classification and link prediction. âĂŞ Identifying optimal models based on accuracy, efficiency, and interpretability [14].

Table 1. Comparison of GNN Model Options

Model	Core Idea	Key Strengths	Applications
GCN	Spectral graph convolutions	Simplicity, interpretability, computational efficiency	Node classification,simpler graph tasks
GraphSAGE	Aggregation of neighborhood information	Scalability, generalization, large-scale applicability	Social networks, large graphs
GAT	Attention-based neighbor weighting	High accuracy, interpretability via attention	Complex graphs, tasks needing explainability

Next, we set the model to evaluation mode. This is important because some layers, like dropout or batch normalization, behave differently during training versus evaluation [15,16]. So by calling model.eval(), we ensure those layers are in the right mode for inference. Next, we compare different GNN models by training each one and recording their loss and training time. Starting with the model comparison section, the code loops through each model in the 'models' dictionary. For each model, it trains it using a 'train model' function and stores the final loss and training duration in the 'results' dictionary. After training all models, performance metrics are compared as shown in Fig. 4, while Figs. 5 and 6 illustrate the dependency and probabilistic graph visualizations.

4.3 Results

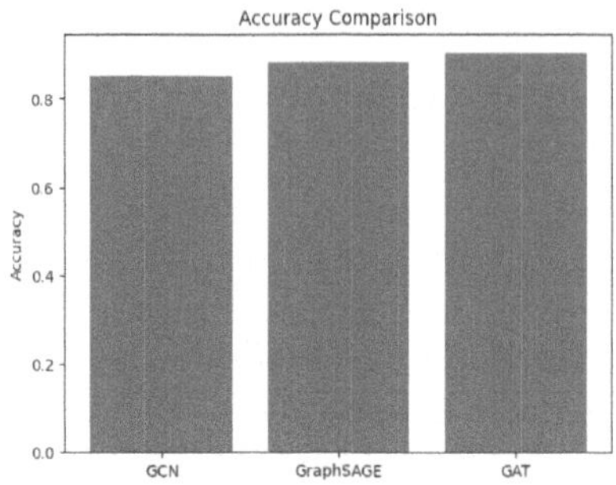

(a) Accuracy comparisons of three models

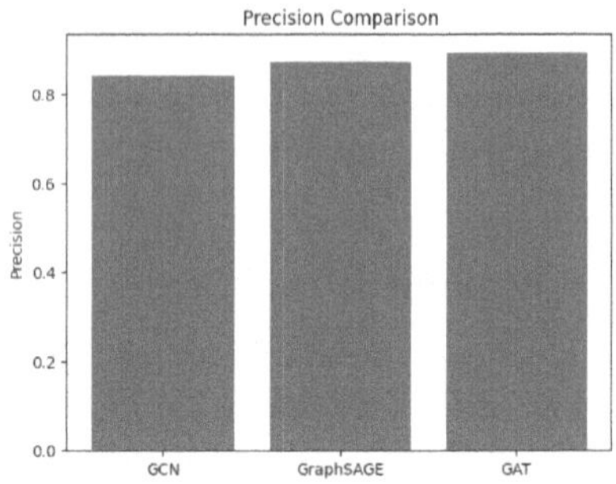

(b) Precision comparison of three models

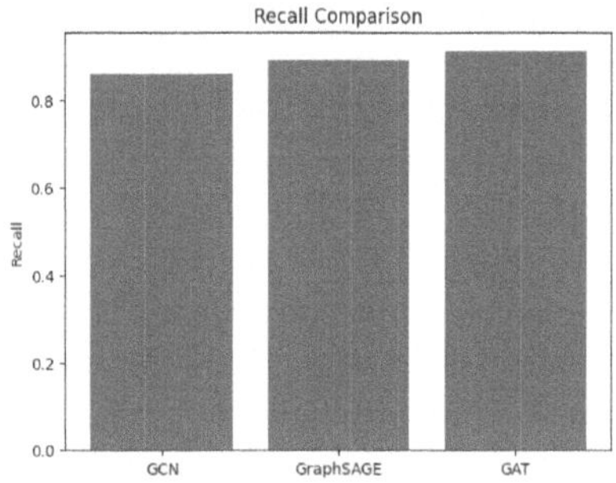

(c) Recall comparison of three models

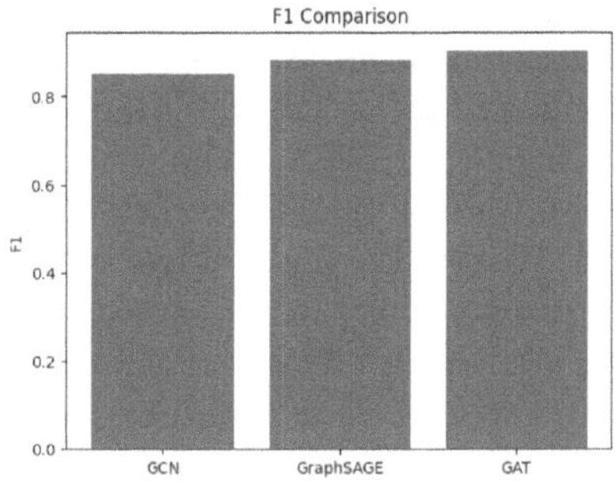

(d) F1 comparison of three models

Fig. 4. Comparison chart of three models based on accuracy, precision, recall and F1 score.

```
    Training GCN...
Training GraphSAGE...
Training GAT...
GCN: Loss = 0.6289, Accuracy = 0.5417
GraphSAGE: Loss = 0.6245, Accuracy = 0.5833
GAT: Loss = 0.6638, Accuracy = 0.5833
Classification Report:
                      precision    recall  f1-score   support

    Failure Analysis       0.75      0.43      0.55        14
Fault Identification       0.50      0.80      0.62        10

            accuracy                           0.58        24
           macro avg       0.62      0.61      0.58        24
        weighted avg       0.65      0.58      0.57        24
```

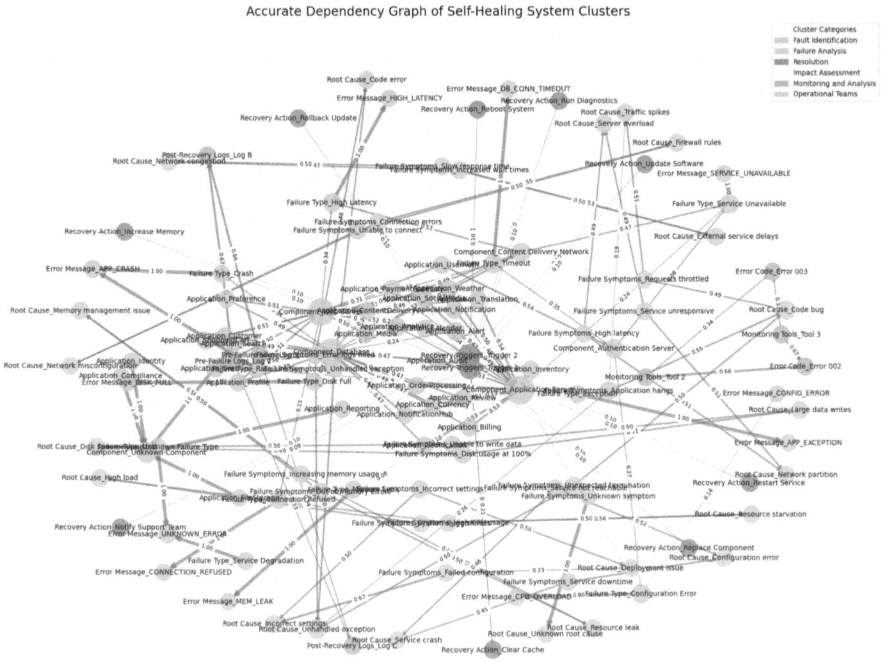

Fig. 5. Full Dependency graph.

Looking at the results, GCN has a loss of 0.6289 and accuracy of 0.5417. GraphSAGE and GAT have slightly lower losses and higher accuracy at 0.5833. But accuracy alone isn't enough, especially with imbalanced classes. The classification report gives more insight.

For "Failure Analysis," precision is 0.75, which means when the model predicts this class, it's correct 75% of the time. However, recall is 0.43, so it only identifies 43% of actual instances. This might indicate the model is conservative in predicting this class. The F1-score is 0.55, which is moderate.

For "Fault Identification," precision drops to 0.50, meaning half the predictions are correct. But recall is higher at 0.80, so it captures most actual instances. The F1 here is 0.62. The macro averages are around 0.6, and weighted averages are slightly lower due to class distribution.

The accuracy of 58% is just the overall correct predictions. But with the classes having different supports (14 vs. 10), the model's performance isn't uniform. The macro avg F1 is 0.58, suggesting average performance across classes, while the weighted avg is 0.57, reflecting class imbalance.

Class 1: Failure Analysis (support = 14) Precision (0.75): When the model predicts "Failure Analysis," it's correct 75% of the time.

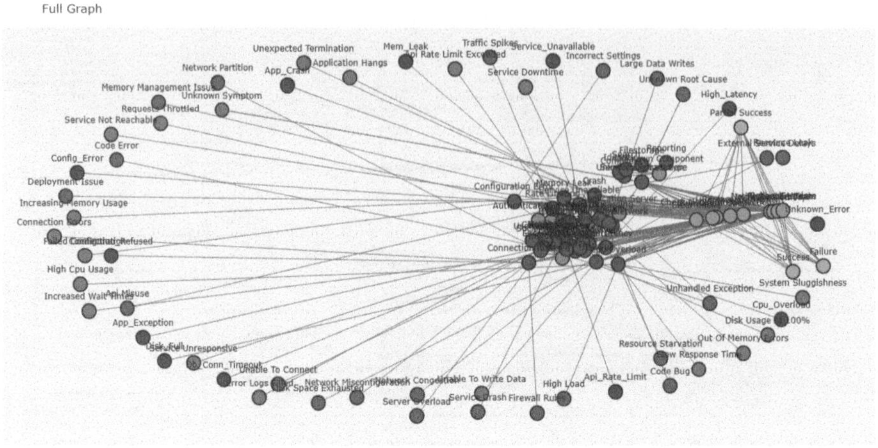

Fig. 6. Explainable and color coded Probabilistic graph.

Recall (0.43): The model only identifies 43%of all true "Failure Analysis" cases.

F1-Score (0.55): Moderate balance between precision and recall.

Issue: High precision but low recall → The model is conservative (avoids false positives but misses many true positives).

Class 2: Fault Identification (support = 10)
Precision (0.50): When the model predicts "Fault Identification," it's correct 50% of the time.

Recall (0.80): The model identifies 80% of all true "Fault Identification" cases.

F1-Score (0.62): Better balance than "Failure Analysis".

Issue: Low precision but high recall → The model is overly generous (catches most true positives but has many false positives).

Figure 7 shows Graph views centered on 'Database' and 'Inventory'. Bottom: Corresponding explainability panels.

Figure 8 is a receiver Operating Characteristic (ROC) curve, which is used to evaluate the performance of a binary classification model. X-axis: False Positive Rate (FPR) - proportion of actual negatives that were incorrectly predicted as positive. Y-axis: True Positive Rate (TPR) or Recall - proportion of actual positives that were correctly predicted. The diagonal dashed line is the line of

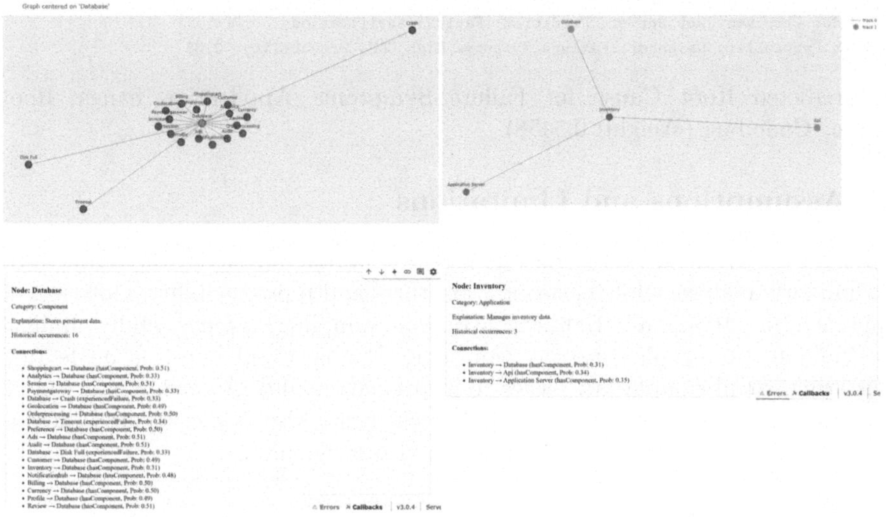

Fig. 7. Top: Graph views centered on 'Database' and 'Inventory'. Bottom: Corresponding explainability panels.

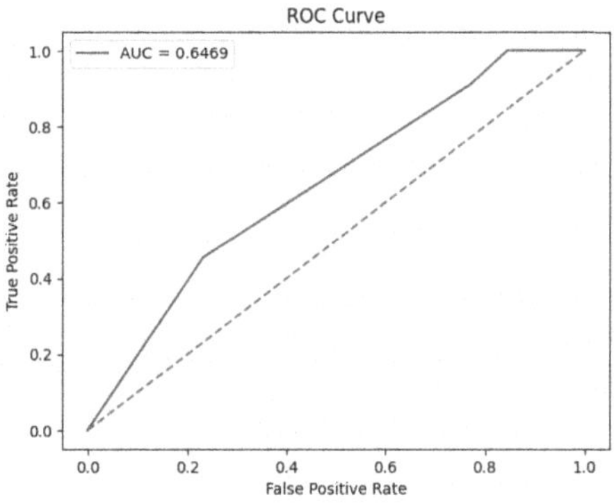

Fig. 8. Receiver Operating Characteristic (ROC) curve.

no-discrimination (i.e., a random classifier). Any classifier performing along this line is doing no better than random guessing. The blue curve represents the performance of your model across various classification thresholds.

```
AUC = 0.6469  #0.6469 indicates that model performs better than random
```

This is the Area Under the Curve, a single scalar value summarizing the ROC curve. AUC ranges from 0.5 (random) to 1.0 (perfect). Next, we Validate if the model's predictions align with the graph's topological relationships (e.g., nodes predicted to belong to a cluster are strongly connected to neighbors in that cluster).

```
    Node: Component_Web_Server, Predicted: Fault Identification,
Highest Probability Neighbor: Failure_Symptoms_High_CPU, Probability: 0.85
```

Predicted Root Cause for Failure Symptoms_Application hangs: Root Cause_Code bug (Weight: 0.5458)

5 Assumptions and Limitations

All these experiments were done on a representative subset of the dataset for preliminary analysis while ensuring robustness and reproducibility. Our current approach (n = 10 and n = 1000 simple random sampling) is purposefully minimal to: Validate the graph construc- tion logic, Enable rapid iteration on feature clustering, small samples are easier to inspect manually). A random state of 42 ensuring the same sample is generated across runs. Also,It was ensured there is no overlap between training, validation, and testing splits.

```
    **VALIDATING SPLITS**
Splits are mutually exclusive.
Training nodes: 84
Validation nodes: 12
Testing nodes: 24
```

The optimizer is Adam with a learning rate of 0.01. Adam is a popular choice because it adapts the learning rate during training, which can lead to faster convergence. [17] The learning rate of 0.01 is a common starting point, but might need tuning depending on the dataset. The loss function is CrossEntropyLoss, which is standard for classification tasks. It measures the difference between the predicted probabilities and the actual labels. Then there's a loop for 200 epochs. Each epoch is a full pass over the training data meaning Iterates over the dataset 200 times. It allows the model to learn patterns by repeatedly adjusting weights. Efficiency Note: We understand a fixed epoch count (200) risks overfitting or under- fitting and it is better to use early stopping (halt training when validation loss plateaus) but for early experimentation we will continue with this experiment.

6 Conclusions

This paper has implemented a bio-inspired approach for autonomous self-healing in software systems. The proposed methodology incorporates techniques such as probabilistic graph theory, machine learning, and redundancy mechanisms to realize self-awareness, damage assessment, and proactive recovery in computational systems. A detailed evaluation methodology was presented consisting of diverse fault injection scenarios, metrics for damage resilience and perpetual testing, as well as comparative analyses against traditional testing approaches. The results of these experiments are presented for prototype model by bridging biological self-healing principles with next-generation computing systems, this pioneering research promises to transform the landscape for building resilient, self-sustaining software capable of immortal computation.

References

1. Molri, K., Shaalan, M.: Towards development and implementation of bioinspired algorithms to enhance self-healing and fault tolerance in critical software systems. In: Submitted to 11th International Conference on Computational Science and Computational Intelligence (CSCI 2024) (2024)
2. Chapman, A.P., Missier, P., Simonelli, G., Torlone, R.: Capturing and querying fine-grained provenance of preprocessing pipelines in data science. In: Proc. VLDB Endow. vol. 13, no. 12, pp. 3149–3161 (2020). https://doi.org/10.14778/3407790.3407831
3. Sancricca, C., Cappiello, C.: Supporting the design of data preparation pipelines. In: Proc. Sistemi Evoluti per Basi di Dati (SEBD) (2022)
4. Lim, C.S., Elnawawi, S., Rippon, L., O'Connor, D.L., Gopaluni, R.B.: Data quality over quantity: pitfalls and guidelines for process analytics. IFAC-PapersOnLine **55**(10) (2022). https://doi.org/10.1016/j.ifacol.2022.10.205
5. Gupta, N., et al.: Data quality for machine learning tasks. In: Proceedings of the 27th ACM SIGKDD Conference on Knowledge Discovery and Data Mining (KDD) (2021). https://doi.org/10.1145/3447548.3467272
6. Gautam, R., Latifi, S.: Comparison of simple missing data imputation techniques for numerical and categorical datasets. In: Proc. (2023)
7. Kaiser, J.: Dealing with missing values in data. J. Syst. Integration **5**(1), 42–51 (2014). https://doi.org/10.20470/jsi.v5i1.129
8. Haq, I., Gondal, I., Vamplew, P., Brown, S.: Categorical features transformation with compact one-hot encoder for fraud detection in distributed environment. In: Proc. Australasian Data Mining Conference (AusDM) (2018)
9. Gnat, S.: Impact of categorical variables encoding on property mass valuation. In: Proc. International Conference on Knowledge-Based Intelligent Information and Engineering Systems (KES) (2021)
10. Ahsan, M., Mahmud, M., Saha, P., Gupta, K.D., Siddique, Z.: Effect of data scaling methods on machine learning algorithms and model performance. Technologies **9**(3), 1–19 (2021). https://doi.org/10.3390/technologies9030052
11. Fey, M., Lenssen, J.E.: Fast graph representation learning with PyTorch Geometric. arXiv preprint arXiv:1903.02428 (2019). https://arxiv.org/abs/1903.02428
12. Wu, J., Sun, J., Sun, H., Sun, G.: Performance analysis of graph neural network frameworks. In: Proc. IEEE International Symposium on Performance Analysis of Systems and Software (ISPASS) (2021). https://doi.org/10.1109/ISPASS51385.2021.00018
13. Wang, X., Vinel, A.: Benchmarking graph neural networks on link prediction. arXiv preprint arXiv:2105.13335 (2021). https://arxiv.org/abs/2105.13335
14. Kaler, T., et al.: Accelerating training and inference of graph neural networks with fast sampling and pipelining. In: Proc. 3rd Conference on Machine Learning and Systems (MLSys) (2021)
15. Xie, X., Madankan, R., Wu, K.: Inference calibration of neural network models. In: Proc. 2022 IEEE International Conference on Knowledge Graph (ICKG), Nanjing, China (2022)
16. Suzuki, M., Nagano, T., Kurata, G., Thomas, S.: Inference-invariant transformation of batch normalization for domain adaptation of acoustic models. In: Proc. Interspeech 2018, Hyderabad, India (2018)

17. Xie, Z., Wang, X., Zhang, H., Sato, I., Sugiyama, M.: Adai: separating the effects of adaptive learning rate and momentum inertia. arXiv preprint arXiv:2006.06865 (2020)
18. Koller, D., Friedman, N.: Probabilistic Graphical Models: Principles and Techniques. MIT Press (2009)
19. Airoldi, E.M.: Getting started in probabilistic graphical models. PLoS Comput. Biol. **3**(12), e252 (2007)
20. Ray, S., Lakdawala, S., Goswami, M., Gao, C.: Learning Graph Neural Networks for Multivariate Time Series Anomaly Detection (2021). http://arxiv.org/abs/2111.08082
21. Nadjak, K., Yin, G.: Recent Developments on Probabilistic Graphical Model Applied in Data Analysis (2020)
22. Deliparaschos, K.M., Michail, K., et al.: Facilitating autonomous systems with AI-based fault tolerance and computational resource economy. Electronics (Switzerland) **9**(5) (2020).
23. Dillig, T., Aiken, A.: Automated error diagnosis using abductive inference. In: Proceedings of the 33rd ACM SIGPLAN Conference on Programming Language Design and Implementation (PLDI), New York, NY, USA, pp. 568–578 . Association for Computing Machinery (2012). https://doi.org/10.1145/2254064.2254087
24. Knab, P., Fluri, B., Gall, H., Pinzger, M.: Interactive views for analyzing problem reports. In: 2009 IEEE International Conference on Software Maintenance, Edmonton, AB, Canada, pp. 309–312 (2009). https://doi.org/10.1109/ICSM.2009.5306339
25. Yeasmin, S., Roy, C., Schneider, K.A.: Interactive visualization of bug reports using topic evolution and extractive summaries. In: 2014 IEEE International Conference on Software Maintenance and Evolution (ICSME), Victoria, BC, Canada, pp. 491–495 (2014). https://doi.org/10.1109/ICSME.2014.80
26. Ghosh, D., Sharman, R., Rao, H., Upadhyaya, S.: Self-healing systems: survey and synthesis. Decis. Support Syst. **42**(4), 2164–2185 (2007). https://doi.org/10.1016/j.dss.2006.05.006
27. Lu, W., Zhu, Y., Ma, C., Zhang, L.: A fault model centered modeling framework for self-healing computing systems. In: Proceedings of the 2011 International Conference on Artificial Intelligence and Computational Intelligence (AICI), pp. 345–349 (2011). https://doi.org/10.1109/AICI.2011.82
28. Jiang, M., Zhang, J., Raymer, D., Strassner, J.: A modeling framework for self-healing software systems. In: 2007 IEEE International Conference on Systems, Man and Cybernetics, Montreal, QC, Canada, pp. 336–341 (2007). https://doi.org/10.1109/ICSMC.2007.4413612
29. Nikolic, J., Jubatyrov, N., Pournaras, E.: Self-healing dilemmas in distributed systems: fault correction vs. fault tolerance. IEEE Trans. Netw. Serv. Manage. **17**(4), 2275–2289 (2020). https://doi.org/10.1109/TNSM.2020.3020014
30. Hamilton, W.L., Ying, R., Leskovec, J.: Representation learning on graphs: methods and applications. IEEE Data Eng. Bull. **40**(3), 52–74 (2017)
31. Cao, S., Lu, W., Xu, Q.: Deep neural networks for learning graph representations. In: Proceedings of the Thirtieth AAAI Conference on Artificial Intelligence (AAAI), Phoenix, AZ, USA, pp. 1145–1152 (2016)
32. Yang, Z., Cohen, W.W., Salakhutdinov, R.: Revisiting semi-supervised learning with graph embeddings. In: Proceedings of the 33rd International Conference on Machine Learning (ICML), New York, NY, USA, pp. 40–48 (2016)

33. Brefeld, U., Getoor, L., Macskassy, S.A.: In: MLG@KDD Proceedings of the Eighth Workshop on Mining and Learning with Graphs, MLG '10, Washington, D.C., USA, 24-25 July (2010)
34. Alonso-Barba, J.I., Nielsen, J., Ossa, L.D.L., Puerta, J.M.: Learning probabilistic graphical models: a review of techniques and applications in medicine. In: Proc. 2012 Int. Conf. on Machine Learning Applications (ICMLA) (2012)

A Framework for Simulating Resilient Cloud-Edge AI Tasking for Geospatial Operations in Contested Environments

Haley Dozier(✉), Raimundo Dos Santos, and Victoria D. Moore

US Army Engineer Research and Development Center - Information Technology Laboratory, Vicksburg, MS 39180, USA
{Haley.R.Dozier,Raimundo.F.DosSantos,Victoria.D.Moore}@erdc.dren.mil

Abstract. The increasing reliance on edge-cloud computing architectures to support geospatial decision-making and battlefield analytics introduces a critical vulnerability in Denied, Degraded, Intermittent, and Limited-bandwidth (DDIL) environments. This paper proposes a potential reinforcement learning-based simulation framework that models task-aware resilience across variable data availability, network conditions, and compute heterogeneity. Using operationally relevant geospatial datasets, the framework will evaluate dynamic AI tasking strategies—such as data offloading, model compression, and adaptive routing under degraded conditions.

Keywords: machine learning · network simulation · reinforcement learning · resilience · edge-cloud computing

1 Introduction

The increasing reliance on edge-cloud computing architectures to support geospatial decision-making and battlefield analytics introduces a critical vulnerability in Denied, Degraded, Intermittent, and Limited-bandwidth (DDIL) environments. Operational tasks such as battle damage assessment, terrain classification, and lidar-based object detection are often computationally expensive. That is, they require significant computational resources and large, high-fidelity data to work effectively. Exploring DDIL conditions in a simulated environment is challenging, as these conditions frequently disrupt data collection, transmission, and processing at the tactical edge.

Reinforcement learning (RL) offers a promising method to explore this complex design tradespace. Constructing a simulation environment where the agent learns to adapt task assignments across a mix of cloud, edge, and high-performance computing (HPC) nodes allows for investigating resiliency in a complex battlespace. This research explores using reinforcement learning to simulate, evaluate, and optimize resilient edge-cloud configurations required to maintain mission-essential AI capability even when complete data availability or network connectivity cannot be guaranteed.

H. R. Arabnia et al. (Eds.): CSCE 2025, CCIS 2932, pp. 272–276, 2026.
https://doi.org/10.1007/978-3-032-22193-3_20

2 Related Work

Reinforcement learning has shown strong potential for adaptive decision-making in complex, mission-driven environments, including prior applications in mission engineering and task allocation under uncertainty [1–3]. However, most existing research isolates a single dimension of system behavior—such as optimizing AI performance under constrained data, modeling network resilience, or scheduling tasks across distributed compute resources [4,6,7]. In contrast, the framework presented here integrates all three: data availability and quality (e.g., missing or degraded raster/lidar data), network reliability (e.g., bandwidth variability, edge-node failures), and compute heterogeneity (e.g., GPU-enabled edge devices, cloud infrastructure, HPC nodes). This holistic view more accurately reflects the operational conditions encountered in contested environments and enables tradespace analysis rather than single-objective optimization.

Previous approaches often rely on rule-based heuristics or deterministic optimization [5,7], which lack adaptability and generalization across scenarios. By contrast, reinforcement learning supports dynamic policy learning, enabling agents to balance competing objectives—such as latency, accuracy, and resource efficiency—under variable conditions.

Finally, while conventional edge-cloud resilience research tends to focus on system uptime metrics (e.g., node availability, throughput, packet loss) [8,9], the approach taken here emphasizes task-aware resilience. This framework is designed to answer operationally relevant questions: How much data loss is tolerable before AI performance degrades? Can alternate data sources compensate for incomplete inputs? What is the minimum threshold of fidelity required to complete the task? These insights reveal critical gaps in current capabilities and inform future development of robust systems and networks.

3 Geospatial Edge-Compute Operations Model Features

3.1 Data

Simulated tasks are drawn from military-relevant, geospatial engineering workflows. Therefore, the datasets that will be used within this framework will include raster-based overhead imagery collected by satellites or Unmanned Aerial Vehicles (UAVs) for classification tasks, vector data representing geospatial overlays used in terrain analysis, and lidar-derived point clouds for 3D structure reconstruction. Additional inputs will include spatio-temporal datasets derived from mobile platforms and sensor time series, as well as network-level telemetry capturing communication throughput, packet loss, and latency variability. Together, these datasets reflect the diversity and complexity of military, geospatial, operational environments. Tasks are paired with synthetic network conditions where edge devices may intermittently lose connectivity, suffer from compute degradation, or receive incomplete or corrupted data.

3.2 Network Conditions

To explore adaptive tasking under constrained compute and network conditions, the simulation-based testbed will integrate realistic operational contexts (e.g., UAV imagery ingestion, real-time damage assessment, lidar-based 3D reconstruction), diverse data modalities (e.g., raster/vector geospatial data, point clouds, sensor time series), and varied network topologies (e.g., high-latency cloud links, intermittent edge connectivity, mobile ad hoc nodes).

3.3 Compute Heterogeneity

Varying combinations of computing systems and processing units, such as constrained GPUs at the edge versus large HPC nodes in the cloud, are considered for model compression (e.g., speed, accuracy, availability, degradation, failure). Emulated environments with varied compute availability, each with differing data access privileges and delays, will explore processing strengths to determine optimal edge cloud configurations for geospatially grounded operational scenarios.

3.4 Reinforcement Learning

The simulation framework be developed utilizing the OpenAI Gym [10] framework and will leverage open source libraries such as stablebaselines [13] to create a reinforcement learning agent that can select actions such as offloading data to cloud or retaining at the edge, choosing alternative data sources when primary collections are unavailable, applying model compression or resolution reduction, and adjusting model fidelity based on compute constraints. The agent's rewards can then be computed based on successful task completion (e.g., percent accurate image classification), resource utilization, and response latency. Additionally, constraints such as minimum viable data thresholds and tolerance to missing data are incorporated into the environment to support realistic decision-making. Through the agent's exploration of the environment, a resilient tradespace can be formalized that characterizes performance across multiple dimensions.

Initial training of the reinforcement learning agent is conducted using model-free reinforcement learning techniques (such as proximal policy optimization [11]), which are well-suited for environments with sparse or delayed rewards and complex action spaces. As the simulation environment matures, future experiments may incorporate model-based reinforcement learning to enable planning under uncertainty and faster convergence in partially observable domains.

4 Example Use Case Scenario

The following scenario is presented as initial proof-of-concept use case designed to demonstrate the core capabilities of the proposed framework. This scenario provides a simplified operational context that allows systematic evaluation of key variables such as compute availability, data degradation, and communication constraints. This foundational example serves to validate the environment design, reinforce the applicability of reinforcement learning for adaptive decision-making, and establish baseline comparisons against heuristic and optimization-based strategies. Future work will expand upon this initial effort by incorporating more complex, multi-agent scenarios, diverse data modalities, and additional real-world mission constraints.

4.1 Scenario

In this scenario, an Unmanned Aerial Vehicle (UAV) collects overhead imagery of a simulated battlefield with the objective of classifying images to assess damage in real time. In this environment, DDIL communication and compute conditions may apply at varying levels. Key operational challenges include intermittent edge compute failures, high-latency and bandwidth-limited cloud access, constrained data transfer requiring tradeoffs in image resolution and compression, and degraded imagery caused by occlusions, frame loss, or environmental interference.

The simulation environment for this scenario includes a configurable data pipeline using the xBD dataset [12], which provides both pre and post disaster imagery for supervised learning and evaluation. Degradation is applied to mimic realistic data loss and compression impacts. Compute options include on-device GPU resources at the edge and remote CPU resources in the cloud. The action space for the reinforcement learning agent includes decisions to offload, compress, defer, or reroute tasks based on available resources and task parameters. The agent state includes observables such as network conditions, compute status, data quality indicators, and task criticality scores.

This scenario was chosen for its tactical ISR relevance, alignment with public datasets, and suitability for early benchmarking. It supports controlled experimentation across key decision variables and enables comparisons with baseline heuristics and deterministic methods. The use case allows exploration of critical questions, such as the data quality threshold for reliable inference, the effectiveness of model compression under constraint, and whether reinforcement learning can outperform static rules when edge compute is intermittently available.

5 Future Work

Future efforts will focus on expanding the framework's adaptability, realism, and operational relevance. Planned extensions include the integration of federated learning for model retraining under DDIL constraints, incorporation of uncertainty-aware and Bayesian reinforcement learning agents, and the development of explainable or causally informed policies to support transparent decision-making.

Operational realism will be expanded through the incorporation of real-world datasets and the integration of simulations derived from geospatial engineering tools and models. This includes the use of high-resolution satellite and UAV imagery, lidar point clouds, and terrain vector data from actual field operations.

Simulation environments will be further enhanced by incorporating outputs from established modeling platforms used in military engineering, such as hydrologic, terrain, or mobility models, enabling scenario generation grounded in realistic mission conditions. These additions will support more accurate task representations, enable performance validation under field-relevant constraints, and ensure that learned policies generalize beyond synthetic test cases.

The framework will also be extended to support multi-agent reinforcement learning for cooperative tasking across distributed assets, as well as scaled deployment to high-performance computing (HPC) clusters for broader scenario exploration and accelerated training. Integration with real-world tools, datasets, and geospatial models will further support transition to applied use.

References

1. Salhi, A., Jabour, J.E., Arnolds, T.L., Ross, J.E., Dozier, H.R.: Leveraging JSBSim and gymnasium: a reinforcement learning approach for air combat simulation. In: Arabnia, H.R., Ferens, K., Deligiannidis, L. (eds) Applied Cognitive Computing and Artificial Intelligence. CSCE 2024. Communications in Computer and Information Science, vol 2251. Springer, Cham (2025)
2. Shukla, I., Dozier, H., Henslee, A.: Learning behavior of offline reinforcement learning agents. In: Proc. SPIE 13051, Artificial Intelligence and Machine Learning for Multi-Domain Operations Applications VI, 130510N (2024)
3. Henslee, A. et al.: Data-driven reinforcement learning for mission engineering and combat simulation. In: Azimov, D. (eds) Proceedings of the IUTAM Symposium on Optimal Guidance and Control for Autonomous Systems 2023. IUTAM 2023. IUTAM Bookseries, vol 40. Springer, Cham (2024)
4. Krichen, M., Abdalzaher, M.S.: Performance enhancement of artificial intelligence: a survey. J. Netw. Comput. Appl. **232** (2024)
5. Yan, M., Yang, R., Zhang, Y., et al.: A hierarchical reinforcement learning method for missile evasion and guidance. Sci. Rep. **12**, 18888 (2022)
6. Graham, E., Gariépy, G., Orpana, H.: System dynamics models of depression at the population level: a scoping review. Health Res. Policy Sys. **21**, 50 (2023)
7. Sharkey, T.C., Pinkley, S.G., Eisenberg, D.A., Alderson, D.L.: In search of network resilience: an optimization-based view. Networks **77**, 225–254 (2020)
8. Satyanarayanan, M., Bahl, P., Cáceres, R., Davies, N.: The case for VM-based cloudlets in mobile computing. IEEE Pervasive Comput. **8**(4), 14–23 (2009)
9. Bonomi, F., Milito, R., Zhu, J., Addepalli, S.: Fog computing and its role in the internet of things. In: Proceedings of the First Edition of the MCC Workshop on Mobile Cloud Computing, pp. 13–16 (2012)
10. Brockman, G., et al.: OpenAI Gym. arXiv (2016). https://arxiv.org/abs/1606.01540
11. Schulman, J., Wolski, F., Dhariwal, P., Radford, A., Klimov, O.: Proximal Policy Optimization Algorithms. CoRR abs/1707.06347 (2017)
12. Gupta, R., et al.: xBD: a dataset for assessing building damage from satellite imagery (2019). arXiv https://arxiv.org/abs/1911.09296
13. Raffin, A., Hill, A., Gleave, A., Kanervisto, A., Ernestus, M., Dormann, N.: Stable-baselines3: reliable reinforcement learning implementations. J. Mach. Learn. Res. (2021)

Simulation-Based Problem Solving: Enhancing Productivity and Decision-Making Across Diverse Real-World Applications

Bahram Asiabanpour(✉)

Texas State University, San Marcos, TX 78666, USA
ba13@txstate.edu

Abstract. This paper explores the integration of simulation-based course projects into a senior-level engineering curriculum as a means to address real-world productivity challenges across diverse domains. Through the application of discrete event simulation tools, students analyze, model, and optimize systems in areas such as sports team scheduling, automotive service operations, and aquaponic agriculture. The paper details the course structure, project methodology, and key pedagogical strategies, highlighting the role of simulation in developing students' technical, analytical, and problem-solving skills. Results demonstrate significant performance improvements and the successful implementation of circular economy principles within complex system models. The findings support the broader adoption of simulation education as a powerful approach to bridging theoretical instruction with industry-relevant practice.

Keywords: Simulation Case Study · Discrete Event Simulation · Modeling

1 Introduction

1.1 Challenges in System Improvement

Improving the performance of complex systems is a central goal across many industries, including manufacturing, healthcare, logistics, and research. Organizations routinely employ a variety of qualitative and quantitative methods to identify inefficiencies, reduce costs, and enhance overall productivity [1].

Qualitative methods often include expert interviews, direct observation, and structured techniques such as Failure Mode and Effects Analysis (FMEA). Quantitative methods may involve Statistical Process Control (SPC), linear programming, or queuing theory, providing data-driven insights into system behavior. In some instances, direct experimentation on real systems is used to test and refine operational changes. While such experimentation can yield highly accurate results, it is often disruptive, costly, and time-consuming [2].

For example, attempting to rebalance a production line by physically testing new equipment configurations may require halting operations, retrofitting facilities, and training personnel. These changes could involve significant financial investment and time—only to potentially conclude that the changes were unnecessary. These risks underscore the need for more efficient and less invasive methods of system analysis.

H. R. Arabnia et al. (Eds.): CSCE 2025, CCIS 2932, pp. 277–289, 2026.
https://doi.org/10.1007/978-3-032-22193-3_21

1.2 Simulation: Benefits and Applications

An increasingly preferred alternative is simulation modeling, which involves constructing a computer-based representation of a dynamic real-world system. This allows analysts to explore and predict system behavior under varying input conditions and evaluate key output parameters—without disrupting the actual system.

Simulation enables informed decision-making by allowing the testing of different scenarios, policy changes, or resource allocations in a safe, low-cost virtual environment. Key advantages include faster iteration cycles, minimized operational disruption, and reduced financial risk [3].

The flexibility and broad applicability of simulation make it a valuable tool in a wide range of sectors, including:

Manufacturing and supply chain management
Transportation and logistics
Healthcare systems
Retail operations
Military planning
Business process optimization

Thanks to its scalability and insight-generating capabilities, simulation modeling has become an essential tool for addressing real-world operational challenges across both industry and academia [4].

1.3 Simulation in Engineering Education

To prepare students for addressing these complex challenges, simulation courses—commonly titled Discrete Event Simulation, Systems Simulation, or Manufacturing Systems Design—are core components of undergraduate engineering programs, particularly in Industrial and Manufacturing Engineering disciplines. These courses aim to build both the theoretical foundation and practical skills necessary for modeling and improving real-world systems.

- A well-structured simulation course typically includes:
- Instructions on the fundamentals of simulation modeling
- Coverage of key supporting topics, including random number generation, statistical distributions, and confidence intervals
- Hands-on training with simulation software (e.g., Arena, Simio, AnyLogic)
- A comprehensive course project, preferably based on an actual system
- A final written report or presentation documenting the problem, model, analysis, and recommendations

Delivering this content effectively within the constraints of a 16-week semester is demanding. Students are expected to master technical software tools and analytical methods while executing a full simulation project—often for the first time. Despite these challenges, such courses offer powerful, real-world preparation that bridges academic learning with industry-relevant application.

1.4 Study Objective

The objective of this research is to:

- Describe the structure and learning outcomes of a simulation-focused engineering course to:
- Present the framework and expectations of simulation-based course projects
- Compare and analyze a range of student-developed simulation models across different domains.
- Share key lessons learned regarding educational value and real-world relevance

1.5 Case Studies in Simulation Projects

This study highlights the educational and practical value of simulation-based course projects in diagnosing and resolving real-world operational issues. By applying discrete event simulation methods, students were able to analyze complex problems, explore performance scenarios, and develop data-informed recommendations.

Three selected case studies demonstrate the diversity and impact of this approach:

Sports Team Preparation
Simulation was used to optimize athlete scheduling and equipment utilization for a Division I football program. The model balanced team practice times, minimized conflicts, and ensured proper recovery periods, improving both performance and facility usage.

Automotive Repair Services
Inspired by firsthand experiences with long service delays, this project identified workflow bottlenecks and resource misallocations at a commercial tire shop. The simulation modeled service times, staffing, and customer flow, proposing more efficient scheduling strategies.

Controlled Aquaponic Systems Research
This project integrated circular economy principles into vertical farming and aquaponics systems. Simulation was used to model fish tanks, plant growth cycles, composting, and food processing, helping identify optimal capacity and resource allocation strategies for sustainable agriculture.

These examples demonstrate how simulation projects reinforce academic learning while equipping students with valuable skills to solve real-world challenges across industries.

2 Method

2.1 Course Content

The simulation course, offered under the title Manufacturing Systems Design, is a required senior-level course for students in both Industrial and Manufacturing Engineering programs. The course is designed to provide students with a comprehensive understanding of discrete event simulation and its practical applications in system design and analysis.

Key topics covered include:

- Fundamentals of simulation modeling
- Random number generation and random variate concepts
- Statistical distributions and confidence intervals
- Techniques for analyzing raw data and fitting appropriate statistical distributions
- Core components of simulation modeling using Arena software, such as: Entity flow and resource management, Scheduling and failure modeling, Capacity constraints and task sharing, and Transportation logic and basic animation features.
- Advanced topics in simulation analysis and optimization using complementary tools such as: OptQuest for optimization, Process Analyzer (PAN) for scenario analysis, and Output Analyzer for statistical comparison of simulation outputs.

This structure ensures that students gain both theoretical knowledge and hands-on experience in simulation modeling, analysis, and decision-making.

2.2 Course Activities and Assessment

The course is structured to include three hours of lecture and two hours of lab per week, providing a balanced mix of conceptual instruction and applied learning.

Student performance is assessed through a combination of the following components:

- Class participation and activities
- Homework assignments
- Quizzes
- Midterm and final examinations
- A comprehensive course project

As a writing-intensive course, a significant emphasis is placed on the final project report, which must be a minimum of 600 words. This reinforces the importance of communication and documentation skills alongside technical competence. The course project not only allows students to apply simulation tools to real-world problems but also serves as a critical component of the course's learning outcomes, encouraging independent thinking, problem-solving, and professional-level reporting.

Project Format

While students may choose from pre-defined case studies with available datasets—such as those offered through the Rockwell Arena Simulation Competition—they are strongly encouraged to select a real-world problem for their course project. Most students have prior professional experience, either through part-time or full-time employment, which helps them identify a relevant topic and partner organization.

Regardless of the business domain (e.g., manufacturing, service, healthcare) or project scale, students are expected to follow a standardized simulation project procedure, illustrated in Fig. 1. The key steps are as follows:

1) Problem Formulation

Students identify a real organization and a recurring operational problem with significant impact (e.g., cost, time, or waste) to justify simulation.

2) Objective and Scope Definition

Clear input variables and output performance measures are set, ensuring project goals are achievable within a semester.

3) Model Conceptualization

Students map the logic and flow of the system, including entities, resources, and decision points, typically using flowcharts.

4) Data Collection and Preparation

Sufficient, unbiased data is gathered and converted into usable formats (e.g., statistical distributions) for accurate modeling.

5) Model Translation

Concepts and data are built into a working simulation model using software such as Arena.

6) Verification

The model is tested for logic and error-free performance to ensure internal consistency.

7) Validation

Simulation results are compared with real system performance; discrepancies are resolved to ensure external accuracy.

8) Experimental Design

Students run what-if scenarios to test system changes and analyze performance metrics such as cost, throughput, and utilization.

9) Optimization and Documentation

Iterative runs help refine the model. Final results are documented in a structured report suitable for academic or professional use.

This structured approach not only reinforces core simulation concepts but also provides students with realistic, hands-on experience in applying simulation to complex systems in various industries. It helps build skills in analytical thinking, model development, and data-driven decision-making—all critical for success in engineering and operations careers.

2.3 Problem Statement for the Case Studies

The following case studies (Table 1), drawn from diverse domains, were selected, formulated, and modeled by students as part of a single-semester simulation course project:

Sports Team Preparation

This project focused on optimizing the workout and training schedule for an NCAA Division I Football Bowl Subdivision (FBS) program. The team, comprising over 100 student-athletes, often faces scheduling conflicts due to overlapping academic commitments, other team activities, and limited access to workout facilities. The simulation model aimed to create a balanced and efficient schedule that:

- Minimizes scheduling conflicts
- Maximizes utilization of limited training equipment
- Ensures adequate rest and recovery periods between workout sessions

The model helped identify scheduling strategies that improve resource allocation and athlete performance without overloading the system.

Automotive Repair Services
Inspired by firsthand experience with service delays at a national chain tire shop, this project addressed inefficiencies in scheduled vehicle maintenance. Despite having set appointments, customers frequently encountered significant waiting times. Simulation analysis revealed that:

- Poor resource allocation
- Inadequate staffing during peak times
- Misaligned scheduling policies

were the root causes of service delays. The simulation model explored alternative staffing plans and resource distribution strategies to improve customer experience and operational efficiency.

Controlled Aquaponic Systems Research
This project explored the integration of circular economy principles into vertical farming and aquaponics systems to support zero-waste agriculture. The objective was to evaluate different process sequences and system configurations to enhance the financial viability of sustainable farming practices (Fig. 2). The simulation model:

- Represented the interconnected stages of aquaponics and post-processing
- Tested capacity and configuration changes at each stage
- Assessed resource efficiency, waste reduction, and system scalability

2.4 Model Construction

All three projects followed the project implementation process shown in Fig. 1 to collect data and logic, implement the simulation model (Fig. 3), validate it and conduct design of experiments to optimize the model using one of the available tools such as Process Analyzer (PAN), Output Analyzer, Opquest, or similar software in Arena software.

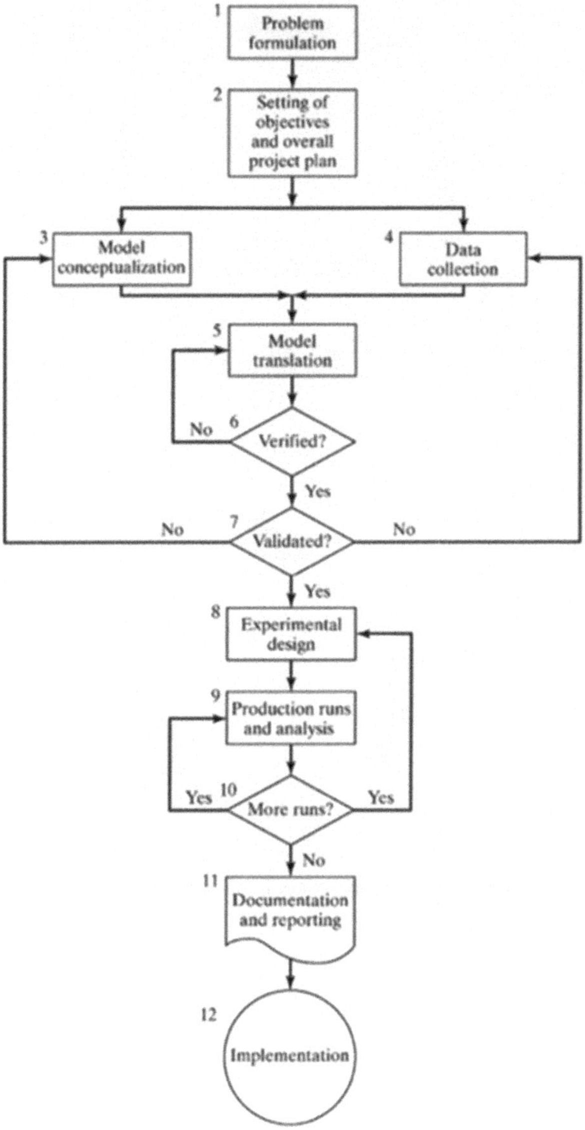

Fig. 1. Standardized simulation project procedure

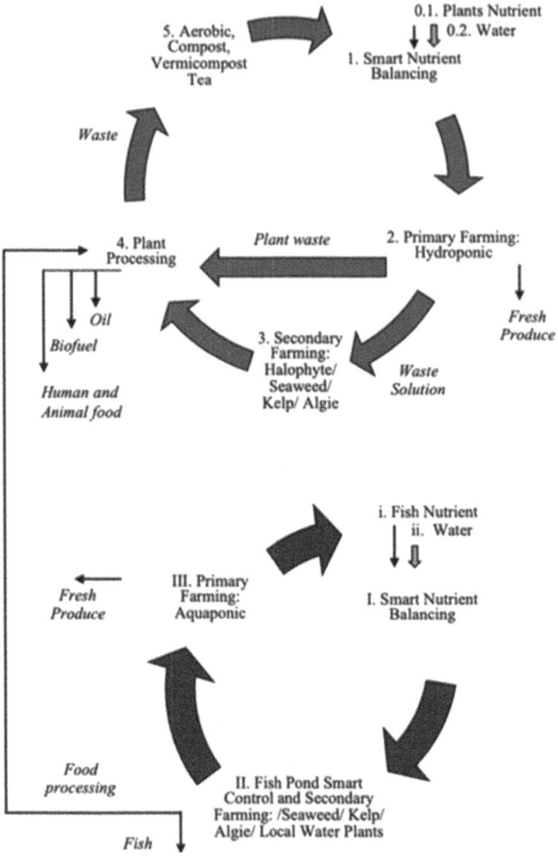

Fig. 2. Proposed circular economy model for vertical farming [5]

Table 1. The summary of three projects' inputs and performance measures

Aspect	Sports Team Preparation	Automotive Repair Shop	Controlled Aquaponic System
Problem	- Long wait times between exercises due to poor scheduling and equipment bottlenecks.	Delays in service appointments caused by poor resource planning and underutilization.	Resource imbalance across different aquaponic stages, impacting process efficiency and system sustainability.
Input Variables	- Athlete group size - Number of groups - Exercise duration at each station	- Service type (air check, tire rotation, repair, replacement) - Number of employees - Number of bays	- Capacity and processing time for fish tanks, plant growth, composting, and food processing
Other Factors	- Varying number of athletes - Weather conditions - Equipment failures	- Equipment failures - Item availability - Vehicle types	- Fish and plant species and maturity - Seasonal and ambient conditions - Type of compost/nutrient treatment
Performance Measures	- Total workout completion time - Efficiency of session flow - Improvements in fitness indicators	- Average time in service - Number of customers waiting in queue	- Cycle time - Resource utilization - Feasibility of system scaling

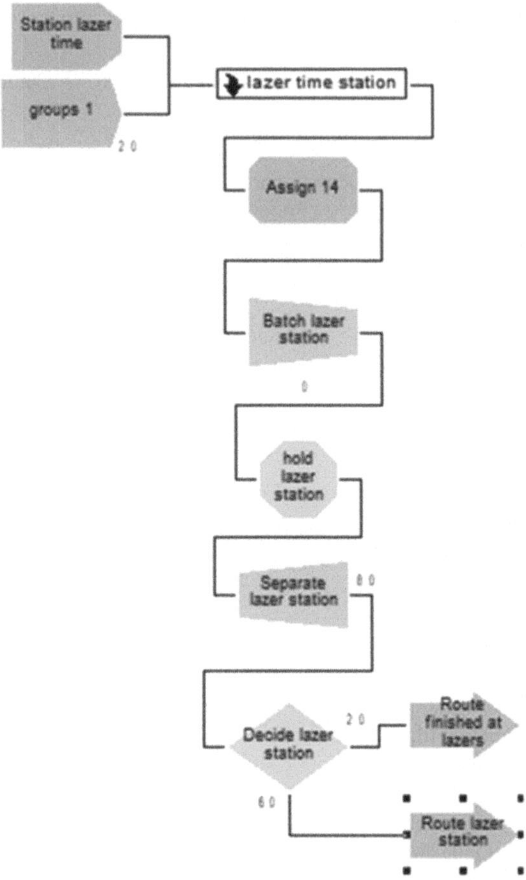

Fig. 3. A portion of logic flowchart of the simulation model

3 Results

3.1 Improvement from the Base Model

- Sport Team Preparation: Results from the Design of Experiments and Process Analyzer (PAN) software analysis showed that changing the size of the group size improve the overall practice time by five minutes. In other words, because the stages of the exercises did not have equal time, unequal size of each group improves the overall time and reduces the idle times for team members.
- Automotive Repair Shop: Results from optimization using employing different numbers of additional workers and adding the fourth bay showed that the cycle time for the customers (vehicles) in system reduces from more than 1 h to 0.3 h. This is more 70% improvement. Regarding number of vehicles waiting, the improvement is even more significant from 6.35 to 0.28 vehicles in average, a 95% improvement.

- Controlled Aquaponic System: This study introduces the vertical farming circular economy model, a computer-based simulation model designed to enhance vertical farming efficiency within the context of a circular economy, with the goal of optimizing resource utilization and reducing waste. The proposed model offers an opportunity to significantly improve overall system efficiency while providing an answer to pressing environmental concerns by addressing challenges such as high investment costs, maintenance expenses, energy consumption, and waste generation.

3.2 Lesson Learned

Over the past 20 years of teaching this simulation course, numerous lessons have been learned and incorporated into the evolving course structure. While software platforms, features, and computing power have advanced significantly, the fundamentals of simulation education have remained consistent. The following key insights have helped optimize course delivery and student learning outcomes:

1. **Starting Projects Early**

One of the main challenges in simulation projects is the timing. Traditionally, students would begin projects after gaining proficiency in the simulation software, often around Week 8, post-midterm. This limited the time available for completing comprehensive projects.

To address this, the revised course structure introduces the project as early as Week 2. In the early weeks, students engage in:

- Identifying personal areas of interest
- Problem definition and team formation
- Initial data collection
- Defining input/output variables
- Mapping logic, entity flow, resource use, and decision-making processes

These preparatory steps can be done without prior software knowledge, allowing students to focus on technical modeling once software training begins around Week 5–6. By Week 8, students are well-equipped to build and test their models with minimal delay.

2. **Reordering Course Topics**

To support earlier project initiation, the sequence of lecture topics has been strategically adjusted. Traditionally, theoretical content such as random number generation, random variates, and statistical distributions is covered early in the semester. However, these topics are not essential for early-stage software modeling, so they have been moved to the final three weeks. This adjustment has created more space early in the semester for students to begin conceptualizing and planning their projects.

3. **Emphasizing Valid Data and Logical Accuracy**

Impressive animations and visually appealing graphs can often disguise flaws in project logic or input assumptions. The validation stage—comparing simulation outputs with real-world system behavior—exposes any discrepancies. Therefore, students are strongly encouraged to:

- accurate and representative data
- raw data into usable formats
- document logic and decision rules within the model

Validation is only meaningful when the underlying assumptions and inputs are sound.

4. **Promoting a Modular Team-Based Approach**

Through experience, teams of three students have proven to be optimal for semester-long simulation projects. To ensure equitable contribution, projects are structured from the outset with a modular architecture—where each team member is responsible for a distinct subsystem. This prevents uneven workload distribution, where one student becomes the primary modeler and others default to documentation or presentation tasks.

5. **Weekly Progress Documentation**

At the start of the project, students may not fully understand how the final deliverable will take shape. To scaffold progress, the course uses a structured platform (e.g., Canvas) for weekly submissions. Students upload ongoing work—such as problem definition, entity flow diagrams, resource plans, and data analysis—incrementally.

By the end of the semester, students find that most of the content needed for the final report and presentation has already been developed and just needs integration and refinement. This approach reduces last-minute effort and improves project quality.

4 Conclusions

- Simulation-based course projects effectively bridge theoretical instruction and practical application.
- Significant performance improvements were achieved across diverse domains such as sports scheduling, automotive repair, and sustainable agriculture.
- Early project initiation and modular team structure contributed to project success within a single semester.
- Emphasis on data validation and modeling logic ensured meaningful simulation outcomes.
- The course structure effectively prepares students with analytical and technical skills applicable across industries.

Acknowledgments. The work was made possible with funding from the US Department of Agriculture (Grant number: 2020-38422-33097, 2020). The authors would like to express their sincere appreciation to USDA and Texas State University for providing funding and access to both infrastructure and laboratories. The funding agency had no involvement in the design of the research, data collection, analysis, interpretation of findings, or the decision to publish the work.

References

1. Crowe, S., Brown, K., Tregay, J., Wray, J.: Combining qualitative and quantitative operational research methods to inform quality improvement in pathways that span multiple settings. BMJ Open Qual. **6**(1), e000095 (2017). https://doi.org/10.1136/bmjquality-2017-000095

2. Thanigasalam, R., Tan, K.K.H., Fahad, O.: Methodological approaches to support process improvement in emergency departments: a systematic review. BMC Health Serv. Res. **19**, 1–14 (2019). https://doi.org/10.1186/s12913-019-4355-4
3. Kelton, W.D., Zupick, N., Ivey, N.: Simulation with Arena, 7th edn. McGraw-Hill (2024)
4. Chowdhury, H., Asiabanpour, B.: A circular economy integration approach into vertical farming with computer-based simulation model for resource optimization and waste reduction. J. Clean. Prod. **470** (2024)
5. Randolph, O., Asiabanpour, B.: Automation of an off-grid vertical farming system to optimize power consumption. In: Advances in Parallel & Distributed Processing, and Applications. Transactions on Computational Science and Computational Intelligence. Springer, Cham (2021). https://doi.org/10.1007/978-3-030-69984-0_74

Center-Surround Improves Multimodal Learning

Marc Estafanous[1(✉)], Evan Mattson[2], and Erhan Guven[3]

[1] Johns Hopkins University, Cleveland, USA
mestafa1@jhu.edu, estafanous@neurobaby.com
[2] Johns Hopkins University, Seoul, South Korea
emattso4@jhu.edu
[3] Johns Hopkins University, Baltimore, USA
eguven2@jhu.edu

Abstract. In vertebrates, visual information is processed first through a commonly themed, fixed pre-processing, i.e., center-surround processing (CSP), before final learned processing. We applied CSP pre-processing to visual and audio data before it is input into neural networks using a single, simple network layer. We compared the final results and learning rate to networks without the layer, networks with an extra layer, and those of earlier center-surround networks. We show that, although no benefit to the CSP layer was found in larger networks, CSP reduces the number of iterations needed to achieve stability and higher accuracy in smaller networks.

Keywords: center-surround processing · convolutional neural networks · retina layer · cochlear layer

1 Introduction

Evolution has had millions of years to experiment with sensory processing. In vertebrates, sensory information is processed first through a commonly themed, fixed pre-processing, i.e., center-surround processing (CSP), before final learned processing.

CSP is most easily explained in vision. The retina is composed of 3 main layers of cells: the photoreceptor layer, the bipolar layer, and the ganglion cell layer.

The photoreceptor layer consists of two kinds of cells: rods (grayscale) and cones (red, green, and blue colors). The photoreceptor layer feeds information to the bipolar layer, which is a preprocessing layer.

Each bipolar cell receives signals from a set of photoreceptors, which form its receptive field. Rather than simply summing the inputs from all the photoreceptors that feed into the cell, the cell will contrast the level of signal from the photoreceptors in the center of its field to the signals from the photoreceptors in the periphery ("surround") of its receptive field. This is what is called CSP.

Submission Type: Short Research Paper.

H. R. Arabnia et al. (Eds.): CSCE 2025, CCIS 2932, pp. 290–303, 2026.
https://doi.org/10.1007/978-3-032-22193-3_22

CSP was first found by Kuffler [6] in mammalian and non-mammalian vertebrate cells by Bartlow [2]. The same pre-processing was also found in invertebrates, specifically arthropods such as horseshoe crabs [12] and Drosophila flies [8]. In addition to CSP in vision, it, or analogous lateral-inhibition processing, has been found in auditory [9,11], and somatosensory processing [10].

We hypothesized that CSP provides an evolutionary advantage by increasing efficiency and accuracy in vision and possibly other topographic sensory inputs in animals. Interestingly, when visualized, early convolutional neural network (CNNs) filters display edge detection properties [16]. Thus, CSP may benefit machine learning architectures, such as CNNs when applied to vision and audio tasks.

To test this hypothesis, we designed a simple, lightweight preprocessing layer that applies CSP to inputs that can be easily added to existing neural architectures. We show that this simple layer can shorten the learning time and improve accuracy in smaller networks for visual and audio processing.

2 Related Work

Early work with neural networks used center-surround processing in models like the Neocognitron [4]. Surprisingly, very little has been done regarding adding CSP to convolutional neural networks. To date, there is one conference-reported paper by Hasani [5], and one pre-print article by Babaiee [1], that look at CSP in the vision field, and one article from Kurogi [7] for audio processing.

In Fukushima's work, the convolutional filters are not uniform magnitude cells in the center and surround, but Gaussian curves. This can potentially lead to various cells contributing more to the edge detection than others. In Babaiee's work, the filters are simply a variation of those used by Fukushima. There is no experimental evidence that this is the case in biological models, so we make the magnitudes uniform, simplifying the kernel's calculation and leading to sharper contrast and edges.

In both papers, the filters are identical for all output channels, so it is unclear what the advantage of having more than one output channel per center-surround type is. In our network, we only output the number of channels that give unique information, thereby reducing the number of calculations necessary.

Fukushima explored using their filters as preprocessing layers in their CS2SM model but found no advantage, so they only applied the filters to the activation maps of existing convolutional layers. In other words, they used the filters in a method similar to that seen with pooling layers rather than having the filters process the incoming images directly. The lack of applying a non-linear activation, such as rectified linear activation, after the filter application, may explain why they failed to see a benefit in using the filters for preprocessing.

Babaiee's networks also require splitting the network into two parallel paths and including residual connections to create OOCS blocks (on-off center-surround blocks). Our approach differs in that we use a single layer, the RetinaLayer, which is a simple add-on layer that requires no change in network design and only changes the number of input channels to the next layer to match the output channels of the RetinaLayer.

Similarly, we also create a single add-on layer that we call the Cochlear layer, applied to the frequency dimension of spectrograms. In the auditory processing field, Kurogi's work in 1991 [7] used a filter to pre-process the fast Fourier transform (FFT) signal in a lateral inhibition layer. The network was not convolutional and did not use backpropagation. Choi et al. [3] used Temporal Convolutions to process the audio signals, but did not do any CSP.

2.1 Contributions of This Work

- We created single convolutional layers that can be added to the front of any convolutional network. These networks are biologically inspired and use simple, fixed, center-surround convolutional filters to improve the learning rate and enhance the performance of small network architectures.
- We show the robustness of the layer by testing it with multiple datasets and multiple modalities.

3 Methods

3.1 Retina Layer

To implement CSP, we will mimic the functionality of the bipolar cells. There are effectively 6 kinds of bipolar cells that respond to the following contrasting inputs using CSP center-surround:

$$\left\{ \begin{array}{c} \text{On-Off} \\ \text{Off-On} \\ \text{Red-Green} \\ \text{Green-Red} \\ \text{Blue-Yellow} \\ \text{Yellow-Blue} \end{array} \right\}$$

The result of using CSP is, in effect, to create an edge-detecting filter. In image processing, one form of edge detector consistent with the center-surround nature of the bipolar cells is called the Laplacian filter. In the RetinaLayer, we create a convolutional kernel that reproduces the connections between a bipolar cell and its photoreceptors. The kernels are all 3x3 Laplacian filters with a center-surround architecture. For On Center-Off Surround and all the color filters, we will be effectively using a kernel of the form[1]:

$$\begin{bmatrix} -1 & -1 & -1 \\ -1 & 8 & -1 \\ -1 & -1 & -1 \end{bmatrix} \tag{1}$$

[1] Also known as an isotropic Laplacian filter.

The Off Center-On Surround filter is that kernel multiplied by −1. This is straightforward for grayscale; we use the Gaussian normalized value for each pixel. For color images, red, green, and blue values are directly obtained from the pixels, but we need to calculate the grayscale and yellow values. Yellow is the average of red and green:

$$\text{Yellow} = (\text{Red} + \text{Green})/2 \tag{2}$$

To get grayscale, we can use the ITU-R 601-2 luma transform [13]:

$$L = R * 0.299 + G * 0.587 + B * 0.110 \tag{3}$$

With grayscale images, we apply the fixed kernel above for both On Center-Off Surround and Off Center-On Surround convolutions, and turn off the gradient so that it is not adjusted during backpropagation. During the forward pass, we apply both kernels to the image and output both channels after applying a rectified linear layer. The latter is important as it mimics the firing of cells vs inactivity, and leads to different information propagating forward between the 2 convolutions. Without it, the 2 layers would have inverse, but otherwise identical, outputs.

We need to process color images slightly differently since we are comparing 2 different colors. We want the center of the filter to apply to one color while the surround will apply to the second, and then we want to add the two colors together[2]:

$$\text{Center Filter: } \begin{bmatrix} 0 & 0 & 0 \\ 0 & 8 & 0 \\ 0 & 0 & 0 \end{bmatrix} \tag{4}$$

$$\text{Surround Filter: } \begin{bmatrix} -1 & -1 & -1 \\ -1 & 0 & -1 \\ -1 & -1 & -1 \end{bmatrix} \tag{5}$$

Using PyTorch, we can take advantage of depthwise separable convolutions. For a good explanation, see the one by Wang [14].

First, if we concatenate the two colors of interest with the center color, we can perform a depthwise convolution using the two filters. This will give us a 2-channel output with the convolution output at each point. Then we apply a pointwise convolution using a filter of shape (2, 1, 1) where each (1, 1) filter = [1], which will add the two output channels together, giving us the sum of the center and surround at each pixel.

During the forward pass, we concatenate the (r, g), (g, r), (b, y), and (y, b). Finally, we pass the resulting output through a rectified linear layer as above. The results of applying the filters and passing them through the rectified linear layer are seen in Fig. 1.

[2] These two filters algebraically add to the standard Laplacian kernel.

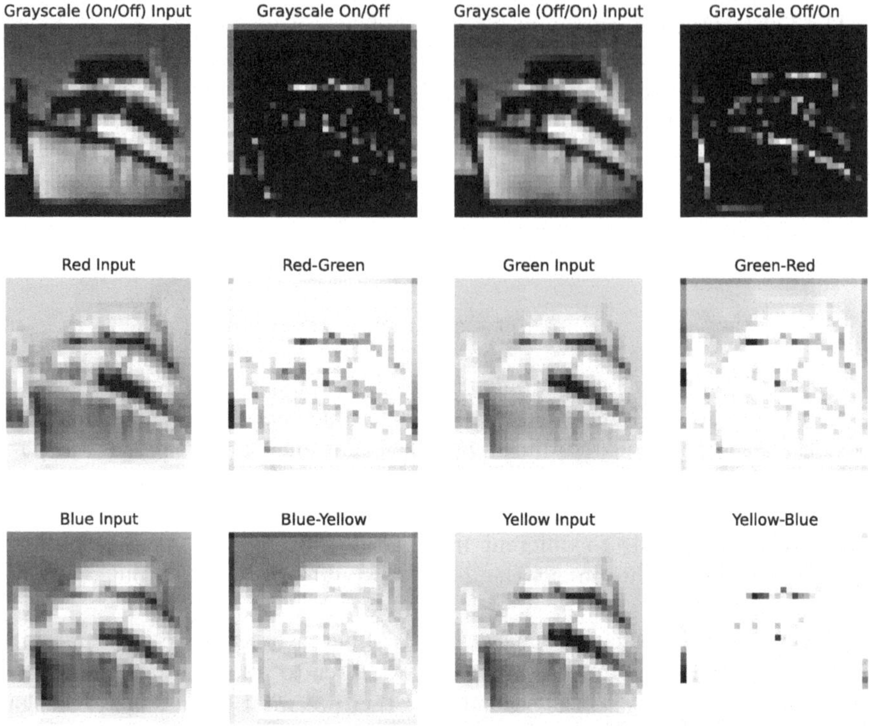

Fig. 1. Center-Surround Filter Effects

When preprocessing an image with the RetinaLayer, the input channels effectively double, but otherwise, a network without the layer would be identical. In Fig. 2, we can visualize the edge enhancement effect of applying the center-surround filters to a color image.

3.2 Cochlear Layer

Sound is translated into an electrical signal in the cochlea through specialized hair cells that respond to different frequencies. These signals are pre-processed via a center-surround mechanism similar to that in vision. On Center-Off Surround cells respond best when the central frequency is not activated with adjacent higher and lower frequency cells, and vice-versa for Off Center-On Surround.

To mimic the outputs of the cochlear hair cells, but reduce the amount of computations, We process this data by converting the waveforms to their respective Mel spectrograms (n fft=2048, win length=320, hop length=160, n mels=128). This gives data that is windowed into 128 frequency bins and 101 timesteps.

To process the auditory signals, we created a layer we call the CochlearLayer. The layer uses the same filters in the RetinaLayer, but flattened to 1-dimension, and we use 1D-convolutions. These filters are then applied along the frequency

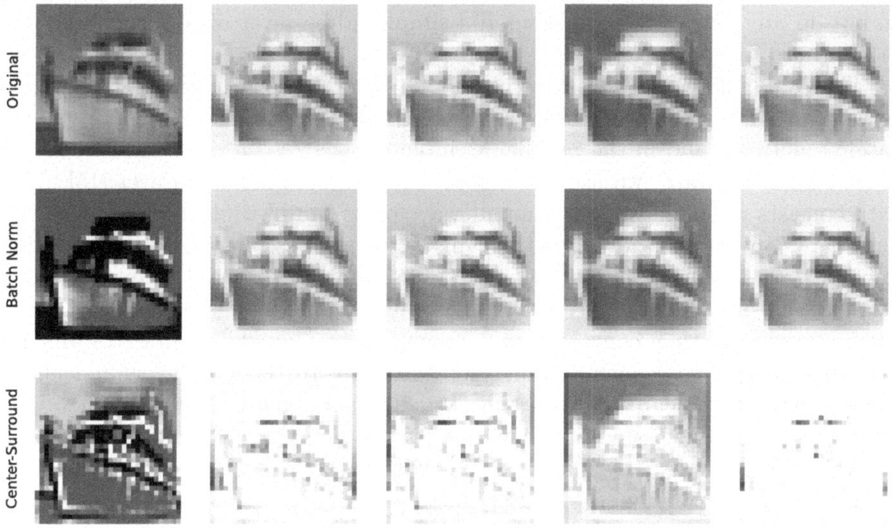

Fig. 2. Normalization (Edge Detection) Effect of Center-Surround Filters

dimension to create the On-Off and Off-On outputs in either 1- or 2-dimensional signals. When applied to 1-dimensional signals, the 2 outputs are concatenated and then normalized. The timesteps are broken up into 101 channels. Using the timesteps as the channels was proposed by Choi et al. [3] in what they call Temporal Convolutions.

3.3 Experimental Setup

Several experiments were run to see the effects of adding a center-surround layer to CNNs.

First, we compare results on a simple network architecture on MNIST, CIFAR-10, and CIFAR-100. The network consists of 4 convolutional layers (64, 128, 256, 512), followed by a pooling layer and then passed through a rectified linear activation. The final layers are linear layers (1024, 512) passed through rectified linear activation, followed by an output layer of appropriate size.

Then we look at adding the RetinaLayer to deeper networks like MobileNet and ResNet in both randomly initialized and pre-trained networks for the CIFAR-10 and CIFAR-100 datasets. Finally, we will compare the RetinaLayer to the on-off center-surround pathways (OOCS) network of Babaiee.

We will test each network on both the original and inverted datasets. To invert the image, we subtract the pixel value from 255. All inputs are normalized through a batch normalization layer within the RetinaLayer.

When adding a RetinaLayer (CS networks), it is possible that simply adding parameters may improve performance. Each network was also tested with an extra convolution network (EC networks) to control for this. The EC networks do not do any extra pre-processing and simply add a layer of equivalent size to the Retina Layer.

The OOCS networks add extra parameters due to the addition of the parallel network architecture, so we compare the RetinaLayer as a direct addition to the baseline network and in the parallel architecture.

For auditory data, we use the Google Speech Commands dataset [15]. The data consists of single-word command waveforms sampled at 16 Hz. The waveforms are converted to Mel Spectrograms. This process bins both the time and frequency axes using a moving window. First, simple, 4 layer, 1D convolutional networks are used to compare the results with and without the CochlearLayer. The networks are then converted to 2D convolutions by adding an extra dimension that turns the frequency dimension into two. In theory, this should allow the convolutions to capture both time and frequency data. Last, the Choi TC-Resnet8 model [3] is tested both with and without CSP.

All networks were tested for accuracy, with performance graphs showing validation accuracy over epochs. Vision models ran for 20 epochs, and audio for 30. Networks were optimized with SGD, trained with a StepLR learning rate schedule, and cross-entropy loss.

4 Results

4.1 Simple CNN

We first look at a simple network architecture to see the effect of adding a RetinaLayer, if any. As we can see in Table 1 and Fig. 3, adding the RetinaLayer led to better performance for all 3 datasets: MNIST, CIFAR-10, and CIFAR100. The RetinaLayer networks also performed significantly better with the inverted images.

Table 1. Simple Net Results

Model	Validation	Test	Test Inverted
MNIST	0.9882	0.9883	0.1133
MNIST CS	**0.9894**	**0.9889**	**0.6442**
MNIST EC	0.9877	0.9888	0.1364
CIFAR 10	0.5964	0.6030	0.1381
CIFAR 10 CS	**0.7051**	**0.7064**	**0.2513**
CIFAR 10 EC	0.4650	0.4681	0.0926
CIFAR 100	0.1616	0.1551	0.0068
CIFAR 100 CS	**0.2575**	**0.2658**	**0.0208**
CIFAR 100 EC	0.0144	0.0150	0.0078

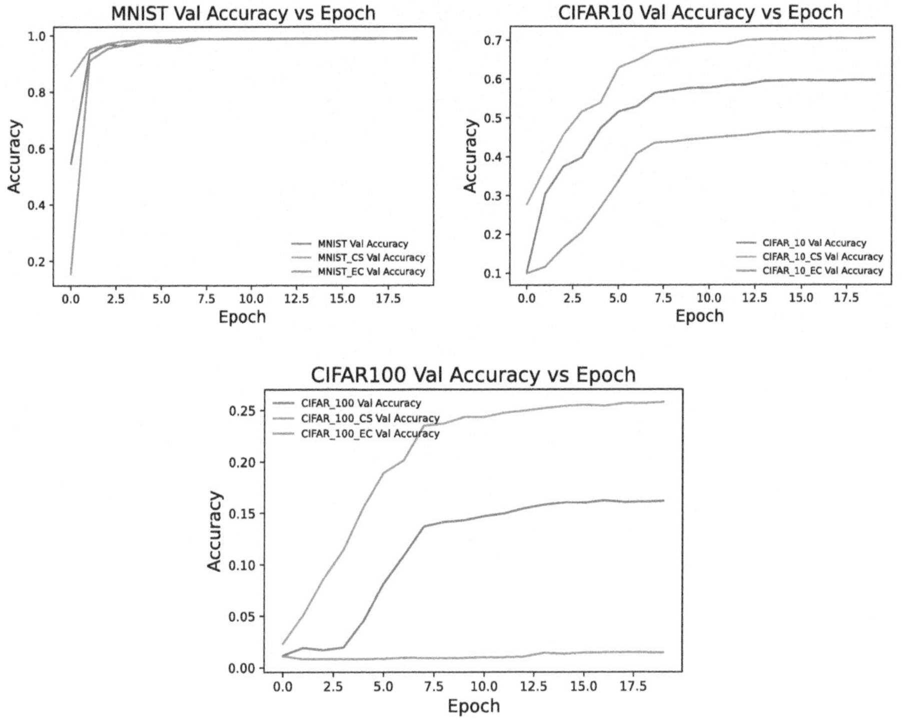

Fig. 3. Simple CNN Results for MNIST (Left), CIFAR-10 (Right), and CIFAR-100 (Bottom).

4.2 Deeper Models

The following experiment is designed to see if the effects of the RetinaLayer persist in deeper models, specifically ResNet-18 (ResNet) and MobileNet small v3 (MobileNet). Here we see that when training the full networks from scratch, there was a slightly increased performance with ResNet, but no benefit to MobileNet by adding the RetinaLayer (Tables 2 and 3, Fig. 4). In fact, with MobileNet, the performance slightly decreased (Fig. 4). However, the RetinaLayer improved the performance with all the inverted datasets (Tables 2 and 3).

Table 2. Resnet Results

Model	Validation	Test	Test Inverted
CIFAR 10 Resnet	0.6440	0.6450	0.1682
CIFAR 10 Resnet CS	**0.6481**	**0.6533**	**0.2075**
CIFAR 100 Resnet	**0.3390**	**0.3344**	0.0268
CIFAR 100 Resnet CS	0.3340	0.3342	**0.0405**

Table 3. Mobilenet Results

Model	Validation	Test	Test Inverted
CIFAR 10 Mobilenet	**0.5492**	**0.5516**	0.1172
CIFAR 10 Mobilenet CS	0.5400	0.5491	**0.1414**
CIFAR 100 Mobilenet	0.1485	**0.1543**	0.0094
CIFAR 100 Mobilenet CS	**0.1487**	0.1490	**0.0111**

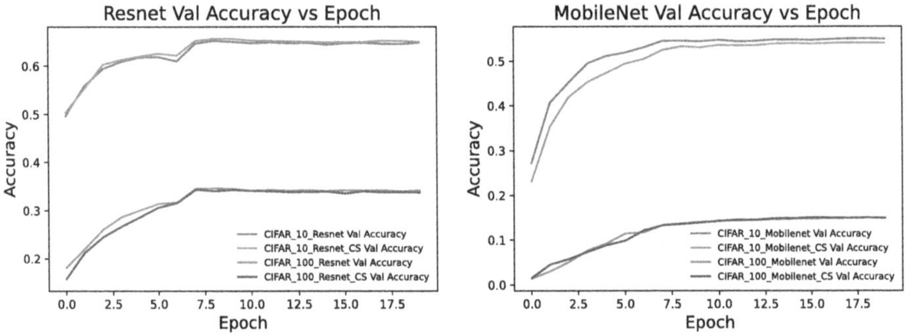

Fig. 4. Resnet (Left) and MobileNet (Right) results for CIFAR-10 and CIFAR-100.

4.3 Transfer Learning

Now, we will look at three types of transfer learning on ResNet models: fine-tuning, feature extraction only, and feature extraction with fine-tuning of the input layer for ResNet (Table 4, Fig. 5). We aim to see if the patterns above persist with previously learned features. Here we see a few interesting things.

The RetinaLayer slightly improved ResNet's performance on CIFAR-10 across all transfer learning methods but decreased it on CIFAR-100. Its effect on the inverted dataset was inconsistent, with only minor differences.

4.4 Vision Prior Art

Next, we will compare the RetinaLayer to the OOCS module previously described. We specifically look at six different architectures:

- Basenet: Babaiee paper convolutional network
- OO: OOCS split architecture
- OO CS: Same architecture but CSP at front of network
- OO CS Split: CSP On-Center and Off-Center applied at split rather than combining in CSP layer
- Basenet CS: Basenet with CSP at front
- OO Skip: OOCS architecture without any pre-processing

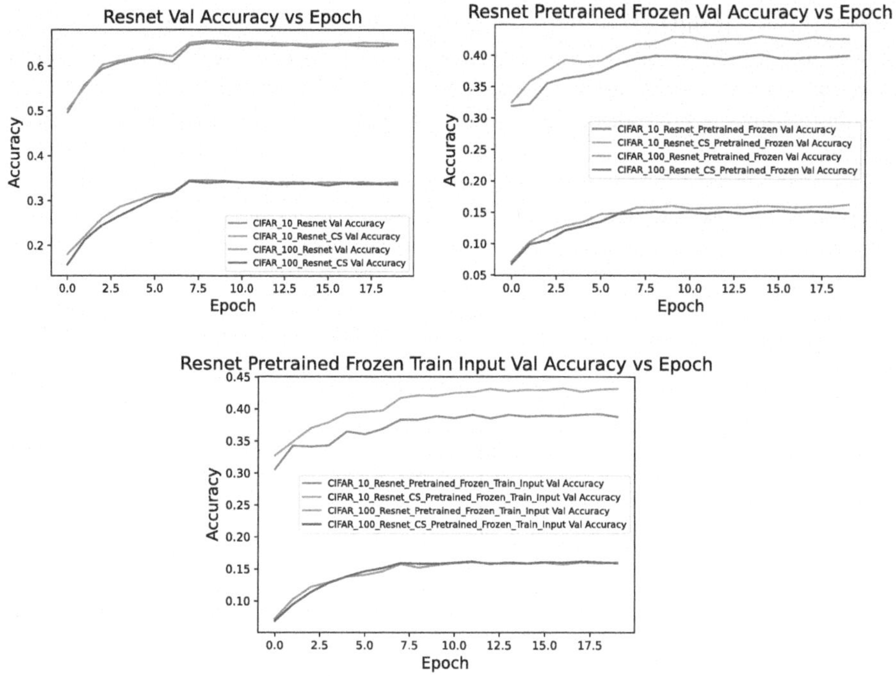

Fig. 5. Transfer Learning Results, Fine Tuning (Left), Feature Extraction Only (Right), Feature Extraction and Fine Tune Input (Bottom).

Here, we see a clear improvement over the prior art on CIFAR-10. There was no significant difference with MNIST, given that all the networks learned the dataset. The only exception is the split architecture, where splitting the RetinaLayer was detrimental (Table 5, Fig. 6). Once again, we see a clear improvement in the results with the inverted data.

4.5 Speech Recognition

Finally, we look at the results of using a CochlearLayer for speech recognition. First, we use a simple CNN that uses 1D convolutions along the frequency dimension, using the temporal dimension as channels. Without the layer, the network only achieved a 65% accuracy rate. With the layer, the accuracy jumps almost 15% to 79% (Table 6).

Next, we turn the 1D convolutions into 2D ones and use Temporal Convolutions [3], i.e., use the time-steps as channels, but add in an extra dimension to turn the frequency dimension into an image of width 1. Doing this did not show any improvement with CSP (Table 6).

Lastly, we use the TC-Resnet8 model. These models show the highest results, with the CSP slightly increasing the accuracy (Table 6).

While these results are still far below the state of the art, or even the results of Choi et al. [3], who achieved 96.6% accuracy, it is clear that the Center-Surround processing enhances the signal to the network. It is important to note that data augmentation was not performed in order to see the results of the CSP on the raw data.

While it is tempting to use a RetinaLayer in a network analyzing the spectrograph, logically, this doesn't make sense because the layer effectively uses edge detection. In a spectrograph, edges are not the signal.

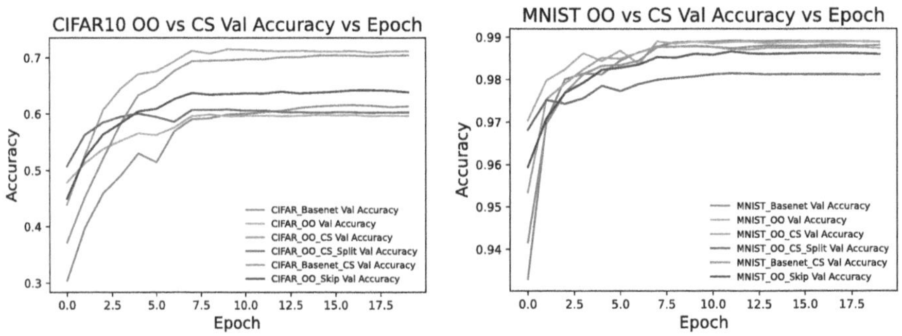

Fig. 6. Prior Art Results, MNIST (Left) and CIFAR-10 (Right)

Table 4. Transfer Learning Results

Model	Validation	Test	Test Inverted
CIFAR 10 Resnet Pretrained	0.6777	0.6827	0.2097
CIFAR 10 Resnet CS Pretrained	**0.6833**	**0.6878**	**0.2592**
CIFAR 100 Resnet Pretrained	**0.4138**	**0.4194**	0.0579
CIFAR 100 Resnet CS Pretrained	0.3907	0.3955	**0.0634**
CIFAR 10 Resnet Pretrained Frozen	0.3999	0.4168	**0.1238**
CIFAR 10 Resnet CS Pretrained Frozen	**0.4264**	**0.4282**	0.1140
CIFAR 100 Resnet Pretrained Frozen	**0.1630**	**0.1597**	0.0216
CIFAR 100 Resnet CS Pretrained Frozen	0.1491	0.1512	**0.0234**
CIFAR 10 Resnet Pretrained Frozen Train Input	0.3877	0.3900	0.1135
CIFAR 10 Resnet CS Pretrained Frozen Train Input	**0.4314**	**0.4251**	**0.1250**
CIFAR 100 Resnet Pretrained Frozen Train Input	**0.1600**	**0.1564**	**0.0274**
CIFAR 100 Resnet CS Pretrained Frozen Train Input	0.1589	0.1545	0.0226

Table 5. Prior Art Results

Model	Validation	Test	Test Inverted
MNIST Basenet	**0.9889**	**0.9887**	0.2774
MNIST OO	0.9888	0.9884	0.1378
MNIST OO CS	0.9873	0.9885	0.5400
MNIST OO CS Split	0.9812	0.9821	**0.6397**
MNIST Basenet CS	0.9881	0.9876	0.3478
MNIST OO Skip	0.9859	0.9851	0.1356
CIFAR Basenet	0.6128	0.6113	0.1566
CIFAR OO	0.5963	0.6053	0.1840
CIFAR OO CS	**0.7110**	**0.7142**	**0.3083**
CIFAR OO CS Split	0.6022	0.6052	0.2264
CIFAR Basenet CS	0.7039	0.7112	0.2707
CIFAR OO Skip	0.6379	0.6412	0.1971

Table 6. Speech Recognition Results

Model	Validation	Test
CNN 1D	0.6771	0.6541
CNN 1D CS	**0.8121**	**0.7911**
CNN TC 2D	**0.8446**	**0.8425**
CNN TC 2D CS	0.8224	0.8045
TC-ResNet8	0.8619	0.8490
TC-ResNet8 CS	**0.8668**	**0.8544**

4.6 Time Complexity Analysis

The fixed 3×3 convolution is applied across the image which yields to $\mathcal{O}(H \times W)$ for gray scale and $\mathcal{O}(C \times H \times W)$ for color images. In practice, making the algorithm linear in complexity. This is in replacement of the CNN, which is normally $\mathcal{O}(C_{in}K^2HWC_{out})$, resulting in the RetinaLayer a much lower complexity algorithm. Note that K is the kernel size, C channels, working on H by W size images.

5 Conclusion

Preliminary testing shows that adding a CSP layer to existing architectures does in fact lead to faster learning and greater accuracy compared to networks with similar numbers of parameters and regular layers, as well as compared to previously reported center-surround architectures. This improvement was only found in smaller architectures, and the benefits were lost with deeper networks.

In theory, the RetinaLayer could be added anywhere within a vision network architecture; however, physiologically, the advantage of this isn't clear, as in biological systems, the edge-detection seems to happen solely as a preprocessing step. There is, however, evidence that the center-surround layers do have direct connections to higher-order centers in the brain, so one thing that can be explored would be to include a look at using the preprocessed output for the skip connections in ResNets and whether smaller ResNet networks can learn.

Similarly, the Cochlear layer also improved the audio processing when applied to the frequency domain of the signals.

It became evident that the benefits of the CSP were lost with deeper layers. This makes sense because edge detection on the original signals is lost as the networks get deeper.

Future work would also explore center-surround, or lateral inhibition, preprocessing in other sensory domains such as somatosensory processing. The use of data augmentation, as well as using the CSP layers with batch-norms within deeper networks, may enhance the utility of CSP layers.

In conclusion, by adding the RetinaLayer and CochlearLayer to the set of available tools for neural networks, we are coming closer to state-of-the-art machine learning with fewer computational resources.

References

1. Babaiee, Z., Hasani, R., Lechner, M., et. al.: On-off center-surround receptive fields for accurate and robust image classification. ArXiv.org (2021). https://arxiv.org/abs/2106.07091. Accessed 13-03-2025
2. Barlow, H.B.: Action potentials from the frog's retina. J. Physiol. **119**, 58–68 (1953)
3. Choi, S., Seo, S., Shin, B., et al.: Temporal convolution for real-time keyword spotting on mobile devices. ArXiv.org (2019). https://arxiv.org/abs/1904.03814. Accessed 13-03-2025
4. Fukushima, K.: Neocognitron: a self-organizing neural network model for a mechanism of pattern recognition unaffected by shift in position. Biol. Cybern. **36**(4), 193–202 (1980)
5. Hasani, H., Soleymani, M., Aghajan, H.: Surround modulation: a bio-inspired connectivity structure for convolutional neural networks. In: Wallach, H., et al. (eds.) Advances in Neural Information Processing Systems 32, pp. 15903–15914. Curran Associates Inc (2019)
6. Kuffler, S.W.: Discharge patterns and functional organization of mammalian retina. J. Neurophysiol. **16**(1), 37–68 (1953)
7. Kurogi, S.: Speech recognition by an artificial neural network using findings on the afferent auditory system. Biol. Cybern. **64**(3), 243–249 (1991). https://doi.org/10.1007/BF00201985. Accessed 13-03-2025
8. Laughlin, S.B.: A simple coding procedure enhances a neuron's information capacity. Z. Naturforsch. **36**(9), 910–912 (1981)
9. Ma, X., Suga, N.: Lateral inhibition for center-surround reorganization of the frequency map of bat auditory cortex. J. Neurophysiol. **92**(6), 3192–3199 (2004). https://doi.org/10.1152/jn.00301.2004. Accessed 12 Sept. 2024
10. Mountcastle, V.B.: Modality and topographic properties of single neurons of cat's somatic sensory cortex. J. Neurophysiol. **20**(4), 408–434 (1957)

11. Okamoto, H., Stracke, H., Draganova, R., Pantev, C.: Asymmetric lateral inhibitory neural activity in the auditory system: a magnetoencephalographic study. BMC Neurosci. **8**(33) (2007). https://doi.org/10.1186/1471-2202-8-33. Accessed 13-03-2025
12. Ratliff, F., Hartline, H.K.: The responses of limulus optic nerve fibers to patterns of illumination on the receptor mosaic. J. Gen. Physiol. **42**(6), 1241–1255 (1959)
13. Rohrer, B.: How to Convert an RGB Image to Grayscale. E2eml.school (2019). https://e2eml.school/convert_rgb_to_grayscale. Accessed 13-03-2025
14. Wang, C.-F.: A basic introduction to separable convolutions. Medium (2018). https://towardsdatascience.com/a-basic-introduction-to-separable-convolutions-b99ec3102728. Accessed 13-03-2025
15. Warden, P.: Speech commands: a dataset for limited-vocabulary speech recognition. ArXiv.org (2018). https://arxiv.org/abs/1804.03209. Accessed 13-03-2025
16. Zeiler, M.D., Fergus, R.: Visualizing and understanding convolutional networks. In: Fleet, D., Pajdla, T., Schiele, B., Tuytelaars, T. (eds.) ECCV 2014. LNCS, vol. 8689, pp. 818–833. Springer, Cham (2014). https://doi.org/10.1007/978-3-319-10590-1_53

Manufacturing Process Improvement Using Discrete Events Simulation

Abdu Shaalan, David Baglee(✉), and Ben Hartop

University of Sunderland, Sunderland SR60DD, UK
{Abdu.shaalan,david.baglee}@sunderland.ac.uk

Abstract. Manufacturing process improvement has been a topic of interest for decades since the introduction of lean applications to increase performance, quality, and reduce cost across various industries. Lean methodologies introduced multiple tools that supported such needs over the centuries and have proven efficiency in improving the process in numerous areas of the manufacturing process and various industries. Discrete events simulation (DES), as a recently introduced tool, was introduced to help apply various lean tools in a simulation format to test the impact of such applications before they take place. This research evaluates the performance of the DES simulation on the manufacturing process of modular housing. The paper investigates different scenarios backed up with lean thinking in reducing various sources of waste within the manufacturing process

Keywords: Discrete Events Simulation · Lean · Process improvement · Line balancing

1 Introduction

Manufacturing systems are described by Black (2000) to be an assembly of manufacturing processes to produce goods for customers, particularly in factories. Similarly, Caggiano (2014) states that manufacturing systems have the goal of production in the manufacturing industry and are comprised of an organisation of different departments, work areas, or processes.

1.1 The Development of Manufacturing Systems

Manufacturing systems have been said to change over time due to the advancement of technology and production, as well as the emergence of new organisational strategies, materials for production, and concerns for the environment (ElMaraghy et al., 2021).

Esmaeilian et al. (2016), mentioned some of these advancements, such as additive manufacturing, Industrial control systems, robotics, management systems, planning and demand management, automated tools, design for manufacturing methodologies, sustainable methodologies and newer advancements, including smart manufacturing where data is used to aid manufacturing, advanced manufacturing methodologies where new methods of manufacturing such as nano manufacturing and additive manufacturing are used to make complex, advanced products.

H. R. Arabnia et al. (Eds.): CSCE 2025, CCIS 2932, pp. 304–315, 2026.
https://doi.org/10.1007/978-3-032-22193-3_23

1.2 Modular Housing

Modular houses are a relatively new concept introduced in the construction industry, where houses are prefabricated in blocks in factories before being transported to a housing estate and being put into their final position and assembled to make the final house assembly. Such an approach is proven to reduce the cost and lead time for completion of the build (Turner, 2022).

The European Commission has funded the "FutureHome" project, which is a modular housing project, with newer design and production methodologies. The project is used to bring many benefits, such as cost and time reduction compared to constructing traditional housing (Wing and Atkin, 2002).

1.3 Modular Housing Factories' Layouts and Processes over Time

In the 1920s, the first modular housing initiative was created, comprising 6 modules put together to make a house, with a steel modular house being built around a similar time, with a steel exterior and structure (Blasco and Fausto, 2024). Blasco and Fausto go further in their analysis of the history of the modular housing manufacturing process, detailing first the post-World War 2 increase in popularity and relevance of modular housing as emergency housing before detailing some of the thoughts behind modular housing, such as ease of transport and assembly.

Marquit and LiMandri (2013) Talk about some of the time that Blasco and Fausto miss in their analysis, stating that modular housing in the 60 s was made of precast concrete modules put together, before moving onto the 80 s, where the design and dimensions were changed, allowing for multistorey designs. It then details a more up-to-date account on modular housing, however, it fails to detail any actual process.

A more beneficial account looking into the actual process was written by Dykstra (2018), detailing assembly lines starting with that of Henry Ford, who mass-produced drywall and did all the plumbing and electricity in the factory. This seems to have been kept until the 1970's where it was changed to meet new regulations, although it is not specified what the changes were. It then details the development of new insulated wall panels in the 1990s before detailing a typical manufacturing process for a modular house, starting with the flooring, followed by walls, ceiling, plumbing and electricity, roofing, then interior and exterior features are added.

1.4 Lean Manufacturing and Line Balancing

Lean methodologies seek to eliminate waste in every process, from manufacturing to administrative processes (Chiarini, 2013). In the manufacturing context that this report is working within, there are seven main wastes, summed up by Shah and Patel, (2018): Defects in the product, Overproduction of product, Inventory, Transportation of materials/products that add to the time of production, Waiting time, Unnecessary motion of employees and Overprocessing of the product.

One of the major tools used in Lean manufacturing is line balancing, described by Rathod et al., (2016) to be an influential tool that optimises the production time by reducing it, arranging the tasks in a process into workstations that have similar work times, making sure that the minimum number of workstations are used and the preceding order of work is kept to.

1.5 Discrete Event Simulation

Discrete event simulation is a digital-rooted technique used for research and modelling purposes that functions by modelling activities along with queues and other similar systems to first model and then assess and optimise either an existing or hypothetical system (Serrano, et al., 2021). This is quite similar to digital twin simulation, which is a virtual version of a real life process, objects and systems, used to connect the real and virtual worlds and model manufacturing processes, allowing companies to see how their processes would work in real life and gather data to make better informed decisions to improve the performance of their process (Javaid et al., 2023). Mohsen et al., (2021) agree with Vázquez-Serrano, Peimbert-García and Cárdenas-Barrón, (2021) on the purpose of Discrete event simulation, describing this to be to reduce the working and idle times, as well as to improve the productivity of a system.

It has even been used in the COVID-19 pandemic to balance hospital resources for different types of patients (Melman et al., 2021).

Discrete event simulation has been found to have benefits in many fields. One such field as found by Fahl and Askari-Nasab (2023) is mining, where they describe the main benefits of Discrete event simulation as the ability for the simulation model to be complex and flexible, the ability to model uncertain and variable behaviours of a real-life system, the ability to model hypothetical scenarios, the ability to train newer employees on a virtual model and the ability to test ideas or processes cheaply without having to bring them in physically.

A combination of simulation, like Discrete event simulation and lean methodologies, has been shown to have a growing interest in recent times (Goienetxea Uriarte, Ng and Urenda Moris, 2019).

Lean methodologies could be used to assess the performance of a system, whilst discrete event simulation could be used to optimise the system (Omogbai and Salonitis, 2016). In a healthcare context, Bal et al. (2017) found that discrete event simulation could be used to verify the effects of lean techniques on a system, in their case, emergency departments.

2 Case Study

The current case study is focused on a local SME that manufactures modular housing for the local community. The company started this operation based on a moral goal of delivering houses to people in urgent need of housing in an efficient manner. The company started operations three years prior to this project being undertaken. The company has a set of designs for their houses and works based on individual projects by themselves while having various suppliers for various elements of the build, manufacturing certain parts in-house.

The company suffers from various sources of waste and delays within its manufacturing process. The main issue the company highlighted that they need to improve is the delivery time of their houses, due to the urgent need to deliver in the shortest time possible once they receive a new order. Various data was collected, including operations data, manufacturing processes, resources for each process, process dependencies, site layout, and flow of processes across the site.

The company highlighted that they are open to increasing manpower to a certain limit and potentially looking at reorganizing the processes, however they cannot change the layout of the factory or add expensive handling equipment due to financial limitations.

The table below shows a sample of the manufacturing processes for Sect. 1, the frame assembly, and Sect. 2, the various process operations, which include the planned and actual times, the required labour, and the idling time as shown below (Table 1).

Initial analysis of the manufacturing process has been carried out, looking into the individual processes, their requirements, and dependencies. The analysis shows a poorly balanced production line, which creates multiple bottlenecks through the process, as shown in the chart below. Such a poorly balanced line created a large waiting time in the process for different processes (Fig. 1).

The initial model of the manufacturing process has been developed using FlexSim software for discrete event simulation. The model includes all the processes' times, required operators, and their dependencies within the given site layout, as shown below (Fig. 2).

Running the simulation based on the company's current operations flow and resources presented a process capacity of 24 completed houses a year. From the company's perspective, they believed that they could improve dramatically and increase their capacity to what they need. The calculations match the company's actual output, which creates certainty of the operations' accuracy.

Approaching the improvement with a lean mindset, the line balancing approach is used in consultation with the company to have certainty about the various dependencies. The company agreed on the ability to employ a certain number of extra employees to improve the delivery time, but they needed evidence that such a cost would have an impact on production capacity. A new model has been created based on the new balanced line to present the expected improvements that could take place.

3 Results and Analysis

After studying the various processes and dependencies of other processes, an overlap initiative has been done on the different processes. After consultation with the company, they agreed that highlighting the targeted change of overlapping certain processes will not contradict the flow of operations and is possible to be carried out without creating any interruptions.

The new structure splits the processes into stations that are made up of different processes that could be done together without creating any interruption.

Below is a revised process flow of the manufacturing process, which presents the creation of various grouped processes into stations that can be executed together without interruption (Table 2).

The improved line balancing shown below presents a grouping of operations into stations, which results in a reduction in the general presentation of the full process

Table 1. Manufacturing process breakdown before improvement

Section 1					
	Planned	Actual			
Task Name	Total Labour Hrs	Working Hours	No.of Technicians	Idle Time	Competency Req'd
Factory Manufacturing	610.2	378.7			
Plot 1	610.2	378.7	1		
Modules	0	0			
Homeless Pod	610.2	378.7			
Op 10 Floor Assembly	10	5			
Affix Edge Beams	0	0	2		
Insulation / Rodent Mesh	4	2	2		General
VCL	1	0.5	2		General
Provision for M&E	0	0	2		
Timber floor batons	1	0.5	2		General
Decking	4	2	2		General
Op 20 Frame Assembly	17.6	8.8			
Sheathing Boards Attached	16	8	2		General
Breather Membrane	1.6	0.8	2		General
Inspection & Sign-off	0	0	0		Manager
Op 30 Roof Assembly	16	8			
Joists	4	2	2		General
Firrings	0	2	2		
OSB Decking	4	2	2		General
Insulation / Single ply membrane	8	2	2		Contractor

(*continued*)

Table 1. *(continued)*

Section 1					
Op 40 Module Assembly	40	10			
Land GF Cassette	8	2	4		General
LSF Panel Erection	16	4	4		General
Land Ceiling Cassette	16	4	4		
SECTION 2					
Op 50 Internal Fit Out	84	54			
Wall Void Insulation	4	2	2	30	General
VCL	4	2	2	30	General
Inspection & Sign-off	0	0	0		Manager
Fire Line plasterboard	32	16	2	16	General
Inspection & Sign-off	0	0	0		Manager
50 mm Internal PIR Insulation	8	4	2	28	
MF Ceiling	16	8	2	24	
MF Wall & Pocket Door	16	8	2	24	General
Pattresses	4	2	2	30	General
Inspection & Sign-off	0	0	0		Manager
Air Tightness Test	0	0	0		Contractor

and creates an improved process flow. The improved flow reduced the maximum time that an operation can take down to sixteen hours from thirty-two hours in the original process flow. The improved flow relies on increasing the number of employees within the accepted limit for the company (Fig. 3).

The improved line was then fed into an enhanced version of the simulation to test the efficiency of the process and measure the difference in capacity over a year's time (Fig. 4).

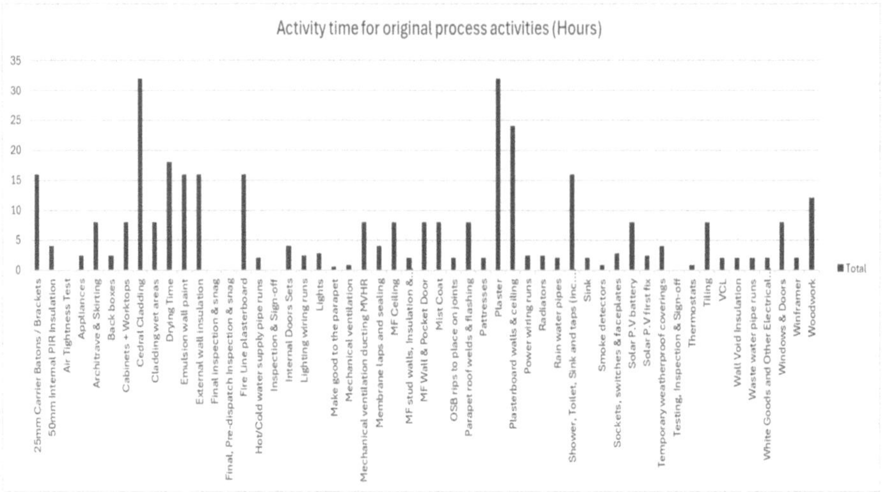

Fig. 1. Current production flow

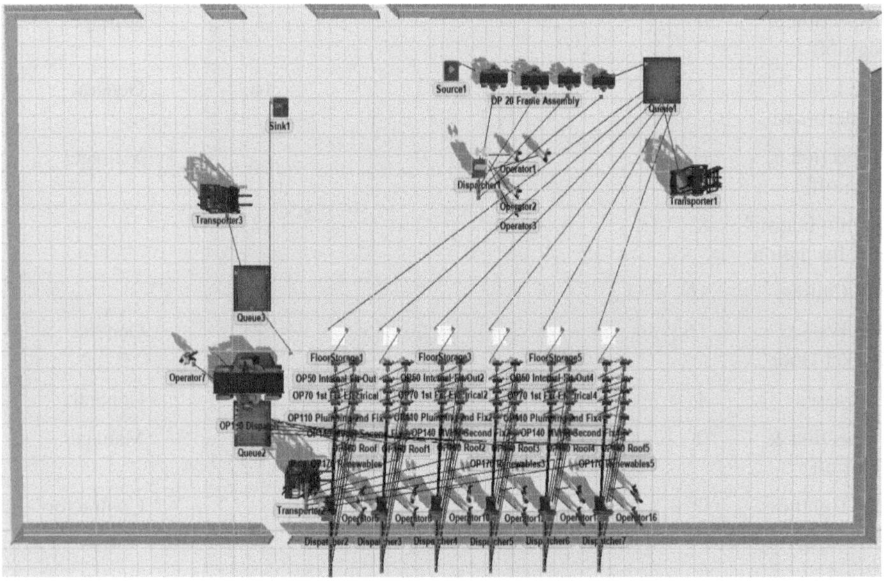

Fig. 2. Current process simulation

The revised simulation presents various impacts on the process including a 35.6% reduction in total process time of the frame assembly which presents better flow optimisation, a 38.9% reduction in various operations processing time, a balance loss improvement of 52.7% which indicates massive reduction in idling time between the different processes, a reduction of 50% in cycle time of the longest process, which is a large contributing factor into balancing the entire manufacturing process, a 89.8% reduction

Table 2. Manufacturing process breakdown after improvement showing new overlapped processes' structure

Process	Process Time	No of Technicians	Competency	Idle Time (Per Station)
Op 10 Floor Assembly	5			
Affix Edge Beams	0	2		
Insulation / Rodent Mesh	2	2	General	
VCL	0.5	2	General	
Provision for M&E	0	2		
Timber floor batons	0.5	2	General	
Decking	2	2	General	
Op 20 Frame Assembly	8.8			
Sheathing Boards Attached	8	2	General	
Breather Membrane	0.8	2	General	
Inspection & Sign-off	0	0	Manager	
Op 30 Roof Assembly	8			
Joists	2	2	General	
Firrings	2	2		
OSB Decking	2	2	General	
Insulation / Single ply membrane	2	2	Contractor	
Op 40 Module Assembly	10			
Land GF Cassette	2	4	General	
LSF Panel Erection	4	4	General	
Land Ceiling Cassette	4	4		
Station 1	2			14
Wall Void Insulation	1	4	General	
VCL	1	4	General	

(*continued*)

Table 2. (*continued*)

Process	Process Time	No of Technicians	Competency	Idle Time (Per Station)
Inspection & Sign-off	0	0	Manager	
Station 2	12			4
Fire Line plasterboard	8	4	General	
Inspection & Sign-off	0	0	Manager	
50 mm Internal PIR Insulation	4	2		
Station 3	13			3
MF Ceiling	8	2		
MF Wall & Pocket Door	4	4	General	
Pattresses	1	4	General	
Inspection & Sign-off	0	0	Manager	

in idling time between process and an increase in the production capacity of 872% which is due largely to the utilisation of resources being improved and reduction of idle time (Table 3).

Table 3. Before and after comparison of process performance

Measurable	Before	After
Section 1: Frame assembly process time	378.7 h	243.7 h
Section 2: Various ops Process time	346.9 h	211.9 h
Balance Loss	78%	36.9%
No of units done per year	25 units	243 units
Cycle time (longest process)	32 h	16 h
Idle Time of Section 2	1221.1 h	124.1 h

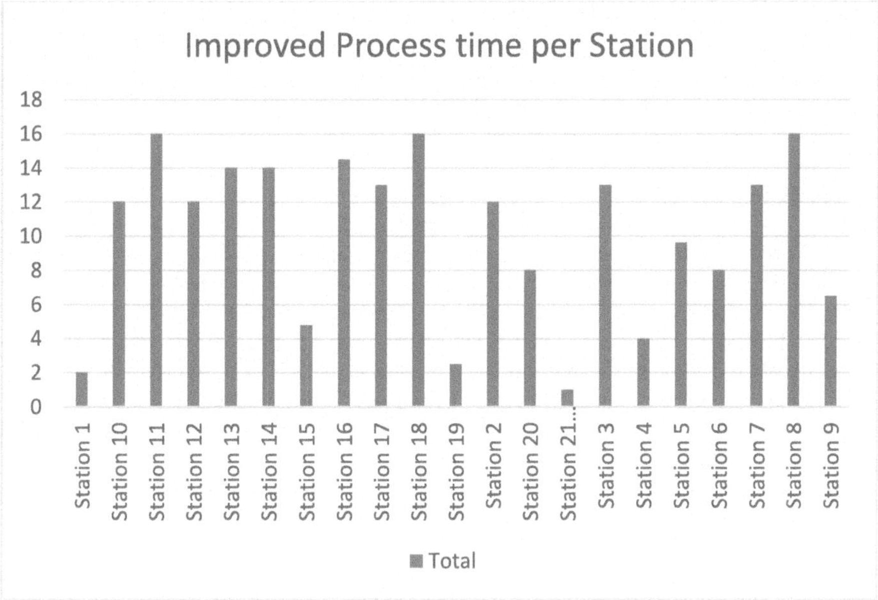

Fig. 3. Improved process flow

Fig. 4. Improved process simulation

4 Conclusion

Following a review of literature surrounding modular housing, discrete event simulation, lean manufacturing and line balancing, A case study has been presented looking into a local SME and how Discrete Event simulation, along with Lean methodologies such as line balancing could and has been used to increase the efficiency and capability of their manufacturing process. As a result of the implemented changes, the company's manufacturing time has been decreased and as a result their capacity and output has been increased.

References

Bal, A., Ceylan, C., Taçoğlu, C.: 'Using value stream mapping and discrete event simulation to improve efficiency of emergency departments', international. J. Healthc. Manag. **10**(3), 196–206. Available at: (2017). https://doi.org/10.1080/20479700.2017.1304323

Black, J.T.: Production Systems flexiblein manufacturing systems. In: P.M. Swamidass (ed.) Encyclopedia of Production and Manufacturing Management. pp. 423–431 Springer US, New York, NY (2000). Available at: https://doi.org/10.1007/1-4020-0612-8_559.

Blasco, M.P. Fausto, I.C.i.: Prefabricated housing construction throughout history, archiDOCT **12**(2), 33–41 (2024)

Caggiano, A.: Manufacturing system. In: Laperrière, L., Reinhart, G. (eds.) CIRP Encyclopedia of Production Engineering, pp. 830–836. Available at:. Springer, Berlin, Heidelberg (2014). https://doi.org/10.1007/978-3-642-20617-7_6562

Chiarini, A.: The seven wastes of lean organization. In: Chiarini, A. (ed.) Lean Organization: from the Tools of the Toyota Production System to Lean Office, pp. 15–30. Available at:. Springer Milan, Milano (2013). https://doi.org/10.1007/978-88-470-2510-3_2

Dalenogare, L.S., et al.: The expected contribution of industry 4.0 technologies for industrial performance. Int. J. Prod. Econ. **204**, 383–394. Available at: (2018). https://doi.org/10.1016/j.ijpe.2018.08.019

De Paula Ferreira, W., et al.: Modelling and simulation in industry 4.0. In: Dingli, A., Haddod, F., Klüver, C. (eds.) Artificial Intelligence in Industry 4.0: a Collection of Innovative Research Case-Studies that Are Reworking the Way we Look at Industry 4.0 Thanks to Artificial Intelligence, pp. 57–72. Available at:. Springer International Publishing, Cham (2021). https://doi.org/10.1007/978-3-030-61045-6_5

ElMaraghy, H., et al.: Evolution and future of manufacturing systems. CIRP Ann. **70**(2), 635–658. Available at: (2021). https://doi.org/10.1016/j.cirp.2021.05.008

Esmaeilian, B., Behdad, S., Wang, B.: The evolution and future of manufacturing: a review. J. Manuf. Syst. **39**, 79–100. Available at: (2016). https://doi.org/10.1016/j.jmsy.2016.03.001

Fahl, S.K., Askari-Nasab, H.: Benefits of Discrete Event Simulation in Modeling Mining Processes (2023). Available at: https://doi.org/10.13140/RG.2.2.23709.69604.

Ghobakhloo, M.: Industry 4.0, digitization, and opportunities for sustainability. J. Clean. Prod. **252**, 119869. Available at: (2020). https://doi.org/10.1016/j.jclepro.2019.119869

Goienetxea Uriarte, A., Ng, A.H.C., Urenda Moris, M.: Bringing together lean and simulation: a comprehensive review. Int. J. Prod. Res. **58**(1), 87–117. Available at: (2019). https://doi.org/10.1080/00207543.2019.1643512

Javaid, M., Haleem, A., Suman, R.: 'Digital twin applications toward industry 4.0: a review', cognitive. Robotics. **3**, 71–92. Available at: (2023). https://doi.org/10.1016/j.cogr.2023.04.003

Marquit, A., LiMandri, C.R.D.: A History of Prefabricated and Modular Housing (2013)

Melman, G.J., Parlikad, A.K., Cameron, E.A.B.: Balancing scarce hospital resources during the COVID-19 pandemic using discrete-event simulation. Health Care Manag. Sci. **24**(2), 356–374. Available at: (2021). https://doi.org/10.1007/s10729-021-09548-2

Mohsen, O., et al.: Discrete-event simulation and data analysis for process flow improvements in a cabinet manufacturing facility. Int. J. Simul. Process. Model. **16**(1), 57–65. Available at: (2021). https://doi.org/10.1504/IJSPM.2021.113075

Omogbai, O., Salonitis, K.: Manufacturing system lean improvement design using discrete event simulation. Procedia CIRP. **57**, 195–200. Available at: (2016). https://doi.org/10.1016/j.procir.2016.11.034

Rathod, B. et al.: Optimization of Cycle Time by Lean Manufacturing Techniques-Line Balancing Approach 4 (2016)

Shah, D., Patel, M.P.: Productivity improvement by implementing lean manufacturing tools. In: Manufacturing Industry, vol. 05, (2018)

Turner, L.: Modular housing: A comprehensive guide, Housing Digital (24 Oct 2022). Available at: https://housingdigital.co.uk/modular-housing-a-comprehensive-guide/. Accessed 22 Apr. 2025

Vachálek, J., et al.: The digital twin of an industrial production line within the industry 4.0 concept. In: 2017 21st International Conference on Process Control (PC), pp. 258–262 (2017). https://doi.org/10.1109/PC.2017.7976223

Vázquez-Serrano, J.I., Peimbert-García, R.E., Cárdenas-Barrón, L.E.: Discrete-event simulation modeling in healthcare: a comprehensive review. Int. J. Environ. Res. Public Health. **18**(22), 12262. Available at: (2021). https://doi.org/10.3390/ijerph182212262

Wing, R., Atkin, B.: FutureHome - a prototype for factory housing. In: In. 19th International Symposium on Automation and Robotics in Construction, Washington, DC, USA. Available at: (2002). https://doi.org/10.22260/ISARC2002/0027

PDPTA'25:31st International Conference on Parallel and Distributed Processing Techniques and Applications

A Simulator for Next Generation SSDs with Networked Backend Architecture

Amir Mirzaei[1], Fatemeh Serajeh Hassani[1(✉)], Atiyeh Gheibi-Fetrat[1], Mina Zabihi[1], Sina Ghorbani-Jabbehdar[1], Mahmoud Reza Kheyrati-Fard[1], Ahmad Javadi Nezhad[1], Seyed Mohammad Hosseini[1], Negar Akbarzadeh[2], and Hamid Sarbazi-Azad[1,2]

[1] Sharif University of Technology, Tehran, Iran
{amir.mirzaei79,mahmoud.kheyrati222,smh.hosseini992}@sharif.edu, fatemeh.serajeh@ce.sharif.edu
[2] Institute for Research in Fundamental Sciences (IPM), Tehran, Iran
azad@ipm.ir

Abstract. Solid-state drives (SSDs) have revolutionized non-volatile storage technology for computer systems and have become widely used in today's digital systems. This is due to SSDs offering high performance with lower power consumption compared to traditional hard disk drives. While data sizes and the demand for higher-capacity storage systems grow, SSDs haven't seen considerable growth in capacity, mainly because it is extremely difficult to scale up the current architecture of SSD devices with reasonable performance. A revolutionary idea is to use a network to network flash chips to solve the scalability issue. Partly due to the absence of an integrated, accurate, and extensible simulator, research on such architectures as the most viable structure for next-generation SSDs has been limited. In this paper, we present MQSimNet, an open-source integrated simulator for SSDs with networked flash chips, offering ease of operation and the possibility of low-effort extensibility.

Keywords: Solid-State Drives (SSDs) · Next-generation networked SSDs · Open source simulator

1 Introduction

Solid-state drives (SSDs) have emerged as the preferred storage medium in modern computing environments, offering substantial improvements in performance, energy efficiency, and reliability over older technologies [11]. Although traditional hard disk drives (HDDs) were once the backbone of storage systems, their mechanical nature imposed inherent limitations in speed, density, and durability—particularly under the demands of data-intensive workloads. SSDs,

---

He is now a Visiting Research Professor at Chosun University under the Brain Pool (BP) Program, funded by the Ministry of Science and ICT through the National Research Foundation of Korea (RS-2023-00284115).

H. R. Arabnia et al. (Eds.): CSCE 2025, CCIS 2932, pp. 319–328, 2026.
https://doi.org/10.1007/978-3-032-22193-3_24

built on flash memory and lacking mechanical parts, avoid these bottlenecks entirely, enabling faster data access and more compact, robust designs.

Despite desirable advantages over HDDs, SSDs face certain limitations. Notably, the storage capacity of single devices is usually lower compared to HDDs, and higher-capacity SSDs come at a premium cost. This limitation is mainly due to how SSDs operate. Generally, increasing the capacity of SSDs leads to degradation of performance, both in terms of latency and throughput, and can potentially reduce the device lifetime. In SSDs, data is stored in flash chips that are grouped together in rows, each row connected to a single flash controller via a channel.

Higher-capacity SSDs often suffer from performance degradation and reduced lifetime due to architectural and physical limitations. Expanding storage involves either enlarging individual flash chips or adding more chips per device. The former—scaling die, plane, block, or page sizes, or using higher-density cells like MLC and QLC—leads to increased manufacturing complexity, higher error rates, and shorter cell endurance, all of which adversely affect reliability and throughput. The latter—integrating more flash chips—faces bottlenecks in channel utilization, as each flash controller typically services only one chip at a time, thereby limiting parallelism and increasing overhead. While adding more channels can improve both capacity and parallel operation, it significantly escalates costs due to the need for more advanced controllers, processing units, and memory resources. These trade-offs underscore the fundamental tension between capacity scaling and sustainable performance in SSD architectures.

As mentioned, the scalability of SSDs is not satisfactory for gaining maximum utilization of flash chips to reach high throughput. This is mostly due to the existence of a single path from each flash chip to Flash Translation Layer (FTL) and blocking operations, which means the most number of operations that can be performed in parallel is equal to the number of unique flash controllers (rows) with queued transactions.

Network-on-SSDs (NoSSD) proposed by Tavakol et al. [17] offers a scalable architecture for SSDs. The proposed method was the first that used an interconnection network for connecting flash chips to the FTL, thus, eliminating physical channel limitations and offering multiple paths between each chip and the FTL, paving the path to higher capacities SSDs as well as increasing possible parallelism and improving performance and throughput of the devices. Although this approach incurs higher costs for lower-capacity SSDs, it can be offset in higher-capacity SSDs by enabling the use of more cost-effective hardware components for other parts of the device. Other studies have also explored interconnection networks to link flash chips [1,18–20], supporting the idea that using interconnection networks in the SSD back-end is an effective and innovative strategy for scaling SSD capacity. Consequently, having a reliable simulator to evaluate these architectures is crucial for advancing research in this area.

The promising potential of the architecture has been overshadowed by research constraints, predominantly due to the unavailability of a reliable and accurate simulation framework. The need for such a simulator is especially critical because there is currently no physical hardware for this architecture to validate simulations against. In this work, we introduce MQSimNet, a flexible simulator that supports various interconnection network architectures in the SSD back-end. To ensure reliable simulation results, MQSimNet integrates two well-established simulators, MQSim [8] for SSD functionality and SuperSim [9] for networking, providing a comprehensive and robust platform. To enhance the simulator's capabilities, we have extended both MQSim and SuperSim, incorporating additional features to support more advanced functionalities in the integrated platform. MQSimNet is both flexible and highly extensible, accommodating multiple network topologies, routing algorithms, and switching methods. Additionally, its modular design allows network and SSD components to be independently extended for customized configurations. The simulator provides detailed insights into both network and SSD operations, enabling comprehensive performance analysis. Unlike previous simulators for networked SSDs, MQSimNet's source code is openly accessible, promoting further research and development in this emerging field.

2 The Structure of SSDs

Figure 1 demonstrates the structure of a modern SSD, composed of two main parts: front-end and back-end. The front end includes the Flash Translation Layer, the Host Interface Layer (HIL), and some Flash Controllers, while the back end comprises arrays of flash memory chips.

Flash Translation Layer: The Flash Translation Layer manages the internal operations of SSDs through an embedded microprocessor, performing key tasks such as address mapping, garbage collection, wear leveling, and cache management. A core function is address mapping, which involves translating logical addresses used by the operating system into physical addresses on the flash memory. Since flash memory does not allow in-place updates, when data is modified, a new physical page is allocated for the updated data while the old page is marked as invalid [1]. This ensures efficient data storage and retrieval while accommodating the constraints of flash memory. The FTL also reclaims unusable space through garbage collection by relocating valid pages and erasing blocks to make them reusable [1]. It extends the device's lifetime through wear leveling, which evenly distributes write operations across memory blocks [14], and enhances performance by caching frequently accessed data in internal DRAM, reducing latency and wear on flash cells [1].

Host Interface Layer: The HIL acts as a bridge between the host system and the SSD controller, facilitating communication between the two components [3]. To achieve this, the HIL utilizes various communication protocols over the system I/O bus. One notable advancement in this area is the introduction of NVMe, which leverages the PCI Express bus to support multiple I/O queues, significantly improving communication efficiency with the host system [1].

Flash Controllers (FC): The Flash Controller is a small embedded processor that manages communication with multiple flash chips via a shared channel using arbitration and control/data signals. During write operations, it randomizes data to reduce error rates, applies ECC encoding for reliability [10], and then sends the data along with a write request to the flash chip. For read operations, it issues a read request, retrieves the data, performs ECC decoding, and derandomizes it to recover the original content.

Flash Chips: Flash chips are connected to a shared channel which is controlled by a flash controller. Each flash chip contains one or more dies that can operate individually, thereby enhancing system throughput by enabling parallel processing within the chip. Each die contains one or more planes, which are subdivisions designed to further increase parallelism. Within each plane, there are a large number of blocks (hundreds to thousands). These blocks are fundamental storage units, and each block is further divided into multiple pages, which are the smallest writable or readable units in flash memory [1]. This hierarchical structure of chip, die, plane, block, and page enables high-density storage and contributes to the performance capabilities of SSDs, though it also introduces complexity in managing access and reducing contention across shared resources.

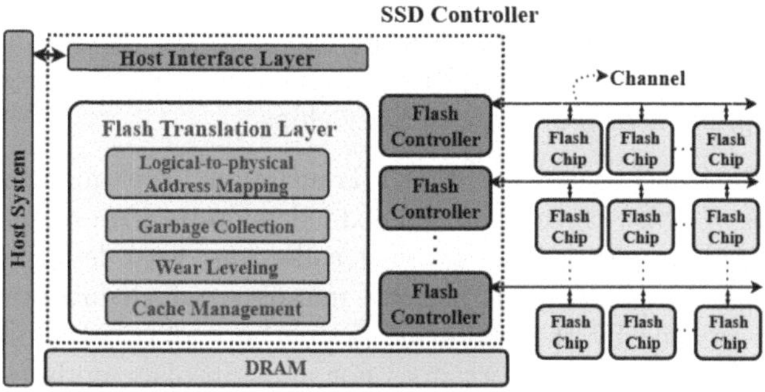

Fig. 1. High-level overview of a solid-state drive.

3 Network-Based SSDs and MQSimNet

Network-based SSD architectures, such as NoSSD, have been proposed to overcome the scalability and parallelism limitations of traditional channel-based designs. By introducing interconnection networks between flash chips and the FTL, these architectures enable multiple communication paths and improve overall throughput. However, the lack of a flexible and accurate simulator has hindered progress in this area.

To address this need, we introduce MQSimNet, an open-source simulator that integrates SSD functionality with interconnection network modeling. It combines two established tools—MQSim for SSD simulation and SuperSim for network simulation—into a unified platform. In the following section, we describe the main components of MQSimNet and how they work together to support the evaluation of networked SSD designs.

3.1 MQSimNet Components

MQSimNet simulates a novel SSD architecture. As such, there are no real-world counterparts to the simulated devices that are yet been built. This lack of real-world devices makes it extremely difficult to verify the proper functionality of this simulator. To counter this issue, MQSimNet was built from two well-known, verified, and time-tested simulators, each responsible for one part of this revolutionary design and a bridge to connect them.

MQSim [8] is designed to simulate almost every part of an SSD device except for communication between the SSD front-end and the back-end, and SuperSim [9] is used to create the remaining communication section of the MQSimNet simulator. As both MQSim and SuperSim have been verified to properly simulate the SSD and interconnection networking, respectively, we are confident that the final simulator proposed in this work would present accurate results.

MQSim: MQSim [8] is a discrete-event, open-source simulator written in C++ and introduced in 2018. It was specifically developed to address critical gaps in SSD modeling by supporting multi-queue (MQ) I/O request processing, accurate steady-state behavior modeling, and comprehensive end-to-end latency estimation. These features make MQSim particularly well-suited for studying modern MQ-enabled SSDs, while also retaining the ability to model traditional SATA-based SSDs. Released under the permissive MIT License, MQSim encourages adoption and extensibility in academic and industrial research.

One of MQSim's models flash memory chips in detail. Considering three major latency components: the transfer of addresses and commands to the memory chip, the execution of read and write operations across various flash technologies (such as Single-Level Cell, Multi-Level Cell, and Triple-Level Cell), and the data transfer between memory chips and the SSD controller. The simulator also incorporates advanced command execution features and accounts for die- and plane-level parallelism constraints. This level of granularity ensures precise modeling of SSD back-end operations.

The front-end modeling in MQSim also stands out for its comprehensiveness. It includes accurate representations of NVMe and SATA host interfaces, with the NVMe interface supporting key features like multi-queue processing and priority classes for queues. Moreover, MQSim also simulates data cache management of the modern SSDs.

Another feature of MQSim is that it supports various workloads and can simulate workloads accurately, achieving performance results that align with real-world, state-of-the-art SSDs within a margin of only 6%-18% error.

SuperSim: SuperSim [9] is an open-source, event-driven interconnection network simulator designed to model the architectural details of large-scale networks with precision, written in C++ and introduced in 2018. SuperSim is dedicated to flit-level simulation, capturing the finest details of router microarchitecture and network behavior. This level of granularity is essential for accurately studying the performance and design trade-offs of networks.

SuperSim's modular architecture supports a wide range of network topologies, routing algorithms, and router microarchitecture. It also includes both oblivious and adaptive routing algorithms, allowing researchers to evaluate a variety of routing strategies under different traffic patterns and workloads. The simulator's ability to isolate network and workload modeling ensures that it can be used to study the network behavior of diverse applications without predefined assumptions, enabling a wide range of experiments.

Network Bridge: To minimize modifications to the base simulators, most of the functionality in MQSimNet was added in separate files and components. The key additions include a network bridge for MQSim, the SuperSim application to communicate with the mentioned network bridge, and a unified event loop.

Instead of considering a constant delay for bus communication in the original implementation of MQSim, in our work, a corresponding message is created and passed to the network bridge. This message is then forwarded to SuperSim, where it traverses the network to its destination. Once the message reaches its destination, it is sent back to the network bridge for processing. The SSD simulator considers the arrival time of this response as the time for the completion of the communication.

The use of both simulators with minimal changes is enabled by the unified event loop. Instead of having a single event loop, our work maintains a separate event queue for each of the core simulators (MQSim and SuperSim). A unified event loop considers the first event of both queues and executes the one that happens earlier. This way, both base simulators can maintain their own queue structure.

New Features and Extensions: To expand the capabilities of MQSimNet and enable more comprehensive exploration of network-based SSD architectures, we introduced several new features to both the MQSim and SuperSim components. In the SSD simulation layer, we implemented dynamic address mapping algorithms as proposed in [21], allowing researchers to evaluate more adaptive and efficient flash resource utilization strategies. On the interconnection network side, we enhanced SuperSim by adding support for pipeline circuit switching and three advanced routing algorithms: East-First, Duato [12], and Tulip [4]. These additions broaden the range of topologies, switching, and routing schemes that can be studied, fostering deeper analysis of performance trade-offs and architectural optimizations in next-generation SSDs.

4 Case Studies

To demonstrate the capabilities of MQSimNet, we present two case studies focused on evaluating performance-critical aspects of SSDs with networked backend architectures. The first explores how different address mapping strategies—static versus dynamic—affect throughput, response time, and end-to-end delay. The second examines the effect of various routing algorithms, including deterministic and adaptive types, on average packet latency. These studies showcase MQSimNet's ability to provide deep architectural insights for optimizing scalable SSD designs. Table 1 outlines the essential parameters utilized in the simulation experiments.

Table 1. Parameters for MQSimNet

SSD Parameters		Network Parameters	
Host Interface	PCIe 3.0 (NVMe 1.2)	Network Topology	Mesh
SSD Capacity	1.5 TB	Routing Algorithm	XY Routing
Channel Width	64 Bytes	Flit Size	64 Byte
NAND Config	8 channels, 8 chips/channel, 2 die/chip, 4 planes/die, 1024 blocks/die, 4KB page	Flits in Packet	512
Read Latency	3 μs	Input Buffer Size	6 KB
Program Latency	100 μs	Output Buffer Size	8 KB
Erase Latency	1 ms	Network Channel Latency	1 ns

4.1 Impact of Address Mapping

In conventional SSDs, static address mapping assigns fixed transaction targets without considering runtime resource availability, leading to poor parallelism and increased latency. In contrast, networked SSDs support dynamic mapping that adapts to resource idleness and congestion. For example, mapping schemes can vary in granularity—some fix both die and plane addresses, while others explore flexibility by fixing only one [21].

Using six MSR Cambridge traces, we compared a static and a dynamic (with fixed die and plane assignments) mapping algorithm across both MQSim and MQSimNet. As shown in Fig. 2, the dynamic strategy significantly improves IOPS and reduces latency by leveraging parallelism more effectively.

4.2 Impact of Routing Algorithm

Routing policies in networked SSDs impact transaction latency by shaping traffic flow through the interconnect. Deterministic algorithms like dimension-ordered routing offer simplicity but suffer under high traffic. Adaptive algorithms such as Duato [2], on the other hand, adjust to network congestion dynamically.

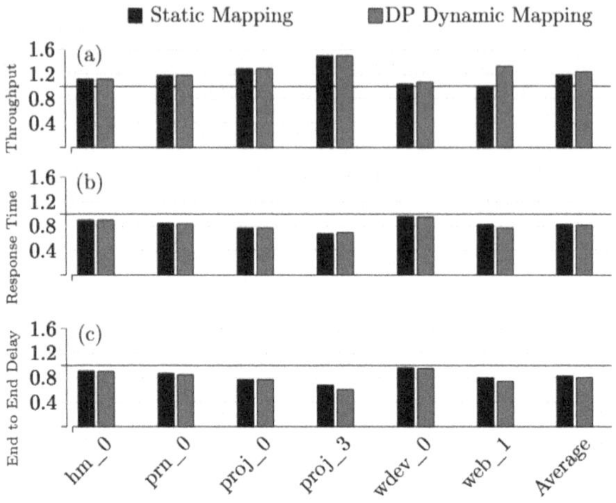

Fig. 2. Obtained results normalized to baseline bus-based SSD; (a) Normalized Throughput, (b) Normalized Device Response Time, and (c) Normalized End to End Request Time.

Simulations comparing dimension-ordered and Duato routing across MSR traces show minor improvements in average latency with Duato (Table 2). However, due to limited traffic, adaptive strategies did not reach full potential—though they are expected to perform better under more diverse or intensive workloads [2].

Table 2. Network Latency in SSD's back-end with dimension-ordered and Duato routing algorithms

Routing	hm_0	prn_0	proj_0	proj_3	wdev_0	web_1	Average
Dimension-ordered	17625.76	24571.76	51125.79	2232.99	25923.49	3243.74	23933.36
Duato	17350.71	24222.59	50725.80	2211.89	25566.43	3213.14	23677.64

5 Limitations

5.1 MQSim Memory Leakage

Despite its strengths, MQSim is not flawless. Notable in memory management, as prolonged simulations can lead to significant memory leakage, sometimes exceeding the size of the simulated data. In the development of MQSimNet, some of the leakage has been patched, yet the issue is not fully resolved. What makes solving this issue particularly difficult is abundance of leakage points in the MQSim engine. Additionally, MQSimNet replaces the core event queue algorithm in MQSim to improve the performance and reduce the memory footprint of the simulator, especially during longer simulations.

5.2 Single Threaded Operation

To assure in order processing of all the events, operations must happen sequentially and in a single thread. This design means that the simulator fails to utilize more than one CPU core, leaving considerable computational power of the modern CPUs unused. Assuming there is enough memory available, executing multiple instances of the simulator, with different configurations, could increase CPU utilization. However, this wouldn't improve the execution time of any individual simulation. Additionally, since large simulations have larger memory requirements, running multiple simulations at once is bound by the memory capacity of the underlying system.

6 Conclusion

In this work, we introduced MQSimNet, a simulator for network-equipped SSD devices that offers fairly accurate results for SSD and network-related operations of such devices. MQSimNet simulates both multi-queue NVMe and SATA SSDs. Relying on MQSim for SSD simulation, MQSimNet faithfully models all individual SSD components, leading to accurate steady-state behavior and end-to-end I/O request latency modeling. Similarly, network modeling is done by SuperSim, which models every individual component and captures the specific behavior of those components, leading to dependable results. The source code of MQSimNet is available at https://shorturl.at/bseOb.

References

1. Nadig, R., Sadrosadati, M., Mao, H., Ghiasi, N.M., Tavakkol, A., et al.: Venice: improving solid-state drive parallelism at low cost via conflict-free accesses. In: Proceedings of the 50th Annual International Symposium on Computer Architecture, pp. 1–16 (2023)
2. Kiasari, A.E., Sarbazi-Azad, H., Rezazad, M.S.: Performance comparison of adaptive routing algorithms in the star interconnection network. In: Eighth International Conference on High-Performance Computing in Asia-Pacific Region (HPCAsia'2005), p. 8. IEEE (2005)
3. Jung, M., Choi, W., Srikantaiah, S., Yoo, J., Kandemir, M.T.: HIOS: a host interface I/O scheduler for solid state disks. ACM SIGARCH Comput. Architecture News **42**(3), 289–300 (2014)
4. Gheibi-Fetrat, A., Akbarzadeh, N., Hessabi, S., Sarbazi-Azad, H.: Tulip: turn-free low-power network-on-chip. IEEE Comput. Architecture Lett. (2023)
5. Modarressi, M., Tavakkol, A., Sarbazi-Azad, H.: Virtual point-to-point connections for NoCs. IEEE Trans. Comput. Aided Des. Integr. Circuits Syst. **29**(6), 855–868 (2010)
6. Tanenbaum, A.S.: Computer Networks, Prentice-Hall International. Upper Saddle River, NJ 2 (1996)
7. Seitz D.: Deadlock-free message routing in multiprocessor interconnection networks. IEEE Trans. Comput. **100**(5), 547–553 (1987)

8. Tavakkol, A., Gómez-Luna, J., Sadrosadati, M., Ghose, S., Mutlu, O.: MQSim: a framework for enabling realistic studies of modern Multi-QueueSSD devices. In: 16th USENIX Conference on File and Storage Technologies (FAST 18), pp. 49–66 (2018)
9. McDonald, N., Flores, A., Davis, A., Isaev, M., Kim, J., Gibson, D.: SuperSim: extensible flit-level simulation of large-scale interconnection networks. In: 2018 IEEE International Symposium on Performance Analysis of Systems and Software (ISPASS), pp. 87–98. IEEE (2018)
10. Cai, Y., Ghose, S., Haratsch, E.F., Luo, Y., Mutlu, O.: Error characterization, mitigation, and recovery in flash-memory-based solid-state drives. Proc. IEEE **105**(9), 1666–1704 (2017)
11. Cho, S., Kim, B., Cho, H., Seo, G., Mutlu, O., Kim, M., et al.: AERO: adaptive erase operation for improving lifetime and performance of modern NAND flash-based SSDs. In: Proceedings of the 29th ACM International Conference on Architectural Support for Programming Languages and Operating Systems, vol. 3, pp. 101–118 (2024)
12. Duato, J., Yalamanchili, S., Ni, L.: Interconnection networks. Elsevier (2002)
13. Hwang, J., Vuppalapati, M., Peter, S., Agarwal, R.: Rearchitecting Linux storage stack for µs latency and high throughput. In: 15th USENIX Symposium on Operating Systems Design and Implementation (OSDI 21), pp. 113–128 (2021)
14. Lim, S., Lee, S., Moon, B.: FASTer FTL for enterprise-class flash memory SSDs. In: 2010 International Workshop on Storage Network Architecture and Parallel I/Os, pp. 3–12. IEEE (2010)
15. NVM Express. NVM Express Base Specification, 8 (2024). Rev. 2.1
16. Serial ATA Revision 3.1 – Gold Revision Serial ATA Int'l Org., 7 (2011)
17. Tavakkol, A., Arjomand, M., Sarbazi-Azad, H.: Network-on-SSD: a scalable and high-performance communication design paradigm for SSDs. IEEE Comput. Archit. Lett. **12**(1), 5–8 (2012)
18. Tavakkol, A., Arjomand, M., Sarbazi-Azad, H.: Design for scalability in enterprise SSDs. In: proceedings of the 23rd international conference on parallel architectures and compilation, pp. 417–430 (2014)
19. Jinhua, C., Feiyu, C., Lu, L., Shiqiang, N., Yang Laurence, T.: SmartNetSSD: exploiting path resources for read performance improvement in network-based SSDs. In: 2024 IEEE 42nd International Conference on Computer Design (ICCD), pp. 356–359. IEEE (2024)
20. Kim, J., Kang, S., Park, Y., Kim, J.: Networked SSD: flash memory interconnection network for high-bandwidth SSD. In: 2022 55th IEEE/ACM International Symposium on Microarchitecture (MICRO), pp. 388–403. IEEE (2022)
21. Tavakkol, A., Mehrvarzy, P., Arjomand, M., Sarbazi-Azad, H.: Performance evaluation of dynamic page allocation strategies in SSDs. In: ACM Transactions on Modeling and Performance Evaluation of Computing Systems (TOMPECS), pp. 1–33. ACM (2016)

Billion Scale Tensors: Compression Methods and Parallel Computations

Sudhindra Gopal Krishna(✉), Sridhar Radhakrishnan, Aditya Narasimhan, and Richard Veras

School of Computer Science, University of Oklahoma, Norman, OK, USA
{sudhi,sridhar,adinaras,richard.m.veras}@ou.edu

Abstract. Tensors, their representations, and computations are gaining popularity with an increasing number of machine learning algorithms for applications. In this paper, we show several techniques for storing compressed sparse tensors. One of our approaches using compressed binary trees (CBTs) shows that the large sparse tensors occupy nearly 1/3 of the space occupied by the storage technique used in *tsparse*. We show how tensor multiplication can be performed *directly on our proposed structure* thereby making it space efficient – allowing us to perform tensor multiplication on extremely large tensors on GPU computing platforms. Our results show that the smaller the block size (up to a point), the larger the size of the representation, and the larger the level of parallelism, and vice versa.

Keywords: Data Compression · Tensor Representation · Algorithm · Matrix Multiplication

1 Introduction

A 1-dimensional tensor in general is referred to as a vector or an array, whereas a 2-dimensional tensor is a matrix. The power of a tensor lies in its ability to concisely capture complex relationships in multidimensional data. Such is the case in physics, quantum chemistry, and more recently in machine learning and graph analytics.

In practice, these tensors can be extremely large in nature and often tend to push the limits of storage and computational power needed to perform analysis. High Performance Computing (HPC) helps parallelize the resource-heavy operations that can be performed using tensors.

This approach of using HPC raises another problem, being able to fit these extremely large datasets into our desired memory for computation. A predominate challenge is blocking these datasets and arranges the computation so that the necessary subset of the data, or working dataset, is in the global when it is needed. One solution to overcome this issue and make maximum use of the bandwidth is to compress the data on the host before transferring the working dataset to the device and directly access the desired data on the compressed

H. R. Arabnia et al. (Eds.): CSCE 2025, CCIS 2932, pp. 329–338, 2026.
https://doi.org/10.1007/978-3-032-22193-3_25

structure without having to decompress. The compressed data allows us to place larger amounts of data in the space limited shared memory that is available on the streaming multiprocessors. By keeping data closer to the processor (rather than accessing the global memory) it allows to overcome memory access latency.

In this paper, we address this problem for performing tensor computations on compressed data using GPGPUs. Our work builds Compressed Binary Trees (*CBT*) – a row by row adjacency matrix compression technique for storing graphs – that are used to perform computations on tensors that have been flattened to matrices.

Our contributions in this work are the following.

- We developed several compression techniques for storing sparse tensors with billions of elements. These techniques use *CBT* as the baseline technique, as shown in Sect. 3.
- We have improved the concept of dividing the matrix into blocks which is amenable to parallel computation in several ways. The computation can now be performed on our compressed blocks as shown in Sect. 4.
- We have provided an approach that refines parallel computation from coarse grain involving row blocks and column blocks in multiplication to finer grain as shown in Sect. 5.
- Our algorithms are such that all computations are performed directly on the compressed structure - there is no need to decompress. This avoids the crucial step in previous algorithms which uses the Expand, Sort, and Compress technique.

2 Related Work

There is extensive body work on compressed sparse matrix formats, which is extensively discussed in [1–4]. In the context of parallel computing, he Coordinate list technique (COO) has been demonstrated to be one of the least efficient formats [3]. Therefore, it has been extended and improved in [2] with bmSparse. Furthermore, the authors in [2] demonstrated that bmSparse is 32 times more efficient than COO.

Compressed Sparse Row (CSR) [5] is another popular compression scheme that has been adapted for a variety of platforms, including GPGPUs [6] and has been adapted by the authors in the compressed context for time evolving graphs in [4,7].

We proceed to discuss more about various matrix multiplications from a parallel processing perspective. We start by exploring the first usage of *CBT* for performing matrix operations. This was done in [8] by sequentially multiplying two binary matrices. The interesting contribution here is that the resultant is also stored in the *CBT* structure directly without usage of any intermediate structures. To improve that work, the authors in [7] extended *CBT* to a value-based sequential matrix-matrix multiplication and compared it with CSR-based matrix-matrix multiplication.

Table 1. Comparing the storage for various Boolean matrices in various representations/compression techniques.

	Number of rows and columns (n)	Number of nonzero values (nnz)	Adjacency matrix	COO	CSR	tSparse (modified bmSparse)	CBT
Friendster	65,608,366	1,806,067,135	489.36 T	26.91 G	13.95 G	13.58 G	4.4 G
Live journal	3,997,962	34,681,189	1.82 T	529.19 M	295.10 M	272.22 M	64.2 M
10 million	10,000,000	19,999,996	11.37 T	305.18 M	228.88 M	171.66 M	59.6 M
100 million	100,000,000	10,000,000	1,136.87 T	152.59 M	839.23 M	267.03 M	47.68 M
1 billion	1,070,000,000	91,070,000,000	127.10 PB	1.32 T	680.51 G	680.51 G	9.5 G

Sparse General Matrix Multiplication (spgemm), being a fundamental kernel, has a multitude of applications and implementations [9–11]. However, one of the challenges of multiplying two sparse matrices is managing the intermediate results of the output matrix.

In order to address that issue, the Expansion, Sorting and Contraction algorithm (ESC) from [12] takes intermediate results during the calculation of matrix multiplication and stores them in a tuple format (index and value) that later is sorted and combined based on the common index positions.

Zachariadis et al. [3] provide a matrix multiplication technique that takes these CUSP and ESC methods and modifies them to an approach called *tSparse*, which uses a modified ESC called Sort-Expand and Compress (SEaC).

The usage of the ESC strategy is not necessary in our multiplication technique as we provide a way that out intermediate results are directly stored as CBT structures.

The storage capacities are further compared in Table 1 considering other datasets (real world and synthetic).

3 Tensor Representation

This paper approaches the storage of tensors in three different ways, a) approaches to store tensors of even dimensions, b) approaches to store tensors of odd dimensions, and c) an approach to store tensors of any dimension.

3.1 Even-Mode Tensors

Figure 1a shows the two ways to compress the even mode tensors. The first one, the process first starts by compressing the outermost dimension A, which denotes all non-zero locations where the corresponding A_i are present. Then, the corresponding A_i, the matrix of the following dimensions. The figure to the right, shows the second approach for compressing an even-mode tensor. In this approach, we first start by compressing the nonzero matrix A, followed by compressing the further dimensions A_is in the same way as a time-evolving graph shown in [13].

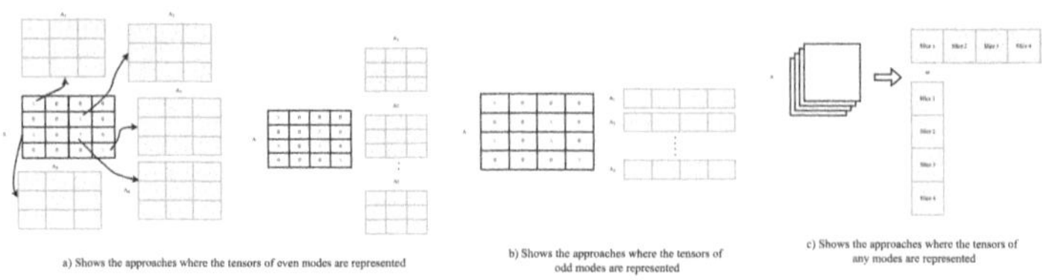

Fig. 1. Shows different approaches to represent tensor, a) shows the ways to represent the tensors of even mode, b) shows the ways to represent odd mode tensors, and c) shows the ways to represent tensors of any mode.

3.2 Odd-Mode Tensors

For the tensor of odd modes, we first compress all but the last dimension using the even-mode tensor approach discussed in Sect. 3.1, and every non-zero row of the last dimension is then compressed using the desired compression algorithm. Figure 1b, illustrates a three-mode tensor, where the nonzero element of the matrix A consists of an array in the third dimension.

3.3 Tensors of any Mode

However, one of the most common methodologies for representing a tensor is to convert any mode tensor into a matrix. The reduction in dimensionality starts by merging the inner dimension with the penultimate dimension repeatedly until the total number of dimensions is equal to two, which is a matrix. This process represents a tensor, as a matrix is referred to as unfolding. For example, consider a three-mode tensor as shown in right of Fig. 1c is of dimension $(I \times J \times K)$, the unfolded representation of the tensor will be represented as a matrix of dimensions $(I \times (J * K))$.

4 Compression Methods

Until now, compression techniques and operations on compressed structures have been limited to matrices [7,8,14]. This paper introduces four techniques to compress the tensors represented as shown in Sect. 3.

4.1 CBT-Leaf_CBT

$CBT - Leaf\_CBT$ is an extension to CBT mentioned by Nelson et al., [14]. In this technique, if the leaf node is equal to 1, the leaf will continue to have more CBTs of the following dimension.

4.2 Time-Evolving CBT

The time-evolving CBT was first introduced in 2019, by Nelson et al., [13]. The first dimension is stored as a regular CBT [14] and the inner dimensions of tensor are stored as a difference between one another as seen in a time-evolving graphs.

4.3 Unfolding CBT

Since a tensor of three-mode and higher are often hard to visualize, one of efficient ways to do it is by spreading out the inner-dimensions of the tensor into the outer-dimension which is often referred to as unfolding. Once the tensor is unfolded into a matrix, the matrix is then compressed one row at a time using *CBT* [14]. This compression technique is referred to as Unfolded *CBT* or *UCBT*.

4.4 Block Compression

This compression technique is designed to store matricized tensor blocks that will serve to improve the temporal cache locality during the tensor operations. This compression technique is called Block Compressed Binary Tree (*BCBT*). Nonzero blocks are continuously stored in the same way as the row-by-row nature of *CBT* [14].

Figure 2a, shows one of the ways in which we can covert a tensor into a matrix, in this approach, the third dimension k, is kept constant and the other two dimensions are merged together to form a high-dimension matrix. Once the tensor is unfolded, the tensor is then split into blocks of desired size, in this case the blocks are divided into the dimensions of size (2×2).

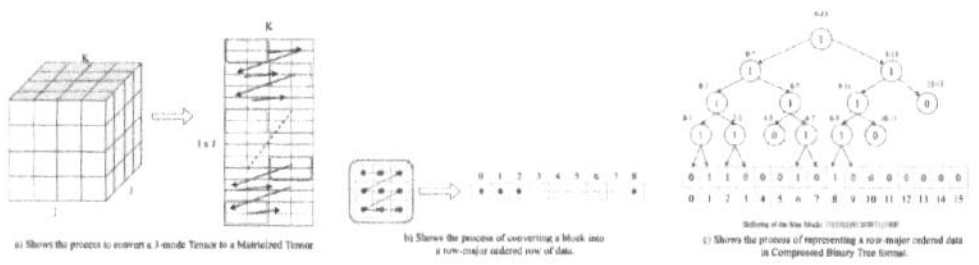

Fig. 2. Shows the process to convert a 3-mode Tensor to a Matricized Tensor, and represent each tensor block as *CBT*.

Figure 2b, shows the procedure to store each block in a compressed format. Before compressing the block, the block is first converted to a row of data using the row-major order. In this example, for simplicity, we have considered the block size to be (3×3).

Once represented as a row, the data is now compressed using *CBT* [14], as shown in Fig. 2c.

4.5 Compression Result

The data used in this paper are generated synthetically. Data generation is modeled after the real-world scenario of a sparse tensor. For the analyses, the data generated are in the scale of tens of million to more than a billion nonzero values in the tensor. We compare our unfolding compression results with the most well-known compression technique for storing matrix, Compressed Sparse Row (*CSR*) [5].

Table 2 shows the various datasets that are used in the analyses and their corresponding memory sizes when we take the corresponding compression approaches. From the table, it does look like the memory required and the time taken to compress are very similar. However, depending on the use of these tensors, the appropriate compression approach must be chosen. The result for Unfold *CBT* on the billion-scale graph is missing due to the extremely high value of the outer dimension.

Table 2. Shows the different odd and even tensor datasets along with their corresponding compression approach and the time taken to compress.

Dimension	NNZ	Raw file Size	CBT_LCBT		Unfold CBT		Block CBT	
			Time	Size	Time	Size	Time	Size
500 × 500 × 400	32,967,574	409 MB	17.19 MB	15.85 s	17.04 MB	24.05 s	17.04 MB	16.61 s
670 × 670 × 450	100,354,540	1.3 GB	40.38 MB	38.27 s	40.11 MB	56.77 s	40.3 MB	36 s
512^3	134,217,728	1.7 GB	0.87 MB	8.18 s	0.81 MB	2.1 s	0.81 MB	2.60 s
$2^{17} \times 2^{17} \times 2^{17}$	993,798,762	19 GB	4.22 GB	1616.57 s	–	–	2.18 GB	868 s

Dimension	NNZ	Raw file Size	CBT_LCBT		Unfold CBT	
			Time	Size	Time	Size
400 × 400 × 300 × 300	53,251,472	864 MB	80.14 MB	38.59 s	79.94 MB	50.48 s
589 × 589 × 322 × 458	66,407,269	1.1 GB	107.71 MB	46.91 s	111.85 MB	67.607 s
256 × 256 × 128 × 128	252,783,285	4.1 GB	155.08 MB	121.2 s	154.07 MB	220.75 s

5 Parallel Computations

Sparse matrices, in general, are highly irregular, which relates to more memory accesses for fewer data. The GPU's efficiency depends on maximizing the amount of data read (lower communication cost) from the host to the device. To achieve maximum computation out of GPU's on the data, we are considering using block-based tensor compression discussed in Sect. 4.4.

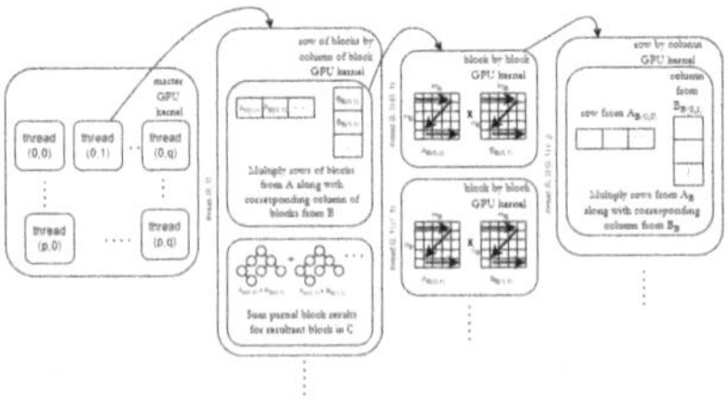

Fig. 3. Shows the two levels of parallelism in the GPU. p and q are the number of blocks on both the dimensions. $p = \frac{n}{n_B}$ $q = \frac{m}{m_B}$.

Here, we have divided the implementation of multiplying two matrices into three algorithms. The Algorithm 1 multiplies two blocks of matrices to obtain a partial result, Algorithm 2 provides the implementation for multiplying a row block of A and a column block of B to obtain a block in C, and Algorithm 3 provides the implementation for multiplying the matrix in parallel.

There are four levels of parallelism here. The first level is where each thread executes a row of blocks from A along with a column of blocks from B. The second level is when a thread takes two blocks (one from A and one from B) to be multiplied. The third deeper level is when a single thread takes an entire row of A and an entire column of B of elements to result in a single resultant value in C. The fourth final level of parallelism occurs when a single element is taken from the row of A to be multiplied with another element of B. Once we find the partial multiplication results of these values, we may use the scan operation to receive the resultant element in C. In this paper, the first two levels of parallelism are implemented. The latter levels are the potential for future work.

5.1 Partial Multiplication

This algorithm takes a block of matrix A, and a block of matrix B as input and computes the partial resultant block of matrix C as shown in Fig. 3. Since these blocks are of compute size, these block matrices are multiplied in parallel, where a row in block A and a column in block B, are multiplied to obtain a value in C. Once all threads finish multiplying the block, it is sent back to Algorithm 2.

Algorithm 1: multiply(nnz_A, nnz_B): A Parallel Partial Matrix Multiplication Algorithm

```
Input: Block in A, Block in B
Output: Partial Block of Resultant Matrix C
begin
    do in parallel:
        for a row of block_A: a do
            for a row of block_B: b do
                if index_a == index_b then
                    rowSum += a×b;
        partialBlock_C += rowSum;
    return partialBlock_C;
```

5.2 Compute Resultant Block

This algorithm computes the result of a block of matrix, this algorithm receives the starting index positions of each block in a row of matrix A, and starting index of each block in a column of matrix B. Since each block is independent of other blocks, these blocks can also be parallelized to obtain the results much faster. The algorithm is tweaked to take a blocked compressed data as an input and the starting index of the block, to obtain all non-zero elements in a row-major order. Each block of A and B is then sent to the Algorithm 1 to obtain the partial resultant of the block. The blocks obtained from each thread are then reduced with respect to their indices to obtain the final result.

Algorithm 2: matrixMultiply(indicesA_tid, indicesB_tid): A Parallel Algorithm for Computing Resultant Block for Matrix C

```
Input: Row Indices of Matrix A, Column Indices of Matrix B
Output: Block of Resultant Matrix C
begin
    /* Number of RowIndices == Number of Column Indices */
    do in parallel: for each block in A and a block in B
        nnz_A = matA[rowBlock].getNNZ()
        nnz_B = matB[columnBlock].getNNZ()
        partialBlock_C += multiply (nnz_A, nnz_B)
    return block_C;
```

Algorithm 3: Parallel Algorithm to Multiply Matrices

```
  Input: Compressed Matrix A, Compressed Matrix B, Index Array id_A, Index
         Array id_B
  Output: Resultant Matrix C
1 begin
2     numThreads = (numRows_C * numColumns_C) / block_size^2
      do in parallel: for each block in C
3         // call Algorithm 2 to compute the resultant of each block
          block_C = matrixMultiply(rowOf_A, columnOf_B)
          bitString_Block_C = block_C.toBitString()
4     return ResultantMatrix_C
```

5.3 Parallel Matrix Multiplication

This algorithm is the final piece of matrix multiplication. Line 2 determines the number of threads required to compute the resultant matrix. From Line 3, each resultant block of C is computed by the thread associated with the row. The thread will handle the row of matrix A and a column of matrix B, and then this thread calls the procedure mentioned in Algorithm 2 to obtain the final result of a block in C. Line 6, then computes the bitstring for the final resultant of the block in C [4]. These bitstrings are then appended one after the other in the order of the blocks in C.

At the lowest level of these algorithms, when multiplying a row and a column to calculate the result element of the resultant matrix, there would be multiple queries to be performed, and this is going to result in multiple neighbor queries. To avoid this, a partial sum technique can be implemented that takes the two CBT structures and merges them by adding the common index values [7].

6 Conclusion and Future Work

In this work, we propose four techniques to store extremely large tensors using the state-of-the-art compression technique, Compressed Binary Tree [13,14]. To utilize the compressed structure, we performed a matrix-matrix multiplication on the matricized tensors to show the operations that are capable on a matrix of such a large scale. Our compression technique also allows one to eliminate the need to use ESC methodologies to update the partially computed matrix. We also show the ability to compress the matricized tensors into blocks of size greater than 8×8 as needed in [2,3]. The multiplication technique can be further improved by constructing CBT on the partial results obtained in the Algorithm 1, and combining these $CBTs$ at the end of the Algorithm 2. This helps to multiply larger blocks, as the partial results are compressed in the computation.

References

1. Langr, D., Tvrdik, P.: Evaluation criteria for sparse matrix storage formats. IEEE Trans. Parallel Distrib. Syst. **27**(2), 428–440 (2015)
2. Zhang, J., Gruenwald, L.: Regularizing irregularity: bitmap-based and portable sparse matrix multiplication for graph data on GPUs. GRADES-NDA 2018. Association for Computing Machinery, New York, NY, USA (2018)
3. Zachariadis, O., Satpute, N., Gómez-Luna, J., Olivares, J.: Accelerating sparse matrix-matrix multiplication with GPU tensor cores. Comput. Electr. Eng. **88**, 106848 (2020)
4. Gopal Krishna, S., Nelson, M., Radhakrishnan, S., Chatterjee, A., Sekharan, C.: On compressing time-evolving networks. In: ALLDATA 2021, The Seventh International Conference on Big Data, Small Data, Linked Data and Open Data, pp. 43–48 (2021)
5. Snay, R.A.: Reducing the profile of sparse symmetric matrices. Bulletin Géodésique **50**(4), 341–352 (1976)
6. NVIDIA: CUDA C Programming Guide (2022). https://docs.nvidia.com/cuda/cuda-c-programming-guide/index.html
7. Krishna, S.G., Narasimhan, A., Radhakrishnan, S., Veras, R.: On large-scale matrix-matrix multiplication on compressed structures. In: 2021 IEEE International Conference on Big Data (Big Data), pp. 2976–2985 (2021)
8. Nelson, M., Radhakrishnan, S., Sekharan, C.N.: Billion-scale matrix compression and multiplication with implications in data mining. In: 2019 IEEE 20th International Conference on Information Reuse and Integration for Data Science (IRI), pp. 395–402 (2019)

9. Lin, P., et al.: Towards extreme-scale simulations for low mach fluids with second-generation trilinos. Parallel Process. Lett. **24**(04), 1442005 (2014)
10. Deveci, M., Trott, C.R., Rajamanickam, S.: Multi-threaded sparse matrix sparse matrix multiplication for many-core and GPU architectures. Technical report, Sandia National Lab.(SNL-NM), Albuquerque, NM (United States) (2018)
11. Wolf, M.M., Deveci, M., Berry, J.W., Hammond, S.D., Rajamanickam, S.: Fast linear algebra-based triangle counting with kokkoskernels. In: 2017 IEEE High Performance Extreme Computing Conference (HPEC), pp. 1–7 (2017)
12. Dalton, S., Olson, L., Bell, N.: Optimizing sparse matrix-matrix multiplication for the GPU. ACM Trans. Math. Softw. (TOMS) **41**(4), 1–20 (2015)
13. Nelson, M., Radhakrishnan, S., Sekharan, C., Chatterjee, A., Krishna, S.G.: Queryable compression on time-evolving web and social networks with streaming. ACM Trans. Web **16**(2) (2021)
14. Nelson, M., Radhakrishnan, S., Sekharan, C.: Queryable compression on time-evolving social networks with streaming. In: 2018 IEEE International Conference on Big Data (Big Data). IEEE BigData 2018, pp. 146–151 (2018)

GPU Accelerated GMRES Solver for Efficient Sparse Linear Systems

Khiem Luong[1], Sabbir Polak[1], Byunghyun Jang[1(✉)], and Shuang Z. Tu[2]

[1] The University of Mississippi, University, MS 38677, USA
{kdluong,mhpolak,bjang}@go.olemiss.edu
[2] Jackson State University, Jackson, MS 39217, USA
shuang.z.tu@jsums.edu

Abstract. The Generalized Minimal Residual (GMRES) algorithm is a cornerstone for solving sparse linear systems in scientific and engineering applications. However, traditional CPU-based implementations struggle to meet performance demands as the scale of these systems increases. In this paper, we focus on implementing a CUDA-based GMRES algorithm to leverage the massive parallelism of modern GPU architectures. The porting process optimizes key computations such as matrixvector multiplication and orthogonalization. Performance analysis shows significant speedups compared to CPU implementations, especially for large sparse matrices. For instance, the execution time for a 23,052 × 23,052 matrix is reduced from 283 s on the CPU to 70 s on the GPU. The results also show that while the GPU implementation has longer execution times for small matrices due to initialization and memory transfer costs, it consistently outperforms the CPU implementation as matrix size increases.

Keywords: GMRES · sparse linear systems · iterative solvers · GPU · CUDA

1 Introduction

Sparse linear systems are fundamental in applied science and engineering, forming the backbone of numerous real-world applications such as computational physics, fluid dynamics, and machine learning [1]. These systems are typically represented by large, sparse matrices in which most elements are zero. This sparsity renders direct solvers such as Gaussian elimination [2] computationally expensive and impractical for large-scale problems.

To address these challenges, iterative solvers such as the Generalized Minimal Residual (GMRES) algorithm have been widely adopted. GMRES iteratively approximates the solution within a Krylov subspace and minimizes the residual at each step, avoiding explicit matrix factorization. This property makes it particularly effective for solving large sparse systems. However, GMRES implementations on conventional CPUs often face scalability challenges due to limited parallelism and high memory bandwidth requirements.

H. R. Arabnia et al. (Eds.): CSCE 2025, CCIS 2932, pp. 339–352, 2026.
https://doi.org/10.1007/978-3-032-22193-3_26

Graphics Processing Units (GPUs) provide a compelling alternative because of their ability to handle massive parallel workloads. Nevertheless, implementing GMRES efficiently on GPUs presents unique challenges, particularly in optimizing sparse matrixvector operations that are central to the algorithm. Frequent memory transfers between the CPU and GPU can also introduce considerable overhead and degrade performance on large matrices. Furthermore, precise thread synchronization is required to maintain data consistency across algorithmic stages, which may incur additional latency when data dependencies span multiple GPU blocks. Addressing these challenges is critical to achieving faster and more scalable solutions for large-scale scientific computations. Therefore, this study aims to implement the GMRES algorithm using CUDA to fully exploit the parallelism of modern GPUs.

CUDA (Compute Unified Device Architecture) is a parallel computing platform and programming model developed by NVIDIA. It enables developers to harness the GPU for general-purpose computation by providing direct access to its instruction set and memory hierarchy. CUDA supports several programming languages, including C/C++, Fortran, Python, and MATLAB, through language extensions that allow developers to express parallelism and direct the compiler to offload computation to the GPU accelerator.

The main contributions of this paper are summarized as follows:

- **Optimized Implementation:** We develop a CUDA-based GMRES algorithm that optimizes key computational operations to effectively leverage the parallel processing capabilities of GPUs.
- **Performance Enhancement:** Our implementation demonstrates significant speedups over traditional CPU-based methods, particularly for large, sparse matrices.
- **Scalability Improvements:** We address scalability issues by minimizing latency and overhead arising from memory transfers and thread synchronization, thereby improving algorithmic efficiency on modern GPU architectures.

2 Related Work

The acceleration of iterative solvers such as GMRES using GPU architectures has been extensively studied in recent years. Early research in this area primarily focused on demonstrating the feasibility of GPU-based solvers for sparse systems. For instance, Couturier and Domas implemented a GPU-based GMRES solver achieving speedups ranging from 8× to 23× across a variety of sparse matrices, with optimizations targeting sparse matrixvector (SpMV) and vector operations [3]. This foundational study demonstrated that GPUs can significantly reduce GMRES execution time, particularly for large matrices, due to their inherent parallelism and high memory bandwidth. However, it mainly emphasized performance potential without thoroughly analyzing trade-offs between speed and accuracy, especially regarding numerical stability and floating-point precision.

Subsequent research explored more advanced optimization strategies to address the limitations of GPU-based sparse solvers. Anzt and colleagues conducted an in-depth analysis of mixed-precision techniques, investigating the impact of using lower-precision arithmetic for computationally intensive operations such as orthogonalization and SpMV [4]. By storing matrix data in reduced precision while performing critical computations in higher precision to preserve accuracy, their approach aimed to minimize memory bandwidth consumption. Their results demonstrated up to a 50% reduction in execution time and highlighted the importance of efficient memory access patterns such as the compressed sparse row (CSR) format, which is widely adopted in iterative solvers for its adaptability. Although effective in reducing runtime, this approach introduces complexity in tuning and maintaining accuracy—factors that are crucial in applications demanding high numerical fidelity.

More recent developments in GMRES implementations have emphasized hybrid-precision and storage-optimized methods. Loe and co-authors investigated mixed-precision strategies and found that hybrid-precision techniques maintain convergence accuracy for most large sparse systems while substantially reducing computational costs [5]. By selectively employing lower precision for computationally intensive tasks, these methods enhance solver performance while preserving numerical stability. Such approaches are particularly beneficial in GPU systems, where memory bandwidth and compute throughput are critical for scalability. Nevertheless, reliance on mixed precision can limit applicability in contexts where single-precision arithmetic is insufficient, necessitating careful evaluation of algorithmic accuracy and the resulting solution quality.

Overall, prior work demonstrates growing interest in optimizing GPU-based solvers for large sparse systems. However, many existing studies leverage GPU capabilities in a relatively generic manner. In contrast, our approach fully exploits the architectural features of modern NVIDIA GPUs through a novel kernel design and optimized memory management. Building on these advances, this paper presents a comprehensive CUDA-based GMRES implementation that integrates fine-grained optimizations across all algorithmic components and kernels, effectively handling matrices of varying sizes and sparsity levels while ensuring consistent numerical stability and improved performance.

3 Methodology

3.1 Original GMRES Algorithm in C

The GMRES (Generalized Minimal Residual) is an iterative method commonly used to solve large, sparse, asymmetric linear systems $Ax = b$. The strength of this algorithm lies in avoiding the computation of the inverse of matrix A by minimizing the residual norm $||Ax - b||$ in the Krylov subspace [6]. This Krylov subspace is constructed from the initial residual $r_0 = b - Ax_0$ where:

$$K_m(A, r_0) = span\{r_0, Ar_0, A^2r_0, ..., A^{m-1}r_0\} \tag{1}$$

GMRES uses the Arnoldi process to build an orthonormal basis for this Krylov subspace. Then, a Hessenberg matrix is solved through QR factorization to find an approximate solution [7]. The main steps in the implementation on CPU include:

Sparse Matrix-Vector Multiplication (SpMV)

- This is a memory-bound operation and takes up most of the computing time.
- Sparse matrix is stored in CSR format to save memory and support fast access to non-zero elements [8].

Orthogonalization Process

- The Modified Gram-Schmidt method is used to maintain the orthogonality of the Krylov basis.
- This step involves numerous dot products and vector updates, which can significantly impact performance when executed sequentially on a CPU.

Hessenberg Matrix Solving

- The small Hessenberg matrix is reduced using Givens rotation to triangular form, making it simpler to solve the resulting system.

Even though developing GMRES on CPU is popular and effective for small to medium-sized systems, they are incapable of scaling larger systems due to limitations in memory bandwidth and sequential nature of the operations.

3.2 Optimization Strategy for GMRES Solver

To take advantage of the high memory bandwidth and enormous parallelism of contemporary GPU architectures, the GMRES algorithm has been ported to GPUs. Unlike a CPU-based algorithm, you can break down the algorithm into independent, parallelizable tasks, which allows the data to flow concurrently on thousands of threads on the GPU and execute the computations simultaneously. This concurrency allows multiple operations to be performed in parallel, boosting up the computations that otherwise would be sequential on traditional CPU systems. The primary aspects of the CUDA implementation include:

Sparse Matrix-Vector Multiplication (SpMV)

- Matrix Format: The sparse matrix is stored in CSR format, where:
  - AA contains the nonzero values.
  - IA stores the starting index of each row in AA.
  - JA contains the column indices of the corresponding nonzero elements.
- Parallelization Strategy: Each thread processes one row of the matrix, computing partial sums for its assigned row. Memory access patterns are optimized to ensure coalesced memory access and reducing global memory latency.

Orthogonalization Process

- CUDA Optimizations:
  - The Modified GramSchmidt process is implemented using warp-level reductions, taking advantage of shared memory to reduce the number of global memory accesses.
  - The use of double precision ensures numerical stability, which distinguishes this method from mixed precision methods.
- Synchronization:
  - Thread synchronization within each block is handled using *__syncthreads()* [9].
  - Kernel-level synchronization is achieved using atomic operations [10], ensuring data consistency during Krylov subspace construction.

Memory Management [11]

- Shared memory is used to store temporary data such as intermediate results from dot products, greatly reducing global memory access latency.
- Global memory is used for large data structures like sparse matrix and vectors.
- Constant memory is used for fixed parameters to speed up access.
- To minimize data transfer, data remains on the GPU throughout the computation, with only the final solution transferred back to the CPU.

Kernel Synchronization. During the Arnoldi process, kernel synchronization ensures correct computation at critical steps, which is achieved through:

- Busy waiting: using *atomicAdd* to control the status of operations [10].
- Independent Kernels: Each kernel handles distinct computation stages, minimizing conflicts between threads.

4 Implementation Details

The CUDA implementation of the algorithm is divided into several specialized kernels that work together to maximize parallel effectiveness and optimize memory usage.

4.1 Sparse Matrix-Vector Multiplication (SpMV)

The matrix-vector multiplication is one of the most computationally expensive components of the algorithm. The goal of this kernel is to compute $w = A \cdot v$ where A is a sparse matrix stored in Compressed Sparse Row (CSR) format, as this format is super efficient to access matrix with large number of non-zero elements.

Each thread computes the dot product of one row of matrix A and accesses the non-zero elements of the current row using $IA[idx]$ and $IA[idx + 1]$, where

idx is the global id of each thread. For each non-zero element $AA[k]$, the corresponding value in $x[j]$ is fetched using $JA[k]$ for column index, and their product is added to the row's sum.

The CSR format helps store the non-zero values in AA sequentially, which minimizes global memory latency. JA and IA are accessed in coalesced manner since each thread reads continuous memory locations for its assigned row. Because each thread handles one row of A, this will help distribute the workload evenly across all threads.

Input

- AA: array contains all non-zero elements of A.
- IA: array stores the cumulative number of non-zero elements up to (not including) the i-th row.
- JA: stores the column index of each element of A.
- x: input vector
- nn: number of rows in A.

Output

- s: resultant vector w, representing $A \cdot x$.

Algorithm 1 CSR Matrix-Vector Multiplication Kernel

Require: AA (nonzero values of matrix A), IA (row pointers), JA (column indices), nn (number of rows), x (input vector)
Ensure: s (result vector $s = A \cdot x$)
Input: AA, IA, JA, nn, x
Output: s
$idx \leftarrow$ threadIdx.x + blockIdx.x × blockDim.x
if $idx < nn$ **then**
  $k1 \leftarrow IA[idx]$
  $k2 \leftarrow IA[idx + 1] - 1$
  $s[idx] \leftarrow 0.0$
  for $k \leftarrow k1$ to $k2$ **do**
    $j \leftarrow JA[k]$
    $s[idx] \leftarrow s[idx] + AA[k] \cdot x[j]$
  end for
end if

4.2 Arnoldi Iteration

This process is responsible for the construction of an orthonormal basis for the Krylov subspace and the construction of the Hessenberg matrix H. In this kernel, we shall use CUDA Dynamic Parallelism (CDP), which allows it to spawn smaller child kernels for smaller tasks [12]. The following are the key components of this process.

Dot Product

- A child kernel is used to compute $h_{ij} = v_i^T w$.
- Shared memory is used to reduce latency by caching partial results.

Vector Update subtracts projections $h_{ij}v_i$ from w

Normalization computes $v_{j+1} = w/||w||$, ensuring the new vector is a unit vector

Hessenberg update givens rotations via trigonometric updates to modify H to maintain its triangular structure [7].

__syncthreads() ensures that all threads complete their tasks within a block before proceeding while *atomicExch* and *atomicAdd* are used for synchronization across all blocks, particularly for shared operations.

Algorithm 2 Dot Product Parallel

```
function my_dot_product_parallel(arr1, arr2, result, n)
shared shared_data[]
tid ← threadIdx.x
idx ← blockIdx.x · blockDim.x + threadIdx.x
stride ← gridDim.x · blockDim.x
sum ← 0
while idx < n do
    sum ← sum + arr1[idx] · arr2[idx]
    idx ← idx + stride
end while
shared_data[tid] ← sum
syncthreads()
repeat
    if tid < blockDim.x/2 then
        shared_data[tid] ← shared_data[tid] + shared_data[tid + blockDim.x/2]
    end if
    syncthreads()
    blockDim.x ← blockDim.x / 2
until blockDim.x ¿ 1
if tid = 0 then
    *result ← shared_data[0]
    atomicExch(sync_flag, 1)
end if
end function
```

4.3 Update Iteration Counter

The kernel updates the total iteration count after completing each Arnoldi process cycle. This count is necessary for tracking convergence and ensures that the algorithm stays within the maximum iteration limits.

4.4 Back Substitution

After constructing the Hessenberg matrix H and solving $H \cdot y = \beta_0 \cdot e_1$ through QR factorization, this kernel performs back substitution to compute the solution y.

4.5 Update Solution

Once the solution y is computed, this kernel updates the approximation of x as $x = x_0 + V \cdot y$ where V is the matrix of Krylov basis vectors.

4.6 Convergence Check

The Convergence Check verifies if the algorithm has reached the needed accuracy or should it require more iterations, it determines whether the residual norm or convergence order meets criteria. If the algorithm has not converged, it must recompute the residual $r_0 = b - A \cdot x$ using the above dot product function and the first Krylov vector $v1 = r_0/||r_0||$ is reinitialized.

5 Experimental Setup

5.1 Hardware and Software Environment

GPU

- Model: NVIDIA GeForce RTX 3090
- CUDA Cores: 10,946
- Memory Size: 24GB GDDR6X
- Memory Bandwidth: 936.2GB/s
- Clock Speed: 1.40 GHz, 1.70 GHz boost
- Compute Capability: 8.6
- TDP (Thermal Design Power): 350W
- Architecture: Ampere [14]
- FP32 Performance: 35.58 TFLOPS

Software

- CUDA 12.6 was used for GPU programming.
- Operating System: Ubuntu 24.04 LTS
- C Library: Linear Algebra PACKage (LAPACK) [15]
- C Library: Basic Linear Algebra Subprograms (BLAS) [16]

5.2 Test Datasets

To evaluate the performance of the CUDA implementation, we tested it on a set of matrices with different sizes, each was input as a Matrix Market Exchange (mtx) file. These matrices were sourced from the SuiteSparse Matrix Collection originated from the work of Tim Davis at the University of Florida [13]. Finally, we compare the execution time between the CPU and GPU version of the algorithm to see how much is the CUDA-based algorithm faster/slower than the traditional C algorithm.

bcsstm07

- Size: 420
- Non-Zero Elements: 7252
- Sparsity: 95.88%

bcsstm27

- Size: 1224
- Non-Zero Elements: 56,126
- Sparsity: 96.25%

bcsstk24

Size: 3562
Non-Zero Elements: 159,910.
Sparsity: 98.74%

bcsstk38

- Size: 8032
- Non-Zero Elements: 355,640
- Sparsity: 99.45%

bcsstk17

- Size: 10,974
- Non-Zero Elements: 428,650
- Sparsity: 99.64%

bcsstk36

- Size: 23,052
- Non-Zero Elements: 1,143,140
- Sparsity: 99.78%

5.3 Evaluation Metrics

The total time taken to solve the sparse linear system using GMRES is measured. The speedup is computed as the ratio between CPU time and GPU time. The residual norm ($||Ax - b||$) is recorded to ensure accuracy after each iteration. To validate the correctness of the GPU implementation, we compute the difference between the solutions given by the CPU and the GPU and ensure that it is less than 10^{-6}.

6 Experimental Results

The experiments aim to evaluate the performance of the CUDA-based GMRES implementation to solve linear systems with high sparsity across various range. The key metrics include execution time and speedup compared to the CPU version of the algorithm. Table 1 summarizes the performance of both implementations across every matrices mentioned in Experimental Setup, highlighting the advantages as well as the limitations of GPU acceleration.

Table 1. Execution times of GMRES on CPU and GPU

Matrix	Size	NNZ	CPU time(s)	GPU time(s)	Speedup
bcsstm07	420	7252	0.001306	0.030679	0.04
bcsstm27	1224	56,126	0.803816	2.172306	0.37
bcsstk24	3562	159,910	5.437634	6.439711	0.84
bcsstk38	8032	355,640	29.478004	21.106660	1.39
bcsstk17	10974	428,650	52.015021	23.376520	2.22
bcsstk36	23052	1,143,140	283.639225	70.076734	4.04

6.1 Execution Time Comparison

Small Matrices. For small matrices like **bcsstm07** (n = 420, NNZ = 7252), **bcsstm27** (n = 1224, NNZ = 56,126) and **bcsstk24** (n = 3562, NNZ = 159,910) the Speedup is 0.04, 0.37 and 0.84 respectively, which mean that the GPU implementation actually performs slower than CPU. This is attributed to the overhead of GPU kernel launches and data transfers, which dominate the computational cost for smaller problems.

Medim-Sized Matrices. As matrix size increases, the GPU begins to reveal its advantage compared to CPU. For **bcsstk38** (n = 8032, NNZ = 355,640), we see a speedup of 1.39, where the GPU begins to achieve a faster speed than that of CPU, indicating that the benefits brought by parallelism are beginning to outweigh the overheads.

Large Matrices. Finally, for larger matrices: **bcsstk17** (n = 10,974, NNZ = 428,650) and **bcsstk36** (n = 23,052, NNZ = 1,143,140), the GPU significantly outperforms the CPU with a speed of 2.22 and 4.04 in respective order. The parallel nature of GPU architecture allows it to handle larger workloads efficiently, especially in large kernels where Sparse Matrix Vector Multiplication and Arnoldi iteration are computed.

6.2 Speedup Analysis

The speedup achieved by GPU is the key component to determine the performance boostup. Speedup is defined as:

$$\textbf{Speedup} = \frac{\text{CPU time}}{\text{GPU time}} \tag{2}$$

The speedup trends observe in the study illustrates the growing advantage of GPU parallelism as the matrix size and number of non-zero elements increase. With small matrices, the speedup is less than 1, showing that CPU implementation has a better speed compared to the GPU version. This is mainly because the kernel launch overhead and data transfer costs still dominate the whole execution. However, as the matrix size grows larger and larger, GPU begins to show its efficiency as it has a relatively equal speed with CPU, with speedup is approximately 1.39 when matrix size is 8032 times 8032. When the matrix grows larger, a significant speedup is observed, where at the maximum point, we see a 4 times faster when comparing the GPU and CPU execution of GMRES algorithm. The trend is visualized in the below visualization.

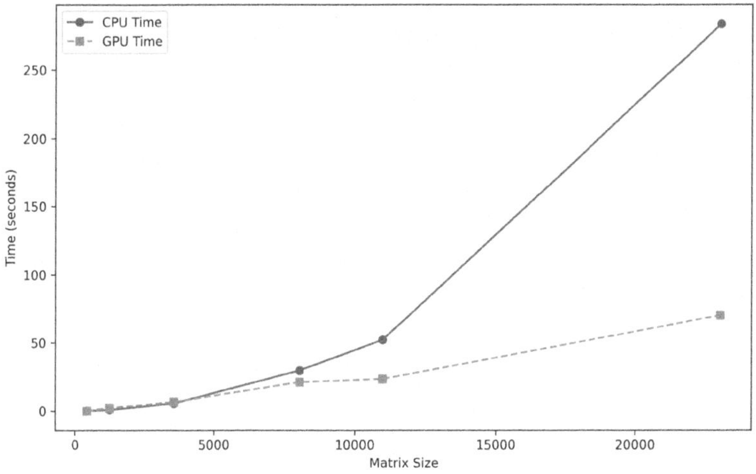

Fig. 1. CPU vs GPU Execution Time.

Figure 1 demonstrates the performance gap between CPU and GPU implementations. We can clearly see the gap is between the two versions grows larger as the matrix size grows larger.

6.3 Summary

- **Threshold** The GPU begins to outperform the CPU at matrix sizes approximately 8000 times 8000 with number of non-zero elements around 350,000. Below this threshold the GPU's fixed overheads overshadow it parallel computational benefits.
- **Maximum Speedup Achieved** With the largest matrix tested (**bcsstk36** - 23,052 elements and 1,143,140 number of non-zero elements), the GPU execution time is 4 times faster than the CPU execution time.
- **Scalability** The speedup trends indicate that the GPU implementation scales well with increasing size, which suggests that further performance gains may even be achieved for even larger matrices.

7 Future Work

Although the GPU shows clear advantages for large matrices, there exist some limitations. For smaller matrices, the cost of launching kernels and transferring data from CPU to GPU and vice versa dominates the overall run time, making the GPU less efficient. Extremely large matrices size could also exceed the GPU's global memory capacity, which requires further optimizations or multi-GPU setups or GPU that works well in supercomputers for more efficient computation.

The Arnoldi Process is one of the key components of the GMRES algorithm, responsible for constructing an orthonormal basis for the Krylov subspace. The current implementation of this process represents a good performance for large matrices, there is still room for improvements. Here we are using atomic operations like *atomicExch* and *atomicAdd* to synchronize threads between kernels. However, with the use of these operations, the threads must wait for each other to complete, which slows down the process. An attempt could be trying to synchronize at warp level. By exploiting the power of GPU warp-level synchronization, threads in the same warp can share data directly without relying on global synchronization.

The memory access pattern also plays a pivotal role in the performance of the Arnoldi iteration kernel. Currently matrices are stored in CSR format, which is efficient for sparse matrix but may cause uncoalesced global memory accesses. Therefore, we shall explore alternative sparse matrix storage formats such as Ellpack (ELL) and Jagged Diagonal Storage (JDS) [17,18].

The current implementation is limited on a single GPU, which cannot handle super large matrices. Thus, the Arnoldi Process could be modified to work across multiple GPUs, matrix and vector could be divided among GPUs and using communication techniques like the Message Passing Interface (MPI) or NVIDIA Collective Communications Library (NCCL) [19,20]. Overlapping computation with MPI would help to minimize the overhead of data transfers between GPUs, allowing to solve the much larger systems than currently possible.

In conclusion, while the Arnoldi iteration performs well enough for current datasets, there exist opportunities to boost its performance further. Optimizing synchronization, improving the memory access pattern, etc. These improvements would not only enhance the execution time but also allow it to handle larger and more complex systems, broadening its applicability in scientific and engineering computations.

Acknowledgments. This study was funded by National Science Foundation #2219543.

References

1. Saad, Y.: Iterative Methods for Sparse Linear Systems, 2nd edn. SIAM, Philadelphia, PA, USA (2003)
2. Duff, I.S., Erisman, A.M., Reid, J.K.: Direct Methods for Sparse Matrices. Oxford University Press, Oxford (2017)
3. Couturier, R., Domas, S.: Sparse systems solving on GPUs with GMRES. J. Supercomput. **59**(3), 1504–1516 (2012)
4. Aliaga, J.I., Anzt, H., Grützmacher, T., Quintana-Ortí, E.S., Tomás, A.E.: Compressed Basis GMRES on High Performance GPUs. arXiv preprint arXiv:2009.12101 (2020)
5. Loe, J.A., Glusa, C.A., Yamazaki, I., Boman, E.G., Rajamanickam, S.: A Study of Mixed Precision Strategies for GMRES on GPUs. arXiv arXiv:2109.01232 (2021)
6. Liesen, J., Strakoš, Z.: Krylov Subspace Methods: Principles and Analysis. Numerical Mathematics and Scientific Computing, Oxford (2013)
7. Gragg, W.B.: The QR algorithm for unitary hessenberg matrices. J. Comput. Appl. Math. **16**(1), 1–8 (1986)
8. Greathouse, J.L., Daga, M.: Efficient sparse matrix-vector multiplication on GPUs using the CSR storage format. In: SC 2014: Proceedings of the International Conference for High Performance Computing, Networking, Storage and Analysis, pp. 769–780 (2014)
9. NVIDIA Corporation: CUDA C Programming Guide, Section 2.2, NVIDIA Developer Documentation (2022). https://docs.nvidia.com/cuda/cuda-c-programming-guide/
10. NVIDIA Corporation: CUDA C Programming Guide, Section 7.14, NVIDIA Developer Documentation (2022). https://docs.nvidia.com/cuda/cuda-c-programming-guide/
11. NVIDIA Corporation: CUDA C Programming Guide, Section 3.2, NVIDIA Developer Documentation (2022). https://docs.nvidia.com/cuda/cuda-c-programming-guide/
12. NVIDIA Corporation: CUDA C Programming Guide, Section 9, NVIDIA Developer Documentation (2022). https://docs.nvidia.com/cuda/cuda-c-programming-guide/

13. Davis, T.A., Hu, Y.: The university of Florida sparse matrix collection. ACM Trans. Math. Softw. (TOMS) **38**(1), 1–25 (2011)
14. Abdelkhalik, H., Arafa, Y., Santhi, N., Badawy, A.H.A.: Demystifying the NVIDIA ampere architecture through microbenchmarking and instruction-level analysis. In: 2022 IEEE High Performance Extreme Computing Conference (HPEC), pp. 1–8 (2022)
15. Anderson, E., et al.: LAPACK Users' Guide. Society for Industrial and Applied Mathematics, Philadelphia, PA, USA (1999)
16. Remington, K., Pozo, R.: NIST Sparse BLAS: User's Guide. Technical Report, NIST (1996). https://gams.nist.gov/spblas
17. Maggioni, M., Berger-Wolf, T.: AdELL: an adaptive warp-balancing ELL format for efficient sparse matrix-vector multiplication on GPUs. In: 2013 42nd International Conference on Parallel Processing, pp. 11–20 (2013)
18. Ekambaram, A., Montagne, E.: An alternative compressed storage format for sparse matrices. In: Yazıcı, A., Şener, C. (eds.) ISCIS 2003. LNCS, vol. 2869, pp. 196–203. Springer, Heidelberg (2003). https://doi.org/10.1007/978-3-540-39737-3_25
19. Jacobsen, D., Thibault, J., Senocak, I.: An MPI-CUDA implementation for massively parallel incompressible flow computations on multi-GPU clusters. In: 48th AIAA Aerospace Sciences Meeting Including the New Horizons Forum and Aerospace Exposition, Orlando, FL, USA, p. 522 (2010)
20. NVIDIA Corporation: NVIDIA Collective Communications Library (NCCL), NCCL Documentation (2023). https://developer.nvidia.com/nccl

Accelerating TVM LLM Inference via Paged KV-Cache and Customized Kernels on RVV

Shou Chen Chiu, Chun Lin Huang(✉), Meng Shiun Yu, Ming Zhang Huang, and Jenq Kuen Lee

Department of Computer Science, National Tsing Hua University, Hsinchu, Taiwan
{scchiu,clhuang,msyu,mzhuang,jklee}@pllab.cs.nthu.edu.tw

Abstract. This paper proposes a method to accelerate large language model (LLM) inference on CPUs using the TVM compiler and MLC-LLM framework. By tensorizing TVM's TensorIR into RISC-V Vector (RVV) intrinsics, we automatically generate efficient vectorized kernels for key operators. Leveraging recent TVM improvements, our framework significantly boosts throughput, during the prefill phase. Experiments show up to 18× speedup in attention and 2.6× more tokens-per-second.

Keywords: TVM · RISC-V · MLC-LLM · KV-Cache · RVV

1 Introduction

Large language models (LLMs) [7] have achieved state-of-the-art results in a wide range of NLP tasks, but their inference latency remains a major bottleneck, especially on resource-constrained platforms. While GPU-based optimizations such as FlashAttention and paged KV-cache [6] have proven effective, they often rely on proprietary libraries like CUDA or Metal, limiting portability to CPU-only environments. This constraint is particularly pronounced in embedded systems and RISC-V-based edge devices, where power and cost concerns make GPU deployment impractical.

To address this gap, we build on the TVM [1,2,5] compiler stack and the MLC-LLM [3] framework to develop an optimized CPU inference path. Compared to traditional TVM flows based on Relay, our approach leverages the newer Relax IR, which simplifies shape handling and enables tighter integration with TensorIR (TIR) [4] for low-level scheduling and hardware-specific code generation. We introduce a paged KV-cache [6] to support long-sequence generation and develop custom RISC-V Vector (RVV) [8,9] kernels optimized for attention and matmul operations.

The RISC-V Vector Extension (RVV) is a modern vector ISA designed to provide flexible and scalable data-level parallelism for RISC-V CPUs. Unlike

Regular Research Paper.

H. R. Arabnia et al. (Eds.): CSCE 2025, CCIS 2932, pp. 353–366, 2026.
https://doi.org/10.1007/978-3-032-22193-3_27

traditional fixed-length SIMD architectures (such as x86 SSE/AVX or ARM NEON/SVE), RVV supports configurable vector lengths, allowing implementations to tailor vector width based on hardware capabilities and design constraints. This scalability is particularly important for emerging RISC-V SoCs with diverse performance and power requirements. RVV also offers advanced features, including predicated execution, strided memory access, and segment loads/stores, making it well-suited for complex workloads such as attention mechanisms and batched matrix multiplications in large language models.

Our results show that a combination of compiler-level control and hardware-aware vectorization can significantly improve LLM inference performance in CPU-centric deployment scenarios.

- We extend existing RVV tensorization techniques by **introducing a schedule-aware, KV-cache friendly variant** tailored for LLM inference. Our approach is designed for efficient execution on 256-bit VLEN cores and offers substantial improvements over baseline scalar TIR implementations.
- We implement a CPU paged KV-cache system for CPU inference, enabling memory-efficient long-context generation.
- We leverage tensorization to lower scheduled TIR blocks into RVV intrinsics, automatically generating high-performance kernels for critical LLM operators.
- We evaluate our approach on RISC-V CPU backends and observe substantial performance improvements over baseline inference. In particular, the Attention computation in Llama2-7B achieves up to 18x speedup, and tokens-per-second throughput increases by 1.7x to 2.6x across the tested models.

The remainder of this paper is structured as follows. We first introduce background knowledge on the MLC-LLM compilation flow targeting RISC-V CPU backends in Sect. 2. Next, we present our optimized inference workflow in Sect. 3, highlighting the use of Relax IR and the paged KV-cache implementation tailored specifically for CPUs. We then describe our approach to generating customized RVV kernels via TVM's tensorization techniques in Sect. 4, with a focus on critical operations such as attention and matrix multiplication. In Sect. 5, we provide detailed experimental results and performance evaluations, comparing various optimization strategies across multiple LLM models. Finally, we summarize our conclusions and discuss potential future research directions in Sect. 6.

2 MLC-LLM on RISC-V CPU Backend

2.1 System Overview

The system presented in this work leverages TVM and MLC-LLM frameworks to efficiently perform large language model (LLM) inference specifically on the RISC-V CPU architecture. TVM is an end-to-end deep learning compilation framework that compiles models through multiple intermediate representations (IRs). However, unlike traditional TVM compilation flows that utilize Relay IR,

MLC-LLM utilizes both TVM's Relax and Tensor Intermediate Representation (TIR) in its compilation flow, enabling flexible high-level modeling as well as fine-grained kernel optimization, specifically tailored for large language models' unique computational patterns, such as prefill and decode stages.

In this integrated compilation flow, models defined at the TIR level are optimized through specialized scheduling, kernel mapping, and low-level vectorization techniques, ultimately producing optimized code tailored explicitly for the RISC-V backend and its vector extension (RVV).

2.2 MLC-LLM Compilation Support for RISCV CPU Targets

The original MLC-LLM compilation flow was designed for GPU backends and did not support CPUs. To address this, support for the LLVM CPU target was introduced, enabling code generation for various CPU architectures, including RISC-V. In addition, several compiler passes originally tailored for GPUs were adapted or given CPU-specific fallbacks to ensure correct and efficient execution. As a result, MLC-LLM can now deploy LLM models on RISC-V CPUs efficiently.

For RISC-V CPUs, the compilation process takes advantage of LLVM's RISC-V backend with vector extension support. Target-specific extensions can be enabled by passing the `mattr` flag (e.g., `"mattr":["+v"]` for the V extension). Vector length (VLEN) is configured using `vector-width=<VLEN>`, allowing the generated code to fully utilize hardware vector capabilities.

3 MLC-LLM Flow

In large language model (LLM) inference, the key-value (KV) cache stores intermediate attention outputs to enable efficient autoregressive decoding. The inference process is generally divided into two stages: the *prefill* phase, which processes the entire input prompt in parallel, and the *decode* phase, which generates one token at a time using previously cached values. Efficient management of the KV-cache is especially important for long-context inference, where memory reuse and locality can significantly impact performance.

3.1 TVM RELAX

MLC-LLM is built on top of the TVM compiler stack, which supports multiple intermediate representations. Earlier versions of TVM relied primarily on **Relay**, a high-level, statically typed functional IR designed for full-graph optimizations. In contrast, **Relax** is a newer IR that supports both static and dynamic shapes, staged compilation, and partial graph lowering. Relax integrates more closely with TensorIR, enabling finer-grained scheduling, shape analysis, and operator fusion at the lower level. This hybrid IR pipeline allows Relax to serve as a more flexible front-end for workloads like LLM inference that benefit from dynamic execution and hardware-specific optimization.

3.2 kv Cache

During the decode phase, the KV-cache holds the attention key and value tensors produced in earlier time steps. These tensors are reused across future token generations, allowing the model to avoid recomputing attention outputs for previously seen tokens. A naïve implementation of the KV-cache typically stores tensors in fixed memory buffers indexed by position, which can lead to memory fragmentation or inefficient access patterns when handling long sequences or batch processing.

3.3 Paged KV-Cache Implementation on CPU

To address the limitations of flat KV-cache memory, we implement a paged KV-cache on CPU backends. In contrast to conventional flat layouts—which often suffer from low cache hit rates due to strided or sparse access patterns during token decoding and increased memory allocation overhead as sequence lengths grow—the paged structure divides the cache into fixed-size blocks (pages). Each page stores key and value slices for a subset of tokens, and a page table maintains the mapping from sequence positions to pages. During decoding, the page table is queried to retrieve relevant entries, while new tokens are appended to available pages. This design improves memory locality, reduces memory movement, and allows cache reuse across batch elements, which is especially beneficial in memory-constrained CPU environments.

To further enhance efficiency, we apply a scheduling strategy to the attention TensorIR by blocking the sequence axes Q_{LEN} and KV_{LEN} with a configurable tiling factor. This creates tiled workloads for both $\mathrm{QK}^{\top}$ and QV computations. A two-dimensional scratchpad buffer is introduced to stage intermediate values, and the computations are organized into `S_gemm` and `O_gemm` blocks for optimized execution.

4 Custom RVV Kernel Generation

To fully leverage the parallel processing capabilities of RISC-V CPUs, we implement custom kernels using the RISC-V Vector Extension (RVV). These kernels are designed to accelerate key operations in LLM inference. Our approach extends TVM TIR (Tensor Intermediate Representation) to emit RVV-compatible vector instructions through pattern-specific scheduling strategies.

4.1 RVV Intrinsic

The RISC-V Vector Extension (RVV) is a flexible SIMD architecture that enables efficient data-parallel execution on RISC-V CPUs. RVV supports configurable vector lengths, allowing implementations to select vector widths that match hardware capabilities and design goals.

RVV supports a rich set of operations, including:

- **Vector Load/Store:** `vle.v`, `vse.v` for sequential memory access.
- **Arithmetic:** `vadd.vv`, `vmul.vv`, `vfmacc.vv` for fused multiply-adds.

In C/C++, these vector operations are accessed via RVV intrinsics defined in `riscv_vector.h`. Table 1 presents a sample of representative examples with RVV intrinsics.

Table 1. Examples of commonly-used RVV C Intrinsics

Intrinsic	Operation	Assembly	Vector Type
`vle32_v_f32m1(ptr, vl)`	Load contiguous 32-bit float vector	`vle32.v`	`vfloat32m1_t`
`vse32_v_f32m1(ptr, v, vl)`	Store contiguous 32-bit float vector	`vse32.v`	`vfloat32m1_t`
`vlse32_v_f32m1(ptr, stride, vl)`	Load strided 32-bit float vector	`vlse32.v`	`vfloat32m1_t`
`vsse32_v_f32m1(ptr, stride, v, vl)`	Store strided 32-bit float vector	`vsse32.v`	`vfloat32m1_t`
`vfadd_vv_f32m1(v1, v2, vl)`	Vector floating-point add	`vfadd.vv`	`vfloat32m1_t`
`vfsub_vv_f32m1(v1, v2, vl)`	Vector floating-point subtract	`vfsub.vv`	`vfloat32m1_t`
`vfmul_vv_f32m1(v1, v2, vl)`	Vector floating-point multiply	`vfmul.vv`	`vfloat32m1_t`
`vfmacc_vv_f32m1(acc, a, b, vl)`	Vector fused multiply-add	`vfmacc.vv`	`vfloat32m1_t`
`vfredsum_vs_f32m1(v, scalar, vl)`	Vector reduction sum	`vfredsum.vs`	`vfloat32m1_t`

The RVV intrinsics listed in Table 1 provide a versatile set of operations for vectorized computation on RISC-V CPUs, supporting efficient data loading/storing patterns (both contiguous and strided), vector arithmetic, fused operations, and reduction patterns, all of which are extensively used in optimizing LLM inference kernels. A simple fused multiply-add (FMA) kernel using RVV intrinsics in C might look like the code in Listing 1.1. This example demonstrates how vector length (`vl`) can be determined dynamically via `vsetvl_e32m1()`, enabling portable vector code that adapts to the actual hardware capabilities. These intrinsics allow precise control over register allocation, loop tiling, and memory access, making them essential building blocks for hand-optimized transformer kernels on RVV-compatible RISC-V CPUs.

Listing 1.1. RVV intrinsics examples for fma

```c
#include <riscv_vector.h>

void vec_fma(const float* a, const float* b, float* out, size_t n) {
    size_t vl;
    for (size_t i = 0; i < n; i += vl) {
        vl = vsetvl_e32m1(n - i);
        vfloat32m1_t va = vle32_v_f32m1(a + i, vl);
        vfloat32m1_t vb = vle32_v_f32m1(b + i, vl);
        vfloat32m1_t vo = vfmacc_vv_f32m1(vb, va, vb, vl); // out = vb + va * vb
        vse32_v_f32m1(out + i, vo, vl);
    }
}
```

4.2 Computation Pattern in Prefill and Decode

The computational workload in LLM inference exhibits distinct patterns in the prefill and decode stages. Prefill involves batched operations over long sequences, including dense matrix multiplications for $QK^\top$ and QV products, as well as softmax reductions. In contrast, the decode phase typically performs small, one-token-at-a-time operations that must still maintain cache locality and low latency. We define TIR scheduling strategies that account for:

- **Vectorization:** Mapping axis-aligned loop structures to RVV `vload/vstore` and arithmetic intrinsics.
- **Unrolling and Loop Fusion:** Reducing loop overhead and improving pipeline efficiency.

4.3 TIR to RVV Kernel Tensorization

To deploy large language models (LLMs) efficiently on RISC-V CPUs, we extend the TVM compiler stack with a backend that lowers scheduled TensorIR (TIR) into RVV (RISC-V Vector) intrinsics. This transformation leverages TVM's tensorization mechanism—a powerful abstraction that allows the compiler to identify compute patterns (e.g., dot products, fused multiply-adds) and replace them with optimized low-level code, often handcrafted or architecture-specific. Tensorization bridges the gap between high-level loop nests and architecture-aware vector or matrix instructions by binding computational blocks to intrinsic templates, ensuring both correctness and efficiency.

In our system, tensorization is applied to TIR programs after meta-scheduling. At this stage, tiling, unrolling, and vectorization decisions have been made, and the TIR representation is amenable to substitution with RVV-specific patterns. Our backend emits RVV intrinsic calls such as `vle.v` and `vse.v` for vector loads and stores, and `vfmacc.vv` or `vadd.vv` for arithmetic operations. These instructions are dynamically sized using `vsetvl`, ensuring portability across hardware implementations with different vector register widths.

Attention Kernel. The attention in transformer inference is responsible for processing the full input sequence and populating the key-value (KV) cache. This involves large batched matrix multiplications and attention score computations, such as evaluating $QK^\top$ and applying softmax followed by a QV product. These operations are compute- and memory-intensive, making them prime candidates for vectorization.

The example below shows an RVV-based kernel written in C, where each iteration computes a fused dot product for Q and K vectors:

We highlight four key regions of Listing 1.2:

- **Line 4** sets the vector length register to `vl=16`. The same binary scales when VLEN changes.

- **Lines 6–13** zero-initialise eight accumulators (`acc0`–`acc7`) that correspond to an 8 × 16 output tile.
- **Lines 15–25** form the compute core: each iteration loads one 16-element slice of `B` (L 16) and fuses multiplyadd into the eight accumulators(one row of `A` times the same `vb` vector). This yields 8 × 16 FMAs per loop step while streaming `A`.
- **Lines 26–34** post-multiply by a scale factor (e.g. Softmax scaling factor). Finally, **Lines 36–44** write the tile back to `C` with a fixed stride of 16, matching the column-major layout expected by the subsequent softmax.

This code highlights the use of fused multiply-accumulate (FMA), which is the key enabler for efficient attention computation on RVV hardware.

Listing 1.2. RVV-based prefill kernel

```
1  #include <riscv_vector.h>
2  extern ""C"" void sgemm_8x16(float *out, const float *a, const
       float *b, const int K, const float *scale) {
3      vfloat32m2_t acc0, acc1, acc2, acc3, acc4, acc5, acc6, acc7;
4      size_t vl = __riscv_vsetvl_e32m2(16);
5      // Init OUT zeros
6      acc0 = __riscv_vfmv_v_f_f32m2(0.f, vl);
7      acc1 = __riscv_vfmv_v_f_f32m2(0.f, vl);
8      acc2 = __riscv_vfmv_v_f_f32m2(0.f, vl);
9      acc3 = __riscv_vfmv_v_f_f32m2(0.f, vl);
10     acc4 = __riscv_vfmv_v_f_f32m2(0.f, vl);
11     acc5 = __riscv_vfmv_v_f_f32m2(0.f, vl);
12     acc6 = __riscv_vfmv_v_f_f32m2(0.f, vl);
13     acc7 = __riscv_vfmv_v_f_f32m2(0.f, vl);
14     // Accumulate
15     for(int k = 0 ; k < K; ++k){
16         vfloat32m2_t vb = __riscv_vle32_v_f32m2(b + 16 * k, vl);
17         acc0 = __riscv_vfmacc_vf_f32m2(acc0, *(a + k + K * 0), vb,
               vl);
18         acc1 = __riscv_vfmacc_vf_f32m2(acc1, *(a + k + K * 1), vb,
               vl);
19         acc2 = __riscv_vfmacc_vf_f32m2(acc2, *(a + k + K * 2), vb,
               vl);
20         acc3 = __riscv_vfmacc_vf_f32m2(acc3, *(a + k + K * 3), vb,
               vl);
21         acc4 = __riscv_vfmacc_vf_f32m2(acc4, *(a + k + K * 4), vb,
               vl);
22         acc5 = __riscv_vfmacc_vf_f32m2(acc5, *(a + k + K * 5), vb,
               vl);
23         acc6 = __riscv_vfmacc_vf_f32m2(acc6, *(a + k + K * 6), vb,
               vl);
24         acc7 = __riscv_vfmacc_vf_f32m2(acc7, *(a + k + K * 7), vb,
               vl);
25     }
26     // Multiply with Scale
```

```
    acc0 = __riscv_vfmul_vf_f32m2(acc0, scale[0], vl);
    acc1 = __riscv_vfmul_vf_f32m2(acc1, scale[0], vl);
    acc2 = __riscv_vfmul_vf_f32m2(acc2, scale[0], vl);
    acc3 = __riscv_vfmul_vf_f32m2(acc3, scale[0], vl);
    acc4 = __riscv_vfmul_vf_f32m2(acc4, scale[0], vl);
    acc5 = __riscv_vfmul_vf_f32m2(acc5, scale[0], vl);
    acc6 = __riscv_vfmul_vf_f32m2(acc6, scale[0], vl);
    acc7 = __riscv_vfmul_vf_f32m2(acc7, scale[0], vl);
    // Store out
    const int out_strides = 16;
    __riscv_vse32_v_f32m2(out + out_strides * 0, acc0, vl);
    __riscv_vse32_v_f32m2(out + out_strides * 1, acc1, vl);
    __riscv_vse32_v_f32m2(out + out_strides * 2, acc2, vl);
    __riscv_vse32_v_f32m2(out + out_strides * 3, acc3, vl);
    __riscv_vse32_v_f32m2(out + out_strides * 4, acc4, vl);
    __riscv_vse32_v_f32m2(out + out_strides * 5, acc5, vl);
    __riscv_vse32_v_f32m2(out + out_strides * 6, acc6, vl);
    __riscv_vse32_v_f32m2(out + out_strides * 7, acc7, vl);
}
```

Matmul Kernel. Matrix multiplication is a cornerstone of LLM architectures, appearing in attention, projection, and feed-forward layers. In our approach, we tensorize small matmul blocks within TIR by matching them to RVV FMA templates, taking into account tiling dimensions and data alignment constraints. This allows the TIR schedule to be directly lowered to RVV kernels that are both bandwidth- and compute-efficient.

A representative C intrinsic example for matrix multiplication is shown in Listing 1.3. The kernel executes a $1 \times 2 \times 64$ matrix tile (one output row, two output columns, 64-wide inner dimension) entirely in vector registers:

- **Line 5** sets `vl=32`, so each `vfloat32m4_t` register holds $32 \times 4 = 128$ bytes but is used here in "m4" grouping (four registers) to cover 64 elements of B.
- **Lines 6–7** preload two 32-element slices of A into `va0` and `va1`; these are reused for both output columns, eliminating extra loads.
- **Lines 10–16** stream B column-pairs: each loop step performs 64 FMAs and advances `b_ptr` by `b_stride`.
- **Line 18** horizontally reduces the accumulator with `vfredusum`, producing the dot-product, and atomically adds it into the output row.

Listing 1.3. RVV $1 \times 2 \times 64$ matrix-tile kernel

```
1  #include <riscv_vector.h>
2  extern "C" void mmt_1x2x64(float *out, int out_off, int out_stride,
3                  float *a, int a_off, int a_stride,
4                  float *b, int b_off, int b_stride) {
5    size_t vl = __riscv_vsetvl_e32m4(32);
6    vfloat32m4_t va0 = __riscv_vle32_v_f32m4(a + a_off, vl);
```

```
    vfloat32m4_t va1 = __riscv_vle32_v_f32m4(a + a_off + 32, vl);
    float *b_ptr = b + b_off;
    float *c_ptr = out + out_off;
    for (int i = 0; i < 2; ++i) {
      vfloat32m4_t acc = __riscv_vfmv_v_f_f32m4(0.f, vl);
      vfloat32m4_t vb = __riscv_vle32_v_f32m4(b_ptr, vl);
      acc = __riscv_vfmacc_vv_f32m4(acc, va0, vb, vl);
      vb = __riscv_vle32_v_f32m4(b_ptr + 32, vl);
      acc = __riscv_vfmacc_vv_f32m4(acc, va1, vb, vl);
      b_ptr += b_stride;
      /* horizontal reduce + accumulate into C */
      float sum = __riscv_vfmv_f_s_f32m1_f32(
                    __riscv_vfredusum_vs_f32m4_f32m1(
                      acc,
                      __riscv_vfmv_s_f_f32m1(0.f, vl), vl));
      c_ptr[i] += sum;
    }
  }
```

This kernel showcases how vectorized matrix blocks can be fused into a single loop structure, improving data locality and reducing scalar loop overhead. By combining TIR's scheduling flexibility with the expressiveness of RVV intrinsics, we achieve significant performance improvements across both prefill and matmul phases. This tensorization framework enables scalable and portable transformer inference across the rapidly growing ecosystem of RISC-V vector-capable processors.

Example: Before vs. After Tensorization. As shown in Listings 1.4–1.5, the tensorized version collapses the inner (2×64) loop nest and delegates computation to an RVV kernel, removing 128 scalar FMAs per iteration.

In Listing 1.4, the baseline TIR code represents a straightforward scalar implementation of a matrix multiplication operation (C += A × B). The nested loops explicitly iterate over each dimension:

- **Line 6** defines loop dimensions and tiling factors explicitly.
- **Lines 7–9** perform scalar computations to accumulate matrix multiplications.

This approach results in significant overhead from scalar operations and inefficient memory access patterns.

In Listing 1.5, the tensorized TIR illustrates the optimization achieved by collapsing inner loops and delegating computationally intensive tasks directly to a custom RVV kernel:

- **Line 6** defines the tensorized loop dimensions and tiling factors.
- **Lines 7–8** define the matmul block and remap the reduction variable.
- **Lines 10–13** invoke a optimized external RVV kernel ('mmt_') that exploits hardware-specific vectorization features. This significantly reduces loop overhead and enhances parallel execution.

This transformation significantly reduces scalar computational overhead by leveraging vector instructions, resulting in substantial runtime improvements.

Listing 1.4. Baseline TIR before tensorization

```
@T.prim_func
def main(A: T.Buffer((20, 2048), "float32"),
         B: T.Buffer((11264, 2048), "float32"),
         C: T.Buffer((20, 11264), "float32")):
    T.func_attr({"global_symbol": "mmt"})
    for i, j_0, k_0, j_1, k_1 in T.grid(20, 5632, 32, 2, 64):
        with T.block("update"):
            vi = T.axis.spatial(20, i)
            vj = T.axis.spatial(11264, j_0 * 2 + j_1)
            vk = T.axis.reduce(2048, k_0 * 64 + k_1)
            C[vi, vj] += A[vi, vk] * B[vj, vk]
```

Listing 1.5. Tensorized TIR invoking RVV kernel

```
@T.prim_func
def main(A: T.Buffer((20, 2048), "float32"),
         B: T.Buffer((11264, 2048), "float32"),
         C: T.Buffer((20, 11264), "float32")):
    T.func_attr({"global_symbol": "mmt"})
    for i, j_0, k_0 in T.grid(20, 5632, 32):
        with T.block("update_o"):
            vi_o, vj_o, vk_o = T.axis.remap("SSR", [i, j_0, k_0])
            T.block_attr({"pragma_import_llvm": metadata["runtime.String"][0]})
            A_1 = T.match_buffer(A[vi_o, vk_o*64:vk_o*64+64], (1, 64))
            B_1 = T.match_buffer(B[vj_o*2:vj_o*2+2, vk_o*64:vk_o*64+64], (2, 64))
            C_1 = T.match_buffer(C[vi_o, vj_o*2:vj_o*2+2], (1, 2))
            T.call_extern("void", "mmt_", C_1.data, C_1.elem_offset, 11264,
                          A_1.data, A_1.elem_offset, 2048,
                          B_1.data, B_1.elem_offset, 2048, 2048)
```

5 Experimental Result

We evaluate three implementation strategies across five LLM models:

- **RV64GC (baseline)**: Non-vectorized scalar implementation; speedup defined as 1.00.
- **Auto Vectorization**: Compiler-driven vectorization.
- **Tensorization**: Support tensorization of key operators using RVV intrinsics.

We specifically evaluate and compare the performance of these implementation strategies during the prefill phase of LLM model inference. To comprehensively understand the benefits provided by these optimizations, we analyze six representative metrics:

- **Attention**: The attention layer, which computes weighted relationships between tokens.
- **MHA_Q_Proj**: Multi-head attention query projection.
- **MHA_Out_Proj**: Multi-head attention output projection.
- **FFN_Up_Proj**: Feed-forward network up projection.
- **FFN_Down_Proj**: Feed-forward network down projection.

- **Token Per Second (TPS)**: Overall throughput of token processing during the prefill phase.

All experiments are conducted on a BananaPi BPI-F3 platform with RISC-V vector extension (VLEN 256 bits). The system runs bianbu 2.0.4 as the operating system. We use mlc_llm 0.20 and TVM 0.20 as the deep learning compiler and runtime, and LLVM 18.1.3 for host compilation and code generation.

Table 2. Overall Speedup Comparison across Models (Prefill Token Per Second)

Model	RV64GC (Baseline)	Auto Vectorization	Tensorization
TinyLlama-1.1B	1.00×	1.70×	2.25×
LLaMA2-7B	1.00×	1.69×	2.60×
LLaMA3-3B	1.00×	1.69×	2.46×
Gemma2-2B	1.00×	1.49×	2.12×
DeepSeek-R1 Qwen-1.5B	1.00×	1.56×	1.71×

Table 2 summarizes the overall throughput improvement—measured in tokens per second (TPS)—across all evaluated models and implementation strategies. The baseline RV64GC implementation (non-vectorized scalar code) is normalized to 1.00× for each model. Auto Vectorization provides moderate speedups ranging from 1.49× to 1.70× depending on the model architecture, while our Tensorization approach yields consistently higher performance, reaching up to 2.6× for LLaMA2-7B. **TinyLlama-1.1B** [10] is a compact model designed for resource-efficient deployment, where tensorization delivers a 2.25× improvement, highlighting its suitability for lightweight inference scenarios. **LLaMA2-7B** [11] and **LLaMA3-3B** [12] represent larger decoder-only architectures with substantial compute demands; these models benefit notably from our optimized RVV kernels, with the latter achieving a 2.46× speedup. **Gemma2-2B** [13], a newer open model with improved training efficiency, also shows significant gains, affirming the generality of our tensorization strategy across model variants. Lastly, **DeepSeek-R1 Qwen-1.5B** [14], a hybrid architecture incorporating techniques from Qwen and DeepSeek's pretraining, shows an observed speedup of 1.71×.

Figures 1–5 present the speedup comparison bar charts for each evaluated model. Figure 1 shows that TinyLlama-1.1B (q4f32) achieves up to 4x speedup in Attention, while other metrics show improvements ranging from 2.2x to 2.7x. Figure 2 shows that Llama2-7B (q4f32) achieves up to 18x speedup in Attention. Other metrics are improved by 2.2x and 2.6x. Figure 3 shows that LLaMA3-3B (q4f32) achieves up to 10x speedup in Attention, while other metrics have speedup between 2.6x and 3x. Figure 4 shows that Gemma2-2B (q4f32) achieves up to 5x speedup in Attention. Other metrics show improvements ranging from 2.1x to 2.5x. Figure 5 DeepSeek-R1 Qwen-1.5B (q4f32) achieves up to 9x speedup in

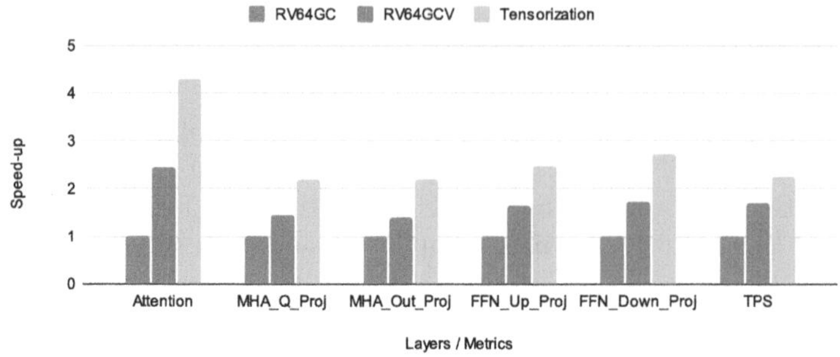

Fig. 1. Speedup comparison for TinyLlama-1.1B.

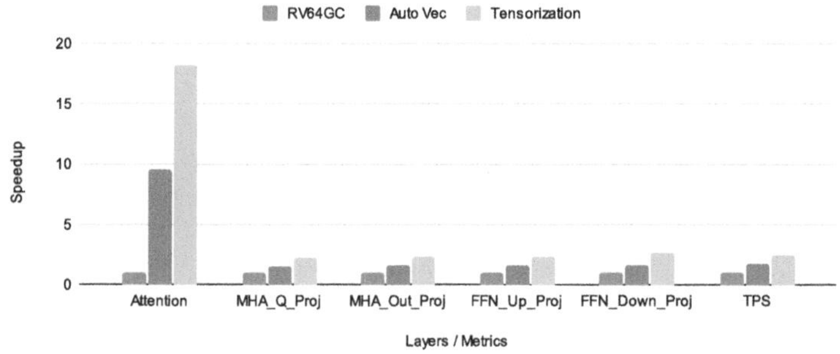

Fig. 2. Speedup comparison for Llama2-7B.

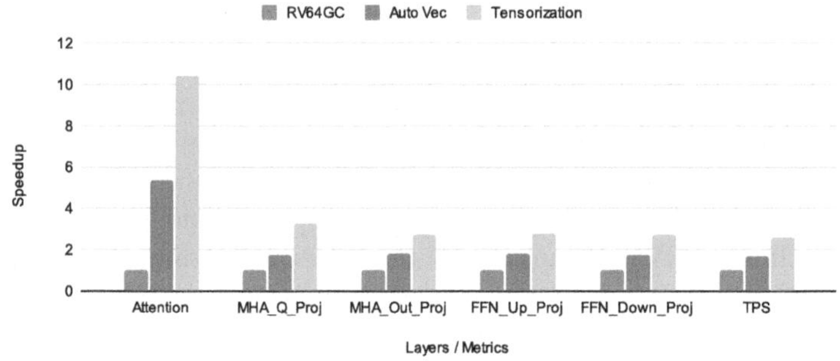

Fig. 3. Speedup comparison for LLaMA3-3B.

Attention and 2.7x in FFN_Down_Proj, while improvements for the other metrics over auto vectorization are marginal.

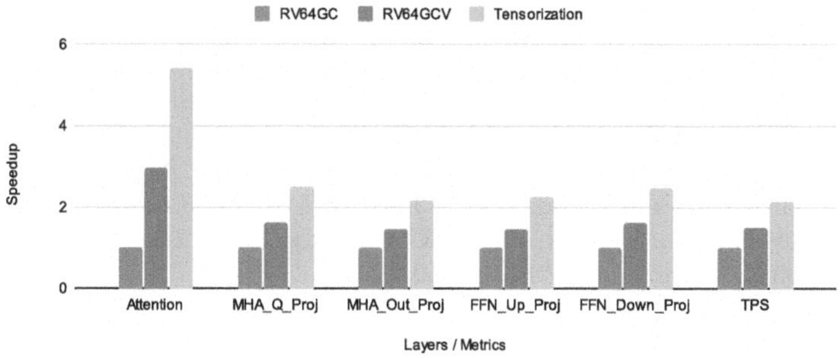

Fig. 4. Speedup comparison for Gemma2-2B.

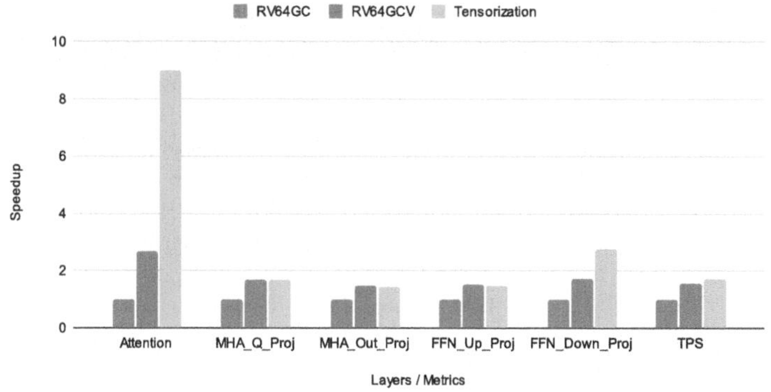

Fig. 5. Speedup comparison for DeepSeek-R1 Qwen-1.5B.

6 Conclusion

In this paper, we presented an optimized approach for accelerating large language model (LLM) inference on RISC-V CPUs by leveraging the TVM compiler stack and the MLC-LLM framework. Specifically, we introduced a paged KV-cache mechanism designed for efficient CPU inference, significantly improving memory utilization and enabling scalable long-context sequence processing. Additionally, we developed customized kernels targeting the RISC-V Vector Extension (RVV), utilizing tensorization to efficiently lower scheduled TensorIR (TIR) into vectorized RVV instructions.

Our experimental evaluations across a range of LLM models—such as TinyLlama-1.1B, Llama2-7B, LLaMA3-3B, Gemma2-2B, and DeepSeek-Qwen-1.5B—demonstrated significant performance gains. Specifically, our RVV-optimized kernels achieve up to 18× speedup in the Attention module, with other submodules observing 2.1× to 3× improvements across models. These results underscore the effectiveness of combining compiler-assisted tensorization, RVV-specific kernel generation, and lightweight runtime optimizations for efficient CPU-based LLM inference.

References

1. Chen, T., Moreau, T., Jiang, Z., et al.: TVM: an automated end-to-end optimising compiler for deep learning. In: 13th USENIX Symposium on Operating Systems Design and Implementation (OSDI '18), pp. 578–594. (2018)
2. Yang, C.C., Chen, Y.R., Liao, H.H., Chang, Y.M., Lee, J.K.: Auto-tuning fixed-point precision with TVM on the RISC-V packed SIMD extension. ACM Trans. Des. Autom. Electron. Syst. **28**(3), 1–21 (2023)
3. MLC Team: MLC-LLM (Software). GitHub Repository (2023–2025). https://github.com/mlc-ai/mlc-llm
4. Feng, S., Hou, B., Jin, H., et al.: TensorIR: an abstraction for automatic tensorised program optimisation. In: Proceedings of the 28th ACM International Conference on Architectural Support for Programming Languages and Operating Systems (ASPLOS '23), pp. 804–817 (2023). https://doi.org/10.1145/3575693.3576933
5. Shao, J., Zhou, X., Feng, S., et al.: Tensor program optimisation with probabilistic programs. In: Advances in Neural Information Processing Systems, vol. 35, pp. 35783–35796 (NeurIPS 2022) (2022)
6. Ge, S., Zhang, Y., Liu, L., Zhang, M., Han, J., Gao, J.: Model Tells You What to Discard: Adaptive KV-Cache Compression for LLMs. arXiv preprint arXiv:2310.01801 (2023)
7. Li, J., Tang, T., Zhao, W.X., Nie, J.Y., Wen, J.R.: Pre-trained language models for text generation: a survey. ACM Comput. Surv. **56**(9), 1–39 (2024)
8. Lin, J.-K., Yang, Y.-L., Lai, H.-M., Lee, J.-K.: Rewriting and optimizing vector length agnostic intrinsics from arm SVE to RVV. In: Proceedings of the 53rd International Conference on Parallel Processing Workshops (ICPP-W 2024, ACM, New York, NY, USA (2024)
9. Li, J.-H., et al.: SIMD everywhere optimization from ARM NEON to RISC-V Vector extensions. In: Proceedings of the RISC-V Summit, Santa Clara, USA (2023). Slides & talk
10. Zhang, P., Zeng, G., Wang, T., Lu, W.: TinyLlama: an open-source small language model (2024). arXiv preprint arXiv:2401.02385
11. Touvron, H., et al.: LLaMA 2: open foundation and fine-tuned chat models, (2023). arXiv preprint arXiv:2307.09288
12. Grattafiori, A.., et al.: The LLaMA 3 herd of models (2024). arXiv preprint arXiv:2407.21783
13. Team, G., et al.: Gemma 2: improving open language models at a practical size (2024). arXiv preprint arXiv:2408.00118
14. Guo, D., et al.: DeepSeek-R1: incentivizing reasoning capability in LLMs via reinforcement learning, (2025). arXiv preprint arXiv:2501.12948

A Cloud-Edge Compute Continuum Experimental Methodology, Applied to a 5G Core Study

Samuel Rac[1], Rajarshi Sanyal[2], and Mats Brorsson[1](✉)

[1] University of Luxembourg, Esch-sur-Alzette, Luxembourg
mats.brorsson@uni.lu
[2] Proximus SA, Bertrange, Luxembourg
https://www.proximus.lu/en, https://www.uni.lu/snt-en/

Abstract. Cloud-native technologies such as Kubernetes have improved resource allocation and the performance of cloud infrastructures. The trend is also to extend cloud-native computing to the edge and beyond to build a Cloud-Edge compute continuum. However, the traditional resource orchestration algorithms do not work well for extending the compute infrastructure outside the data center, and it is also difficult to test a heterogeneous cloud infrastructure without building it.

To address these challenges, we propose a new methodology to aid in deploying, testing, and analyzing the effects of application placement in a heterogeneous Cloud environment. With this methodology, we can simulate any combination of deployment scenarios and monitor metrics in accordance with the placement of the application in the cloud-edge continuum. Edge devices may be simulated, but as we use Kubernetes, any device which can be attached to a Kubernetes cluster could be used. We have applied our methodology to the problem of network function placement of an open-source 5G core implementation. We have used three different 5G application scenarios as use cases and three different cloud architectures and report on changes in key metrics when different 5G network functions are placed in different locations, all done with the methodology in a public cloud.

Keywords: Edge-cloud continuum · Experimental Methodolog · 5G · Edge Computing · Kubernetes · Application placement · Open-source testbed

1 Introduction

Cloud-native technologies, such as Kubernetes [6], have significantly improved the way to allocate infrastructure resources to applications. For developers of distributed applications, deployment is greatly simplified as the individual components, typically embodied as Docker containers, are automatically mapped to nodes in the cluster that make up the infrastructure. This technology also has

H. R. Arabnia et al. (Eds.): CSCE 2025, CCIS 2932, pp. 367–385, 2026.
https://doi.org/10.1007/978-3-032-22193-3_28

the potential to improve resource utilization and reduce over-provisioning, which is otherwise common. Overall it leads to shorter deployment times and reduced costs for infrastructure.

Taking Kubernetes as an example, the different nodes that make up a cluster may differ in compute capacity (e.g., in the number of cores and memory capacity) and in architecture (e.g., IA64 vs. ARM). The Kubernetes scheduler can still make a good mapping of containers to nodes, provided that the deployment manifest indicates the minimum requirements of each container. Even containers requiring the use of specific hardware resources, such as GPU or FPGA, can be handled, but it obviously makes the problem of finding an optimal placement harder.

Edge and fog computing [14] have been introduced to enable the deployment of (parts of) applications closed to the end-user in order to lower end-to-end latency, reduce data sent over the network, or improve privacy by keeping the data local. While this has obvious benefits, it also introduces new challenges. A software component can no longer execute anywhere in the compute infrastructure as the Edge nodes typically require specific formats and explicit placement. While data center nodes typically are homogeneous in architecture, Edge nodes come in many different forms and architectures. We need to extend the cloud-native paradigm from the data center to the edge. From the developer's perspective, deploying an application taking advantage of the edge should be as easy as deploying it in a cloud data center. However, the best placement of software components is often not clear and extensive experimentation is needed, both for the placement and for finding the right system architecture.

The 5th generation (5G) of the cellular telecommunication network is amenable to being deployed in an edge-to-data-center continuum (in contrast to previous generations, which needed much more specialized equipment). The main talked-about benefits of the 5G technology are enhanced Mobile Broadband (eMBB), Ultra-Reliable Low Latency Communication (URLLC), and massive Machine Type Communication (mMTC).

To achieve eMBB and URLLC, applications need to be deployed at the 5G edge close to base stations (gNB) and 5G devices. Then, it is important to understand the behavior of 5G Network Functions (NFs) when deployed in heterogeneous system architectures, including with different kinds of nodes.

The 5G core is built using *network functions* (NFs) that build up a service-based architecture that allows for control and user plane separation, i.e., control and user plane NFs can be deployed separately in different locations. The User Plane Function (UPF) links gNB to a Data Network (the internet in most cases) can then be deployed close to the end-user.

In this paper, we present a novel methodology to build testbeds that are particularly well suited to run experiments on 5G network function placement on a heterogeneous cloud infrastructure. When deploying the 5G core in a heterogeneous cloud, there can be a plethora of possible architectural options based on the location choices of the NFs within the network areas/zones. However, we chose three of the most pertinent combinations (elaborated in Sect. 3.2). To simulate different use cases, we define three realistic use cases: i) Augmented Reality, ii) Industrial IoT, and iii) Massive IoT. We evaluate different placement options for the use cases across three system architectures.

In this methodology, we leverage the power of public cloud infrastructures and Kubernetes. In order to mimic the cloud system we want to test, we map the nodes in the cluster to evaluate nodes with similar capabilities in the public cloud. This is, of course, crude but serves our purpose. More importantly, we can simulate different geographical localities of subsets of nodes by controlling the latency and bandwidth available in communication links between nodes. Thanks to that, we use Kubernetes, the 5G core can be deployed unchanged from one experiment to another. The only difference is the Kubernetes pod taints used to guide the placement of network functions. We also use standard tools for monitoring purposes for performance evaluations.

Using this methodology alleviates the tedious and time-consuming process of building large physical testbeds while the software development process can be kept the same as a real environment. In addition, experiments are easily reproducible.

We have initially used this methodology to investigate the placement of specific 5G components pertaining to the user or control plane in the central cloud, at the network edge, or in an intermediate local data center. However, the methodology is general and can be used in any other setting involving the edge to data center continuum. One example is the deployment of a cloud multiplayer gaming system. Since the methodology leverages Kubernetes, it can run every containerized application. In that manner, the testbeds generated by this methodology will be application agnostic.

1.1 Related Work

Goshi et al. describe a testbed that highlights Inter-NF dependencies [11]. Kube5G is a cloud-native 5G testbed designed to handle the whole 5G stack [5]. COPA is an orchestration framework for networking running above the Kubernetes layer [18]. However, these three testbeds (and the others referenced in their study) are not meant for the evaluation of placement and performance of the applications with respect to heterogeneous system architectures. It is not possible to simulate the impacts of geographical distances between nodes on networking (e.g., latency) or the bandwidth restrictions. In contrast, our methodology enables the deployment of reproducible experiments in a public or private cloud without the costs and constraints of handling a country-sized network.

The *AccessOpt* architecture detailed in Sect. 3.2 is based on many studies [12,15–17]. These studies describe multi-layered 5G architectures. They are respectively based on areas (National, Region, Local, antenna vicinity), geographical topologies, logical layers (Infrastructures, Network Function, Service, and Orchestration), and other application layers.

Sarrigiannis et al. describe a two-tier architecture (Cloud and Edge) for VNF placement with an NFV orchestrator [19]. Contrary to their approach, we leverage Kubernetes, the state-of-the-art orchestration framework. It renders the flexibility to scale up and down on-demand or automatically. Exploiting Kubernetes, intricate architectures requiring complex interactions between nodes either at the control or user plane can be set up and tested.

Ejaz et al. present a 3 tier architecture (Cloud IoT, Edge IoT, and Local Edge IoT) to improve reliability for mission-critical processes, based on iFogSim simulator [9]. This study helped us to define our system architectures. However, the iFogSim simulator does not allow deploying a real containerized application.

Edgenet, as described by Şenel et al. [8], provides a global distributed Kubernetes cluster, but it is not suitable as a testbed for 5G core or other edge-based applications as it cannot be configured, and there is not access to the Edge nodes.

Enoslib [7] is another suggestion to facilitate experimentation with distributed systems. It is a general tool to facilitate reproducible experimentation and is thus orthogonal to our methodology, which could be used as the backend in an Enoslib experiment. We have so far not seen it beneficial to use Enoslib.

1.2 Our Contributions

Our main contributions are (i) a methodology to study the impacts of deploying applications in a heterogeneous cloud environment [13], and (ii) a performance analysis of a 5G core installation while studying three 5G use cases deployed using different system architectures on a testbed generated by our methodology.

The testbeds developed with our methodology can run standard containerized applications in a cloud environment where different system architectures can be simulated by controlling networking properties and leveraging different virtual machines available in the host cloud representing different node architectures. Latency and bandwidth can be tuned to simulate distances between nodes or edge-related bandwidth limitations. The testbed can be used to set up reproducible edge computing experiments quickly.

The rest of the paper is organized as follows: in Sect. 2 we describe in more detail the fundamentals of our methodology. In Sect. 3, we describe in more detail the 5G scenario and the use cases explored. Finally, the experiments, and their results are described in Sects. 4 and 5, respectively, before concluding the paper.

2 Methodology

Our methodology relies on two main components: *cloud-native technologies* and *tools to simulate many architectural options* in a cloud environment. Testbeds according to this methodology can be deployed in public, private, or hybrid clouds. The tools and scripts needed for this are publicly available on github [13].

2.1 Cloud-Native Technologies

A testbed is a distributed computer cluster with the ability to simulate heterogeneous architectures (i.e., with many kinds of nodes: different hardware and location). This framework relies on some well-known cloud-native technologies like containers and Kubernetes.

Containerization. We use Docker containers which greatly simplify application deployment [3]. With a very lightweight virtualization layer, this technology has become a standard to package applications for deployment. They have a small overhead and can be easily managed and deployed. In the edge computing scope, containers can help to deal with the inherent heterogeneity. The container abstraction alleviates the complexity of deploying software on nodes with different CPU architecture (e.g., an edge node). A container image can have multiple implementations to target most of the possible target architectures.

Stateless applications can be scaled up/down more effortlessly than stateful applications; there is no need to cope with the state consistency. Thus, it is easier to containerize stateless applications and scale them up/down. E.g., 5G Network Functions can have a stateless implementation [2] and take advantage of the containers' benefits. In the experiments Sect. 4 all of the 5G NFs are stateless and packaged into containers.

Container Orchestration. To quickly deploy, scale up/down and manage containerized applications in a cloud environment, we use Kubernetes, the state-of-the-art container orchestration tool, as mentioned earlier. Kubernetes manages pods, the atomic unit manageable by Kubernetes. Pods are composed of at least one container. It is possible to assign a pod or a set of pods to any node manually or automatically (Kubernetes pod scheduler is designed to be easily customizable). A custom Kubernetes scheduler can be used to develop new scheduling methodologies and may be used in our methodology.

Monitoring. Cloud-native technologies contain a large set of tools for monitoring vast infrastructures. Prometheus[1] collects and exposes many metrics (CPU usage, memory, networking, and other metrics). In our testbed, we leverage Prometheus to aggregate data from nodes and expose it as a time series. Automatically, logs, network traces (running *Wireshark*[2] in a side-car container), and other metrics are effortlessly recorded and stored to be able to collect experimental metrics.

In addition, a custom scheduler can use all the metrics collected to make better decisions. E.g., the scheduler can fetch networking metrics (like bandwidth or latency between nodes) to lower latency between an application and its end-user. A 5G system scheduler could, for instance, use the user equipment (UE) location or closest antenna information.

Kubernetes Limitations. The Kubernetes scheduler is a powerful tool. It can find a proper application placement when looking at available resources or node taints. However, network performance is not taken into account. It is not an issue while working with a traditional data center with homogeneous nodes, but it becomes a limitation when dealing with some edge computing use cases.

[1] https://prometheus.io/.
[2] https://www.wireshark.org/.

E.g., it is challenging to achieve ultra-low latency without considering at which geographical position an application is deployed.

2.2 Architecture Simulation

In this section, we explain how we can simulate different system architectures on top of Kubernetes. This is a key feature for designing new infrastructures or developing new application placement strategies in the edge computing scope.

Configurability of Network Capacity and Latency. To simulate a system architecture, we need to be able to configure the network capacity and latency between nodes. Configurable latency is a key feature of our methodology. It enables the simulation of the distance between two nodes, e.g., between a data center and an edge node. Theoretically, the more the distance, the higher will be the latency. We can also configure the network bandwidth between the nodes. This can be useful to simulate edge use cases, especially with bandwidth restrictions. In the case of 5G, this capability can help tune and evaluate the use cases pertaining to eMBB and MIoT.

The control of these parameters is achieved by means of *traffic control*[3] (tc). It is a utility program that can reconfigure the Linux kernel packet scheduler. It can add latency on received packets, change maximum bandwidth and other networking parameters. We use it because it is lightweight and does not consume too much CPU, which is ideal for our experiments. *Traffic control* can run inside a container as a side-car, modifying the pod properties one by one. With this tool, we can have a different configuration for every pod in the cluster.

Different Kinds of Nodes. In our setup, Kubernetes nodes are deployed on instances with different resource allocations (CPU, Memory), reflecting different compute capabilities at the edge compared to in the data center. In addition, some nodes specifically meant for hosting the application (e.g., online gaming, 5G slices) would have hardware accelerators like GPU or FPGA, but this is not done in our experiments reported here. The nodes are labeled according to their properties (resources, location, hardware accelerator) and follow a naming convention. These labels help to select where to deploy an application according to system requirements.

Application Placement. The Kubernetes scheduler can use the above-described labels. Associating an application to a node can be done manually or automatically (implementing a custom scheduling policy). Manual application placement is based on Kubernetes *taints* and *tolerations*, i.e., checking node labels and application permissions to know the candidate nodes where an application is authorized to be deployed. We can define a rule to force application deployment on a specific node using *Pod affinity*.

[3] https://linux.die.net/man/8/tc.

Figure 1 gives an overview of the architecture simulation in a testbed setup. Nodes are labeled according to their kind, and networking between pods is configurable.

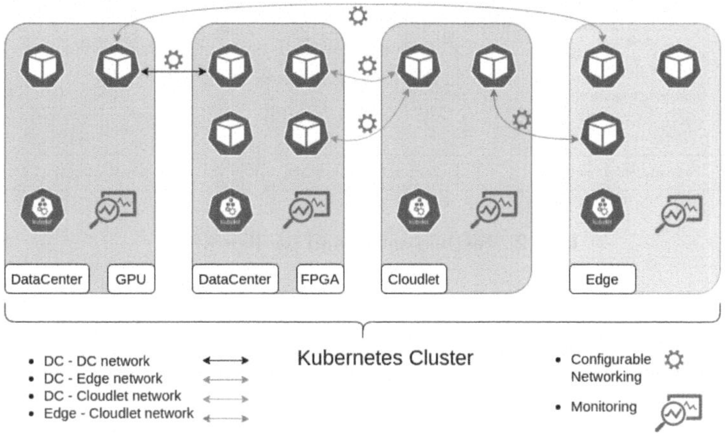

Fig. 1. A testbed setup. Each coloured box represents a kind of node. Communication links with a "cog" represents links with configurable latency and bandwidth.

2.3 Testbed Configuration and Deployment

We describe the manifests, scripts, and configuration files needed to control a testbed experiment.

The *configuration file* stores information about network parameters (latency/bandwidth) controlling the *tc* (traffic control) running as sidecar in each pod. It also stores cluster information (e.g., master node IP, pod subnetworks) and node parameters (e.g., taints, tolerations, labels). A script initializes the cluster state based on the configuration file.

The *Kubernetes manifests* (YAML files) store experiment information, applications to deploy on the testbed, as well as a description of the placement strategies. Application *affinities* and *tolerations* can be parameterized in manifests as well as the selected scheduler. Additional scheduler and monitoring tools deployments are also defined in these manifests.

Finally, a sequence of *scripts* are used to set up the cluster, but they are also used to manage the experiment life cycle. They can deploy application pods, start pcap (Wireshark) traces recording, stop the experiments (deleting the pods), and collect the results.

Figure 2 illustrates a testbed setup and configuration. The configuration file defines the cluster's desired state and manifests the applications to deploy. There are scripts to manage the cluster according to configuration files and manifests. Configured networking between pods is handled by running tc on each pod.

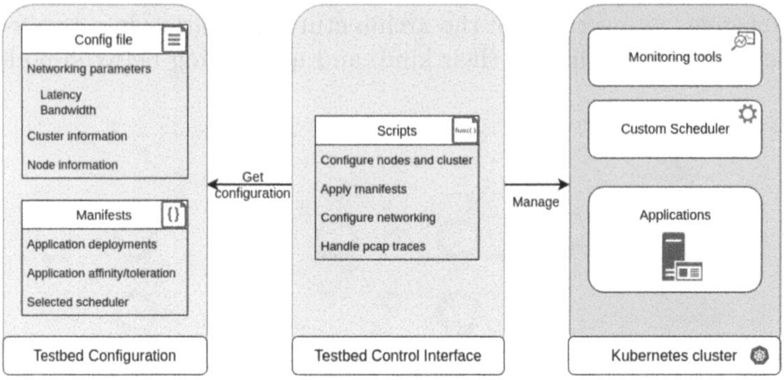

Fig. 2. Testbed setup and configuration.

The scripts, manifests, and configuration files that make up the core of the methodology are released open source [13]. Thus, more technical details can be found in the code repository. Thus, it is possible to run new experiments or reproduce the results detailed in the following sections.

3 Deploying a 5G System

The methodology has been developed to create testbeds to can run edge computing experiments. The following sections describe how we conduct a study on a complete 5G core system implementation, studying the effects of 5G network function placement in different system architectures and for different use cases.

3.1 5G Network Functions on the Testbed

A complete description of a 5G System (access network, devices, and core) is out of the scope of this paper, but some familiarity with the core components is necessary to understand the study. The 5G core consists of a number of Network Functions (NFs). The gNodeB (gNB) represents the radio access network (RAN) to which user equipment (UE, e.g., phones) is connected over cellular radio.

We have used an open-source 5G core [10] and implemented each NF in a container. Most of the details about NFs are not important for this study, but we detail three of them: AMF, SMF, and UPF. These are essential to understanding how the system architectures are defined. The AMF (Access and Mobility management Functions) handles incoming connections and session requests of UEs and manages mobility (handover between two cells). The UPF (User Plane Function) handles user data traffic. The UPF is directly connected to a Data Network (Internet or Application Server). The SMF (Session Management Function) establishes PDU sessions (Protocol Data Unit) for the UEs. A PDU session is a data tunnel that links a UE to a data network (DN) through a UPF. This session is attached to a *network slice* (reserved virtual networking capabilities);

e.g., it is possible to reserve bandwidth for a session to guarantee QoS. A UE can be connected to up to five sessions at the same time. Other 5G NFs always stay in the data center in this study. E.g., UDM (Unified Data Management) and AUSF (Authentication Server Function) act as front-end to the database and thus need quick access to the database.

3.2 System Architectures

In this study, we use three different kinds of nodes: *Data center*, *Edge* and *Cloudlet* nodes, and define three system architectures comprising of different node types and topology. One architecture is used as a reference reproducing the traditional approach where all NFs are deployed in a data center, while the others use an edge node close to the gNB and a cloudlet node in-between the edge and the data center. We then experiment with different placement of the UPF, SMF, and AMF network functions in the different architectures and study the effect on system performance.

Figure 3 shows the *baseline* system architecture where all network functions are placed in a single data center with homogeneous nodes. The RAN elements (gNB and UEs) are simulated and run on different nodes, not included in the simulated architecture, to not interfere with the NF placement study. One node is dedicated to the gNB, and another one is for UEs. These elements also run into containers on the same Kubernetes cluster to simplify experiments. Node *taints* prevent NFs from running on these nodes. Links between nodes are called N2 to N6 as defined in 5G standard architecture [2]. In the Baseline architecture, links within the cluster have no extra latency penalty, while the N2 and N3 links are given 20 ms extra latency to account for communication to the (relatively) remote gNB. Since the Baseline architecture's nodes are homogeneous, NFs can be placed anywhere without any effects.

The Baseline architecture cannot support eMBB and URLLC use cases well (e.g., cloud gaming applications or AR/VR both need ultra-low latency and high bandwidth). For this, a UPF needs to be deployed closer to the gNB to lower latency and higher bandwidth on the N3 link. To this effect, we define Edge nodes that are located close to the gNB and therefore have very low latency to it. The UPF can be placed on an Edge node which will lower the end-user latency and improve bandwidth once the session has already been established.

The LatOpt system architecture, shown in Fig. 4, is a well-known architecture. It should enable eMBB and URLLC use cases, significantly improving link N3 latency and throughput. With this architecture, the UPF is deployed on an edge node close to the gNB. Other NFs are running on data center nodes. The UPF is designed to be used in this configuration and achieve the CUPs.

The AccessOpt system architecture is similar to LatOpt architecture but includes Cloudlet nodes. This architecture wants to be a simplified implementation of the multi-layered 5G architectures mentioned in Sect. 1.1. Investigating the effects of this architecture could provide valuable information to implement more complex ones. Cloudlet nodes are closer to the data center nodes than edge nodes. Several gNBs may be connected to one Cloudlet node. AMF and SMF are

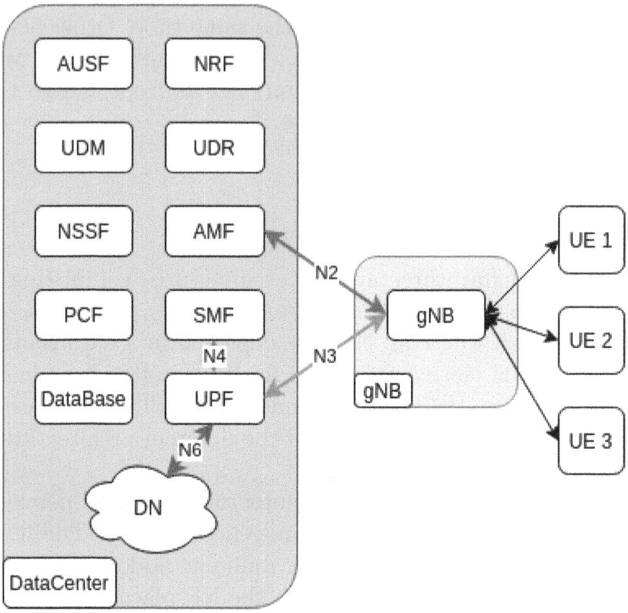

Fig. 3. Baseline: System architecture I.

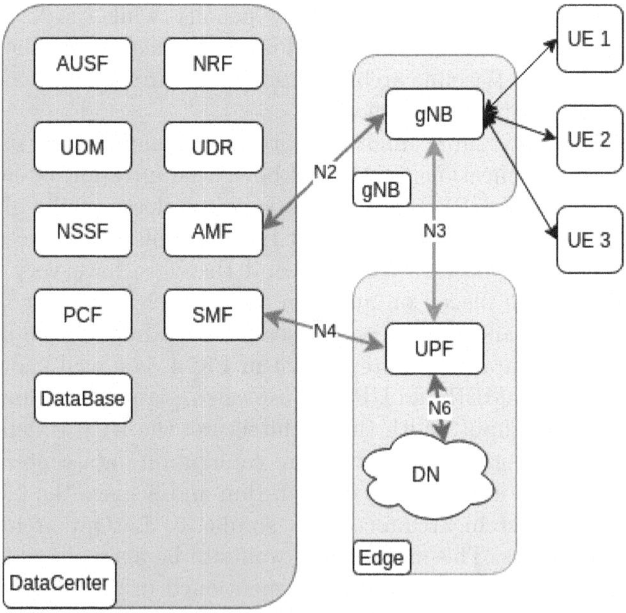

Fig. 4. LatOpt: System architecture II, optimized for end-user latency and bandwidth.

deployed on Cloudlet nodes because they handle UE connection, session management, and mobility procedures. Thus, Cloudlet nodes can handle UE's massive mobility (many UEs moving from one gNB to another) while keeping reasonable latency with other NFs located in the data center. Figure 5 shows AccessOpt architecture. Deploying AMF and SMF on Cloudlet nodes should improve UE registration, mobility, and PDU session establishment procedures performances.

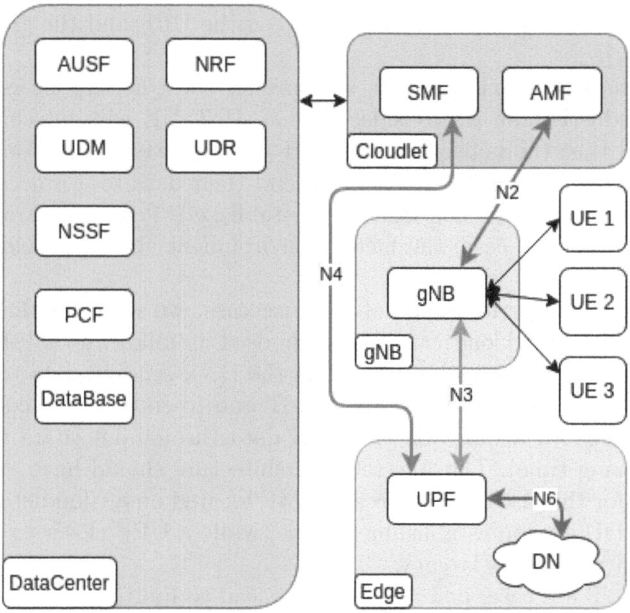

Fig. 5. AccessOpt: System architecture III, optimized for session throughput.

3.3 Use Cases

In order to experiment with major 5G features (eMBB, URLLC, and mMTC), we introduce three use cases related to 5G. We investigate different NF placement, as discussed, on the above-described system architectures using these use cases: Augmented Reality (AR), Industrial IoT (IIoT, e.g., a smart factory with sensors), and Massive IoT (MIoT). These use cases are designed to generate a specific workload on different network functions in the 5G core. Studying these three use cases will bring valuable knowledge for i) building new infrastructures including slices at the 5G edge, and ii) developing new scheduling methodologies for placing NFs.

The AR and IIoT use cases are detailed in-depth by Siriwardhana et al. in [20]. They experiment with 5G devices in a smart factory. 5G connectivity is needed to stream high-definition videos to an AR screen and to offload smart sensor data to a server respecting low latency. In a large factory, a private 5G network can be an alternative to a WiFi network. It could be cheaper and easier to deploy. We adapt the workload and the experiment duration to the capabilities of the testbed. However, note that in our study, the 5G core and its NFs are not simulated but are real operation-grade elements.

In the AR use case, a UE should receive a high-quality video with low latency. We look at the UE end-to-end latency to evaluate different system architectures. The LatOpt architecture should improve this metric with respect to the baseline architecture by reducing the distance between the UPF and the gNB (manipulating latency).

For the Industrial IoT use case, we consider the UEs as sensors in a smart factory. In industry 4.0, we consider that an IIoT UE will not change of network cell and that the network is acquired at UE power up. Periodically, these devices will establish a data session and send their data to a processing server. Before sharing data, a session has to be established. Power constraints are not considered in this use case, the factory environment should provide energy to devices.

To evaluate the performance of this use case, we measure the end-to-end latency. The IIoT workload can be decomposed as follow: establishing a PDU session (to contact a processing server via the DN), sending data to the server, and getting the server's response. The IIoT end-to-end latency comprises two main parts: network acquisition time and data throughput (data transfer and server processing time). The AccessOpt architecture should have an impact on E2E latency for this use case. AMF and SMF located on a Cloudlet node should reduce the PDU session establishment time, while a UPF closer to gNB should reduce the data session's latency.

In the MIoT use case, power constraints lead to limiting UE uptime to save battery. In this case, we considered tiny IoT devices with a battery designed to last many years. They spend most of their time powered off to save battery. When they do need to share data, they power up, acquire a network, establish a PDU session, transmit lightweight data, and turn it off again. When millions of devices simultaneously power up and acquire the network, the control plane manages a heavy workload. To support it, the Control Plane needs to be boosted, that is why the AMF and SMF functions are deployed closer to gNBs in the AccessOpt architecture. Many instances of AMF and SMF can be deployed at this location as requests may be shared among them. The study of the AMF request load balancer is outside of the scope of this study. Alawe et al. have already investigated this problem [4]. The UE registration time is an important metric because it can induce registration time-out failures. Ultra-low latency for registration may not be impactful for end users, but when too many requests are received simultaneously, requests may expire due to a long handling time.

A different network *slice* is defined for each use case. UEs use these slices to be connected to different DN depending on their use case. Different SST (Slice/Service Type) values are defined in the configuration files [13]. Table 1 summarizes the specifics of each use cases.

Table 1. Use cases and their characteristics.

Use cases	Favoured System architecture	Type of workload	KPIs
AR (Smart Factory)	Baseline or LatOpt	High data rate on the UP	E2E latency
IIoT (Smart Factory)	Baseline or AccessOpt	PDU session establishment process + Low data rate the UP	E2E latency
MIoT (Massive IoT)	Baseline or AccessOpt (+ load balancer)	Registration + PDU session establishment process + Low data rate on the UP	Time to register + establish a PDU session

Table 2. Additional latency used in different system architectures

System Architecture	N2 (ms)	N3 (ms)	N4 (ms)	N6 (ms)	DC-Cloudlet (ms)
Baseline	12.5	12.5	0	0	0
LatOpt	12.5	1	12.5	0	0
AccessOpt	3.5	1	3.5	0	9

4 Experimental Methodology

In this section, we outline the experimental setup and parameters of the experiments, such as additional latency and use case workload.

4.1 Experimental Setup

To test all use cases, we run all the experiments in a public cloud environment. We use a self-managed Kubernetes cluster with one master node and seven worker nodes. All of these machines have 2 CPUs and 4 GB of RAM.

On this cluster, we run the open-source 5G core free5GC [10]. Every Network Function (NF) runs inside its own pod. User Equipment (UE) and gNodeB are simulated using an open-source RAN simulator [21].

4.2 Additional Latency

As described above, we can set an additional latency between two nodes to reflect the physical latency in the target system architecture. Table 2 summarizes the additional latencies used in experiments. These are the additional latencies to what is already experienced in the physical cloud infrastructure.

4.3 Workload Parameters

Table 3 summarizes the use cases' workload parameters of the different experiments. The IIoT and MIoT use cases workload should mainly be managed by the Control Plane (respectively on SMF and AMF). In contrast, the User Plane (UPF) should support the AR use case workload.

Table 3. Use case Workloads.

Use Case	Workload size	#UEs
AR	460 Mbit of video stream sent to the UE	3
IIoT	PDU session establishment requests + 640 kB of data	20
MIoT	UE registration requests + PDU session establishment requests + 100 kB of data	50

5 Results

Results in this section are twofold: (i) Resource usage plots of network functions, to ensure the proper progression of the experiments, (ii) the presentation of the KPIs of the use cases for the selected architectures. We then analyze the connections between the placement of network functions and the KPIs.

5.1 Resource Usage

Monitoring the resource usage when running experiments is necessary to follow the experiments' progression. In addition, monitoring data can be recorded and could be part of the results. Our methodology proposes using automation to record multiple metrics on the testbed and to automatically generate figures.

To illustrate the monitoring capabilities and study the network functions' behavior, we analyze the variations of the CPU usage of the MIoT use case. Figure 6 shows CPU consumption of the Control Plane NFs for the MIoT use case. The y-axis represents the CPU-time rate (time that a process spends on CPU) for each control plane NFs' pod. The CPU consumption of the AMF is higher when the UEs power up and try to acquire the network. This figure also shows that CPU consumption is higher for the UDM (Unified Data Management); it is the database's front end that is frequently queried during the UE registration procedure. Other NFs involved in the session establishment procedure also increase their CPUconsumption. The NFs have the expected behavior, more CPU is consumed when requests are handled. Requests and the network traffic are automatically recorded and stored in pcap traces. This information confirms that the experiment follows the procedure specifications defined in the standard [1]. This data is available for the other use case experiments, and the same analysis can be conducted.

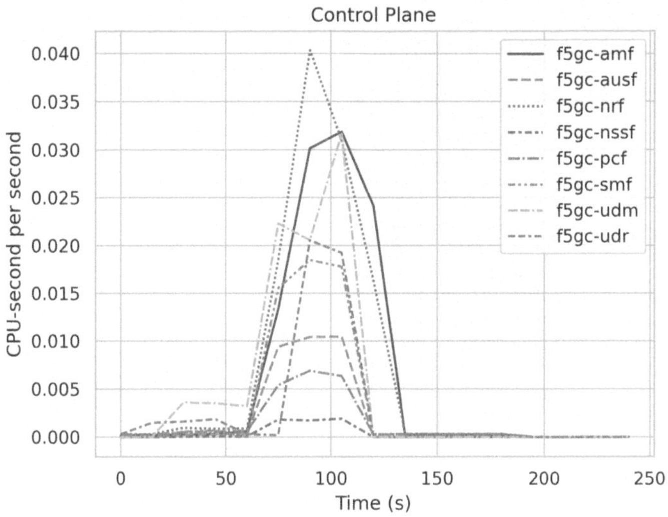

Fig. 6. Control Plane CPU rate - MIoT use case/Baseline architecture.

Other metrics about memory or networking are available. These metrics can describe many objects such as containers, pods, or nodes. Studying resource usage automatically allows monitoring experiments and gathering results. In addition, these metrics can be used directly by a custom scheduler.

5.2 KPIs

In this section, we compare different KPI values. For each use case, we run several experiments using different system architectures. Then, we compare the performance by looking at the recorded KPI values. This provides insights into the best architecture to adopt for the use case.

Each use case has a different workload. Table 3 details the characteristics of each workload. We repeat the described workload three times (once every 5 min). Figures 7, 8 and 9 shows the mean KPI values for each use case according to the chosen architecture. These KPIs compile the network interactions recorded in pcap (Wireshark) traces during the experiments.

Figure 7 shows a significant difference in end-to-end latency for the AR use case. This KPI value is four times lower when using the LatOpt architecture. This improvement can be explained by positioning the UPF closer to the gNB. Latency on the link N3 is lower with the LatOpt architecture as well as end-to-end latency. This demonstrates the ability of the testbed by replicating well-known use cases.

The end-to-end latency for the IIoT use case is shown in Fig. 8. The AccessOpt architecture provides E2E latency almost four times lower than the Baseline architecture. E2E latency is divided into the time to achieve the PDU session establishment procedure and data traffic duration (transport and processing

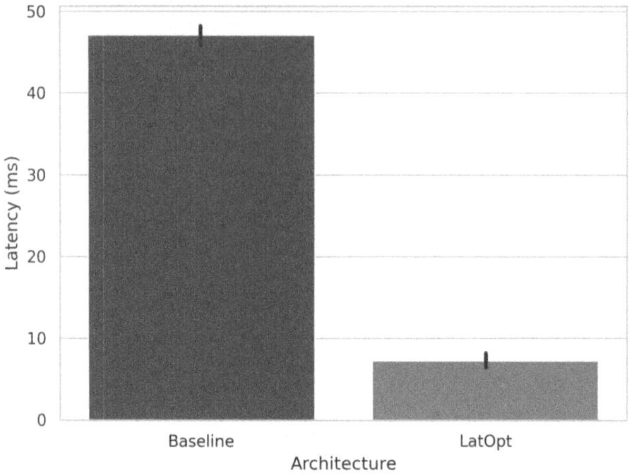

Fig. 7. End-to-end latency: AR use case.

time). Both are significantly improved with AccessOpt. Establishing a new data session takes more time than transmitting data. Almost half of the requests go from AMF or SMF to the data center during the session establishment procedure, and the others go to the edge. Then having less latency to the edge improves the time to complete the procedure. With the AccessOpt architecture, the AMF is close to the edge nodes and on the same machine as SMF. This proximity explains the better KPI value for the AccessOpt architecture. Like in the AR use case, the UPF lowers the latency of the data session. The placement of AMF, SMF, and UPF in the AccessOpt architecture reduces the E2E latency significantly.

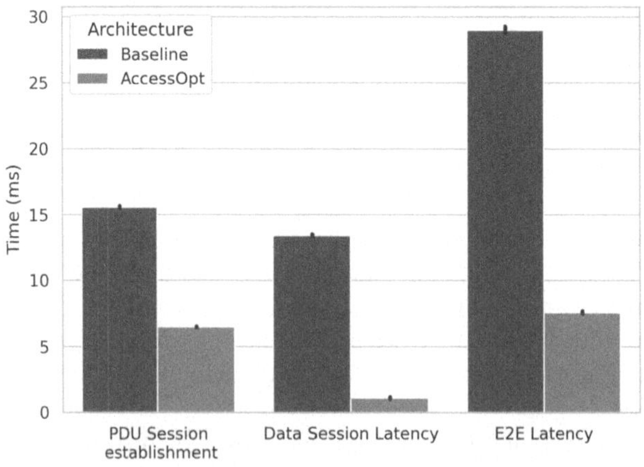

Fig. 8. End-to-end latency: IIoT use case.

Figure 9 shows a significant difference in KPI values when using the Baseline and the AccessOpt architectures. The total procedure with the baseline architecture is 13 times faster than AccessOpt. UE registration procedure is 14 times faster on the Baseline architecture than on AccessOpt. However, the PDU session establishment procedure is ten times faster on the AccessOpt architectures. However, session establishment represents only 0.06% of total time for AccessOpt and 8% for Baseline. Therefore PDUsession establishment time has a limited impact on AccessOpt architecture's total performance. Registration procedures have to be complete before a session can be established. During the registration procedure, AMF mainly addresses NFs located in the data center (close to the database). This procedure will take more time to achieve with AccessOpt architecture, where AMF is far from the data center. It is contrary to the data session establishment procedure. Traffic is balanced between NFs in the Datacentre and at the Edge. Then, placing the AMF on a cloudlet node gives better performance for this procedure.

When the latency between the cloudlet and data center nodes becomes too high, it causes a systematic registration time-out. Only a few UEs can register before all registration timers are triggered when latency becomes high. In that case, UEs will try two more times to register without success. The UEs' procedure retries impact the CPU consumption of the control plane because a UE will initialize many procedures.

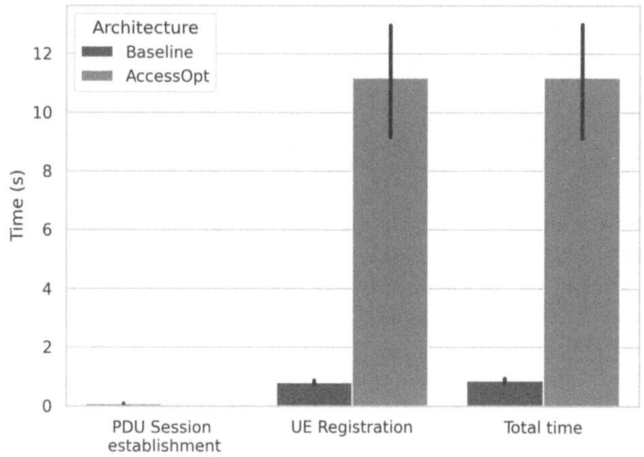

Fig. 9. Duration of different procedures in the MIoT use case.

In these 5G usecases, our methodology helps choose an architectural design by comparing KPIs. The AR and the IIoT use cases show significant improvements in their KPIs when deployed on an architecture different from Baseline. However, the KPI of the MIoT use case is not improved. Results are better on the reference architecture. These results confirm that placing UPF at the Edge improves latency. Also, these experiments show that it is better to place AMF in a data center to achieve the registration procedure and place it at the Edge (or nearby) for the session establishment procedure.

6 Conclusion

Our methodology permits studying edge computing use cases using an existing cloud infrastructure (either public or private). To experiment with edge computing use cases, we need to consider the inherent heterogeneity of these infrastructures. This is possible with control of nodes' characteristics and networking.

We deploy three 5G use cases on our testbed, testing different system architectures. The detailed analysis of some 5G processes highlights the importance of AMF and SMF placement. To achieve the UE registration procedure, they should be placed close to the data center to get better KPIs performances. However, they can be placed closer to the edge nodes and gNBs to establish new PDU to improve KPIs.

We aim in the next steps to experiment with new customized Kubernetes schedulers, which can make use of all the metrics collected to perform the placement of network functions automatically for different use cases.

Acknowledgments. This work has been partly funded by the Luxembourg National Research Fund (FNR) under contract number 16327771 and has been supported by Proximus Luxembourg SA.

References

1. 3GPP: Procedures for the 5g system (5gs). Technical Specification (TS) 23.502, 3GPP (2021), version 17.2.1
2. 3GPP: System architecture for the 5g system (5gs). Technical Specification (TS) 23.501, 3GPP (2021), version 17.2.0
3. Ahmed, A., Pierre, G.: Docker container deployment in fog computing infrastructures. In: 2018 IEEE International Conference on Edge Computing (EDGE), pp. 1–8. IEEE (2018)
4. Alawe, I., Hadjadj-Aoul, Y., Ksentini, A., Bertin, P., Darche, D.: On the scalability of 5g core network: the amf case. In: 2018 15th IEEE Annual Consumer Communications & Networking Conference (CCNC), pp. 1–6. IEEE (2018)
5. Arouk, O., Nikaein, N.: Kube5g: a cloud-native 5g service platform. In: GLOBECOM 2020–2020 IEEE Global Communications Conference, pp. 1–6 (2020). https://doi.org/10.1109/GLOBECOM42002.2020.9348073. Accessed 16 Nov 2025
6. Brewer, E.A.: Kubernetes and the path to cloud native. In: Proceedings of the Sixth ACM Symposium on Cloud Computing, p. 167. SoCC '15, Association for Computing Machinery, New York, NY, USA (2015). https://doi.org/10.1145/2806777.2809955. Accessed 16 Nov 2025
7. Cherrueau, R.A., et al.: Enoslib: a library for experiment-driven research in distributed computing. IEEE Trans. Parallel Distrib. Syst. **33**(6), 1464–1477 (2022). https://doi.org/10.1109/TPDS.2021.3111159. Accessed 16 Nov 2025

8. Şenel, B.C., Mouchet, M., Cappos, J., Fourmaux, O., Friedman, T., McGeer, R.: Edgenet: a multi-tenant and multi-provider edge cloud. In: Proceedings of the 4th International Workshop on Edge Systems, Analytics and Networking, pp. 49–54. EdgeSys '21, Association for Computing Machinery, New York, NY, USA (2021). https://doi.org/10.1145/3434770.3459737. Accessed 16 Nov 2025
9. Ejaz, M., Kumar, T., Ylianttila, M., Harjula, E.: Performance and efficiency optimization of multi-layer iot edge architecture. In: 2020 2nd 6G Wireless Summit (6G SUMMIT), pp. 1–5 (2020). https://doi.org/10.1109/6GSUMMIT49458.2020.9083896. Accessed 16 Nov 2025
10. free5GC (2022). https://www.free5gc.org/
11. Goshi, E., Jarschel, M., Pries, R., He, M., Kellerer, W.: Investigating inter-nf dependencies in cloud-native 5G core networks. In: 2021 17th International Conference on Network and Service Management (CNSM), pp. 370–374 (2021). https://doi.org/10.23919/CNSM52442.2021.9615565. Accessed 16 Nov 2025
12. Gupta, N., Sharma, S., Juneja, P.K., Garg, U.: SDNFV 5G-IoT: a framework for the next generation 5G enabled IoT. In: 2020 International Conference on Advances in Computing, Communication Materials (ICACCM), pp. 289–294 (2020). https://doi.org/10.1109/ICACCM50413.2020.9213047, iSSN: 2642-7354
13. HetBed: (2022). https://github.com/srac0/HetBed. Accessed 16 Nov 2025
14. Laroui, M., Nour, B., Moungla, H., Cherif, M.A., Afifi, H., Guizani, M.: Edge and fog computing for iot: a survey on current research activities & future directions. Comput. Commun. **180**, 210–231 (2021)
15. Patounas, G., Foukas, X., Elmokashfi, A., Marina, M.K.: Characterization and identification of cloudified mobile network performance bottlenecks. IEEE Trans. Netw. Serv. Manag. **17**(4), 2567–2583 (2020). https://doi.org/10.1109/TNSM.2020.3018538. Accessed 16 Nov 2025
16. Rahimi, H., Zibaeenejad, A., Safavi, A.A.: A novel IoT architecture based on 5G-IoT and next generation technologies. In: 2018 IEEE 9th Annual Information Technology, Electronics and Mobile Communication Conference (IEMCON), pp. 81–88 (2018). https://doi.org/10.1109/IEMCON.2018.8614777. Accessed 16 Nov 2025
17. Recse, A., Szabo, R., Nemeth, B.: Elastic resource management and network slicing for iot over edge clouds. In: Proceedings of the 10th International Conference on the Internet of Things. IoT '20, Association for Computing Machinery, New York, NY, USA (2020). https://dl.acm.org/doi/10.1145/3410992.3411015. Accessed 16 Nov 2025
18. de Resende, H.C.C., Schimuneck, M.A.K., Both, C.B., Wickboldt, J.A., Marquez-Barja, J.M.: COPA: experimenter-level container orchestration for networking testbeds. IEEE Access **8**, 201781–201798 (2020). https://doi.org/10.1109/ACCESS.2020.3035619. Accessed 16 Nov 2025
19. Sarrigiannis, I., Kartsakli, E., Ramantas, K., Antonopoulos, A., Verikoukis, C.: Application and network vnf migration in a mec-enabled 5G architecture. In: 2018 IEEE 23rd International Workshop on Computer Aided Modeling and Design of Communication Links and Networks (CAMAD), pp. 1–6 (2018). https://doi.org/10.1109/CAMAD.2018.8514943. Accessed 16 Nov 2025
20. Siriwardhana, Y., Porambage, P., Ylianttila, M., Liyanage, M.: Performance analysis of local 5G operator architectures for industrial internet. IEEE Internet Things J. **7**(12), 11559–11575 (2020). https://doi.org/10.1109/JIOT.2020.3024875. Accessed 16 Nov 2025
21. UERANSIM (2022). https://github.com/aligungr/UERANSIM. Accessed 16 Nov 2025

Design and Evaluation of a Cost-Aware Dynamic Load Balancer for Distributed Environments

Satish Penmatsa[1(✉)] and P. Krishna Kanth Varma[2]

[1] Framingham State University, Framingham, MA 01701, USA
spenmatsa@framingham.edu

[2] SRKR Engineering College, Bhimavaram, AP 534204, India

Abstract. In modern distributed and cloud-native systems, minimizing the cost of compute-intensive workloads has become a critical objective, especially under usage-based pricing models. This paper presents a dynamic, cost-aware load balancing strategy designed to reduce the monetary cost incurred by users for utilizing shared computational resources. The approach is based on a central-server node model that includes communication costs when transferring jobs to remote processing nodes. The proposed dynamic strategy is evaluated against existing static load balancing methods through simulations conducted across varied system configurations. Results demonstrate that the dynamic approach adapts more effectively to changing workloads and system conditions, achieving greater cost-efficiency.

Keywords: Cost-Aware Load Balancing · Distributed Systems · Dynamic Resource Allocation

1 Introduction

The rapid growth of cloud computing, edge computing, and hybrid distributed systems has fundamentally changed how organizations deploy, scale, and manage workloads. Users now have access to vast pools of shared computational resources that can be provisioned on demand. However, with this flexibility comes a growing concern about cost efficiency, as cloud services are typically billed based on usage such as CPU hours, memory consumption, storage, and data transfer. This makes monetary cost a key consideration in system and application design [1, 2].

In these heterogeneous environments, workloads vary in intensity and resource needs, and compute nodes differ in processing capacity, availability, and pricing. Additionally, communication overheads, such as inter-node data transfer fees or regional egress charges, further complicate job allocation decisions [3]. As a result, traditional load balancing methods that focus on optimizing performance metrics like response time or throughput may fail to minimize actual costs incurred by users, especially in multi-user, cost-sensitive settings [4, 5]. To address this, we present a dynamic, cost-aware load balancing strategy (CostAwareDLB) that adapts to changing system conditions and pricing differences. We use a central server node model that includes communication

H. R. Arabnia et al. (Eds.): CSCE 2025, CCIS 2932, pp. 386–396, 2026.
https://doi.org/10.1007/978-3-032-22193-3_29

costs incurred when jobs are transferred to other nodes for remote processing. The proposed strategy explicitly aims to minimize the total cost to users rather than focusing on traditional performance metrics.

Prior research has explored a broad range of load balancing strategies in distributed systems, addressing goals such as latency reduction [3], fairness in resource allocation [6, 7], energy efficiency [8], and fault tolerance [9]. These strategies have contributed significantly to improving system performance, reliability, and resource utilization across a variety of environments. However, the landscape of distributed computing has shifted considerably with the widespread adoption of cloud-based pay-per-use models, making cost-aware scheduling a growing area of interest.

Recent studies have begun to address this shift by incorporating dynamic pricing models for cloud resources, cost-aware offloading in edge-cloud scenarios, and economic models that consider user behavior in job placement decisions [10–12]. These approaches reflect an increasing awareness of the financial dimension of resource allocation, especially as cloud users must now consider not just performance, but also monetary cost, in their workload management strategies.

As cloud platforms continue to evolve, leading providers such as Amazon Web Services (AWS), Microsoft Azure, and Google Cloud Platform have introduced diverse pricing models, including on-demand, reserved, and spot instances. These pricing options offer flexibility but also introduce additional complexity for users, who must carefully weigh cost, availability, and reliability when selecting resources. In this context, dynamic load balancing strategies that adapt to both workload variability and pricing fluctuations are becoming increasingly essential. Furthermore, the rise of multi-cloud and hybrid cloud deployments, where organizations utilize resources across different providers and geographic regions, adds another layer of heterogeneity to pricing and performance. In such environments, the ability to incorporate cost-awareness into job scheduling is not just advantageous, but is crucial for minimizing user expenses while maintaining service quality.

Our work contributes by proposing an adaptive load balancing approach that explicitly minimizes user-incurred costs in multi-user, heterogeneous environments. We conduct simulations under varying system loads and configurations to compare the cost-efficiency of the proposed dynamic strategy with traditional static approaches. Results show that proposed scheme consistently reduces overall user costs and adjusts effectively to changing workload patterns, making it a suitable solution for cost-sensitive distributed computing systems.

The remainder of the paper is structured as follows. Section 2 describes the system and cost models used in this study. Section 3 presents the proposed load balancing procedure. Section 4 outlines the simulation setup and discusses the results, including a comparison of the proposed CostAwareDLB scheme with other existing approaches. Finally, Sect. 5 concludes the paper with a summary of key findings.

2 System and Cost Modeling

The system model consists of a heterogeneous distributed computing environment with n nodes connected through a communication network, as shown in Fig. 1.

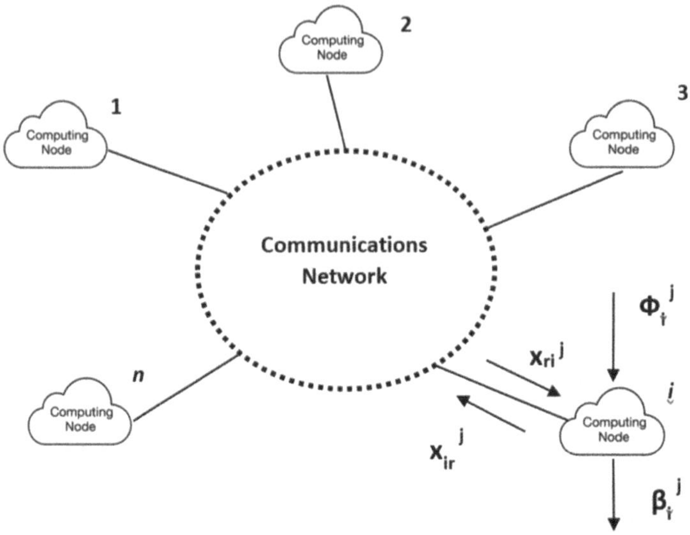

Fig. 1. System Model

Let the service rate of node i be represented by μ_i. Each node receives jobs from m distinct user classes. The arrival rate of jobs from user j to node i is denoted by ϕ_i^j, while ϕ^j denotes the total arrival rate of jobs from user j across all nodes. The overall arrival rate of jobs into the system is represented by Φ. Let β_i^j is the job processing rate (load) of user j at node $i$and $\beta_i = \left[\beta_i^1, \beta_i^2, \ldots, \beta_i^m\right]^T$. The service time of an I/O device is denoted by t_{IO}.

Each computing node follows a central-server model [13] as shown in Fig. 2 with components including a scheduler, processor, and a set of I/O devices. The scheduler is the entry point for all incoming jobs to a node. It decides whether a job should be processed locally by the processor or forwarded to another node in the network. Let p_0 represent the probability that a job completes after leaving the processor, and p_1 represent the probability that it proceeds to request I/O service. The ratio $\frac{p_1}{p_0}$ thus indicates the average number of I/O requests per job. The job flow rate of user j from node r to node i is denoted by x_{ri}^j. We assume that both the computing nodes and the communication network follow exponential service time distributions, and that job arrivals conform to a Poisson process, as described in [14].

Let k_i represent the constant that maps execution time to the amount of resources consumed at node i, and let k_c denote the constant that translates communication delay into the corresponding network resource usage. The price per unit resource that user j pays on node i is given by p_i^j and the price for consuming a unit resource of the communication network by user j is given by p_c^j. The pricing that users must pay to access the resources is determined using a bargaining-based game-theoretic approach [15]. In this framework, software agents representing the user and the resource owner engage in a non-cooperative bargaining game characterized by incomplete information and alternating offers. The objective for both parties is to maximize their respective

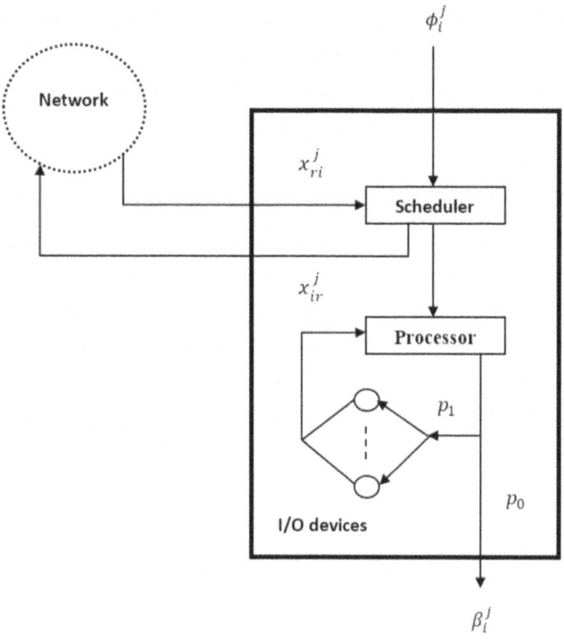

Fig. 2. Node Model

profits. As a result, the game becomes one of negotiating how to split the difference between the user's maximum willingness to pay and the owner's minimum acceptable price.

Based on the above assumptions, the mean cost for a user j job processed at node i is given by [14]:

$$F_i^j\left(\beta_i^j, p_i^j\right) = \frac{k_i p_i^j}{\left(\mu_i - \sum_{k=1}^m \beta_i^k\right)} + \frac{p_1}{p_0} t_{IO} \tag{1}$$

The mean communication cost for a user j job is given by:

$$G^j\left(\lambda^j, p_c^j\right) = \frac{k_c p_c^j t}{\left(1 - t\sum_{k=1}^m \lambda^k\right)}, \sum_{k=1}^m \lambda^k < \frac{1}{t} \tag{2}$$

where t is the mean communication time for sending or receiving a job form one node to the other for any user, λ^j is the job traffic through the network of user j, and λ is the total traffic over the communications network.

The problem of minimizing the mean cost of the entire system can be expressed as:

$$\min D(\beta, \lambda, p) = \frac{1}{\Phi} \sum_{j=1}^m \left[\sum_{i=1}^n \beta_i^j F_i^j\left(\beta_i^j, p_i^j\right) + \lambda^j G^j(\lambda^j, p_c^j)\right] \tag{3}$$

subject to the constraints:

$$\beta_i^j \geq 0 \tag{4}$$

$$\sum\sum_{i=1}^{n}\beta_i^j = \phi^j \tag{5}$$

$$\sum_{j=1}^{m}\beta_i^j < \mu_i \tag{6}$$

The non-linear optimization problem formulated in Eq. 3 can be addressed using the Karush-Kuhn-Tucker (KKT) conditions [16], which provide necessary conditions for optimality in constrained optimization problems. By applying the KKT theorem, we obtain a set of optimal load values $\beta_i = \left[\beta_i^1, \beta_i^2, \ldots, \beta_i^m\right]^T$ that minimize the total cost incurred for executing user jobs across the distributed system. These optimal loads represent a *static* allocation baseline, offering a cost-minimizing reference configuration under the assumption of known and fixed system parameters. While the solution assumes steady-state conditions, it provides valuable insight into the ideal distribution of workloads and serves as a foundation for comparison against dynamic, adaptive load balancing strategies under variable system conditions.

3 Cost-Aware Dynamic Load Balancing

In this section, we present the dynamic, cost-aware load balancing strategy (CostAwareDLB).

The user j marginal computing cost $f_i^j\left(\beta_i^j, p_i^j\right)$ and marginal communication cost $g^j\left(\lambda^j, p_c^j\right)$ are defined as:

$$f_i^j\left(\beta_i^j, p_i^j\right) = \frac{\partial}{\partial \beta_i^j}\sum\sum_{k=1}^{m}\beta_i^k F_i^k\left(\beta_i^j, p_i^j\right)$$

$$\Rightarrow f_i^j\left(\beta_i^j, p_i^j\right) = \frac{k_i p_i^j \mu_i}{\left(\mu_i - \sum_{k=1}^{m}\beta_i^k\right)^2} + \frac{p_1}{p_0}t_{IO} \tag{7}$$

$$g^j\left(\lambda^j, p_c^j\right) = \frac{\partial}{\partial \lambda^j}\sum_{k=1}^{m}\lambda^k G^k\left(\lambda^j, p_c^j\right) = \frac{k_c p_c^j t}{\left(1 - t\sum_{k=1}^{m}\lambda^k\right)^2} \tag{8}$$

Let r_i denote the mean service time of a job at node i and N_i^j denote the average number of jobs of user j at node i. The *marginal computing cost* of a user j job at node i from Eq. 7 can be expressed in terms of r_i and N_i^j (using Little's law [14]) as:

$$f_i^j\left(\beta_i^j, p_i^j\right) = k_i p_i^j r_i (1 + \sum_{k=1}^{m} N_i^k)^2 + \frac{p_1}{p_0}t_{IO} \tag{9}$$

Let ρ denote the average utilization of the communications network where $\rho = t\sum_{k=1}^{m}\lambda^k$. Rewriting Eq. 8 in terms of ρ, we have:

$$g^j\left(\lambda^j, p_c^j\right) = \frac{k_c p_c^j t}{(1-\rho)^2}, \rho < 1 \tag{10}$$

Let n_i^j denote the number of jobs of user j at node i at a given instant and $\rho\prime$ denote the utilization of the communications network at a given instant. Rewriting Eq.'s 9 and 10 in terms of these instantaneous variables, we have:

$$f_i^j\left(\beta_i^j, p_i^j\right) = k_i p_i^j r_i \left(1 + \sum_{k=1}^{m} n_i^k\right)^2 + \frac{p_1}{p_0} t_{IO} \tag{11}$$

$$g^j\left(\lambda^j, p_c^j\right) = \frac{k_c p_c^j t}{(1 - \rho\prime)^2}, \rho\prime < 1 \tag{12}$$

The functions f_i^j and g^j represent the estimated marginal virtual costs for user j at node i. Specifically, f captures the cost associated with processing at the node, while g reflects the cost incurred due to communication overhead in the network. These cost functions serve as dynamic indicators of how resource consumption affects the user's overall expenditure. The CostAwareDLB dynamic cost-aware load balancing scheme aims to achieve equilibrium by equalizing the marginal virtual processing costs across all nodes for each user. By continuously monitoring and adjusting job allocations based on these estimates, the system responds to variations in load, pricing, and network conditions. This ensures that users are not only distributed efficiently across the system but are also directed toward nodes where the cost-benefit trade-off is most favorable. In doing so, the strategy minimizes user expenses while adapting to changing system dynamics.

Each node i periodically shares information with all other nodes, broadcasting both the current number of user j jobs in its local queue (n_i^j's) and the corresponding arrival rates (ϕ_i^j's). This shared information enables every node to independently solve the non-linear optimization problem described in Eq. 3, using the arrival rate data to compute (static) optimal load distributions. These optimal loads are then translated into queue thresholds T_i^j (using Little's Law [14]) representing the target number of jobs of user j that node i should ideally hold. When a job from user j arrives at node i, the node compares the current queue length n_i^j against its threshold T_i^j. If $n_i^j > T_i^j$, the node is considered overloaded for user j's jobs, and the arriving job is redirected to a less loaded node for remote processing. Conversely, if $n_i^j \leq T_i^j$, the job is retained and processed locally. To decide where to offload the job when the node is overloaded, node i compares its current load with that of other nodes using the same broadcast information. If $f_i^u > f_j^u + g^u$, then node i is said to be more heavily loaded than node j for a user u job. The node with the lowest relative load for user j is selected as the destination for remote processing. This dynamic and decentralized approach ensures that job allocations adapt in real time to changes in arrival rates and queue states, promoting balanced system behavior and improved cost efficiency.

4 Performance Evaluation

This section presents the experimental results and compares the performance of CostAwareDLB with that of other existing schemes. We simulated a distributed computing environment consisting of 32 heterogeneous nodes serving 20 distinct users. To model heterogeneity across the system, the nodes were assigned varying service rates such that the fastest node operates at a rate ten times greater than that of the slowest node. This variation allows us to capture realistic disparities in processing capabilities commonly found in cloud and distributed environments. The total job arrival rate in the system is determined by the product of the system's utilization (or load factor) and the aggregate service rate of all nodes. To reflect diverse user behavior, the total job arrival rate is distributed unevenly across the 20 users, simulating scenarios where some users generate significantly more traffic than others. The mean communication delay between nodes is assumed to be 1 ms, capturing a modest but non-negligible network overhead for remote job transfers.

For benchmarking purposes, we also implemented a Proportional load balancing scheme (PROP_M) [2, 17] and a static Global Optimal System-wide Cost-based Scheme (GOSPC-CS) [11, 18]. In PROP_M, each user distributes their jobs across computing nodes in proportion to the nodes' service rates, without accounting for dynamic system conditions. This static allocation provides a baseline for evaluating the adaptability and cost-awareness of the CostAwareDLB scheme. The goal of GOSPC-CS is to minimize the total cost of executing all user jobs across the system, thereby providing a system-optimal solution under static assumptions.

Figure 3 illustrates the impact of system utilization (i.e., system load) on the performance of the load balancing schemes when there is no overhead associated with job transfers. Here, job transfer overhead is defined as the fraction of a node's service time consumed in sending or receiving a job. Under low system loads (10% to 30%), the average cost per job for GOSPC-CS and CostAwareDLB appears relatively similar. However, even at these lower loads, PROP_M tends to overcharge users by disproportionately assigning jobs to slower nodes, leading to inefficient cost distribution. As the system load increases, so does the pressure on node utilization, revealing clearer differences among the schemes. CostAwareDLB consistently outperforms the static schemes by assigning jobs in a way that minimizes user costs. This advantage becomes more evident at higher loads. For example, at 80% utilization, CostAwareDLB achieves an average cost approximately 35% lower than that of GOSPC-CS. This improvement is largely due to CostAwareDLB's use of real-time system state information, which enables smarter job redirection to lower-cost nodes, optimizing both resource usage and user pricing.

Figure 4 shows the impact of system utilization on performance when the job transfer overhead is set to 5%. As seen previously, at lower utilization levels, GOSPC-CS and CostAwareDLB offer similar average prices to users, while PROP_M consistently results in higher costs due to its proportionate allocation strategy. As the system becomes more heavily utilized, CostAwareDLB demonstrates a clear advantage by leveraging real-time load information from all nodes to make more cost-effective job assignments. For example, at 70% system utilization, CostAwareDLB achieves an average cost that is approximately 37% lower than that of GOSPC-CS.

Figure 5 illustrates the impact of system utilization on the performance of the load balancing schemes when the job transfer overhead is set to 10%. As expected, the mean cost for all schemes increases due to the higher communication overhead. At low system loads, GOSPC-CS and CostAwareDLB continue to yield similar pricing outcomes. However, in the medium load range, CostAwareDLB achieves a notable advantage,

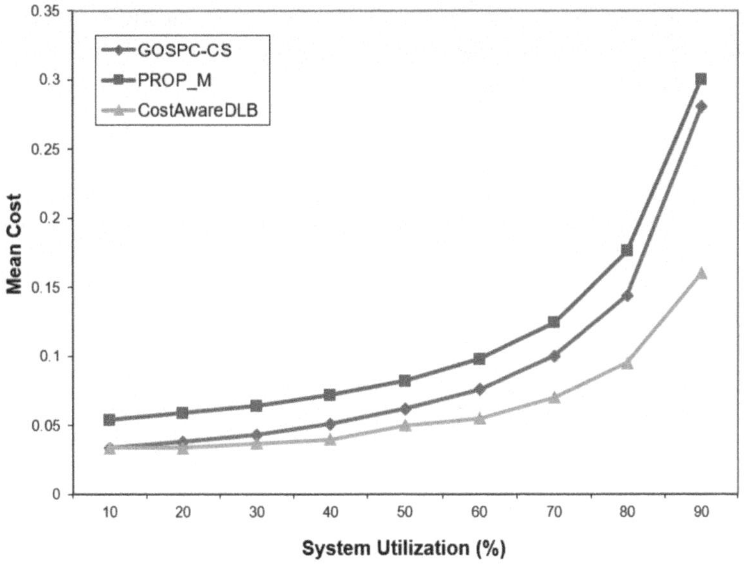

Fig. 3. System Utilization vs Mean Cost (Overhead = 0)

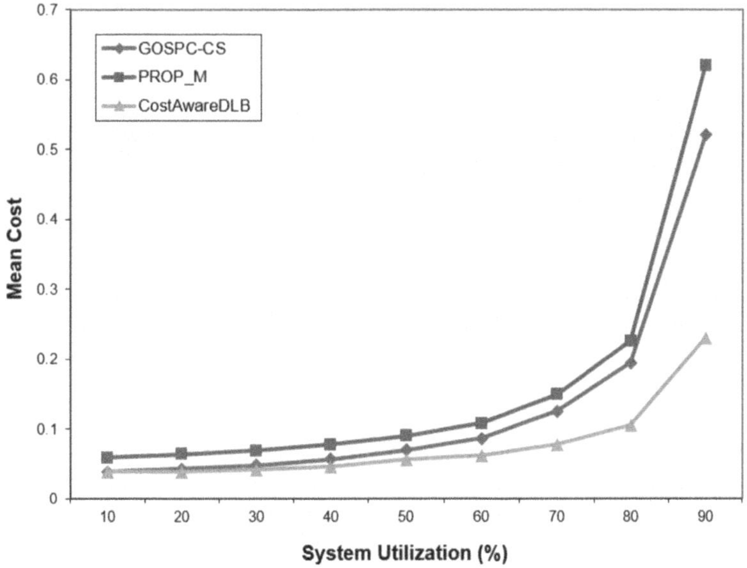

Fig. 4. System Utilization vs Mean Cost (Overhead = 5%)

reducing the average cost by approximately 30% to 40% compared to GOSPC-CS. At high utilization levels, this advantage persists, with CostAwareDLB maintaining a cost reduction of around 20% to 36% relative to GOSPC-CS. For overhead values exceeding 10%, further analysis revealed that CostAwareDLB continues to deliver significantly lower expected prices for system utilizations up to 70%, gradually converging to the performance of the static schemes as utilization approaches its upper limit.

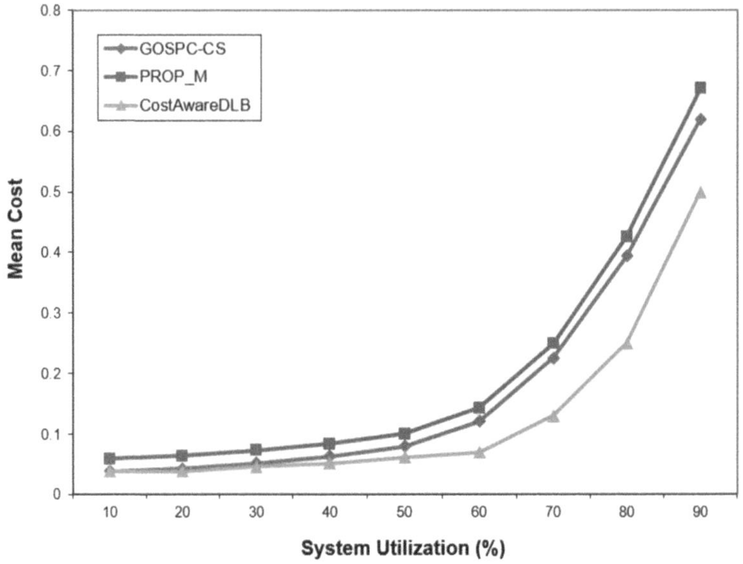

Fig. 5. System Utilization vs Mean Cost (Overhead = 10%)

We now examine how speed skewness, or the degree of heterogeneity in node processing capabilities, affects the performance of the CostAwareDLB scheme. Speed skewness is defined as the ratio between the maximum and minimum service rates of the nodes in the system. To study this effect, we modeled a distributed environment with 32 computing nodes, where the slower nodes have a baseline service rate of 1, and the faster nodes vary in service rate to create different levels of heterogeneity. This variation ranges from a ratio of 1 (representing a homogeneous system) to 20 (indicating high heterogeneity). The overall system utilization is fixed at 60%, and all other simulation parameters are consistent with those used in the setup for Fig. 3.

Figure 6 shows how the mean cost per job varies with increasing speed skewness. When the system is nearly homogeneous, CostAwareDLB performs similarly to GOSPC-CS, with little difference in the mean cost. However, as heterogeneity increases, CostAwareDLB begins to outperform GOSPC-CS more significantly. For example, under moderate skewness (e.g., a speed ratio of 12), CostAwareDLB achieves a mean cost that is approximately 33% lower than GOSPC-CS. At higher skewness levels (e.g., a ratio of 14 or more), the cost advantage grows further, reaching up to 40% lower than GOSPC-CS. These results highlight the strength of CostAwareDLB in heterogeneous environments. By dynamically adapting to variations in processing speed and load, it is better equipped to allocate jobs cost-effectively, especially when the gap between fast and slow nodes becomes more evident.

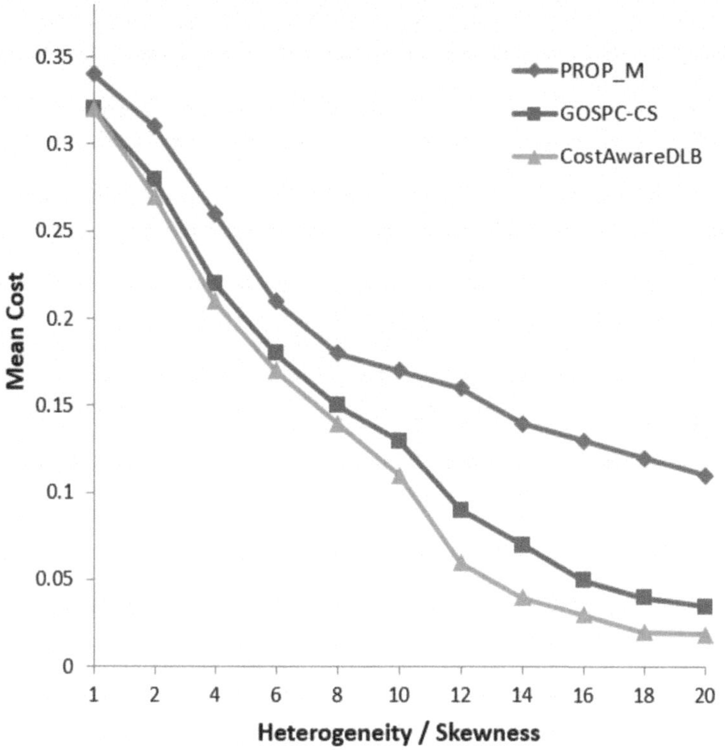

Fig. 6. Heterogeneity vs Mean Cost

5 Conclusions

This paper presented CostAwareDLB, a dynamic, cost-aware load balancing strategy designed for heterogeneous distributed systems operating under usage-based pricing models. Unlike traditional schemes that focus primarily on performance metrics such as response time or throughput, CostAwareDLB explicitly minimizes the monetary cost incurred by users while maintaining efficient resource utilization. The proposed approach leverages real-time system state information and pricing parameters to make intelligent job allocation decisions that adapt to varying workloads and node capabilities. A detailed simulation-based evaluation demonstrated that CostAwareDLB consistently outperforms static schemes such as GOSPC-CS and PROP_M, especially under medium to high system utilization and in environments with high node heterogeneity. Future work may explore extending the model to incorporate energy efficiency, fault tolerance, and multi-objective optimization in real-world deployments.

References

1. Buyya, R., Srirama, S.N., Casale, G., et al.: A manifesto for future generation cloud computing: research directions for the next decade. ACM Comput. Surv. **51**(5), 1–38 (2018)

2. Hussain, M., Luo, M.-X., Hussain, A., et al.: Deadline-constrained cost-aware workflow scheduling in hybrid cloud. Simulation Modelling Practice and Theory **129**, 102819, ISSN 1569-190X, Dec. 2023
3. Chiaro, C., Monaco, D., Sacco, A., Casetti, C., Marchetto, G.: Latency-aware Scheduling in the Cloud-Edge Continuum, pp. 1–5. IEEE Network Operations and Management Symposium, Seoul, Republic of Korea (2024)
4. Xu, J., Palanisamy, B.: Cost-Aware Resource Management for Federated Clouds Using Resource Sharing Contracts. In: IEEE 10th International Conference on Cloud Computing, pp. 238–245, Honololu, HI, USA (2017)
5. Cheng, F., Huang, Y., Tanpure, B., et al.: Cost-aware job scheduling for cloud instances using deep reinforcement learning. Clust. Comput. **25**, 619–631 (2022)
6. Kishor, A., Niyogi, R., Veeravalli, B.: Fairness-aware mechanism for load balancing in distributed systems. IEEE Trans. Serv. Comput. **15**(4), 2275–2288 (2022)
7. Grosu, D., Chronopoulos, A.T.: Noncooperative load balancing in distributed systems. J. Parallel Distributed Comput. **65**(9), 1022–1034 (2005)
8. Medara, R., Singh, R.S., Sompalli, M.: Energy and Cost Aware Workflow Scheduling in Clouds with Deadline Constraint. Concurrency and Computation: Practice and Experience, March 12, 2022
9. Mohammadian, V., Darwesh, A.: Fault-tolerant load balancing in cloud computing: a systematic literature review. IEEE Access (2021)
10. Mohammad, F.-M., Mostafa, G.-A., Shakarami, A.: A cost-aware IoT application deployment approach in fog computing. Cluster Comput. **28**(3), January 2025
11. Pal, S., Agrawal, K.K., Kasi, B.: Evolving towards optimal cloud resource allocation and cost management: an in-depth analysis. In: IEEE 1st International Conference on Advances in Computing, Communication and Networking (ICAC2N), pp. 289–295, Greater Noida, India (2024)
12. Wan, X., Yin, J., Guan, X., Bai, G., Choi, B.-Y.: A pricing based cost-aware dynamic resource management for cooperative cloudlets in edge computing. In: 27th International Conference on Computer Communication and Networks (ICCCN), pp. 1–6, Hangzhou, China (2018)
13. Zhang, Y., Hakozaki, K., Kameda, H., Shimizu, K.: A performance comparison of adaptive and static load balancing in heterogeneous distributed systems. In: Proc. IEEE 28th Annual Simulation Symposium, pp. 332–340, Phoenix, AZ (1995)
14. Jain, R.: The Art of Computer Systems Performance Analysis: Techniques for Experimental Design, Measurement, Simulation, And Modeling", Wiley-Interscience (1991)
15. Ghosh, P., Roy, N., Das, S.K., Basu, K.: A pricing strategy for job allocation in mobile grids using a non-cooperative bargaining theory framework. J. Parallel Distributed Comput. **65**(11), 1366–1383 (2005)
16. Kameda, H., Li, J., Kim, C., Zhang, Y.: Optimal Load Balancing in Distributed Computer Systems. Springer Verlag, London (1997)
17. Chow, Y.C., Kohler, W.H.: Models for dynamic load balancing in a heterogeneous multiple processor system. IEEE Trans. Comput. **C-28**(5), 354–361 (1979)
18. Penmatsa, S.: Global optimal load balancing in distributed utility computing systems. J. Global Inf. Technol. **8**(1&2), 12–19, ISSN 1931-8162 (2013)

“PDPTA’25 International Workshop on Mathematical Modeling and Problem Solving (MPS) Co-chairs:”

Employment Method of Regression Machine Learning to Forecast Cherry Blossoms

Miho Chiyonobu[1] and Masami Takata[2(✉)]

[1] Shiga University, Hikone, Shiga 5228522, Japan
miho-chiyonobu@biwako.shiga-u.ac.jp
[2] Nara Women's University, Nara, Nara 6308506, Japan
takata@ics.nara-wu.ac.jp

Abstract. This study combines weather conditions and regression machine learning to forecast cherry blossoms. Somei Yoshino (Yoshino cherry) trees are widely planted in Japan. Therefore, cherry flowers bloom almost simultaneously in neighboring areas. To align the schedule of cherry blossom–related events in advance to coincide with the peak blooming period, forecasting the blooming date in advance is important. To examine conditions and methods suitable for advanced forecasting of blooming dates, we used random forest, extreme Gradient Boosting (XGBoost), and support vector regression (SVR) to forecast actual blooming dates. Experimental results showed that using the highest temperature data for advanced forecasting in February yielded a high accuracy rate. Additionally, the findings demonstrated the feasibility of creating a nationwide forecasting model without city–specific training.

Keywords: random forest · eXtreme Gradient Boosting · Support Vector Regression

1 Introduction

Cherry blossoms are a springtime tradition in Japan. Most cherry trees in Japan are Somei Yoshino (Yoshino Cherry). Somei Yoshino propagates by grafting and cutting. Therefore, they possess the same genes and bloom simultaneously as those in neighboring areas.

Hanami is a cultural event where viewers enjoy eating, drinking, and socializing while appreciating cherry browsing in bloom and it remains widely celebrated across Japan. During Hanami season, cherry blossom viewing spots across Japan attract large crowds. However, the period during which cherry blossoms are in bloom is limited. The time from bloom to full bloom is at most seven days, and the time from full bloom to the beginning of fall is approximately one week. This means the window for enjoying the beauty of cherry blossoms, from bloom to fall, is relatively short–ranging from roughly 10 days to 2 weeks. Rainfall and strong winds can further shorten the viewing period. Therefore, planning

H. R. Arabnia et al. (Eds.): CSCE 2025, CCIS 2932, pp. 399–407, 2026.
https://doi.org/10.1007/978-3-032-22193-3_30

events to coincide with these brief periods is necessary. Event scheduling is an important factor, with most events finalized by the end of February.

Forecasting cherry blossoms bloom is crucial for cherry blossom viewing. Private weather service providers use their forecasting formulas with temperature observations and forecast data to predict blooming dates [1]. However, at early February, forecasting bloom dates may have large error margins. Weather data, such as temperature, which are important for forecasting, are affected by climate change due to global warming. Therefore, rather than statistical data analysis, bloom day forecasting using AI [2] and neural networks [3] has been investigated.

In this study, we propose a regression machine learning method for forecasting cherry blossoms. The regression methods used included random forest, extreme Gradient Boosting (XGBoost) [4], and support vector regression (SVR) [5]. In the experiments, the highest, lowest, and average temperatures were used as meteorological data. Periods from January only, February only, and February to March were compared.

2 Relationship Between Cherry Blossom and Temperature

Temperature differences significantly influenced cherry tree flowering. The flower buds of cherry trees form in the summer. They remain dormant from fall to winter and then during midwinter, they are placed in a low–temperature state. The buds are then awakened from dormancy at warmer temperatures, which leads to blooming.

The 600 Celsius law is a famous cherry blossom forecast. The 600 Celsius law is effective for tree specimens in Tokyo. In the 600 Celsius law, February 1, when dormancy is broken on, is set as the starting point of the bloom forecast, and the highest temperature after February 1 is added to the forecast. The date when the total temperature finally reaches 600 Celsius is set as the forecasted flowering date.

The accuracy rate of the 600 Celsius law is compared for Japan to verify whether there are location differences and how the climate has changed in recent years.

The flowering dates for each city were obtained from the Japan Meteorological Agency (JMA) [6]. The prefectural capitals of all prefectures, except Okinawa, where Somei Yoshino was not planted, were sampled. Kumagaya City in Saitama Prefecture, Choshi City in Chiba Prefecture, Hikone City in Shiga Prefecture, and Shimonoseki City in Yamaguchi Prefecture, which were not observed in the prefectural capital, were sampled as representative sites. The years considered were 1991-2023 and 2014-2023.

The difference in the number of days between the bloom date and the 600 Celsius law represents the error.

Let e be the number of years within 5 days before or after the error. Let d denote the total number of years. The accuracy rate t is defined as follows:

$$t = 100\frac{e}{d}. \tag{1}$$

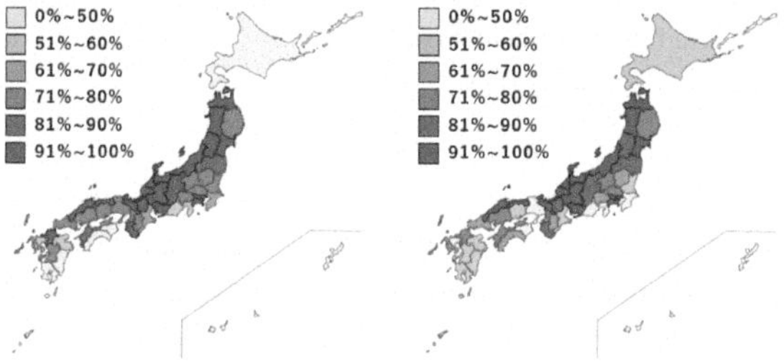

(a) 1991–2023 (b) 2014–2023

Fig. 1. Accuracy rate of 600 Celsius law [%].

Figure 1 presents the accuracy rate of 600 Celsius law. Figure 1(a) shows the target for all 33 years and (b) shows the target for 10 years. The darker the color, the higher the accuracy rate, as shown in Figs. 1. In Fig. 1, the accuracy rate is higher in Tokyo and several locations on the Sea of Japan side. However, the accuracy rate was lower in the Pacific location and Kyushu. The accuracy rates shown in Fig. 1(b) are lower than that in Fig. 1(a).

In Fig. 1, the location differences in the accuracy rate can be confirmed. Thus, in addition to the relationship between cherry browning and temperature, this location should also be considered. The accuracy rates for the 33–and 10–year periods differed only slightly. Therefore, forecasting can be achieved using data from the most recent years rather than relying on data from longer periods.

3 Regression Machine Learning

Regression machine learning involves using continuous values to make forecasts from one number to another. Regression analysis is a statistical technique that reveals the causal relationship as an equation describing the influence of relevant factors and data on the forecasted outcome.

Forecasting cherry blossoms requires multiple explanatory variables. Therefore, multiple regression analysis was performed using the following equation:

$$y = b + W_1x_1 + W_2x_2 + \cdots + W_nx_n,$$

where y is the objective variable, x_i $(i : 1 \leq i \leq n)$ is the explanatory variable, b is the intercept, W_i is the regression coefficient, and n represents the number of explanatory variables.

Random forest combines ensemble learning, bagging, and decision trees to generate forecasts using decision trees with multiple branching patterns. The advantages include efficient learning even when the dimensionality of features, which are data affecting the forecast object, increases, and no requirement for normalization and standardization of features. The accuracy may be difficult to improve with limited training data. The three main types of parameters of the random forest are as follows:

- $n_{estimators}$: The number of decision trees
- max_{depth}: Depth of the decision trees
- $max_{features}$: Number of features

XGBoost [4], a gradient–boosting regression tree, combines boosting and decision trees in ensemble learning. Boosting uses the results of a previous model to train a new model with smaller residuals. Learning new models improves overall accuracy. Subsequently, weights were assigned to each decision–tree model based on its accuracy and aggregated to create a model.

The seven main types of parameters are set as follows:

- max_{depth}: Depth of the decision trees
- sub_{sample}: Percentage of training data randomly extracted from the decision tree
- $colsample_{bytree}$: The percentage of the randomly extracted features
- λ: L2 Regularization term
- α: L1 Regularization term
- η: Learning rate
- γ: Additions and subtractions of the loss reduction

The regularization term suppresses the overlearning of the model and improves generalization performance. The L1 regularization selects the necessary features by shifting the weights of unnecessary features closer to 0. L2 regularization reduces the influence of a single feature by lowering the coefficients of features with large weights.

SVR [5] is a regression implementation of a support vector machine used in classification problems. It uses a blind loss function ε.

The three main types of parameters in the SVR are as follows:

- Kernel Functions
- C: Regularization coefficient
- ε: Deadweight coefficient

Kernel functions include kernels with Gaussian functions, linear kernels with linear functions, and polynomial kernels with polynomial functions. The larger the regularization factor C, the smaller the allowable error. The insensitivity coefficient ε determines error tolerance.

4 Experiment

This section compares the accuracy rates of weather data and regression machine learning methods for forecasting blooms.

In Sect. 4.1, the experimental environment is described and Sect. 4.2 introduces the datasets. In Sect. 4.3, the accuracy rates are compared when the maximum, average, and minimum temperatures are used as the weather data. In Sect. 4.4, a relationship between the locations used for training and those used for testing is examined. Subsequently, in Sect. 4.5, the influence of the different periods of the data is verified.

4.1 Experimental Environment

Table 1. Computer environment

CPU	Intel Xeon CPU 2.30GHz
GPU	NVIDIA Tesla T4
Memory	12GB
OS	Ubuntu 22.04.03 LTS
Lib	scikit-learn 1.2.2

Table 1 shows the computer environment. The accuracy was computed using Eq. (1). When the results obtained by each regression method were expressed as decimals, they were rounded to the nearest whole number.

The parameters of the random forest are as follows:

- $n_{estimators} = 100$
- max_{depth}: unlimited
- $max_{features}$: unlimited

The parameters of the XGBoost are as follows:

- $max_{depth} = 6$
- $sub_{sample} = 1$
- $colsample_{bytree} = 1$
- $\lambda = 1$
- $\alpha = 0$
- $\eta = 0.3$
- $\gamma = 0$

The SVR parameters are as follows:

- Linear kernel
- $C = 1.0$
- $\varepsilon = 0.1$

4.2 Dataset

The observation area excluded Okinawa, where some Yoshino trees could not be grown. Thus, 46 prefectures were covered.

Weather data were provided as explanatory variables for the regression. Weather data were sourced from historical weather data [7] of the JMA. The dataset included the maximum, average, and minimum temperatures for each prefecture. The data were acquired from January to March. The number of years is assumed to be from 1996 to 2020. Data for February 29 of the leap year were excluded.

Cherry–bloom blooming dates were obtained from the JMA list of cherry–bloom blooming dates. The dates obtained are expressed as the number of days elapsed since March 1.

In Sects. 4.3 and 4.4, 10 years of data (2006–2015) is used as the training data and 5 years of data (2016–2020) is used as the test data.

4.3 Relationship with Weather Data

In this section, the accuracy rates for the different weather datasets are compared. Weather data for February and March were used as explanatory variables. Because all observation sites were used in the training data, $d = 10 * 46$ in Eq. (1).

Table 2. Computation time[sec.]

	Learning time	test time
Random forest	2.667	0.009
XGBoost	1.245	0.002
SVR	0.030	0.008

Table 2 lists the computation times. There was no significant difference in computation time regardless of which regression method was used.

Table 3. Accuracy rate for weather data [%]

Temperature	Maximum	Average	Minimum
Random forest	82	72	72
XGBoost	71	73	72
SVR	73	62	46

Table 3 lists the accuracy rates of the weather data. In Table 3, the accuracy rate in the maximum temperature is the best.

Therefore, maximum temperature is appropriate for forecasting cherry tree blooms.

4.4 Relationship with Location

In Sect. 2, the 600 Celsius law shows location differences. Therefore, the accuracy rates of the learning data in the following 2 locations were compared:

1. Its forecasting location
2. All location

The explanatory variables were the maximum temperatures in February and March.

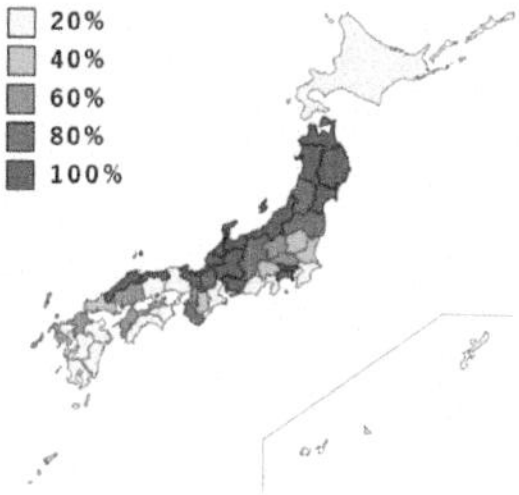

Fig. 2. Accuracy of 600 Celsius law (2016–2020).

Figure 2 shows a map of Japan for five years under the 600 Celsius law. The darker the color, the larger e, which means the number of years within 5 days before or after the error in Eq. (1). Figures 3 and 4 show a color map in e. Table 4 presents the accuracy rates for each training data.

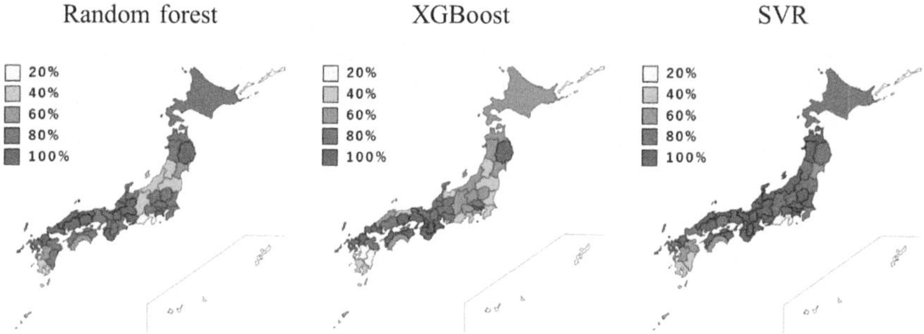

Fig. 3. Accuracy in training data 1.

From Figs. 2 and 3, the accuracy of regression machine learning is better than that of the 600 Celsius law. 600 Celsius Law was based on data from Tokyo. Therefore, location differences were expected. Training data 1 was trained and tested using the data from its location, which improved the accuracy of each regression.

In Fig. 4, when data from all locations are trained together, rather than restricting the locations, the accuracy is better. In Table 4, the accuracy rate of

Table 4. Accuracy rates[%]

Training data	1	2
Random forest	79	82
XGBoost	70	71
SVR	87	73

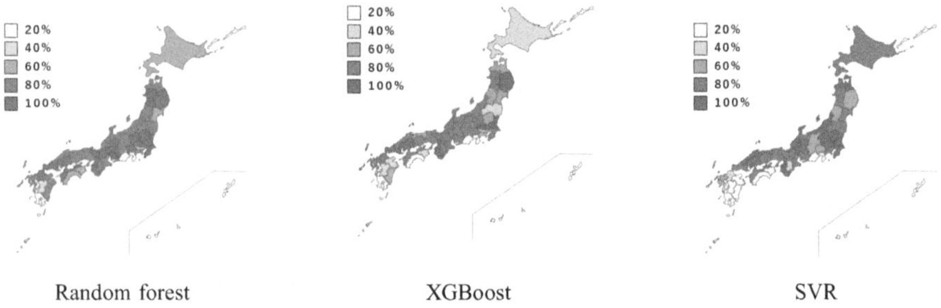

Fig. 4. Accuracy in training data 2.

training data 2 in the random forest or XGBoost exceeds that of training data 1. Therefore, it was not necessary to set the training data for each location.

Thus, forecasting cherry blooms in any location in Japan is possible.

4.5 Relationship with Explanatory Variables

To determine the effect of different numbers of explanatory variables, the experiment was conducted with the following three types of explanatory variables:

1. February and March
2. February
3. January

Obtaining an accurate forecast of cherry flowers at the earliest possible time is preferable. Accordingly, we did not conduct an experiment in which March was the only explanatory variable.

Table 5. Accuracy rate in explanatory variables.[%]

Explanatory	February and March	February	January
Random forest	82	80	64
XGBoost	71	75	62
SVR	73	71	56

Table 5 lists the accuracy rates of the explanatory variables. From Table 5, the accuracy rate for explanatory variable 2 is not significantly different from the accuracy rate for explanatory variable 1. The accuracy of explanatory variable 3 was low. Therefore, the meteorological data for January are insufficient.

Therefore, forecasting using only February meteorological data is effective.

5 Conclusion

This study adopted regression machine learning, including random forest, XGBoost, and SVR to forecast cherry tree blooming. The temperature data, observation points, explanatory variables, and the number of years required for the regression were confirmed experimentally. The results of the experiments are as follows: First, only the maximum temperature was required for the weather data. Second, learning using data from neighboring forecast locations is effective. Thus, accuracy can be improved by selecting various locations. Using only meteorological data from February was enough to achieve satisfactory accuracy.

Acknowledgment. This work was supported by JST SPRING (JPMJSP2115).

References

1. Cherry Blossom Forecast. https://n-kishou.com/corp/news-contents/sakura/?lang=en
2. Cherry Blossom Day, Shimadzu, 2020. https://www.shimadzu.co.jp/today/20200326-1.html (in Japanese)
3. Dan, Y., Kawai, A.: A study on the prediction of cherry blossoms bloom date using artificial neural networks. In: The 24th Annual Conference of the Japanese Society for Artificial Intelligence, 2010, vol. 2D1-4, pp. 1–4 (2010)
4. xgboost, GitHub. https://github.com/dmlc/xgboost
5. Pandit, P., Krishnamurthy, K.N., Bakshi, B.: Prediction of crop yield and pest-disease infestation. AI Edge IoT-based Smart Agric. **2022**, 375–393 (2022)
6. Cherry Blossom Date, Japan Meteorological Agency. https://www.data.jma.go.jp/sakura/data/sakura003_07.html (in Japanese)
7. Historical Weather Data Search, Japan Meteorological Agency. https://www.data.jma.go.jp/obd/stats/etrn/ (in Japanese)

A Proposal of an Operational Model of Autonomous Delivery Mobility Systems Utilizing Medium-Accuracy Maps Generated from Driving Trajectories

Eriko Toma[1(✉)], Atsuyuki Kamei[1], and Masami Takata[2]

[1] Advanced Technology R&D Center, Mitsubishi Electric Co., Amagasaki 661-8661, Hyogo, Japan
Toma.Eriko@dy.MitsubishiElectric.co.jp
[2] Nara Women's University, Nara 630-8506, Nara, Japan

Abstract. With the rise of telework, interest in relocating to rural areas has increased. However, the lack of shopping facilities and inconvenient public transportation remain significant challenges. To resolve these issues, we propose an operational model for autonomous delivery mobility systems to enhancing e-commerce services in rural suburbs. The autonomous delivery mobility system ensures safe by utilizing remote monitoring and a high-accuracy map. Additionally, to maintain service continuity during the high-accuracy map update periods, we employ a medium-accuracy map. This map is generated from the driving trajectories of the autonomous delivery mobilities. It also helps reduce the human resources required for monitoring. To verify the feasibility of this operational model, we generated a medium-accuracy map from in-vehicle driving trajectories and evaluated their accuracy.

Keywords: Autonomous Delivery Mobility · Medium-Accuracy Map · Driving Trajectories

1 Introduction

The advancement of remote work and telecommuting has increased interest in relocating to rural areas rather than concentrating in some large cities like Tokyo [1]. However, since telework does not eliminate the need to go to the office, both of natural environments and good access to offices are required. Therefore, suburban and regional cities within about an hour's commute are becoming realistic options.

To create a flow of people from urban areas to rural areas, it is necessary to address issues such as the lack of shopping facilities in rural areas and the inconvenience of public transportation to and from office areas. Therefore, we propose enhancing logistics services in rural suburban areas using autonomous delivery mobilities. In our proposed operational model, autonomous delivery mobilities will utilize high-accuracy maps to safely navigate and gather surrounding information without significant investment in

H. R. Arabnia et al. (Eds.): CSCE 2025, CCIS 2932, pp. 408–416, 2026.
https://doi.org/10.1007/978-3-032-22193-3_31

infrastructure. Additionally, to ensure that the model is reassuring for elderly residents, we will implement remote monitoring to support in case of any accidents.

When using high-accuracy maps, their aging is one of the most important issues, because roads are changed constantly. To maintain the service during high-accuracy map update periods, we consider using medium-accuracy maps generated from the driving trajectories obtained through the manual driving mode of our operational model. The medium-accuracy map has some locational errors but represent the current road situations. We show our operational model and describe a method of generating medium-accuracy maps with its experimental result.

In this paper, we summarize the challenges of operating autonomous delivery mobility in Sect. 2, and explain our operational model in Sect. 3. In Sect. 4, we evaluate the feasibility of the proposed model by generating medium-accuracy maps from the driving trajectories obtained from the vehicles. Finally, in Sect. 5, we conclude the paper with a summary and discuss future challenges.

2 Challenges in Operating Autonomous Delivery Mobilities

Autonomous delivery robots are expected to play significant roles in various fields. With the growth of e-commerce, the demand for logistics has increased, leading to the consideration of adopting autonomous delivery robots [2, 3].

In rural suburban areas of Japan, the autonomous delivery mobility for the last mile can be expected to improve logistics services. However, considering the shortage of manpower in these regions, it is unrealistic to expect extensive infrastructure for the mobility such as numerous vehicle detection sensors and surveillance cameras along every road, to be installed for the implementation of autonomous delivery mobility. Securing the manpower and funds for maintenance and updates of the system are also difficult.

One method to obtain surrounding information is to utilize high-accuracy maps. High-accuracy maps are being developed primarily for highways, and the main arterial roads in regional urban areas are included in the plans. However, those updates are still considered challenging due to the cost and time involved.

High-accuracy lane-level maps used for autonomous driving must achieve an accuracy of 25 cm, and they are measured by sensor mounted vehicles called MMS (Mobile Mapping System) [4, 5]. Even if these high-quality high-accuracy maps, however, they cannot represent recent road changes which occurred after their creations, until their next updates. It is a problem how to continue delivery services with the incomplete pre-update maps.

To shorten the update period for high-accuracy maps, research is being conducted on collecting and utilizing the driving trajectories of general-purpose vehicles as update information [6–8]. The positional accuracy of GNSS sensors installed in general-purpose vehicles has larger errors and reliability issues compared to RTK positioning MMS. Therefore, it has been proposed to improve accuracy by statistically processing multiple driving trajectories [8]. Research has shown that by collecting lidar data in addition to GNSS sensor data and statistically processing them by lane, an accuracy of 0.5m can be achieved with data from 20 runs.

By statistically improving the accuracy of driving trajectories measured in the same lane, it is possible to generate partially usable high-accuracy driving centerlines. However, since the accuracy depends on the GNSS sensor's reception environment, generating uniformly accurate maps is challenging. Therefore, a cautious approach is taken regarding the practical use of high-accuracy maps for in-vehicle safety applications. We call these revised high-accuracy maps “medium-accuracy maps”. While they include some low-accuracy parts and do not guarantee uniform accuracy, they do achieve approximately 1m accuracy in certain areas.

3 Proposal for an Operational Model of Autonomous Delivery Mobility

In this chapter, we describe the proposed operational model of autonomous delivery mobility.

The proposed model assumes the following conditions (hereafter referred to as the "proposed model assumptions"):

(a) The autonomous delivery mobility operates by referencing high-accuracy maps.
(b) The autonomous delivery mobility is equipped with D-GPS positioning sensors.
(c) The high-accuracy maps are provided by a map supplier and are quality-assured through human verification processes.
(d) The autonomous delivery mobility is remotely monitored by humans, allowing for manual control in case of emergencies and real-time location tracking.

The proposed model assumptions are designed to establish an operational model that ensures safety and provides peace of mind. Even in areas with a high population of elderly residents, explaining proposed model assumption (d) can reduce adoption barriers by showing that human intervention is always available and support can be provided in case of any issues. This model is easy to implement in rural suburban areas with many elderly residents and a shortage of labor, aiming to improve logistics services and attract younger generations from urban areas.

A key challenge in meeting these conditions is maintaining service continuity when updates to the high-accuracy maps are needed. Since updating these maps takes time, it is desirable to have a method that ensures safety while placing minimal demands on human resources during this period.

Therefore, when discrepancies between the high-accuracy maps and reality occur, we will continue the service through manual driving by utilizing remote monitoring, without relying on the high-accuracy maps. Additionally, we aim to reduce the workload of the monitoring personnel and minimize human resource requirements by using medium-accuracy maps generated from the driving trajectories of manual driving. The proposed model assumption (b) aims to ensure the acquisition of self-positioning at a level that can identify the driving lane and maintain the accuracy of the medium-accuracy maps.

This operational model defines three modes for the autonomous delivery mobility: autonomous driving mode, manual driving mode, and remote hands-off mode. These three modes are switched and operated according to the state of the high-accuracy maps, as shown in the sequence diagram in Fig. 1. The term "Remote Monitoring Personnel" in Fig. 1 refers to the staff providing remote monitoring services.

In autonomous driving mode, the high-accuracy map matches the real-world environment, allowing the autonomous delivery mobility to move towards its destination without any issues. This mode places the least burden on the monitoring personnel, who only need to pay attention to any alerts indicating system abnormalities.

In manual driving mode, the monitoring personnel constantly control the autonomous delivery mobility manually. This mode places the highest burden on the monitoring personnel, as they must continuously hold the controller, take full responsibility for speed, route, and situational judgment, and ensure the safety of the surroundings.

In remote hands-off mode, the autonomous delivery mobility operates by referring to a medium-accuracy map instead of a high-accuracy map, similar to the autonomous driving mode. However, unlike the high-accuracy map, the medium-accuracy map lacks information such as lane markings and road shoulders, and only includes unevenly accurate driving centerline shape information. This raises concerns about misrecognition of self-positioning and deviations from the drivable area. Therefore, the monitoring personnel must always sit in front of the controller, constantly monitor the surroundings of the mobility and be ready to switch to manual driving at any time. On the other hand, partial automation of steering and speed adjustments can reduce the burden on the monitoring personnel.

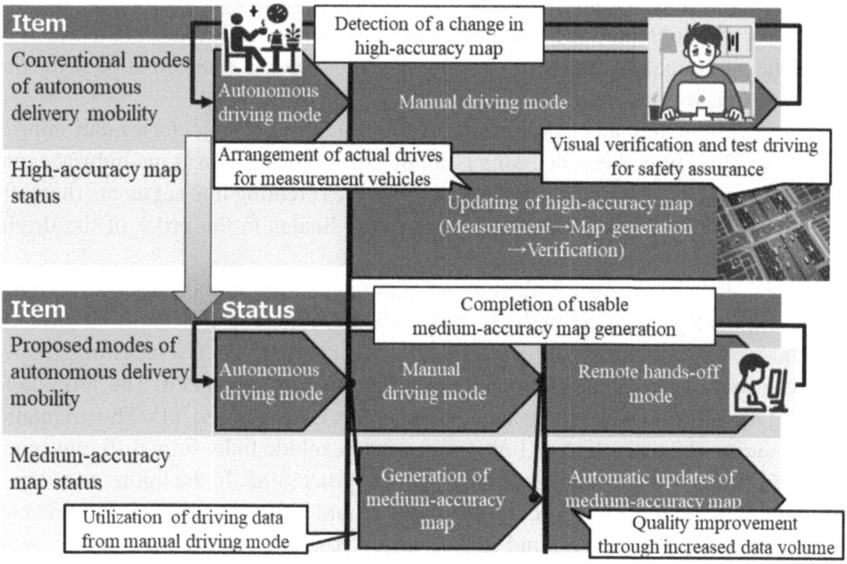

Fig. 1. The operation mode switching image

4 Evaluation of Medium-Accuracy Maps Using GNSS Data from D-GPS Positioning

In this chapter, we evaluate the feasibility of generating and utilizing medium-accuracy maps using trajectories obtained through remote operation of autonomous delivery mobility. Instead of using trajectories from manual driving through remote operation, we generate medium-accuracy maps using GNSS data from D-GPS positioning collected while driving on public roads, and we perform accuracy evaluations. In order to evaluate accuracy, high-accuracy maps generated from MMS survey data are used. The evaluation value is calculated by determining the error between the lane centerlines of the generated medium-accuracy map and the high-accuracy map.

The evaluation data was collected by driving multiple times on Hyogo Prefectural Road 141 Kuroishi-Sanda Line. This area has few tall buildings, is located in the suburbs of a regional city, and does not include tunnels, making it relatively favorable for GNSS reception.

Assuming the remote operation of delivery mobility, GNSS data from D-GPS positioning was collected using an onboard device. Since the same section was driven multiple times, each journey was segmented and assigned an ID to ensure that no single lane was driven multiple times within a single journey. The data consists of five journeys collected over two days, June 12 and 13, 2018, with an average travel time of 28 min and 21 s and an average distance of 15.2 km per journey. The earliest time of data collection was 11:52:30 (hh:mm:ss), and the latest was 17:46:05.

GNSS data was obtained at 1-s intervals, and data deemed to be incorrectly measured, based on the measurement data while stationary and the accuracy information at the time of measurement, was deleted.

It is known that statistical processing of multiple driving trajectories can improve accuracy [8]. Therefore, this processing is applied to utilize the data as medium-accuracy map data. Specifically, the generation method involves creating line segments (hereafter referred to as "links") by connecting position coordinates in the order of the driving trajectories (Fig. 2).

From a point of any given link (link α), a perpendicular line of arbitrary length is drawn, and links that intersect with this perpendicular line are extracted (link group β). Links whose orientations are within a certain threshold are then extracted (link group γ), and the centroid of the intersections within link group γ is calculated. The formula for calculating the centroid when there are n intersections is given in Eq. (1). The orientation judgment during the extraction of link group γ is to exclude links from different roads.

Figure 2 illustrates the concept of the statistical processing. In the figure, the perpendicular line refers to the perpendicular from link α, and links α, δ, and ε, which intersect with this perpendicular, correspond to link group β. Link ε is excluded based on the orientation judgment, so link group γ consists of links α and δ.

The Points $P_1(x_1, y_1), \cdots, P_n(\mathrm{x}_n, \mathrm{y}_\mathrm{n})$ represent intersections.

$$\text{The centroid of these intersections} = \left(\frac{\sum_{i=1}^{n} x_i}{\mathrm{n}}, \frac{\sum_{i=1}^{n} y_i}{n}\right) \tag{1}$$

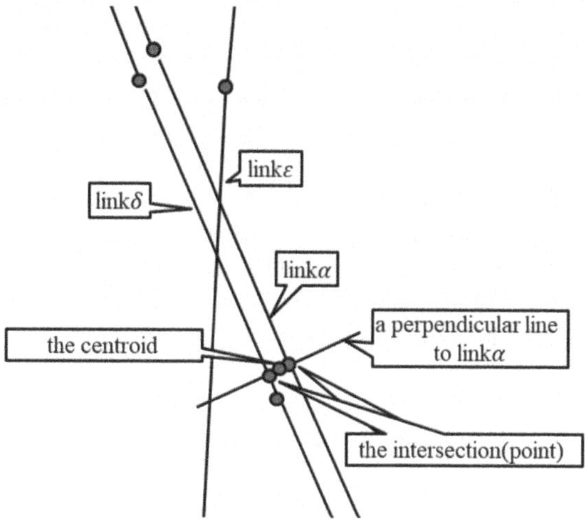

Fig. 2. The statistical processing of multiple driving trajectories

The length of the perpendicular line can impact the accuracy of the integrated driving trajectories. If the perpendicular line is too long, it may integrate trajectories from other lanes, leading to decreased accuracy. Conversely, if it is too short, it may not find enough integration targets, and without a large amount of data, the accuracy improvement may not be achieved. Additionally, the more intersections used to calculate the centroid, the more reliable the driving centerline is considered to be. We compared the accuracy based on the length of the perpendicular line and the number of intersections to determine if a driving centerline at a practical level for real-world operation could be generated using the evaluation data.

Based on the results from [9], the GNSS data collected using D-GPS positioning while driving in the same lane on the highway showed an average deviation of about 0.10 m, a standard deviation of about 0.74 m, and a maximum deviation of about 2.03 m. On the other hand, when calculating the differences with the GNSS data collected while driving in the adjacent lane, the average deviation was about 3.12 m, the standard deviation was about 0.54 m, and the minimum deviation was about 1.04 m. The lane width is 3.5 m, and the measurements were taken in areas with relatively good GNSS reception, excluding tunnel sections.

Using these results as a reference, we generated medium-accuracy maps with two perpendicular distance settings: 1.5 m and 2.0 m for each side. When the perpendicular lines are 1.5 m, statistical processing is performed within the range of 3.0 m, and when the perpendicular lines are 2.0 m, statistical processing is performed within the range of 4.0 m. To evaluate the generated medium-accuracy map, we calculated the errors relative to the lane centerline of a high-accuracy map based on MMS survey data (hereafter referred to as the MMS lane centerline).

The method for calculating the errors is as follows (Fig. 3): From each vehicle position, perpendicular lines 5 m in length extending in both the left and right directions at 90° to the direction of travel are drawn, and the intersections with the MMS lane centerline are determined. If multiple intersections exist, the one with the shortest distance is used.

The distance between each position coordinate and the intersection is calculated as the error (e). If the intersection is on the left side of the direction of travel, the error is considered positive; if it is on the right side, the error is considered negative.

The average (u) is calculated using only the position coordinates where the error could be determined; if no intersection exists, it is treated as non-calculable. Additionally, the standard deviation (s) of the error (e), the root mean square error (*RMSE*), the minimum error (absolute value), and the maximum error (absolute value) were also calculated. The method for calculating the standard deviation (s) is shown in Eq. (2), and the method for calculating the RMSE is shown in Eq. (3). In these equations, (e) refers to the error at each position coordinate.

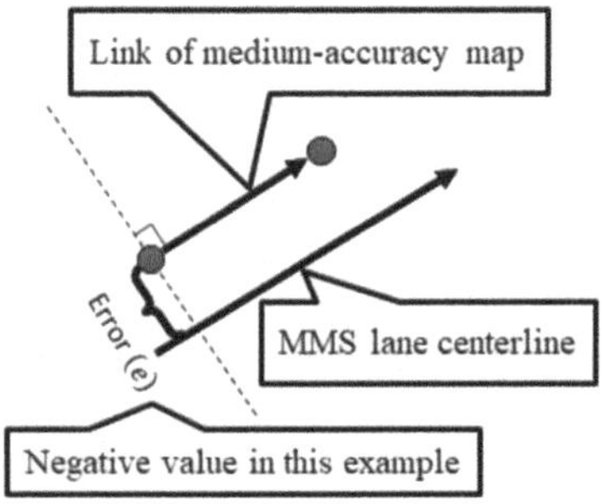

Fig. 3. The method for calculating the errors

$$s = \sqrt{\frac{1}{n}\sum_{i=1}^{n}(e_i - u)^2} \tag{2}$$

$$\mathrm{RMSE} = \sqrt{\frac{1}{n}\sum_{i=1}^{n}{e_i}^2} \tag{3}$$

The results within the range of 3.0 m are shown in Table 1, and the results within the range of 4.0 m are shown in Table 2. ‘Intersect.’ refers to the number of intersection points used to determine the centroid in Fig. 2. ‘Eval.’ indicates the number of points where the error with the MMS lane centerline could be calculated. On the other hand, ‘Err.’ indicates the number of points where the error with the MMS lane centerline could not be calculated. For the generated medium-accuracy map, intersection points for error calculation are generated at intervals of approximately 1m along the link.

Table 1. The evaluation results of the medium-accuracy map generated within the range of 3.0m (u:Average s:Sample standard deviation)

Intersect	Distance(km)	Eval	Err	u (m)	s(m)	RMSE (m)	Min (m)	Max (m)
2	7.7	8002	928	−0.14	0.79	0.80	0.0008	2.13
3	4.05	4195	28	−0.36	0.71	0.80	0.00008	1.63
4	3.67	3796	0	−0.27	0.68	0.73	0.0001	1.62
5	0.81	833	0	−0.57	0.90	1.07	0.0862	1.60
All	16.24	16826	956	−0.25	0.76	0.80	0.00008	2.13

Table 2. The evaluation results of the medium-accuracy map generated within the range of 4.0m (u:Average s:Sample standard deviation).

Intersect	Distance(km)	Eval	Err	u (m)	s(m)	RMSE (m)	Min (m)	Max (m)
2	7.35	7617	961	−0.26	0.54	0.60	0.0002	2.13
3	1.58	1665	36	−0.35	0.60	0.69	0.00002	1.52
4	2.46	2542	3	−0.32	0.71	0.78	0.0006	1.62
5	6.12	6290	0	−0.57	0.58	0.81	0.0001	1.61
All	17.50	18114	1000	−0.39	0.60	0.71	0.00002	2.13

According to the results in Tables 1 and 2, the generated distance within the range of 4.0 m is longer by 17.50 km. Regarding accuracy, since the distance to the nearest MMS lane centerline is calculated, there may be cases where the distance to a different adjacent lane is calculated, resulting in an overestimation of accuracy. Therefore, while it is a reference value, the RMSE showed better accuracy within the range of 4.0 m.

5 Conclusion

In this paper, we propose an operational model for autonomous delivery mobility with remote monitoring using high-accuracy maps. In the proposed model, we utilize medium-accuracy maps generated from driving trajectories obtained through remote manual control as a method to maintain service during high-accuracy map update periods. This approach aims to reduce the workload of monitors and decrease human resource requirements through remote hands-off mode.

In order to verify the feasibility of the proposed operational model, we generated a medium-accuracy map by statistically processing GNSS data obtained from D-GPS positioning of the vehicle. One map was generated from data within a range of 3.0 m and another from data within a range of 4.0 m. As a result of the evaluation, it was confirmed that the medium-accuracy map within the range of 4.0 m generated 17.50 km. Additionally, although the error between the medium-accuracy map and the MMS lane centerline is a reference value, the accuracy within the 4.0 m range was better than that within the range of 3.0 m, with an RMSE of 0.71 m.

In the future, we plan to compare the maps within the ranges of 4.0 m and 3.0 m, extract sections with non-matching shapes, and visually inspect them for accuracy. In this paper, we evaluated the medium-accuracy map within 5 m of the MMS lane centerline. We also plan to extract the medium-accuracy map within the lane width and examine the length and continuity of the extracted sections. Additionally, we intend to investigate the reasons behind the tendency for the measurement data to shift in the negative direction.

Disclosure of Interests. The authors have no competing interests to declare that are relevant to the content of this article.

References

1. Kubo, T.: Local Response to the "Sponge-fication" of Urban Space: Case of a Middle-sized City in Japan: Annals of the Association of Economic Geographers, vol. 67, No.2, pp. 118–124 (2021). (in Japanese)
2. Lemardele', C., Estrada, M., Page's, L., Bachofner, M.: Potentialities of drones and ground autonomous delivery devices for last-mile logistics: transportation research. Part E, logistics and transportation review, vol.149, p. 102325:1–102325:51 (2021)
3. Mathew, N., Smith, S.L., Waslander, S.L.: Planning paths for package delivery in heterogeneous multirobot teams. IEEE Trans. Autom. Sci. Eng. **12**(4), 1298–1308 (2015)
4. Kitagawa, T., Tsuchida, N., Yasui, Y.: High-accuracy map creation technology (special issue: realizing social IoT through dynamic maps and their applications): Syst. Control Inf. **60**(11), 475–480 (2016). (in Japanese)
5. Koyama, H., Shibata, Y.: Development of Dynamic Maps for Autonomous Driving (Special Issue: Realizing Social IoT through Dynamic Maps and Their Applications): Systems, Control and Information, vol. 60, No. 11, pp. 463–468 (2016) (in Japanese)
6. Kojima, Y.: Accurate map generation method using a standard GPS and an in-vehicle camera data—accurate positioning using virtually increased GPS Satellites Taken from Multiple Driving Data: IPSJ J. **54**(1), 103–115 (2013). (in Japanese)
7. Yamauchi, H.: A Road Map Making Probe System by Integration of Road Shapes with Roadside Hue Information: IPSJ J. **52**(1), 257–268 (2011). (in Japanese)
8. Massow, K., et al.: Deriving HD maps for highly automated driving from vehicular probe data. In: 2016 IEEE 19th International Conference on Intelligent Transportation Systems (ITSC), pp. 1745–1752 (2016)
9. Toma, E., Fujiwara, M., Kamei, K., Joe, K.: Accuracy Verification of Lane Center Lines Generation System According to Driving Lane Matching Judgment of In-vehicle Camera Images: Electronics, Information and Systems Institute of Electrical Engineers of Japan (Web), Vol. 2023, pp. ROMBUNNO.OS1-2-4 (WEB ONLY) (2023) (in Japanese)

Correction Method for Text Errors in Early-Modern Japanese Books Using BERT

Hiyori Kanetaka[1(✉)], Miho Chiyonobu[2], Yuki Takemoto[3], Yu Ishikawa[4], and Masami Takata[5]

[1] Graduate School of Humanities and Sciences, Nara Women's University, Nara 630-8506, Nara, Japan
kanetaka-hiyori0203@lics.nara-wu.ac.jp

[2] Data Science and AI Innovation Research Promotion Center, Shiga University, Hikone 522-8522, Shiga, Japan
chiyonobu-miho@biwako.shiga-u.ac.jp

[3] College of Information Science and Engineering, Ritsumeikan University, Osaka 530-0018, Osaka, Japan
y-tkmt@fc.ritsumei.ac.jp

[4] Faculty of Data Science, Kyoto Women's University, Kyoto 605-8501, Kyoto, Japan
ishikaway@kyoto-wu.ac.jp

[5] Division of Human Life and Environmental Sciences, Research Group of Information and Communication Technology for Life, Nara Women's University, Nara 630-8506, Nara, Japan
takata@ics.nara-wu.ac.jp

Abstract. In recent years, the digitization of books has been promoted to improve accessibility and convenience. However, early-modern Japanese books published from the Meiji to early Showa periods (1868–1935) differ in many ways from modern publications. While research on character recognition systems specialized for early-modern books has progressed, recognition errors still occur. In this paper, we propose a method for detecting and correcting misrecognized characters in early-modern Japanese books. Our method employs Bidirectional Encoder Representations from Transformers (BERT). The experimental results show that in 90.6% of the detected misrecognition, the top five correction candidates contain the correct character.

Keywords: Error Correction · Early-Modern Book · Character Recognition · BERT

1 Introduction

It is difficult to prevent deterioration of printed materials over time. In addition, searching for and accessing the information from them requires considerable time and effort. Therefore, printed materials should be digitized. The primary method of digitization is text conversion using Optical Character Recognition (OCR) software. OCR is a technology that reads printed or handwritten text from image data and converts it into digital text. However, most existing OCR systems are designed for standardized character sets used

H. R. Arabnia et al. (Eds.): CSCE 2025, CCIS 2932, pp. 417–426, 2026.
https://doi.org/10.1007/978-3-032-22193-3_32

in modern printed books. Hence, it is difficult to accurately recognize texts from books published before character sets had been standardized as they often contain inconsistent or irregular character shapes.

Some characters used in early-modern Japanese books are difficult to recognize using existing OCR systems. Early-modern Japanese books have been published from the Meiji to early Showa periods (1868–1935). Unlike modern books, early-modern Japanese publications do not follow standardized character sets or typographical conventions. In addition, fonts and character shapes vary by publisher and year of publication. These factors make it difficult to recognize early-modern characters correctly with existing OCRs [1]. Consequently, OCRs specialized for early-modern books, which use CNN [2], have been developed [3, 4]. The National Diet Library of Japan developed an OCR processing program that extracts text data from scanned images of early-modern Japanese books [3]. The character recognition accuracy has been improving year by year, achieving more than 90% [5]. With the training data consisting of manually collected early-modern characters, and modern printed characters, the recognition rate of OCR has achieved approximately 97% [4].

Despite these advancements, the recognition accuracy is not yet perfect; several misrecognized characters are still found per 100 characters. Given the vast number of early-modern Japanese books, it is manually detecting and correcting all such recognition errors is both time-consuming and labor-intensive. Although research has been conducted to diversify and increase training data to further improve recognition rates [6, 7], the recognition accuracy remains imperfect.

In this paper, we detect and correct misrecognized characters in text data recognized from early-modern Japanese books. For this purpose, we use Bidirectional Encoder Representations from Transformers (BERT). This method consists of three stages: erroneous sentence detection, recognition error detection, and correction of those words. For the detection of erroneous sentences, we use a classifier fine-tuned from a pre-trained BERT model. The fine-tuning is performed using both correct and erroneous sentences from early-modern books. Error detection is carried out by matching words in the input sentences with those found in the training data. For correcting misrecognitions, the words containing the detected errors are replaced with special [MASK] tokens, and the correct words are predicted using Masked Language Modeling (MLM) task of BERT.

2 Related Work

2.1 Error Correction After OCR in Cursive Handwriting

Yasin et al. use Transformer [9]-based Neural Machine Translation (NMT) for sentence -by-sentence correction of recognition errors in OCR output [10]. NMT is a machine translation method using neural networks. In [10], the translation method of NMT is applied to the conversion of erroneous sentences to correct ones. The target of the correction is the OCR output of handwritten Urdu documents in cursive script, a language mainly spoken in Pakistan and India. The training and evaluation data used are subtitles from an Urdu news channel and text data collected from the news channel's Twitter/X account. The system creates erroneous sentences from the collected text data by mimicking recognition errors made by OCR. After removing special characters and duplicate sentences, characters are randomly inserted, deleted, and replaced. The process of creating erroneous sentences for each sentence is performed nine times, creating a large amount of training data. In training, the encoder of Transformer receives the erroneous sentence and the decoder receives the correct sentence paired with the erroneous sentence. Then, the model is able to output the correct sentence from the erroneous sentence. The performance is evaluated by calculating the reduction in Levenshtein distance between the corrected and the original correct sentence, compared to the distance between the erroneous and the correct sentence. The experimental results report that the distance between the corrected and original correct sentences reduces to 56.92%.

2.2 Correcting English Prepositional Errors Using BERT

Nakatani et al. proposed a method for detecting and correcting prepositional errors in English sentences using Masked Language Model (MLM) task [11] of BERT. The target error types include substitution, omission, and insertion of prepositions.

Substitution errors occur when an incorrect preposition is used in place of the correct one. To avoid the substitution errors, the input sentence is first parsed for parts of speech. Prepositions in the sentence are then replaced with [MASK], except when the word following "to" is in its base verb form. MLM task of BERT is used to predict the most likely replacements based on contextual probabilities.

Omission errors are cases where necessary preposition is missing. These are handled by inserting [MASK] immediately before each word in the input sentence following part-of-speech tagging and computing the likelihood of a preposition appearing at that position. Candidate corrections are generated similarly to substitution errors. In this step, [MASK] is not inserted immediately before or after certain word types, such as infinitive "to", base verbs, auxiliary verbs, symbols, interjections, and determiners.

Insertion errors are the presence of unnecessary prepositions. These are corrected by masking the suspect preposition and evaluating whether removing improves sentence plausibility. To delete the preposition, no candidate word is inserted in its place.

Error detection performance is evaluated using the F1 score; the harmonic mean of precision and recall. Correction performance is assessed based on the rate of successful corrections.

Experimental results show that substitution error detection achieves an F1 score of 0.908 and a correction success rate of 87.7%. Omission error detection yields an F1 score of 0.821 and a correction success rate of 92.5%. For insertion errors, the F1 score is 0.797.

3 Proposed Method

In this section, we propose a method for detecting and correcting recognition error in early-modern books after character recognition. The proposed method is divided into three stages: erroneous sentence detection, recognition error detection, and recognition error correction. The flow of the proposed method is shown in Fig. 1. Chinese character misrecognition is an important problem that needs to be solved because misrecognition is common low-frequency characters in the training data and for characters that are similar in shape. Therefore, the purpose of this paper is to detect and correct misrecognized Chinese characters.

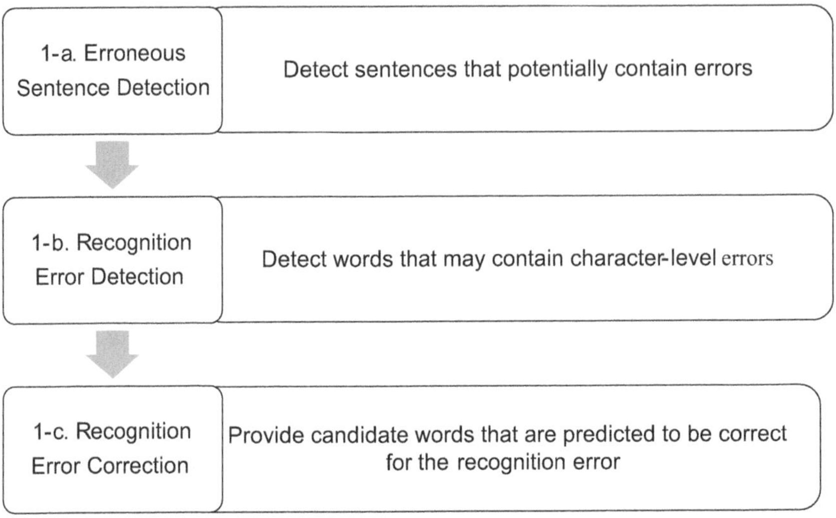

Fig. 1. Flow of the proposed method

Section 3.1 describes the method for detecting erroneous sentences in step1-a and recognition errors in step 1-b, and Sect. 3.2 describes the method for correcting recognition errors in step 1-c.

3.1 Method for Detecting Erroneous Sentences and Recognition Errors

This section describes the erroneous sentence detection in step 1-a. In step 1-a, sentences containing misrecognitions caused by OCR are detected. The detection is performed using a classifier with a fine-tuned pre-trained model of BERT. A pre-trained BERT model specialized for early-modern books does not currently exist; therefore, a new model is constructed. BERT has two pre-training tasks: the MLM task, which predicts original tokens from masked tokens [MASK] based on their context, and the Next Sentence Prediction (NSP) task, which determines whether two given sentences are consecutive or not. The MLM task has two positive points as follows. First, the purpose of this research is to detect and correct recognition errors. Second, it is crucial for accurate word-level prediction. Therefore, the MLM task is employed in the proposed method. The model is trained using the Trainer module from the Transformers library. Unlabeled text data extracted from early-modern Japanese books are used as training data. For tokenization in the MLM task, SentencePiece [12] is employed. The tokenizer is trained on the same dataset and converts input sentences into token sequences represented by numeric IDs suitable for model input. Through the process, a domain-specific pre-trained model is constructed.

Fine tuning uses labeled data in which correct and erroneous sentences are shuffled. A correct sentence has no recognition errors, while an erroneous sentence contains one or more recognition errors. To create labeled data, a correct sentence is used only if it consists of three or more words after tokenization. The contextual representation of the data is important when using BERT to detect erroneous sentences based on contextual information. Therefore, extremely short sentences are excluded from the fine-tuning dataset.

The procedure for generating erroneous sentences is shown in Fig. 2. In step 2-a, all Chinese characters contained in the dataset are collected and stored in a list one by one. In step 2-b, each sentence is segmented into words. Sentences that consist of three or more words and contain at least one *jukugo* are retained. In Japanese, a *jukugo* refers to a word composed of two or more Chinese characters that together form a single meaning. In step 2-c, one *jukugo* is selected from the retained sentences, and one *jukugo* is randomly chosen from the *jukugo* extracted in step 2-b. Finally, in step 2-d, the second or later characters of the selected *jukugo* are randomly replaced with Chinese characters sampled from the list obtained in step 2-a. Erroneous sentences are generated by embedding the recognition errors generated through steps 2-a to 2-d into the original sentence.

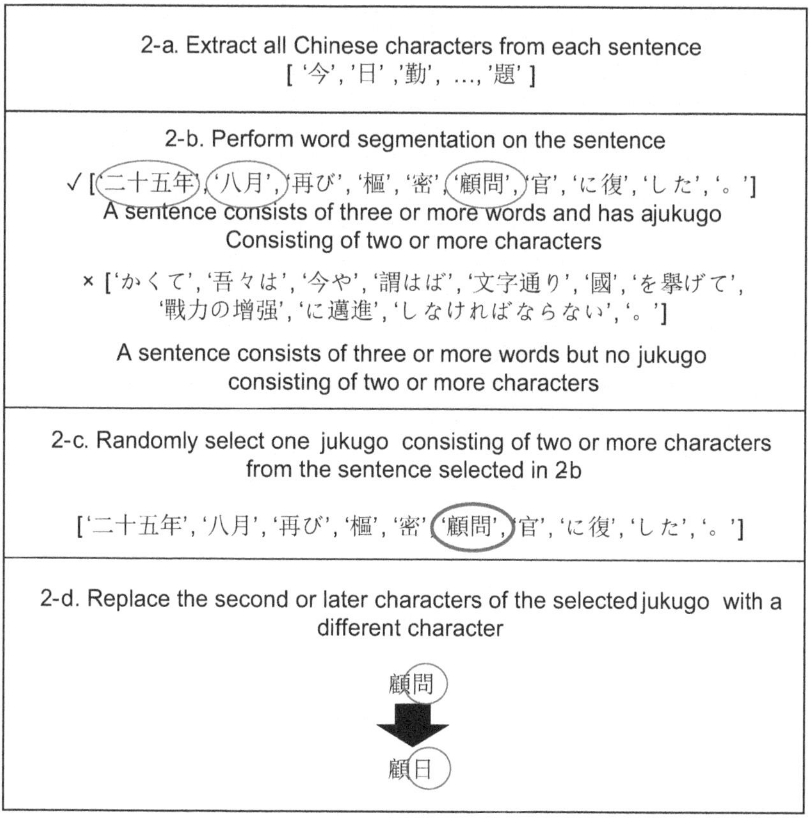

Fig. 2. Procedure for generating erroneous sentences

In the error detection process of step 1-b, words containing recognition errors are extracted. The recognition errors targeted for detection in this paper are limited to character substitution errors, where one Chinese character is mistakenly replaced by another Chinese character. A *jukugo* corpus is used for the detection process. The corpus is created by extracting *jukugo* and words formed by consecutive Chinese characters from the data used in pre-training, after processing with SentencePiece. In the erroneous sentence detection, the sentences identified as containing errors are segmented into words. *Jukugo* consisting of two or more Chinese characters, as well as words formed by connecting consecutive Chinese characters, are compared with the *jukugo* corpus. Words not in the *jukugo* corpus are detected as recognition errors and replaced with the [MASK] token.

3.2 Method for Correcting Recognition Errors

In step 1-c, recognition error correction is performed by generating a list of candidate words predicted to be correct for each detected error. The correction process combines the BERT pre-trained model and its MLM task, which is constructed in Sect. 3.1, with filtering based on recognition errors. The OCR accuracy for early-modern books has achieved an F-score of over 0.9 [3, 4]. Therefore, consecutive misrecognitions rarely occur within a single *jukugo*. Hence, from the predicted words obtained from the MLM task, words that start or end with the same character as the erroneous character in the detected *jukugo* are filtered. Thus, the approach is expected to provide more appropriate correction candidates. Figure 3 outlines the flow of the process, while Fig. 4 provides an example of an erroneous sentence. Sentence in Fig. 4 means, "Today, Japan is also in a period of a new cultural formation." The part enclosed in red is an erroneous *jukugo*, and its correct *jukugo* are written below. In step 3-a, the first and last characters of the erroneous *jukugo* are obtained. In step 3-b, the erroneous part is replaced with the [MASK] token. In step 3-c, the MLM task predicts words that could fill the [MASK] token, ranked by their probability. In step 3-d, from the predicted words, those that begin with the same first character or end with the same last character as that of the erroneous *jukugo* are selected. Finally, as shown in step 3-e, the top n candidates obtained are used as the correction candidates.

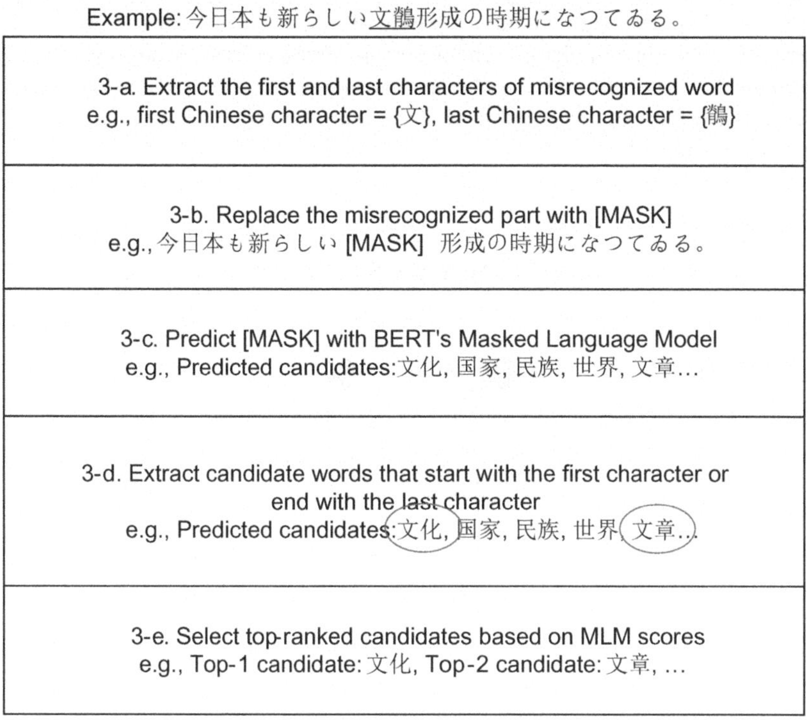

Fig. 3. Method for recognition error correction

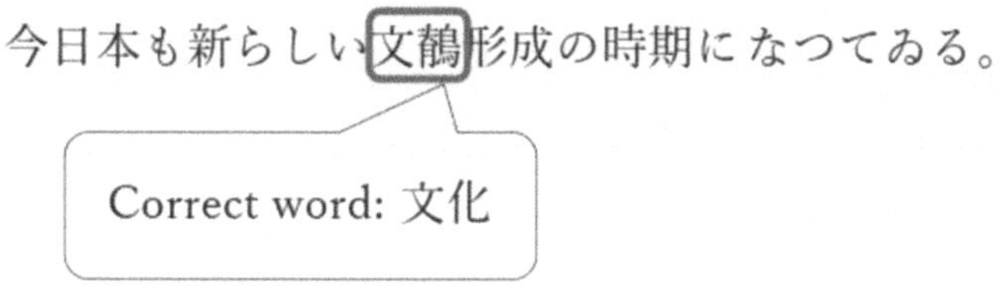

Fig. 4. The example of an erroneous sentence

4 Experiment

In this section, experiments on recognition error detection and correction for early-modern books are conducted to evaluate the effectiveness of the proposed method. Section 4.1 describes the experimental environment, and Sect. 4.2 presents the experimental results.

4.1 Experimental Environment

The dataset consists of digital texts of early-modern Japanese books generated by NDLOCR and made publicly available through the Next Digital Library of the National

Diet Library [13]. The digital data are provided in a plain text format, with one line per page. The data contain illegible characters and extraneous symbols as shown Fig. 5. Therefore, extraneous symbols and character strings are first removed. Then, sentences containing page numbers or illegible characters are excluded. Consequently, 282,893 sentences are obtained.

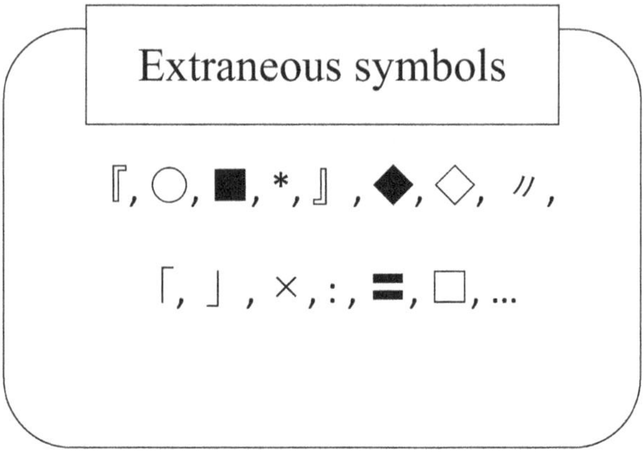

Fig. 5. The example of extraneous symbols

As the pre-trained model used for recognition error correction, 280,000 sentences are selected from the collected dataset, and 279,997 sentences are used for training after removing those that are similar to the evaluation data.

The evaluation data for recognition error correction consists of 500 erroneous sentences generated by using the method described in Sect. 3.1, based on 2,893 sentences not used in the training data.

The experimental environment is shown as follows:

- OS: Ubuntu 20.04.6 LTS
- GPU: NVIDIA GeForce RTX 4090
- CUDA: CUDA 10.1
- Libraries

  Torch 2.3.1
  Transformers 4.40.1

4.2 Results and Discussion

In the experiment, to validate the effectiveness of the recognition error correction in the proposed method, the results of the proposed method (MLM with filtering) are compared with the results of the MLM only method. In this paper, recognition error correction presents a list of candidate words predicted to be correct for the erroneous parts. In the experiment, the top five word candidates for the erroneous parts are output as correction candidates. Accuracy is the probability that the correct word is included among the top-*n* candidates.

The results of the experiment are shown in Table 1. For evaluation, a prediction is considered correct if the correct word is present within the top five candidates. In Table 1, the method combining the MLM task and filtering significantly outperforms the MLM-only method in terms of accuracy. In Table 1, the method combining the MLM task and filtering significantly outperforms the MLM-only method in terms of accuracy. It can be attributed to the fact that predictions based solely on context may allow for multiple words that fit the meaning of the sentence. In other words, multiple words might be correctly inferred from the context, and the model may return a word that is not the original correct word but still semantically appropriate as a correction candidate. As a result, it may not be recognized as correct by the evaluation metrics, limiting the improvement in accuracy. On the other hand, the proposed method filters the prediction candidates from the MLM task under the assumption that the first and last characters of the *jukugo* containing recognition errors are correct. The proposed method allows for a more appropriate narrowing down of the predicted vocabulary, resulting in a significant improvement in accuracy.

Table 1. The results of the recognition error correction

Method	Accuracy
MLM + Filtered	90.6%
MLM	34.8%

Even with the proposed method, there are two types of cases where accurate prediction remains difficult. The first case occurs when there are many *jukugo* that share common Chinese characters and have similar meanings. In such situations, it becomes difficult for the model to distinguish between the similar *jukugo*, resulting in closely competing scores in the MLM task. As a result, the correct *jukugo* may not appear within the top five candidates. The second case involves *jukugo* that are difficult to predict from context, such as proper nouns. This is likely because the occurrence of proper nouns in the training data is extremely low. That prevents the correct word from being generated as a candidate during the MLM task. In both cases, erroneous candidates tend to remain in the top ranks even when using the proposed method. The issues could potentially be addressed by expanding the training data or fine-tuning the model.

Therefore, the proposed method is considered effective, achieving a correction accuracy of 90.6% for correcting recognition errors.

5 Conclusion

In this paper, we propose a method for detecting and correcting recognition errors in early-modern Japanese books following character recognition using BERT. Existing OCR systems do not achieve sufficient accuracy for early-modern Japanese texts. While OCR models specialized for such texts have been proposed, the recognition accuracy remains imperfect. Therefore, it is necessary to detect and correct recognition errors in the text data after character recognition. The proposed method consists of erroneous sentence detection, recognition error detection, and recognition error correction. In the correction stage, candidate corrections are generated using the MLM task of BERT, followed by a filtering process. Base on experimental results, the proposed method achieves a correction accuracy of 90.6%.

Furthermore, although our method leverages the unique structure of Japanese *jukugo*, we believe it could also be applied to other languages with similar characteristics, such as Chinese.

References

1. Ashida, N., Takata, M., Sasaki A., Kamo, H., Nide, N., Joe, K.: Construction of a paper classification system using SVM. In: Proceedings of the 2007 International Conference on Parallel and Distributed Processing Technologies and Applications (PDPTA'07), vol. 2, pp. 759–765 (2007)
2. LeCun, Y., Bottou, L., Bengio, Y., Haffiner, P.: Gradient-based learning applied to document recognition, Proc. Inst. Electr. Electron. Eng. **86**(11), 2278–2324 (1998)
3. NDLOCR. https://github.com/ndl-lab/ndlocr_cli. Accessed 19 Apr 2025
4. Yasunami, S., Koiso, N., Takemoto, Y., Ishikawa, Y., Takata, M., Joe, K.: Applying CNNs to early-modern printed Japanese character recognition. In: Proceedings of the 2019 International Conference on Parallel and Distributed Processing Technologies and Applications (PDPTA'19), pp. 189–195 (2019)
5. OCR text conversion of digitized materials in FY2021. https://lab.ndl.go.jp/data_set/ocr_en/r3_text. Accessed 21 Apr 2025
6. Kosaka, K., Awazu, T., Ishikawa, Y., Takata, M. and Joe, K.: An effective and interactive training data collection method for early-modern Japanese printed character recognition. In: Proceedings of the 2015 International Conference on Parallel and Distributed Processing Techniques and Applications (PDPTA'15) 2, pp. 276–282 (2015)
7. Fujisaki, N., Ishikawa, Y., Takata, M., Joe, K.: Crawling low appearance frequency character images for early-modern Japanese printed character recognition. Advances in Parallel & Distributed Processing, and Applications, pp. 683–695 (2021)
8. Devlin, J., Chang, M.-W., Lee, K., Toutanova, K.: BERT: Pre-training of Deep Bidirectional Transformers for Language Understanding, arXiv preprint arXiv:1810.04805 (2018)
9. Vaswani, A., et al.: Attention Is All You Need. In: Advances in Neural Information Processing Systems 30, pp. 5998–6008 (2017)
10. Yasin, N., Siddiqi I., Moetesum, M., Rauf, S., A.: Transformer-Based Neural Machine Translation for Post-OCR Error Correction in Cursive Text, Document Analysis and Recognition-ICDAR 2023 Workshops, 14194, pp. 80–93 (2023)
11. Nakatani, S., Uwano, S., Ohta, M.: A method of English prepositional error correction support by BERT, DEIM2022. Session **H41–5**, 18–24 (2022). (In Japanese)
12. SentencePiece. https://github.com/google/sentencepiece. Accessed 19 Apr 2025
13. Next Digital Library. https://lab.ndl.go.jp/dl. Accessed 21 Apr 2025

Efficient Implementation of the QR Algorithm for Complex Matrices

Miho Chiyonobu[1(✉)], Masami Takata[2], Kinji Kimura[3], and Yoshimasa Nakamura[4]

[1] Shiga University, Shiga, Japan
miho-chiyonobu@biwako.shiga-u.ac.jp
[2] Research Group of Information and Communication Technology for Life, Nara Women's University, Nara, Japan
takata@ics.nara-wu.ac.jp
[3] Faculty of Engineering, University of Fukui, Fukui, Japan
kkimur@u-fukui.ac.jp
[4] Faculty of Data Science, Osaka Seikei University, Osaka, Japan
nakamura-yo@osaka-seikei.ac.jp

Abstract. The QR algorithm is a method for calculating singular values and vectors, offering a faster and more efficient way to approximate singular values. Early implementations of the QR algorithm for Singular Value Decomposition (SVD) were constrained by past computing systems with small amounts of memory, requiring a repetitive series of complex matrix multiplications that was time–consuming, especially for large and complex matrices. By maximizing modern computational capabilities, this study proposes an efficient implementation of the QR algorithm that uses real matrix multiplication to the maximum extent for the SVD of complex matrices. In this paper, we compare the computation time and accuracy between the conventional method and our proposed method.

Keywords: Singular Value Decomposition · QR Algorithm · Complex matrices

1 Introduction

In numerical analysis, as datasets become more complex and grow in dimensionally, the challenges associated with high–dimensional data have become increasingly obvious. These challenges include overfitting, increased computation time and decreased computation accuracy. Addressing these issues requires dimensionality reduction techniques that preserve the structure and information within the data.

The Singular Value Decomposition (SVD) is a fundamental mathematical tool in numerical linear algebra that is widely used in various algorithms, including dimensionality reduction, solutions to least squares problems and machine learning applications. By decomposing a matrix into singular values and singular

H. R. Arabnia et al. (Eds.): CSCE 2025, CCIS 2932, pp. 427–439, 2026.
https://doi.org/10.1007/978-3-032-22193-3_33

vectors, SVD provides an excellent structure for analyzing and simplifying high-dimensional data. For example, in principal component analysis (PCA), SVD enables the identification of principal components, allowing for efficient data representation and processing. However, the efficient computation of SVD, particularly for large and complex matrices, faces numerical difficulties and remains a critical area of research in numerical linear algebra.

The QR algorithm [3–7] s an iterative method used to compute singular values and vectors of a matrix in an alternative manner. It has been implemented for SVD and has proven to be a faster method for SVD computation. Its stability and efficiency make it suitable for handling the computational complexities of SVD. However, earlier computing systems were constrained by limited memory and processing power, necessitating the use of algorithms that minimized resource usage. Early methods were designed to perform SVD with complex matrix multiplication, which significantly increased the computation time. These challenges are especially obvious for large complex matrices.

With advancements in modern computing systems, larger memory capacities and faster processing speeds have enabled the optimization of computations, allowing for faster and more accurate calculations.

This paper proposes an efficient implementation of the QR algorithm for complex matrices in computing SVD. By maximizing modern computational capabilities, using real matrix multiplication to the maximum extent for the SVD of complex matrices, the proposed method improves both the efficiency and accuracy of SVD computations.

2 The Singular Value Decomposition

SVD is among the most important matrix factorizations, especially for applications in data science. SVD unlocks the solution to a variety of least squares/regression problems, and is also a fundamental tool for dimension reduction (including PCA). SVD is not just a practical tool; it also enables deep theoretical insights. This section introduces SVD and describes its applications.

2.1 Formal Definition

Let m and n be arbitrary; we do not require $m \geq n$. Given that $A \in \mathbb{C}^{m\times n}$ is not necessarily of full rank, the SVD of A is a factorization $A = U\Sigma V^*$ where $U \in \mathbb{C}^{m\times n}$ is unitary, $V \in \mathbb{C}^{n\times n}$ is unitary, and $\Sigma \in \mathbb{R}^{n\times n}$ is diagonal. In addition, it is assumed that the diagonal entries of σ_j are nonnegative and in decreasing order; that is $\sigma_1 \geq \sigma_2 \geq \cdots \geq \sigma_p \geq 0$, where $p = \min(m, n)$.

2.2 Derivation of the Singular Value Decomposition: Full Rank Case

We seek to derive the SVD of a general rectangular matrix. To simplify the initial derivation, assume that $A \in \mathbb{C}^{m\times n}$ with $m \geq n$ and that all the columns of A

are linearly independent. This last condition implies that $rank(A)$ is as large as possible, $\text{rank}(A) = n$, so the dimension of the column space is $n : \dim(\mathcal{R}(A)) = n$.

For reduced SVD, full-rank A, suppose that $A \in \mathbb{C}^{m\times n}$ has $\text{rank}(A) = n$, with $m \geq n$. Then we can write $A = U\Sigma V^*$, where the columns of $U \in \mathbb{C}^{m\times n}$ and $V \in \mathbb{C}^{n\times n}$ are orthogonal in unitary space, $U^*U = I \in \mathbb{C}^{n\times n}, V^*V = I \in \mathbb{C}^{n\times n}$, and $\Sigma \in \mathbb{R}^{n\times n}$ is zero everywhere except for entries on the main diagonal.

2.3 The Dyadic Form of the SVD

We are now prepared to develop an analog for the full–rank rectangular matrices. Consider the reduced SVD, $A = U\Sigma V^*$, and multiply $U\Sigma$ to obtain

$$\begin{bmatrix} | & | & & | \\ \boldsymbol{u}_1 & \boldsymbol{u}_2 & \dots & \boldsymbol{u}_n \\ | & | & & | \end{bmatrix} \begin{bmatrix} \sigma_1 & & & \\ & \sigma_2 & & \\ & & \ddots & \\ & & & \sigma_n \end{bmatrix} = \begin{bmatrix} | & | & & | \\ \sigma_1\boldsymbol{u} & \sigma_2\boldsymbol{u}_2 & \dots & \sigma_n\boldsymbol{u}_n \\ | & | & & | \end{bmatrix}.$$

Further, we can write $A = (U\Sigma)V^*$ as

$$\begin{bmatrix} | & | & & | \\ \sigma_1\boldsymbol{u}_1 & \sigma_1\boldsymbol{u}_2 & \dots & \sigma_n\boldsymbol{u}_n \\ | & | & & | \end{bmatrix} \begin{bmatrix} - & \boldsymbol{v}_1^* & - \\ - & \boldsymbol{v}_2^* & - \\ & \vdots & \\ - & \boldsymbol{v}_n^* & - \end{bmatrix} = \sum_{j=1}^{n} \sigma_j \boldsymbol{u}_j \boldsymbol{v}_j^*.$$

Now for any matrix $A \in \mathbb{C}^{m\times n}$ with $m \geq n$ and linearly independent columns we can write A as the weighted sum of outer products. Suppose that $A \in \mathbb{C}^{m\times n}$ has $\text{rank}(A) = n$ with $m > n$. Then we can write

$$A = \sum_{j=1}^{n} \sigma_j \boldsymbol{u}_j \boldsymbol{v}_j^*, \tag{1}$$

where the columns $\boldsymbol{u}_1, ..., \boldsymbol{u}_n \in \mathbb{C}^m$ are orthonormal and $\boldsymbol{v}_1, ..., \boldsymbol{v}_n \in \mathbb{C}^n$ are orthonormal, and $\sigma_1 \geq \sigma_2 \geq \cdots \geq \sigma_n$. This expression (1) is called the dyadic form of the SVD. The matrices $\boldsymbol{u}_j\boldsymbol{v}_j^* \in \mathbb{C}^{m\times n}$ are not generally projectors, but they have similar interpretations. When computing the action of A upon a vector $\boldsymbol{x} \in \mathbb{C}^n$,

$$A\boldsymbol{x} = \left(\sum_{j=1}^{n} \sigma_j \boldsymbol{u}_j \boldsymbol{v}_j^* \right) \boldsymbol{x} = \sum_{j=1}^{n} \sigma_j (\boldsymbol{v}_j^* \boldsymbol{x}) \boldsymbol{u}_j.$$

the scalars $\boldsymbol{v}_j^*\boldsymbol{x}$ are the coefficients of the best approximation to $\boldsymbol{x}$ from $\text{span}(\boldsymbol{v}_j)$. Now, this coefficient is multiplied against the left singular vector $\boldsymbol{u}_j$ and scaled by the singular value σ_j.

2.4 The Full SVD

We still require $A \in \mathbb{C}^{m \times m}$ to be a rectangular matrix with $m \geq n$ and linearly independent columns. In the reduced SVD, the matrix $U \in \mathbb{C}^{m \times n}$ had orthonormal columns, so $U^*U = I$ but if $m > n$ the columns of U cannot form an orthonormal basis for $\mathbb{C}^m$, so $UU^* \neq I$.

Here, we seek to augment the matrix $U \in \mathbb{C}^{m \times n}$ with $m - n$ additional column vectors, to give a full set of m orthonormal vectors in $\mathbb{C}^m$. To find these extra vectors: For $j = n + 1, ..., m$, pick

$$\boldsymbol{u}_j \perp \text{span } \boldsymbol{u}_1, ..., \boldsymbol{u}_{j-1},$$

with $\boldsymbol{u}_j^* \boldsymbol{u}_j = 1$. Then define

$$\tilde{U} = \begin{bmatrix} | & & | & | & & | \\ \boldsymbol{u}_1 & \dots & \boldsymbol{u}_n & \boldsymbol{u}_{n+1} & \dots & \boldsymbol{u}_m \\ | & & | & | & & | \end{bmatrix} \in \mathbb{C}^{m \times m}.$$

We have constructed $\boldsymbol{u}_1, \dots, \boldsymbol{u}_m$ to be orthonormal vectors, so $\tilde{U}^*\tilde{U} = I$. As $\tilde{U} \in \mathbb{C}^{m \times m}$, this orthogonality also implies $\tilde{U}^{-1} = \tilde{U}^*$.

We are now ready to replace the rectangular matrix $U \in \mathbb{C}^{m \times n}$ in the reduced SVD with the square matrix $\tilde{U} \in \mathbb{C}^{m \times n}$ in the reduced SVD. To do so, we also need to replace $\Sigma \in \mathbb{R}^{n \times n}$ with some $\tilde{\Sigma} \in \mathbb{R}^{m \times n}$ such that $U\Sigma = \tilde{U}\tilde{\Sigma}$. The simplest approach is to obtain $\tilde{\Sigma}$ by appending zeros to the end of Σ, thus ensuring that there is no contribution when the new entries of $\tilde{U}$ multiply against the new entries of $\tilde{\Sigma}$:

$$\tilde{\Sigma} = \begin{bmatrix} \Sigma \\ 0 \end{bmatrix} \in \mathbb{R}^{m \times n}.$$

Finally, we arrive at the main result, full SVD, for the case where $\text{rank}(A) = n$.

For full SVD, full-rank A, suppose that $A \in \mathbb{C}^{m \times n}$ has $\text{rank}(A) = n$, with $m \geq n$. Then we can write $A = \tilde{U}\tilde{\Sigma}V^*$ where the columns of $\tilde{U} \in \mathbb{C}^{m \times m}$ and $V \in \mathbb{C}^{n \times n}$ are orthonormal, $\tilde{U}^*\tilde{U} = I \in \mathbb{C}^{m \times m}, \tilde{V}^*\tilde{V} = I \in \mathbb{C}^{n \times n}$, and $\tilde{\Sigma} \in \mathbb{R}^{m \times n}$ is zero everywhere except for entries on the main diagonal.

3 Matrix Bidiagonalization

Matrices can be bidiagonalized by applying complex Householder reflections to the left and right.

First, by using complex Householder reflections, we find the QR decomposition of A:

$$A = QR, Q \in \mathbb{C}^{m \times n}, R \in \mathbb{C}^{n \times n}.$$

Next, we perform bidiagonalization on the complex upper triangular matrix R using the complex Householder Reflection.

Assume that the matrix has been bidiagonalized up to the $k-1$–th step:

$$R^{(k-1)} \equiv \begin{bmatrix} d_1 & f_1 & & & & \\ & \ddots & \ddots & & & \\ & & d_{k-1} & f_{k-1} & & \\ & & & r_{kk}^{(k-1)} & \cdots & r_{kn}^{(k-1)} \\ & & & \vdots & \ddots & \vdots \\ & & & r_{nk}^{(k-1)} & \cdots & r_{nn}^{(k-1)} \end{bmatrix}.$$

Note that $R^{(0)} \equiv R$. Next, we proceed with bidiagonalization for the k–th step. Define $\boldsymbol{w}_k^L$ as

$$\boldsymbol{w}_k^L \equiv \begin{bmatrix} 0 \\ \vdots \\ 0 \\ r_{kk}^{(k-1)} - d_k \\ r_{k+1,k}^{(k-1)} \\ \vdots \\ r_{nk}^{(k-1)} \end{bmatrix} \in \mathbb{C}^n, d_k \equiv \pm\sqrt{\sum_{i=k}^{n} \left| r_{ik}^{(k-1)} \right|^2}.$$

Multiply $R^{(k-1)}$ on the right side of matrix H_k^L,

$$H_k^L \equiv I_n - \frac{1}{d_k\left(d_k - \frac{r_{kk}^{(k-1)} + \left(r_{kk}^{(k-1)}\right)^*}{2}\right)} \boldsymbol{w}_k^L \left(\boldsymbol{w}_k^L\right)^* \in \mathbb{C}^{n\times n}. \tag{2}$$

d_k is reversed from the sign $r_{kk}^{(k-1)}$ to avoid loss of precision due to digit cancellation. We then obtain

$$H_k^L R^{(k-1)} = \begin{bmatrix} d_1 & f_1 & & & & \\ & \ddots & \ddots & & & \\ & & d_{k-1} & f_{k-1} & & \\ & & & d_k & \hat{r}_{k,k+1}^{(k-1)} & \cdots & \hat{r}_{kn}^{(k-1)} \\ & & & & \vdots & \ddots & \vdots \\ & & & & \hat{r}_{n,k+1}^{(k-1)} & \cdots & \hat{r}_{k,k+1}^{(k-1)} \end{bmatrix}.$$

Next, we define w_k^R as

$$\boldsymbol{w}_k^R \equiv \begin{bmatrix} 0 \\ \vdots \\ 0 \\ \hat{r}_{k,k+1}^{(k-1)} - f_k \\ \hat{r}_{k,k+2}^{(k-1)} \\ \vdots \\ \hat{r}_{kn}^{(k-1)} \end{bmatrix} \in \mathbb{C}^n, f_k \equiv \pm \sqrt{\sum_{j=k+1}^{n} \left| \hat{r}_{kj}^{(k-1)} \right|^2}.$$

Multiplying H_k^R to the right side of $H_k^L R^{(k-1)}$,

$$H_k^R \equiv I_n - \frac{1}{f_k \left(f_k - \frac{\hat{r}_{k,k+1}^{(k-1)} + \left(\hat{r}_{k,k+1}^{(k-1)}\right)^*}{2} \right)} \boldsymbol{w}_k^R \left(\boldsymbol{w}_k^R\right)^* \in \mathbb{C}^{n \times n}. \tag{3}$$

$$H_k^L R^{(k-1)} H_k^R = \begin{bmatrix} d_1 & f_1 & & & & \\ & \ddots & \ddots & & & \\ & & d_k & f_k & & \\ & & & r_{k+1,k+1}^{(k)} & \cdots & r_{k+1,n}^{(k)} \\ & & & \vdots & \ddots & \vdots \\ & & & r_{n,k+1}^{(k)} & \cdots & r_{nn}^{(k)} \end{bmatrix} \equiv R^{(k)}. \tag{4}$$

Similar to d_k, f_k is reversed from the sign $\hat{r}_{k,k+1}^{(k-1)}$.

By performing the above transformations for $k = 1, \ldots, n$, we obtain:

$$H_n^L \cdots H_1^L R H_1^R \cdots H_{n-1}^R = \begin{bmatrix} d_1 & f_1 & & \\ & \ddots & \ddots & \\ & & \ddots & f_{n-1} \\ & & & d_n \end{bmatrix} \equiv B \in \mathbb{R}^{n \times n}. \tag{5}$$

However, after $k = n-1$, the complex Householder Transformation from the right side is not necessary; for $k = n$, this algorithm can perform up to $k = n - 1$.

Because the above transformation matrices H_k^L, H_k^R are unitary matrices, $\tilde{U} \equiv H_1^L \cdots H_n^L, \tilde{V}_1^R \equiv H_1^R \cdots H_{n-1}^R$ can be satisfied, and the real bidiagonalized matrix B can be obtained. The calculations for $\tilde{U}, \tilde{V}$ are, for example, for $\tilde{U}$, we can first define the unit matrix of size $n \times n$ and then start multiplying $H_n^L, H_{n-1}^L, \ldots, H_1^L$ from the left side. The two-dimensional array used to store the complex upper triangular matrix R can be reused to store $\tilde{V}$ or $\tilde{U}$.

4 QR Iteration

Next, we discuss the diagonalization of a real bidiagonal matrix $B \in \mathbb{R}^{n\times n}$. In this section, we describe the implicitly shifted QR algorithm, which is currently the most commonly used method.

The standard algorithm for finding singular values of a real bidiagonal matrix B,

$$B = \begin{bmatrix} d_1 & f_1 & & \\ & \ddots & \ddots & \\ & & \ddots & f_{n-1} \\ & & & d_n \end{bmatrix}.$$

is the QR algorithm applied implicitly to B^TB. The algorithm computes a sequence B_i of real bidiagonal matrices starting from $B_0 = B$ as follows. From B_i, the algorithm computes a shift σ_i which is usually taken to be the smallest eigenvalue of the bottom 2×2 block of $B_i^T B_i$. Then, the algorithm performs an implicit QR factorization of the shifted matrix

$$B_i^T B_i - \sigma_i I = QR,$$

where Q is orthogonal and R is upper triangular. From this, it computes a real bidiagonal B_{i+1} such that

$$B_{i+1}^T B_{i+1} = RQ + \sigma_i I.$$

as (i) increases, (B_i) converges to a diagonal matrix with singular values on the diagonal.

The roundoff errors in this algorithm are generally on the order of $(\varepsilon\|B\|)$, where (ε) is the precision of the floating–point arithmetic used. This means we can expect absolute errors in the computed singular values of the same order. In particular, tiny singular values of (B) could be changed completely.

In this section, we present a variation of this standard algorithm that computes all the singular values of a real bidiagonal matrix, even the tiniest ones, with guaranteed high relative accuracy. We call this the "implicit zero–shift QR" algorithm because it corresponds to the above algorithm when $(\sigma = 0)$. However, it is organized such that each entry of (B_{i+1}) is computed from (B_i) to nearly full machine precision. The singular values of (B_i) and (B_{i+1}) all agree with high relative accuracy. When (B_i) has finally converged to a diagonal matrix, these diagonal entries must therefore also be accurate singular values for the initial $(B = B_0)$.

The final algorithm is a hybrid of the standard QR and implicit zero–shift QR. Standard QR is used when the condition number of the real bidiagonal matrix B (the ratio of the largest to smallest singular values) is modest. In this case, the roundoff errors are guaranteed to make acceptably small perturbations in the smallest singular values of the real bidiagonal matrix B. If the condition number is large, we use implicit zero–shift QR instead.

5 Conventional Method and Proposed Method

In this section, we explain the details of our proposed method in implementing the QR algorithm for SVD computations designed for complex matrices. Our proposed method implements matrix bidiagonalization via complex Householder reflections, QR decomposition using complex Householder reflections and the QR algorithm in approximating singular values and corresponding singular vectors.

5.1 Summary of Conventional Method

The conventional method involves the following steps:

1. Obtaining complex Householder reflectors from the bidiagonalization of the complex upper triangular matrix R into the real bidiagonal matrix B.
2. Complex matrix?-matrix multiplication is performed via Level–3 BLAS [2] routines to determine the values of P_1 and P_2.
3. Computing the SVD of the real bidiagonal matrix B via Givens rotations and, simultaneously, performing complex matrix–matrix multiplications via Level–3 BLAS routines to apply the Givens rotations to P_1 and P_2.

5.2 Summary of Proposed Method

The proposed method involves the following steps:

1. Obtaining complex Householder reflectors from the bidiagonalization of the complex upper triangular matrix R into the real bidiagonal matrix B.
2. Computing SVD of the real bidiagonal matrix B to determine the values of U' and $(V')^\top$ via real matrix–matrix multiplication via Level-3 BLAS routines.
3. Complex matrix–matrix multiplication is performed via Level–3 BLAS routines to determine the values of Q_1 and Q_2.

5.3 Decompositions of Matrix A

We know that the SVD of matrix A is expressed as:

$$A = U\Sigma V^*, A \in \mathbb{C}^{m\times n}.$$

where U and V^* are unitary matrices, and Σ is a diagonal matrix containing the singular values of A. In QR decomposition, by using complex Householder reflections, matrix A decomposes into a matrix Q and a complex upper triangular matrix R:

$$A = QR, Q \in \mathbb{C}^{m\times n}, R \in \mathbb{C}^{n\times n},$$

where $Q^*Q = I$.

5.4 Obtaining Complex Householder Reflectors

In our proposed method, first, we obtain complex Householder reflectors. The complex upper triangular matrix R can be transformed into P_1BP_2, where both matrices P_1 and P_2 are unitary matrices, and matrix B is a real upper bidiagonal matrix:

$$H_n^L \cdots H_1^L R H_1^R \cdots H_{n-1}^R = B, \tag{6}$$

because H_k^L and H_k^R are unitary matrices, which means $H_k^L H_k^L = I$ and $H_k^R H_k^R = I$, the complex upper triangular matrix R can be expressed as:

$$R = H_1^L \cdots H_n^L B H_{n-1}^R \cdots H_1^R. \tag{7}$$

From the above equation, we obtain the following complex Householder reflectors: $H_1^L, \cdots, H_n^L, H_1^R, \cdots, H_{n-1}^R$.

In the conventional method, first, we compute $R = P_1BP_2$, where $P_1 = H_1^L \cdots H_n^L$ and $P_2 = H_{n-1}^R \cdots H_1^R$.

5.5 Computing the Singular Value Decomposition of Matrix B

Next, we compute the following singular decomposition for the real bidiagonal matrix B:

$$B = U' \Sigma (V')^\top. \tag{8}$$

By using the Givens rotation, the singular values of the real bidiagonal matrix B can be computed as:

$$G_z^L \cdots G_2^L G_1^L B G_1^R G_2^R \cdots G_z^R = \Sigma, \tag{9}$$

because the real Givens rotation matrix is orthogonal, which means $G_k^L (G_k^L)^\top = I$ and $G_k^R (G_k^L)^\top = I$, the real bidiagonal matrix B can be expressed as:

$$B = (G_1^L)^\top (G_2^L)^\top \cdots (G_z^L)^\top \Sigma (G_z^R)^\top \cdots (G_2^R)^\top (G_1^R)^\top. \tag{10}$$

By comparing (8) and (10), we understand that $U' = (G_1^L)^\top (G_2^L)^\top \cdots (G_z^L)^\top$ and $(V')^\top = (G_z^R)^\top \cdots (G_2^R)^\top (G_1^R)^\top$. In the proposed method, the SVD of the real bidiagonal matrix B is computed to determine the values of $U' = (G_1^L)^\top (G_2^L)^\top \cdots (G_z^L)^\top$ and $(V')^\top = (G_z^R)^\top \cdots (G_2^R)^\top (G_1^R)^\top$ using real matrix–matrix multiplications via Level–3 BLAS routines.

In conventional method, in the above computation, for each calculation of complex numbers, using Level–3 BLAS, we obtain:

$$P_1^{(0)} = P_1,\ P_1^{(1)} = P_1^{(0)} (G_1^L)^\top,\ P_1^{(2)} = P_1^{(1)} (G_2^L)^\top,\ \ldots,\ P_1^{(z)} = P_1^{(z-1)} (G_z^L)^\top,$$
$$P_2^{(0)} = P_2,\ P_2^{(1)} = (G_1^R)^\top P^{(0)},\ P_2^{(2)} = (G_2^R)^\top P^{(1)},\ \ldots,\ P_2^{(z)} = (G_z^R)^\top P_2^{(z-1)}.$$

Thus, the following equation is satisfied;

$$R = P_1BP_2 = P_1 (G_1^L)^\top (G_2^L)^\top \cdots (G_z^L)^\top \Sigma (G_z^R)^\top \cdots (G_2^R)^\top (G_1^R)^\top P_2 = P_1^{(z)} \Sigma P_2^{(z)}.$$

5.6 Multiplying Matrices

In the proposed method, the obtained complex Householder reflectors and singular vectors are used to obtain Q_1 and Q_2 through Level–3 BLAS routines, with complex matrix-matrix multiplication as follows:

$$Q_1^{(0)} = U', \quad Q_1^{(1)} = H_n^L Q_1^{(0)}, \quad \ldots, \quad Q_1^{(n)} = H_1^L Q_1^{(n-1)},$$
$$Q_2^{(0)} = (V')^\top, \quad Q_2^{(1)} = Q_2^{(0)} H_{n-1}^R, \quad \ldots, \quad Q_2^{(n-1)} = Q_2^{(n-2)} H_1^R.$$

Thus, the following equation is satisfied;

$$R = H_1^L \cdots H_n^L B H_{n-1}^R \cdots H_1^R = H_1^L \cdots H_n^L U' \Sigma (V')^\top H_{n-1}^R \cdots H_1^R = Q_1^{(n)} \Sigma Q_2^{(n-1)}.$$

6 Numerical Experiments

6.1 Numerical Experiments Environment

The numerical experiments are conducted using the following computers. The computational environments used for the numerical experiments are shown in Table 1.

Table 1. Computational Environment

CPU	Intel(R) XEON(R) Silver 4116 CPU @2.10 GHz
OS	Rocky Linux release 9.3 (Blue Onyx)
Memory	192GB
Compiler	Intel FORTRAN Compiler ifx 2024.02
Library	Intel Math Kernel Library

For these numerical experiments, we compare the computation time, and the computation accuracy in terms of the orthogonality of the left and right singular vectors, between conventional method and our proposed method. Below are the details for every method applied in these numerical experiments:

- Method 1: Conventional Method
  This method computes the desired singular values by using the QR iteration, uses Givens rotations and performs SVD through level–3 BLAS routines, and complex matrix multiplications.
- Method 2: Proposed Method
  This method uses complex Householder reflectors, focusing on computing the SVD using efficient Level–3 BLAS routines, and real matrix multiplications to the greatest extent.

The input matrices for the numerical experiments are as follows: All the elements of the complex upper triangular matrix R are complex and are generated randomly. The size of the matrices are 2500×2500, 5000×5000, 7500×7500, and 10000×10000.

The computation time in these experiments is defined as the total time taken to compute the desired singular values and their corresponding left and right singular vectors. The computation accuracy measures how closely the results match the true SVD by measuring the orthogonality of the left and right singular vectors, and reconstruction the input matrix. The computational accuracy is evaluated using the following equations: $\|U^*U - I\|_F$, $\|V^*V - I\|_F$, and $\|A - U\Sigma V^*\|_F$. Theoretically, these values should be equal to zero. Therefore, the closer the values are to zero, the higher the accuracy of the methods. Here, matrices U and V are constructed with the desired right and left singular vectors of A such as $U = (u_1, u_2, \ldots, u_n)$ and $V = (v_1, v_2, \ldots, v_n)$.

6.2 Experimental Results

Figure 1 shows the results of the numerical experiment's computation time, and Fig. 2, 3 and 4 show the results of the computation accuracy.

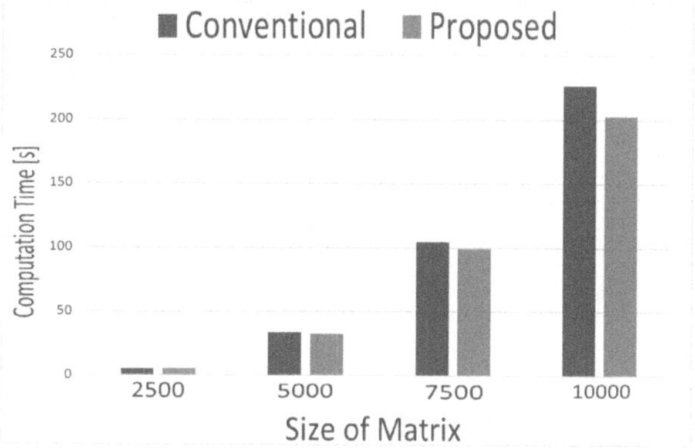

Fig. 1. Computation Time, [s].

6.3 Evaluation of the Numerical Experiments

On the basis of the results presented in Fig. 1, for the computation time of each method, our proposed method computes SVD faster than the conventional method. As the size of the matrix increases, the computation time for both methods also increases. However, the rate of increase is smaller for our proposed method, showing its improved scalability. This pattern is particularly noticeable

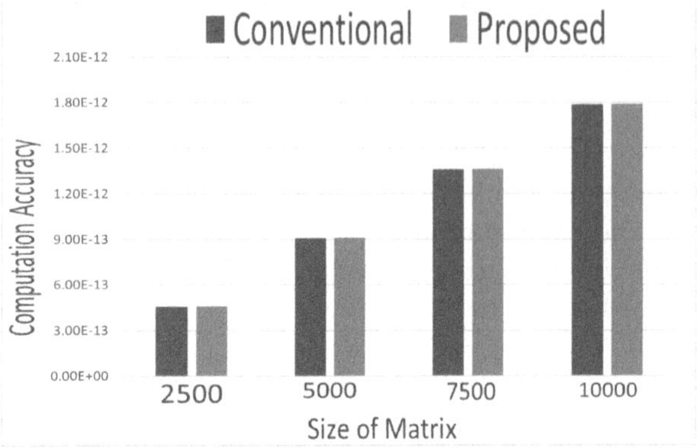

Fig. 2. Computation Accuracy, $||U^*U - I||_F$.

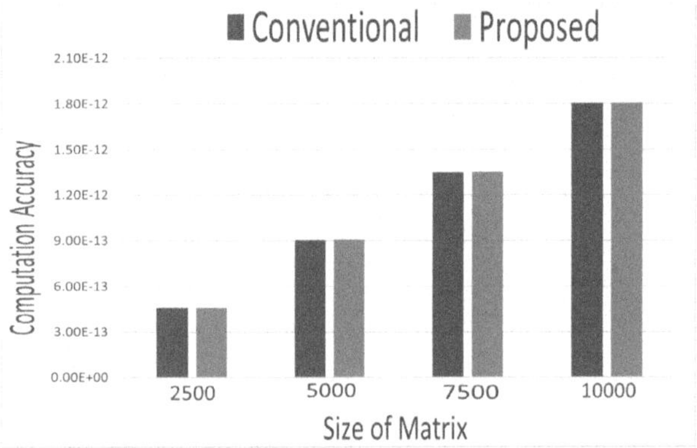

Fig. 3. Computation Accuracy, $||V^*V - I||_F$.

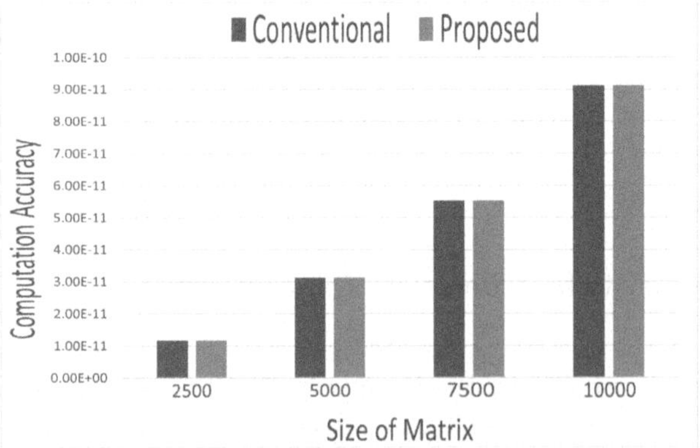

Fig. 4. Computation Accuracy, $||A - U\Sigma V^*||_F$.

for higher–dimensional matrices and specifically for higher performance computers.

Next, in terms of the computational accuracy, as shown in Fig. 2, 3 and 4, there were no computational failures for either method. All the computed accuracy values were close to zero, indicating high accuracy. Furthermore, the computational accuracy of both methods are almost identical, confirming that our proposed method achieves faster computation without sacrificing accuracy.

7 Conclusion

This paper presented a new method for computing the SVD of complex matrices. The numerical experiments proved that our proposed method's computation time is reduced by a small amount, which indicates an improvement in computational efficiency. Additionally, the better the computer's performance, the better the efficiency of our proposed method. Furthermore, for computational accuracy in terms of the orthogonality of the desired left and right singular vectors and the reconstruction of original input matrix, our proposed method maintains the orthogonality of the singular vectors and does not face computational failure. Therefore, these results prove that our proposed method is an efficient alternative method for computing the SVD of complex matrices.

For future work, we plan to conduct further experiments with matrices of even higher–dimensions, using computers with even higher performance, to further evaluate the efficiency and potential limitations of the proposed method. In addition, evaluating the performance of the proposed method when iy is applied to quaternion matrices is necessary.

References

1. Abdi, H., Williams, L.J.: Principal component analysis. Wiley Interdiscip. Rev. Comput. Stat. **2**(4), 433–459 (2010)
2. Basic Linear Algebra Subprograms, Netlib. http://netlib.org/blas/index.html
3. Demmel, J.: Applied Numerical Linear Algebra. SIAM, Philadelphia (1997)
4. Demmel, J., Kahan, W.: Accurate singular values of vidiagonal matrics. SIAM J. Sci. Stat. Comput. **67**, 191–229 (1994)
5. Francis, J.G.F.: The QR transformation a unitary analogue to the LR transformation part 1. Comput. J. **4**, 265–271 (1961)
6. Golub, G., Kahan, W.: Calculating the singular values and pseudo-inverse of a matrix. SIAM J. Numer. Anal. **2**, 205–224 (1965)
7. Golub, G., Reinsc, C.: Singular value decomposition and least squares solutions. Numer. Math. **14**, 403–420 (1970)

GraphBioisostere: General Bioisostere Prediction Model with Deep Graph Neural Network

Sho Masunaga, Kairi Furui, Apakorn Kengkanna, and Masahito Ohue(✉)

School of Computing, Institute of Science Tokyo, Yokohama, Kanagawa, Japan
{masunaga,furui,kengkanna}@li.comp.isct.ac.jp, ohue@comp.isct.ac.jp

Abstract. Lead optimization to improve pharmacokinetics and toxicity while maintaining biological activity is an important and costly stage in the drug discovery process, requiring computational approaches for increased efficiency. We propose GraphBioisostere, a bioisostere prediction model that uses graph neural networks. The proposed model leverages a large-scale matched molecular pair dataset constructed from the ChEMBL database and directly learns bioisosterism without target information by considering entire chemical structures. Our evaluation demonstrates that GraphBioisostere achieves superior bioisostere prediction performance compared to approaches that consider only substituents. Furthermore, it outperforms conventional LightGBM-based methods, and models directly learning potency changes failed to discriminate bioisosteres, highlighting the importance of specifically learning bioisosterism. Additionally, models pre-trained on target-independent bioisostere prediction exhibited excellent transfer learning performance for potency change prediction against specific targets. This suggests that GraphBioisostere acquires useful representations of the relationship between chemical structure and activity. Our research provides a tool to evaluate the potential of structural changes in molecular pairs to maintain activity independently of targets, contributing to improved efficiency in the drug discovery process.

Keywords: Bioisostere · Graph neural network · Deep learning · Drug discovery

1 Introduction

Drug development typically costs over 1 billion dollars [36] and takes more than 10 years [32], making computational approaches to reduce these resources a critical challenge in drug discovery. Lead compound optimization is a crucial stage in the drug discovery process. This phase requires enhancing pharmacokinetic properties and reducing toxicity while maintaining or improving the biological activity of compounds [23,24].

S. Masunaga and K. Furui—These authors are equally contributed.

H. R. Arabnia et al. (Eds.): CSCE 2025, CCIS 2932, pp. 440–449, 2026.
https://doi.org/10.1007/978-3-032-22193-3_34

Bioisosteres represent a key concept for achieving this goal [10,23]. Bioisosteric replacement involves substituting part of a bioactive molecule with a substructure having similar physicochemical properties that elicits a similar biological response against the target protein [10,23]. Bioisosteres are sets of compounds related through such replacements. The concept of bioisosteres is closely linked to Matched Molecular Pair (MMP) analysis [14,31,34,37]. MMPs are pairs of compounds that can be interconverted by a single chemical transformation [14,34], and when this transformation maintains similar activity, the pair of substituents is considered bioisosteric. Conversely, when an MMP exhibits a significant change in activity, it is termed an "activity cliff" [27,34], and identifying substituent combinations that avoid such activity cliffs leads to effective bioisostere identification.

Previous research has introduced various tools for bioisosteric replacement [6,8,9,35]. Particularly, MMP-based bioisostere prediction using deep learning [10,19] has gained significant attention. In Ertl's work [10], a neural network was developed to learn inherent relationships between molecular fragments using training data constructed from the ChEMBL database. However, this approach only learns information about substituents without adequately considering how surrounding chemical environments influence bioisosterism. Additionally, DeepBioisostere is a deep generative model designed to create appropriate bioisosteric replacements for controlling multiple molecular properties [19]. While DeepBioisostere focuses on optimizing molecular properties, it doesn't directly address activity. Consequently, an external binding affinity prediction model was required to evaluate bioisostere activity.

Meanwhile, research on predicting potency changes in MMPs [12,13,25,31] continues to advance. These studies enable more efficient learning and enhancement of MMP activity by directly predicting potency changes between molecular pairs. However, existing models for predicting potency changes in MMPs are typically specialized for specific target proteins and cannot be applied when target information is unavailable [3,25].

In this study, we propose GraphBioisostere, a general bioisostere prediction model that considers the entire molecule and directly predicts the likelihood of maintaining similar biological activity. This approach aims to be applicable even to novel targets or compounds with unknown interaction mechanisms. By leveraging graph neural networks (GNNs), we aim to effectively capture structural features of molecules and achieve more accurate bioisostere prediction. This approach allows for evaluating the potential of structural modifications to preserve biological activity even without specific target information, contributing to more efficient drug discovery processes.

2 Methods

2.1 Construction of MMP Dataset

In this study, we constructed an MMP dataset for bioisostere prediction by extracting assay data from the ChEMBL35 database [4] and implementing the Hussain and Rea algorithm [15] for molecular pair generation.

First, we extracted IC_{50} assays with high confidence (`confidence_score=9`) targeting single proteins from binding assays. We further selected only assay data with IC_{50} values ranging from 0 to 10,000 nM and removed entries containing relational operators. After standardization processes including salt removal, selection of the largest fragment, and neutralization of molecules, we selected compounds with molecular weights below 800 and extracted only unique compounds for each assay.

Next, from the extracted assay data, we constructed an MMP dataset by implementing the Hussain and Rea algorithm [15] using OpenBabel [29], following an approach similar to the Swissbioisostere methodology [2,35]. First, molecular structures were fragmented by cutting up to three bonds. Cuttable bonds were defined as single bonds that are not part of a ring or aromatic system, have at least one carbon at one end, and do not have hydrogen at either end. Then, MMPs were defined when only one fragment differed between two molecular pairs. Additionally, for single cuts, only pairs where the different fragments were smaller than the common part were included; for multiple cuts, only pairs where the number of atoms in the different fragments was 15 or fewer were included. By using only compound pairs within the same assay and targeting the same target, we ensured consistent experimental conditions for activity measurements. As a result, we constructed an MMP dataset consisting of 850,246 compound pairs from 112,107 unique compounds and 1,908 targets obtained from 12,853 assays.

MMPs were classified as bioisosteres if they satisfied $|\Delta p\mathrm{IC}_{50}| < 0.3$ ($p\mathrm{IC}_{50} = -\log_{10}(\mathrm{IC}_{50})$). This threshold was established based on previous studies [5,16,21,22] indicating that experimental error typically falls within $|\Delta p\mathrm{IC}_{50}| < 0.3$.

2.2 Model Architecture

In this study, we developed GraphBioisostere, a GNN-based bioisostere prediction model that takes molecular pairs as input, utilizing MMGX [18]. We utilized a 3-layer GNN encoder based solely on atom graph representations to derive latent variables from the node and edge features of molecules.

Figure 1 shows an overview of the model. First, to represent molecular structures as atom-level molecular graphs, we calculated 30-dimensional node features and 11-dimensional edge features using DeepChem's [30] default features. GraphBioisostere performs classification using the difference between output embedding representations of molecular pairs obtained from the MMGX encoder based on a siamese network [28,38]. Specifically, for two molecular graphs G_A and G_B, we first obtain embedding representations $\mathbf{f}_A$ and $\mathbf{f}_B$ using a common encoder:

$$\mathbf{f}_A = \mathrm{Encoder}(G_A), \quad \mathbf{f}_B = \mathrm{Encoder}(G_B) \tag{1}$$

Next, we calculate the absolute difference of these embedding representations and perform classification through a multilayer perceptron (MLP) head:

$$\mathbf{f}_{\mathrm{AB}} = |\mathbf{f}_A - \mathbf{f}_B| \tag{2}$$

In addition to the absolute difference of molecular pair embeddings, we also evaluated using the element-wise product of embeddings and concatenated representations. When using concatenated representations, the input dimension of the MLP is twice the embedding dimension. We refer to each pair representation integration approach as GraphBioisostere (diff), GraphBioisostere (product), and GraphBioisostere (concat).

$$\hat{y}_{AB} = \mathrm{MLP}(\mathbf{f}_{\mathrm{AB}}) \tag{3}$$

The MLP consists of two fully connected layers with ReLU activation functions and outputs the prediction probability for two classes—whether the pair is a bioisostere or not. Cross-entropy loss was used for training the classification model.

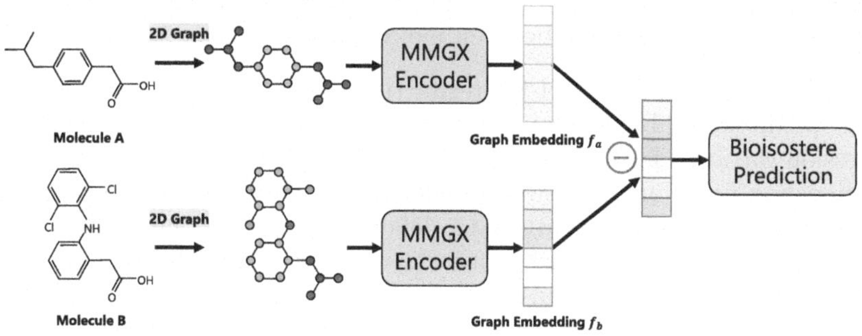

Fig. 1. Overview of GraphBioisostere.

2.3 Experiment

Next, we describe the experimental procedure. The Adam optimizer [20] was applied with a learning rate of 1×10^{-3} for model training. Learning rate scheduling was performed using cosine annealing [26]. Early stopping was applied when the ROC-AUC score on the validation data did not improve for 100 consecutive epochs, with training conducted for a maximum of 1,000 epochs.

Additionally, we performed 5-fold cross-validation based on targets to evaluate the model's generalization performance to unknown protein targets. Data was grouped according to protein target IDs, and data splitting was performed based on these targets.

It should be noted that our MMP dataset contains instances where the same molecular pair may be classified differently as a bioisostere or not depending on different assays or targets. During training, these data were used as is. This approach implicitly teaches the model how likely a molecular pair is to generally function as a bioisostere. During evaluation, only unique MMPs with a single label were used.

For comparison with whole-molecule approaches, we also evaluated fragment-based methods where the matched substructure is removed and only the two substituents are used as input.

2.4 GBDT-Based Model

In this study, we implemented gradient boosting decision trees based on LightGBM [17] as a baseline for comparison with GraphBioisostere. Models were trained and evaluated in the following three scenarios:

- LGBM-Classifier: A bioisostere prediction model that classifies whether a molecular pair is a bioisostere ($|\Delta p\mathrm{IC}_{50}| < 0.3$) or not.
- LGBM-Regressor: An absolute potency change prediction model that predicts the $|\Delta p\mathrm{IC}_{50}|$ value between molecular pairs.
- LGBM-Regressor (no-Abs): A potency change prediction model that directly predicts the $\Delta p\mathrm{IC}_{50}$ value between molecular pairs.

It should be noted that LGBM-Regressor (no-Abs) makes fundamentally meaningless predictions about relative activity without using target information. Regression was used for continuous potency change prediction, and binary classification was used for bioisostere prediction as the objective function. Training was conducted using LightGBM's default parameters, with early stopping ($N_{round} = 100$) performed using root mean squared error (RMSE) for regression and ROC-AUC for classification on validation data. As features, we used concatenated 2,048-dimensional Morgan fingerprints with radius 2 (ECFP4) generated using RDKit [1]. To ensure consistent outputs when the order of molecular pairs was swapped at input, training and validation data were augmented to include swapped pairs.

3 Results and Discussion

3.1 Performance Evaluation of Bioisostere Prediction Model

Figure 2 shows the ROC-AUC scores for GraphBioisostere and LGBM models for each target. The results demonstrate that GraphBioisostere achieved superior overall performance. This suggests that GraphBioisostere, which directly utilizes molecular structure information, is more suitable for bioisostere prediction than fingerprint-based LGBM approaches. In particular, the GraphBioisostere (diff) model achieved the highest ROC-AUC score, indicating that the siamese network-based approach using the difference of molecular pair embedding representations was most effective.

Among LGBM-based models, LGBM-Classifier showed higher performance than LGBM-Regressor. Additionally, LGBM-Regressor (no-Abs) showed an ROC-AUC of around 0.5, indicating performance equivalent to random prediction. This suggests that simply predicting activity differences is insufficient for determining whether compounds are bioisosteres, and it is important to directly learn whether a meaningful difference exists.

Figure 3 shows the performance when calculating ROC-AUC for each target for each model. Similarly, GraphBioisostere outperformed LGBM-based models, with GraphBioisostere (diff) achieving the highest performance. While LGBM-Regressor (no-Abs) showed a median around 0.5 with no predictive ability, LGBM-Classifier and LGBM-Regressor showed similar performance. It should be noted that even the best-performing GraphBioisostere (diff) has cases with ROC-AUC < 0.5 in about 25% of instances. The decreased prediction accuracy for some targets is a natural outcome from a biological perspective, as the influence of substituents varies depending on the target protein. Therefore, there is an inherent limitation in making high-accuracy predictions in all cases for the effect of specific substitutions on activity without target information. Nevertheless, GraphBioisostere's higher overall performance compared to LGBM-based models suggests that it can effectively learn general trends of bioisosteres from molecular structures.

Next, we discuss individual prediction results from GraphBioisostere. Figure 4 shows examples of predictions for molecular pairs in the test set that have labels different from the training data. True positive (TP) examples correctly predict that small substitutions have minimal impact, and true negative (TN) examples correctly predict that activity differences occur due to functional groups. On the other hand, the false positive (FP) example represents an activity cliff where the presence or absence of a hydroxyl group significantly changes activity. Additionally, in the false negative (FN) example, the model failed to predict that the position change of a trifluoromethyl group resulted in only a slight activity difference. Since the effect of substituents strongly depends on the binding pocket environment of the target protein, substitutions that generally tend not to change activity may not always show the same phenomenon with individual targets. This highlights a certain limitation in predicting activity maintenance without target information.

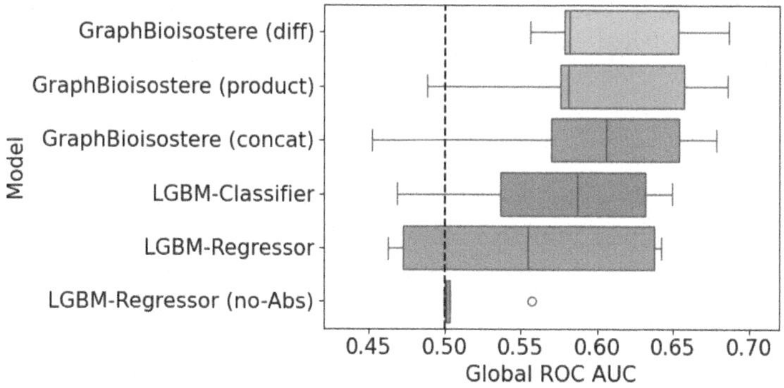

Fig. 2. Distribution of ROC-AUC scores for bioisostere prediction. The box plot shows ROC-AUC scores for GraphBioisostere and LightGBM-based models.

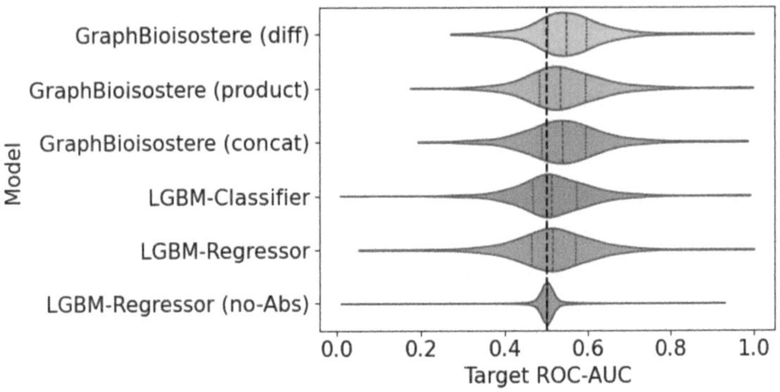

Fig. 3. Distribution of ROC-AUC scores for cross-validation for each target protein. The box plot shows ROC-AUC scores for GraphBioisostere and LightGBM-based models. Only targets containing 50 or more molecule pairs in the test data are used.

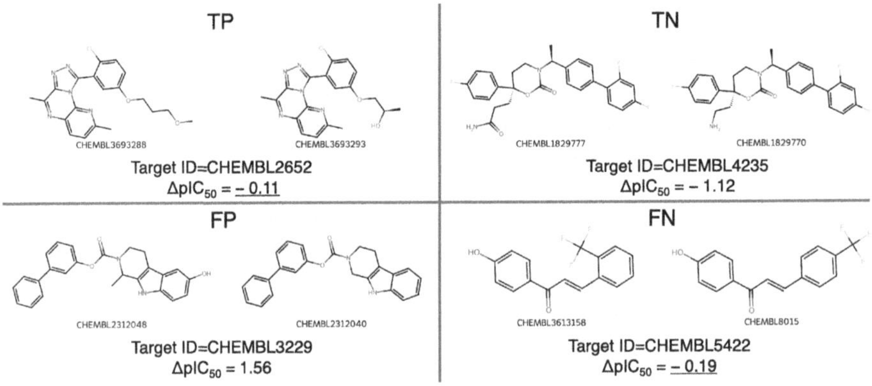

Fig. 4. Examples of predictions for molecular pairs in the test set with labels different from the training data. Top left: Correctly predicted example of a bioisostere, top right: Correctly predicted example of a non-bioisostere, bottom left: Example incorrectly predicted as a bioisostere, bottom right: Example incorrectly predicted as a non-bioisostere.

Also, Fig. 5 shows examples of the same substitution patterns having different labels in training and test data. In the left case, the substitution of a pyridine ring with a chlorobenzene ring appears as a bioisostere in the test set but as a non-bioisostere in the training set. In the right case, the substitution of a piperidine group with a methoxy group appears as a non-bioisostere in the test set but as a bioisostere in the training set. Interestingly, the model made accurate predictions for these cases by considering the entire molecule, though it was difficult to explain the predictions from chemical and biological perspectives. This demonstrates the black-box nature of GNN models and suggests that

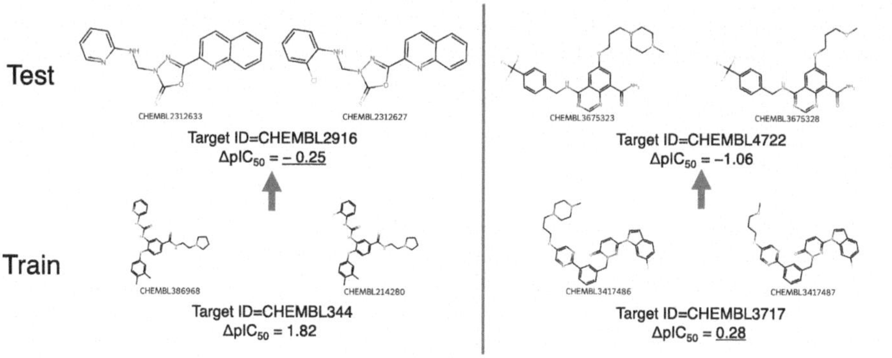

Fig. 5. Examples from the test set where molecular pairs have the same substitution as in training data but with reversed labels, which were correctly predicted. Left: An example where it is a non-bioisostere in the training set but a bioisostere in the test set. Right: An example where it is a bioisostere in the training set but a non-bioisostere in the test set.

incorporating explainable AI (XAI) technologies [18] represents an important future challenge.

4 Conclusion

In this study, we developed GraphBioisostere, a bioisostere prediction model using GNN from a large-scale MMP dataset constructed from the ChEMBL database. Experimental results showed that GraphBioisostere demonstrated higher prediction performance than LGBM-based methods, confirming that it can improve bioisostere prediction accuracy by effectively capturing molecular structural features. We also found that directly predicting potency changes does not provide useful insights into whether compounds are bioisosteres. These results indicate that the developed bioisostere prediction model can serve as a valuable tool for evaluating the potential of structural modifications to maintain activity even without target information. Future research could focus on acquiring richer latent representations through other representation learning techniques such as contrastive learning [11,33] or metric learning [7] to improve bioisostere prediction accuracy. Additionally, important challenges include revealing the basis of bioisosterism through explainable AI [18] and developing optimization frameworks that improve synthetic feasibility and ADME properties while maintaining activity based on the developed model [19]. This research provides a novel approach to the important drug discovery challenge of evaluating bioisosterism and is expected to contribute to the advancement of future drug discovery research.

Acknowledgments. This work was financially supported by the Japan Science and Technology Agency FOREST (Grant No. JPMJFR216J), the Japan Society for the Promotion of Science KAKENHI (Grant Nos. JP23H04880, JP23H04887, JP24KJ1091), and the Japan Agency for Medical Research and Development Basis for Supporting Innovative Drug Discovery and Life Science Research (Grant No. JP25ama121026).

References

1. RDKit: Open-source cheminformatics. https://www.rdkit.org
2. Alessandro, C., Antoine, D., Marta, A.S.P., Olivier, M., Vincent, Z.: SwissBioisostere 2021: updated structural, bioactivity and physicochemical data delivered by a reshaped web interface. Nucleic Acids Res. **50**(D1), D1382–D1390 (2022)
3. Beck, J.M., Springer, C.: Quantitative structure-activity relationship models of chemical transformations from matched pairs analyses. J. Chem. Inf. Model. **54**(4), 1226–1234 (2014)
4. Blackshaw, J., et al.: Chembl database release 35 (2009). https://doi.org/10.6019/chembl.database.35
5. Brown, S.P., Muchmore, S.W., Hajduk, P.J.: Healthy skepticism: assessing realistic model performance. Drug Discov. Today **14**(7–8), 420–427 (2009)
6. Cao, X., Yang, H., Liu, C., Zhang, R., Maienfisch, P., Xu, X.: Bioisosterism and scaffold hopping in modern nematicide research. J. Agric. Food Chem. **70**(36), 11042–11055 (2022)
7. Coupry, D.E., Pogány, P.: Application of deep metric learning to molecular graph similarity. J. Cheminform. **14**(1), 11 (2022)
8. Dick, A., Cocklin, S.: Bioisosteric replacement as a tool in anti-HIV drug design. Pharmaceuticals (Basel) **13**(3), 36 (2020)
9. Ertl, P.: World Wide Web-based system for the calculation of substituent parameters and substituent similarity searches. J. Mol. Graph. Model. **16**(1), 11–13, 36 (1998)
10. Ertl, P.: Identification of bioisosteric substituents by a deep neural network. J. Chem. Inf. Model. **60**(7), 3369–3375 (2020)
11. Fang, Y., et al.: Knowledge graph-enhanced molecular contrastive learning with functional prompt. Nat. Mach. Intell. **5**(5), 542–553 (2023)
12. Fralish, Z., Chen, A., Skaluba, P., Reker, D.: DeepDelta: predicting ADMET improvements of molecular derivatives with deep learning. J. Cheminform. **15**(1), 101 (2023)
13. Fralish, Z., Reker, D.: Finding the most potent compounds using active learning on molecular pairs. Beilstein J. Org. Chem. **20**(1), 2152–2162 (2024)
14. Griffen, E., Leach, A.G., Robb, G.R., Warner, D.J.: Matched molecular pairs as a medicinal chemistry tool: miniperspective. J. Med. Chem. **54**(22), 7739–7750 (2011)
15. Hussain, J., Rea, C.: Computationally efficient algorithm to identify matched molecular pairs (mmps) in large data sets. J. Chem. Inf. Model. **50**(3), 339–348 (2010)
16. Kalliokoski, T., Kramer, C., Vulpetti, A., Gedeck, P.: Comparability of mixed IC_{50} data - a statistical analysis. PLoS ONE **8**(4), e61007 (2013)
17. Ke, G., et al.: LightGBM: a highly efficient gradient boosting decision tree. In: Advances in Neural Information Processing Systems, vol. 30 (2017)
18. Kengkanna, A., Ohue, M.: Enhancing property and activity prediction and interpretation using multiple molecular graph representations with MMGX. Commun. Chem. **7**(1), 74 (2024)

19. Kim, H., Moon, S., Zhung, W., Lim, J., Kim, W.Y.: DeepBioisostere: discovering bioisosteres with deep learning for a fine control of multiple molecular properties. arXiv [q-bio.BM] (2024)
20. Kingma, D.P., Ba, J.: Adam: a method for stochastic optimization. arXiv [cs.LG] (2014)
21. Kramer, C., Kalliokoski, T., Gedeck, P., Vulpetti, A.: The experimental uncertainty of heterogeneous public K(i) data. J. Med. Chem. **55**(11), 5165–5173 (2012)
22. Landrum, G.A., Riniker, S.: Combining IC50 or Ki values from different sources is a source of significant noise. J. Chem. Inf. Model. **64**(5), 1560–1567 (2024)
23. Langdon, S.R., Ertl, P., Brown, N.: Bioisosteric replacement and scaffold hopping in lead generation and optimization. Mol. Inform. **29**(5), 366–385 (2010)
24. Leach, A.G., et al.: Matched molecular pairs as a guide in the optimization of pharmaceutical properties; a study of aqueous solubility, plasma protein binding and oral exposure. J. Med. Chem. **49**(23), 6672–6682 (2006)
25. de la Vega de León, A., Bajorath, J.: Prediction of compound potency changes in matched molecular pairs using support vector regression. J. Chem. Inf. Model. **54**(10), 2654–2663 (2014)
26. Loshchilov, I., Hutter, F.: SGDR: stochastic gradient descent with warm restarts. In: International Conference on Learning Representations (ICLR) (2017). https://openreview.net/forum?id=Skq89Scxx
27. Maggiora, G., Vogt, M., Stumpfe, D., Bajorath, J.: Molecular similarity in medicinal chemistry: miniperspective. J. Med. Chem. **57**(8), 3186–3204 (2014)
28. McNutt, A.T., Koes, D.R.: Improving $\Delta\Delta G$ predictions with a multitask convolutional Siamese network. J. Chem. Inf. Model. **62**(8), 1819–1829 (2022)
29. O'Boyle, N.M., Banck, M., James, C.A., Morley, C., Vandermeersch, T., Hutchison, G.R.: Open Babel: an open chemical toolbox. J. Cheminform. **3**(1), 33 (2011)
30. Ramsundar, B., Eastman, P., Walters, P., Pande, V., Leswing, K., Wu, Z.: Deep Learning for the Life Sciences. O'Reilly Media (2019)
31. Turk, S., Merget, B., Rippmann, F., Fulle, S.: Coupling matched molecular pairs with machine learning for virtual compound optimization. J. Chem. Inf. Model. **57**(12), 3079–3085 (2017)
32. Van Norman, G.A.: Drugs, devices, and the FDA: Part 1: an overview of approval processes for drugs. JACC Basic Transl. Sci. **1**(3), 170–179 (2016)
33. Wang, Y., Wang, J., Cao, Z., Barati Farimani, A.: Molecular contrastive learning of representations via graph neural networks. Nat. Mach. Intell. **4**(3), 279–287 (2022)
34. Wassermann, A.M., Bajorath, J.: Chemical substitutions that introduce activity cliffs across different compound classes and biological targets. J. Chem. Inf. Model. **50**(7), 1248–1256 (2010)
35. Wirth, M., Zoete, V., Michielin, O., Sauer, W.H.B.: SwissBioisostere: a database of molecular replacements for ligand design. Nucleic Acids Res. **41**, D1137-1143 (2013)
36. Wouters, O., Mckee, M., Luyten, J.: Estimated research and development investment needed to bring a new medicine to market, 2009–2018. JAMA **323**(9), 844–853 (2020)
37. Yang, Z., Shi, S., Fu, L., Lu, A., Hou, T., Cao, D.: Matched molecular pair analysis in drug discovery: methods and recent applications. J. Med. Chem. **66**(7), 4361–4377 (2023)
38. Zhang, Y., et al.: Similarity-based pairing improves efficiency of Siamese neural networks for regression tasks and uncertainty quantification. J. Cheminform. **15**(1), 75 (2023)

GBDT-Based Model and Web Tool for Prediction of Blood-Placental Barrier Permeability of Small Molecules

Masahito Ohue(✉) and Kairi Furui

School of Computing, Institute of Science Tokyo, Kanagawa, Japan
ohue@comp.isct.ac.jp, furui@li.comp.isct.ac.jp

Abstract. The extent to which a drug administered to a mother reaches the fetus is evaluated by the permeability of the blood-placenta barrier. Knowledge of a compound's blood-placenta barrier permeability is not only crucial for the development of safe drugs but also provides guidelines for treating pregnant women. In this study, we employ gradient boosting decision trees (GBDT) to predict blood-placenta barrier permeability with relatively low computational cost. Two types of publicly available data were used to construct separate regression models: (i) *in vivo* data, where the fetal–maternal blood concentration ratio (F/M ratio) measured in umbilical and maternal blood at birth is transformed via logarithm (logFM), and (ii) *ex vivo* data from human placental perfusion experiments providing a clearance index (CI). In both cases, the proposed LightGBM-based method outperformed previous approaches, and we further developed a web service to provide predictions based on the constructed models. PBPredictor, a prediction tool, is accessible as a web application via the following URL: https://pbpredictor.net.

Keywords: Blood-Placental Barrier · Permeability Prediction · Gradient Boosting Decision Trees · LightGBM · PBPredictor

1 Introduction

The extent to which a drug administered to a mother transfers to the fetus is evaluated by its ability to pass through the blood-placenta barrier. Determining the blood-placenta barrier permeability of candidate compounds is crucial for developing safe drugs and also serves as a guideline for treating pregnant women [1]. However, because the human placenta exhibits species-specific characteristics that are not reproducible in animal models [2], evaluation using human tissue models is necessary.

Two major experimental approaches have been used to assess placental transfer. One is to measure the concentration of the compound in umbilical cord (fetal) blood versus maternal blood at birth, yielding the fetal–maternal blood concentration ratio (F/M ratio). The common logarithm of this ratio is denoted as

H. R. Arabnia et al. (Eds.): CSCE 2025, CCIS 2932, pp. 450–455, 2026.
https://doi.org/10.1007/978-3-032-22193-3_35

logFM and serves as a direct *in vivo* indicator of permeability. A limitation of this approach is that data are available only for compounds known to be safe [3]. Alternatively, the human placental perfusion model provides an *ex vivo* method where the transfer rate (clearance) of a compound from the maternal side to the fetal side is measured. The clearance index (CI) is defined as the ratio of the compound's clearance relative to that of the control compound, antipyrine [4]. Although the placental perfusion experiment can be applied to a wide range of compounds, CI is only an indirect indicator of permeability.

In this study, we use the existing logFM data and placental perfusion experiment data to predict blood-placenta barrier permeability. Although several studies have attempted to predict permeability using machine learning methods [5–8], the predictive accuracies were not satisfactory and software implementations were limited. Here, we focus on gradient boosting decision trees (GBDT), which allow high-accuracy predictions with relatively low computational cost. Specifically, we construct separate regression models for logFM and CI using LightGBM [11], and we compare our predictions to those reported in the literature. In addition, we have implemented a web service that provides predictions based on the constructed models.

2 Materials and Methods

2.1 Datasets

Two endpoints representing blood-placenta barrier permeability were considered:

logFM Dataset. The logFM value is the base-10 logarithm of the fetal–maternal blood concentration ratio obtained from umbilical and maternal blood at birth. We used logFM values for 55 compounds compiled by Takaku *et al.* [5]. Previous studies applied multiple linear regression [5] and Lasso regression [6] to this dataset.

CI Dataset. The clearance index (CI) is defined as the ratio of a compound's clearance (measured via the human placental perfusion model) relative to that of antipyrine [4]. Our CI dataset consists of 88 compounds compiled by Giaginis *et al.* [7], with previous predictions obtained using partial least squares [8].

2.2 Prediction Model Construction

Molecular descriptors were computed using Mordred [9] (which calculates over 1,600 2D and 213 3D descriptors using RDKit). Three-dimensional conformations were generated with RDKit's ETKDGv2 method [10]. Each dataset was split into training and test sets following the partitioning strategy of previous studies. Regression models were built using LightGBM [11]. Hyperparameter tuning was performed on the training set via leave-one-out cross validation (LOOCV) using the LightGBM Tuner provided by Optuna [12]. To alleviate overfitting observed in preliminary logFM predictions (LOOCV $R^2 = 1$ on training but much lower test performance), Lasso regression-based feature selection was applied on the training data to select five descriptors for model input.

2.3 Evaluation Metrics

Model performance was evaluated using the coefficient of determination (R^2) and the root mean squared error (RMSE). LOOCV RMSE on the training set served as the objective function during hyperparameter tuning.

2.4 Web Service Implementation

Based on the LightGBM models, we developed a web service that computes predictions of logFM and CI from input SMILES strings. The front-end is implemented using Vue.js [13], while the back-end is built in Python with Flask [14]. A REST API is available at https://pbpredictor.net/api/predict?smiles=[str] to return predictions in JSON format.

3 Results and Discussion

3.1 Prediction Performance

Table 1 shows the prediction results for logFM and Table 2 for CI. Our LightGBM-based models (called PBPredictor) outperformed the previous method (Wang *et al.* [6]). In particular, while the previous method [6] exhibited degraded performance on the test set relative to training, our models maintained similar accuracy on both, indicating good generalization.

Table 1. Prediction results for logFM.

	PBPredictor (LightGBM)		Wang *et al.* [6]	
	R^2	RMSE	R^2	RMSE
Training (LOOCV)	**0.716**	**0.181**	0.633	0.206
Test Data	**0.720**	**0.191**	0.557	0.241

Table 2. Prediction results for CI. Note that values in parentheses for Zhang *et al.* [8] correspond to training on the full dataset.

	PBPredictor (LightGBM)		Zhang *et al.* [8]	
	R^2	RMSE	R^2	RMSE
Training (LOOCV)	0.175	0.269	(0.906)	(0.090)
Test Data	**0.624**	**0.158**	0.171	0.234

3.2 Selected Descriptors

The five descriptors selected via Lasso regression for the logFM model were: `AATSC1c`, `MAXsCH3`, `ZMIC1`, `Lipinski`, and `PEOE_VSA6`. For the CI model, the selected descriptors were: `ATSC1se`, `AATSC0c`, `GATS3v`, `PPSA3`, and `DPSA3`. These descriptors, many related to molecular size and lipophilicity, are consistent with known properties affecting placental transfer [15]. Notably, `AATSC1c` and `ZMIC1` were also selected in previous studies [6], supporting their relevance to blood-placenta barrier permeability. Although similar physicochemical properties have been linked to blood–brain barrier permeability [16], our analysis (using ADMET Predictor [17]) did not reveal a strong correlation between predicted blood–brain barrier permeability and either logFM or CI.

3.3 Web Service Example

Figure 1 shows a screenshot of the PBPredictor web service, where users input SMILES strings (one per line) to obtain predictions for logFM and CI. In addition, a REST API is available for direct programmatic access. For example, a request such as

Fig. 1. Screenshot of the PBPredictor web service (https://pbpredictor.net).

```
https://pbpredictor.net/api/predict?smiles=CC(=O)NC1=CC=C(C=C1)O
```

returns a JSON response like

{"logFM":0.0919, "CI":0.5330, "smiles":"CC(=O)NC1=CC=C(C=C1)O"}.

4 Conclusions

We demonstrated that a GBDT-based approach using LightGBM can accurately predict blood-placenta barrier permeability, as measured by logFM and CI, outperforming previous methods. The robustness of the predictions, evidenced by comparable performance on training and test sets, coupled with low computational cost, makes this method well suited for real-time applications. The PBPredictor web service further facilitates access to these predictions, providing a valuable tool for researchers and drug developers. Future work may include multi-label learning to simultaneously model both endpoints and further investigation of additional molecular descriptors.

Acknowledgments. This work was financially supported by the Japan Science and Technology Agency FOREST (Grant No. JPMJFR216J), the Japan Society for the Promotion of Science KAKENHI (Grant Nos. JP23H04880, JP23H04887, JP24KJ1091), and the Japan Agency for Medical Research and Development Basis for Supporting Innovative Drug Discovery and Life Science Research (Grant No. JP25ama121026).

References

1. Myren, M., et al.: The human placenta–an alternative for studying fetal exposure. Toxicol. In Vitro **21**, 1332–1340 (2007)
2. Giaginis, C., et al.: Current toxicological aspects on drug and chemical transport and metabolism across the human placental barrier. Exp. Opin. Drug Metab. Toxicol. **8**, 1263–1275 (2012)
3. Fukata, H., et al.: Necessity to measure PCBs and organochlorine pesticide concentrations in human umbilical cords for fetal exposure assessment. Environ. Health Perspect. **113**, 297–303 (2005)
4. Smith, J.A., et al.: Utilization of an ex vivo human placental perfusion model to predict potential fetal exposure to carboplatin during pregnancy. Am. J. Obstet. Gynecol. **210**(275), e1-9 (2014)
5. Takaku, T., et al.: Quantitative structure-activity relationship model for the fetal-maternal blood concentration ratio of chemicals in humans. Biol. Pharm. Bull. **38**, 930–934 (2015)
6. Wang, C.-C., et al.: Prediction of human fetal-maternal blood concentration ratio of chemicals. PeerJ **8**, e9562 (2020)
7. Giaginis, C., et al.: Application of quantitative structure-activity relationships for modeling drug and chemical transport across the human placental barrier: a multivariate data analysis approach. J. Appl. Toxicol. **29**, 724–733 (2009)
8. Zhang, Y.-H., et al.: Prediction of placental barrier permeability: a model based on partial least squares variable selection procedure. Molecules **20**, 8270–8286 (2015)

9. Moriwaki, H., et al.: Mordred: a molecular descriptor calculator. J. Cheminform. **10**, 4 (2018)
10. Riniker, S., Landrum, G.A.: Better informed distance geometry: using what we know to improve conformation generation. J. Chem. Inf. Model. **55**, 2562–2574 (2015)
11. Ke, G., et al.: LightGBM: a highly efficient gradient boosting decision tree. In: Advances in Neural Information Processing Systems, vol. 30, pp. 3146–3154 (2017)
12. Akiba, T.: Optuna: a next-generation hyperparameter optimization framework. In: Proceedings of the ACM SIGKDD International Conference on Knowledge Discovery and Data Mining, pp. 2623–2631 (2019)
13. Vue.js. https://vuejs.org. Accessed 7 Feb 2025
14. Flask. https://flask.palletsprojects.com. Accessed 7 Feb 2025
15. Joshi, A.A., et al.: Placental ABC transporters: biological impact and pharmaceutical significance. Pharm. Res. **33**(12), 2847–2878 (2016). https://doi.org/10.1007/s11095-016-2028-8
16. Abbott, N.J., et al.: Structure and function of the blood-brain barrier. Neurobiol. Dis. **37**, 13–25 (2010)
17. ADMET Predictor, version 10.0. https://www.simulations-plus.com/. Accessed 7 Feb 2025

Visualizing Phishing Email Features Through Sentiment Analysis

Takeshi Matsuda[1,2(✉)] and Michio Sonoda[2]

[1] Department of Information Science, Hannan University, Matsubara, Japan
[2] National Cyber Training Center, NICT, Tokyo, Japan
d-matsuda@hannan-u.ac.jp

Abstract. In recent years, many cyber attacks have tended to be profit-oriented, and phishing scams have become a problem as one method of harvesting personal information, such as credit card information. This study tried to extract the features of phishing emails without using specific keywords. We had focused our attention on the transitions of emotional features of sentences.

Keywords: Phishing emails · emotional features · unknown words · UMAP

1 Introduction

Technologies for exploiting personal information and distributing malware via email and SMS have evolved rapidly in recent years. The authors proposed a modeling method that visualizes the features of phishing emails by year, and we showed a change in attack methods [1]. A variety of detection methods have been proposed for this type of scam email, utilizing the words contained in the scam email as features, and it can be said that these methods have a certain effect. However, in recent years, there has been an increasing need to be wary of technologies in which attackers abuse generated AI and avoid detection by randomizing spam messages.

The detection method for scam emails not only uses the feature words included in them but can also use the features of email addresses, domains, and attachment files. However, due to a lack of information literacy, some people may not notice information other than the features contained in phishing emails. In addition, the method of analyzing text features can be expected to be applied in other fields as well.

This study investigates a method to extract the features of misleading text that always appears in phishing emails and prompts users to enter personal information, using sentiment analysis techniques. This makes it possible to consider methods for detecting phishing emails that do not rely on specific word information.

H. R. Arabnia et al. (Eds.): CSCE 2025, CCIS 2932, pp. 456–464, 2026.
https://doi.org/10.1007/978-3-032-22193-3_36

This study investigates a method to extract the features of misleading text that always appears in phishing emails and prompts users to enter personal information, using sentiment analysis techniques. This makes it possible to consider methods for detecting phishing emails that do not rely on specific word information. However, since sentence embeddings are not obtained from the embeddings of each word, and are not trained on phishing features, this study also investigates to what extent it is possible to capture phishing features using such general trained LLM (large language models).

2 Conventional Studies

This section introduces a related study on the theme of scam emails. In recent years, various methods using machine learning and deep learning have been proposed.

The paper [2] discusses the detection of phishing scams using Japanese SMS. The paper [2] discusses detection accuracy using machine learning algorithms such as Bayesian and K-nearest neighbor methods by weighting TF-IDF values using an English SMS dataset translated into Japanese.

A deep learning approach is also proposed instead of using a human-modeled feature space. In the paper [3], 100% accuracy was achieved in a spam email detection method using LSTM, showing a marked performance improvement compared to traditional machine learning techniques.

Some studies also use features other than the text of the email to detect scam emails, as in the studies mentioned above. Papers [4,5] discuss filtering scams by managing domains and IP addresses on mail servers. Also, the paper [6] discusses attackers' tactics to induce recipients to take action by categorizing human emotions that can be read from the text as positive or negative.

Detection methods using Large Language Models, which have evolved significantly in recent years, are also proposed. The paper [7] discusses the possibility of detecting phishing emails using LLM by creating prompts using information from the headers and body of EML-formatted emails and feeding them into various LLMs.

Research is also being conducted to detect AI-generated spam emails. The paper [8] discusses the differences between manually created and AI-generated emails using open-source software such as MALLNET, UDAT, and a deep neural network such as LSTM, in response to a large number of AI-generated emails.

The study [9] is known regarding sentiment analysis using BERT model. A model called GoEmotions is introduced that classifies 58,000 English Reddit comments into 27 emotion categories. In this study, we attempt to extract features of phishing emails by utilizing these 27 emotion labels together with the 384-dimensional sentence embedding vector obtained by BERT.

3 Proposed Method and Result

Phishing emails contain elements that make the recipient anxious. Therefore, this study uses a model that extracts emotions from text, compares normal business emails with phishing emails, and proposes a data classification method that features the transition of emotions within the text. The data analysis procedure proposed in this study is as follows.

i) Separate the sentences with punctuation or line breaks, and obtain the document embedding for each. This research used Bert.
ii) At the same time, obtain 27 types of emotion labels for the corresponding sentences using an emotion analysis model.
iii) Construct a 3-dimensional vector that features the emotion transition of the sentences before and after the sentence of interest.
iv) Use the 3-dimensional vector constructed in 3 to find commonalities between phishing emails and business emails.

The data used in this study were 4,617 phishing emails and 421 business emails observed in 2023 (Table 1).

Let us summarize the results obtained from the steps so far. First, summarize the emotion label data and its frequency information contained in business emails and phishing emails in a graph.

Comparing Fig. 1 and 2, we can see that the label "caring" is most prevalent in both business and phishing emails, while various emotion labels are attached to phishing emails. Moreover, the emotion label set for business emails is a subset of the emotion label set for phishing. We consider a two-dimensional vector consisting of a pair of two consecutive emotion labels to investigate how this characteristic changes with the transition in emotion between two consecutive sentences.

In the case of two-dimensional emotion pairs, 14 pairs were obtained from business emails (Fig. 3), and 72 pairs were obtained from phishing emails. Figure 4 shows the frequency information of the top 14 pairs out of the 72 pairs. Let us compare business emails and phishing emails by using these two-dimensional emotion labels. First, the two-dimensional emotion labels obtained from business emails are also included in phishing emails. However, there are two-dimensional emotion labels that are only observed in phishing emails, and the number of sentences with these labels is 282 (Table 2).

Specifically, by using two-dimensional emotion labels that only appear in this phishing campaign, the following sentences were extracted:

- We have placed some restrictions on card usage
- We were unable to update your Amazon membership card information
- We monitor card usage 24 h a day, 365 days a year
- Please call us immediately at (03)-****-****
- Please access the following

Table 1. Emotion Label of GoEmotions

num	emotion label
1	admiration
2	amusement
3	anger
4	annoyance
5	approval
6	caring
7	confusion
8	curiosity
9	desire
10	disappointment
11	disapproval
12	disgust
13	embarrassment
14	excitement
15	fear
16	gratitude
17	grief
18	joy
19	love
20	nervousness
21	optimism
22	pride
23	realization
24	relief
25	remorse
26	sadness
27	surprise

However, since the data also includes short word-level data that is likely to be included in normal business emails, it is necessary to augment the data from normal business emails.

- Also
- this is
- for that reason

The number of sentence emotion labels in phishing emails is greater than that in business emails, so it is likely that the emotion label sets also have a more

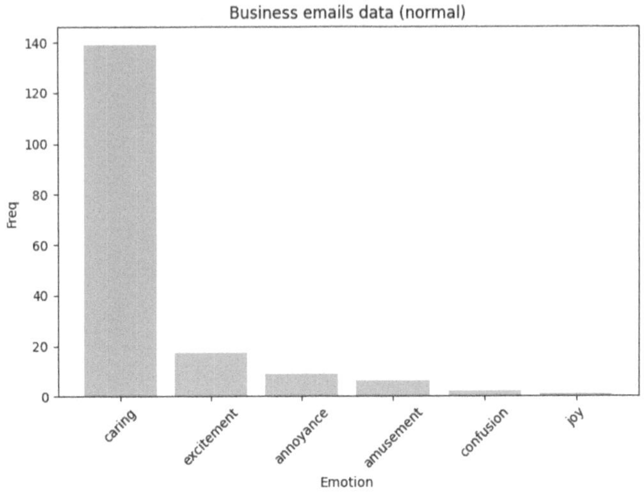

Fig. 1. Frequency of emotional information in business emails

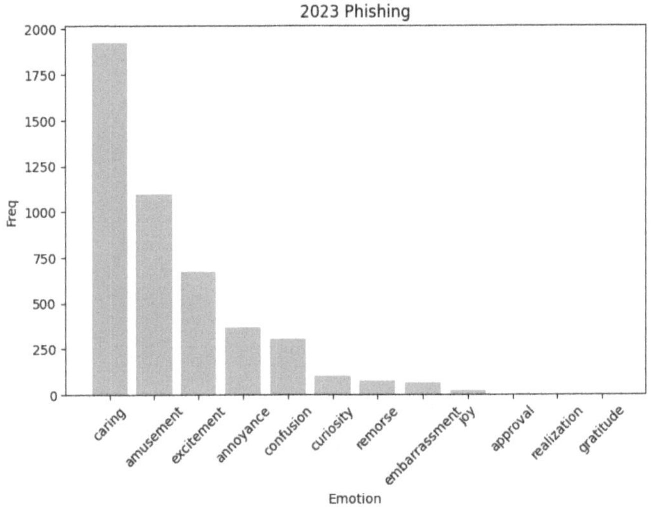

Fig. 2. Frequency of emotional information in phishing emails (2023)

complex structure, with a greater number of patterns than in business emails. In fact, when emotion label pairs were set to three consecutive sentences, 106 patterns of three-dimensional emotion vectors were calibrated, and 828 sentence data items that were only observed in phishing emails were identified. Below is a portion of that data.

- Thank you very much.
- Account Specialist

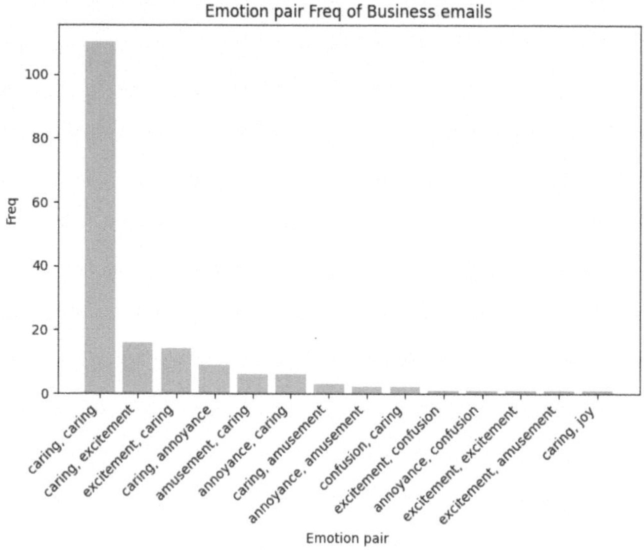

Fig. 3. Frequency of emotional pairs in business emails.

Table 2. Comparison of emotion pairs in business and phishing emails

Email Type	Number of Emotion Pairs	Characteristics
Business Email	14 pairs	Emotion pairs also found in phishing emails
Phishing Email	72 pairs	Contains unique emotion pairs not found in business emails
Phishing-Only Emotion Pairs	-	Found in 282 sentences and Emotion pairs observed only in phishing emails

- If you have not logged in for more than two years
- Before Sunday, October 30, 2022
- Due to tax law
- Amazon Prime free trial is free, but

4 Phishing Detection Technology

4.1 Unknown Word Detection

It is still necessary to increase the data on normal sentences - in this case, business email sentences - but the results of the previous chapter confirm that phishing emails and regular business emails not only have many things in common, but also that there are emotion label vectors that only appear in phishing emails. This means that by analyzing sentences with such emotion label vectors, it is possible to collect information on words contained in phishing emails

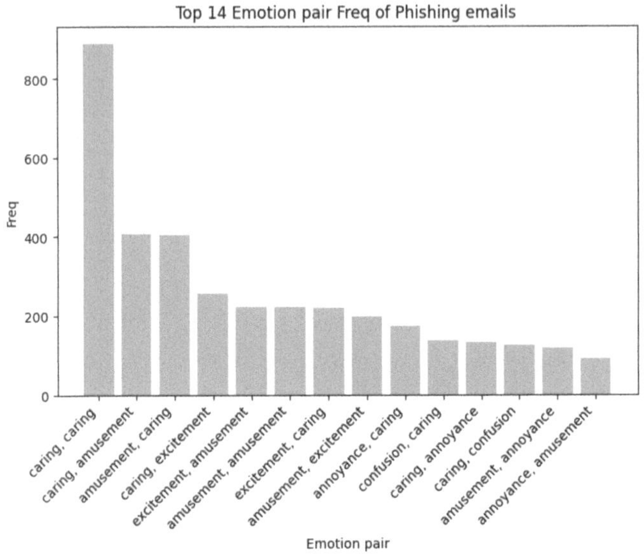

Fig. 4. Frequency of emotional pairs in phishing emails (2023)

observed up to that day. Even if the amount of normal sentences is increased, the number of patterns in the emotion label vectors of phishing emails is quite large, so there is a possibility that noise information will be included, but it is thought that there is a high possibility that sentences with similar characteristics will be captured, regardless of whether a given sentence is a phishing email or not.

When it comes to detecting phishing emails using machine learning, it is possible that detection will not work well due to new words being used. Our proposed method also obtains information on unknown words after new types of phishing emails are distributed, but detection techniques using regular machine learning require the collection of phishing data. Our method used in this research can automatically label a given text as phishing or not, and if the text contains a word that has never been observed before, it can be treated as an unknown word. However, a final human check is still required. Therefore, it may be considered that using this method can improve the speed at which we can respond to unknown attacks.

The phishing email data used in this study was observed in 2023. As candidates for unknown data, 20 pieces of data were extracted from phishing emails observed after April 2025, and the differences in phishing characteristics between 2023 and 2025 were considered. From phishing data from April 2025, 247 three-dimensional emotion vectors were obtained. The number of 2023 phishing data is 4,613.

Comparing the data from 2023 and 2025, there were 293 patterns of three-dimensional emotion vectors, of which only 6 patterns were newly observed in

2025. 210 patterns were observed only in 2023, but this is due to the difference in the number of data (Table 3).

Table 3. Comparison of phishing email data between 2023 and 2025

Year	Number of Data	Number of 3D Emotion Vectors	Common Patterns	New Patterns in 2025	Patterns Only in 2023
2023	4613	4613	293	–	210
2025	20	247	293	6	–

According to previous research [1], it has been reported that the characteristics of phishing scams change significantly from year to year. Therefore, it is thought that unknown phishing patterns may appear in the patterns of three-dimensional emotion vectors that are difficult to observe as characteristics of normal sentences.

4.2 Issues with Detection Technology Using Trained Language Models

Finally, we consider the challenges of detecting phishing emails using the proposed method. Our proposed method uses sentence embedding vectors and emotion labels, so it is possible to build technology to detect phishing emails without using word embedding vectors. However, the emotion label vector proposed in this study completely includes the features of normal sentences in the phishing data features, so it is thought that it will be difficult to classify whether a given sentence is phishing or not as it is.

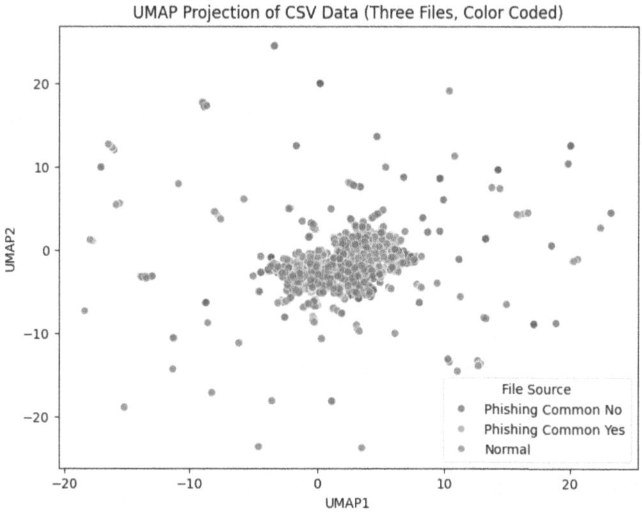

Fig. 5. Frequency of emotional pairs in phishing emails (2023)

To verify the above, we used UMAP to visualize how phishing and business emails are classified using the sentence embedding vectors and 3D sentiment vectors obtained by BERT.

From Fig. 5, it can be expected that, under current circumstances, it is difficult to determine whether an arbitrary sentence is phishing or not. Although this method was able to show that some sentences only appear in phishing, in order to prepare for unknown attacks, it is believed that a sentence embedding method specialized for phishing characteristics is necessary.

5 Conclusions

This study considered a method for extracting the features of phishing emails using a trained language model and sentiment analysis. Our future work will consider methods for extracting features of sentence structure specific to phishing.

References

1. Matsuda, T., et al.: Spam email clustering by ordered pair of modality. In:: 2023 15th International Congress on Advanced Applied Informatics Winter (IIAI-AAI-Winter), pp. 290–295 (2023)
2. Imai, K., et al.: A study on Japanese SMS spam filtering methods (in Japanese). In: The 84th National Convention of IPSJ, no. 1, pp. 531–532 (2022)
3. Eryılmaz, E.E., et al.: Filtering Turkish spam using LSTM from deep learning techniques. In: 2020 8th International Symposium on Digital Forensics and Security (ISDFS) (2020)
4. Sakuraba, S., et al.: Sender reputation construction method and feedback loop using sender authentication. IPSJ J. **64**(1), 13–23 (2023). (In Japanese)
5. Oda, C., et al.: A study on aggregation of email transfer and avoidance of queue congestion using a transparent SMTP proxy. In: Information Processing Society of Japan Transactions on Multimedia, Distributed, Cooperative, and Mobile Symposium, vol. 1, pp. 1479–1485 (2021)
6. Quang, P.T., et al.: Investigation of induction cyber attack detection based on emotional analysis. In: Computer Security Symposium 2017, pp. 399–405 (2017)
7. Koide, T., et al.: ChatSpamDetector: leveraging large language models for effective phishing email detection (2024). arXiv:2402.18093v1 [cs.CR]
8. Eze, C.S., Shamir, L.: Analysis and prevention of AI-based phishing email attacks. Electronics **13**(10), 1839 (2024)
9. Demszky, D., Movshovitz-Attias, D., Ko, J., Cowen, A., Nemade, G., Ravi, S.: GoEmotions: a dataset of fine-grained emotions (2020). https://arxiv.org/abs/2005.00547

Hardware/Software Co-design for a Multi-core Post-Quantum Cryptography CRYSTALS-Kyber Accelerator

Kien Tran-Hoang[1(✉)] and Hironori Nakajo[2]

[1] Department of Electrical Engineering and Computer Science, Tokyo University of Agriculture and Technology, Tokyo, Japan
s241057v@st.go.tuat.ac.jp

[2] Division of Advanced Information Technology and Computer Science, Tokyo University of Agriculture and Technology, Tokyo, Japan
nakajo@cc.tuat.ac.jp

Abstract. This study introduces a hardware/software co-design-based CRYSTALS-Kyber accelerator implemented on an FPGA using a RISC-V-based vector co-processor, focusing on optimizing multiplication operations for enhanced resource efficiency and proposing a possibility in high-speed design for CRYSTALS-Kyber using a multi-core approach. Implemented on the FPGA, the design utilizes 7,668 flip-flops, 13,683 look-up tables, 44 block random access memory, and six digital signal processing blocks, achieving an operational frequency of 100 MHz. Using techniques such as parallelization and loop unrolling, we achieved a balance between resource utilization and computational speed. Our findings suggest the possibility of implementing many cores on Kyber's processing unit in the hardware to accelerate lattice-based post-quantum cryptography (PQC).

Keywords: CRYSTALS-Kyber · RISC-V · FPGA · Vector co-processor · Harware/Software co-design

1 Introduction

Quantum computing, particularly the quantum computers, has recently garnered significant attention from researchers worldwide owing to the potential threat they pose to classical cryptosystems. Shor's algorithm, proposed in 1994, theoretically demonstrated that a sufficiently powerful quantum computer could break the most widely used public key encryption systems such as Rivest–Shamir–Adleman (RSA), Digital Signature Algorithm (DSA), and insecure variants of Elliptic Curve Cryptography (ECC). Consequently, the National Institute of Standards and Technology (NIST) initiated a standardization process for post-quantum cryptography (PQC) in 2016. This initiative aimed to solicit, evaluate, and standardize one or more quantum-resistant public-key cryptographic

H. R. Arabnia et al. (Eds.): CSCE 2025, CCIS 2932, pp. 465–478, 2026.
https://doi.org/10.1007/978-3-032-22193-3_37

algorithms that are secured against both potential threats from quantum and classical computers. CRYSTALS-Kyber key encapsulation mechanism (KEM) is the standardized algorithm selected after three selection rounds by the National Institute of Standards and Technology (NIST) in July 2022. Kyber's security is based on the difficulty of solving the Learning with Errors (LWE) problem over module lattices. The performance of the CRYSTALS-Kyber cryptographic scheme is heavily dependent on the efficiency of polynomial multiplication operations, which are at the core of its key generation, encapsulation, and decapsulation processes. Kyber employed the number theoretic transform (NTT), a technique that significantly reduces computational complexity, to accelerate these operations.

The NTT reduces the complexity of polynomial multiplication from $O(n^2)$ as the classical schoolbook polynomial multiplications, to $O(n \log(n))$. The NTT-based approach involves three main steps: transforming the input polynomials into the NTT domain, performing element-wise multiplications in that domain, and subsequently applying the inverse NTT (INTT) to convert the results back to the standard polynomial domain. The transformation pipeline is critical in determining the overall performance of a cryptographic system.

Recent studies have generally categorized optimization strategies for NTT computation into two main approaches. The first approach adopts a pipeline architecture for NTT transformations by organizing butterfly cores in a sequential chain, in which each core is responsible for performing operations specific to a single NTT or INTT stage. However, this method leads to a large area overhead for the NTT. The second approach uses a parallel architecture with multiple cores to accelerate the NTT computations. This approach faces the challenge of increased memory access, which typically leads to bottlenecks. Recent research on Kyber architecture has proposed increasing temporary memory usage to address this challenge.

This study explored a novel design strategy for a scalable parallel architecture with multiple cores to address bottleneck problems by implementing a vector processor architecture.

1.1 Related Works

After the development of a standard algorithm [1], the PQC Kyber was applied and developed in several aspects. In [2], software implementation was performed, and a memory-efficient high-speed implementation on Cortex-M4 was proposed; however, it exhibited high memory consumption and slow processing speed. A pure-hardware implementation was proposed in [8,9], and [11] to achieve high performance while satisfying resource constraints with a trade-off of flexibility. In [12] and [13], an optimized NTT hardware design is proposed with a flexible architecture. Moreover, [10] RISC-V instruction-set architecture uses hardware-software co-design for flexible implementation; however, operations can only be performed sequentially, and the operation speed is slow. Furthermore, the architecture in [7] utilized 2×2 butterfly cores, whereas that in [3] utilized a set of two unified butterfly cores that enabled the development of high-speed aspects through multi-core integration. However, a memory bottleneck remained when the number of cores increased. Therefore, efficient hardware-software co-design with the multi-core implementations of Kyber still lack to develop in both high-speed and flexible aspects.

1.2 Our Contributions

Some methods to overcome the memory bottleneck were proposed in [4], including the use of a vector processor. In this study, a scalable and parallelized NTT accelerator architecture was proposed for Kyber-512 and Kyber-768. The proposed architecture provides a high-performance set of components, including polynomial sampling, NTT, and point-wise multiplication, which are suitable for high-performance applications that require low latency and prioritize quantum-resistant security. The contributions of this study are as follows.

1. A vector processor-based vector architecture, that supports parallel execution of hash sampling and polynomial operations, was proposed.
2. A control unit was proposed to control the parallel operations between the hash unit and processing unit, as well as to optimize the compress/decompress process.
3. This architecture was applied to both the Server and Client sides to create a complete device.
4. This study was implemented on an Alveo U250 FPGA for evaluation and comparison with previous studies.

The remainder of this paper is organized as follows. In Sect. 2, we discuss the background information about the CRYSTALS-Kyber algorithm. Section 3 describes the hardware and software architectures of this study, including its design methodology and implementation. We discuss our results and compare them with those of previous work in Sect. 4. Finally, Sect. 5 concludes the paper and suggests directions for future research.

2 Background

2.1 Kyber Algorithms

In this study, all of the CRYSTALS-Kyber's operations are on the polynomial ring $R_q = Z_q[X]/(x^n + 1)$ with two security levels including Kyber-512 and Kyber-768. In addition, the parameter set was selected corresponding to the latest version of Kyber, which is $(n, q) = (256, 3329)$ for all its levels. Kyber's key encapsulation mechanism (KEM) is defined as follows, where *sk* stands for secret key, *pk* for public key, and *ct* for ciphertext:

- **Key Generation**: This process results in a pair of keys (*sk*, *pk*) by selecting $\mathbf{s}$ and $\mathbf{e}$ from binomial sampling, and $\mathbf{A}$ from a uniform distribution. Subsequently, *pk* can be received by compressing $\hat{\mathbf{t}}$ with $\hat{\mathbf{t}} = \hat{\mathbf{A}} \cdot \hat{\mathbf{s}} + \hat{\mathbf{e}}$ and $sk = \hat{\mathbf{s}}$.

- **Encryption**: Seed and binomial sampling were used to select $\mathbf{r}$, $\mathbf{e_1}$, and $\mathbf{e_2}$. Furthermore, the inverse matrix of $\hat{\mathbf{A}}$ could be sampled from a uniform distribution. Then, ct = (Compress($\mathbf{u}$), Compress($\mathbf{v}$)), whereas: $\mathbf{u} = \text{INTT}(\hat{\mathbf{A}}^{\mathbf{T}} \cdot \hat{\mathbf{r}}) + \mathbf{e_1}$ and $\mathbf{v} = \text{INTT}(\hat{\mathbf{t}}^{\mathbf{T}} \cdot \hat{\mathbf{r}}) + \mathbf{e_2} + \mathbf{m}$.
- **Decryption**: Plaintext $\mathbf{m}$ is computed by $\mathbf{m}$ = Compress($\mathbf{v}$ - INTT($\hat{\mathbf{s}}^{\mathbf{T}} \cdot \hat{\mathbf{u}}$), whereas $\mathbf{u}$ and $\mathbf{v}$ are taken from the ciphertext.

Keccak. Keccak hash function forms the basis of the SHA-3 family of cryptographic hash functions which is used not only for hashing, but also for generating pseudorandom matrices, sampling noise polynomials, and deriving shared secrets during key encapsulation. The generating of $\mathbf{s}$, $\mathbf{e}$, $\mathbf{r}$, $\mathbf{e_1}, \mathbf{e_2}, \hat{\mathbf{A}}, \hat{\mathbf{A}}^{\mathbf{T}}$ were assigned to the Keccak core function. Its efficiency and versatility are critical to the security and performance of the entire cryptographic scheme. Keccak core supports several function modes specified in the SHA3 standard including SHAKE-128, SHAKE-256, SHA3-256, and SHA3-512. It requires performing 24 rounds to form 1600 bits and consumes 79 cycles.

2.2 Number Theoretic Transform (NTT)

The centerpiece of NTT is a fast Fourier transform (FFT) applied to a finite field. Let f be a polynomial as defined in Eq. 1.

$$f(x) = (f_0, f_1, ..., f_{255}) \in R_q \tag{1}$$

NTT(f) is defined as shown in Eq. 2.

$$\begin{aligned} \hat{f} &= (\hat{f_0} + \hat{f_1}X, \hat{f_2} + \hat{f_3}X, ..., \hat{f}_{254} + \hat{f}_{255}X) \\ \hat{f_{2i}} &= \sum_{j=0}^{127} f_{2j}\zeta^{(2br_7(i)+1)j} \\ \hat{f}_{2i+1} &= \sum_{j=0}^{127} f_{2j+1}\zeta^{(2br_7(i)+1)j} \end{aligned} \tag{2}$$

with $\zeta = 17$ being the first primitive 256-th root of unity modulo q, and br_7 being the bit reversal function. In addition to the theoretical formula, the pseudo-code of the NTT is presented in Algorithm 1. Moreover, the multiplication of two polynomials f and g is calculated by performing $\hat{h} = \hat{f} \cdot \hat{g}$ then conducting the inverse NTT process to convert the result into the normal domain, as shown in Eq. 3.

$$\hat{h} = \hat{h}_{2i} + \hat{h}_{2i+1}X = (\hat{f}_{2i} + \hat{f}_{2i+1}X)(\hat{g}_{2i} + \hat{g}_{2i+1}X) \tag{3}$$

To optimize this multiplication, point-wise multiplication is applied as shown in Eq. 4.

$$\begin{aligned} \hat{h}_{2i} &= \hat{f}_{2i}\hat{g}_{2i} + \hat{f}_{2i+1}\hat{g}_{2i+1}\,\zeta^{2\,\mathrm{br}(i)+1} \\ \hat{h}_{2i+1} &= \hat{f}_{2i}\hat{g}_{2i+1} + \hat{f}_{2i+1}\hat{g}_{2i} \end{aligned} \tag{4}$$

Furthermore, every coefficient of the polynomials after the multiplication or addition operations was reduced with respect to prime q by the modular reduction function, as shown in Algorithm 2.

Algorithm 1. NTT Algorithm Based on Cooley–Tukey algorithm

```
  Input: polynomial f(x) ∈ Z_q[X]/(X_n+1)
  Input: n-th primitive root of unity ω_n ∈ Z_q
  Output: f̂(x) = NTT(f) ∈ Z_q[X]/(X_n+1)
x ← 1
for i from 128 down to 2 by i/2 do
   for j from 0 to 255 by i + k do
      W ← ROM[x]
      for k from j to i + j do
         T ← W.f[i + k] mod q
         f[i + k] ← f[k] - T mod q
         f[k] ← f[k] + T mod q
      end for
      x ← x + 1
   end for
end for
```

Algorithm 2. Barrett Reduction Modulus q = 3329

```
  Input: q = 3329,a ∈ [0, q^2)
  Output: x = a mod q
v ← ((1 ≪ 26) + (q/2)) / q
x ← (v.a + (1 ≪ 25)) ≫ 26
x ← x.q
x ← a - x
return x
```

2.3 RISC-V Vector Extensions

The RISC-V Vector Extension (RVV) is an extended RISC-V instruction set. RVV provides 32 vector registers, and the size of the elements to be stored in them can be configured as 8-, 16-, 32-, or 64-bit. Various RVV-based processors have recently been developed. Perotti et al. developed a vector architecture known as the Ara processor, which supports RVV version 1.0 2022 [5]. Several other commercial cores are available. For instance, ARM released X925, a core that supports scalable vector extension (SVE).

The processor must be customizable to be compatible with the proposed design; therefore, an open-source RVV core was used in this study.

2.4 RV32[I][E] Processor: CV32E40X

CV32E40X is an in-order 4-stage processor that implements RV32I and RV32E, and was developed by the Swiss Federal Institute of Technology in Zurich (ETH) and the University of Bologna. In addition, the source code is available on GitHub, which is written in the SystemVerilog language and uses the OpenHW Group's CORE-V eXtension Interface to communicate with Vicuna, a co-processor that supports RVV.

2.5 RVV Co-processor: Vicuna

Vicuna is a co-processor that implements the RVV developed by TU Wien, Austria. The core was released in June 2021, with an implementation based on Version 1.0 of RVV [6]. Vicuna supports vector element widths of 8, 16, and 32 bits, and implements all vector loads and stores, vector integers, and other typical types of vector instructions. The vector instructions were sent from the CV32E40X to Vicuna and executed in parallel by distributing the processing across pipelines. Each pipeline has a vector load and store unit, vector arithmetic and logical unit, vector slide unit, vector multiplier, and vector indexing unit. The number of pipelines is determined by the length of the vector and width of the data element. The available vector lengths are 128, 512, and 2048 bits. Vicuna and CV32E40X were customized for evaluation. A brief block diagram of the system constructed using CV32E40X and Vicuna is shown in Fig. 1.

3 Hardware/Software Architecture

Full hardware implementation significantly improves the performance of the architecture compared with a hardware/software codesign approach; however, this is at the expense of a longer development time, reduced flexibility, and the requirement of customized data paths tailored to specific protocol-level operations. Leveraging an instruction set processor results in a more compact and simpler design, although it tends to be slower and offers greater control and programmability.

3.1 Software

Our software program, which is run in Vicuna, is divided into three phases: key generation, decryption, and encryption. The key generation phase is shown in

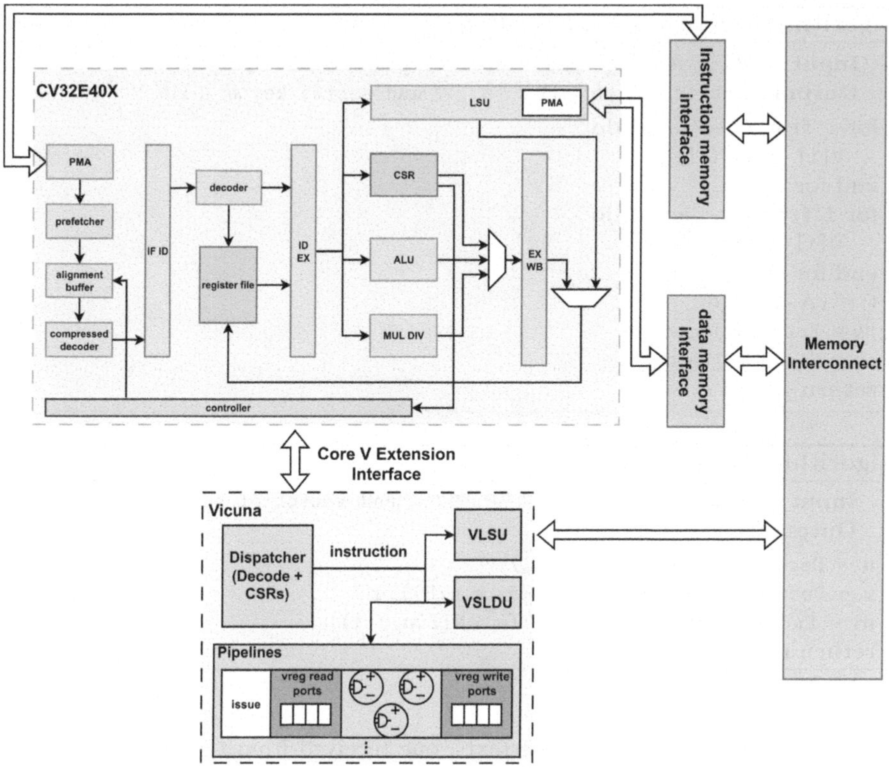

Fig. 1. Brief block diagram of system constructed CV32E40X and Vicuna.

Algorithm 3. Furthermore, the matrix −vector multiplication $\hat{\mathbf{A}} \cdot \hat{\mathbf{s}}$ for Kyber-768 is shown in Eq. 5. The matrix dimensions and number of polynomials were three for Kyber-768, two for Kyber-512, and four for Kyber-1024. Point-wise multiplication was applied to each multiplication operation.

$$\begin{aligned} \hat{\mathbf{A}} \cdot \hat{\mathbf{s}} &= \begin{bmatrix} \hat{\mathbf{A}}_{00} & \hat{\mathbf{A}}_{01} & \hat{\mathbf{A}}_{02} \\ \hat{\mathbf{A}}_{10} & \hat{\mathbf{A}}_{11} & \hat{\mathbf{A}}_{12} \\ \hat{\mathbf{A}}_{20} & \hat{\mathbf{A}}_{21} & \hat{\mathbf{A}}_{22} \end{bmatrix} \cdot \begin{bmatrix} \hat{\mathbf{s}}_{00} \\ \hat{\mathbf{s}}_{10} \\ \hat{\mathbf{s}}_{20} \end{bmatrix} \\ &= \begin{bmatrix} \hat{\mathbf{A}}_{00} \cdot \hat{\mathbf{s}}_{00} + \hat{\mathbf{A}}_{01} \cdot \hat{\mathbf{s}}_{01} + \hat{\mathbf{A}}_{02} \cdot \hat{\mathbf{s}}_{02} \\ \hat{\mathbf{A}}_{10} \cdot \hat{\mathbf{s}}_{10} + \hat{\mathbf{A}}_{11} \cdot \hat{\mathbf{s}}_{11} + \hat{\mathbf{A}}_{12} \cdot \hat{\mathbf{s}}_{12} \\ \hat{\mathbf{A}}_{20} \cdot \hat{\mathbf{s}}_{20} + \hat{\mathbf{A}}_{21} \cdot \hat{\mathbf{s}}_{21} + \hat{\mathbf{A}}_{22} \cdot \hat{\mathbf{s}}_{22} \end{bmatrix} \end{aligned} \tag{5}$$

The operations in polynomial multiplication are reduced with respect to prime q. However, the system transitions to wait mode for the ciphertext from the opponent side to change its status into the decryption phase. The decryption phase is presented in Algorithm 4.

However, an encryption phase was performed to verify the authenticity of the plaintext after decrypting the ciphertext. Subsequently, a comparison was

Algorithm 3. Kyber: Key Generation

Input: matrix $\hat{\mathbf{A}} \in \mathbf{R}_q^{kxk}$ and vector of polynomials $\mathbf{s},\mathbf{e} \in \mathbf{R}_q^k$
Output: public key $pk \in \mathbf{B}^{(12.k.n/8)+32}$ and secret key $sk \in \mathbf{B}^{12.k.n/8}$

```
for i from 0 to k - 1 do
    ŝ[i] = NTT(s[i])
end for
for i from 0 to k - 1 do
    ê[i] = NTT(e[i])
end for
t̂ = (Â · ŝ) + ê
pk = Encode(t̂) mod q
sk = Encode(ŝ) mod q
return pk and sk
```

Algorithm 4. Kyber: Decryption

Input: ciphertext $ct \in \mathbf{B}^{(d_u.k.n/8)+(d_v.n/8)}$ and vector of polynomials $\mathbf{s} \in \mathbf{R}_q^k$
Output: $\mathbf{m} \in \mathbf{B}^{32}$

```
u = Decompress(Decode_du(ct),d_u)
v = Decompress(Decode_dv(ct + (d_u.k.n/8)),d_v)
m = Encode(Compress(v - INTT(ŝ^T · NTT(u)),1))
return m
```

performed between the two ciphertexts, one received from the opposing side in the decryption phase, and the other created in the encryption phase based on the plaintext decrypted in the decryption phase. However, to improve the efficiency of the program, instead of the two ciphertexts, a comparison is performed between Compress($\mathbf{u}$,d_u) and Compress($\mathbf{v}$,d_v) after the encryption phase and $(\mathbf{u}, \mathbf{v})$ received in the decryption phase after the decoding process. The encryption phase is described in Algorithm 5.

Furthermore, the compression or decompression algorithm for the decryption/encryption phase is described by Eq. 6:

$$Compress(x,d) = (\frac{2^d.x}{q}) \bmod 2^d \quad Decompress(x,d) = (\frac{q.x}{2^d}) \tag{6}$$

3.2 Hardware

The overall communication between our device and the CRYSTALS-Kyber is shown in Fig. 2. Our complete device comprises two parts: server and client, which is a half-duplex system. Communication is established between our device and the external components. Additionally, a system, including a Vicuna vector processor and a CV32E40X scalar processor, was used simultaneously on both the server and client sides. The proposed architecture on the server side is illustrated in Fig. 3.

Algorithm 5. Kyber: Encryption

Input: inverse matrix $\hat{\mathbf{A}}^{\mathbf{T}} \in \mathbf{R}_q^{kxk}$ and vector of polynomials $\hat{\mathbf{t}}, \mathbf{r}, \mathbf{e}_1 \in \mathbf{R}_q^k$
Input: polynomial $\mathbf{e_2} \in \mathbf{R}_q$ and plaintext $\mathbf{m} \in \mathbf{B}^{32}$
Output: Compress($\mathbf{u}$,d_u) and Compress($\mathbf{v}$,d_v)

```
for i from 0 to k - 1 do
    r̂[i] = NTT(r[i])
end for
u = INTT(Â^T · r̂) + e1
v = INTT(t̂^T · r̂) + e2 + Decompress(Decode(m),1)
return u and v
```

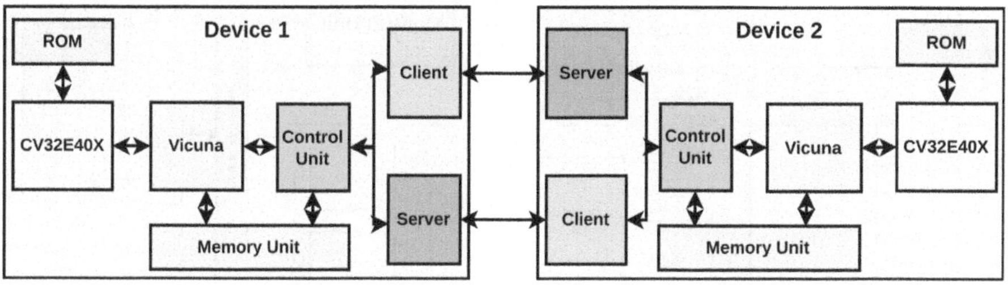

Fig. 2. Communication between devices.

Hash Unit. Keccak unit is configured to support four function modes, including SHAKE-128, SHAKE-256, SHA3-256, and SHA3-512. An input fifo was developed to interface with the Keccak core with a 32-bit data bandwidth. Keccak core's output was interfaced with two fifos that stored the value for matrix $\hat{\mathbf{A}}/\hat{\mathbf{A}}^{\mathbf{T}}$ and polynomials $\mathbf{s}$, $\mathbf{e}$, $\mathbf{r}$, $\mathbf{e_1}$ and $\mathbf{e_2}$ while the elements of $\hat{\mathbf{A}}/\hat{\mathbf{A}}^{\mathbf{T}}$ were sampled from 12 pseudo-random integers and the elements of $\mathbf{s}$, $\mathbf{e}$, $\mathbf{r}$, $\mathbf{e_1}$, and $\mathbf{e_2}$ were sampled from six pseudo-random integers. The sizes of the two fifos were determined as 24×256 and 24×64 respectively. It took 24 rounds for the Keccak core to obtain an output stream with 1600 bits. The sampling process schedule is illustrated in Fig. 4.

Control Unit. The control unit (CU) was designed based on the flow of our software program, including key generation, decryption, and encryption. In key generation, the CU determined the flow data $\hat{\mathbf{t}} = \hat{\mathbf{A}} \cdot \hat{\mathbf{s}} + \hat{\mathbf{e}}$ from memory through the encode function to share the ciphertext. In decryption, this block determines the flow of the ciphertext received in the memory to prepare for the decryption process. During the encryption phase, a comparison and evaluation were performed to determine the authenticity of the plaintext obtained during the decryption phase. Moreover, the CU controls the access between other blocks with memory, such as read/write operations from Vicuna in three phases, as mentioned in the software subsection, or read/write operations from the hash unit, CV32E40X processor, and receiver.

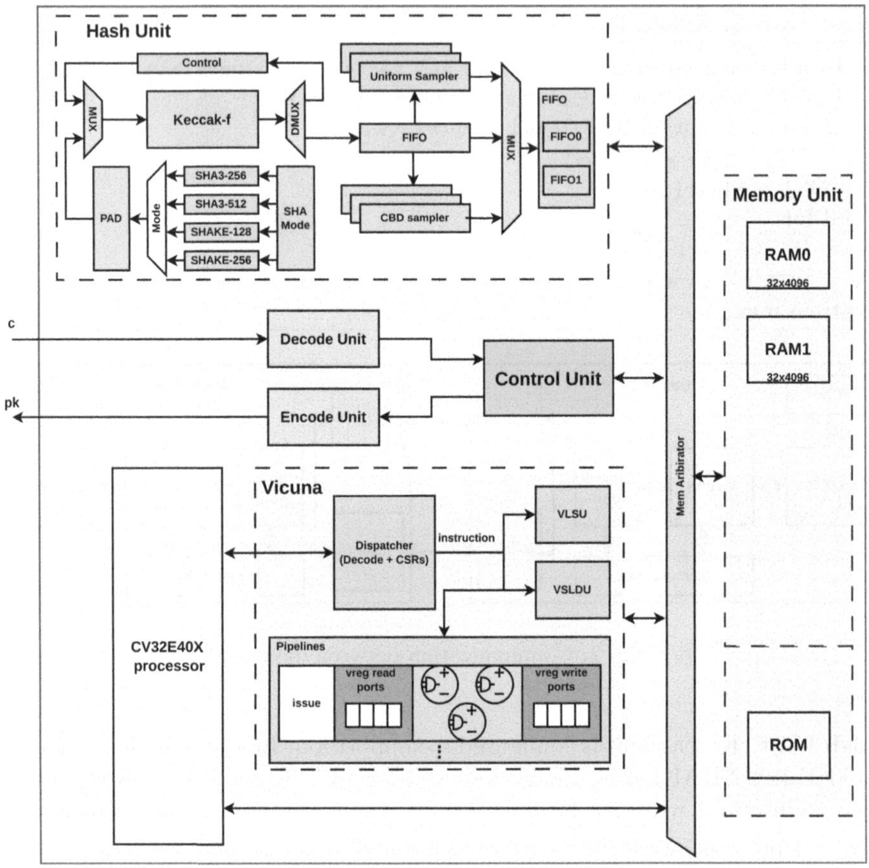

Fig. 3. Overall system architecture.

CV32E40X and Vicuna. Only the CV32E40X scalar processor is connected to the read-only memory (ROM) through a memory arbitrator and is directly connected to Vicuna, but it is not connected to the random access memory (RAM). After loading the software program stored inside the ROM, CV32E40X sent the instructions to Vicuna. Vicuna played an important role in the overall system.

Memory Arrangement. The memory was divided into RAM0 and RAM1. RAM0 was only for storing the value of the seed for the hash unit, such as $\rho, \sigma, hash(pk), \mathbf{r}, hash(ct), r'$ for initializing the symmetric primitives of rejective sampling and CBD. RAM1 involves two partitions: 0 and 1. The input data for Vicuna were stored in Partition 0 as $\hat{\mathbf{A}}, \hat{\mathbf{A}}^{\mathbf{T}}, \mathbf{s}, \mathbf{e}, \mathbf{r}, \mathbf{e_1}$, and $\mathbf{e_2}$, and the output data from Vicuna as the three phases' results, in particular, $\hat{\mathbf{t}} = \hat{\mathbf{A}} \cdot \hat{\mathbf{s}} + \hat{\mathbf{e}}$ and the secret key (sk) are stored from the key generation phase until used for the

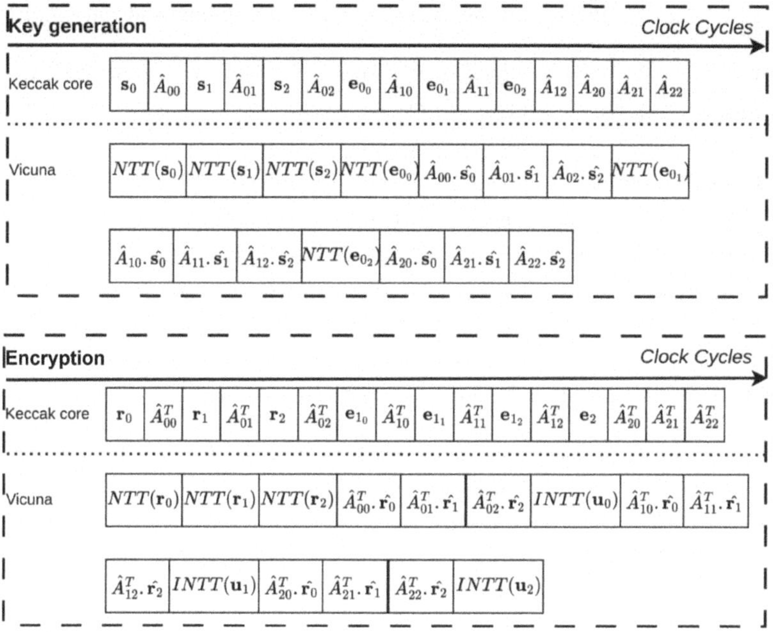

Fig. 4. Elaborate scheduling for sampling and NTT procedures.

decryption and encryption phases. The sizes of RAM0 and RAM1 were 32 × 4096 bits.

4 Experimentation

The proposed architecture was implemented on the Alveo U250 FPGA platform (part number xcu250-figd2104-2L-e) and was modeled using Verilog on the Xilinx Vivado 2021.2 design tool for evaluation as well as comparison with related studies in terms of speed and hardware performance. All results were obtained after place-and-route (PAR). We conducted a comparison between our architecture and the pure hardware implementations, as well as the hardware/software co-design. As shown in Table 1 and Table 2, our design has advantages and disadvantages compared with the design proposed here. Our proposed scheme occupies 13k lookup tables (LUTs), 7k flip-flops (FFs), six digital signal processing blocks (DSPs), and 44 block random access memories (BRAMs); it runs at 100 MHz and takes 434 μs to perform the whole Kyber protocol. Compared to the architectures in [10] and [15] proposed by the hardware/software method, the proposed scheme required much less resource utilization in lookup tables (LUTs) and achieved a speedup factor of 34x compared to its leading counterpart in HW/SW designs, which is [10]. In addition, our design achieves a speedup factor of 50.04× compared to its leading counterpart in SW designs

Table 1. Resource utilization comparison for Kyber-768 implementation on FPGA.

Work	Method	Platform	LUT	FF	Slice	DSP	BRAM
Batros et al. [2]	SW	Cortex-M4	–	–	–	–	–
Banerjee et al. [10]	HW/SW	Artix-7	15K	4K	4K	11	14
Bishes-Niasar et al. [7]	HW	Artix-7	16K	6K	4K	9	6
J. Zhang et al. [14]	HW	UltraScale	18K	6K	3K	8	9
Fritzmann et al. [15]	HW/SW	Zynq-7000	24K	11K	N/A	21	32
Xing et al. [3]	HW	Artix-7	7K	5K	2K	2	3
This work	HW/SW	Alveo U250	13K	7K	3K	6	44

Table 2. Simulate-based comparison with related works for Kyber-768.

Work	Method	Platform	Frequency [MHz]	Total Time [μs]	Speedup Ratio
Batros et al. [2]	SW	Cortex-M4	100	21,720	50.04
Banerjee et al. [10]	HW/SW	Artix-7	25	14,760	34.01
Bishes-Niasar et al. [7]	HW	Artix-7	200	209	0.48
J. Zhang et al. [14]	HW	UltraScale	355	51	0.12
Fritzmann et al. [15]	HW/SW	Zynq-7000	–	–	–
Xing et al. [3]	HW	Artix-7	161	111	0.25
This work	HW/SW	Alveo U250	100	434	1.00

[2]. Moreover, the design implemented with the RISC-V instruction-set architecture, as in [7] and [14], took 2.07 and 8.5 times faster than our approach. The [7] and [14] run at frequencies of 200 MHz and 335 MHz, especially in their works proposed by the pure hardware method, which explains why [7] and [14] can achieve better performance. However, compared with the architectures proposed by the same HW/SW method, our approach achieved better performance and consumed fewer resources. In addition, our study implemented four cores in the Vicuna processor; implementing eight, 16, or more cores can achieve better performance in terms of the high-speed aspect compared with compact hardware architectures.

5 Conclusion

The threat from quantum computers is real owing to the major efforts of researchers and technology companies in developing them, and enhancing security levels in applications for embedded systems or in the semiconductor industry is a necessity. In this study, we proposed a post-quantum multi-core cryptosystem for CRYSTALS-Kyber based on a vector processor. Implementing efficient components has increased the performance compared with those of state-of-the-art software and hardware/software implementations. Our future work will focus on lightweight PQC implementations that are suitable for embedded systems and can be applied in the semiconductor industry.

Acknowledgments. This research was supported by JSPS Grant-in-Aid for Scientific Research (C) No. 24K14874.

References

1. J. Bos, L. et al.: CRYSTALS - kyber: a CCA-secure module-lattice-based KEM. In: IEEE European Symposium on Security and Privacy (EuroS&P), pp. 353–367 (2018). https://doi.org/10.1109/EuroSP.2018.00032
2. Botros, L., Kannwischer, M.J., Schwabe, P.: Memory-efficient high-speed implementation of kyber on cortex-M4. In: Buchmann, J., Nitaj, A., Rachidi, T. (eds.) AFRICACRYPT 2019. LNCS, vol. 11627, pp. 209–228. Springer, Cham (2019). https://doi.org/10.1007/978-3-030-23696-0_11
3. Xing, Y., Li, S.: A compact hardware implementation of CCA-secure key exchange mechanism CRYSTALS-KYBER on FPGA. IACR Trans. Cryptograph. Hardware Embed. Syst. **2021**(2), 328–356 (2021). https://tches.iacr.org/index.php/TCHES/article/view/8797/8397
4. Efnusheva, D., Cholakoska, A., Tentov, A.: A survey of different approaches for overcoming the processor - memory bottleneck. Int. J. Inf. Technol. Comput. Sci. **9**(2), 151–163 (2017). https://doi.org/10.5121/ijcsit.2017.9214
5. Cavalcante, M., Schuiki, F., Zaruba, F., Schaffner, M., Benini, L.: Ara: a 1-GHz+ scalable and energy-efficient RISC-V vector processor with multiprecision floating-point support in 22-nm FD-SOI. IEEE Trans. Very Large Scale Integrat. (VLSI) Syst. **28**(2), 530–543 (2020). https://doi.org/10.1109/TVLSI.2019.2950087
6. Platzer, M., Puschner, P.: Vicuna: a timing-predictable RISC-V vector coprocessor for scalable parallel computation. In: 33rd Euromicro Conference on Real-Time Systems, Leibniz International Proceedings in Informatics, vol. 196, pp. 1:1–1:18 (2021). https://doi.org/10.4230/LIPIcs.ECRTS.2021.1
7. Bisheh-Niasar, M., Azarderakhsh, R., Mozaffari-Kermani, M.: Instruction-set accelerated implementation of CRYSTALS-Kyber. IEEE Trans. Circ. Syst. I: Reg. Papers **68**(11), 4648–4659 (2021). https://doi.org/10.1109/TCSI.2021.3106639
8. Guo, W., Li, S.: Highly-efficient hardware architecture for CRYSTALS-kyber with a novel conflict-free memory access pattern. IEEE Trans. Circ. Syst. I: Reg. Pap. **70**(11), 4505–4515 (2023). https://doi.org/10.1109/TCSI.2023.3306347
9. Guo, W., Li, S.: Split-radix based compact hardware architecture for CRYSTALS-kyber. IEEE Trans. Comput. **73**(1), 97–108 (2024). https://doi.org/10.1109/TC.2023.3320040
10. Banerjee, U., Ukyab, T.S., Chandrakasan, A.P.: Sapphire: a configurable crypto-processor for post-quantum lattice-based protocols. IACR Trans. Cryptograph. Hardware Embed. Syst. **2019**(4), 17–61 (2019). https://doi.org/10.13154/tches.v2019.i4.17-61
11. Huang, Y., Huang, M., Lei, Z., Wu, J.: A pure hardware implementation of CRYSTALS-KYBER PQC algorithm through resource reuse. IEICE Electron. Exp. **17**(17), 20200234 (2020). https://doi.org/10.1587/elex.17.20200234

12. Mert, A.C., Karabulut, E., Ozturk, E., Savas, E., Becchi, M., Aysu, A.: A flexible and scalable NTT hardware: applications from homomorphically encrypted deep learning to post-quantum cryptography. In: 2020 Design, Automation & Test in Europe Conference & Exhibition, pp. 346–351 (2020). https://doi.org/10.23919/DATE48585.2020.9116470
13. Mert, A.C., Karabulut, E., Ozturk, E., Savas, E., Aysu, A.: An extensive study of flexible design methods for the number theoretic transform. IEEE Trans. Comput. **71**(11), 2829–2843 (2020). https://doi.org/10.1109/TC.2020.3017930
14. Zhang, J., et al.: Super-K: a superscalar CRYSTALS-KYBER processor based on efficient arithmetic array. IEEE Trans. Circuits Syst. II Express Briefs **71**(9), 4286–4290 (2024). https://doi.org/10.1109/TCSII.2024.3382772
15. Fritzmann, T., Sigl, G., Sepúlveda, J.: RISQ-V: tightly coupled RISC-V accelerators for post-quantum cryptography. IACR Trans. Cryptograph. Hardware Embed. Syst. **2020**(4), 239–280 (2020). https://doi.org/10.13154/tches.v2020.i4.239-280

SESCA: An Enhanced Sine-Cosine Algorithm with Sigmoid-Based Nonlinear Mapping for Optimization

Yang Cao[1(✉)], Xingbang Du[1], Rui Zhong[2], Jun Yu[3], and Masaharu Munetomo[2]

[1] Graduate School of Information Science and Technology, Hokkaido University, Sapporo, Japan
{yang.cao.y4,xingbang.du.d1}@elms.hokudai.ac.jp
[2] Information Initiative Center, Hokkaido University, Sapporo, Japan
{zhongrui,munetomo}@iic.hokudai.ac.jp
[3] Institute of Science and Technology, Niigata University, Niigata, Japan
yujun@ie.niigata-u.ac.jp

Abstract. Metaheuristic algorithms have been widely employed in complex optimization problems due to their simplicity and efficiency. Amnstrates promising performance; however, it can suffer from issues like premature convergence and suboptimal solution oscillation. To address these challenges, this paper proposes an improved variant named Sigmoid-Enhanced Sine-Cosine Algorithm (SESCA). The key innovations in SESCA is the Sine-Cosine Algorithm (SCA) demoigmoid-based nonlinear modulation, enhancing search accuracy and convergence stability. Experimental results on CEC2022 benchmark optimization problems verify that SESCA outperforms the traditional SCA significantly, showing enhanced robustness and convergence speed.

Keywords: Metaheuristic algorithms · Sigmoid · Sine-Cosine Algorithm

1 Introduction

Metaheuristic algorithms, inspired by natural phenomena such as biological evolution, animal behavior, and physical processes, are widely used in various fields, including engineering design, energy management, machine learning, and finance, due to their powerful global optimization capabilities and adaptability to diverse problem landscapes [1–3]. These algorithms include Particle Swarm Optimization (PSO) [4], Genetic Algorithms (GA) [5], and Differential Evolution (DE) [6], among others. Each of these methods exhibits unique strengths and limitations, motivating continuous development and hybridization to overcome inherent deficiencies.

H. R. Arabnia et al. (Eds.): CSCE 2025, CCIS 2932, pp. 479–492, 2026.
https://doi.org/10.1007/978-3-032-22193-3_38

The Sine-Cosine Algorithm (SCA), inspired specifically by trigonometric sine and cosine functions, has attracted attention due to its intuitive mathematical representation and competitive performance in solving diverse optimization problems [7]. Its simplicity, few parameters, and effective exploration and exploitation balance make SCA appealing to researchers [8]. However, despite these advantages, the conventional SCA suffers from notable drawbacks such as convergence instability, excessive oscillations around optimal solutions, and susceptibility to premature convergence [9]. These limitations can significantly degrade the optimization accuracy and robustness of SCA, particularly in high-dimensional or complex optimization scenarios [10].

To address these challenges, researchers have explored modifications such as adaptive parameter adjustments, hybridization with other metaheuristics, and improved update strategies [11]. Building on these ideas, this study introduces an advanced variant, termed the Sigmoid-based Enhanced Sine-Cosine Algorithm (SESCA). SESCA incorporates a sigmoid-based nonlinear mapping function into the original SCA to dynamically regulate solution updates. This improvement helps SESCA navigate the optimization landscape more effectively, reducing oscillations and mitigating premature convergence. The main contributions of this study are summarized as follows:

- Introduction of a **sigmoid-based nonlinear mapping** to modulate the solution update, effectively reducing excessive oscillations and enhancing solution stability.
- Comprehensive performance validation using benchmark optimization problems, including extensive experiments on the **CEC2022 benchmark suite**, demonstrating SESCA's superior capability and robustness compared to conventional SCA and other metaheuristic algorithms.

This paper elaborates the methodological enhancements introduced by SESCA, provides a comprehensive analysis of its performance against standard benchmark functions, and demonstrates its superior capability compared to the conventional SCA.

The remainder of this paper is organized as follows. Section 2 provides a brief overview of the original Sine-Cosine Algorithm. Section 3 describes the proposed SESCA in detail. Section 4 outlines the experimental setup and evaluation. Section 5 discusses the results and provides performance analysis. Finally, Sect. 6 concludes the paper and outlines potential directions for future research.

2 Sine-Cosine Algorithm

The Sine-Cosine Algorithm (SCA) is a metaheuristic optimization algorithm inspired by the trigonometric sine and cosine functions, first introduced by Mirjalili in 2016 [12]. The algorithm balances exploration and exploitation dynamically through sine and cosine-based position updating mechanisms. The effect of sine and cosine on Eqs. (1) and (2) is shown in Fig. 1. The primary steps of the SCA algorithm are as follows:

1. **Initialization**: A set of initial candidate solutions is randomly generated within the given search space.
2. **Solution updating phase**: The algorithm updates the position of each candidate solution using the sine function as Eq. (1):

$$X_{i,j}^{t+1} = X_{i,j}^{t} + r_1 \cdot \sin(r_2) \cdot |r_3 \cdot P_j - X_{i,j}^{t}| \tag{1}$$

   or using the cosine function as Eq. (2):

$$X_{i,j}^{t+1} = X_{i,j}^{t} + r_1 \cdot \cos(r_2) \cdot |r_3 \cdot P_j - X_{i,j}^{t}| \tag{2}$$

   Here, r_1 is a step-size factor decreasing over iterations, and r_2, r_3 are random parameters used to enhance the stochastic exploration behavior. The term P_j represents the global best solution's position for the j-th dimension.
3. **Iteration**: The process continues until a maximum number of iterations or convergence criteria are met, after which the best-found solution is output.

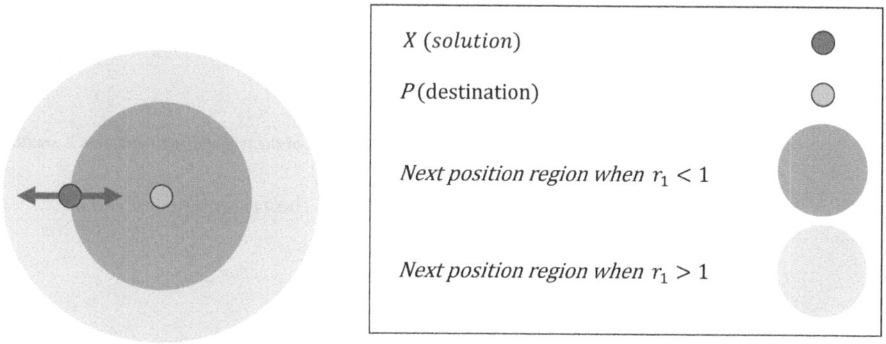

Fig. 1. Impacts of the trigonometric operators in Eqs. (1) and (2) on updating positions.

Although SCA has a simple structure and is easy to implement, it suffers from drawbacks such as oscillatory convergence and susceptibility to local optima. Thus, the SESCA algorithm introduced in this study aims to address these shortcomings.

3 Our Proposal: Sigmoid-Enhanced Sine-Cosine Algorithm

To overcome the drawbacks of traditional SCA, such as premature convergence and solution instability, we propose the Sigmoid-Enhanced Sine-Cosine Algorithm (SESCA), which innovatively incorporates sigmoid-based nonlinear mapping. These enhancements significantly improve the balance between exploration and exploitation, resulting in more stable and accurate convergence behavior. As shown in Fig. 2 the sigmoid function enables the trigonometric output to have smoother values, which allows the algorithm to converge better to the optimal solution in the later stages of exploration. Algorithm 1 is the pseudo-code for SESCA.

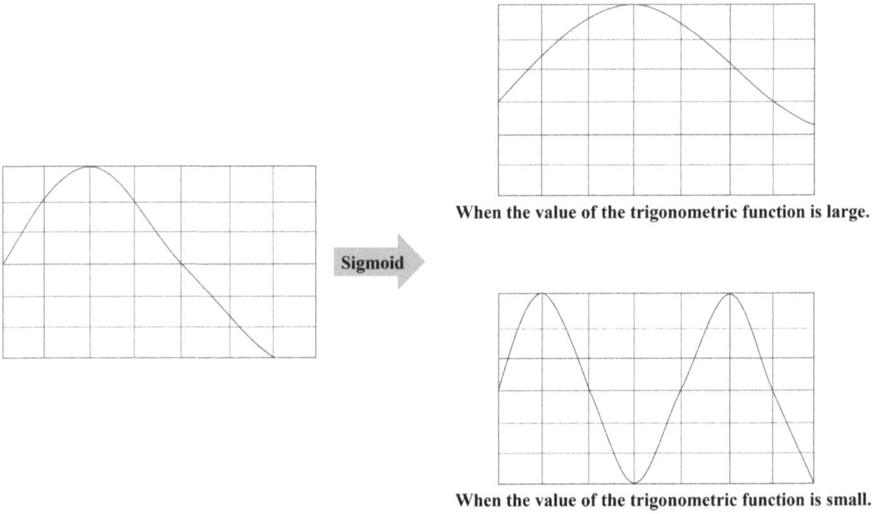

Fig. 2. The sigmoid function smoothes the value of the trigonometric output.

3.1 Initialization

SESCA initializes a population consisting of N candidate solutions X_i^0 randomly within a predefined search space $[LB, UB]$, where each solution is D-dimensional as Eq. (3):

$$X_i^0 \in [LB, UB], \quad i = 1, 2, \ldots, N \tag{3}$$

The fitness values $f(X_i^0)$ of each solution are computed, and the iteration count t is initialized to 0.

3.2 Global Best Determination

In each iteration, SESCA identifies the global best solution P as Eq. (4):

$$P = \arg\min_i f(X_i^t) \tag{4}$$

3.3 Adaptive Step Size Calculation

A dynamic step size decay factor a is introduced to balance exploration and exploitation as Eq. (5):

$$a = 2 - \frac{2t}{\text{MaxIter}} \tag{5}$$

This factor ensures aggressive exploration initially, progressively refining to precise exploitation as iterations proceed.

3.4 Solution Update Mechanism

SESCA updates each individual X_i^t as follows:

1. **Random Parameter Generation**: Define parameters as Eq. (6):

$$r_1 = a, \quad r_2 \sim U(0, 2\pi), \quad r_3 \sim U(0, 2), \quad r_4 \sim U(0, 1) \tag{6}$$

2. **Trigonometric Base Selection**: Compute the trigonometric base as Eq. (7):

$$\text{base} = \begin{cases} \sin(r_2), & \text{if } r_4 < 0.5, \\ \cos(r_2), & \text{otherwise} \end{cases} \tag{7}$$

3. **Sigmoid-based Nonlinear Mapping**: Apply sigmoid transformation to achieve nonlinear modulation as Eq. (8):

$$\sigma(\text{base}) = \frac{1}{1 + \exp(-\text{base})}, \quad \text{factor} = 2\sigma(\text{base}) - 1 \tag{8}$$

4. **Candidate Solution Update**: Compute candidate solutions via Eq. (9):

$$X_{i,j}^{\text{new}} = X_{i,j}^t + r_1 \cdot \text{factor} \cdot \left| r_3 \cdot P_j - X_{i,j}^t \right| \tag{9}$$

5. **Boundary Correction**: Candidate solutions are kept within bounds $[LB_j, UB_j]$ using a reflective boundary correction strategy.
6. **Acceptance Criterion**: SESCA adopts a selective update strategy as Eq. (10) :

$$X_{i,j}^{t+1} = \begin{cases} X_{i,j}^{\text{new}}, & \text{if } f(X_i^{\text{new}}) < f(X_i^t), \\ X_{i,j}^t, & \text{otherwise} \end{cases} \tag{10}$$

3.5 Iterative Optimization

The algorithm repeats the process, incrementing the iteration count until a predefined stopping criterion (e.g., maximum iterations) is met.

Algorithm 1: SESCA Algorithm

Population size: N, Dimension: D, Max iteration: T_{Max}, Search space: $[LB, UB]$;
Initialize iteration counter $t = 0$, randomly initialize population $X^{(t)}$;
while $t < T_{Max}$ **do**
  Calculate fitness $f(X_i^{(t)})$ for all individuals;
  Determine the global best solution using Eqs. (4);
  Compute the adaptive factor using Eqs. (5);
  for *each individual* $X_i^{(t)}$ **do**
    for *each dimension* j **do**
      Generate random numbers $r_2 \sim U(0, 2\pi)$, $r_3 \sim U(0, 2)$, $r_4 \sim U(0, 1)$;
      if $r_4 < 0.5$ **then**
        $base = \sin(r_2)$;
      else
        $base = \cos(r_2)$;
      end
      Compute the factor using Eqs. (8);
      Calculate the candidate solution using Eqs. (9)
      Apply boundary correction (reflective):
      $X_{i,j}^{new} = reflect(X_{i,j}^{new}, LB_j, UB_j)$;
    end
    Evaluate fitness $f(X_i^{new})$;
    if $f(X_i^{new}) < f(X_i^t)$ **then**
      $X_i^{(t+1)} = X_i^{new}$;
    else
      $X_i^{(t+1)} = X_i^{(t)}$;
    end
  end
  Update $t = t + 1$;
end
Return the best solution P;

4 Numerical Experiments

4.1 Experimental Settings

To evaluate the performance of the proposed SESCA, 12 benchmark functions from the CEC2022 suite are employed. The comparison involves several well-known metaheuristic algorithms (MAs), including ES, PSO, DE, and CRO implemented via the MEALPY library [13–15], as well as the original SCA. The evaluation is performed on problem dimensions of 10 and 20. For the CEC2022 benchmark, the maximum number of fitness evaluations (FEs) is defined as $1000 \times D$, where D represents the problem dimensionality. To account for stochastic variability, each algorithm is independently executed 20 times. The parameter settings for SESCA, detailed in Table 1, and the parameters of the competitive algorithms were derived from the optimal configurations reported in previous studies [13].

4.2 Experimental Results

Tables 2 and 3 summarize the performance outcomes on the 10-dimensional and 20-dimensional CEC2022 benchmark problems. For each of the 12 test functions, the results include the average (mean) and standard deviation of fitness values obtained by each algorithm. A lower mean indicates that an algorithm

Table 1. Parameter settings for SESCA.

Parameter	Value
Population size (N)	200
Dimension size (D)	10, 20
Lower bound (LB)	-100 (for each dimension)
Upper bound (UB)	100 (for each dimension)
Random parameters (r)	$r_2 \sim U(0, 2\pi)$, $r_3 \sim U(0, 2)$, $r_4 \sim U(0, 1)$

consistently locates solutions closer to the global optimum, suggesting superior performance. Likewise, a smaller standard deviation reflects greater reliability and convergence stability across multiple runs. In contrast, higher standard deviation values may reveal fluctuating solution quality, implying potential issues with convergence consistency or robustness.

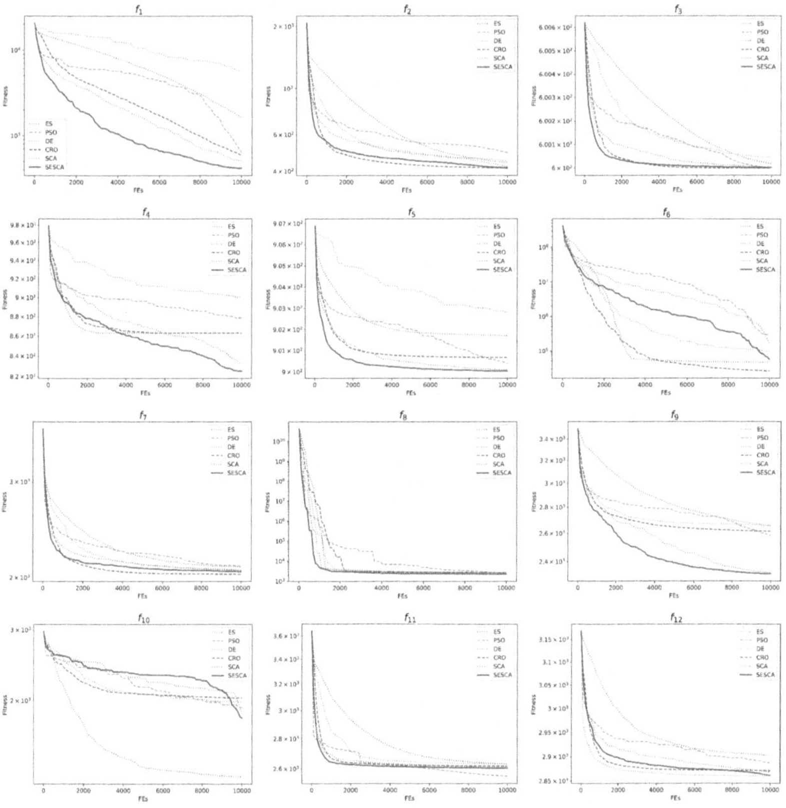

Fig. 3. Convergence plot in 10-D CEC2022.

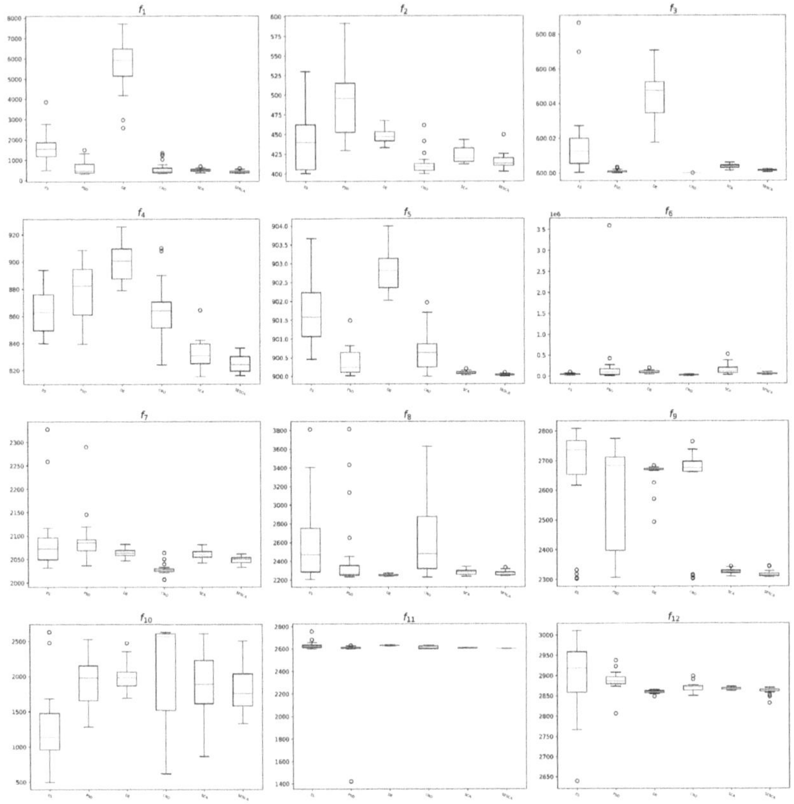

Fig. 4. Boxplot in 10-D CEC2022.

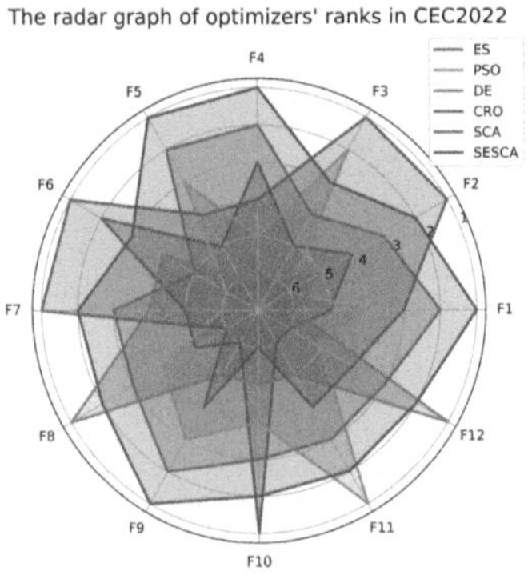

Fig. 5. Radar graph of optimizers' ranks in 10-D CEC2022.

In these tables, the comparison between SESCA and other algorithms is annotated as follows: a "+" indicates SESCA significantly outperforms the com-

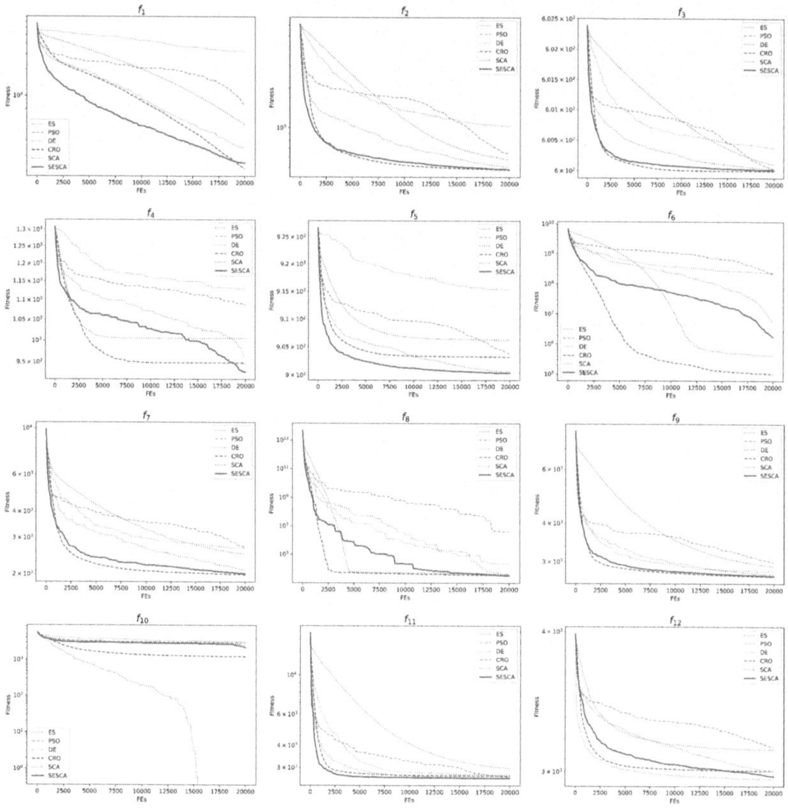

Fig. 6. Convergence plot in 20-D CEC2022.

pared method (p-value < 0.05); a "–" denotes that SESCA performs significantly worse; and "≈" implies no statistically significant difference (p-value >= 0.05). These symbols reflect the outcomes of statistical significance testing and indicate whether observed performance differences are likely due to algorithmic improvements rather than random variation.

For the 10-dimensional (10D) CEC 2022 tests, Fig. 3 shows how each algorithm's solution quality improves over iterations, revealing their convergence trends on the 12 benchmark functions. Figure 4 complements this by presenting boxplots of the final fitness values, which expose the spread of results and any outliers. To summarise overall performance, Fig. 5 provides a radar chart ranking that compares all algorithms across the full test suite.

For the 20-dimensional (20D) CEC 2022 tests, the same sequence of analyses is given: Fig. 6 traces convergence behaviour, Fig. 7 delivers boxplots of final fitness distributions, and Fig. 8 offers a radar-chart overview of algorithm rankings under the higher-dimensional setting.

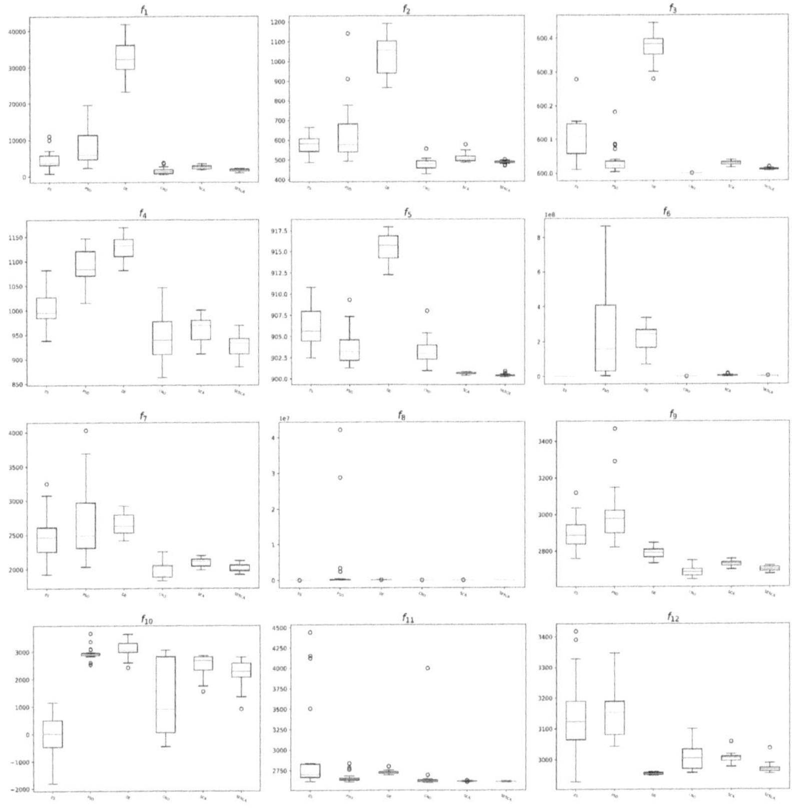

Fig. 7. Boxplot in 20-D CEC2022.

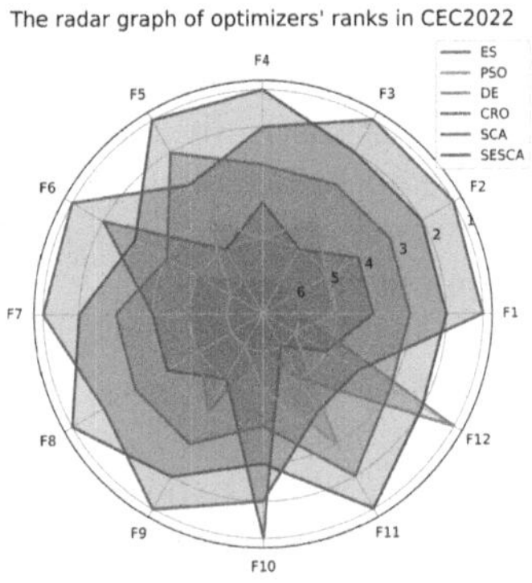

Fig. 8. Radar graph of optimizers' ranks in 20-D CEC2022.

Table 2. Experimental results and statistical analysis in 10-D CEC2022.

Func.		ES	PSO	DE	CRO	SCA	SESCA
f_1	mean	1.613e+03 +	6.342e+02 ≈	5.620e+03 +	5.867e+02 +	5.131e+02 +	**4.171e+02**
	std	7.279e+02	3.600e+02	1.260e+03	2.852e+02	8.577e+01	6.216e+01
f_2	mean	4.396e+02 ≈	4.903e+02 +	4.482e+02 +	**4.133e+02** ≈	4.235e+02 +	4.158e+02
	std	3.725e+01	4.365e+01	9.042e+00	1.452e+01	9.416e+00	9.887e+00
f_3	mean	6.000e+02 +	6.000e+02 −	6.000e+02 +	**6.000e+02** −	6.000e+02 +	6.000e+02
	std	2.157e-02	9.301e-04	1.239e-02	2.283e-05	1.267e-03	4.425e-04
f_4	mean	8.633e+02 +	8.789e+02 +	9.004e+02 +	8.635e+02 +	8.324e+02 +	**8.253e+02**
	std	1.479e+01	1.893e+01	1.451e+01	2.123e+01	1.065e+01	6.248e+00
f_5	mean	9.017e+02 +	9.004e+02 +	9.028e+02 +	9.007e+02 +	9.001e+02 +	**9.000e+02**
	std	8.471e-01	3.668e-01	5.092e-01	5.353e-01	3.965e-02	2.100e-02
f_6	mean	4.717e+04 −	2.877e+05 ≈	9.840e+04 +	**2.621e+04** −	1.549e+05 +	5.715e+04
	std	1.868e+04	7.646e+05	3.863e+04	1.213e+04	1.202e+05	1.870e+04
f_7	mean	2.092e+03 +	2.095e+03 +	2.064e+03 +	**2.029e+03** −	2.061e+03 +	2.049e+03
	std	7.180e+01	4.985e+01	9.419e+00	1.220e+01	9.537e+00	7.148e+00
f_8	mean	2.631e+03 +	2.470e+03 ≈	**2.252e+03** −	2.648e+03 +	2.283e+03 ≈	2.270e+03
	std	4.533e+02	4.407e+02	8.488e+00	4.356e+02	2.840e+01	2.513e+01
f_9	mean	2.657e+03 +	2.583e+03 +	2.656e+03 +	2.616e+03 +	2.328e+03 +	**2.319e+03**
	std	1.775e+02	1.698e+02	4.440e+01	1.550e+02	8.609e+00	1.003e+01
f_{10}	mean	**1.291e+03** −	1.923e+03 ≈	1.979e+03 ≈	2.032e+03 ≈	1.858e+03 ≈	1.811e+03
	std	5.090e+02	3.419e+02	1.934e+02	6.920e+02	4.336e+02	3.244e+02
f_{11}	mean	2.632e+03 +	**2.552e+03**−	2.631e+03 +	2.616e+03 +	2.607e+03 +	2.603e+03
	std	3.435e+01	2.598e+02	2.863e+00	1.216e+01	1.738e+00	6.215e-01
f_{12}	mean	2.902e+03 +	2.887e+03 +	**2.860e+03** −	2.871e+03 +	2.868e+03 +	2.862e+03
	std	8.530e+01	2.421e+01	3.776e+00	1.024e+01	2.796e+00	8.311e+00
+/≈/−:		9/1/2	6/4/2	9/1/2	7/2/3	10/2/0	–
Avg. ranks:		4.42	4.08	4.50	3.25	2.92	**1.83**

5 Discussion

On the 10-dimensional CEC2022 benchmark, SESCA demonstrated strong superiority over competing algorithms. Specifically, SESCA achieved statistically better performance ("+") in 41 out of all pairwise comparisons, showed no significant difference ("≈") in 10 cases, and was outperformed ("−") in only 9 instances. Its average ranking score across all benchmark functions was 1.83, securing the top position among all algorithms tested.

In the 20-dimensional setting, SESCA maintained its leading performance. It outperformed other methods ("+") in 48 cases, performed similarly ("≈") in 5, and was outperformed ("−") in only 7 comparisons. Once again, it achieved the best average rank of 1.83.

These results clearly indicate that SESCA is not only competitive but consistently effective across both low- and high-dimensional problems. Its stable top-ranking average, coupled with a dominant number of statistically significant wins, highlights the algorithm's robustness, convergence reliability, and strong global search capability. The small number of "−" cases further confirms that

Table 3. Experimental results and statistical analysis in 20-D CEC2022.

Func.		ES	PSO	DE	CRO	SCA	SESCA
f_1	mean	4.635e+03 +	7.656e+03 +	3.259e+04 +	**1.425e+03** −	2.501e+03 +	1.678e+03
	std	2.837e+03	4.425e+03	4.914e+03	9.096e+02	4.951e+02	3.186e+02
f_2	mean	5.779e+02 +	6.393e+02 +	1.031e+03 +	**4.818e+02** ≈	5.098e+02 +	4.872e+02
	std	5.066e+01	1.524e+02	9.702e+01	3.212e+01	2.150e+01	7.199e+00
f_3	mean	6.001e+02 +	6.000e+02 +	6.004e+02 +	**6.000e+02** −	6.000e+02 +	6.000e+02
	std	6.208e-02	4.099e-02	4.237e-02	4.797e-05	6.162e-03	2.560e-03
f_4	mean	1.005e+03 +	1.089e+03 +	1.130e+03 +	9.462e+02 ≈	9.612e+02 +	**9.280e+02**
	std	3.758e+01	3.508e+01	2.623e+01	4.856e+01	2.733e+01	2.182e+01
f_5	mean	9.063e+02 +	9.039e+02 +	9.154e+02 +	9.033e+02 +	9.006e+02 +	**9.004e+02**
	std	2.341e+00	2.140e+00	1.762e+00	1.597e+00	1.097e-01	1.420e-01
f_6	mean	4.168e+05 −	2.329e+08 +	2.153e+08 +	**1.011e+05** −	5.791e+06 +	1.738e+06
	std	9.240e+04	2.436e+08	7.717e+07	3.440e+04	4.216e+06	7.443e+05
f_7	mean	2.486e+03 +	2.689e+03 +	2.660e+03 +	**1.990e+03** ≈	2.098e+03 +	2.009e+03
	std	3.215e+02	5.476e+02	1.517e+02	1.068e+02	6.384e+01	6.369e+01
f_8	mean	4.431e+03 +	3.873e+06 +	2.372e+04 +	3.533e+03 ≈	3.780e+03 +	**3.271e+03**
	std	1.696e+03	1.079e+07	2.178e+04	1.372e+03	5.806e+02	4.253e+02
f_9	mean	2.901e+03 +	3.003e+03 +	2.792e+03 +	**2.690e+03** −	2.731e+03 +	2.701e+03
	std	9.000e+01	1.532e+02	3.174e+01	3.043e+01	1.356e+01	1.390e+01
f_{10}	mean	**-74.7** −	2939 +	3099 +	1224 ≈	2519 +	2185
	std	7.760e+02	2.348e+02	3.038e+02	1.294e+03	3.664e+02	5.113e+02
f_{11}	mean	2.976e+03 +	2.663e+03 +	2.726e+03 +	2.691e+03 +	2.620e+03 +	**2.613e+03**
	std	5.643e+02	5.856e+01	2.388e+01	3.002e+02	3.901e+00	2.583e+00
f_{12}	mean	3.140e+03 +	3.156e+03 +	**2.954e+03** −	3.005e+03 +	3.004e+03 +	2.973e+03
	std	1.328e+02	7.908e+01	3.515e+00	3.979e+01	1.626e+01	1.707e+01
+/≈/−:		10/0/2	12/0/0	11/0/1	3/5/4	12/0/0	–
Avg. ranks:		4.08	5.08	5.08	1.92	3.00	**1.83**

SESCA rarely fails against its peers, making it a highly dependable choice for solving complex optimization problems.

6 Conclusion

In this paper, we proposed SESCA, a Sigmoid-based Enhanced Sine-Cosine Algorithm designed to overcome the limitations of the original SCA, such as unstable convergence and excessive solution oscillation. By introducing a nonlinear mapping mechanism based on the sigmoid function, SESCA significantly improves both the stability and precision of the optimization process.

Extensive experiments were conducted on the CEC2022 benchmark suite in both 10- and 20-dimensional settings. The results demonstrated that SESCA consistently outperforms several state-of-the-art metaheuristic algorithms, achieving the best average rank and the highest number of statistically significant wins in pairwise comparisons. These findings confirm SESCA's strong global search capability, robustness, and adaptability to complex optimization problems.

In future work, SESCA could be extended to solve multi-objective and constrained optimization problems. Moreover, integrating learning-based or self-adaptive parameter control mechanisms may further enhance its performance across diverse problem landscapes.

Acknowledgment. This work was supported by JST SPRING, Grant Number JPMJSP2119 and JSPS KAKENHI Grant Number 21A402 and 24K15098.

References

1. Muazu, A.A., Hashim, A.S., Sarlan, A.: Review of nature inspired metaheuristic algorithm selection for combinatorial t-way testing. IEEE Access **10**, 27404–27431 (2022)
2. Lai, G.J., Li, T., Shi, B.J.: RRT-based optimizer: a novel metaheuristic algorithm based on rapidly-exploring random trees algorithm. IEEE Access **13**, 42744–42776 (2025)
3. Cao, Y., Yu, J., Zhong, R., Munetomo, M.: Forecasting renewable energy and electricity consumption using evolutionary hyperheuristic algorithm. Sci. Rep. **15** (2025)
4. Khan, R.A., Yang, S., Fahad, S., Khan, S.U.: Kalimullah: a modified particle swarm optimization with a smart particle for inverse problems in electromagnetic devices. IEEE Access **9**, 99932–99943 (2021)
5. Raj, B., Ahmedy, I., Idris, M.Y.I., Noor, R.M.: A hybrid sperm swarm optimization and genetic algorithm for unimodal and multimodal optimization problems. IEEE Access **10**, 109580–109596 (2022)
6. Gao, T.Y., Jiao, Y.C., Zhang, Y.X., Zhang, L.: A hybrid self-adaptive differential evolution algorithm with simplified Bayesian local optimizer for efficient design of antennas. IEEE Trans. Antennas Propag. **73**(1), 391–404 (2025)
7. El-Kenawy, E.S.M., et al.: Advanced ensemble model for solar radiation forecasting using sine cosine algorithm and newton's laws. IEEE Access **9**, 115750–115765 (2021)
8. Fan, Y., Zhang, S., Yang, H., Xu, D., Wang, Y.: An improved future search algorithm based on the sine cosine algorithm for function optimization problems. IEEE Access **11**, 30171–30187 (2023)
9. Wang, M., Lu, G.: A modified sine cosine algorithm for solving optimization problems. IEEE Access **9**, 27434–27450 (2021)
10. Gupta, N.K., Kar, M.K., Singh, A.K.: Design of a 2-DOF-PID controller using an improved sine-cosine algorithm for load frequency control of a three-area system with nonlinearities. Prot. Control Mod. Power Syst. **7**(3), 1–18 (2022)
11. Al-Faisal, H.R., Ahmad, I., Salman, A.A., Alfailakawi, M.G.: Adaptation of population size in sine cosine algorithm. IEEE Access **9**, 25258–25277 (2021)
12. Mirjalili, S.: SCA: a sine cosine algorithm for solving optimization problems. Knowl.-Based Syst. **96** (2016)
13. Van Thieu, N., Mirjalili, S.: MEALPY: an open-source library for latest metaheuristic algorithms in python. J. Syst. Archit. (2023)

14. Van Thieu, N., Barma, S.D., Van Lam, T., Kisi, O., Mahesha, A.: Groundwater level modeling using augmented artificial ecosystem optimization. J. Hydrol. **617**, 129034 (2023)
15. Ahmed, A.N., Van Lam, T., Hung, N.D., Van Thieu, N., Kisi, O., El-Shafie, A.: A comprehensive comparison of recent developed meta-heuristic algorithms for streamflow time series forecasting problem. Appl. Soft Comput. **105**, 107282 (2021)

Incorporating Angular Information Into GNNs for Protein-Protein Interaction Re-ranking

Yukinobu Matsuno[1], Nobuaki Yasuo[2], and Masakazu Sekijima[1](✉)

[1] Department of Computer Science, Institute of Science Tokyo, Yokohama 226-8501, Japan
matsuno.y.af@m.titech.ac.jp, sekijima@comp.isct.ac.jp

[2] Graduate Major in Materials and Information Sciences, Institute of Science Tokyo, Tokyo 152-8550, Japan
yasuo.n.0a87@m.isct.ac.jp

Abstract. Many proteins are known to regulate cellular functions through interactions with other proteins (Protein-Protein Interaction). Therefore, the structure of protein complexes is useful information for structure-based drug discovery. Experimental methods such as X-ray crystallography exist, but determining complex structures requires enormous costs and expenses. Therefore, docking methods that predict complex structures using computers have been developed. The evaluation of structures obtained through docking is often inaccurate when relying solely on docking score functions, leading to the development of re-ranking methods for re-evaluating docking structures. Among these, a method using Graph Neural Networks (GNNs) to learn protein-protein interactions based on graph structures has been proposed. However, existing GNN-based re-ranking methods do not consider edge angle information, resulting in an inability to fully capture three-dimensional structural features. In this study, we aimed to improve prediction accuracy by employing an architecture that considers angle information. As a result, we successfully achieved higher accuracy with the model incorporating angle information compared to the model without angle information.

Keywords: Protein-Protein Interaction (PPI) · Graph Neural Network (GNN) · Protein Docking · Angle-aware Representation

1 Introduction

Proteins do not necessarily function alone; they often interact with other proteins to form complexes that participate in the transmission of information and metabolic control within living organisms. Therefore, elucidating the structure of protein–protein interactions (PPIs) is crucial for understanding the life sciences and for drug discovery. From the perspective of Structure-Based Drug Design (SBDD) in particular, PPI interfaces represent attractive targets for

H. R. Arabnia et al. (Eds.): CSCE 2025, CCIS 2932, pp. 493–503, 2026.
https://doi.org/10.1007/978-3-032-22193-3_39

novel inhibitor design. However, experimental methods such as X-ray crystallography can be very time-consuming and costly due to the need for protein production, crystallisation and beamline-based acquisition of diffraction intensity data. Although docking simulations are important, they are not sufficiently accurate, making re-ranking essential. Furthermore, protein structures are not static but fluctuate over time. Kamada et al. applied wavelet transform to molecular dynamics (MD) simulations, demonstrating that proteins move collectively between multiple conformations rather than remaining in a single structure [1]. Furthermore, Yoshino et al. identified a novel cryptic binding site in spermidine synthase from Trypanosoma cruzi using an MD-derived structural ensemble [2]. Through virtual screening and experiments, they discovered a new inhibitor and determined its co-crystal structure. While this study is an example of SBDD targeting a single protein rather than PPI, it shows that it is useful to consider the diversity of dynamic structures rather than relying solely on static crystal structures. While the "importance of dynamic ensembles" is thus demonstrated, the mainstream approach in actual drug discovery applications still involves handling numerous static candidate structures obtained via docking, and there remains room for improvement in the accuracy of their re-ranking. In particular, prior research using GNNs (Graph Neural Networks) has succeeded in extracting features from PPI interfaces, but existing GNN-based re-ranking methods generally overlook edge-angle information, making it challenging to fully capture the three-dimensional features of PPI interfaces. This study does not perform dynamic modelling itself, but rather aims to improve re-ranking accuracy by focusing on static docking structures. Specifically, it seeks to improve prediction accuracy by explicitly incorporating edge angle information into existing GNN architectures to capture the three-dimensional features of PPI interfaces more accurately. First, we review existing approaches to protein complex structure prediction and re-ranking. Next, we summarise the characteristics of GNN-based methods, including DeepRank-GNN [3]. Finally, having identified the challenges of current methods, we present the novel architecture proposed in this study that incorporates angle information.

1.1 Protein Complex Structure Prediction

Although experimental methods such as X-ray crystallography are available for determining protein complex structures, these methods can be time-consuming and expensive. In silico methods for predicting these structures include AlphaFold-Multimer [4], docking simulations and molecular dynamics (MD) methods. In protein-protein docking, rigid body docking methods such as ZDOCK [5] treat proteins as rigid bodies, whereas flexible docking methods consider their flexibility. In this study, we analyse data from rigid body docking and a small amount of flexible docking, as well as MD simulations.

1.2 Protein Docking Re-ranking

Using only the docking score function to seek the most plausible docking model from among the created docking models results in many models that are not close to the natural structure ranking high, leading to low accuracy. Therefore, a method called re-ranking is used to re-evaluate the structures obtained from docking, using a new evaluation function to re-rank the docking models. One example of a re-ranking method is ZRANK2 [6], which uses a linear combination of van der Waals forces, electrostatic forces, and desolvation energy for evaluation. Recently, deep learning–based methods have been extensively studied. These include DOVE [7] using CNN and DeepRank-GNN [3] using GNN. In this study, we focused on DeepRank-GNN using GNN.

1.3 DeepRank-GNN

DeepRank-GNN [3] is a method that treats complex structures as graphs and performs re-ranking. DeepRank-GNN [3] has achieved state-of-the-art performance. BM5 [8] dataset is used for training. Two types of graphs are created. One is an intra-protein graph linking C_α atoms within the same protein as edges. The other is a graph linking C_α atoms between different proteins. GAT (Graph Attention Networks) [9] is used to extract features from each of the two graphs. The features obtained from the two graphs are combined. Finally, a fully connected layer is used to obtain the output.

1.4 Existing GNN Methods

GCN. GCN [10] is a GNN that utilizes convolution operations, and GAT (Graph Attention Networks) [9] and others are additions to this framework. Convolution on graphs cannot be performed simply because the data does not have a fixed shape like image data. Convolution in GCN is performed by applying a function to adjacent nodes and updating node features using the sum of the results.

$$h_i^{(l+1)} = \sigma\left(\sum_{j\in N(i)} \frac{1}{c_{ij}} W^{(l)} h_j^{(l)}\right) \tag{1}$$

Here, $h_i^{(l)}$ is the node feature at layer l, W is the weight parameter for node features, c_{ij} is the product of the roots of the degrees of nodes i and j, and σ is the activation function.

GAT. GAT is a framework that calculates the importance of edges and uses that importance in the aggregation of node features in GCN. Recent ranking methods such as DeepRank-GNN [3] and GNN-DOVE [11] use this method.

$$e_{ij} = a(W_h h_i, W_h h_j) \tag{2}$$

$$\alpha_{ij} = \mathrm{softmax}_j(e_{ij}) = \frac{\exp(e_{ij})}{\sum_{k \in N(i)} \exp(e_{ik})} \tag{3}$$

$$h_i^{(l+1)} = \sigma\left(\sum_{j \in N(i)} \alpha_{ij} W^{(l)} h_j^{(l)}\right) \tag{4}$$

e_{ij} is the attention coefficient of edge ij connecting nodes i and j, a is a function for calculating attention, which is often a single-layer neural network, and α_{ij} is the importance of edge ij. Node features are calculated using the importance and Eq. (4).

1.5 Issues with Existing Research

DeepRank-GNN [3] and other existing studies using GNN have the issue that the angle information of two edges is not considered when aggregating nodes. This is because, as shown in Fig. 1, both graphs are processed in the same way in GNN. Therefore, we considered that changing the GNN processing based on the angle between the two edges could improve accuracy. Specifically, for the two graphs shown in Fig. 1, we considered that angle information could be taken into account by using different weights during feature calculation for each graph and the same weight during feature calculation for graphs with similar edge angles.

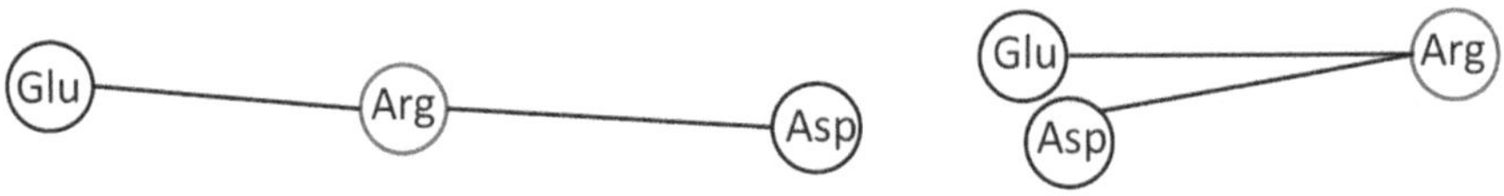

Fig. 1. Graphs with different edge angles

2 Proposed Method

Figure 2 shows an overview of this study. In this study, similar to DeepRank-GNN [3], we apply GNN to graphs with edges added between proteins and graphs with edges added between proteins obtained from a docking model, and output prediction values. In this study, we modified the node aggregation part of the GNN in the architecture of DeepRank-GNN [3].

2.1 Graph Definition

The graph definition is the same as that used in DeepRank-GNN [3]. The nodes of the graph are C_α atoms, and the edges are determined by the distance between C_α atoms. We define the graph with edges between C_α atoms within 3 Å of each other in the same protein as the protein-internal graph, and the graph with

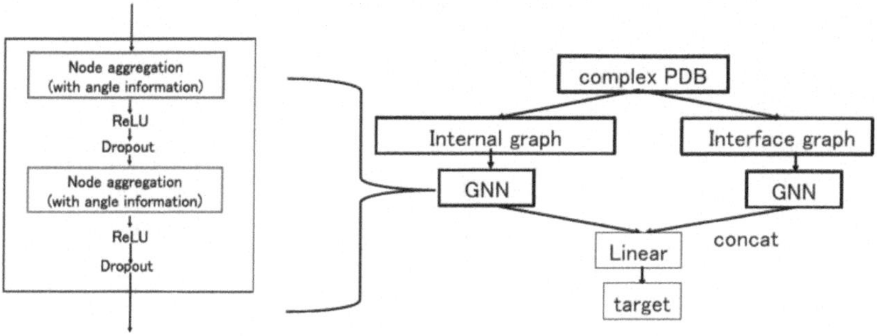

Fig. 2. Overview of this study

edges between C_α atoms within 8.5 Å of each other in different proteins as the protein-interaction graph. The protein-internal graph models the 3D structure of two proteins, while the protein-interaction graph models the interaction surfaces between two proteins.

2.2 Features

Features are the same as those used in DeepRank-GNN [3]. The features used are shown in Table 1. Polarity is classified into nonpolar, positively charged, negatively charged, and uncharged polarities. BSA (Buried Surface Area) is the solvent contact area lost due to the formation of new contact interfaces. PSSM (Position-specific scoring matrix) is constructed based on information obtained from multiple sequence alignments. In alignment, the sequences of different proteins at the same position are compared, and the probability of different amino acids appearing at each position is calculated. This is considered to preserve evolutionary information. Cons (Conservation score–from PSSM) is a score indicating how well amino acids are conserved at a specific position. ic (Information content–from PSSM) is an indicator of information content, and amino acids at positions with high ic are evolutionarily conserved. These regions may be functionally important or evolutionarily conserved.

2.3 GNN

To address the issue that conventional GNNs do not consider angle information, we used a message passing neural network (MPNN) that considers edge angles, as proposed in GearNet [12], a protein representation learning method, in our GNN. By grouping edges by angle and sharing weights among each group, we performed node aggregation that considers angle information. First, we define a relationship R between edges in the original graph G. The relationship between edges ij and kj is determined by the angle between them. The edge angle relations R are divided into n intervals from 0° to 180°, and each pair of adjacent edges is assigned to one of the n intervals. The message function $m_{ij}^{(l+1)}$ of each edge is

Table 1. Graph features

Feature	Description	Number of parameters	Type
Residue type	One-hot encoded	20	Node feature
Charge		1	Node feature
Polarity	One-hot encoded	4	Node feature
BSA		1	Node feature
PSSM		20	Node feature
Cons		1	Node feature
ic		1	Node feature
Distance		1	Edge feature

calculated using Eq. (5). In other words, the edge feature of ij is obtained by aggregating the edge features of the adjacent edges kj that have j as a node. The weight W'_r of the aggregation function is determined by the angle relationship $r \in R$ of the edges. In other words, the weight W'_r of the aggregation function has n different weights. Edges with smaller angles share the same weight, and edges with larger angles share the same weight. Finally, the node feature of node i is updated by message passing.

$$m_{ij}^{(l+1)} = \sigma(\sum_{r \in R} W'_r \sum_{kj \in N^r(ij)} m_{kj}^{(l)}) \tag{5}$$

$$h_i^{(l+1)} = \sigma(W_h \sum_{j \in N(i)} \left(h_j^{(l)} + FullyConnected\left(m_{ji}^{(l+1)}\right)\right)) \tag{6}$$

Here, m_{ij} is the message at edge ij, and the edge features are updated by this message. Let us explain what kind of processing is performed in Fig. 3. When updating the feature (message) of edge e1 connecting nodes v1 and v2, the features of e2, e3, and e4 shared by node v1 are used. The angle relationship of the edges is divided into green, blue, and light blue zones based on the angle from e1. The weight W'_r of the aggregation function used for e2 is from the blue zone. The weight W'_r of the aggregation function used for e3 and e4 is from the light blue zone. In other words, e3 and e4 are aggregated to e1 using the same light blue zone weights, while e2 is aggregated to e1 using different blue zone weights from e3 and e4. The same process is performed for all edges, and the obtained features are used to update the node features.

2.4 Dataset

In this study, we trained a docking model using the Docking Benchmark Version 5 (BM5) [8] dataset created by DeepRank [13]. The BM5 dataset is designed for docking and contains 231 protein complex structures and the protein structures that compose them. DeepRank performed docking on 140 complexes from this

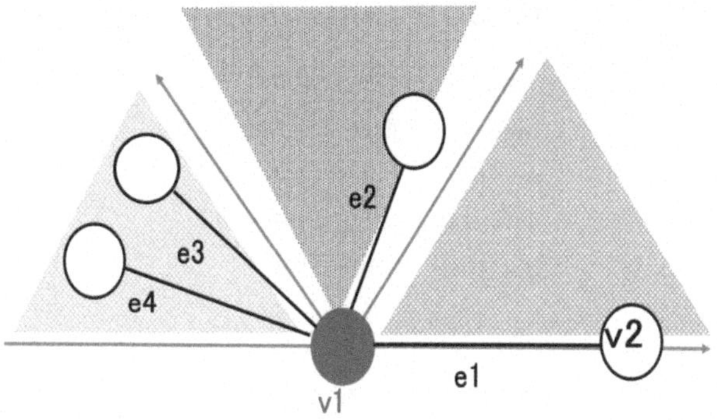

Fig. 3. Example of a graph divided by angle

dataset, excluding those containing three or more proteins. Using HADDOCK [14], 25,300 docking models were created for each complex. This dataset includes 22,000 rigid body docking data points, 1,600 docking data points considering the flexibility of protein main chains and side chains, and 1,600 MD (molecular dynamics) simulation data points in water solvent. All of these data points are results of docking in the unbound-unbound configuration. Additionally, the dataset includes 50 bound-bound docking data sets that consider the flexibility of the protein main chains and side chains, along with 50 MD simulation data sets in an aqueous solvent. Due to computational time constraints, the number of docking models per complex was reduced to 1/100 for the experiments. The dataset was divided into train:validation:test = 8:1:1 using protein complexes as units, and the best model was selected from the train dataset and the validation dataset, and the model was evaluated using the test dataset.

2.5 Labeling of Predicted Structures

For each predicted structure obtained from HADDOCK [14], fnat was calculated, and if the value was 0.3 or higher based on the CAPRI evaluation criteria in Table 2, it was classified as a positive example structure, otherwise it was classified as a negative example structure. Pairs of amino acid residues in proteins where the distance between any two atoms is 5 Å or less are considered contact residue pairs. fnat is the ratio of contact residue pairs in the predicted structure that are correct in the native structure.

$$f_{nat} = \frac{\text{number of contact residue pairs in the predicted structure that are present in the native structure}}{\text{number of contact residue pairs in the native structure}} \tag{7}$$

2.6 Evaluation Metrics

In this study, we used ROC-AUC and Success Rate as evaluation metrics for re-ranking prediction. ROC-AUC is the area under the ROC curve and is one of the

Table 2. CAPRIevaluation

Evaluation	Conditions
high	fnat ≥ 0.5
medium	$0.3 \leq$ fnat < 0.5
acceptable	$0.1 \leq$ fnat < 0.3
incorrect	fnat < 0.1

evaluation metrics for binary classification problems. In this study, we used the average ROC-AUC value for each complex. Success Rate(N) is the percentage of complexes that contain at least one positive example structure among the top N predicted structures.

3 Experiments and Results

3.1 Learning Method

BM5 train dataset was used for training. The optimization method was Adam, the batch size was 128, the learning rate was 0.001, and training was performed for 20 epochs.

3.2 Experimental Environment

As shown in Table 3, the experiments in this study were conducted using a single NVIDIA A6000 GPU (with 48GB of memory) and an Intel(R) Core(TM) i9-9900X CPU. The operating system used was Ubuntu 22.04.3 LTS, and training took approximately 13 h.

Table 3. Experimental Environment

GPU	NVIDIA A6000 1 unit Memory 48GB
CPU	Intel(R)Core(TM)i9-9900X
OS	Ubuntu 22.04.3LTS
Training time	13 h

3.3 Verification Method

Verification was performed by comparing a baseline MPNN that does not consider angles, MPNN models with angle divisions of 6 and 8 that consider angles, a DeepRank-GNN model trained on a dataset 100 times larger than the original dataset [3], and a DeepRank-GNN model trained on the same dataset as the original study [3].

3.4 Results

As shown in Tables 4 and 5, the proposed MPNN(angle6) method achieved the highest ROC-AUC value (0.950) and outperformed the baseline methods in terms of success rate. Notably, MPNN(angle6) demonstrated equivalent or superior performance to DeepRank-GNN, confirming the effectiveness of incorporating angle information into the GNN framework. These results suggest that this approach improves re-ranking accuracy and increases the proportion of correct structures in the top predictions.

Table 4. AUC on the BM5 dataset

	ROC-AUC
MPNN(no_angle)(Baseline)	0.900
MPNN(angle8)	0.931
MPNN(angle6)	0.950
DeepRank-GNN	0.927
DeepRank-GNN_100data	0.941

Table 5. Success Rate on the BM5 Dataset

	TOP1	TOP5	TOP10	TOP30
MPNN(no_angle)(Baseline)	0.533	0.867	0.933	0.933
MPNN(angle8)	0.733	0.867	0.933	0.933
MPNN(angle6)	0.867	0.933	0.933	0.933
DeepRank-GNN	0.800	0.933	0.933	0.933
DeepRank-GNN_100data	0.800	0.867	0.867	0.933

3.5 Discussion

Since MPNN with angle information performed better than MPNN(no_angle) without angle information, it can be considered that angle information is effective for re-ranking protein-protein interactions. The reason why MPNN(angle6) was more accurate than MPNN(angle8) is not because increasing the number of divisions allows for more detailed angle information to be considered, but because even a slight shift in the angle of an edge can change the assigned weight, making stable learning difficult. Increasing the number of divisions may also increase the number of parameters and complicate the model. These verifications were not performed in this study.

4 Conclusion

4.1 Conclusion of This Study

This study addresses the shortcoming of existing graph neural network (GNN) methods for protein-protein interaction (PPI) interfaces, which fail to consider the angular information between two edges during node aggregation. To address this issue, we developed a novel message passing neural network (MPNN) by applying the node aggregation technique used in GearNet [12]. The angular-aware MPNN achieved higher accuracy than the baseline MPNN and demonstrated the highest accuracy among existing studies. These results demonstrate the effectiveness of incorporating angular information into graph-based models for capturing the three-dimensional characteristics of PPI interfaces. This study is significant because it shows that adding geometric features (edge angles) can substantially improve prediction accuracy while focusing on static docking structures and not directly handling dynamic ensembles. These findings suggest that GNNs incorporating angular information could serve as a general framework for improving the accuracy of evaluating protein-protein docking models. Their application to related tasks in structure-based drug discovery is anticipated.

4.2 Future Work

A key challenge moving forward is evaluating the model using all available data. Since DeepRank-GNN achieves higher accuracy when trained on larger datasets, similar improvements are expected for the model in this study. Furthermore, while this study only involved training three types of angle segmentation parameters, optimising these parameters could lead to further accuracy improvements. However, the architecture used in this study causes the weights to change abruptly, even with slight differences in the edge angle, which could lead to unstable learning. Therefore, exploring architectures in which weight changes more smoothly with angle could be a fruitful area for further improvement. In recent years, attempts have been reported to enhance model performance by refining structural features and search strategies. These include reinforcement learning methods utilising graph representations for molecular optimisation [15], as well as molecular generation methods incorporating Monte Carlo tree search for multi-objective optimisation [16]. Similarly, the introduction of angular information and architectural improvements in this study are expected to lead to a more accurate capture of geometric and structural features.

Acknowledgements. This research was partially supported by the Research Support Project for Life Science and Drug Discovery (Basis for Supporting Innovative Drug Discovery and Life Science Research (BINDS)) from AMED under Grant Number JP25ama121026 and the Japan Society for the Promotion of Science (JSPS) under KAKENHI Grant Numbers 25H01574 and JP24H01760.

References

1. Kamada, M., Toda, M., Sekijima, M., Takata, M., Joe, K.: Analysis of motion features for molecular dynamics simulation of proteins. Chem. Phys. Lett. **502**(4–6), 241–247 (2011). https://doi.org/10.1016/j.cplett.2010.12.028
2. Yoshino, R., et al.: Discovery of a hidden Trypanosoma cruzi spermidine synthase binding site and inhibitors through in silico, in vitro, and X-ray crystallography. ACS Omega **8**(29), 25850–25860 (2023). https://doi.org/10.1021/acsomega.3c01314
3. Réau, M., Renaud, N., Xue, L.C., Bonvin, A.M.: DeepRank-GNN: a graph neural network framework to learn patterns in protein–protein interfaces. Bioinformatics **39**(1), btac759 (2023)
4. Evans, R., et al.: Protein complex prediction with AlphaFold-multimer. biorxiv, pp. 2021–10 (2021)
5. Chen, R., Li, L., Weng, Z.: ZDOCK: an initialstage proteindocking algorithm. Proteins: Struct., Funct., Bioinf. **52**(1), 80–87 (2003). https://doi.org/10.1002/prot.10389
6. Pierce, B., Weng, Z.: A combination of rescoring and refinement significantly improves protein docking performance. Proteins: Struct., Funct., Bioinf. **72**(1), 270–279 (2008)
7. Wang, X., Terashi, G., Christoffer, C.W., Zhu, M., Kihara, D.: Protein docking model evaluation by 3D deep convolutional neural networks. Bioinformatics **36**(7), 2113–2118 (2020)
8. Vreven, T., et al.: Updates to the integrated protein-protein interaction benchmarks: docking benchmark version 5 and affinity benchmark version 2. J. Mol. Biol. **427**(19), 3031–3041 (2015)
9. Velickovic, P., Cucurull, G., Casanova, A., Romero, A., Lio, P., Bengio, Y., et al.: Graph attention networks. Stat **1050**(20), 10–48550 (2017)
10. Kipf, T.N., Welling, M.: Semi-supervised classification with graph convolutional networks. arXiv preprint: arXiv:1609.02907 (2016)
11. Wang, X., Flannery, S.T., Kihara, D.: Protein docking model evaluation by graph neural networks. Front. Mol. Biosci. **8**, 647915 (2021)
12. Zhang, Z., et al.: Protein representation learning by geometric structure pretraining. arXiv preprint: arXiv:2203.06125 (2022)
13. Renaud, N., et al.: DeepRank: a deep learning framework for data mining 3D protein-protein interfaces. Nat. Commun. **12**(1), 7068 (2021)
14. De Vries, S.J., Van Dijk, M., Bonvin, A.M.: The haddock web server for data-driven biomolecular docking. Nat. Protoc. **5**(5), 883–897 (2010)
15. Erikawa, D., Yasuo, N., Suzuki, T., Nakamura, S., Sekijima, M.: Gargoyles: an open source graph-based molecular optimization method based on deep reinforcement learning. ACS Omega **8**(40), 37431–37441 (2023). https://doi.org/10.1021/acsomega.3c05430
16. Suzuki, T., Ma, D., Yasuo, N., Sekijima, M.: Mothra: multiobjective de novo molecular generation using monte Carlo tree search. J. Chem. Inf. Model. **64**(19), 7291–7302 (2024). https://doi.org/10.1021/acs.jcim.4c00759

Growth Monitoring of Mini Tomatoes Using Color Analysis and Cumulative Temperature to Predict Maturity Degree

Yan Lyu[1], Kyuki Shibuya[2], Yoshiki Gama[2], Yoshiki Hatanaka[2], Warut Timprae[1], Poltak Sandro Rumahorbo[1], Shinya Yamanaka[1], and Shinya Watanabe[1](✉)

[1] Muroran Institute of Technology, Muroran, Hokkaido 050-8585, Japan
sin@muroran-it.ac.jp
[2] Asai Nursery, Inc., Tsu, Mie 514-2221, Japan

Abstract. This study proposes an original approach for automated growth monitoring of mini tomatoes by integrating image-based skeleton extraction, segmentation detection, and environmental data analysis. This approach accurately predicts growth percentage using color hue angles and cumulative temperature. Experimental results confirm the usefulness of segmentation and skeleton extraction for precise fruit identification and demonstrate the effectiveness of linear regression models in correlating hue angles with growth percentages. This approach enhances growth monitoring efficiency, reduces labor costs, and supports future cultivation planning through improved data management.

Keywords: Greenhouse tomato · Image processing · Color analysis · Maturity degree

1 Introduction

Mini tomatoes are a representative high-value greenhouse crop, which requires uniformity of shape, size, and color [1]. However, because of the variations in light, temperature, and microclimate conditions, individual fruits often exhibit different growth rates and ripening patterns. It makes continuous growth monitoring essential. Meanwhile, labor shortages in agriculture further exacerbate these challenges.

As of 2020, the number of agricultural workers in Japan, totaling 1,363,000, has diminished by 20% from 2015, when it was 1,757,000, indicating a growing scarcity of personnel in agriculture [2]. The population aged 65 and older is 70% (949,000 individuals) of the total, and the segment of the population aged 49 and under represents 11% (147,000 individuals). Younger individuals are increasingly reluctant to pursue careers in agriculture. Locating fresh agricultural laborers is challenging. Automated greenhouse monitoring has become a necessity rather than an option.

H. R. Arabnia et al. (Eds.): CSCE 2025, CCIS 2932, pp. 504–515, 2026.
https://doi.org/10.1007/978-3-032-22193-3_40

Computer vision has been developed to reduce labor dependency in agriculture. However, most existing approaches rely on fixed-camera setups and controlled lighting conditions, making them impractical for real-world greenhouse environments. These methods typically perform one-time ripeness classification, failing to provide continuous growth tracking. Environmental factors such as natural light variations, occlusions, and plant structural complexity further hinder the robustness of these approaches. In summary, current solutions lack adaptability to real-world agricultural settings, where dynamic conditions significantly impact fruit growth.

In response to these challenges, we present an image-based growth monitoring system. The proposed system integrates skeleton extraction, segmentation detection, and color analysis to automatically estimate the number, color, and position of mini tomatoes to show their growth status. The system enables growth percentage estimation for each fruit, individual growth tracking, fruit condition visualization, and historical data recording for further analysis and cultivation planning.

This system reduces reliance on labor-intensive inspections, enhances data-driven planting management, and provides valuable data support for future planning. With remote monitoring capabilities, just a few personnel can oversee the entire greenhouse, ensuring sustainability and productivity while reducing labor costs and improving operational efficiency. With this monitoring system, only a few personnel are needed to oversee the entire greenhouse, which ensures sustainability and productivity while reducing labor costs and improving efficiency management.

2 Related Works

Monitoring plant growth and fruit development is crucial in modern agriculture, especially for greenhouse crops such as mini tomatoes, which require meticulous environmental regulation to guarantee consistency in size, shape, and color. Conventional techniques depend on manual inspections, which are labor-intensive, susceptible to discrepancies, and more unsustainable due to the global reduction in agricultural labor [3]. Researchers have investigated automated monitoring systems with computer vision, deep learning, and the integration of environmental information to address these challenges.

The previous research concentrated on recognizing and classifying fruit by conventional image processing methods such as color thresholding and edge detection [4]. Deep learning has made it easier to accurately divide and recognize fruit using convolutional neural networks (CNNs). This makes it possible to identify growth stages accurately [5,6]. YOLO-based models have shown strong real-time effectiveness in agricultural applications, allowing fruits to be automatically recognized and separated in complex situations [7,8]. Faster R-CNN [9] and Mask R-CNN [10] have been employed in segmentation in fruit detection tasks, offering high accuracy but often requiring extensive labelled datasets for training. With the improvement of AI technology, many studies have tried to combine computer vision with environmental data like temperature and humidity [4,11,12]. However, most prior research is directly designed for large-scale field crops, which is limited in adaptability to greenhouse-specific conditions.

Color analysis and cumulative temperature are two critical elements in automated agriculture. Cumulative temperature is employed to assess the development of plants [13]. These models combine average temperature data exceeding a threshold to predict phenological stages. In industrially used tomato farming, cumulative temperature is also used to evaluate the amount of time and make further plans [14]. Because of the absence of direct phenotypic measurements, the cumulative temperature is commonly used for making plans rather than daily monitoring.

Reference [15] investigated tomato ripening using CIELAB color representation, comparing multiple color indices, including hue, chroma, color index, and a/b. Their results demonstrated that hue provided the highest range of values, effectively distinguishing between ripening stages. However, their study relied on colorimeter-based manual measurements, requiring human intervention and limiting automation. León et al. applied CIELAB color space in food quality assessment and proposed computational methods for RGB-to-LAB conversion [16]. Ref. [17] estimates fruit maturity by feature concatenation of data acquired from two imaging modes: visible-light and hyperspectral imaging systems. However, the high cost associated with hyperspectral imaging hardware limits its applicability in commercial greenhouse environments. With CIELAB, Caroline et al. successfully predicted the maturity degree of tomatoes [18]. However, the images were captured using a Canon camera in a controlled laboratory environment, where lighting conditions were fixed, and no background interference was present. In contrast, greenhouse environments contain various background interferences, making real-world applications more challenging.

This paper proposes a monitoring system to manage the growth information and estimate mini tomatoes' growth percentage for the greenhouse environment. Unlike earlier image processing methods that only considered a single fruit, our model employs YOLOv8 for segmentation and skeleton extraction for accurate fruit localization and structural analysis. In addition, our model combines the image information and cumulative temperature instead of a single element in prior research. Our system is more comprehensive and adaptable for daily monitoring in the greenhouse, as it considers fruits, clusters, and environmental data.

3 Methodology for Growth Monitoring Based on Tomato Color

In this chapter, we introduce the methodology employed to assess the growth of mini tomatoes. We present the segmentation and skeleton extraction procedures for detecting fruit and plant structures, followed by a color analysis and growth percentage estimation.

3.1 Process Framework

The proposed system uses advanced image processing and environmental data to monitor the mini-tomato growth percentage. This approach combines segmentation detection, skeleton extraction, and color analysis for growth percentage estimation. The complete procedure is depicted in Fig. 1.

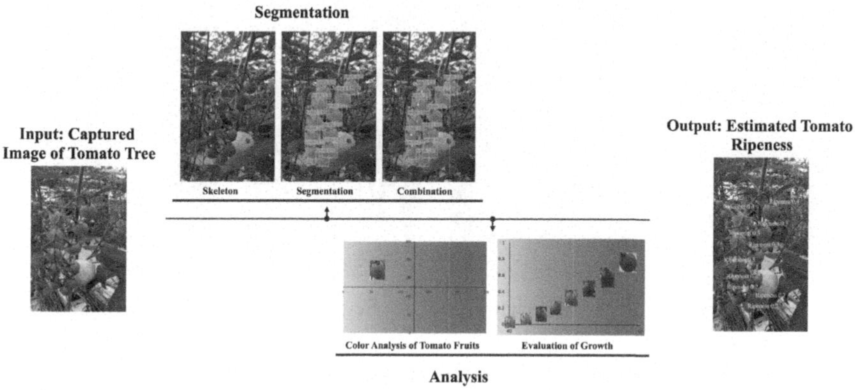

Fig. 1. Flow chart of our methodology of the growth monitor

We employ segmentation detection to identify individual fruits and skeleton extraction to detect the key points of fruits and the overall structure of the cluster. This method allows estimation of fruit positions, total fruit count, and cluster structure, which facilitates further analysis.

As tomato growth accompanies the color changing from green to red, color is an important element of fruit maturity evaluation. The monitor we designed analyzes the color condition of a single fruit and classifies it into several levels, as defined by the Asai Nursery.

Previous studies have shown that during the growth period from anthesis to physiological maturity, a specific amount of heating degree-days must accumulate for tomatoes to reach maturity [19]. This concept of heating degree-days is closely related to the cumulative temperature adopted in this study. We modelled the maturity degree as a percentage from 0% (unripe) to 100% (fully ripe) with the actual and target cumulative temperature. We incorporated the relationship between color progression and cumulative temperature to estimate the maturity degree of mini tomatoes. Such a linear relation allows the monitoring system to forecast growth percentage solely from color data instead of manual checking.

Overall, the system employs segmentation and skeleton methods to detect tomato fruits and clusters and color analysis to summarize the growth status of tomatoes. Details of each part are introduced in the following chapters. This system can receive growth information, including the number of fruits, individual and cluster-level color data, and predicted growth percentage. Such insights support growth monitoring and further planning by data management, reducing the need for frequent greenhouse visits.

3.2 Skeleton, Segmentation, and Combination

(a) Original (b) Skeleton (c) Segmentation (d) Combination

Fig. 2. Result samples of the skeleton, segmentation and combination.

YOLOv8 models are adopted for the segmentation and skeleton extraction tasks due to their state-of-the-art real-time object detection and segmentation performance. Figure 2b and 2c show the respective segmentation and skeleton extraction results of Fig. 2a. For further analysis, these two results are combined into a single image, as shown in Fig. 2d, instead of using two separate result images. The final image precisely determines fruit positions, numbers, and cluster growth structures. These data support both fruit-level and cluster-level growth analysis, providing a robust foundation for further studies.

3.3 Color Analysis of Tomato Fruits

For automatic color level estimation, we transmit color to a numeric representation. Asai Nursey's reference classifies tomatoes from green to red into 10 levels, as seen in Fig. 3a.

As the light condition in the greenhouse is uncontrollable, we adopt the CIELAB color space [20] to represent color information. The CIELAB color space separates lightness (L) from chromaticity (a and b). The 'a' channel represents the green-to-red spectrum, while 'b' represents the blue-to-yellow spectrum, enabling robust color differentiation in various lighting conditions.

$$HUE = \operatorname{atan2}(b, a) \tag{1}$$

As defined in Eq. 1, the HUE angle is computed using the a and b values of CIELAB color space. We employ the HUE angle to arrange color edges for different levels based on these values. Figure 3b shows that the HUE angle is

(a) Standard of tomato color levels

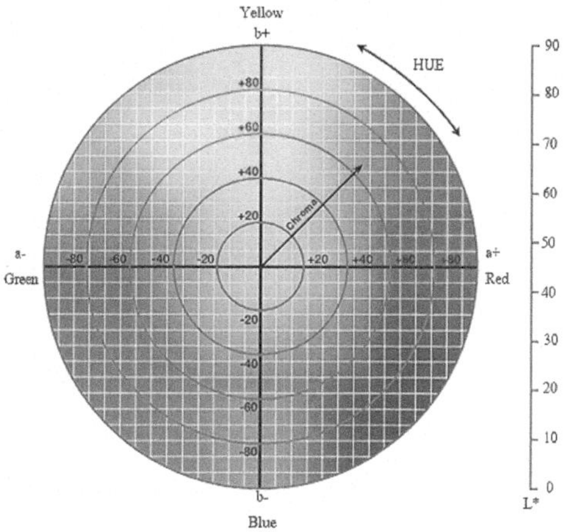

(b) CIELAB color space and HUE angle.

Fig. 3. Tomato color levels and CIELAB color space.

a chromaticity-based metric that stays the same for the same perceived color even if a and b values change. The circle arrangement shows that the same HUE angle represents the same color, no matter how big or small the a and b are. This approach effectively reduces the influence of varying lightness in greenhouse environments and enhances the robustness of ripeness detection under natural illumination conditions.

However, in actual greenhouse situations, objects like branches and leaves cause confusion into the color measurement. Analysis of the color distributions presented in Fig. 4a revealed that the majority of regions displayed uniform color values, however a minor subset of data points exhibited substantial deviations attributable to obstructions.

We employed a statistical method to eliminate outliers in the a and b color channels. We calculated the standard deviation and mean of all a and b values inside the segmented fruit region, identifying outliers as points that differed by more than three standard deviations from the mean in either channel.

Let a_i and b_i denote the a and b values of each pixel, and μ_a, σ_a, μ_b, σ_b represent their respective means and standard deviations. The filtering condition can be formulated as Eq. 2. Only pixels satisfying both conditions were retained for further color analysis.

$$|a_i - \mu_a| < 3\sigma_a \quad \text{and} \quad |b_i - \mu_b| < 3\sigma_b \tag{2}$$

This method effectively removes extreme values caused by occlusions such as stems, leaves, and lighting artifacts, while preserving the main color distribution of the fruit surface. As illustrated in Fig. 4b, the distribution after filtering became more concentrated.

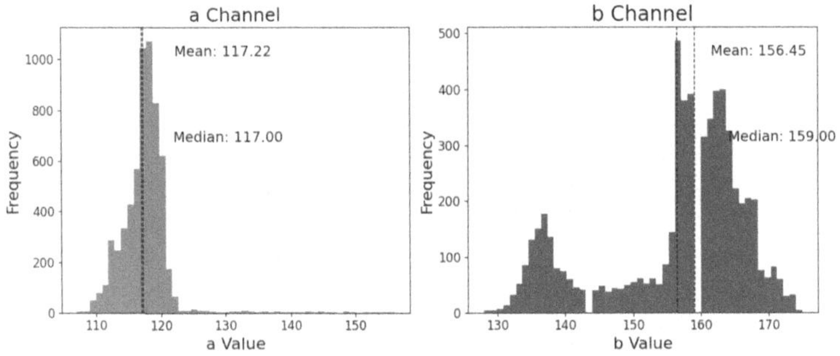

(a) Original distribution of a and b of CIELAB.

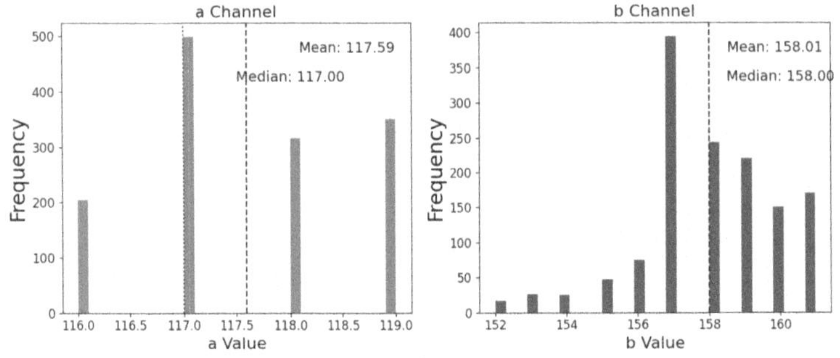

(b) Filtered distribution of a and b of CIELAB.

Fig. 4. Comparison of distribution of original color data and filtered color data.

We set up a reliable metric that balances the differences between the standard and actual data based on the HUE angle to make consistent classification easier. As shown in Fig. 3a, the colors defined in the reference chart for adjacent maturity levels are visually similar, making them difficult to distinguish. To reduce this ambiguity and enhance classification reliability, we merged neighboring levels into broader categories (e.g., L1+L2, L3+L4, L5+L6). In addition, Levels 7 and above (L7+) were grouped together to represent the optimal harvest stage.

3.4 Evaluation of Growth

Cumulative temperature (CT) is the daily average temperature accumulated from fruit set to harvest, which has been proven to be a critical metric for estimating crop development stages. To evaluate the growth percentage with colour information, we establish the linear relationship between the HUE angle and cumulative temperature. CT is calculated as Eq. 3, where $T_{avg,i}$ is the daily average temperature, T_{base} is the baseline temperature (10°C), and n is the number of days.

$$CT = \sum_{i=1}^{n} (T_{avg,i} - T_{base}) \tag{3}$$

Asai Nursery employs CT in cultivation management to plan annual schedules by estimating the number of days from fruit set to harvest. Depending on the tomato variety, the reference temperature from fruit set to harvest is approximately 1000°C. For instance, if the daily average temperature is 20°C, the estimated time from fruit set to harvest would be 1000°C / 20°C = 50 d, providing a framework for annual planning. Based on this, we normalize the CT with the reference temperature of mini tomato planting, 1000°C, to represent the maturity degree.

In this chapter, we evaluate the maturity degree with color information. We incorporate the linear relation between the HUE angle and growth percentage, which is calculated with the reference and cumulative temperature. The HUE angle offers a robust representation of color condition, with larger angles corresponding to the unripened stage (green fruit) and smaller angles representing the ripened stage (red fruit).

4 Experiments and Results

In this chapter, we introduce the experimental configuration and assessment outcomes. We describe the dataset preparation and the experiment results, including fruit-detecting accuracy, color level prediction and growth percentage estimation.

4.1 Dataset and Experiment Settings

We compiled a dataset from video circularly captured in Asai Nursery by personnel to validate the suggested methodology, concentrating on a single tomato cluster. The footage covers 40 d from June 6 to July 16, 2024, during which the average temperature was 25°C, providing optimal growing conditions for mini tomatoes.

The footage was first split into separate frames. Consequently, unclear images with inadequate framing or conflicting viewpoints were eliminated to maintain the dataset's quality. The selected images represent different maturity degrees while ensuring data integrity. Furthermore, we employed all frames of the same day in the training or testing dataset to avert similar images from influencing the validation of the proposed strategy. We ultimately generated a dataset including 250 high-quality images for training and validating the segmentation and skeleton detection model.

To support model training, we annotated the images using Roboflow, labeling both tomato masks for segmentation and key points for skeleton detection. The annotated data were subsequently used to train YOLOv8-based models.

4.2 Skeleton and Segmentation Results

Table 1. Performance metrics for segmentation and skeleton. P: Precision, R: Recall. The mAP95 refers to mAP50-95.

Class	Box				Mask			
	P	R	mAP50	mAP95	P	R	mAP50	mAP95
ball	0.953	0.995	0.943	1	0.953	0.995	0.995	0.843
tomato	0.991	0.996	0.995	0.811	0.991	0.996	0.995	0.763
Avg.(segmentation)	0.995	0.975	0.995	0.877	0.995	0.975	0.995	0.803
Avg.(skeleton)	0.971	1	0.991	0.769	0.974	0.972	0.981	0.588

The skeleton and segmentation extraction models demonstrated strong effectiveness in recognizing and analyzing tomato fruits and cluster structure, as shown in Table 1. The segmentation model achieved a precision of 0.995 and a recall of 0.975, with mAP50-95 scores of 0.877 for bounding boxes and 0.803 for masks. The "ball" class achieved nearly perfect accuracy, benefiting from its distinct shape. The "tomato" class had a marginally lower mask mAP50-95 of 0.763, due to data variation or object occlusion.

The YOLOv8-based model enabled the skeleton extraction model to identify key points of clusters and single fruits, achieving a precision of 0.971. Despite a relatively lower mAP5095 of 0.588, the model effectively localized structural features across various samples.

Our fine-tuned model enables automated monitoring by identifying fruits and analyzing their structural relationships. This is crucial for estimating maturity degree and supporting greenhouse management.

4.3 Color Analysis and Growth Evaluation Results

As shown in Table 2, the model achieved a color level classification accuracy of 83%. The table also provides the hue angle ranges for each maturity level group. We observed that certain adjacent levels, such as L5+L6 corresponding to a HUE range of $40^\circ - 50^\circ$. The two levels are both visually indistinguishable and numerically close in HUE angle. This supports our decision to merge such levels during classification, as the small perceptual and numerical gap between

Table 2. Color level classification accuracy

Color Level	HUE Angle Range	Accuracy	Manurity Degree Range
All(L3-L7)		83%	
L1 + L2	120°–140°	N/A	<0.52
L3 + L4	50°–90°	81%	0.52 ˜0.79
L5 + L6	40°–50°	96%	0.80 ˜0.83
L7+	0°–40°	64%	0.83+ (could be cut)

them makes them inherently difficult to distinguish. Therefore, level merging is not only a simplification strategy, but also a necessary adjustment based on the nature of the color progression in mini tomato ripening.

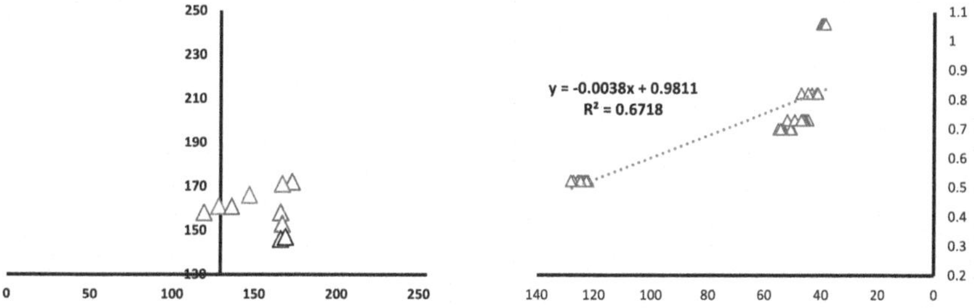

(a) Plotting of different color levels (b) HUE angle and the maturity degree

Fig. 5. (a) shows the positions of different color levels on the axes of a and b. The x-axis and the y-axis present a and b of CIELAB, respectively. (b) is the relationship between the HUE angle and the maturity degree. The x-axis represents the HUE angle (degrees), and the y-axis indicates the growth percentage.

As shown in Fig. 5, a linear regression model was established to quantify the relationship between HUE angle and maturity degree by plotting the data points. The resulting model is represented by Eq. 4, where y represents the maturity degree and x is the HUE angle. The coefficient of determination ($R^2 = 0.67$) indicates a moderate correlation between HUE angle and maturity degree. Furthermore, Table 2 provides the maturity degree ranges corresponding to each merged HUE angle, reinforcing the consistency between color features and growth stages. This suggests that the HUE angle can serve as a reasonably effective predictor of mini tomato maturity degree.

$$y = -0.0038x + 0.9811 \tag{4}$$

In this part, we integrated cumulative temperature and HUE angle into a unified model for maturity degree prediction. This comprehensive approach combines chromaticity features and environmental information, offering a robust framework for growth monitoring. By leveraging both metrics, the proposed method enables estimation of mini tomato maturity degree, thereby supporting informed decision-making in cultivation planning.

5 Conclusion

In this study, we monitored the growth of mini tomatoes from June 6 to July 16, focusing on the relationship between color levels and cumulative temperature. Given the close association between maturity degree and temperature, the original 10-level color grading system was restructured to reduce misclassification caused by subtle differences between adjacent levels. Similar levels were grouped (e.g., L1+L2, L3+L4), and L7+ was consolidated based on the harvest criteria provided by Asai Nursery. The proposed model demonstrated reliable performance in color level estimation, achieving an overall accuracy of 83% across all levels, with the highest accuracy of 96% observed for the merged category L5+L6.

The proposed system enables remote monitoring of fruit condition, accurate estimation of color levels, and maturity degree. This approach contributes to efficient greenhouse management by reducing labor costs, allowing a small number of personnel to monitor the entire facility. Moreover, by continuously collecting growth data over time, the system holds potential for constructing growth rate models to support predictive analytics and long-term cultivation planning.

Despite its advantages, two practical challenges remain. First, variations in lightness due to weather, time, and regional conditions can still affect color-based maturity estimation. Second, physical noise such as support structures and surrounding leaves, whose colors differ greatly from the fruit, may interfere with color analysis. Since the color-based maturity degree estimation relies on highly accurate color information, such interference must be mitigated. In this study, we proposed an outlier removal method based on standard deviation filtering; however, it may not be sufficiently robust under complex greenhouse conditions. Future work will focus on developing more reliable filtering strategies to adapt to diverse noise patterns and improve the stability of color measurements under real-world conditions.

Acknowledgement. This work was supported by Council for Science, Technology and Innovation (CSTI), Cross-ministerial Strategic Innovation Promotion Program (SIP), the 3rd period of SIP "Creation of new ways of learning and working in a post-COVID-19 era" Grant Number JPJ012347 (Funding agency: JST).

References

1. D'Amico, A., De Boni, A., Ottomano Palmisano, G., Acciani, C., Roma, R.: Environmental analysis of soilless tomato production in a high-tech greenhouse. Cleaner Environ. Syst. **11**, 100137 (2023)

2. Ministry of Agriculture, Forestry and Fisheries of Japan. Special Feature: Changing (Shifting) Agricultural Structure in Japan (2023). https://www.maff.go.jp/j/wpaper/w_maff/r3/r3_h/trend/part1/chap1.html
3. Japan International Research Center for Agricultural Sciences (JIRCAS). Key Numbers on the World's Agri-food Systems (2024). https://www.jircas.go.jp/en/program/proc/blog/20241127
4. Pathare, P.B., Opara, U.L., Al-Julanda Al-Said, F.: Colour measurement and analysis in fresh and processed foods: A review. Food Bioprocess Technol. **6**, 36–60 (2013)
5. Sa, I., Ge, Z., Dayoub, F., Upcroft, B., Perez, T., McCool, C.: Deepfruits: a fruit detection system using deep neural networks. Sensors **16**(8), 1222 (2016)
6. Bhargava, A., Bansal, A.: Fruits and vegetables quality evaluation using computer vision: a review. J. King Saud Univ.-Comput. Inform. Sci. **33**(3), 243–257 (2021)
7. Jocher, G., Chaurasia, A., Stoken, A.: YOLOv8: Real-time object detection and segmentation (2023). https://github.com/ultralytics/ultralytics. Accessed 18 Feb 2025
8. Zhu, T., et al.: A method for detecting tomato canopies' phenotypic traits based on improved skeleton extraction algorithm. Comput. Electron. Agric. **214**, 108285 (2023)
9. Cheng, B., Wei, Y., Shi, H., Feris, R., Xiong, J., Huang, T.: Revisiting RCNN: on awakening the classification power of faster RCNN. In: Proceedings of the European Conference on Computer Vision (ECCV), pp. 453–468 (2018)
10. He, K., Gkioxari, G., Dollár, P., Girshick, R.: Mask R-CNN. In: Proceedings of the IEEE International Conference on Computer Vision, pp. 2961–2969 (2017)
11. Cheng, Z.: Multi-modal fusion and multi-task deep learning for monitoring the growth of film-mulched winter wheat. Precision Agric. , 1–25 (2024)
12. Peng, Y., Lu, R.: Modeling multispectral scattering profiles for prediction of apple fruit firmness. Trans. ASAE **48**(1), 235–242 (2005)
13. Bonhomme, R.: Bases and limits to using 'degree day' units. Eur. J. Agron. **13**(1), 1–10 (2000)
14. Ayenan, M.A.T., et al.: Accelerating breeding for heat tolerance in tomato (solanum lycopersicum l): an integrated approach. Agronomy **9**(11), 720 (2019)
15. López Camelo, A.F., Gómez, P.A.: Comparison of color indexes for tomato ripening. Hortic. Bras. **22**, 534–537 (2004)
16. Leon, K., Mery, D., Pedreschi, F., Leon, J.: Color measurement in l a b units from rgb digital images. Food Res. Int. **39**(10), 1084–1091 (2006)
17. Garillos-Manliguez, C.A., Chiang, J.Y.: Multimodal deep learning and visible-light and hyperspectral imaging for fruit maturity estimation. Sensors **21**(4), 1288 (2021)
18. da Fonseca, C.S., Nhantumbo, B.G., Ferreira, Y.M., da Silva, L.A.: and Anderson G Costa. Computational vision for tomato classification using a decision tree algorithm. *Engenharia Agrícola***45**, e20240124 (2025)
19. Marcelis, L.F.M., Elings, A., Visser, P.H.B., Heuvelink, E.: Simulating growth and development of tomato crop. Acta Hort. **821**, 101–110 (2009)
20. Luo, M.R.: Cielab. In: Encyclopedia of Color Science and Technology, pp. 251–257. Springer (2023)

MPIcam: A Deep Learning Based Real-Time Medicinal Plant Identification System for Rural Healthcare in Bangladesh

Shabnur Anonna Akhy[1,2(✉)], Hayaru Shouno[1], Mayen Uddin Mojumdar[2], Tahir Hussain[1], Md Bilayet Hossain[2], Shah Md Tanvir Siddiquee[2], and Narayan Ranjan Chakraborty[2]

[1] Graduate School of Informatics and Engineering, Department of Informatics, The University of Electro-Communications, Tokyo 182-8585, Japan
{a2495007,f2240014}@gl.cc.uec.ac.jp, shouno@uec.ac.jp

[2] Department of Computer Science and Engineering, Daffodil International University, Dhaka 1216, Bangladesh
{mayen.cse,hossain15-5821,Tanvir.cse}@diu.edu.bd, narayan@daffodilvarsity.edu.bd

Abstract. Plant-based herbal medicine has played a vital role in traditional healthcare in Bangladesh, especially in rural areas lacking access to modern medical care. However, manual identification of medicinal plants presents considerable difficulties, as it is time-consuming and usually requires expert knowledge. To address this issue, we developed the Medical Plant Identification Camera (MPIcam), a web-based application that enables real-time plant identification through leaf image capture. Designed with a simple and user-friendly interface, MPIcam is accessible even to users with minimal technical experience. The system employs deep learning (DL) techniques based on Convolutional Neural Networks (CNNs). The dataset, which consisted of 9,150 images from six different categories of medicinal plant species, was split 80% for training and the remaining 20% equally between testing and validation. We applied modifications to the suggested methods: VGG16, DenseNet201, MobileNetV2, Xception, and ResNet50. Based on the evaluation of the models, DenseNet201 achieved the highest test accuracy of 99.00%, followed by ResNet50 (98.59%), MobileNetV2 (97.99%), Xception (95.58%), and VGG16 (93.17%). We used the best-performing model in MPIcam with Streamlit to build a simple and easy-to-use web interface for identifying plants automatically. The proposed system offers a practical solution for researchers, herbalists, and the general public to accurately identify medicinal plants and understand their associated health benefits.

Keywords: Medicinal-Plant Identification · Automated System · Deep Learning

H. R. Arabnia et al. (Eds.): CSCE 2025, CCIS 2932, pp. 516–528, 2026.
https://doi.org/10.1007/978-3-032-22193-3_41

1 Introduction

Since ancient times, medicinal plants have been a major source of substances used to treat illnesses, and it is critical to recognize and classify medicinal herbs for better healthcare [24]. Researchers claimed that almost 80% of people are dependent on herbal plants for their health and wellness [24]. In ancient times, people were not dependent on technology, and advanced medical systems were not prevalent. Consequently, to meet their medical needs, people prepared home remedies using various medicinal plants. However, with changing times, people are increasingly relying on technology, which is affecting their ability to retain traditional knowledge. This growing dependence on technology is associated with a decline in human knowledge about medicinal plants. Thus, there is a significant decline in public awareness of traditional herbal remedies, and these practices are gradually disappearing.

However, situations occasionally arise in which people are temporarily disconnected from technology and require medical treatment. Unfortunately, in such cases, access to hospitals, pharmacies, and doctors may be unavailable. Basic treatment can be provided if knowledge of home remedies using medicinal plants is available. Besides, many people in modern society do not recognize the correct medicinal plants nor understand which plants are beneficial for specific diseases [24]. Consequently, in critical situations, individuals are unable to obtain appropriate treatment from environmental medicinal plants and must rely solely on hospitals, pharmacies, and medical specialists. To overcome this challenge, we developed a real-time application that helps users recognize the correct medicinal herbs and learn about the plant's benefits. Image recognition technology has become more sophisticated and is utilized in various kinds of industries, for example, face identification, object detection, medical imaging, etc., as computer vision technology has advanced and gained popularity [8,27]. People will be able to identify and utilize therapeutic herbs in any serious situation. This application can assist in providing initial first aid treatment and will significantly benefit society. Since medicines are essential for curing different types of diseases and maintaining a healthy lifestyle [30], it is crucial for people seeking important herbs to ensure their accurateObjective identification.

To bridge this research gap, this study aims to evaluate the performance of five advanced deep learning algorithms (DenseNet201, VGG16, MobileNetV2, ResNet50, and Xception) using real-field images of medicinal plants. Among these techniques, DenseNet201 achieved the highest accuracy of 99.00%. The main goal of this study is to reduce reliance on human vision for identifying medicinal plants by developing automated system. **The major contributions of this paper are:**

- The study introduces a real-time, automated system using DL, (specifically CNNs) that enables non-experts to identify Bangladeshimedicinal plants through leaf images.

- MPIcam eliminates the reliance on expert knowledge or human observation for identifying herbal plants, thereby enhancing accessibility to herbal medicine in remote or emergency situations.

In earlier studies, traditional classifiers such as Support Vector Machines (SVM), K-Nearest Neighbors (KNN), and Random Forests were commonly employed for plant identification based on leaf features like vein patterns and leaf margins. However, these methods often suffer from limitations, including poor performance on small or limited datasets. In contrast, Convolutional Neural Networks (CNNs) have demonstrated superior capabilities in automatically extracting complex and high-level features from images [6]. To enhance interpretability in deep learning models, Explainable AI (XAI) frameworks such as SHapley Additive exPlanations (SHAP) and Local Interpretable Model-agnostic Explanations (LIME) have been applied to analyze model predictions and risk factors [1,7].

The remainder of this paper is structured as follows: Sect. 2 reviews related work in the field. Section 3 details the proposed research methodology. Section 4 presents the experimental results along with a discussion. Finally, Sect. 5 concludes the paper and outlines potential directions for future research.

2 Related Works

For more than sixty years, researchers have worked toward enabling machines to understand and interpret visual information [23]. The use of DL algorithms and image pre-processing techniques for image classification, plant disease detection [20,25], and identification in agriculture has been an active area in recent years. Investigators can utilize pre-trained DL models, transfer learning approaches, or custom-built models in their work. Several studies have explored the use of CNNs to detect and classify various types of plants, leaves, crops, fruits, and vegetables based on images [10].

One notable study introduced AyurLeaf, a deep learning-based CNN model designed to classify medicinal plants by analyzing leaf features such as shape, size, color, and texture [25]. This study utilized a secondary dataset, where the SVM classifier achieved the highest accuracy of 96.76% [13], and several optimization techniques were applied to improve model stability [5]. Another approach employed the VGG16 architecture for the classification of herbal leaves from images [24]. Besides, a separate study used YOLOv5 to identify therapeutic plants, achieving a classification accuracy of 83.00% on a Philippine dataset containing four common medicinal plant species. However, that work lacked the development of an automated application, limiting its real-world usability [27].

To tackle this obstacle, [23] developed a smartphone application which capable of identifying the medicinal benefits of a plant leaf by analyzing its image. They used a dataset of 30 Indian medicinal leaf species and applied preprocessing techniques such as resizing, scaling, and data splitting. A custom CNN model was employed, achieving 94.00% accuracy. The app interface was designed using Android Studio [23].

Table 1. Comparison and gap analysis of prior work on medicinal plant identification

Reference	Model	Pre-Processing	Accuracy	Gap Analysis
[2]	MobileNetV2	Resizing, Splitting	98.05%	No detection system
[11]	Faster R-CNN	Resizing	67.34%	Single approach
[18]	DenseNet201	Smoothing, Sharpening	93%	No application
[19]	VGG16	RGB conversion, Filtering	98.7%	No application
[22]	Inception v3	Splitting, Resizing	95%	No application
[24]	VGG16	Resizing, Splitting	97%	Not deployed
[29]	DenseNet201	Histogram Equalization	98.58%	No implementation
[31]	DENN	Scaling, Enhancement	98.5%	No use-case
Our work	DenseNet201	Optimization, Histogram Equalization	99.00%	MPIcam application

Similarly, another study implemented an automated mobile application for medicinal flora recognition, experimenting with various DL models, including CNN, SVM, PNN, and FNN. Among these, the CNN model achieved the highest accuracy of 99.70%. Flutter was used to design the application's graphical user interface [14]. In [15], the PB3C (Big BangBig Crunch) algorithm achieved an accuracy of 93.20%, showcasing the effectiveness of CNNs in plant species identification. In the same way, [32] proposed a custom ANN model that achieved 98.30% accuracy, despite challenges posed by features like leaf morpho-colorimetry and visible/near-infrared spectroscopy. On the flip side, [21] presented an IoT-based approach with a DCNN, which outperformed standard CNNs by achieving 98.45% accuracy. In addition, another study argued that conventional CNNs remain effective, with a custom MNN model achieving 85.15% accuracy offering faster performance compared to MobileNet [9].

Moreover, [30] introduced the SDAMPI algorithm for identifying immunity-boosting medicinal plants, attaining 96.00% accuracy. Pre-trained CNN models such as VGG16 were employed by [28,33], while [26] explored transfer learning with ResNet50, VGG16, and MobileNet2, with ResNet50 achieving the best performance at 91.00%. However, most of these studies lacked a deployable application. By contrast, [2] developed a fully functional, user-friendly application for herbal plant recognition. Correspondingly, [3] presented a mobile app that classifies herbs based on geometric features. [16] applied MobileNetV2 for classifying diseases, medicinal plants, and fruits, demonstrating improved learning rate optimization and multi-functional detection. Furthermore, feature selection methods such as EFS were also employed in recent models [5], which gained popularity due to the depth and complexity of modern architectures. Table 1 presents a comparison and gap analysis of existing works.

In conclusion, based on an exhaustive literature review, we found that no automated application currently exists in Bangladesh to assist the general public in accurately identifying medicinal plants. To address this gap, this work focuses on developing an automated application capable of detecting medicinal plants without relying on human visual identification.

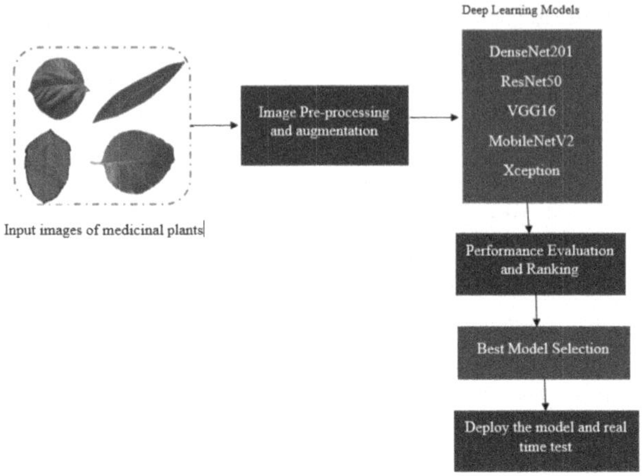

Fig. 1. The overall process used in this study to identify medicinal plant species using leaf

3 Methodology

3.1 Data Acquisition

This study utilized leaf images from six Bangladeshi medicinal plant species, collected from local fields in Ashulia, Savar, Dhaka. Traditional herbal plants are utilized for enhancing immunity [30]. Figure 1 illustrates the medicinal plant identification workflow.

3.2 Data Pre-processing

This study employs comprehensive pre-processing techniques, including file format optimization, histogram equalization, background removal, data cleaning, data augmentation, and gamma correction.

3.3 Hyperparameter Setting

To train our DCNN models, this study uses custom data. 80% of the dataset was used in the training procedure. In order to track model performance and avoid overfitting, an additional 10% of the data was allocated for validation at the beginning of each epoch. Additionally, a completely separate dataset of 10% was used for testing to provide an objective assessment of the model's performance. Besides, new and real data is used in the test to check if the model works well with different stuff it hasn't seen before. For accurate gradient estimations, a batch size of 32 was utilized throughout the training phase, even though it required more memory. The "softmax" function is also used in the output layer to map the final layer's output and enhance the predictability of the model. To make sure the models always give the same results, we start the randomness from a specific

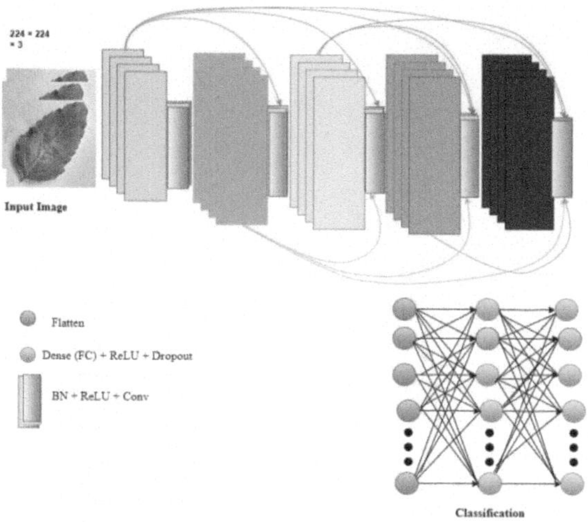

Fig. 2. Architecture of Proposed Model DenseNet201

number, which is 64. In order to ensure consistent training and evaluation for accurate performance comparison, the model's parameters are modified through training based on input data and the optimization process.

By utilizing ImageDataGenerator's "horizontal flip" feature, more training data will be available to the model, helping in its capacity to identify features independent of horizontal movements and enhancing the handling of test data with comparable movements. For multiclass classification, the "categorical" class mode was employed, which allowed models to understand connections between classes and predict multiple classifications. Images were utilized with 0.2–20% zoom in and out, and the images were randomly rotated with 20% shifting along the X and Y axes. However, we applied the "Adam" optimizer function, which is an improvement on the stochastic gradient descent optimization technique. This function adjusts learning rates for each parameter, corrects estimator bias in the gradient's first and second moments, and improves model stability and performance during training.

3.4 Leaf Features Extraction Analysis

Feature extraction plays an important role in detecting features in digital images such as edges, shapes, or motion in DL research.

All medicinal plant leaves are not the same age. There are mixed-age leaves, like pre-mature, semi-mature, and mature. Selecting these three conditions for each species of medicinal plant allows for an in-depth study because the leaves appear differently at various stages of growth. The types of medicinal plants for this research are neem, moringa, Malabar nut, holy basil, arjun, and green chiretta. Utilizing the features that a neural network was trained on before is quick and efficient when performed via feature extraction. This research's main

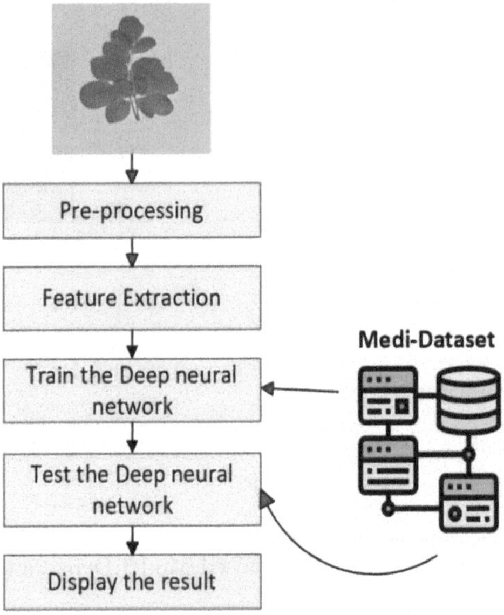

Fig. 3. The process of classification approach

objective is to develop an automated system for identifying the accurate medicinal plants that are deployed by transfer learning models. Additionally, transfer learning serves as a feature extraction and shape extractor, increasing data efficiency, enhancing generalizations, and enabling domain adaptation from input data. It offers two key benefits: (i) higher model performance (ii) better data and resource efficiency. It reduces the training time and increases sustainable computational resources. The most popular pretrained models are InceptionV3, DenseNet201, VGG16, VGG19, ResNet50, ResNet121, Xception, MobileNetV2, and DenseNet121 [4,12]. Figure 2 represents the architecture of the best-selected model, and Table 2 shows the DenseNet201 classification report.

Table 2. Classification Report of DenseNet201 Model

Class Name	Precision	Recall	F1-score	Support
Arjun	1.00	1.00	1.00	84
Holy Basil	1.00	1.00	1.00	84
Green Chiretta	1.00	0.99	0.99	84
Malabar Nut	0.99	1.00	0.99	84
Moringa	1.00	1.00	1.00	84
Neem	1.00	1.00	1.00	84

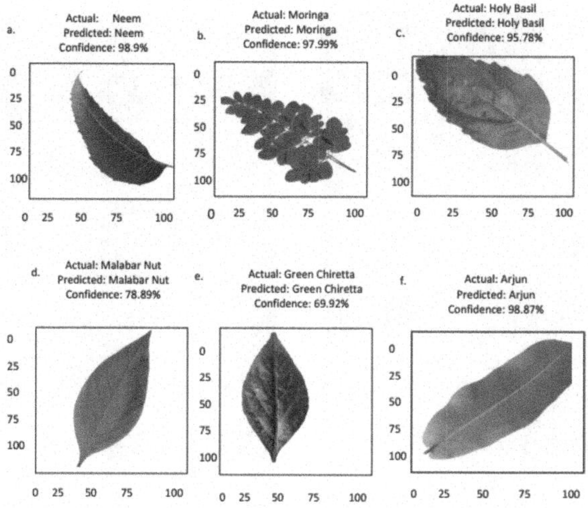

Fig. 4. Evaluate the efficacy of the trained DenseNet201 model for automated medicinal plant identification based on leaf

4 Experimental Result and Discussion

Advanced, automated, and interpretable diagnostic tools are necessary for clinical decision-making due to the rapid growth of medical imaging technologies [17]. A total of 9,150 medicinal plant leaf images were used in this study. The dataset was divided into training sets (80%), validation sets (10%), and testing sets (10%). The images were captured using an OPPO A76 smartphone. The original image resolution of 1380×780 pixels was resized to 224×224 pixels to align with the input requirements of the DenseNet201 model.

The DenseNet201 model was trained using the Adam optimizer with a learning rate of 0.001 over 50 epochs. The training process employed a batch size of 32 and utilized the categorical cross-entropy loss function. Data augmentation techniques, including rotation, zoom, and horizontal flipping, were applied to enhance the model's generalization capabilities. Experiments were conducted on a Windows 10 system equipped with an 11th Gen Intel(R) Core(TM) i5-11400 CPU @ 2.60 GHz, 32 GB RAM, and Intel(R) UHD Graphics 730 GPU. Additionally, Google Colab was utilized for data analysis and model training, leveraging its GPU acceleration capabilities. The trained DenseNet201 model achieved a test accuracy of 99.00%, outscored other evaluated models such as ResNet50, MobileNetV2, Xception, and VGG16. This high accuracy underscores the robustness and suitability of the model for real-time medicinal plant identification. A web-based application was developed using Streamlit, integrating the trained DenseNet201 model saved in.h5 format. This application allows users to upload or capture leaf images and receive immediate identification results, facilitating accessible and efficient plant recognition. Finally, this study introduced an automated application for detecting accurate Bangladeshi medicinal plants

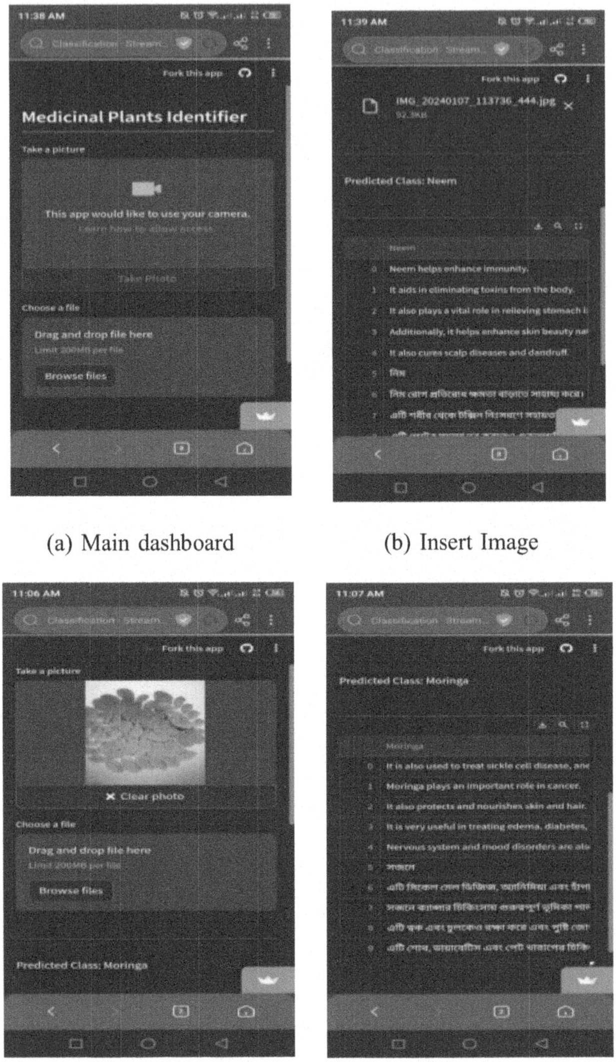

(a) Main dashboard (b) Insert Image

(c) Real-time testing (d) Output screen

Fig. 5. Real-time testing interfaces of MPIcam.

that overcomes the previous research gap and it has already been mentioned in Table 1.

4.1 Discussion

In this work, the author examined five transfer learning models for detecting medicinal plants: DenseNet201, MobileNetV2, ResNet50, VGG16, and Xception.

Based on prior research, these models are selected for training. In comparing the training of models, DenseNet201 achieved better accuracy than other models. However, DenseNet201 obtained 99.00% accuracy on the test set, demonstrating its exceptional performance. While the other four models VGG16 obtained 93.17%, MobileNetV2 obtained 97.99%, ResNet50 obtained 98.59%, and Xception obtained 95.58% test accuracy. This comparison of model performances is shown in Table 3.

The automated system integrates correctly with the DenseNet201 model. Because of DenseNet201's sophisticated CNN design, it could capture the characteristics of the therapeutic plant precisely. Precision and recall scores of 1.00 for most classes in the confusion matrix demonstrated DenseNet201's reliable performance. However, the implemented automated application could help the common people and the healthcare system to identify accurate Bangladeshi medicinal plants easily. Users can take an instant photo and identify the plant name along with its facility by using the MPIcam application. Additionally, users can upload photos from their device gallery to identify medicinal plants. The system determines the relevant plant species by extracting leaf features and classifying them using pre-trained models.

Table 3. Comparison of CNN model performances

CNN Models	Accuracy (%)
VGG16	93.17
Xception	95.58
MobileNetV2	97.99
ResNet50	98.59
DenseNet201	99.00

After post-processing, the output is displayed on the screen, and the application automatically makes a decision. As a result, users can accurately identify medicinal plants through leaf feature extraction and obtain reliable results with ease, allowing them to utilize the plants according to their needs. Future research can explore larger datasets and alternative models to improve the identification process as well as distinguish between normal and diseased leaves.

4.2 Model Deployment-MPIcam

For model deployment, the best-performing DenseNet201 model was saved in .h5 format and integrated into a Python-based environment using Streamlit for real-time interaction. This lightweight web framework enabled the development of a simple and user-friendly interface for automated plant identification. To evaluate the model's predictive capability, we used both the training data and a separate set of new images for testing. The DenseNet201 model successfully identified medicinal plant species, demonstrating its robustness and reliability.

Figure 3 illustrates the flow of the classification process within the application. Figure 4 presents the model's efficacy in identifying medicinal plants based on leaf input, and Fig. 5 displays real-time testing results from the deployed Streamlit application.

5 Conclusion

This study developed an automated application that can quickly and accurately identify Bangladeshi medicinal plants without human effort. We evaluated five deep learning models, including VGG16, ResNet50, Xception, MobileNetV2, and DenseNet201, using a primary dataset. From the models tested, DenseNet201 performed the best with a 99.00% accuracy. By applying DenseNet201 with transfer learning and image pre-processing, the system enables precise classification of herbal leaf images. However, the application was built using Python and the open-source Streamlit framework, integrating the DenseNet201 model for reliable, real-time plant identification. This tool benefits the general public, healthcare professionals, and younger users who may struggle to identify medicinal plants. At present, this system can recognize only six herb classes. Moreover, this application requires a strong internet connection, which may not be available in remote or hilly regions. In future work, we plan to resolve this complexity by developing an Android-based offline version of the system to ensure accessibility in any area. Also, expand the dataset to include more medicinal plant species and utilize advanced AI techniques. Additionally, the system will be improved to distinguish between dangerous and non-dangerous plants, enhancing its safety for medical and first-aid applications.

Acknowledgments. This study was funded by Shouno Lab. The authors would like to thank the lab for providing computational resources and a supportive research environment. Their continuous guidance and encouragement were instrumental in completing this work.

Data Availability Statement. The dataset used in this study is available upon request. Interested researchers may contact the corresponding author for the access.

Disclosure of Interests. The authors declare that they have no competing interests.

References

1. A novel ai-driven model for student dropout risk analysis with explainable ai insights. Comput. Educ. Artifi. Intell. **8**, 100352 (2025). https://doi.org/10.1016/j.caeai.2024.100352, https://www.sciencedirect.com/science/article/pii/S2666920X24001553
2. Abdollahi, J.: Identification of medicinal plants in ardabil using deep learning: identification of medicinal plants using deep learning. In: 2022 27th International Computer Conference, Computer Society of Iran (CSICC), pp. 1–6. IEEE (2022)

3. Acharya, B., Ghosh, A., Panda, S., Hu, Y.C.: Automated plant recognition system with geographical position selection for medicinal plants. Adv. Multimedia **2023** (2023)
4. Aggarwal, M., et al.: Pre-trained deep neural network-based features selection supported machine learning for rice leaf disease classification. Agriculture **13**(5), 936 (2023)
5. Akhy, S.A., Mia, M.B., Mustafa, S., Chakraborti, N.R., Krishnachalitha, K.C., Rabbany, G.: A comprehensive study on ensemble feature selection techniques for classification. In: 2024 11th International Conference on Computing for Sustainable Global Development (INDIACom), pp. 1319–1324 (2024). https://doi.org/10.23919/INDIACom61295.2024.10498364
6. Akter, R., Hosen, M.I.: Cnn-based leaf image classification for bangladeshi medicinal plant recognition. In: 2020 Emerging Technology in Computing, Communication and Electronics (ETCCE), pp. 1–6. IEEE (2020)
7. Al Mamun, A., Akhy, S.A., Mustofa, S., Mia, M.B., Sarkar, P.D., Chakraborty, N.R., Ali Khan, M.A
8. Alhudhaif, A., et al.: A particle swarm optimization based deep learning model for vehicle classification. Comput. Syst. Sci. Eng. **40**(1), 223–235 (2022)
9. Amuthalingeswaran, C., Sivakumar, M., Renuga, P., Alexpandi, S., Elamathi, J., Hari, S.S.: Identification of medicinal plant's and their usage by using deep learning. In: 2019 3rd International Conference on Trends in Electronics and Informatics (ICOEI), pp. 886–890. IEEE (2019)
10. Bi, Y., Xue, B., Mesejo, P., Cagnoni, S., Zhang, M.: A survey on evolutionary computation for computer vision and image analysis: Past, present, and future trends. IEEE Trans. Evol. Comput. **27**(1), 5–25 (2022)
11. Cynthia, S.T., Hossain, K.M.S., Hasan, M.N., Asaduzzaman, M., Das, A.K.: Automated detection of plant diseases using image processing and faster r-cnn algorithm. In: 2019 International Conference on Sustainable Technologies for Industry 4.0 (STI), pp. 1–5. IEEE (2019)
12. Dara, S., Tumma, P.: Feature extraction by using deep learning: a survey. In: Second International Conference on Electronics, Communication and Aerospace Technology (ICECA), pp. 1795–1801. IEEE (2018)
13. Dileep, M., Pournami, P.: Ayurleaf: a deep learning approach for classification of medicinal plants. In: TENCON 2019–2019 IEEE Region 10 Conference (TENCON), pp. 321–325. IEEE (2019)
14. Dong, J., Fuentes, A., Yoon, S., Kim, H., Park, D.S.: An iterative noisy annotation correction model for robust plant disease detection. Front. Plant Sci. **14** (2023)
15. Ghosh, S., Singh, A., Kumar, S.: Pb3c-cnn: an integrated pb3c and cnn based approach for plant leaf classification. Intel. Artif. **26**(72), 15–29 (2023)
16. Gulzar, Y.: Fruit image classification model based on mobilenetv2 with deep transfer learning technique. Sustainability **15**(3), 1906 (2023)
17. Hussain, T., et al.: Effresnet-vit: a fusion-based convolutional and vision transformer model for explainable medical image classification. IEEE Access (2025)
18. Ibrahim, N.M., et al.: Transfer learning approach to seed taxonomy: a wild plant case study. Big Data Cognitive Comput. **7**(3), 128 (2023)

19. Islam, M., Ria, N.J., Ani, J.F., Masum, A.K.M., Abujar, S., Hossain, S.A.: Deep learning based classification system for recognizing local spinach. In: Troiano, L., et al. (eds.) Advances in Deep Learning, Artificial Intelligence and Robotics. LNNS, vol. 249, pp. 1–14. Springer, Cham (2022). https://doi.org/10.1007/978-3-030-85365-5_1
20. Jiang, P., Chen, Y., Liu, B., He, D., Liang, C.: Real-time detection of apple leaf diseases using deep learning approach based on improved convolutional neural networks. IEEE Access **7**, 59069–59080 (2019)
21. Jogi, K.S., Prasad, R.: Detecting the plant species using deep-convolutional neural network (d-cnn) with internet of things (iot). In: 2023 Third International Conference on Artificial Intelligence and Smart Energy (ICAIS), pp. 66–70. IEEE (2023)
22. Kavitha, K., Sharma, P., Gupta, S., Lalitha, R.: Medicinal plant species detection using deep learning. In: 2022 First International Conference on Electrical, Electronics, Information and Communication Technologies (ICEEICT), pp. 01–06. IEEE (2022)
23. Krishna, D.S.S.V., Kumar, E.V., Goud, E.M.: A novel approach to identify medicinal plant based on image processing (2023)
24. Mardiana, B.D., Utomo, W.B., Oktaviana, U.N., Wicaksono, G.W., Minarno, A.E., et al.: Herbal leaves classification based on leaf image using cnn architecture model vgg16. Jurnal RESTI (Rekayasa Sistem dan Teknologi Informasi) **7**(1), 20–26 (2023)
25. Muneer, A., Fati, S.M.: Efficient and automated herbs classification approach based on shape and texture features using deep learning. IEEE Access **8**, 196747–196764 (2020)
26. Narvekar, C., Rao, M.: Flower classification using cnn and transfer learning in cnn-agriculture perspective. In: 2020 3rd International Conference on Intelligent Sustainable Systems (ICISS), pp. 660–664. IEEE (2020)
27. Pargaien, A.V., Singh, D., Chauhan, M., Negi, H., Chilwal, B., Pargaien, N.: Identification of plant leaves having anti-diabetic property using machine learning. In: 2023 2nd International Conference on Applied Artificial Intelligence and Computing (ICAAIC), pp. 195–200. IEEE (2023)
28. Sharrab, Y., Al-Fraihat, D., Tarawneh, M., Sharieh, A.: Medicinal plants recognition using deep learning. In: 2023 International Conference on Multimedia Computing, Networking and Applications (MCNA), pp. 116–122. IEEE (2023)
29. Singh, H., Singh, R., Goel, P., Singh, A., Sharma, N.: Automatic framework for vegetable classification using transfer-learning. Int. J. Electr. Electron. Res **10**(2), 405–410 (2022)
30. Thanikkal, J.G., Dubey, A.K., Thomas, M.: An efficient mobile application for identification of immunity boosting medicinal plants using shape descriptor algorithm. Wireless Pers. Commun., 1–17 (2023)
31. Vallabhajosyula, S., Sistla, V., Kolli, V.K.K.: Transfer learning-based deep ensemble neural network for plant leaf disease detection. J. Plant Dis. Prot. **129**(3), 545–558 (2022)
32. Xue, J., et al.: Automated Chinese medicinal plants classification based on machine learning using leaf morpho-colorimetry, fractal dimension and visible/near infrared spectroscopy. Inter. J. Agricult. Biol. Eng. **12**(2), 123–131 (2019)
33. Zargar, H.H., Zargar, S.H., Mehri, R., Tajidini, F.: Using vgg16 algorithms for classification of lung cancer in ct scans image. arXiv preprint arXiv:2305.18367 (2023)

Author Index

H. R. Arabnia et al. (Eds.): CSCE 2025, CCIS 2932, pp. 529–531, 2026.
https://doi.org/10.1007/978-3-032-22193-3

The manufacturer's authorised representative in the EU is Springer Nature Customer Service Centre GmbH, Europaplatz 3, 69115 Heidelberg, Germany. If you have any concerns regarding our products, please contact ProductSafety@springernature.com

Printed and bound by CPI Group (UK) Ltd, Croydon, CR0 4YY
05/10/2026
02228031-0009